HISTORY OF THE AMERICAN CINEMA

Volume 1

TO 1907

Film poster, ca. 1900.

HISTORY OF THE AMERICAN CINEMA

CHARLES HARPOLE, GENERAL EDITOR

1
THE EMERGENCE OF CINEMA: THE AMERICAN SCREEN TO 1907

Charles Musser

CHARLES SCRIBNER'S SONS
MACMILLAN LIBRARY REFERENCE USA
Simon & Schuster Macmillan
NEW YORK

Simon & Schuster and Prentice Hall International
LONDON · MEXICO CITY · NEW DELHI · SINGAPORE · SYDNEY · TORONTO

Library of Congress Cataloging-in-Publication Data
Musser, Charles.
   The emergence of cinema: the American screen to 1907 / by Charles
Musser.
      p.   cm.—(History of the American cinema; v. 1)
   Includes bibliographical references and index.
   ISBN 0-684-18413-3 (alk. paper)
   1. Silent films—United States—History and criticism.   2. Motion
pictures—United States—History.   3. Motion picture industry—
United States—History.   I. Title.   II. Series.
PN1993.5.U6H55 vol. 1
[PN1995.75]   90-48307
                                                              CIP

                        ISBN 0-684-18413-3

                   Charles Scribner's Sons
            An Imprint of Simon & Schuster Macmillan
                         1633 Broadway
                      New York, NY 10019-6785

                          Impression

                       3 4 5 6 7 8 9

Advisory Board

The Cinema History Project and the
History of the American Cinema
have been supported by grants from the
National Endowment for the Humanities and the
John and Mary R. Markle Foundation.

For my parents

Contents

General Preface

*T*he *History of the American Cinema* is a narrative, analytic, chronological treatment of our film heritage in an anticipated ten volumes. Within its loosely decade-by-decade plan, the scheme of organization of each volume has been determined by the special conditions of the period under discussion and the requirements of sound scholarship. Thus, readers should not look for the same degree of concentration on specific topics from volume to volume. Each author has attempted to render a dispassionate and clear historical vision of an era, accommodating so far as possible both the author's individual research and the soundest findings available in the existing literature. Much of the research in these pages appears for the first time, and the illustrations have been selected for their rarity as well as for their aptness.

The series is intended for a wide readership, including students, scholars, archivists, and professionals, as well as the interested general public. The general reader will be served by the organized overviews of each time period, and the scholar will find the thorough documentation valuable both in teaching and in extending the findings of the series. The archivist will be particularly interested in these books' implicit advice concerning the films and film records that demand preservation and dissemination. The industry professional may be especially interested in following marketing trends dating back to the earliest motion pictures and the conception and development of film styles that now permeate cinema practice. With this broad audience in mind, the authors have attempted to make their volumes as comprehensive as the current state of material resources and publishing constraints will allow. Since the very intellectual foundations of this series rest on the evolutionary nature of the scholarly process, it is our hope that the present contributions to knowledge will evoke an even fuller literature of cinema history from those who follow.

Film history involves three major forces: technology, social and economic conditions, and style and aesthetics. The technological apparatus defines and limits everything that appears on the screen. Technology has also made cinema an expensive medium. Films cannot be made without significant financial investment, and in capitalist America films are almost always made with the hope of profit. Financial and social pressures affect every aspect of cinema history. Finally, filmmaking is an art, and each volume in this series records the development of its many styles. The three forces interact in intimate ways, and the examination of this interaction is one of the many unique qualities of the series.

Our purview is the films and film industry of the United States and those foreign films and filmmakers that impinge most directly on the American experience. Our concentration is on the traditional narrative feature film, the documentary, and the "avant-garde," "experimental," or "art" film. Excluded, or treated in less detail, are most military, scientific, and industrial films. By concentrating on the major forms, we have sought to render history with a depth and clarity not possible on a broader front—to take readers from pre-production (including securing financing) to production (including scriptwriting as well as editing and printing of the release prints) to distribution (including wholesale marketing) to exhibition and consumption (including viewers' reception of films and the audience's impact on the shaping of later cinema).

In a discipline where theory has tended to outstrip historical investigation as the dominant mode of inquiry, the need for a carefully researched and comprehensive history is obvious. Vigorous research based in semiotics, feminist studies, and a broad spectrum of politically and ideologically rooted disciplines has enriched our understanding of the nature of cinema. But few theorists would deny that intellectual investigation ought to be based on a solid knowledge of the past. The *History of the American Cinema* has been conceived to provide just such a historical foundation. The individual authors attempt to outline as much of the past as can be traced through existing records, in some cases breaking new scholarly ground in their examination of the earliest filmmaking equipment, memoirs, business documents, archives, the oral recollections of the few surviving film pioneers, and, above all, the crumbling celluloid remnants of our film heritage. They also interpret the evidence they gather, while acknowledging that the order imposed on a subject emerges ultimately from our own schemata, not necessarily those of the past itself.

From the first it was obvious that no one scholar could hope to address the entire first century of American film. To embrace not only the traditional aesthetic of the narrative feature film but also the technological and socioeconomic factors at work throughout the industry, a broad-based team approach was deemed essential. To that end I organized a planning conference, which was held near Carbondale, Illinois, in November 1980, with funding provided by the National Endowment for the Humanities, the Markle Foundation, and Southern Illinois University.[1] Out of that meeting emerged commitments to research, advise, and write for the projected series. Fortuitously, the conference also drew a representative of Charles Scribner's Sons, Publishers, and Marshall De Bruhl of the Reference Division soon offered the publishing contract that officially launched the project. Dedicated funding for the initial three volumes was secured from the National Endowment for the Humanities in 1981, and the Society for Cinema Studies endorsed the project the same year. At the NEH, Harold Cannon was the first to encourage the project, and David Wise has observed the development of the series from its first application. Mary Milton at the Markle Foundation was also an early friend of the project, and Markle provided key planning funding in the early years. The grants administration offices of Southern Illinois University, the University of Texas at Dallas, the Ohio State University, and the University of Central Florida have given funding, leave time, and graduate

1. The conference participants were Jeanne Allen, Robert C. Allen, Roy Armes, Richard Blumenberg, Eileen Bowser, Marshall Deutelbaum, Jack Ellis, John Fell, Jane Feuer, Lucy Fischer, Ian Jarvie, Stuart Kaminsky, E. Ann Kaplan, Gorham "Hap" Kindem, Richard Koszarski, James Leahy, Jay Leyda, Jayne Loader, Timothy Lyons, John Mercer, Bill Nichols, Donald Staples, Birgitta Steene, and Howard Suber.

student research assistantships. David R. Holdridge of James Madison University volunteered a personal donation. Michael McGinley, Charles E. Smith, and Karen Day have each in turn carried the series forward at Scribners. To John Fitzpatrick of Scribners has come the job of preparing the manuscripts for publication. His steady hand has been of great help.

A host of graduate students assisted the project over the years. For expediting the planning conference, helping to prepare the manuscripts, and assisting with funding proposals and library research, profound thanks are due, in order of service, to: Rebecca Thompson, Fred Marx, Michelle Edmonds, Kelly Yuen, Michael Presnell, Darien Smith, Diane Welch, Andrew Short, Susan Tong, Paul Cornelius, Mary Charlotte Johnson, and Chester Gallant. I have fond memories of the camaraderie we shared.

Development of the series also benefited from the generous cooperation and interest of the American Film Institute, the Motion Picture Producers Association of America, and, early on, a number of scholars from abroad who lent a valuable international perspective. Ian Jarvie and E. Ann Kaplan deserve special thanks as coordinators of the Advisory Board, which provided guidance at many points. Beyond the Board proper, John Fell contributed wise counsel and invaluable research guidance. The authors' acknowledgments in each volume of the series expand further on the great and selfless contributions made by scores of film studies professionals.

Personally, I must pay tribute to Jay Leyda, my mentor and friend and to whose memory I dedicate my own work on this series. Both an unrelenting researcher and a thoughtful and generous teacher, Jay was the kindest and the strongest intellectual I have known. In my personal life, I have been sustained by Carole Harpole and our son, Andrew, and by Hank and Kathrine, and Beanie and Nell. Above all I thank Mary, whose most special friendship has enriched my life and work.

CHARLES HARPOLE
General Editor

Acknowledgments

This work culminates more than a dozen years of research, reflection, and writing on America's early cinema. Inevitably such an enterprise leaves me deeply indebted to numerous individuals and institutions. My gratitude begins with Charles Harpole, who gave me the opportunity to undertake the book at hand and guided it through to successful completion. John Fell, who was originally scheduled to be its author, kindly sponsored me as his replacement and provided invaluable advice. The writers of volumes two and three, Eileen Bowser and Richard Koszarski, offered useful information, insightful criticisms, and psychological support. I could not have chosen better collaborators.

Extensive, in-depth research on a historical period is only possible when the requisite materials have been acquired, preserved, and made available by museums and archives. Not only does the Museum of Modern Art in New York City have extensive holdings related to early cinema, but its staff has long played a special nurturing role for me as for many others. Here I would like to thank Curator Eileen Bowser as well as Charles Silver, Jon Gartenberg, Mary Lea Bandy, Clive Phillpot, Janice Ekdahl, Peter Williamson, Ron Magliozzi, John Johnson, Nancy Barnes, and Jyette Jensen. In the course of my many visits to the Library of Congress to see films and scan microfilm, Paul Spehr, Patrick Sheehan, Pat Loughney, Kathy Loughney, Barbara Humphries, Madeleine Matz, and Emily Sieger often went out of their way to help. The staffs of the UCLA Film and Television Archive (particularly Robert Rosen and Robert Gitt), the British Film Institute (particularly David Francis, Roger Holman, and Elaine Burrows), and the George Eastman House (particularly John Kuiper, the late George Pratt, Jan-Christopher Horak, and Paolo Cherchi-Usai) all extended their hospitality in ways that aided my research. Responding to my pleas, Sam Gill and Anthony Slide at the Academy of Motion Picture Arts and Sciences gave me access to the Charles Clarke/William Selig Collection. Many individuals at these institutions share a deep commitment to early cinema and have facilitated serious work in this field. George Pratt, who shared his discoveries and taught me how to research local newspapers, deserves special mention. Likewise, Pat Loughney brought obscure holdings to my attention and then inconvenienced himself to take many photographs for this book.

Sustained historical work is made possible by a community of scholars. In my case, Domitor (the Society for Early Cinema), the Society for Cinema Studies, the Columbia University Seminar on Film and Interdisciplinary Interpretation, the Magic

Lantern Society of the United States and Canada, the Thomas A. Edison Papers at Rutgers University, the Film Division at Columbia University, and the Department of Cinema Studies at New York University have all provided an important sense of fellowship. Tom Gunning, Miriam Hansen, George Pratt, Alan Williams, John Mercer, William Welling, and Dan Greenberg served as thoughtful readers of this manuscript and helped me refine it. X. Theodore Barber, who is currently writing a dissertation on the magic lantern in America, kindly reviewed the opening chapter. Reese Jenkins reviewed chapter 2. Linda Kowall enhanced my understanding of Sigmund Lubin's activities, while Veyda Semarne reviewed relevant sections on the Lumière brothers. Robert Sklar and the late Jay Leyda directed my energies into profitable areas of inquiry and provided crucial advice and criticism as well. André Gaudreault, Janet Staiger, Noël Burch, Judith Mayne, Roberta Pearson, Robert C. Allen, Martin Sopocy, and David Levy have all shared ideas, criticisms, and information with me at key moments. Their work, as well as the contributions of others mentioned above, deserves more mention in these pages than I can give.

Related projects helped immensely. With Reese Jenkins and the Thomas A. Edison Papers staff, I gathered together early motion-picture catalogs to produce *Motion Picture Catalogs by American Producers and Distributors, 1894–1908: A Microfilm Edition* (1985), which was an invaluable resource. With support from Wilder Green and Sam McElfresh at the American Federation of the Arts, Jay Leyda and I curated the 1986 "Before Hollywood" show and catalog that made available many important films from this era. Carol Nelson involved me in a book and film project on traveling exhibitor Lyman H. Howe. My own work on Edwin S. Porter and the Edison Manufacturing Company provided a firm base from which to develop the wider scope of this project. An earlier, shorter version of chapter 1 appeared in the *Quarterly Review of Film Studies*.

Mention should be made here of two conventions observed in the present volume, though not in other parts of the series. First, the word "theater/theatre" is given throughout in the former spelling (except in direct quotations). Usage varied in the early period for both the trade and the press, but it has seemed best to simplify matters for the modern reader. Also, I have adopted the convention recommended by the Thomas A. Edison Papers of using uppercase letters for companies, such as Vitagraph and Biograph, but lowercase for the particular inventions they operated, such as the vitagraph and the biograph. This distinction is observed here even when (as in the preceding examples) the names were frequently, if inconsistently, capitalized during the period.

One boon to my research efforts has been living in the "golden triangle" formed by three research branches of the New York Public Library that I visited almost daily: the Library for the Performing Arts at Lincoln Center, the Annex at Forty-third Street and Tenth Avenue, and the Main Research Library at Forty-second Street. Mimi Bowling, Ed Pershey, and Faye Whitaker at the Edison National Historic Site and Florence Bartoshesky at the Baker Library of Harvard Business School have likewise been of great assistance. Paula Jescavge at New York University's Elmer Holmes Bobst Library arranged for the interlibrary loan of endless reels of microfilm. Personnel at the Federal Archive and Record Centers in Bayonne, Philadelphia, and Chicago helped give me important access to court records. Lynne Kirby, Richard Balzer, Charles Hummel, Françoise Levie, Marc Wanamaker, Carey Williams, and Joyce Jesionowski kindly provided illustrations. Among the many who extended themselves on behalf of this volume are Kathy Oberdeck, Germaine Lacasse, Hiroshi Komatsu, Willaim K. Everson, George Hall, Susan Kemplar, Raymond Fielding, Martin Sopocy, Herbert Reynolds, Cal Pryluck, H. Mark Gosser, Robert Haller, Elizabeth Gorla, and Alexis Krasilovsky. The students in my seminar at Yale University also provided a forum for me to develop and clarify some of the ideas that follow. John Fitzpatrick, Miriam Rosen, and Karen Day at Scribners were wonderfully patient, sensitive, and supportive as they proceeded with the publication of this book.

Above all, I extend heartfelt appreciation to the friends and colleagues who have tolerated my obsessions for so long. In these days of word processors, no one need be thanked for typing this manuscript except my Macintosh computer. Nevertheless, Lynne Zeavin had to live with this undertaking almost as much as I did (and with few of the compensations!). She has offered intriguing observations from her own field of psychology as well as the many pleasures of daily life. In this regard I am particularly fortunate.

CHARLES MUSSER, 1990

*

For the second and third printings, I have been able to make a few modest corrections and additions. In this regard, I would like to thank Paolo Cherchi-Usai, Robert Klepner, Richard M. Bueschel, and Tom Gunning for pointing out small inaccuracies.

In addition, work by X. Theodore Barber on the magic lantern and Gregory Waller on moviegoing and filmmaking in Lexington, Kentucky, has required me to add important information about prior lantern showings and filmmaking by William Selig. Barber's dissertation, "Evenings of Wonders: A History of the Magic Lantern Show in America," is essential reading for those wishing more information on this subject and will soon be published in book form. I also thank Scribners for its eagerness to incorporate these changes—an attitude that exemplifies the very best in American publishing

C.M., 1993

HISTORY OF THE AMERICAN CINEMA

Volume 1

TO 1907

Introduction

*T*his book, the first in a multivolume history of American film, looks at the initial twelve years of cinema, from 1895 to the fall of 1907. Here, *cinema* refers to projected motion pictures and their sound accompaniment, but two closely related developments must also be considered. First, there is the history of *screen practice*—projected images and their audio complement—which dates back to the seventeenth century and includes the magic lantern, a precursor of the modern slide projector. As the title of this book suggests, cinema was neither "born" nor a "new art form": it emerged out of, even as it soon dominated, screen practice. For this reason, the first chapter briefly traces the history of earlier projected images as they originated in Europe and subsequently developed within the United States. Second, this volume is concerned with the history of *motion pictures*, which includes not only cinema but forms of exhibition that did not involve projection. Of these exhibition formats, individualized or peephole viewing was the most important. The history of commercial motion pictures in fact began in 1894 with Edison's peephole kineto-scope, while the mutoscope, a peephole flip-card device, was an important presence during the late 1890s and early 1900s. The cinema, the screen, motion pictures—these involve distinct though overlapping practices.

Although the cinema was to become known affectionately as "the movies" or "the flicks," in the 1890s and early 1900s it was called "animated photographs," "moving pictures," and sometimes even "life-model motion pictures." Today, some turn-of-the-century terminology may seem foreign or quaint, while other expressions retain the seeming freshness of contemporary idiom. Correspondingly, as Judith Mayne has pointed out, turn-of-the-century images appear to combine similar qualities of strangeness and familiarity.[1] Whatever the case, these films and the corresponding practices do not readily open themselves to our understanding: they are frequently strange and familiar in unexpected ways. The methods of production and representation were so different from today's mainstream cinema that apparent parallels can readily deceive rather than illuminate. But, properly understood, the foreignness of the earlier period gives us a remarkable perspective on present-day moving images, whether those of Hollywood and its blockbusters, television and the evening news, or American independents and avant-garde explorations. The purpose of this study is not to revel in the seeming eccentricities of early cinema (the label historians often apply to this period and the one used here as well) but to make its methods under-standable within the context of its own norms and practices.

Any multivolume history must justify its periodization. While starting with the "beginnings" is logical enough, it remains to explain why this volume ends around September 1907. Here a combination of factors must be cited. The brief economic recession that started in October 1907 encouraged important changes in the organization of the industry, including the formation of various patent-based alliances that culminated in the Motion Picture Patents Company. Moreover, the modes of representation and production began to change in new and far-ranging ways late in 1907. Finally, although American cinema experienced many transformations between 1895 and 1907, there were also fundamental continuities that make it appropriate to see the period as a coherent one.

Elements of Stability in Early Cinema

Early cinema enjoyed a distinctive "mode of reception." The ways in which specta-tors understood and appreciated motion pictures regularly took one of three basic forms, none of which was privileged or preferred. First of all, the film's subject or narrative was often already known by the spectators. Especially with the aid of a brief cue (such as a main title) to identify the well-known story or event, viewers brought this special knowledge to bear on the film. When the Biograph Company showed filmed excerpts of Joseph Jefferson performing his famous stage role in *Rip Van Winkle*, for example, the audience's familiarity with the play was assumed. Early cinema thus evidenced a profound dependence on other cultural forms, including the theater, newspapers, popular songs, and fairy tales.

Alternatively, the spectator might rely on the exhibitor to clarify the film's narra-tive or meaning through a live narration and other sounds (music, effects, even dialogue added by actors from behind the screen). PARSIFAL (Edison, 1904) and William Selig's films of Armour & Company (the meat-packing concern) were in-tended to be presented with a lecture. The exhibitor's spiel usually did more than simply clarify, however: it conveyed the showman's own interpretation of these images or rendered them subordinate to his authorial vision.[2]

Finally, spectators might easily find themselves in a position where they had to understand the film story without recourse to either special knowledge or the ex-hibitors' aid. Here, the representational system sharply limited the filmmakers' abil-ity to present a self-sufficient narrative. Certain genres, such as Méliès' trick films, did not require the spectator to discern a coherent plot, since their narratives were not based on a logical progression of events. Some pictures—for example, chase films such as MEET ME AT THE FOUNTAIN (Lubin, 1904)—told simple stories that could be readily understood. Others, such as A KENTUCKY FEUD (Biograph, 1905), relied heavily on intertitles to explain the story line.

Since the mechanisms for audience comprehension were so diverse, one might wonder what they shared. Here, if only for a moment, early cinema is worth defining negatively: its representational system could *not* present a complex, unfamiliar nar-rative capable of being readily understood irrespective of exhibition circumstances or the spectators' specific cultural knowledge. In practice, a significant number of films left their viewers somewhat mystified and confused. Often, the key to following the narrative was not widely known or exhibitors failed to perform their job, but it was also not unusual for filmmakers to exceed the capacities of their representational system. This does not mean that cinema lacked an array of conventions that facilitated audience comprehension of projected images, for spectators were generally familiar with various strategies for conveying meaning (certain genres, certain gestures by actors or relations between shots). Rather, these conventions only operated effectively within strict limits.

The early cinema's system of representation became more elaborate over time but did not fundamentally change. Once again, it was not until 1907 that the system began to break down. This mode of representation was predominantly *presentational* in its acting style, set design, and visual composition as well as in its depiction of time, space, and narrative. Rooted in theatrical discourse, the concept of a presentational style was originally used to describe a method of acting that dominated the American and English stage during most of the nineteenth century. Actors not only played to the audience but used highly conventionalized gestures to convey forceful emotions. The style was frontal and relied on indication. Among many late-nineteenth-century practitioners of high theatrical art, the presentational style was superseded by one that emphasized greater verisimilitude and restraint. The older representational techniques continued, however, in diverse cultural forms, including not only such popular theatrical genres as melodrama and burlesque but the magic lantern, cartoon strips, and early cinema.

The presentationalism of early cinema is most obvious in the pro-filmic elements (the mise-en-scène) and the manner in which they were organized vis-à-vis the camera and the audience. Lacking words, actors often resorted to extensive pantomime to convey their thoughts or actions, pushing the use of conventionalized gestures to an extreme. Within scenes, time and space were likewise indicated rather than rendered in a verisimilar manner. In LOST IN THE ALPS (Edison, 1907), the time it takes for actions to occur offscreen (*i.e.*, "offstage") is radically condensed. The mother, looking for her children, leaves but quickly returns. Yet the audience knows that this search took much longer than was actually depicted. The passage of time is thus signaled and dealt with in terms that satisfied old-style theatrical conventions (in the naturalistic theater that was replacing this system, meanwhile, such indicating was much less acceptable).

The same type of indicating also characterized the production design for many of these films. Schematic sets eschewed all illusionism. For HOW THEY ROB MEN IN CHICAGO (Biograph, 1902), a simple flat identifies the type of location without actually trying to simulate it. The fact that the same backdrop was shot with the same frontal camera framings for many other Biograph films amply demonstrates its iconic nature. Elaborately painted theatrical drops were also commonly integrated into these films, but again, they only suggest depth and perspective. Their effect was quite different from that of full three-dimensional sets or real locations for exterior scenes. Studio sets were routinely used for exteriors as well as interiors, reflecting not only a theatrical tradition but a continuing practice of indication.

Early cinema's presentational approach was also, as Tom Gunning has pointed out, concerned with display, exhibitionism, and the offering of spectacular, realistic, or novel effects.[3] As in DR. DIPPY'S SANITARIUM (Biograph, 1906), set designs often sacrificed realistic perspectives for an opening up of the space and mise-en-scène. In a film such as GRANDPA'S READING GLASS (Biograph, 1902), objects are shown in close-up "as if" viewed through a magnifying glass. But this "as if" is based not on verisimilitude but on display, for the objects were photographed against plain backgrounds that removed them from the mise-en-scène, further isolating them for the spectator. This style often involved an acknowledgment of the camera and the spectator. The genre of facial-expression films, for example, usually entailed a single close-up of a performer confronting the camera. In FACIAL EXPRESSION BY LONEY HASKELL (Biograph, 1897), the performer grimaces into the camera and shares the humorous results with his audience. The viewer is a voyeur but not, as in later cinema, apparently effaced. The compositional dynamics of many chase films, such as the immensely popular PERSONAL (Biograph, 1904), in which pursuer and pursued run toward and past the camera, offer another form of this display.

Cinema's pervasive presentational style was not limited to fiction films with their recognizable theatrical antecedents or parallels. The train (EMPIRE STATE EXPRESS [Biograph, 1896]) or cavalry (CHARGE OF THE SEVENTH FRENCH CUIRASSIERS [Lumière, 1896]) rushing toward the camera and visually assaulting the spectator was equally characteristic. Since speeches, parades, and inaugurations were subjects that involved conscious uses of display and spectacle, this approach was readily applied to the making of actualities (*i.e.*, films of actual events). These events replicated and reinforced a tendency toward frontal compositions. Nonetheless, it was with actualities that the presentational style was most vulnerable. FEEDING THE BABY (Lumière, 1895) or HERALD SQUARE (Edison, 1896) captured the phenomenal world as it unfolded in resolutely real time. Camera movement, which became increasingly common after 1897 but was initially used only for actualities, further emphasized the existence of offscreen space and a real world beyond the edges of the frame. Here the cinema offered a verisimilar approach that was compatible with naturalistic theater.

What Georges Sadoul describes as the snapshot quality of these films[4] and their application to fiction filmmaking in the early 1900s might have undermined the strong presentational tendencies of early cinema much sooner except for the fact that the system of representation was resolutely syncretic in its combination and juxtaposition of different mimetic means. In many films, such as FRANCESCA DI RIMINI (Vitagraph, 1907), exteriors were taken both in specially constructed studio sets and on location. Even within many sets, some props and design elements were rendered with paint, while others were three-dimensional or real objects. In THE BOLD BANK ROBBERY (Lubin, 1904), a real lamp is used, but the light rays are painted on the wall. Filmmakers thus routinely shifted between different levels of representing reality. This syncreticism can be contrasted with later cinema's predominant emphasis on mimetic consistency. To be sure, artifice such as backdrops would continue to be used, but the goal was increasingly to meld the juncture of different mimetic means until they became seamless. Early cinema was predominantly syncretic, presentational, and nonlinear, while later classical Hollywood cinema favored consistency, verisimilitude, and a linear narrative structure, particularly in its dramas and light comedies.

The presentational approach was also apparent in the way narratives were depicted. Many narratives were highly conventionalized and operated within genres far narrower than those found in later cinema. The bad-boy and fire-rescue genres are only two examples.[5] The spectator knows that the bad boys will engage in a series of humorous, mischievous acts; only the specific form of their mischief is in doubt. In other instances, as Noël Burch points out, stories were not told "as if for the first time" insofar as they were assumed to be a part of the viewers' previous knowledge.[6] Since the films did not usually create or convey a complex original story in themselves, the producers' energies could be directed elsewhere. The filmmakers assembled spectacular images that evoked the story rather than telling the story in and of itself; indeed, images jumped from high point to high point with crucial causal connections left unarticulated. This was also true for magic-lantern images, while a similar presentationalism was enjoying its greatest success in the theater. The repertoire of plays, Janet Staiger indicates, was limited and well known to the audience: "Sets, props and costume were conventional and spare; the drama was less the plot and more the actor and the individual interpretation of the plot."[7]

With melodrama continuing the presentational approach on the turn-of-the-century stage, it is not surprising that cinema quickly appropriated many of its characteristics. As Roberta Pearson reports, character motivation was notably absent in both melodrama and early film.[8] In both cases, characters "do not carry the full weight of real life" and "are devoid of any individuality."[9] In THE PAYMASTER (Biograph, 1906), the factory manager embodies evil as he tests the good paymaster and the mill girl. Moreover, chance rather than a realistic or "organic" development of events propels the plot, which is therefore subject to dramatic, striking reversals: a chance discovery of the stolen money exposes the factory manager's scheme at the crucial moment. Film companies also adopted the common melodramatic technique of double titles, as with Vitagraph's ADVENTURES OF SHERLOCK HOLMES; OR, HELD FOR A RANSOM (1905) or Selig's TRACKED BY BLOODHOUNDS; OR, A LYNCHING AT CRIPPLE CREEK (1904). Both play and film titles played a key naming function, and the titles of play acts and film scenes within the respective productions also had a common orienting or identifying role.[10]

One of the pre-1907 cinema's most distinctive features was its nonlinear temporality in the arrangement of scenes. The relationship between the outgoing and incoming shots could take several forms. As seen in the seminal LIFE OF AN AMERICAN FIREMAN (Edison, 1902–1903), filmmakers often relied on temporal repetitions, returning to earlier points in time to pick up their story. The same actions or event could thus be shown from multiple viewpoints, as in THE LAUNCHING OF THE U.S.S. BATTLESHIP "CONNECTICUT" (Biograph, 1904), wherein the launching was shown three times, each time for a different camera position. In other instances, different lines of action that occurred simultaneously were shown successively; in THE KLEPTOMANIAC (Edison, 1905), for example, the concurrent lives of two women are presented one after the other, rather than shifting back and forth between the two.

By 1908–1909, temporal repetition, early cinema's solution to the problem of simultaneity, was superseded by a linear progression and parallel editing. Linear continuities with matching action across the cuts did appear, however, in a few early films, such as THE ESCAPED LUNATIC (Biograph, 1903), which contains a cut to a different camera position just as the lunatic throws a guard off the bridge. Yet employment of this type of continuity was exceptional, and spectators could not assume that a film story would unfold in simple chronological order. This nonlinear organization of shots was consistent with the general framework of reception discussed above. While repeated actions or narrative cues sometimes provided sufficient information for the spectator to follow the flow of events and relationships between shots, in other cases, help had to come from external sources—either the exhibitor or the spectator's previous knowledge of the story.

In contrast to this temporality, the spatial relations constructed through editing are much more familiar to the modern viewer. Exterior/interior relations, the establishing shot and closer view, even the point-of-view shot, all appear with some frequency in early cinema. Indeed, all had well-established antecedents in screen history. Although extensive creation of a spatial world through successive close-ups within a scene, shot/counter-shots, and cuts on the glance was part of a later repertoire of cinematic techniques, none of the spatial constructions that appeared in early films were later excluded by Hollywood. Rather, pre-1907 methods of constructing a spatial world through editing became more frequent, subtle, and suggestive of mood in later years.

Although many aspects of film production changed between 1895 and 1907, the organization of work within the small studios remained relatively constant. Here again, early filmmaking activities were organized in many different ways. The most characteristic method of production, however—which might be called the collaborative system—usually involved two men, the stage manager and cameraman, who worked together in an informal and nonhierarchical manner. Throughout this period, America's film companies were often started or at least staffed with collaborative teams. J. Stuart Blackton and Albert E. Smith of Vitagraph, Edwin S. Porter and George Fleming at Edison, William Paley and William Steiner of Paley & Steiner, and Wallace McCutcheon and Frank Marion of Biograph are only some examples. Such collaborative methods of work were also evident in the invention of cinema's "basic apparatus"—the camera and projector.

Within this system, and unlike the dominant post-1907 production methods that organized staff along more hierarchical lines of authority and accountability, early filmmaking involved little specialization. The originator(s) of a story would often direct the actors, appear in the films, operate the camera, develop the exposed raw stock, cut the negative, and—if necessary—run the projector. This knowledge of all aspects of the craft was what distinguished these pre-1907 filmmakers from their more specialized successors.[11]

Finally, it must be recalled that film production occurred within a white, virtually all-male world. Even female roles were often played by men—either professional female impersonators like Gilbert Saroni in THE OLD MAID HAVING HER PICTURE TAKEN (Edison, 1901) or employees like the bookkeeper who played "the wife's choice" in THE SERVANT GIRL PROBLEM (Vitagraph, 1905). The selection of narrative elements and the application of presentational techniques consistently enhanced the element of male voyeurism. The display of normally concealed female anatomy was common, particularly in Biograph productions. Many short comedies were made by men, for men, and revealed a number of the preoccupations and assumptions of this "homosocial" world that was just beginning to break down.[12]

Changing Methods of Production and Representation

Despite many stable elements, the cinema underwent a staggering array of fundamental changes between 1895 and 1907. During the first months of widespread projection, short (one-shot) films were enjoyed primarily for their ability to reproduce lifelike motion and exploit isolated presentational elements. While such comparatively non-narrative uses of film continued and developed in what Tom Gunning has called "the cinema of attractions," many exhibitors began to organize these short films into multishot narratives. Although arranging these scenes was the chief responsibility of exhibitors during the 1890s, production companies had largely assumed control over this process (i.e., editing) by 1903–1904. The era of storefront motion-picture theaters or "nickelodeons," which began in 1905–1906, involved a new organization of exhibition that had profound effects on all other aspects of film practice.

Change creates new necessities, new opportunities, and new practices even as it eliminates old ones. In many respects, the introduction of a single fundamental change—the adaptation of Edison's moving pictures to projection—precipitated a series of shifts and transformations within the field of screen entertainment that could be likened to a row of falling dominos. While nothing inherent in the medium necessitated this rapid succession of innovations, the economic and cultural dynamics of American society in general and screen practice in particular pressured the film industry to change along the general lines that it did. Perhaps a somewhat different kind of development would have taken place if William Kennedy Laurie Dickson had remained with Thomas Edison or if a patents company had been established in the 1890s. Yet even here the differences would have been limited. Motion-picture practices did not evolve as they did because of the extraordinary genius of a few individuals but because significant numbers of people recognized new commercial and artistic opportunities implicit in previous change and so, in turn, further altered the practice of cinema.

In seeking to explain the underlying dynamics of a rapidly changing film practice and to provide an account of the American screen before 1907, this volume does not dwell on the theoretical and methodological framework.[13] In some respects it remains rather "old-fashioned" in that it is very concerned with who did what, where, and when. The reasons why something was done and its significance or relation to the larger industry are carefully investigated. Nonetheless, this narrative treatment functions within a carefully worked-out historical model. A central aspect of this model explores the interaction between cinema's mode of production (how the cinema is made) and the mode of representation (how a story is told or a subject represented). The gradual shift in editorial responsibility from exhibitor to producer in the early 1900s, for example, allowed for new ways of articulating a narrative. As filmmakers explored the new representational possibilities resulting from this shift, the commercial success of these innovative pictures provided further impetus for centralizing the control of editing inside the production companies.

In examining the cinema's production methods, we must begin by looking at how films were made, shown, and appreciated: in other words, by looking at the production companies, the exhibitors, and the spectators. Although the spectators' relationship to the screen experience remained relatively constant through 1907, the interactions between image production and exhibition underwent multiple transformations. Each shift involved complex adjustments between the two areas. It is not coincidental that most of the leading filmmakers from the early 1900s had previous experience in exhibition: Edwin S. Porter, James White, J. Stuart Blackton, Wallace McCutcheon, and William Paley—to name only a few. Since distribution is at the interface of film production and exhibition, it is hardly surprising that it too underwent substantial changes. Although the industry had autonomous sales agents and a few exchanges from the outset, many distribution functions were performed by either producers (who commonly sold their films directly to "the trade") or exhibitors (who rented films to theaters as one part of their service package). Only after key postproduction responsibilities were assumed by the film producers did the development of the rental system become possible and specialized distribution companies or "exchanges" emerge as important factors in the field.

The Industry

To address such dramatic changes, it is expedient to organize this volume chronologically. Chapters deal with the activities of the industry's principal production and exhibition companies during relatively short periods of time—a few months to a few years. While several important businesses blossomed only briefly as the film industry began, greater continuity is evident by the late 1890s. Since change was instituted on a company-by-company basis, commercial enterprises rather than individuals usually provide the most appropriate unit of inquiry and organization. The collaborative method of work, the eventual recognition of the production company as the author of a screen narrative, and the fact that the individuals responsible for many films were rarely publicized and even now frequently remain unknown: all these factors justify such an organizing principle.

The ten corporations that formed the Motion Picture Patents Company (discussed in the next volume) were all active by mid 1907. The two that became preeminent in this organization also played crucial roles throughout the earlier period. The Edison Manufacturing Company introduced commercial, modern motion pictures to the world. Its owner, Thomas A. Edison, achieved immense influence through both his company's activities and his use of patent litigation as a commercial weapon. The American Mutoscope & Biograph Company (originally named the American Mutoscope Company, and often referred to as the Biograph Company after its biograph projector) was the most commercially successful American film enterprise during the late 1890s and again in 1904–1905. A large and well-financed corporation, it mounted an effective challenge to Edison's patent claims and was perhaps the only entity in the United States that could have done so. The multifaceted rivalry between the two organizations colored the entire industry.

Although substantial information from this period—paper documentation as well as a large number of films—survives for both companies, much more has been written about the Edison enterprise. Interest has focused on the invention of motion pictures at the Edison laboratory and its early commercial history. Additional work has been done on Edwin S. Porter, the earliest American filmmaker to enjoy a significant reputation, who was an Edison employee from late 1900 to 1909.[14] Although Biograph has been understandably associated with the D. W. Griffith years (1908–1913), the company's role in the earlier period was crucial.[15] This volume seeks to redress that imbalance with a careful examination of Biograph's activities.

Other Patents Company members played significant but ultimately less central roles in the pre-1907 period. Sigmund Lubin, who did business under his own name, and William Selig, who formed the Selig Polyscope Company, as well as American Vitagraph, which was owned by J. Stuart Blackton, Albert E. Smith, and William T. Rock, were all involved in both production and exhibition by 1898. Here again, more has been written about Vitagraph than about either Lubin or Selig, and so this volume makes a particular effort to trace the activities of the latter two.[16] The Kleine Optical Company, run by George Kleine, entered the motion-picture field in 1896 and served as a leading sales agent for domestic and foreign producers throughout the period covered by this study.

Only two production companies allied with the Motion Picture Patents Company were not active by the 1890s. These late additions, however, were headed by men who had owned and/or managed important film businesses before the turn of the century and finally entered the production field in early 1907. The Kalem Company was owned by George Kleine and two former Biograph employees, Frank Marion and Samuel Long. The Essanay Film Manufacturing Company was formed by George Spoor, who ran a leading exhibition service, and Gilbert M. Anderson, an actor and director who had previously worked for four other American producers. These companies thus represented a consolidation of earlier achievements even though they did not enjoy prominence until the period covered by the next volume in this series, *The Transformation of Cinema*. The Patents Company also had two foreign members whose films already enjoyed wide popularity in the United States during the 1890s and early 1900s: Georges Méliès and Pathé Frères. To better exploit this popularity, both firms established sales offices in New York City during 1903–1904 and played influential roles in the American industry. Carefully examined, the activities of these recurring figures through 1907 offer fundamental insights into the rapidly changing industry.

These leading businesses did not, of course, begin to constitute the entire industry. Numerous individuals enjoyed noteworthy if more modest careers within the time frame considered here. Among those acquiring some production experience were William Paley, the Miles brothers, Burton Holmes, and Lyman H. Howe. Many other enterprises were influential but short-lived. This is particularly true of cinema's first two or three years, when the Lambda Company, Eidoloscope Company, Vitascope Company, Lumière Agency, and International Film Company played influential roles. Figures such as William Fox, Carl Laemmle, and the Warner brothers entered the field at the beginning of the nickelodeon era, but they were to achieve their greatest success in subsequent years. Many minor figures whose careers are interesting and illuminating cannot be considered—at least not systematically—within the limited framework of this study.

Exhibition poses a particular problem for the historian. No records survive for many, perhaps most, of the screenings that occurred in this early era. Tracing and assessing them is extremely difficult, and conclusions must be couched in tentative terms. Nonetheless, the research done for this volume suggests that motion pictures were a much more important part of American life during their first ten years than has been widely recognized. Moreover, the types of exhibition sites were more diverse than usually acknowledged, at least by those focusing on vaudeville exhibition. Films were often shown between acts of plays, in black tents at carnivals, as complete evenings of entertainment in the local church or opera house, as part of an illustrated lecture, and in storefront theaters. This study seeks to outline the scope of these diverse exhibition sites and practices, which were often subject to financial instability and frequent shifts in their relative importance.

As will be seen, there was considerable regional variation in exhibition. Since vaudeville was never popular in the South, people in that area usually had to rely on carnivals and a few traveling exhibitors to see films before the nickelodeon era. In

contrast, small-time vaudeville was so popular in the Pacific Northwest that it im-
peded the introduction of the more specialized motion-picture theaters. This volume, however, highlights those locales that best help to explain the overall
development of the industry. Activities occurring in a relatively few large cities along
the East Coast and in the Midwest influenced the course of film practice much more
than activities outside of these centers. While much still needs to be learned and said
about exhibition in many areas of the United States, such an undertaking is beyond
the scope of this study.

Grappling with the diversity of exhibition is mild, however, compared to questions
about spectatorship. The specialized motion-picture spectator, the regular filmgoer,
was developing only at the end of this period. Moreover, there were no professional
moviegoers—*i.e.*, film reviewers—whose biases and attitudes we might trace as
cinema developed. Occasionally, cultural reporters or theatrical reviewers would
comment on the films or note a strong reaction by fellow spectators (a scream or
offhand remark by someone in a neighboring seat). More often, the likely response
or interpretation of an image can only be established circumstantially. An image
implies or constructs one or more hypothetical spectators, but these imaginary spectators were often contradicted by real ones. Films directed at male spectators were
also watched by women, whose presence often challenged and reinterpreted the
all-male discourse. Bad-boy films were directed at adult, middle-class males who
were expected to recall the carefree days of childhood. Yet, when shown to children
and working-class immigrants, they became potentially subversive.

Spectators must almost inevitably be treated in groups, their presence inferred
from the exhibition site, ticket price, and other indirect evidence. Here the purpose
is not only to explore the way spectators understood the films but to break down the
assumption that cinema appealed almost exclusively to lovers of commercial popular
culture and was ignored or opposed by other groups. In fact, the situation was far
more complex, for motion pictures were also enjoyed by members of conservative
religious groups and proponents of genteel culture; it was the rise of the story film
and the nickelodeon that turned the cinema into a form overwhelmingly oriented
toward amusement.

In the various relationships between the films and the key groups that make up
film practice (spectators, exhibitors, and film producers), cinema's social and ideological role becomes apparent. Here a double movement can be defined. First, as
this study shows, the ideological viewpoints of society in general, various socioeconomic groups more specifically, and the filmmakers in particular were articulated in
the films themselves. Although these films generally expressed middle-class beliefs,
the American middle class was then extremely heterogeneous. Thus the critical, yet
often defensive, "old middle class" perspective of many Porter–Edison films can be
contrasted with the exuberant, urban "new middle class" viewpoint found in many
Biograph and Vitagraph subjects. Lubin films generally articulated a distinctive if
sometimes eccentric laissez-faire anarchism that was undoubtedly shaped by the
Jewish producer's experiences as part of an ethnic minority in the United States. This
ideological vantage differs again from the cinema of reassurance practiced by Lyman
Howe or the elitist social, cultural, and economic assumptions of Burton Holmes.

Motion pictures also helped to reshape the culture and society that produced
them. Responses are often difficult to gauge, particularly because the system of
representation and the subsequent forms of presentation allowed spectators diverse

and particularly active roles in constructing a film's meaning. Yet the cinema's impact on American life cannot be attributed merely to the films. As Robert Sklar has pointed out, the moviegoing experience itself fostered new modes of behavior, leisure, desire and consciousness.[17] By the end of this period, cultural observers were beginning to recognize that the cinema was threatening if not transforming many of American society's most cherished and long-standing values.

Because there has been no previous book-length overview of American early cinema, many central developments and countless facts either are not well established or are coming to light now for the first time. Extensive new research has often revised previous assessments, thus requiring careful documentation of sources. These materials are diverse and clearly not all are equally reliable. Historian Terry Ramsaye, who had access to people and documents no longer in existence, thrived on lively tales that have sometimes proved fanciful. Yet, he often recounts momentous events that are reconcilable with the known facts even though they cannot be absolutely verified. Such sources should not be ignored, but they must be used cautiously, for as Robert C. Allen suggests, many assertions about the cinema have been passed from one historian to another without ever being verified or challenged.[18] Whenever possible, this study has sought to rely on primary source material.

To avoid excessive or unnecessary footnoting, certain rules have been applied. Primary source references are grouped by paragraph where possible. Information about exhibitions in individual cities or at particular theaters was generally established by systematic searches of local newspapers (usually the theater page of Sunday editions). These papers are listed in the bibliography and are cited only if a quotation or elusive piece of information is being provided. Titles of newspaper articles have been retained only where they serve a descriptive function. When documenting the activities of the Edison Manufacturing Company, Lyman Howe and his traveling exhibition companies, or American Vitagraph before 1901, few footnotes are used. Appropriate citations as well as more information on these subjects may be found in my two other books and one lengthy article.[19] The present volume builds on these works, seeking to complement their more focused perspectives with a broader overview. The still-numerous citations will enable interested readers to verify facts and interpretations and will open up primary sources for future research. It is hoped that this book will provide a starting point for future historians as well as a useful resource for those seeking a general understanding of American cinema before 1907.

PART 1

Before Cinema

A hand-painted lantern slide in which the character confronts the audience. A presentational approach is evident in these nonphotographic images.

1

Toward a History of Screen Practice

Starting points always present problems for the historian, perhaps because they imply a "before" as well as an "after." For the film historian, "the invention of cinema" is customarily viewed as the creation of a new form of expression, a new art form. Such a perspective presupposes not only cinema proper but "pre-cinema," an area of historical inquiry that raises significant methodological and ideological issues. This chapter (and the entire volume) questions the value of that starting point and the historical models it supports. Nonetheless, it does not seek to forsake starting points entirely nor, as Jean-Louis Comolli has done, to offer the possibility of so many starting points that the notion of a beginning is not only diffused but ultimately avoided.[1] Rather, it suggests an alternative perspective, one that places cinema within a larger context of what we shall call the history of *screen practice*.

In such a history, cinema appears as a continuation and transformation of magic-lantern traditions in which showmen displayed images on a screen, accompanying them with voice, music, and sound effects. In fact, this historical conception of cinema was frequently articulated between 1895 and 1908. The *Optical Magic Lantern Journal* of November 1896, for example, observed that "The greatest boom the lantern world has ever seen is that which is still reverberating throughout the land— the boom of the living photographs." In *Animated Pictures* (1898), C. Francis Jenkins wrote:

> It has frequently been suggested that the introduction of chronophotographic apparatus sounded the death knell of the stereopticon, but with this opinion I do not agree. The fact is, the moving picture machine is simply a modified stereopticon or lantern, i.e. a lantern equipped with a mechanical slide changer. All stereopticons will, sooner or later, as are several machines now, be arranged to project stationary pictures or pictures giving the appearance of objects in motion.

These observations were echoed by Henry V. Hopwood in *Living Pictures* (1899): "A film for projecting a living picture is nothing more, after all, than a multiple lantern slide."[2] In essence, these writers were emphasizing continuities where recent film histories have tended to see difference. It is this sense of continuity that must be reasserted if we are to understand transformation as a dialectical process.

The origins of screen practice—as distinct from either earlier uses of projected images or the later introduction of cameras—can be traced back to the mid 1600s and the demystification of those magical arts in which observers confused the "lifelike" image with life itself. The much later invention of motion-picture projection was only one of several major technological innovations that transformed screen practice in the course of its history—the development of the magic lantern during the 1650s, the adaptation of photography to projection around 1850, and the synchronization of film with recorded sound, which achieved permanent commercial standing in the late 1920s.

In contrast to this historical model, most histories of cinema and pre-cinema apply three different levels of inquiry to what are seen as discrete and successive historical phases (often but not always by making use of a biological metaphor). First, there is the history of invention, which is associated with pre-cinema. As presented by Jacques Deslandes and Kenneth Macgowan, the historical paradigm is formulated in terms of, and based on, court cases disputing patent rights, where lawyers argued the fine points of technological priority for their industrialist clients.[3] This phase culmi-   . nates with the invention of the "basic apparatus," the camera/projector that made cinema possible. With the advent of cinema, the focus then shifts to a history of technique, the development of basic procedures such as the interpolated close-up and parallel editing (many of which were part of the screen repertoire before cinema came into existence). Only in the third stage do these historians focus their attention on film as art, as culturally significant work.

The three-stage historical treatment implies a kind of technological determinism in which film language is a product of technology and film art exists within the framework of that language. The model presented here, in contrast, argues that screen practice has always had a technological component, a repertoire of representational strategies, and a social-cultural function, all of which undergo constant, interrelated change. This model refines a second historical approach that explores film's debt to other forms of cultural expression and sees the motion picture as a new medium/technology in need of a content and an aesthetic. In early, methodologically crude studies such as Robert Grau's *The Theatre of Science* and Nicholas Vardac's *Stage to Screen*, cinema is treated as a void that adopted the essentials of a theatrical tradition and then pushed them to new extremes in the "photoplay." John Fell and Erwin Panofsky have argued that film borrowed freely from many different forms of popular culture, including comic strips, dime novels, popular songs, the magic lantern, and theater. More recently, Robert Allen's work has foregrounded the connections between film and vaudeville. Thus, in the nature (technology) vs. nurture (cultural context) debate, these authors have emphasized the cultural determinants.[4]

The continuities of screen practice offer an alternative to tabula rasa assumptions of a new "medium." At the same time, moments of profound transformation (such as the adaptation of photographic slides or Edison's moving pictures to the screen) allow for new possibilities, for an influx of new personnel, and for disruption and considerable discontinuity. When the screen enters a period of flux, it is particularly receptive to new influences from other cultural forms; it is at such moments that its cultural interconnectedness becomes most apparent and perhaps important. During periods of comparative stability, the screen continues to function in relation to other cultural forms, but because the nature of these connections does not change so drastically, they appear less obvious or are taken as givens. A history of the screen can offer a more fruitful model for analyzing those cultural borrowings that Fell and others rightly see as crucial. Such influences, however, existed before there was cinema. Cinema did not emerge out of the chaos of various borrowings to find its true or logical self: it is part of a much longer, dynamic tradition, one that has undergone repeated transformations in its practice while becoming increasingly central within a changing cultural system.

A history of the screen also helps to define the subject of "pre-cinema." In the past, the boundaries of pre-cinema were limited by preoccupations with technology and invention, and an obvious teleology. Once this framework is demolished pre-cinema loses its specificity; anything that the historian might subsequently consider relevant to our understanding of cinema as a cultural, economic, or social practice becomes a fitting subject of inquiry. Thus, a work such as Michael Chanan's *The Dream That Kicks* explores the pre-cinema development of photography, music halls, consumption, patent law, and cultural institutionalization.[5] While shedding light on the world in which motion pictures "appeared," the book often functions simply as a cultural history of nineteenth-century England. Certainly such history is fascinating and important. Certainly context is crucial. But what is being contextualized? Something that does not yet exist. Simply put, it is a history of screen practice that provides the context with an appropriate object and so gives the field a necessary focus and framework for historical inquiry.

A history of the screen is not new in itself. Historians such as Olive Cook have argued the case of Hopwood and the *Optical Magic Lantern Journal*—that cinema is an extension of the magic lantern.[6] Unfortunately, they do so by arguing that the invention of the magic lantern is the crucial technological innovation and so the appropriate starting point. Such a starting point is no different from the invention of cinema chosen by most film historians: both begin with a technology, not with a cultural practice; both see the technology as determining practice, not as a component part of this practice. Here the work of Athanasius Kircher (1601–1680), a German-born Jesuit priest and scientist, proves to be crucial. A proper reading of his texts makes it clear that the practical use of screen technology was more important than the technology itself. Furthermore, it was this practice that provided a framework in which technological innovation became possible.

Kircher and the Demystification of the Projected Image

While recent research has clearly shown that Kircher did not invent the magic lantern, his *Ars magna lucis et umbrae* still occupies a privileged place at the start of the screen's history.[7] In the first edition of *Ars magna* (1646), Kircher described a "catoptric lamp" he used to "project" ("reflect" might be the more accurate word) images onto a wall in a darkened room. While this lamp was an improvement over earlier devices of a similar nature, Kircher's improvements were less important than his militant stance toward the demystification of the projected image. He laid out the apparatus for all to see (at least all who had access to his book), not only through description but by illustration. He also urged practitioners (exhibitors) to explain the actual process to audiences so that these spectators would clearly understand that the show was a catoptric art (involving reflection and optics), not a magical one. Kircher's

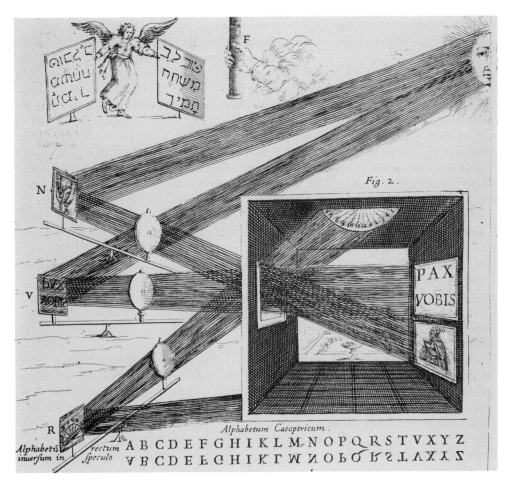

Kircher's room for projected images (1646).

argument suggests a decisive starting point for screen practice: when the observer of projected/reflected images became the historically constituted subject we now call the spectator. The history of the pre-screen is therefore concerned with the period before this demystification took place, the period when projecting apparatus were used to manipulate the unsuspecting spectator with mysterious, magical images.

Kircher actually offers a historical section in *Ars magna* that is a history of the pre-screen thus defined. When such an instrument was used in the time of King Solomon, he points out, the rabbis thought it was magic. And, he adds, "We've read of this art in many histories in which the common multitudes look on this catoptric art to be the workings of the devil." Again and again he warns his readers that in the past these techniques produced "such wonderful spectacle that even those considered philosophers were not infrequently brought under suspicion of being magicians" (pp. 792–794). Since someone practicing the devil's art might suffer torture and a slow death, such accusations were not to be taken lightly.

Kircher's text indicates that the revelation of the technical base of projection to the audience was a necessary condition of screen entertainment. The instrument of projection had to be made manifest within the mode of production itself, so that projected images did not appear as magic but as "art." Images were subsequently described as "lifelike," not as life itself. This demystification, however, cannot be assumed. Into the nineteenth century, mediums used projected images, concealed their source, and claimed these images were apparitions. Indeed, the potential for deception remained an underlying concern of early cinema, which enjoyed an even greater level of technical illusionism. R. W. Paul's THE COUNTRYMAN'S FIRST SIGHT OF THE ANIMATED PICTURES (1901) and Edwin Porter's UNCLE JOSH AT THE MOVING-PICTURE SHOW (1902) spoof the country rube who lacks the cultural framework needed to distinguish an image from real life.

The genesis of the screen coincided with a profound transformation in Western culture, particularly in Holland (where magic-lantern inventor Christiaen Huygens was working), and in England. As Christopher Hill argues, the English Revolution of the 1640s marked the end of the Middle Ages in key areas of English social, economic, and cultural life. The resulting political and social structure was much more open to—and even encouraged—capitalist production. Accompanying this development was an intellectual revolution that moved from proof by authority toward rationalism.[8] While the emergence of the screen as a form of entertainment resulted from social and cultural changes often referred to as the seventeenth-century Scientific Revolution, it was not merely rapid progress in science and technology that made this emergence possible. As belief in ghosts declined, as witch burnings ceased, the apparent logic and effectiveness of projecting apparatus as instruments of mystical terror also diminished.

The demystification of the screen established a relationship between producer, image, and audience that has remained fundamentally unaltered ever since. Kircher's own description of his primitive (yet amazingly elaborate!) catoptric lamp suggests ways in which continuities of screen practice can be traced to the present day, even though the means and methods of production have been radically altered. The illustration accompanying Kircher's text shows how images were "projected" into a darkened room. Words or other images were etched or painted upside-down and backward onto a mirror. A lenticular glass or lens was placed between the mirror and the wall on which the image was to be thrown. The sun usually provided the necessary illumination, although Kircher claimed that artificial light could be used if necessary. It was possible to use several catoptric lamps at the same time, so that both writing and images appeared on the wall independently yet simultaneously. The images were colored with transparent paints (to "increase the audience's astonishment"). Theaterlike scenes incorporating movement also could be made. Kircher suggested:

> Out of natural paper make effigies or images of things that you want to exhibit according to their shape, commonly their profile, so that by the use of hidden threads you can make their arms and legs go up and down and apart in whatever way you wish. With these shapes fastened on the surface of the mirror it will work as before, projecting the reflected light along with the shadow of the image in a dark place (*Ars magna*, p. 794).

Kircher offered other ways to present moving images: "If you wish to show live flies, smear honey on the mirror and behold how the flies will be projected on the wall through the surface of the mirror with extraordinary size." Finally, objects could be moved using a magnet behind the mirror. Already Kircher emphasized the combination of words and images, the use of color and movement, the possibility of narrative, and the special relationship between theater and the screen that has continued to this day. While the manner in which these fundamental elements were used, as well as the technology that produced them, has changed radically over the intervening three hundred years, their existence within the repertoire of screen entertainment has not.

The Magic Lantern

The inaccuracies generally found in film histories that discuss the magic lantern's origins should come to an end as information presented in H. Mark Gosser's thoroughly researched article on the subject is taken into account.[9] By 1659 the Dutch scientist Christiaen Huygens had developed a simple *lanterne magique*. His key innovation substituted images painted on glass for those etched on mirrors. Instead of reflecting sunlight off the image surface, he used an artificial light source to shine directly through the glass. Although Huygens sketched some skeletons as possible images for projection, he did not exploit the magic lantern for its commercial possibilities. This was first done by Thomas Walgensten, a Danish teacher and lens grinder who lived in Paris during the 1660s. There, he developed his own magic lantern and, by 1664, gave exhibitions. Walgensten subsequently traveled through Europe presenting lantern shows to royalty in Lyons (1665), Rome (mid to late 1660s), and Copenhagen (1670).

In the second edition of *Ars magna* (1671), Kircher described Walgensten's "magic or thaumaturgic lantern" and attempted to illustrate it. He maintained that his own catoptric lamp was the equal of Walgensten's magic lantern: it could "display in lifelike colors all that they are accustomed to show with [Walgensten's] mobile lamp" and "show the same images even when there is no sunlight through a concave mirror" (pp. 768–770). He further insisted that his own shows were actually preferred by audiences. The main difference between the two was "only" the technology.

In discussing this new magic-lantern technology in the second edition of *Ars magna*, Kircher was much less concerned with the demystification of projected images than with issues of narrative. Referring to his own use of the catoptric lamp, he wrote, "At our college we are accustomed to exhibiting new pictures to the greatest wonder of the audience. Indeed, it is most worthwhile seeing, for with its aid whole satiric scenes, theatrical tragedies, and the like can be shown in a lifelike way." The magic lantern, however, performed these same tasks more efficiently: it became much easier for the exhibitor to present a succession of images that could be used for storytelling purposes. With the magic lantern, a long glass slide containing eight discrete scenes could be passed between the light source and the lens, one image at a time, as in the *Ars magna* illustration. The enlarged images appeared on the screen: "Whence it is obvious," according to Kircher, "that if you have four or five such parallelograms, each of which repeats different images, you can display whatever you wish in a dark room" (pp. 768–770).

Telling a story with a series of images had many precedents, including illustrated books and wall paintings, and these provided suitable models for early screen practitioners. Even in these early stages, the screen was used to present two quite different

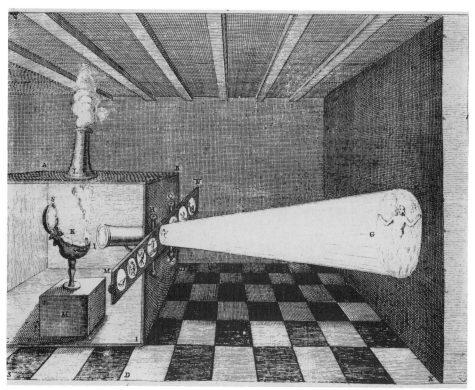

Walgensten's magic, or thaumaturgic, lantern as illustrated in Kircher's Ars magna *(1671). Note that the lens is shown incorrectly, behind the glass slides rather than in front, and that the images are not properly inverted.*

types of material. If Kircher enjoyed presenting satirical scenes and theatrical tragedies, his fellow Jesuit Andreas Tacquet used a catoptric lamp to give an illustrated lecture about a missionary's trip to China.[10] Fictional narratives and documentary programs were part of the screen's repertoire from the outset.

Although Kircher has been faulted for not emphasizing the differences between the magic lantern and his own catoptric lamp, he may not have fully realized the implications of this new technology. He probably lacked the firsthand experience with the magic lantern which might have convinced him that the Huygens and Walgensten apparatus were much more flexible, efficient, and inexpensive than his own.[11] The magic lantern liberated screen practitioners from the elaborate setups and specialized rooms of Kircher's college or other select sites. At the same time, certain effects that Kircher achieved with his catoptric lamp were no longer possible with Walgensten's magic lantern (the magnet technique, the use of live flies). Like later technological improvements, this one created new possibilities but also eliminated old ones.

The second edition of Kircher's *Ars magna* offered not only an explanation of the magic lantern but new descriptions of other optical devices, notably a peephole viewer he called the "Magia Catoptrica," with which a spectator could see "the same things projected by the lantern." Eight scenes were painted on a circle of glass that the spectator revolved so as to bring a succession of images to the eyepiece, which

Kircher's magia catoptrica, *a peephole device for looking at images.*

made the images seem larger. "I usually show the Lord's passion in this way, as figure KL shows," remarked Kircher. "This method can also be used to show any story painted in the sections of the glass" (p. 771). The two instruments shared many elements—including subject matter—but had distinctive qualities as well. One encouraged collective viewing, the other private spectatorship and voyeuristic satisfaction. These two ways of seeing images were to produce closely related, overlapping practices that paralleled each other throughout the period covered by this volume.

The magic lantern provided a technological leap that made possible the new era of traveling exhibitions heralded by Walgensten. According to Kircher, Walgensten not only traveled with his lantern but sold a number of similar devices to Italian princes. After the initial period of novelty, however, the magic lantern passed from the hands of royalty into those of common showmen. These exhibitors were soon touring Europe, presenting their entertainments at fairs—a pattern of exhibition that continued into the twentieth century.[12]

An emerging capitalism had little apparent use for the magic lantern during the first hundred years after its invention. Olive Cook's research suggests that many eighteenth-century lantern shows presented versions of miracle plays that were many centuries old. This budding form kept alive a folk culture that was marginalized by those very changes within society that, paradoxically, had made possible screen entertainments. X. Theodore Barber has shown that "Magick Lanthorn" exhibitions were given periodically in Philadelphia, New York City, and Boston from the 1740s onward, usually in homes, coffeehouses, or commerical establishments.[13] When John Brickell gave his show at Mr. Pacheco's Ware-House in Martfield Street, it included

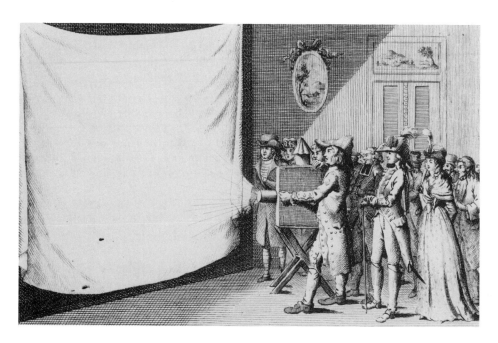

Magic-lantern projection usually occurred before small groups in the eighteenth century.

upwards of 30 humorous and entertaining Figures, larger than Men or Women; at the Rising Sun, the Friendly Travelers, the Pot Companions, the blind Beggar of Gednal Green and his Boy, the merry Piper dancing a Jigg to his own dumb Musick, the courageous Fencing Master, the Italian

Étienne Gaspar Robertson's fantasmagorie show as depicted in his Mémoires *(1831).*

Mountebank or famous infallible Quack, the Man riding on a Pig with his Face toward the Tail, the Dutchman scating on the Ice in the midst of Summer; with a great variety of other Figures equally diverting and curious, too tedious to mention. (*New York Evening Post*, 8 September 1746)

It was only in revolutionary France that the screen's possibilities were first effectively exploited—both ideologically and commercially—by the newly victorious bourgeoisie. In particular, Étienne Gaspar Robert (Robertson) was giving fantasmagorie (magic-lantern) performances at the Pavilon d'Échiquier in Paris by 1799, at the high point of the Revolution. Three years later he began to present his shows at a former Capuchin convent.

Robertson and the Fantasmagorie

Robertson's exhibitions reflected the anticlerical outlook of the Revolution while exploiting the Capuchin convent's residual associations of sacredness to create a mood of uneasy fear in the spectators, who filed through a series of narrow passageways into the main chapel, where the performances took place. By showtime, Robertson wrote in his memoirs, "everybody had a serious, almost mournful expression on their faces and spoke only in whispers."[14] He then appeared and directed some preliminary remarks to his audience:

> That which is about to happen before your eyes, messieurs, is not frivolous spectacle; it is made for the man who thinks, for the philosopher who likes to lose his way for an instant with Sterne among the tombs.
>
> This is a spectacle which man can use to instruct himself in the bizarre effects of the imagination, when it combines vigor and derangement: I speak of the terror inspired by the shadows, spirits, spells and occult work of the magician: terror that practically every man experienced in the young age of prejudice and which even a few still retain in the mature age of reason (Robertson, *Mémoires*, vol. 1 [Paris, chez l'auteur et Librarie de Wurtz, 1831], pp. 278–279).

Robertson's remarks played on the simultaneous realization that the projected image was only an image and yet one that the spectator believed was real.[15]

After Robertson completed his extended speech, the lights were extinguished and the mood heightened still further by sound effects (rain, thunder, and chimes sounding the death toll). An apparition approached the spectators until they were ready to scream—at which point it disappeared. This was followed by a series of sad, serious, comic, gracious, and fantastic scenes (the adjectives are Robertson's). Some pandered to the audience's political sentiments. In one, Robespierre left his tomb, wanting to return to life (as the sans-culottes had wished soon after his execution). Lightning struck and reduced the "monster" and his tomb to powder. After the elimination of this "spectre of the Left," images of the cherished dead were shown: Voltaire, Lavoisier, Rousseau, and other heroes of the bourgeoisie (pp. 283–284). In this "Age of Reason," magic was secularized and turned into a source of entertainment, with a church functioning as an exhibition site.

Fantasmagorie/phantasmagoria exhibitors developed elaborate methods for creating effects and motion. Slides were projected from behind the screen, with several

different lanterns used simultaneously to produce a composite image. A large stationary lantern often displayed a background on which figures projected from smaller
lanterns could move. Operators of these small lanterns roamed about behind the
screen to change the relative size and position of their images. The operator even
controlled the intensity of light: when he approached the screen, the amount of
projected light was reduced so the image would not brighten. Obviously, elaborate
coordination and skilled technicians were needed to give a successful exhibition. By
contrast, glass images for such exhibitions could be produced by a solitary painter.
These production methods are almost the reverse of modern screen entertainments,
where exhibition requires one (largely unskilled) projectionist, but production requires the coordination of many skilled artists and technicians. At the beginning of
the nineteenth century, each show was unique, having much in common with a stage
performance, but by the beginning of the sound era, screen exhibitions were completely standardized. Exploring the transformation of these production practices
during the period between 1800 and 1930 is a crucial task for screen historiography
and the "film" historian.

Robertson's exhibitions established a sophisticated, adult, urban audience for theatrical lantern entertainments. The Industrial Revolution begun in England and the
political revolution in France ensured the rapid spread of similar productions. Robertson later complained that his many imitators presented their shows across Europe
without offering him financial compensation. Paul de Philipsthal gave phantasmagoria performances in London from October 1801 through April 1803, then in Edin-
burgh. Barber reports that a "tremendous spectacle of Phantasmagory" was given at
a covered rotunda at Mount Vernon Garden in New York City. Screenings occurred
three times a week (Tuesday, Thursday, and Saturday evenings) at eight o'clock from
late May through early June 1803. The *New York Chronicle Express* reported that
these shows featured phantoms that "appear at a great distance, and become gradually larger, and at last disappear from the spectator" (30 June 1803). Showmen
Bologna and Tomlinson, claiming to have previously entertained enthusiastic crowds
in London, gave what they called the first phantasmagoria exhibition in the United
States at the City Hotel in New York City on 7 November 1803. The partners
advertised their phantasmagoria thus:

> *Wonderful display of Optical Illusions.* Which introduces the Phantoms,
> or Apparitions of the Dead and Absent, in a way more completely illusive,
> than has ever yet been witnessed, as the objects freely originate in the air,
> and unfold themselves under various forms, and sizes such as imagination
> alone has hitherto painted them, occasionally assuming a figure and most
> perfect resemblance of the heroes and other distinguished characters of
> past and present times. This Spectrology professes to expose the practices
> of artful imposters and exorcists, and to open the eyes of those who still
> foster an absurd belief in *Ghosts or Disembodied Spirits* (*New York
> Evening Post*, 4 November 1803, p. 3).[16]

The phantasmagoria was included in a three-part lantern show along with the "Skiagraphic" and "Brilliancies of Perrico." These latter two were apparently more traditional lantern shows with the equipment located in front of the stage. The skiagraphic
included scenes of an African forest and an "extensive view of the Western Ocean,
storms arise, calms succeed, cloudy and serene skies alternately, ships in different

Operators working backstage at a phantasmagoria show.

situations of sailing; after which an Atlantic Hurricane and shipwreck." *The Magician; or, the Metamorphic Grotto of Merlin* was a trick subject that showed "the wonderful changes of the place, and transmigration of its numerous objects." *The French Cook; or, Confusion in an English Hotel* was a short comedy.

Bologna and Tomlinson, charging one dollar for admission, promised an evening that "will prove highly interesting to the spectator, and give more general satisfaction than any species of Entertainment hitherto offered in this, or any other country." Unfortunately, as the *New York Evening Post* reported on 8 November, their debut was marred by difficulties, "part of the Machinery having been badly constructed through the hurry of the first representations" (p. 3). By the second showing, two days later, these problems were solved, and with adults soon charged fifty cents and children admitted at half price, their performances continued, shifting to the Union Hotel in December.

Bologna and Tomlinson may have soon returned to England, for the phantasmagoria did not debut in other American cities until somewhat later. Bostonians could not see the phantasmagoria until 18 June 1804, when a Mr. Bates performed at the Columbian Museum. His program, as reported in the *Boston Gazette* of 28 June 1804, included the following projections: "The Æriel Progression of Old Father Time—A Female Spirit, rising from the Tomb—The King of Terror—The Ghost and Hamlet—Washington—The President of the United States—A Bust of Dr. Franklin—An Egyptian Pigmy Idol, which instantaneously changes to a Human

Skull." It was preceded by *The World as It Goes; or, A Touch at the Times*, a medley written and performed by Bates, consisting of character sketches, whimsical anecdotes, and comic songs. The evening concluded with Chinese fireworks. Admission was fifty cents. In the view of one enthusiastic critic:

> The novel performance created a very surprising and pleasing effect; as the objects diminished on the eye of the spectator in an inconceivable and wonderful manner. Some of the Figures, indeed did not seem so perfect as others; the most particularly effective and striking were those of *Time*, a *Female Spirit, Hamlet, Washington*, and the *Bust of Franklin*; all of which formed striking resemblances of the objects they were intended to represent, and received general plaudits of approbation, and as we are given to understand, Mr. Bates had no direct model to frame the exhibition from—but formed it entirely from conjecture and surmise, we highly commend his ingenuity and trust (on repetition of the performance) he will, for public liberality, receive its recompense (*Independent Chronicle* [Boston], 21 June 1804, p. 2).

Bates was apparently an American moving into a European-dominated practice. As Charles Pecor has demonstrated, the phantasmagoria quickly became a popular form of amusement, presented in such cities as Philadelphia (by April 1808), Baltimore, Providence, Cincinnati, Savannah, and Lexington.[17]

One of the most successful early exhibitors operating in the United States was a Mr. Martin, who gave his first American show at Boston's newly rebuilt Columbian Museum in early December 1806. His programs included the "Merry Dance and Balancing, on the Slack Rope, by an *Automaton*, representing a natural Boy of 5 years of age" and "curious experiments on the various gases—viz—*Vital, Combustible and Mephitical*.[18] The phantasmagoria performance then began, including a scene from *Romeo and Juliet* in which the two lovers "appear dying as in reality." It ended with:

> FROLIC DANCING and Multiplication of WITCHES. By this extraordinary and magical illusion, one Phantom will multiply to an innumerable number of them, in such a manner that the whole room will appear full of these extraordinary dancers (*Boston Gazette*, 29 December 1806, p. 3).

Like Bates, Martin made the lantern only one part of a multifaceted program and likewise embraced a wide variety of subject for his phantasmagoria performances. Their use of the museum as a venue would be continued by many exhibitors (ultimately including those showing film) in the years ahead.

Martin's performance was applauded for its novelty, and his transparencies were considered "superior to any thing of the kind, ever exhibited in this country."[19] Within six weeks, this "celebrated artist of the *théâtre de la Nouveauté* in Paris" experienced what may have been the first projector-related fire in American screen history, destroying both his apparatus and the museum. Six people were killed and the damage was estimated at twenty thousand dollars.[20] Destitute, Martin advertised in the paper for a loan that would enable him to acquire a new outfit. The plea may

E. ROBERTSON'S
Exhibition
At the EUTERPIAN HALL 410, Broadway.
Every Evening at 8 o'clock precisely.—Doors open at half-past 7.

PROGRAMME.

HYDRAULIC EXPERIMENTS,
OR
Mixture of Fire and Water.

The Evening's Entertainments will commence with the NEW EXHIBITION OF HYDRAULICS, which will be displayed by Mr. Robertson. At his will, by an ingenious combination, the water assumes the most agreeable figures; under his hand, it is at one time, a BASKET, at another a BUTTERFLY, then it takes the appearance of a REFLECTOR and seems to play in the midst of hundreds of lights, which it reflects without extinguishing.

Among other brilliant pieces, he will this evening exhibit the following —

THE TURKISH SMOKER,
A small Automaton Figure, whose only power of action is by the means of water.

THE CAPRICES OF THE LADIES,
THE LANTERN OF DIOGENES,
THE PNEUMATIC PUMP,
THE ASCENDING EGG,
Upon the point of a Waterspout &c. &c. He will terminate his experiments, by elevating an

ILLUMINATED LUSTRE,
UPON THE JET D' EAU.

Each of which by the quantity of water put into operation will tend to cool the hall in a very great degree, and add much to the comfort of the audience; after which

Mr. J. MARIANO CABOLIS,
Lately arrived from Paris with Mr. E. Robertson, will appear for the first time in America and will execute the well known comic dance of

LA POLICHINELLE,
With appropriate music and dresses.

The whole to conclude with

New Optical Illusions, or
Robertson's Phantasmagoria.

Mr. Robertson will use his utmost exertion to merit the approbation of the public, and support the reputation which his Father, the celebrated Professor Robertson, of Paris, acquired by the invention of these Extraordinary Spectacles, and for which he obtained patents from the governments of both France and Holland. These Exhibitions are not in the slightest degree calculated to produce fright even with the youngest persons; on the contrary, they excite the curiosity of the Philosopher, amuse and astonish every body, and tend to convince all ranks of society, the juvenile parts in particular, that such

Apparitions, Spectres, Phantoms, or Shadows
As have appeared or may appear, are the effect of Optical, Dioptrical, or Catoptrical illusions.

Mr. Robertson will present the most agreeable allegories connected with morality, history, and mythology, or selected from anecdotes, and the most approved novels, recalling to the mind of the spectator important events and distinguished individuals. Among the different scenes and objects which will be presented this evening, are

THE THUNDER STORM,
THE DRUM OF THE EUMENIDES,
THE VISIONS,
HIS SATANIC MAJESTY,
Frederick THE GREAT at Spandaw,
French Brandy, Jamaica Rum, English Gin,
(Portraits drawn from Nature.)
MEDUSA'S HEAD,
Love Shaves Every Body,
THE BALLOON AND PARACHUTE,
The Dance of the Chinese,
Doctor Young Interring his Daughter,
THE HEAD WITH THE REVOLVING GLORY,
And the Rose of Love, a much admired Allegory.
To conclude with
THE SHADE OF A DEPARTED HERO.

☞ The eminent Professor of Music, Mr. LOUIS MAJOR, will preside at the

PIANO FORTE
Every evening of Mr. R's. Exhibition. The Hall is spacious and well aired.

The front seats reserved exclusively for Children.

Tickets of admission 50 cents.
Children under 10 years of age, half price.

have been successful, for he was exhibiting again by April 1808 and subsequently performed in New York, Philadelphia, Savannah, and Baltimore. While at this last city in 1811, Martin offered his equipment for sale and probably retired from the peripatetic life of a showman.

Europe continued to be the center of magic-lantern activity. In England, Henry Langdon Childe devoted his entire life to giving magic-lantern shows after having started his career as a painter for Paul de Philipsthal in 1802. By the 1830s he had developed and perfected the technique of "dissolving views," in which one picture faded out as the next one faded in. The images were aligned on the screen and the light remained at a constant intensity, creating a smooth, gradual transition. This permitted a wide variety of effects that had not previously been possible.[21] The magic lantern was also enhanced after Sir Goldsworthy Gurney developed a new illuminant—limelight—in 1822. A flame created by applying a mixture of oxyhydrogen gas to a small cylinder of lime was first used in 1826 for lighthouses but was quickly adopted by showmen. Most equipment and hand-painted slides continued to be imported into the United States from England and France.

By the 1820s, magic-lantern exhibitions were frequently a part of programs offered at museums like Peale's Museum and Gallery of Fine Arts at 252 Broadway in New York City.[22] In 1825–1826, Eugène Robertson, the son of Étienne Gaspar Robertson, visited the United States and attracted wide attention with his balloon ascents. During his stay, he also gave phantasmagoria exhibitions accompanied by scientific demonstrations and hydraulic experiments. He offered similar exhibitions on a return trip in 1834.[23] Such presentations were common through the 1840s and later.

The Stereopticon: Projecting Photographic Images

The development of photography did not give lanternists immediate access to projected photographic images: this had to wait for the development of the albumen and collodion processes in the late 1840s. These new techniques enabled a photographic image to adhere to a glass surface, whereas previous methods (daguerreotypes and talbotypes) had used either a silver-plated copper surface or paper as a base. When John A. Whipple and William B. Jones of Boston patented an albumen process (using egg whites as an adhering agent) in June 1850, they had been using it for several years. The Langenheim brothers, William and Frederick, who had also been working with the albumen process, played an important role in the introduction of photographic lantern slides.[24]

During the 1840s, the Langenheims facilitated the introduction of several new photographic processes into the United States. Interested in the paper photography developed by William Henry Fox Talbot, they became its exclusive agents in the United States. While licensing the talbotype process was not commercially rewarding, the venture encouraged them to adopt and to improve the albumen process. Employing glass as a support for the emulsion, the Langenheims began making photographic lantern slides, for which they claimed:

> The new magic-lantern pictures on glass, being produced by the action of
> light alone on a prepared glass plate, by means of the camera obscura,

must throw the old style of magic-lantern slides into the shade, and supersede them at once, on account of the greater accuracy of the smallest details which are drawn and fixed on glass from nature, by the camera obscura, with a fidelity truly astonishing. By magnifying these new slides through the magic lantern, the representation is nature itself again, omitting all defects and incorrectness in the drawing which can never be avoided in painting a picture on the small scale required for the old slides (*Art-Journal* [London], April 1851, p. 106).

By 1851 they were exhibiting slides at London's Crystal Palace Exhibition, where these "hyalotypes" received extensive praise. Subjects included buildings and landmarks in Philadelphia (United States Custom House, Pennsylvania State Penitentiary), Washington (Smithsonian, the Capitol), and New York (Croton aqueduct) as well as portraits of well-known Americans. These were mounted in rectangular wooden frames that measured 3⅝ × 6⅞ inches with a 2¾- or 3-inch circular opening for the image. From the outset, many of these stereopticon slides, which cost four to five dollars apiece, were hand-colored. For a tour of South America in 1852, Frederick Langenheim used such slides in a four-part program that included "1. Views of Niagara Falls; 2. Interesting Views of the United States and other countries of the world; 3. Microscopic Views magnified two thousand times; 4. Magical and Comical Pictures."[25]

In 1850 the Langenheims also introduced the stereoscope into the United States. This peephole-viewing instrument owed its immense popularity to the illusion of depth that was created when the spectator looked at two pictures of an object, each taken from a slightly different perspective. These stereo views were often transfer printed onto ground glass so the spectator could hold them up to the light. Since the Langenheims and other dealers sold both stereoscopic views and lantern slides, they often cut the double images in half and projected individual slides with a magic lantern. Because these slides were so frequently used in the lantern, Americans often called the projector of photographic slides a "stereopticon."[26]

P. E. Abel and T. Leyland exhibited the Langenheims' slides at the Concert Hall in Philadelphia on 22 December 1860, calling their magic lantern a "stereopticon." Images from Europe and North America were shown—initially without a lecturer, though one was soon added. The rapidly approaching Civil War distracted potential patrons, and the stereopticon closed after twelve weeks, only to reopen in Boston on 8 July 1861. Chemist John Fallon of Lawrence, Massachusetts, developed an improved stereopticon and exhibited it with considerable success in the 1860s. Leyland supervised the Brooklyn, New York, debut of this "scientific wonder of the age" at the Atheneum on 14 April 1863. Although audiences were embarrassingly small at first, the city's leading citizens (including Mayor Martin B. Kalbfleisch and Charles J. Sprague) urged Fallon and Leyland to remain "so that all may enjoy its beauties and profit by its instructions." It ultimately ran almost continuously for six weeks, with a twenty-five-cent admission fee. The evening debut consisted of "a choice selection of landscapes, architectural views and sculptures gathered from travels in the most illustrious parts of Europe, Asia and our own country," and one reviewer suggested that "you can imagine yourself borne away on the enchanted carpet of the Arabian tale, and brought where you can look down upon the veritable Paris, and Rome, and Egypt." Leyland soon made almost daily program changes, devoting each illustrated lecture to a specific country or region: "Great Britain," "France," "Switzerland and the Rhine," and "Italy." For another popular program, the "wall photographer" exhibited photographs of statuary. These evening shows—with Wednesday and Saturday matinees at reduced fee—reportedly were "attended by the learned and scientific portion of society as well as others." For the last ten days of its run, Fallon's stereopticon was presented under the auspices of the Central Congregational Sunday School.[27]

While strong ties between the stereopticon and the cultural elite were being forged in Brooklyn, P. T. Barnum hastened to appropriate the invention for his own amusement purposes in Manhattan. On 4 May 1863, the "Great English Stereopticon" opened as the principal attraction at his American Museum with "photographic views of scenery, celestial and animated objects, buildings, portraits, &c, &c." For this "new pleasure," which Barnum claimed to have cost thousands of dollars, "the picture stands out upon a curtain with the same perspective that is seen in nature, and thousands of people can see it at the same time."[28] After two weeks, the stereopticon was being shown between acts of Dion Boucicault's drama *Fauvrette*.

Fallon's "great work of art, the stereopticon" opened in Manhattan on 15 June at Irving Hall, where it ran for five weeks. Returning the following May, the showman gave exhibitions every evening (with matinees on Wednesdays and Saturdays) for seven weeks. His collection included one thousand slides, and programs changed each week. The return engagement commenced with "Celebrated Places and Statuary," which included portraits of various Union Army generals. A subsequent screening offered local views—images of New York harbor, a recent fair, and the new Worth Monument.[29] The final week was devoted to a program on the war, "The Army of the Potomac," which used photographs taken by Alexander Gardner, the official photographer for the army of the Potomac, and a corps of his associates. Advertisements announced:

> The views illustrate the army from the first battle of Bull Run up to its present position under the commands of Gen. McDowell, Gen. McClellan, Gen. Burnside, Gen. Hooker, Gen. Meade and Lieut. Gen. Grant are vouched for by all our generals, and bring the battle fields, their incidents and localities, before us in the most faithful and vivid manner, each view being reproduced on a canvas covering a surface of over 600 square feet (*New York Daily Tribune*, 27 June 1864, p. 3).

The journalistic praise accorded the stereopticon evokes the amazement that greeted the first screen images and anticipates the later enthusiasm for the novelty of projected motion pictures. "The dead appear almost to speak; the distant to overcome space and time and be close and palpable," noted the *New York Tribune*. When Professor Cromwell acquired Fallon's stereopticon and returned to New York City in the late 1860s, a publicist wrote:

> It will be seen that the [stereopticon] exhibition differs from the exhibition of painting [on glass], in that it presents us with a literal transcription of the actual, heightened into all the beauty and effect of the *chiaro obscuro*, by the combination of optical laws so feebly hinted at in the Magic Lantern. Stereoscopic Pictures are placed before us which are the exquisite shadows of the photograph, freighted with all the minute details of the subject as it really exists, not a flat monochromatic shadow, but a rounded, glowing picture, thrown up into splendid relief with all its marvelous accuracy magnified, all its tints preserved, and the whole character, subtle and sublime of the existing thing itself, reproduced in a

splendid shaft of artificial life, so that for the moment, we seem to be looking at bold picturesque facts and not ingenious and shadowy fancies (*A Guide to Cromwell's Stereopticon*, introduction by A. C. Wheeler [New York, *ca.* 1869], p. 8).

Audiences, accustomed to projected images painted on glass, were overwhelmed by the realism of life-size photographs on the screen.

The shift from painted images to photography was one aspect of the complex transformation of screen practice occurring shortly after midcentury. Before the stereopticon, the screen had been strongly associated with the phantasmagoria's mystery and magic. In the minds of a growing group of enthusiasts, the application of photography to projection provided the lantern with a new scientific basis. Photographic slides not only enhanced the lifelike quality of the screen image but offered a much more accurate record of reality. For popular scientific demonstrations, reality itself was often projected on the screen via specially constructed slides in which small living insects were able to move about. Professor Henry Morton designed "Refraction; or, Prisms and Lenses," his February 1866 illustrated lecture at Philadelphia's Academy of Music, as much for its aesthetic effect as for the information it conveyed:

> A little aquarium containing living fish and plants was placed in the lantern, and an immense image thrown upon the screen. Salt water was then poured into the aquarium, as it gradually mixed with the fresh, it refracted the light at all surfaces of contact, thus producing beautiful, changing, cloud-like shadows on the screen, and also causing a great commotion among the frightened fish, lizards, &c., which greatly amused the audience to see their singular acrobatic and gymnastic evolutions and contortions (*Philadelphia Photographer* 3 [1866], p. 119).

The technique Kircher had used to show "live flies" was thus resurrected in a new form. Crystals, leaves, and microscopic materials were also commonly shown, usually sandwiched between two pieces of glass.[30]

Photography provided the first key element of standardization in screen practice. With the ability to make multiple copies of a single image, slide producers now had a process of manufacture that was much more efficient than hand painting, and this development was accompanied by corresponding advances in lithography, which was also used to make lantern-slide images. Multiple photographic images could be smaller than painted slides yet provided greater detail and were much cheaper to produce. Lanterns could be scaled down, made more portable, and sold for less. Screen practitioners had begun to adopt methods of industrial manufacture.

Slide production and exhibition increasingly became specialized, independent branches of an industry whose relations were characterized by the maturing system of capitalism. Until after the Civil War, magic lanterns and slides were only one line of goods sold by the optical trade. John McAllister opened a Philadelphia shop dealing in optical goods in 1796. Renamed McAllister & Brother when it was taken over by his grandsons (W. Y. and T. H.) in 1855, the enterprise became the country's first major dealer in lanterns. In 1865, T. H. McAllister moved to New York City and set up his own business, which came to specialize in lanterns, slides, and related supplies. By the 1880s, McAllister was best known for its calcium-light lanterns, which cost between $100 and $450.[31] T. H. McAllister would subsequently deal in motion-picture projectors and films as well.

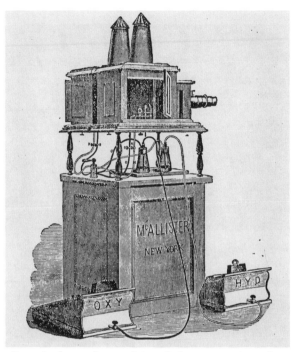

Illustration of an "oxy-hydrogen" or calcium-light stereopticon from T. H. McAllis-ter's 1885 catalog.

In 1850 Daniel H. Briggs of Abington, Massachusetts, found himself painting slides for his own lectures, then a common practice. Fellow exhibitors were soon buying his highly regarded slides, and the demand for these hand-painted glass images became greater than he could supply. In 1853 he learned of the collodion process developed by Frederick Archer and adopted it as a way to increase the efficiency of his production. He prospered and moved to Norton, Massachusetts, where his son, Casper W. Briggs, assumed active management of the slide business in 1868. Exhibition was forgotten and the focus placed on manufacture and sales.

C. W. Briggs moved his business to Philadelphia in 1872 and two years later purchased the Langenheims' business when William died and Frederick retired. The Briggs firm, which remained the dominant American slide producer through World War I, specialized in drawings that were then photographed and usually hand-tinted. Among the many artists employed by the firm, the best known was Joseph Boggs Beale, who had established a reputation as a magazine illustrator. From about 1890 to 1917 he made roughly 1,800 drawings, or an average of less than two a week. Beale's biographer, Terry Borton, indicates that approximately six hundred images were of historical events (recent or past), focusing on subjects like the American Revolution or the Boer War. Another six hundred slides were religious. Others were made for secret societies or emphasized temperance themes or comic incidents. Many of these images reworked and evoked well-known paintings, such as Emanuel Leutze's *Washington Crossing the Delaware* (1851), but most were original, based on art direction provided by Briggs. The addition of color was often critical to these slides' visual effect, although the manner of execution varied widely according to the range of tints employed, as well as the talents and care of the colorists. Briggs had a

Sequence of twelve magic-lantern slides painted about 1890 by Joseph Boggs Beale for "The Raven" by Edgar Allan Poe. Each of the twelve lines from the poem is affixed to the appropriate slide with a printed label, suggesting the point at which the exhibition might cut or dissolve to the new image.

While I nodded, nearly napping, suddenly there came a tapping.

Here I opened wide the door; darkness there, and nothing more.

In there stepped a stately raven of the saintly days of yore.

Tell me what thy lordly name is on the Night's Plutonian shore!

Straight I wheeled a cushioned seat in front of bird, and bust, and door.

But whose velvet-violet lining, with the lamp-light gloating o're, She shall press, ah, nevermore!

Then, methought, the air grew denser, perfumed from an unseen censer.

Of this home by Horror haunted—tell me truly, I implore—

"Prophet!" said I, "thing of evil!— prophet still, if bird or devil! . . ."

It shall clasp a sainted maiden whom the angels name Lenore—

"Get thee back into the tempest and the Night's Plutonian shore! . . ."

And my soul from out that shadow that lies floating on the floor. Shall be lifted— nevermore!

dozen women working on the slides, which were often passed down the line, with each woman specializing in a different color.[32]

Beale's slides embody a strong presentational approach. In illustrating a narrative, Beale selected melodramatic high points and drew them with heightened emotional effect and gestures. This is evident in a twelve-slide rendering of Edgar Allan Poe's poem "The Raven," which he made around 1890. The series is theatrical in style: the character's posture and gestures recall a histrionic acting tradition, while the entire tale unfolds within the confines of one setlike room. The "fourth wall," where the spectator is supposedly sitting, is never shown; the foreground remains empty; and a proscenium arch is likewise suggested. Nevertheless, the viewpoint offered the spectator is a mobile one. The perspective shifts, "moving in" and "panning" from right to left for the first three slides and "pulling back" for the fourth. This spatial instability creates a mood of unease and disorientation well suited to the poem. It also sets up the next slides, in which specters appear. Specifically the progressions from slides four to five and then from seven through ten retain single perspectives and display excellent continuity. By dissolving from one view to the next, the exhibitor could thus create a particularly haunting succession of images.

A reading of Poe's poem was meant to accompany these images, and lines suggesting the cues on which to "cut" were placed along the edge of each slide. The reader who compares the images to the text will note that the slides of specters are projected in quite rapid succession in comparison with the others. The passage of time is suggested by the interaction of verse and image, with the text perhaps dominant. Individual exhibitors would have varied these impressions through the pace of verbal delivery and successive slides, or might have more fundamentally determined them by dropping lines and rearranging or even repeating slides. Temporality, however, is underdeveloped—suggested or indicated by this string of frozen moments rather than rendered continuously in some analogous or verisimilar form.

Philadelphia functioned as the center of the American photographic and lantern-slide industries for several decades. Optician Lorenzo J. Marcy, for example, patented a series of improvements on the magic lantern in the late 1860s, then moved from Newport, Rhode Island, to Philadelphia. There he marketed his sciopticon, a double-wick lantern that burned kerosene oil and generated a stronger light (as much as ten times the brilliance) than previous oil-burning projectors. Small and inexpensive (forty-five dollars), it enjoyed considerable popularity. Other Philadelphia lantern and slide dealers included M. F. Benerman and Edward L. Wilson, T. J. Harbach, and the optician Sigmund Lubin. Lubin established his business in 1882. Within five years he had fourteen employees and a reputation as a "sharp, shrewd businessman." On more than one occasion he was in court contesting a claim. Although he went bankrupt in the late 1880s, he managed to recover and eventually assumed a prominent role in the motion-picture industry.[33]

French and English lantern suppliers had a large share of the American market. In 1874, Benerman & Wilson acquired the American agency for Levy & Company, a French firm whose photographic slides were considered among the best in the world. These images were almost exclusively actuality scenes of various sights throughout the world. To promote them, Wilson wrote and published a series of "lantern journeys"—lectures that could either accompany the slides or be read while privately examining the corresponding stereoscopic views. Levy slides cost a dollar each, while others sold for as little as seventy-five cents (before discounts). A one-hundred-dollar outfit with sciopticon and one hundred slides was meant to "enable everybody to go into the exhibition business." Benerman & Wilson also published the *Magic Lantern*, one of the country's earliest trade journals for lantern enthusiasts. It was started in September 1874 by partner and chief editor Edward L. Wilson, who was already editor of the *Philadelphia Photographer*.[34]

Although New York City was of only secondary importance in the lantern world, it claimed several noteworthy enterprises. Besides T. H. McAllister, E. and H. T. Anthony prospered as producers and dealers in stereoscopic views and lantern slides. Charles B. Kleine opened a small optical firm in 1865 and soon was selling stereopticons. Two sons followed him into the business, including future movie producer George Kleine, who moved to Chicago and opened the Kleine Optical Company in 1893.[35] By then, Chicago had become another important commercial center in the "optical trade," serving as a distribution point for the sale of lanterns and slides throughout the Midwest.

Although early screen practices varied, all methods shared certain underlying characteristics in terms of both production and exhibition. As one approach, manufacturers produced negatives or lithographic masters from which they could make large quantities of slides. Reliance on photography became more pronounced after the late 1870s with the introduction of factory-coated gelatin plates, which further reduced the cost of manufacturing slides and increased the sensitivity of emulsions. Exhibitors bought these slides either individually or in sets. Having selected the images, they sequenced the slides and then projected them with an accompanying lecture, music, and perhaps even sound effects. Using another approach, lantern exhibitors frequently made their own slides, either by photography or by painting on glass. Photographers such as J. W. Bryant supplemented their regular income with evening lantern shows. In an article titled "How I Push the 'Show' Business," Bryant reported:

> At the beginning of winter I commenced preparing for the lantern entertainments, and although I employ three assistants, and work constantly in the [photography] gallery myself, I am making more clear money from the evening entertainments than from my regular business.
>
> In addition to the slides obtained from [Benerman & Wilson], I make slides of my best negatives, being careful to take those best known and most respected. My experience is, there is nothing that pleases better than portraits of persons well known by the audience. I also display outdoor pictures, taken of scenery, public buildings, and private residences, which I have taken in and around this city; in short, anything I can get of a local character (*Magic Lantern*, April 1875, p. 9).

Like many showmen, Bryant hired an advance man who booked engagements for him at Sunday schools, churches, lodges, societies, and public schools.

In the selection and juxtaposition of images, which is a key aspect of the process we now call editing, exhibitors could impose different degrees of continuity and discontinuity. As photographic slides became more widely used, their organization relied less on principles of diversity and variety and more on what one commentator called "the continuous plan":

> The continuous plan is liked best. By that we mean the arranging of your exhibition into one or more parts, and so connecting the pictures

that they are made to illustrate some one subject continuously. The old-fashioned, spasmodic, hitchy way, of showing first a view of Paris, say, then a comic slide, and then a scripture scene, and then another Paris view, and so on, is without interest. You should interest your audience at once, and then keep up the interest. You would grow very tired if you were travelling, and had to jump out and change cars every mile or two. You want to keep on—the scene to change, yet all the time working towards the completion of some interesting story or journey (*Magic Lantern Journal*, February 1875, p. 7).

Spatial continuities became important in the later part of the nineteenth century. Surviving documentation, some as early as 1860, indicates that in sequencing photographic views, practitioners were often preoccupied with the creation of a spatial world.[36] As travel lectures became more elaborate, they often placed the traveler/photographer within the space constructed by a narrative. Thus, spatial relations between the slides—such as cut-ins, exterior/interior, point-of-view, and shot/counter-shot—became codified within the framework of the travel genre. Edward Wilson's lectures from the mid 1870s to the mid 1880s indicate frequent dissolves from exterior to interior and continued spatial references on a reduced scale: "We are looking in the opposite direction from our last picture" is a typical remark. The later travel lectures of John Stoddard, who was active in the 1880s and 1890s, included shots of the traveler/lecturer in his railway car that were intercut with scenes of the countryside through which he was traveling. In some instances, the spectator saw Stoddard in his car, then saw what he had seen out the window. Such connections between images were usually made explicit through the lecture.[37]

The lanternists' preoccupation with the faithful duplication of reality and the creation of a seamless spatial world remained limited, however, and disparate mimetic techniques were routinely juxtaposed in the course of a program. Lithographic and photographic slides, for example, were frequently integrated into one program. In travel lectures like Stoddard's program on Japan, actuality material and studio photographs were combined in the same sequence.[38] This syncretism might even occur within the same slide. Slide producers often placed actors against sets that combined real objects and objects painted on the backdrop; sometimes the actors were shot against a white background and the milieu subsequently drawn in. When the opportunity later arose, these showmen did not hesitate to juxtapose moving and static images.

Illustrated Lectures and Their Authors

In the eyes of spectators and critics, the exhibitor, not the slide producer, was the author. It was the presenter's role that shaped the material, and as with John Stoddard, it was his art that the newspapers reviewed. Stoddard delivered his first lecture, without illustrations, at a Boston church in the spring of 1877, but two years later, he started his professional career with illustrated talks on St. Petersburg, Moscow, and Spain. His second "season," 1880–1881, with its elaborately illustrated account of the recent passion-play performance in Oberammergau, Germany, established him as a prominent lecturer. By the following season he was playing all major

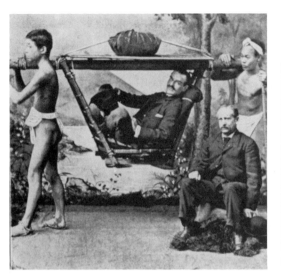 

Two slides from John Stoddard's illustrated lecture on Japan (1893).

cities from Chicago to Boston and receiving $250 a lecture. For many years he was content to purchase his slides from Levy & Company and other dealers, but eventually he began surveying the firm's collection in advance and then hired local photographers to take special views that he needed and he alone could use. While his programs during the 1880s were limited to Europe and the Mediterranean, in 1890 he traveled through Mexico and in 1891 went around the world. By 1893–1894 he was giving a five-part course of lectures that included two sessions on Japan, one on China, and two on India.[39]

The large fraternity of illustrated travel lecturers also included E. Burton Holmes, who would subsequently incorporate motion pictures into his programs. Born into a cosmopolitan Chicago family in 1870, Holmes left school at age sixteen and traveled to Europe with his grandmother. A camera fanatic, he gave his first travel lecture, "Through Europe with a Kodak," before the Chicago Camera Club in 1890. It was a success and was repeated the next year. After traveling to Japan (and meeting Stoddard on the trip), the young man embarked on a professional career, beginning with a lecture at the 350-seat Recital Hall in Chicago on 15 November 1893. As he toured other Midwestern cities, Holmes was applauded for his delivery, the quality of his photographic work, and the beautiful hand-tinting of his slides. The *Milwaukee Sentinel* judged his presentations "among the treats of the season." "In the first lecture," explained Holmes in the program of his first professional lecture, "the audience is taken to the heart of the Real Japan, far beyond the reach of foreign innovations. The experiences of three Americans on a tramp of over three hundred miles through the interior provinces, are vividly described and illustrated." Oscar Depue, then working for a Chicago supplier of optical goods, was hired to project the slides at Recital Hall; he subsequently remained as the lecturer's full-time operator and longtime associate. By the 1895–1896 season Holmes had a full course of five programs just like Stoddard.[40]

As the documentary tradition matured in the era between Reconstruction and the Spanish-American War, the travel lecture provided the dominant paradigm. From within the travel genre, however, there emerged examples of what we would now call ethnographic programs, such as "Land of the Eskimos," delivered by Lieutenant Robert Edwin Peary in 1894. These explorations of distant places and seemingly primitive, impoverished peoples were mirrored by an investigation of another group of "others" who lived much closer to home. In 1888 former police reporter Jacob Riis almost single-handedly launched the social-issue screen documentary, which prospers, now primarily on television, to this day. His ground-breaking exhibition, "The Other Half: How It Lives and Dies in New York," made use of new photographic techniques utilizing a flash. It enabled Riis to go into New York City's slums and to capture photographically those people who lived in dark alleyways and basements amid destitution and disease. His illustrated lectures shocked the well-to-do and did much to stimulate the burgeoning movement for social reform. In exploring differences of class, ethnicity, race, and even gender, in focusing on the dislocations between the private and public spheres that were symptomatic of the daily life of the poor, and by conveying a powerful sense of claustrophobia through the succession of enclosing images, Riis challenged the implicit assumption of a metropolitan experience shared by all city dwellers, articulated in previous illustrated lectures on urban life delivered by the Langenheims and their successors.[41]

Alexander Black of neighboring Brooklyn explored the growing urban landscape of his city in a less disturbing manner. Enjoying an excellent local reputation in the early 1890s, Black became well known for his illustrated lecture sometimes called "Life Through a Detective Camera" and other times "Ourselves as Others See Us." Relying on "instantaneous photography" and hidden camera work, Black constantly reworked the presentation so that audiences would see a different program on return dates. He not only took his own slides but authored *Photography Indoors and Out: A Book for Amateurs*, which was published by Houghton, Mifflin in 1893. He ultimately distinguished himself from his colleagues by writing, photographing, and presenting a full-length fiction "picture play," *Miss Jerry*, which premiered in New York City on 9 October 1894.

Unlike Stoddard, Black was committed to an aesthetic of seamless realism. As he subsequently described his achievement in the preface to *Miss Jerry* (published by Scribners in 1897):

> In this triangular partnership between the art of fiction, the art of the tableau vivant and the science of photography, I have sought to test certain possibilities of illusion with the aim always before me, that the illusion should not, because it need not and could not safely be that of photographs from an acted play, nor that of an artist's illustrations, but the illusion of reality. If it is the function of art to translate nature, it is the privilege of photography to transmit nature. Thus, I sought to illustrate art with life (p. ix).

Although Black thought of his exhibition as a kind of play, the camera enabled him to use a wide range of exterior locations. Interiors were generally sets, though real locations were used in at least one instance (the office of Chauncey Depew, president of the New York Central & Harlem River Railroad). For each scene, many stills were usually taken from a single camera position. These were shown on the screen at the rate of three or four a minute with one dissolving into the next, thus providing not

Miss Jerry (*1894*).

an illusion of motion but an indication of the characters' actions and movements. For his monologue, Black played all the different parts and changed his voice to mimic each character. The enthusiasm that greeted this undertaking encouraged him to produce additional picture plays, including *A Capital Courtship,* set in Washington, D.C., and *Miss America.* As Terry Ramsaye has remarked, they anticipated many aspects of the feature film by almost twenty years.[42]

Although stereopticon lecturers (as well as photographers) were overwhelmingly men and represented the world as they saw and understood it, they directed their exhibitions to mixed-sex audiences. Travel scenes, by focusing on landscapes and local customs, were generally non-erotic and appealed to spectators in non-gender-specific ways. However, the exhibitor often became a strong figure of identification for his audiences. Men commonly saw these authoritative world travelers as individuals to respect and even emulate. Women's admiration not uncommonly turned into infatuation with their matinee idols.

The propriety of illustrated lectures appealed to two important cultural groups in American life. The first was the refined culture associated with *Harper's Weekly* and polite literature. In the form and ideological attitudes of Stoddard's lectures, one finds the social, cultural, and aesthetic concerns underlying Frederick Olmsted's vision of Central Park in New York: harmony, cultivated sensibility, propriety, genteel elitism.[43] It was places like the Brooklyn Institute of Arts and Sciences, one of the nation's foremost cultural institutions, that most warmly received Stoddard and Black. Black, who had the same agent as Mark Twain—Major James Burton Pond—

also exhibited on the Lyceum circuit, which sponsored popular middle-brow cultural events.

The second group that embraced the illustrated lecture consisted of church-based institutions. Churches regularly sponsored cultural events, usually as an alternative to corrupting amusements (melodramas, musicals, and so forth) at the local theater or small-town opera house. They were engaged in a more or less explicit crusade for the souls of the community. Ministers considered the illustrated lecture to be just one of many weapons in their arsenal and frequently presented them. In Orange, New Jersey, the Reverend J. Lester Wells gave a Riis-inspired "flash-light lecture" on "Lower Jersey City and the People's Palace" at the Orange Valley Congregational Church. According to the *Orange Chronicle*, "He projected upon canvas a series of stereopticon views which graphically portrayed the changes which have been going on in lower Jersey City, showing how the population has almost entirely changed in the past few years, the wealthy moving away and the industrial classes taking their places." Two weeks later, the First German Presbyterian Church in the same town offered a stereopticon lecture on the World's Fair and Alaska.[44]

These two groups did not constitute a monolithic bulkwark of middle-class culture; at various points, genteel culture with its underlying humanistic philosophy was in conflict with the evangelical nature of many Protestant denominations. Yet a deep compatibility was often evident. Alexander Black, for example, periodically delivered his picture plays at church-sponsored events. In the mid 1890s, on the eve of projected motion pictures, it was these two groups that provided the most receptive audiences for screen images. By contrast, producers of popular, urban commercial entertainment rarely employed the stereopticon.

Vaudeville houses seldom hired showmen to project lantern-slide images in their theaters in the mid 1890s. In St. Louis, for example, over a hundred programs for a leading variety theater during the 1870s refer to the magic lantern only twice, for a two-week engagement in November–December 1874, when Professor Schaffner of the Royal Polytechnic in London showed "dissolving views and comic illustrations." Similarly, in Boston during the fall of 1894, stereopticon slides appeared in vaudeville houses only once. At the New Lyceum, reported the *Boston Herald*, Professor George H. Gies "gave his first presentation in this city of his beautiful art pictures, and to say that they were admired and appreciated but mildly expresses the effect they had upon the audiences. The pictures they presented are exact copies of the originals, and are the most fascinating of paintings." The following fall, projected views in Boston vaudeville houses were advertised only twice. In October, Howard and Emerson "sang a number of descriptive songs illustrated with beautiful dissolving views" at Benjamin F. Keith's theater; two months later, Professor Gies presented "Beautiful Dissolving Views" there. Although New York managers showed greater interest, the increasing use of the stereopticon (particularly for illustrated songs) by vaudeville and popular theater would more or less coincide with their adoption of moving pictures in 1896–1897. In some localities, such as San Francisco, the two forms of screen entertainment made virtually simultaneous appearances.[45]

Moving Images for the Screen

The cinema (projected motion pictures) was the culmination of long-standing efforts to present ever more lifelike moving images on the screen. As we have seen, lantern exhibitors had always had an array of procedures for creating movement—whether by projecting shadows of living things or by moving multiple lanterns around behind the screen—but the repertoire of such techniques increased during the nineteenth century. The diverse ways of making images move at midcentury were suggested by Benjamin Pike, Jr.'s, 1848 *Catalogue of Optical Goods:*

> The person who manages the lantern must fasten it to his middle with a leather strap passed through the loop soldered to the back of the lantern, and holding the lantern with one hand adjust the top with the other. He should now go up pretty close to the screen and draw out the tube until the image is perfect, which, of course, will be very small; then walk slowly backward and slide the tube in at the same time to keep the image distinct.
>
> To give motion effect to the images, a variety of movable sliders are made for this purpose, many of which produce very curious appearances; but with the usual sliders the images may be made to travel in a circular, elliptical or other direction by moving the lantern in the corresponding way. . . . A shivering motion may be given to the images by giving the lantern a sudden shake. . . . By standing at the bottom of stairs a figure may be made to appear to be going up by giving the lantern a slight angular motion. . . . In the same way this figure may be made to lie on the floor and rise to a sitting or standing posture (quoted in George Kleine, "Progress in Optical Projection in the Last Fifty Years," *Film Index,* 28 May 1910, p. 10).

Some slides had levers to make portions of the image move. Rack-and-pinion and pulley systems produced slides that could be rotated without restriction. In one particularly popular comic slide, a rat crawls across a sleeping man and into his open mouth. Chromatropes had design patterns that were rotated using the pulley system.

Panoramic slides were twelve to fourteen inches long and consisted of a single image. They were moved slowly through the slide holder. Dioramic paintings with moving figures had two pieces of glass, "on one of which the scene is painted and the other the figures. The glass containing the figures is moved in a groove, and the figures, vessels, etc., pan across the scene."[46] Slip slides allowed an image to be quickly altered. On one such slide of a man's full figure, the head of a pig replaced the human head. As this example suggests, slip slides were generally used to create mystical or comic effects. In 1866 L. S. Beale developed the choreutoscope, a ratchet device with a front shutter that allowed six images of a skeleton to be projected in rapid succession. (See illustration on page 45.) The results suggested a moving image.[47] This repertoire of techniques enabled exhibitors with multiple lanterns at their disposal to present elaborate screen narratives.

Photography, with its realistic aesthetic and its scientific basis, seemed incompatible with such methods of image movement. Instead, the search for movement using photographic techniques was directed toward solutions based on the illusion of movement and the persistence of vision. Once again, two Philadelphians from the world of photography came to the fore, both of whom experimented with the presentation of a series of photographs in such a way as to create "moving pictures."[48] The first was Coleman Sellers, chief engineer for William Sellers & Company, a manufacturer of machinery and machinists' tools. In 1861 Sellers patented the kinematoscope, an improvement on the stereoscope that showed movement through a succession of images. As he explained in his patent application:

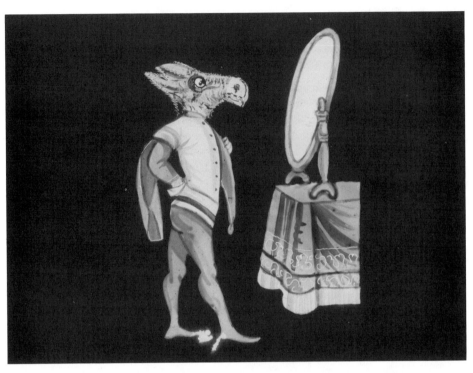

A nineteenth-century slip slide.

Beale's choreutoscope.

What I aim to accomplish is . . . to so exhibit stereoscopic pictures as to make them represent objects in motion such as the revolving wheels of machinery, and various motions of the human body, adding to the wonders of that marvelous invention "the stereoscope" a semblance of life that can only come from motion. It is to breathe into the statuelike forms of the stereograph, as it were, the breath of life. It may have occurred to many the possibility of effecting this desirable result, and the "phantasmascope" gives a clue to the manner of accomplishment of it. That is, that it must be done by viewing in succession a series of pictures (taken in different positions of the moving object) with sufficient rapidity to insure the image of one being retained on the retina until the next one is brought into view (Patent No. 31,357, exhibiting stereoscopic pictures of moving objects, issued 5 February 1861).

Although acknowledging his debt to the children's toy that was best known as the zoetrope (*i.e.*, the "phantasmascope"), Sellers concluded that "the pictures should be entirely at rest during the moment of vision or that motion should be in a direction of the line of vision." He designed several instruments that could be used to show such pictures. If simple, repetitive actions such as sawing or rocking were being shown only three different photographs were needed: the two extreme positions and one in between. These could then be shown as a recurring series in a simple drumlike instrument. For complicated actions, he designed a more complex instrument with "the series of pictures [attached] flatwise to an endless band of cloth." The technical state of photography, however, imposed certain limitations on what Sellers could achieve. Lengthy time exposures meant that each shot had to be taken individually and with the subject in static positions.[49] Developed at the early stages of the Civil War, the kinematoscope was never marketed commercially.

Some of Coleman Sellers' principles were applied to projection by Henry Renno Heyl in 1870. Once again the intimate relationship between peephole, privatized viewing and group reception within a theatrical context was continued. Improving upon a mechanism that was invented by O. B. Brown of Malden, Massachusetts, Heyl called his modified magic lantern a "phasmatrope." This wheel-like attachment held sixteen photographic slides mounted radially along its outer edge. The pictures

Coleman Sellers with his kinematoscope.

The wheel section of Heyl's phasmatrope, used for mounting and displaying slides.

were successively passed along in front of the light source (using an intermittent mechanism and a shutter) with the views repeated as many times as the exhibitor desired. Heyl made at least three series of photographs for his projection device and showed them at the Philadelphia Academy of Music on 5 February 1870, as part of a benefit for the Young Men's Society of St. Mark's Evangelical Lutheran Church. According to the program, these included "a representation of little *All Right* [a popular Japanese acrobat] in a number of his daring feats" and "a characteristic address from *Brother Jonathan* [the 1870 name for Uncle Sam] to the audience." For this second piece, a series of photographs were taken of an "actor" with his lips in different positions. When these were projected, he appeared to be speaking to the audience. This was accompanied by synchronous dialogue delivered from behind the screen:

> Ladies and Gentlemen:
> We are tonight to see for the first time, photographs of persons shown upon a screen by the aid of a magic lantern, the figures appearing to move in most lifelike ways. How this effect is produced we cannot briefly explain, but you will have the evidence of your own eyes to convince you that this new art will rapidly develop into one of the greatest merit for instruction and enjoyment.
> This beginning of greater things is not an imported product but it was perfected right here in Philadelphia, where it adds one more to the list of first inventions of real merit that stand to the credit of the City of Brotherly Love.

Two images for Heyl's phasmatrope. Each position was posed separately.

The photographs were made at 1208 Chestnut Street in the studio of
Mr. O. H. Willard, which place may now be well named "The Cradle of
the Motion Picture."

Another series of a waltzing couple is the only one to survive. For this, the costumed
dancers (Heyl was the man) were photographed in four positions and the photographs were repeated four times to fill out the sixteen slots.[50]

The phasmatrope provided only one portion of the Academy of Music entertainment, which opened with various stereopticon views of Niagara Falls in winter,
Yosemite Valley, and Alpine glaciers, as well as illustrations of the legend of Rip Van
Winkle. Magical and comic illusions were created by the phantasmagoria, but *tableaux vivants* and shadow pantomimes were also among the offerings given for that
evening's cultivated program. Although Heyl subsequently claimed that 1,500 paying customers enabled the organizers to clear $350 for the church coffers, he does not
appear to have exploited the phasmatrope's commercial potential. A somewhat similar device was developed by the Englishman John Arthur Roebuck Rudge in 1875.[51]
In all these instances, a series of photographs were shown in rapid succession to
create some degree of illusory movement even though the photographs were not
taken as part of a continuous series—because they could not be. This important
advance in photographic methods was achieved by Eadweard Muybridge.

Eadweard Muybridge and Photographic Projections of Animals in Motion

Eadweard Muybridge was an English-born photographer who settled in the American West during the 1860s.[52] He undertook many commissioned works both in his
hometown, San Francisco, and on extensive trips to such wide-ranging sites as the
Yosemite Valley, Alaska, and Central America. The final product of this work took
different forms, including the illustrated lecture. In this respect, the photographer
was not unusual—until he was approached by California industrialist Leland Stanford
in 1872. Stanford was interested in proving that at one point in a horse's stride all four
feet were off the ground, contrary to conventional renderings by painters and the
consensus of experts. Photography was to provide the evidence. Muybridge made a
series of individual photographs, a few of which were promising, but his work in this
area was seriously interrupted by a murder trial (he killed his wife's lover) and
self-imposed exile in Central America during most of 1875.

Muybridge's work on photographing horses in motion was resumed in 1877, again
under Stanford's sponsorship. A battery of cameras was constructed, but activating
the shutter mechanisms proved to be a serious problem. Results were inconsistent.
John D. Isaacs, a technical expert for Stanford's Central Pacific Railway, was brought
in and designed elaborate electromagnetic shutters for each camera. These were
triggered when the horse broke a thread that was stretched across the track in its path
and the magnets were connected.[53] The photographs were taken against a white
background with black vertical lines to delineate the space. Each shot was exposed
for approximately $\frac{1}{500}$ of a second, and the exposures were separated by approximately $\frac{1}{25}$ of a second. Since the exposures were activated by animals snapping the
strings, the time between shots was not a standard unit. By June 1878 the system was

working smoothly as horses Sallie Gardner and Abe Edgington raced and trotted down the track.

To reap the rewards of this invention, Muybridge delivered the first of many illustrated lectures on the subject at the San Francisco Art Association on 8 July.[54] According to the *San Francisco Chronicle*:

> The attendance was not so large as might have been expected, considering the unique manner in which the subject was treated and the ability with which the illustrations were described. The stride of Abe Edgington, and of the still more celebrated trotter Occident, was depicted in a clear manner in ten photographs as each passed a space of ground measuring some 21 feet, at a 2:20 to 2:24 gait, and the strange attitudes assumed by each animal excited much comment and surprise, so different were they from those pictures representing our famous trotters at their full stride. But that which still more aroused astonishment and mirth, was the action of the racer at full gallop, some of the delineations being seemingly utterly devoid of all naturalness, so complex and ungraceful were many of the positions, where on the race track beauty, elegance, and symmetry are all so combined. After showing some of Governor Stanford's celebrated trotting stock, Mr. Muybridge supplemented the equine series by a very pretty set of pictures delineating life and scenes in Central America, concluding with a perfect panorama of San Francisco and the surrounding country. Altogether it was a very pleasant entertainment, and Mr. Muybridge showed himself to be a clever and lucid lecturer on a very difficult subject, while his remarks on the Central American series were humorous and excelled in descriptive powers (9 July 1878, p. 3).

The exhibition focused on various aspects of Muybridge's work. Already the serial images of horses in motion were dissolved on and off the screen with sufficient rapidity to suggest their sequential nature. To emphasize the importance of this work, Muybridge contrasted his photographs with artists' renderings of horses in motion.[55] This approach formed the core of a presentation that he would develop over the following years.

During 1878 and 1879, Muybridge's work in serial photography moved forward on several fronts. While continuing to lecture occasionally, he returned to his cameras (increasing their number to twenty-four) and photographed sequences of dogs, deer, oxen, and other animals as they walked or ran along the track. Series were also taken of athletes as they leaped, wrestled, performed somersaults, and ran. Again with Leland Stanford's financial backing and encouragement, Muybridge constructed an elaborate mechanism that was attached to the magic lantern. The machine, initially called the zoogyroscope but eventually renamed the zoopraxiscope, exhibited series of images so as to reconstitute the motion his camera had analyzed. The device projected images on a constantly turning glass wheel, while a disk with series of slits turning in the opposite direction acted as a primitive shutter. Lacking an intermittent mechanism, it was, in this respect at least, less developed than Heyl's phasmatrope. As a result, these circular slides contained not actual photographs but colored, elongated drawings that compensated for the moving shutter. Although the innovations and significance lay in the images rather than in how they were projected, few people were familiar with earlier devices such as Heyl's; it could be argued that in a sense Muybridge actually set back the technology of rapidly projecting successive images.

A circular glass plate used for projecting on Muybridge's zoopraxiscope.

The zoopraxiscope had its commercial debut at the San Francisco Art Association on 4 May 1880. Admission cost fifty cents, and the exhibition was extended, eventually running over nine days. The *San Francisco Chronicle* reported that "the effect was precisely that of animals running across the screen." Another reviewer declared, "Mr. Muybridge has laid the foundation of a new method of entertaining the people, and we predict that his instantaneous photographic, magic lantern zoetrope will make the round of the civilized world." Other lectures on the West Coast followed, and in the summer of 1881 Muybridge left for Europe, where he gave many well-attended exhibitions of his work.[56]

Returning to the United States in June 1882, Muybridge gave his well-honed presentation before prestigious American audiences: the Turf Club and the Union League in New York City, the Academy of Fine Arts and the Franklin Institute in Philadelphia. Still the nation's center for photography, Philadelphia extended a particularly warm reception, which led to a resumption of Muybridge's photographic work at the University of Pennsylvania from May 1884 through December 1885. During this period he took approximately two hundred thousand images. Dry plates

Muybridge's zoopraxiscope.

replaced the wet-plate collodion system, and a black background with a grid system replaced the earlier white wall. Serial images of an action were commonly taken from several different angles simultaneously. Many focused on human actions and activities that were performed by subjects wearing minimal clothing or none, and while taken for "scientific purposes," these images had a strong erotic component. The results of this work—more than 20,000 figures of moving men, women, children, animals, and birds—were published in 1887 as *Animal Locomotion*, but they also enabled Muybridge to return to the lecture circuit with new images at his disposal.

One of Muybridge's expanded lectures was given in Orange, New Jersey, on 25 February 1888. Although, as will be seen in chapter 2, it helped to stimulate Thomas Edison into thinking about a new motion-picture system, the evening program addressed much more than technology. According to the *Orange Chronicle* of 3 March 1888, Muybridge began by analyzing the movements of the horse and comparing them with various paintings, after which "pictures of lions, elephants, camels, rhi-

Muybridge lecturing on animal locomotion at the Royal Society in London (1889).

nocerousses, buffaloes, tigers, deer, elks, kangeroos, dogs, hogs, and a vast variety of other animals were shown, the law of locomotion being uniform without exception." He then made a strategic move that reflected Darwin's theory of evolution: he presented photographs of scantily clad people, treating them much as he had the animals. The final blow of a fight was shown, as was "a series of pictures of female dancers pirouetting, which called down repeated applause."[57]

Responses varied among the six hundred spectators, but some were deeply disturbed by the choice of subjects. One patron protested to the *Orange Journal*:

> Yet it may well be asked whether the realm of animated nature does not furnish illustrations of locomotion besides those found in the "sporting world." All that were used on that occasion were taken from the horse as seen on the turf, or man in the ring. At least these were the prominent motions—running, boxing, athletic games—all of which were interesting to those who have a taste for such sports, but not so to many others.
>
> But a more important question is as to the propriety of exhibiting semi-nude human figures to a promiscuous assembly.
>
> Whether the object in view may not be entirely defeated by the shock to the delicate sensibilities.
>
> To be sure, it is said by persons of cultivated taste that a prudish, squeamish shrinking from nudity argues a low grade of intelligence—that *nature* is always more to be admired than *art*. But suppose certain persons should undertake to appear in our streets and assemblies *in puri naturalibus*, could they appeal to artistic taste in arrest of judgment as criminals or lunatics? Yet what better than this is a life size and life like representation of the nude human form, on canvass before a mixed assemblage?
>
> Among savages such exhibitions are entirely natural and expected, but in civilized society they are shocking to the moral sentiment, indecent and demoralizing (3 March 1888, p. 2).

There is little doubt that Muybridge intended to provoke such a reaction from his audiences. Within the framework of refined Victorian culture, he challenged the beliefs of conservative religious groups and established new parameters for discourse: his presentations were subversive not only of traditional assumptions about animal locomotion but of conventional religious and moral wisdom. As one of the screen's many practitioners, Muybridge integrated these moving images into a larger program that had cultural significance far beyond its contribution to the development of motion-picture technology.

Nineteenth-century screen practice evidenced extraordinary vitality in the growing fraternity of producers and exhibitors, the changing methods of production, and the diverse means of representation. There were an increasing number of ways to present movement on the screen, but all were extremely limited in what they could show. As the last decade of the century began, an overall solution to the problem had yet to be found, even though many were working on the challenge: Louis Le Prince, William Friese-Greene, Ottomar Anschütz, Étienne-Jules Marey, and finally, Thomas Edison. Although this goal—what we now call "the cinema" or projected motion pictures—was readily achievable once more sensitive photographic emulsions and flexible celluloid film became available, it did not happen all at once. As had been the case with previous innovations in image making, modern motion pictures were shown first in a peephole device rather than on the screen. Both the motion-picture camera that exposed these films and the peephole device that first showed them were developed at the Edison laboratory.

2

Thomas Edison and the Amusement World

*I*n "inventing" modern motion pictures, Thomas Alva Edison and William Kennedy Laurie Dickson developed a complex communications system—not a single invention but a whole group of inventions. While this achievement occurred within the framework of multifaceted influences—the work of Muybridge, Étienne-Jules Marey, and others; Edison's own prior accomplishments also shaped their thinking, the process of invention, and the way the developing motion-picture system was initially employed. In the 1870s Thomas Edison had established himself as the businessman's inventor. He was hired to make various improvements on the telegraph for Western Union, Jay Gould, and other financial powers then striving for dominance in the fields of communication and transportation. One of Edison's inventions, the quadruplex, could send four messages over one wire at the same time (two in each direction), an innovation that saved companies millions of dollars. He also worked on the talking telegraph, or telephone, improving its transmitter and its ability to function over long distances. His most impressive invention in the communications field was undoubtedly the phonograph, and its development and use eventually served him as a model for the development of a motion-picture system.

Edison earned his reputation as an inventor of utilitarian devices employed for the organization of large-scale enterprises.[1] Yet even practical communications technology sometimes provided entertainment in mid-nineteenth-century America. In the 1840s Professor James B. Brown and Dr. A. T. Johnson's "Grand Exhibition of Nature and Art" demonstrated the telegraph and a wide range of other inventions, including Colt's submarine battery, the Boston fire alarm bell, and an "Electronome: Or shocking Machine, of great power, for applying Electro-Magnetism to the human body." In the late 1870s telephone concerts presented "speech, music, imitations &c., over a long wire."[2] The musician or elocutionist, who was outside the visible and audible reach of the audience, directed sound into the telephone speaker for reproduction by a receiver in the hall. Always accompanied by lectures that explained the scientific and technical basis of the inventions, such demonstrations revealed one aspect of an "operational aesthetic," which Neil Harris finds characteristic of nineteenth-century American culture.[3] This approach focused attention on the structure of some technology or activity in a way that encouraged audiences to learn how it worked. For Americans, exhibitions of this type had become a form of recreation; they were part of a culture of enlightenment that included the illustrated lecture discussed in the previous chapter. Advocates considered them elevating experiences capable of winning citizens away from those rival amusements that were corrupting and base.

The Phonograph Becomes a Source of Entertainment

Insofar as the phonograph provided Edison with a model for his subsequent motion-picture endeavors, it merits careful attention here. When first invented, the phonograph was predictably seen as another communications device with a fundamentally utilitarian purpose. In the summer of 1877, during the course of experimentation at his Menlo Park, New Jersey, laboratory, Edison encountered certain unexpected phenomena that enabled him to invent an instrument for recording and playing back sound. He called this device the phonograph: the term, derived from the Greek, meant "sound writer." As Reese Jenkins points out, he initially explored three different formats for storing the sound information: in two cases waxed paper or tin

Edison and his tin-foil phonograph (1878).

foil were wrapped around a cylinder or shaped into a disk, while the third possibility involved a paper tape similar to stock-ticker tape, with which Edison was intimately familiar.[4] In the end, he pursued cylinders wrapped in foil. A short time after constructing and testing this novel recorder, the inventor gave a demonstration at the offices of *Scientific American*.[5] The public was amazed, and a whirlwind of publicity culminated in an impromptu entertainment for President Rutherford Hayes at the White House. Almost overnight, Edison became a popular hero dubbed "the Wizard of Menlo Park."

Everyone believed that the phonograph's long-term value was as a business machine. But because it was still too primitive to be employed "for the practical uses of commerce," the instrument was exhibited as a technological novelty. The Edison Speaking Phonograph Company was organized in the first part of 1878 to market and exhibit the new invention. James Redpath, founder of a Lyceum bureau in Boston, organized this aspect of the machine's exploitation. Showmen were assigned territories for their exhibitions, which consisted of practical demonstrations accompanied by elaborate explanations: another instance of the operational aesthetic at work. Only a few hundred exhibition phonographs were built; these used tin foil, wrapped around a cylinder, as a recording material. The instrument was hand-cranked, during both recording and playback. Each impression (the stylus making indentations on the foil) could be used only a few times before its quality degenerated beyond recognition. At exhibitions, the phonograph reproduced speeches and natural sounds as well as music. People were brought onstage to speak into the mouthpiece and then heard their voices emanate from a funnel attached to the phonograph.[6] As a Massachusetts newspaper reported in 1878:

> The experiments were intensely interesting. The operator repeated the juvenile poem,
>
> > "Mary had a little lamb,
> > Its fleece was white as snow,"
>
> and immediately as he reversed the crank, it was repeated through a pasteboard tunnel, giving all the inflections of his voice. A cornet player performed several tunes, placing his cornet over the mouthpiece, and they were all repeated with wonderful accuracy. Someone sang in the mouthpiece and the singing was reproduced. Imitations of crowing, barking, cat calls, whistling and singing, were also repeated, affording much mirth (*Cape Ann Advertiser*, 24 May 1878).

The craze lasted for a little less than a year; once the pool of customers had been exhausted, the novelty failed. Edison then turned his attention to another problem, incandescent light.

After a five-year period during which the phonograph had all but disappeared from commercial use, Alexander Graham Bell and several colleagues unveiled a vastly improved recording system. Tin foil was replaced by a wax-coated cardboard cylinder, and Edison's rigid needle by a free-floating stylus. Impressions were made by "engraving," which meant removing materials from the cylinder rather than simply indenting. The new system utilized much narrower grooves, allowing for more playing time. Acknowledging their debt to Edison, the Bell associates reshuffled the name of his invention and called their own machine the graphophone. They also

Edison and his key associates for the improved phonograph project (1888). Seated (left to right): Fred P. Ott, Edison, and George E. Gourand. Standing: W. K. L. Dickson, Charles Batchelor, A. Theodore E. Wangemann, John Ott, and Charles Brown.

sought a commercial alliance with the Menlo Park inventor, but Edison angrily refused and embarked on his own improvements. His "perfected phonograph," although still requiring further refinement before it could function reliably in practical situations, was unveiled in May 1888.[7] That spring Jesse Lippincott, a successful industrialist, gained control of the recording industry, first acquiring the marketing rights for the graphophone and then for Edison's phonograph. These rights were dispersed on an exclusive basis among approximately thirty regional subcompanies, including the Holland brothers, who controlled the Canadian territory.[8] These subcompanies were to lease (not sell) the machines to their customers for forty dollars a year, exclusive of batteries and other sundries.

The perfected phonograph was expected to fulfill the invention's promise as a useful business machine. Low-paid personnel could simply transcribe an executive's dictation off the cylinder. The new instrument was hailed as "a stenographer which will take with unfailing accuracy from the most rapid dictation, which never goes out to 'see a man,' which is ready for work at any hour of the day, which repeats its notes as often as may be desired, which is never dissatisfied, sick or 'looking for a raise.' "[9]

It could even do away with letter writing. Businessmen could send correspondence via a phonogram, as these cylinders were often called, and so save the time and expense of having letters typed on still-primitive typewriters. Like the quadruplex and the telephone, the phonograph was meant to increase communication efficiency and decrease the costs of running an office. Yet subcompany managers encountered resistance when they marketed the phonograph as a respectable business machine. Phonograph agents testified to the practical difficulties that inexperienced people had in operating the machine. Managers soon realized that only by using the phonograph as a source of entertainment could they make money.[10] This idea took two forms: the phonograph concert and the nickel-in-the-slot phonograph, forms of presentation that paralleled projection and various peephole devices.

Phonograph concerts continued the demonstrations given for the Edison Speaking Phonograph Company. Initially, many of these exhibitions took place in storefronts, sites used by traveling museums and related amusements. During the first part of 1890 Lyman Howe and a partner traveled through eastern Pennsylvania presenting their phonograph in stores and small rooms. Open continuously each afternoon and evening, they gave concerts lasting about half an hour for an admission fee of ten cents. Their varied selections included music, speeches, and on-the-spot recordings of local personalities. These early concerts were "visited by people from every walk in life . . . and [the phonograph] excited the wonder and curiosity of all who heard it."[11] The well-to-do often came more than once.

Concerts given in lecture halls, opera houses, and churches usually lasted two hours or more. As early as February 1889, Edison associates gave a phonograph concert at Commonwealth Hall in East Orange, New Jersey, for the benefit of the Calvary Methodist Episcopal Church. This entertainment, as reported in the *Orange Chronicle,* also included a lecture on the Moors of Spain illustrated by stereopticon slides. When Howe became a solitary exhibitor in late 1890, he adopted the longer format and charged twenty-five cents for admission. Like Howe, showmen leased (and later bought) their phonographs from a subcompany and then traveled through a designated territory giving exhibitions. According to phonograph showman M. C. Sullivan, these concerts required "all the tact and versatility of the man who manipulates the instrument." He had to introduce each selection in a way that maximized its effectiveness yet melded these individual recordings into a coherent program "governed by the well known laws of dramatic practice." While a concert should have a beginning, middle, and end, it still depended on variety principles for its construction. "Serious incidents," advised Sullivan, "should be of short duration and made powerful. Comic incidents should be numerous and carefully mingled with the serious." Novelty was also important. "Sounds from nature," such as cackling hens and crowing roosters, amused audiences simply because they were incongruous and unexpected in a lecture hall. As a climax to the evening, a local band or minister often performed for the phonograph; the playback always left audiences "awed by mystery and amazement."[12]

Coin-operated phonographs (the precursor of the modern-day jukebox) became popular during 1890. In February the Automatic Phonograph Exhibition Company was incorporated to "manufacture, lease, use, and sell a nickel-in-the-slot machine by means of which the dropping of a coin in the slot will operate a mechanism which will cause a phonograph or phonograph-graphophone, to produce the sound recorded upon its cylinder." For five cents an individual could listen to a recording through

One of the Ohio phonograph parlors that opened in 1890.

earphones. By that summer, a dozen were installed at different locations in Richmond, Virginia. The Missouri Phonograph Company placed forty-eight machines in Kansas City and realized as much as fifteen hundred dollars per month.[13] The Ohio Phonograph Company found it more profitable to group its machines in arcades. At the second annual convention of local phonograph companies of the United States, James L. Andem, president of the Ohio company, explained:

> We commenced putting out the Automatic Company's machines, and confined it to the largest cities, such as Cincinnati and Cleveland. The receipts at first were quite large, but the cost of inspection was very heavy, the cylinders were easily damaged and thrown out of adjustment, and people treated the machines in a pretty rough manner at times. We finally grouped them together in what we call a system of arcades. . . . We found there that by putting the machines in groups of ten, having an attendant present to make change and keep the machines in the best adjustment in which they can be kept, the receipts were larger (*Proceedings of the Second Annual Convention*, pp. 58–59).

A Cleveland arcade was opened with twelve phonographs on 15 September 1890, and another in Cincinnati followed less than two months later. These served as models for the many phonograph parlors (and later, kinetoscope parlors) that soon appeared throughout the country. By June 1891 over a third of the country's 3,200 phonographs were being used as nickel-in-the-slot machines.[14] Most others were still employed for business purposes, but over the next several years entertainment became their dominant purpose.

The nickel-in-the-slot phonograph and the phonograph concert appealed to antagonistic cultural groups. The first type was located in saloons, hotels, and railroad stations, sometimes offered racy stories, and was occasionally subject to censorship.[15] Part of the "slot machine" phenomenon, it was strongly opposed by religious and civic groups as morally corrupting. Not long after its appearance, the nickel-in-the-slot phonograph with its multiple users was called a health hazard: infectious diseases were said to spread via the earphones.

By contrast, religious organizations, which frequently opposed the "ordinary phonograph," sponsored phonograph concerts to raise money. (For handling publicity, providing exhibition space, and drawing upon their members and friends, such groups received 30 to 40 percent of the gross receipts.) Commonly located in

Program for a Lyman H. Howe phonograph exhibition. Selections included music from Gilmore's band as well as recordings made by Howe himself.

LYMAN H. HOWE'S
Phonograph Concerts.

"Was the most pronounced success ever given in Buffalo and was a revelation to all that heard it.
— Buffalo Christian Advocate, April 5, '94.

CLARENCE S. WEISS, Advance Representative.

IN THE GRAND OPERA HOUSE

For the Benefit of the Westminster Presbyterian Church.

Tuesday Evening, December 18, 1894.

General Admission, - - - - 35 and 50 Cents.

churches and presided over by ministers, these exhibitions featured sermons or hymns and involved group participation. In their format and selections, they continued the evening concert tradition of music, song, and recitations delivered by church members with occasional assistance from a visitor. Yet for Edison and the phonograph companies, the nickel-in-the-slot machine was far more profitable. While the Ohio Phonograph Company had over sixty nickel-in-the-slot devices, four phonograph exhibitors covered the entire state.[16] Cultural prejudices were forgotten in the face of commercial opportunity, and when Edison sought to extend his phonograph into the visual realm, the inventor developed a method of exhibition modeled after the arcade machine—the peephole kinetoscope.

Edison and the Invention of Modern Motion Pictures

While Edison struggled to turn his phonograph into a viable commercial machine, he "talked up" its myriad possibilities to the press. One possible application had been suggested to him by Eadweard Muybridge, who, it will be recalled, exhibited his zoopraxiscope at the nearby Orange Music Hall on Saturday, 25 February 1888. Two days later, Muybridge met with Edison at his laboratory. There the photographer-lecturer proposed that they combine his projecting machine with the inventor's phonograph. Edison was intrigued. A few months later, a journalist visiting the West Orange laboratory reported:

> Mr. Edison said that Prof. Muybridge, the instantaneous photographer, had visited him lately and had proposed to him a scheme which, if carried to completion, will afford an almost endless field of instruction and amusement. The photographer said that he was conducting a series of experiments recently and had almost perfected a photographic appliance by which he would be enabled to accurately reproduce the gestures and the facial expression of, for instance, Mr. Blaine in the act of making a speech. This was done, he said by taking some sixty or seventy instantaneous photographs of each position assumed by the speaker, and then throwing them by means of a magic lantern upon a screen. He proposed to Mr. Edison that the phonograph should be used in connection with his invention, and that photographs of Edwin Booth as Hamlet, Lillian Russell in some of her songs, and other artists of note should be experimented with. Mr. Edison, he said, could produce with his instrument the tones of the voice while he would furnish the gestures and facial expression. This scheme met with the approval of Mr. Edison and he intended to perfect it at his leisure (*New York World*, 3 June 1888, p. 16).

Perhaps finding some free time a few months later, Edison began to recognize the limitations of Muybridge's techniques. The images were hand-drawn and few in number. In terms of efficiency, reproducibility, and ease of use, Muybridge's system could not compare with his phonograph. Reworking the idea until it became his own, Edison was later to deny that Muybridge had ever shared it with him.[17]

While Edison wondered what to call his proposed invention, he was determined the name would share the same ending as his phono*graph*. He first proposed "motograph," but his patent lawyer, Eugene A. Lewis, advised against the mixing of two languages—*moto* from the Latin and *graph* from the Greek. Lewis then consulted ex-governor Daniel H. Chamberlain, who spoke ancient Greek and suggested "kinesigraph." Not satisfied, Edison turned to *Webster's Dictionary*, found the term *kinet* or *kineto*—Greek for "movement"—and adopted it, with the result that the machine to take motion pictures was called a kinetograph and the one that showed them a kinetoscope, derived from the Greek word *scopos*, "to watch."

Edison's drawing of the micro-kinetoscope, from his October 1888 caveat.

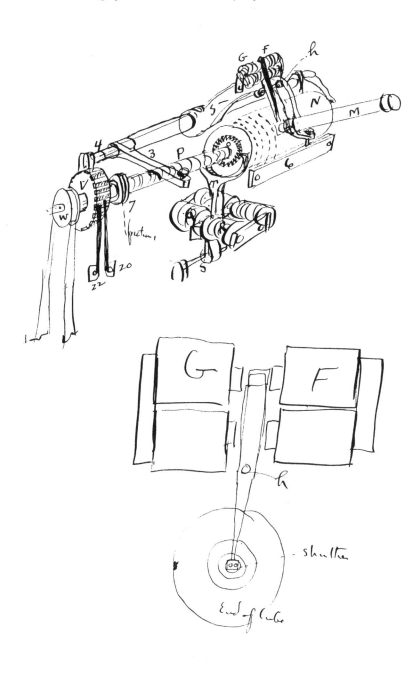

For Thomas Edison and his associates, the phonograph provided a familiar frame of reference as they pursued the development of a motion-picture system. As Edison wrote in October 1888: "I am experimenting upon an instrument which does for the Eye what the phonograph does for the Ear, which is the recording and reproduction of things in motion, and in such a form as to be both Cheap practical and convenient. This apparatus I call a Kinetoscope 'Moving View.' " Such parallelism could also prove a stumbling block, however. Edison's initial idea was to have approximately 42,000 images, each about $\frac{1}{32}$ of an inch wide, on a cylinder that was the size of his phonograph records. These were to be taken on a continuous spiral with 180 images per turn. The spectator would look at the pictures through a microscope while also listening to sound from the phonograph. Each cylinder would contain twenty-eight minutes of pictures. In March and August 1889 Edison filed two additional caveats that tried to solve some of the problems inherent in his initial formulation. The image surfaces were to be flat, and the cylinders made of glass and wrapped with photographic film.[18]

Tracing and accurately dating the various stages of invention that finally led to a commercially successful form of motion pictures is no easy task for the historian. As Gordon Hendricks has demonstrated in *The Edison Motion Picture Myth*, Edison and his associates distorted the record in their efforts to sustain both the inventor's patents and his legend. They testified that Edison's motion-picture achievements occurred years earlier than was actually the case. Newspaper accounts, however, provide a useful source of dating because the inventor, as we have seen with the phonograph, was quick to present his successful accomplishments to the press and prominent members of the public. (Indeed, newspaper accounts were often submitted in patent interference and infringement cases as evidence of an idea's "reduction to practice.") Unsuccessful experiments, such as the various applications of the photographic-cylinder idea, are more difficult to document for several reasons. They did not quickly become part of the public record; later testimony distorted what took place, and many relevant documents were lost or destroyed. Hendricks' exhaustive research, however, has uncovered important clues to the sequence of events and the time frame in which they occurred (even if the author's virulent anti-Edison attitude frequently hampered his ability to offer credible conclusions).

William Kennedy Laurie Dickson Becomes Edison's Motion-Picture Expert

As was the case with other important innovations in motion-picture technology, the kinetograph was the result of a collaboration. Some historians, most notably Terry Ramsaye, have favored Edison's role; others, particularly Gordon Hendricks, have championed Dickson. Similar historiographic differences, as we shall see in the next two chapters, have arisen around the invention of projection technology. The process of invention via collaboration is complex and almost always difficult to document in detail because it relies on the exchange of ideas. The so-called expert may often need the perspective of his or her less specialized partner. The informal process of give and take, the very ability to shape ideas jointly: these are qualities that often yield successful results yet make it impossible to give credit to one member of the team over another. Indeed, the overriding aspect of these inventive processes was the collaborative framework in which they occurred.

In February 1889 the Edison laboratory opened a kinetoscope account, coinciding with the writing of Edison's second caveat. Pattern makers, machinists, and blacksmiths may have spent the next several months building a model that conformed to Edison's idea of a photographic cylinder. Charles A. Brown and W. K. L. Dickson were brought into the kinetograph effort by late June.[19] Edison may have chosen Dickson reluctantly, since he was the inventor's key associate on the laboratory's priority undertaking at the time, the iron-ore-milling project, as well as its preeminent photographer. But if Dickson was overcommitted, he was probably the only staff member with the necessary expertise.

Initially, Dickson and Brown were applying the photographic emulsion directly onto the cylinders. As Dickson later recalled, "The photographic portion of the undertaking was seriously hampered by the defects of the materials at hand, which, however excellent in themselves, offered no substance sufficiently sensitive. How to secure clear-cut outlines, or indeed any outlines at all, together with the phenomenal speed, was the problem which puzzled the experimenters."[20] Various emulsions were tried, but each was lacking in light sensitivity or had excessive grain for the microscopic images.

During the summer of 1889 Dickson and Brown devoted virtually all their time to the kinetoscope project. After Edison had left for Europe and the Paris Exposition in early August 1889, they constructed a special building for this and other photographic work.[21] Soon they were experimenting with cylinders wrapped with celluloid sheets that carried a photographic emulsion—much as Edison had wrapped his orig-

Surviving films from Edison's cylinder experiments showing "monkeyshines."

A cylinder used for Edison's and Dickson's early motion-picture experiments.

inal phonograph with tin foil.[22] Three photographic sheets similar to those used for these experiments survive; they show an Edison employee dressed in white, placed against a black background and performing an array of movements or "monkey-shines" for the camera.[23] When Edison returned that October, he saw some results from Dickson's cylinder experiments. While these were somewhat disappointing, the inventor himself had a new approach to pursue.

During his visit to Paris, Edison had met Étienne-Jules Marey and become acquainted with the Frenchman's methods of photographing continuous series of images on a film strip that was moved along intermittently in front of a single camera lens. This approach pointed toward a conceptual break from the too-literal application of phonograph-kinetoscope parallels. It sent Edison back to earlier design methods, including the ticker-tape-like method of organizing information that he had briefly considered in 1877 while developing his "sound writer." Shortly after his return, Edison drew up a new caveat for motion pictures that reflected these conceptual advances (which were thus also regressions to earlier methods of design, presumably stimulated by a brief exchange with Marey). "Figure 46 is a Kinetoscope. The sensitive film is in the form of a long band passing from one reel to another in front of a square slit as in figure 47. On each side of the band are rows of holes exactly opposite each other & into which double toothed wheels pass. . . . Fig 48 gives rough idea of positive feed mechanism of course this principle can be applied to cylinders covered with the photo material as well as in bands."[24]

Actual production of an instrument based on these principles, however, was almost a year and a half away. Edison and his experimenters were trying to develop a complete kinetograph/kinetoscope system, and Marey's achievements did not seem

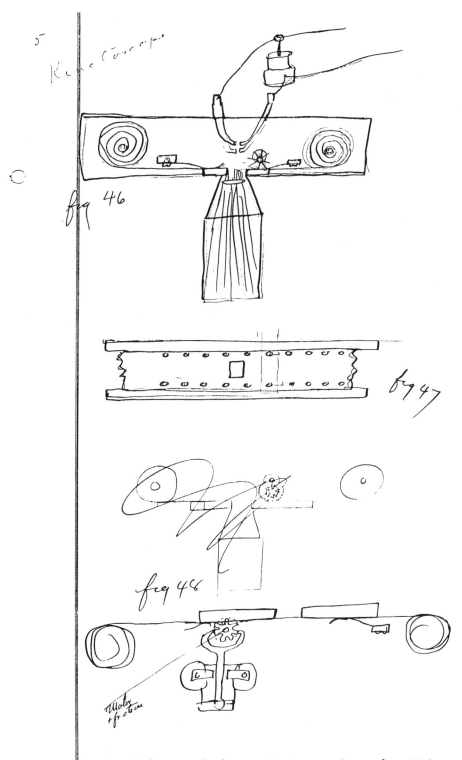

Edison's drawings for his post-Paris caveat (November 1889).

The photographic building at Edison laboratory (constructed 1889).

to suggest an effective method of exhibition. Dickson, no longer restricted to the cylinder idea, briefly reconsidered the disk method of organizing his images. He turned to the tachyscope of Ottomar Anschütz, a device that displayed a series of fourteen to twenty-four images placed along the edge of a disk in a manner somewhat similar to Heyl's phasmatrope. The disk moved continuously, with the images illuminated by a strobe effect. This work occurred in late 1889 and early 1890.[25] The cylindrical and circular motifs evident in the phonograph and Muybridge's disks for the zoopraxiscope combined to bar the way to a quick solution. Moreover Edison's return from Paris meant that Dickson and Brown had little time to devote to the kinetoscope, since Dickson now rejoined Edison on the ore-milling experiments.

It was not until October 1890 that Dickson returned to the motion-picture project. This time, he worked closely with a new assistant, William Heise, whose expertise in advancing rolls of paper tape through an automatic telegraph made him a valuable new partner.[26] The new twosome briefly pursued the cylindrical experiments but was soon working to develop a horizontal-feed motion-picture camera from Edison's Marey-inspired caveat.[27] By then, they were familiar with the work of William Friese-Greene, who claimed to have taken a continuous series of photographs from a single point of view at the rate of ten shots per second.[28] Finally, on 20 May 1891, Edison unveiled a peephole viewing machine to a large group attending a convention of the Federation of Women's Clubs: "They saw, through an aperture in a pine box standing on the floor, the picture of a man. It bowed and smiled, and took off its hat naturally and gracefully. Every motion was perfect, without a hitch or a jerk."[29] The person in the film was Dickson (and the description recalls the subject he supposedly showed to Edison on the latter's return from Paris in 1889).

Charles Kayser and the horizontal-feed kinetograph.

A newspaper cut of Edison's experimental kinetoscope (1891).

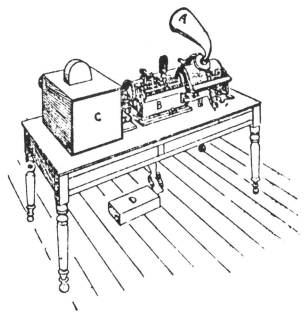

A. Funnel. **B.** Phonograph. **C.** Kinetograph.
D. Battery.

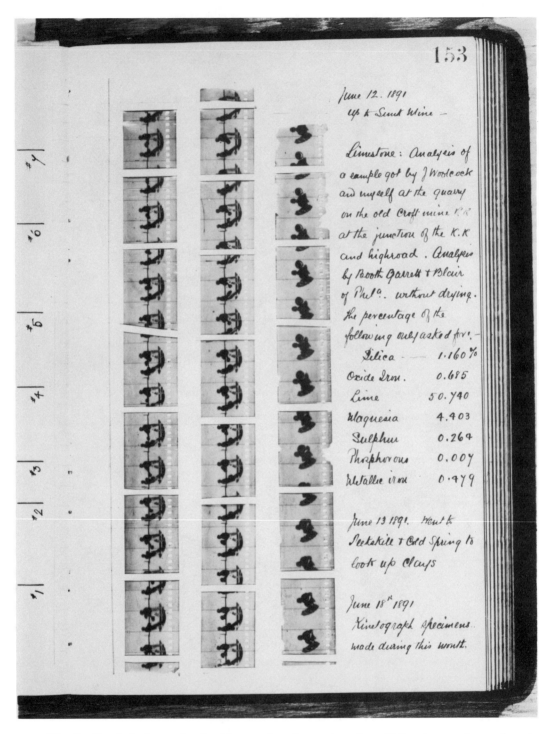

Charles Batchelor's notebook with samples of negatives from Edison's experimental motion-picture subjects. Other references on the page pertain to Edison's ore-milling efforts.

The club members were quickly followed by reporters. Edison claimed that his films were shot at the rate of forty-six frames a second, probably an exaggeration but one that was meant to distinguish his machine from those of competitors like Friese-Greene. "The trouble with all attempts heretofore made to reproduce action and motion by photographs," Edison told a reporter, "was that the photographs could not be taken in series with sufficient rapidity to catch accurately the motion it was desired to reproduce." Edison was excited about the results. "Now I've got it. That is, I've got the germ or base principle. When you get your base principle right, then it's only a question of time and a matter of details about completing the machine." And, the reporter noted, Edison "ran up stairs with the step of a boy" as he prepared to show the machine.[30]

The films at these May demonstrations were only three-quarters of an inch wide and were taken with a horizontal-feed apparatus rather than the vertical-feed system that would characterize modern motion pictures. Positive filmstrips were made from the original camera negatives. A single row of small perforations ran along the bottom edge of the films (these were inverted, top down, however, as they ran through the camera). Images on the film were circular, a technique common to magic-lantern slides. Different subjects were filmed against black backgrounds in a manner recalling Muybridge's earlier photographs. Several showed James Duncan, a laborer at the laboratory who was assigned to the project as an inexpensive and genial subject; these included a close-up of him smoking a pipe, which was designed to capture his facial expressions. Others were of athletes from Newark, New Jersey. Variety in camera framing and the focal plane were assumed from the outset.[31]

Edison did not wait for refinements before beginning the process of patenting this work. In June 1891 Dickson and Edison's lawyers started preparing two patent applications for a motion-picture camera or kinetograph, and one for a peephole-viewing device or kinetoscope. These were submitted on 24 August to the U.S. Patent Office, inaugurating a process of review, claim and counterclaim, suit and countersuit that was to last for over twenty years. Similar applications were not submitted to patent offices overseas. While Edison later claimed that this "oversight" was meant to save money, it seems more plausible that he realized that his broad

Frames from one of Edison's ¾-inch (19-mm) films.

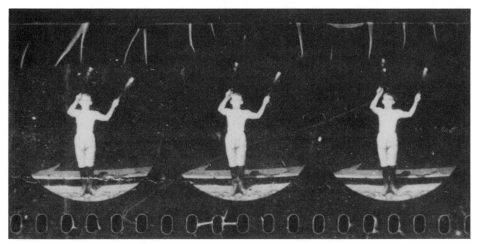

patent claims would be challenged and defeated overseas, where similar work had already been done and was well known.[32]

With the basic principles established, Dickson improved the system, adopting wider strips of film that were less susceptible to breakage. In early November, he ordered raw stock that was 1½ inches wide, 50 feet long, and ⁵⁄₁₀₀₀ of an inch thick. Already this order was for film of two different sensitivities, one for negatives and another for positive film prints. This order to the Eastman Dry Plate and Film Company was not filled until early December—and then only in an unsatisfactory manner, since the emulsion did not stick to the celluloid base. A month later, Dickson was still waiting for usable stock to arrive (such technical difficulties and delays eventually caused him to switch to film stock made by the Blair Camera Company). Meanwhile, Dickson had ordered two lenses for his camera (one "of telescopic character to bring more distant objects clearly and larger to the front . . . say a horse race 200 to 500 feet off large enough to be clearly defined in a 1″ picture") and a third for a viewing device. Rubberized trays and drums were also ordered for developing the film.[33]

By late 1891 the inventors were well on their way to completing a vertical-feed motion-picture camera. Firm evidence of this, however, did not appear until October 1892, when frames of motion-picture subjects were published in the *Phonogram*. Two were of men wrestling and fencing; another showed Heise and Dickson standing against a black background and shaking hands for the benefit of the camera. The presentational approach that would characterize most films made for Edison's peephole kinetoscope was already evident.[34]

Commercial Moving Pictures

In October 1892, shortly after completion of the 1½-inch vertical-feed system (the basis for today's 35-mm film gauge), Edison's secretary, Alfred O. Tate, began to arrange for commercial exploitation of the kinetoscope at the World's Columbian Exposition in Chicago. To meet the anticipated demand for film subjects, Edison built a studio at West Orange. Dickson designed the building to revolve on a graphite core in order to follow the sun. Begun in December, the studio was finished in February and was fully outfitted by May 1893. The studio, known as the "Black Maria"—a slang expression for the patrol wagon it was said to resemble—was rarely used at first because the design and manufacture of kinetoscopes experienced many delays. These viewing devices, electrically powered (often by batteries), although outwardly quite simple, could not be taken for granted. They needed to hold and repeatedly present a substantial amount of film without causing significant wear to the pictures. A new prototype for showing the 1½-inch film gauge was not even completed until shortly before its first public demonstration at the Brooklyn Institute of Arts and Sciences on 9 May 1893. For this occasion, a lecture-demonstration was given by George Hopkins of the institute. Afterward members of the audience stood in line and peered into the machine to see BLACKSMITH SCENE, the first commercial-length modern motion-picture subject to be publicly exhibited. Taken in the Black Maria, it showed three men (Edison employees) hammering on an anvil and passing a bottle of beer around as they worked.[35]

Perhaps after some further adjustments were made in the prototype, Edison con-

In a self-reflexive moment, Dickson and Heise congratulate each other over their production of the first modern films.

THE KINETOGRAPH.

A NEW INDUSTRY HERALDED.

It is difficult for those not familiar with the phonograph to conceive the extent of its field of operations, or the diversity, one might almost say the inconsistency, of the functions it fills. It is like the "harp of a thousand strings" of which we read.

Its latest role is by no means the least wonderful, and though this instrument has already achieved conquests in the sphere of industry that may be denominated vast, the greatest is yet to come; and when it stands forth before the world, will make such gigantic strides as were never previously witnessed.

At the opening of the Columbian Exposition there will appear a dual instrument, two steeds of almost infinite capacity in their special powers, whose performances it will tax the human eye and ear to follow.

The Edison Kinetograph is an instrument intended to reproduce motion and sound simultaneously, being a combination of a specially constructed camera and phonograph. The camera used in connection with this instrument will take forty-six pictures a second, which is 2,760 pictures a minute, or 165,600 in an hour. The rapid photographing of these pictures upon a long band of extremely light, sensitive film creates the illusory spectacle of real motion of the figures, and when to this visual impression The Phonograph is called to

join its voice, we have a combination of effects upon both auditory and optic nerves. This specially constructed camera is attached electrically to a phonograph and their combined movements are simultaneously registered, and thus we have the duplex sensation of vision and sound.

Now the advantages of the kinetograph

Boxing.

A page from The Phonogram, *announcing Edison's successful realization of the long-promised kinetoscope.*

BLACKSMITH SCENE

tracted for twenty-five machines in late June. These were not completed until March 1894. Only the prototype was available for possible exhibition at the Chicago World's Fair, and this was too valuable to send.[36] Edison was quoted as saying, "I was very anxious to have one on exhibition at the fair but we will not have it finished in time."[37] On 1 April, with the completion of the first twenty-five kinetoscopes, Edison shifted his motion-picture business to a commercial entity, the Edison Manufacturing Company (often referred to as the Edison Company). Up until this date, his kinetoscope account showed the following expenses:

Kinetoscope experiment	$21,736.25
Labor, etc. on twenty-five kinetoscopes	1,227.48
Photographing building	516.64
Revolving photograph building (Black Maria)	637.67
TOTAL	$24,118.04[38]

The transition from experimentation to production was made easier by continuity in personnel: W. K. L. Dickson remained in charge of the motion-picture business, assisted by William Heise. The approaching completion of the kinetoscopes spurred the Edison group to serious film production. In early January 1894 Dickson filmed EDISON KINETOSCOPIC RECORD OF A SNEEZE: a few days later, on January 9, it was copyrighted as a photograph. This brief subject, meant for magazine publicity, was a close-up of Edison employee Fred Ott against a black background, facing the camera and in the process of sneezing. Other full-length films made during the winter included AMATEUR GYMNAST, showing a Newark athlete doing a backward somersault, and THE BARBERSHOP, in which a customer gets a lightning-fast shave for five cents. On 6 March Dickson and Heise "kinetographed" the famous Austrian strong man Eugene Sandow, who posed in the Black Maria and then met Edison in lieu of a $250 fee.[39] Bodybuilder Sandow represented an ideal of manly physique and strength. For one film, the strong man stripped to a loincloth and assumed an array of positions that showed off his physique. In cinematography as in photography, Dickson had a well-trained eye. His camera framed Sandow just above the knees; against the black background, Sandow's muscular frame drew all of the viewer's attention.

The rebuilt Edison kinetograph (camera), now at the Henry Ford Museum, Dearborn, Michigan.

The kinetoscope.

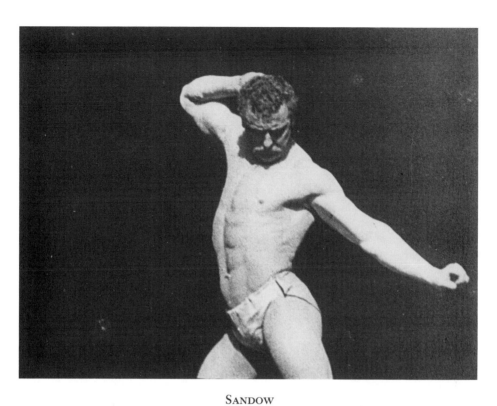

Sandow

Barbershop Scene

The first films had been made by men, primarily for men, and of men, but these conditions were to change soon after Sandow's appearance. Carmencita, a Spanish dancer who had become a star on the variety stage, did a provocative dance for the camera, twirling so that her dress rose and exposed her legs. As commercial exhibition became imminent, other subjects more appropriate for mixed-sex audiences were made, including HIGHLAND DANCE, with a couple doing a Scottish fling, and ORGAN GRINDER. The films, which were approximately 46 feet long and shot at approximately 40 frames per second, lasted less than 20 seconds.

Dickson and Heise kinetographed over seventy-five motion pictures in 1894, and virtually everyone drew on some type of popular commercial amusement. Among the many vaudeville and variety performers they filmed were the contortionist Madame Edna Bertoldi, the facial contortionist George Layman, and the Glenroy Brothers, a burlesque boxing team. Professor Henry Welton's animals appeared in THE WRESTLING DOG and THE BOXING CATS. Dancer Annabelle Whitford [Moore] made the first of many appearances in the Black Maria by mid August in ANNABELLE BUTTERFLY DANCE and ANNABELLE SERPENTINE DANCE. Members of Buffalo Bill's Wild West Show visited the studio at least four times during the fall, yielding BUFFALO BILL, INDIAN WAR COUNCIL, BUCKING BRONCHO (photographed in a corral to the rear of the studio), and ANNIE OAKLEY. Five films were taken of Charles Hoyt's musical comedy *A Milk White Flag*, including BAND DRILL and FINALE OF 1ST ACT, HOYT'S "MILK WHITE FLAG." The latter showed thirty-four persons in costume, which was "the largest number ever shown as one subject in the Kinetoscope."[40]

Sex and violence figured prominently in American motion pictures from the outset. In fact, such subjects were consistent with the individualized, peephole nature of the viewing experience: they showed amusements that often offended polite and/or religious Americans. COCK FIGHT was taken close up against a black background that made the roosters stand out. Terriers were filmed attacking rats. Petit and Kessler appeared in WRESTLING MATCH, while Madame Ruth did the hoochie-coochie for DANCE DE VENTRE. Women dancers often wore skimpy attire. Although many of these films appealed specifically to male voyeurism, they also attracted women with brief glimpses of the usually forbidden world of masculine amusement. Given this sexually charged material, kinetoscope exhibitors periodically experienced forms of censorship. In Asbury Park, New Jersey, a summer resort dominated by conservative Protestants, the mayor forbade the showing of Carmencita's dance film. In San Francisco, the Society for the Suppression of Vice had a kinetoscope exhibitor arrested for showing allegedly indecent pictures.[41]

The methods of film production and exhibition owed much to nineteenth-century photographic practices and, most important, to the phonograph. Phonograph performers were usually placed in a recording studio that isolated them from miscellaneous sounds. Correspondingly, the Maria, with its black walls, eliminated extraneous visual distractions. This dark background also placed its subjects in bold relief in a manner that recalls Eadweard Muybridge's serial views. Neither phonograph nor kinetograph, however, was always restricted to such controlled settings. Some recordings—for instance, church chimes—were made on location, while Dickson and William Heise filmed the tightrope walker Juan Caicedo outside the studio with the wire "stretched in the open air directly north of the building."[42] While the kinetoscope has similarities with the viewing instruments for stereoscopic photo-

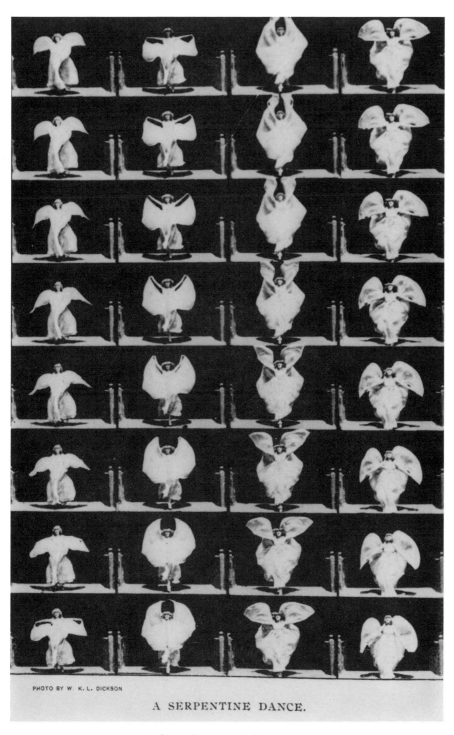

PHOTO BY W. K. L. DICKSON

A SERPENTINE DANCE.

A dance by Annabelle (1894).

Dickson's photograph of the Black Maria in late 1894.

Heise filming in the Black Maria. From Century Magazine, *June 1894. The use of the phonograph (at left) was for publicity and experimental purposes only.*

graphs, its immediate commercial counterpart was the nickel-in-the-slot phonograph. Both kinetograph and phonograph focused on the same types of subject matter, material drawn from America's increasingly vibrant urban popular culture.

Marketing and Exploiting the Kinetoscope

On 1 April 1894, as the kinetoscope business was finally getting under way, Edison hired William E. Gilmore to replace Alfred O. Tate as his business chief. Gilmore became vice-president and general manager of the Edison Manufacturing Company, which handled Edison's motion-picture business over the next eighteen years. (It also manufactured such items as batteries, dental equipment, and later, x-ray machines.) Edison relied on three outside groups to market his kinetoscope and films, the first and most prominent of which was a consortium of entrepreneurs that became known as the Kinetoscope Company. It included Alfred O. Tate, phonograph executives Thomas Lombard and Erastus Benson, Norman C. Raff, Frank R. Gammon, and Andrew Holland.[43] Through Tate, they had a long-standing order for the first twenty-five kinetoscopes. These were finally finished in the spring of 1894. Shipped to the Holland brothers on 6 April, the first ten machines were installed at 1155 Broadway in New York City.[44] A different film subject was placed in each kinetoscope; these were printed on a translucent film base that provided an excellent surface for the film to catch and soften the light. Manufactured by the Blair Camera Company, this frosted stock was the standard film for all kinetoscopes.

With the opening of the Holland brothers' kinetoscope parlor on Saturday, 14 April 1894, the history of commercial motion pictures began. At twenty-five cents a ticket to see one row of five machines, or two tickets to see all ten, they had netted about $120 by evening, and this before any advertising had appeared. A second kinetoscope parlor followed in Chicago on 17 or 18 May, when the Hollands installed another ten machines at a Masonic temple. The remaining five had a San Francisco premiere on 1 June at Peter Bacigalupi's phonograph parlor.

In its 1 April 1895 statement, the Kinetoscope Company estimated the cost of running a first-class kinetoscope parlor at about five hundred dollars a month:

Rent	$300
Manager and attendants	140
Electricity and lights	75

Gross receipts through 1 April 1895 were $16,171.56 for its New York parlor and less than half that amount, $7,409.84, for the one in Chicago. Other exhibitions run by the group were of a more temporary nature. One in Atlantic City, New Jersey, and another in Washington, D.C., for example, were located in phonograph parlors owned by the Columbia Phonograph Company, which was also responsible for their operation. Atlantic City receipts fluctuated between $73.75 and $193 a day in July 1894; the Kinetoscope Company kept 55 percent, while Columbia assumed many expenses.[45]

Edison initially sold kinetoscopes and films to a variety of customers for $250 a machine. Purchasers included Thomas L. Tally (whose family owned a phonograph parlor in Los Angeles although he was then based in Waco, Texas) and Walter Isaacs, both of whom would later play significant roles in the film industry. Kinetoscopes were often placed in summer amusement parks, such as Eagle Rock in Orange, where the novelty had its New Jersey commercial debut on 8 July 1894. It soon became apparent, however, that unrestrained, disorganized exhibition threatened to harm effective marketing, and in mid-August the Kinetoscope Company, headed by Norman Raff and Frank Gammon, was granted exclusive rights for selling regular kinetoscopes within the United States and Canada. They agreed to purchase approximately ten machines a week from Edison for $200 apiece: they then sold these for between $325 and $350 each. The Raff and Gammon partnership sold kinetoscopes only with territorial restrictions—a method similar to that previously employed by the North American Phonograph Company.[46]

The Edison Manufacturing Company gradually built relations with a second group headed by Franck Z. Maguire and Joseph D. Baucus, who made their first purchases in mid July and subsequently opened a kinetoscope parlor in Brooklyn. That September they acquired the exclusive rights to sell and exhibit the kinetoscope overseas—so long as they worked the territory to Edison's satisfaction. They were expected to dispose of thirteen machines per week for six months and eight machines a week thereafter. Incorporating the Continental Commerce Company for overseas activities, the partners operated from an office at 44 Pine Street, New York City. Their European activities commenced 17 October 1894 with the opening of a kinetoscope parlor in London that took in between seventeen and eighteen pounds a day. By early November, they had kinetoscopes operating at four other locations in the city. As Maguire wrote to Edison at the time, the invention was being treated "in the most friendly and enthusiastic way" by the British press, and arrangements were quickly made for openings in other European cities.[47]

A third group, eventually called the Kinetoscope Exhibiting Company, was started by Otway Latham, who managed the Tilden Company, a pharmaceutical business with offices in New York City. On 16 May 1894 he deposited $1,000 toward the purchase of ten kinetoscopes, each costing $245.[48] He soon enlisted the aid of his brother, Gray; his father, Woodville; and an old college friend and fellow Tilden Company employee, Enoch J. Rector. They wanted to show films of prize fights—an idea Edison had mentioned in the press but one that had not been realized because of the kinetoscope's limited capacity for film. It may have been Otway Latham who proposed a solution: to expand the kinetoscope's capacity so that it could show 150 feet of film and slow down the rate of taking exposures to 30 frames per second. Running time was thus increased to slightly more than a minute, allowing each machine to show an abbreviated boxing round.

The first subject for the Latham–Rector enterprise was a six-round boxing match between Michael Leonard and Jack Cushing. The fighters, after waiting all week for a clear day, traveled to the Black Maria on Friday, 15 June. Dickson and Heise filmed the event, which received immediate front-page publicity in the New York papers. Leonard, a popular pugilist, received $150, while his rival got $50. According to the *New York World,*

> The rounds were to last one minute only. That was necessary as the kinetograph could not be arranged to work more than one minute at a time. There were to be six rounds and between each round the men were to rest

seven minutes while the men in charge of the kinetograph prepared it to receive new impressions (*New York World,* 16 June 1894, p. 1).

The papers did not report the fight's outcome, the *World* explained, because "Mr. Edison and the six wise men were too excited to remember just what happened, and the accounts of the two fighters vary." The uncertainty was clearly designed to encourage boxing afficionados to pay sixty cents to see the fight—ten cents a round— and learn the results "first-hand."

In July, Otway Latham and Enoch Rector officially changed their May order from ten regular to twelve large-capacity (150-foot) kinetoscopes. In early August, Latham paid the Edison Manufacturing Company $700, enough for the first six machines. Another $450 payment in mid August may have been for the films, which would have enabled them to open their parlor at 83 Nassau Street and exhibit THE LEONARD–CUSHING FIGHT. Meanwhile, Latham and Rector found a major new source of financing in their employer, Samuel Tilden, Jr., who was heir to a large fortune left to him by his uncle, a former governor of New York. In mid August, Otway Latham placed an order for seventy-two special kinetoscopes at $300 a machine, not including films and batteries. The next set of six was to be delivered in early September, and the third, two weeks later.[49]

New financing allowed the group to produce a more ambitious subject of international interest. They arranged a fight between heavyweight champion James Corbett, then appearing in the Broadway play *Gentleman Jack,* and New Jersey pugilist Peter

THE LEONARD–CUSHING FIGHT

Courtney. The champion was purportedly guaranteed $5,000 if he could knock out Courtney in the sixth round. The fighter also signed a royalty agreement that proved even more profitable: he was to receive $150 per week (later reduced to $50) for each set of films on exhibition in the kinetoscopes. The bout came off on 7 September as planned. Corbett delivered a knockout blow in the sixth round and newspapers reported the event in great detail. Prize fighting, however, was forbidden in New Jersey, as in the rest of the country. Perhaps because this kinetoscope fight involved the heavyweight champion, a knockout, and extensive publicity, Judge David A. Depue in Newark started a grand-jury investigation. Edison was subpoenaed but denied any involvement or knowledge of the event—even though his presence was reported in the press. The matter was eventually dropped, and CORBETT AND COURTNEY BEFORE THE KINETOGRAPH (better known as THE CORBETT–COURTNEY FIGHT) achieved wide popularity.[50]

The Kinetoscope Exhibiting Company opened its second parlor at 587 Broadway in New York City. On 14 September Rector inspected the finished machines at the West Orange laboratory, prior to their expected delivery that afternoon, and by 23 September, the enlarged kinetoscopes were in operation. The parlor soon had to shut down, however, since, as Latham explained in a letter to Gilmore, the films were "breaking as fast as we put them on." This mechanical problem was quickly solved, however, and the Kinetoscope Exhibiting Company went on to open parlors in Boston, Chicago, St. Louis, and San Francisco, after which the machines went on tour. Arrangements were also made with Maguire & Baucus for exhibitions overseas. Despite these initial successes, Otway Latham displayed few organizational skills and his conflicting instructions soon strained relations with the Edison firm, with the result that he was removed as manager. The exhibitions nevertheless proved popular and profitable—at least for Corbett. By August 1896 he had received $13,307. Even after projection caught on, the films remained in use, and Samuel J. Tilden, Jr., was forced to keep paying Corbett: the final sum exceeded $20,000.[51]

The Edison Manufacturing Company enjoyed great prosperity in the year following the introduction of the peephole kinetoscope. From 1 April 1894 through 28 February 1895, motion picture sales totaled:

Kinetoscope sales	$149,548.64
Film sales	$25,882.10
Kinetoscope sundries	$2,416.49
	$177,847.23

Profits came to $85,337.83. The three groups were responsible for approximately 80 percent of these sales. By the end of February 1895 Maguire & Baucus had purchases totaling $71,810.44; Otway Latham and the Kinetoscope Exhibiting Company, $14,270.45, and the Raff & Gammon and Kinetoscope Company people, $57,536.66. This last group's gross profit on sales through 15 March was

Kinetoscopes	$25,794.31
Films	$2,870.91
Batteries	$602.40
	$29,267.62

For the following business year (28 February 1895–1 March 1896), however, total sales for Edison's film-related business fell to $49,896.03 and profits to $4,140.94;

A bar doubles as a kinetoscope parlor. These enlarged kinetoscopes mostly showed films of the Corbett–Courtney fight.

ANNABELLE BUTTERFLY DANCE (1895). *The C at right indicates that the film was produced by the Continental Commerce Company.*

while kinetoscope sales remained substantial into the spring of 1895, they slumped precipitously that summer and never recovered.[52]

With the approaching winter of 1894–1895, production activities declined but included FIRE RESCUE SCENE, a spectacle with smoke effects that showed firemen saving a family from its burning home, and CHINESE LAUNDRY SCENE, a shortened vaudeville routine in which a "Chinaman" eludes an Irish cop through an impressive display of acrobatics. The latter film, featuring the two Italian performers Robetta and Doreto, was an early attempt at ethnic comedy. Filmmaking picked up briefly in early spring with scenes taken from plays (QUARTETTE from *Trilby*), musical revues (JAMES GRUNDY from *The South Before the War*), and Barnum and Bailey's Circus (DANCE OF REJOICING with Samoan Islanders, PRINCESS ALI). Once sales declined, however, filmmaking was again curtailed. To encourage new activity, the wholesale price for kinetoscopes was cut in May to $127.50, with machines retailing for not more than $250. In fact, this did little to spur business. Another flurry of film production occurred in late August and September as Raff & Gammon employee Alfred Clark was assigned responsibility for making new subjects. Several were historical, including JOAN OF ARC and THE EXECUTION OF MARY, QUEEN OF SCOTS, which Heise shot outdoors near the West Orange laboratory. THE EXECUTION OF MARY, QUEEN OF SCOTS used "stop-motion substitution" to show the decapitation of Mary (played by Robert

EXECUTION OF MARY, QUEEN OF SCOTS *(August 1895). A splice appears near the bottom of the upper frame.*

Thomae, secretary and treasurer of the Kinetoscope Company): just before the be-heading took place, the camera stopped, Thomae was replaced by a dummy, and the filming resumed. When the two takes were spliced together, the interruption was not evident to the spectator and appeared as one continuous shot. This stop-motion sub-stitution, along with the depiction of historical subject matter, were significant inno-vations; even so, Clark's film subjects commanded only modest sales, and very few additional pictures were made in the following months.[53]

Edison and his associates tried to revive their motion-picture business in April 1895 with the introduction of the long-promised kinetophone, combining kineto-scope and phonograph. The spectator looked through a peephole viewer and listened

An experimental sound film that was never released. Dickson plays the violin into the phonograph horn.

simultaneously to a recording through earphones. Subjects were usually dances or musical numbers, which required only loose synchronization. Pictures were rarely if ever made especially for the kinetophone. The only surviving exception, usually identified as DICKSON EXPERIMENTAL SOUND FILM, was never shown commercially. Taken in the Black Maria, it shows Dickson playing the violin as two men dance. Kinetophones began to be sold for as much as four hundred dollars, but the demand was small and only forty-five had been made by early 1900.[54]

Edison's motion-picture business faced multiple difficulties by summer 1895. Maguire & Baucus encountered serious competition in England, where Robert W. Paul was making duplicate kinetoscopes and his own original films, and these activities were safe from legal action because of Edison's failure to patent his motion-picture inventions overseas. While the Kinetoscope Exhibiting Company continued its operations, its attempts to take films of another championship fight were repeatedly frustrated. Raff & Gammon's orders declined not only because the novelty of kinetoscope motion pictures was fading but because, as Raff wrote to Dickson in January 1896, "other parties got out machines and sold them at low figures."[55] The principal domestic imitation was made by Charles E. Chinnock, a former Edison associate. On the market by early 1895, these Chinnock kinetoscopes were placed in the Eden Musee and other amusement centers. Raff & Gammon were eventually forced to sell machines for one hundred dollars apiece (seventy dollars wholesale), which greatly reduced their profit margin. Volume also dropped, and late in the business year there were months when they did not sell a single machine.

The declining kinetoscope business was reflected in personnel changes. W. K. L. Dickson, increasingly disenchanted with his situation at the Edison laboratory, left the inventor's employ in April 1895, and Alfred Clark returned to the phonograph business late in the year. James White and Charles Webster, who had worked for the Holland brothers and then exhibited their own kinetoscopes, sold their machines. White also reembraced the recording industry, while Webster took Clark's place at Raff & Gammon.[56] With Raff & Gammon ready to sell or even liquidate the Kinetoscope Company, Edison's motion-picture novelty might have suffered the fate of the tin-foil phonograph—had it not been rescued by projection.

3

Projecting Motion Pictures: Invention and Innovation

*T*he idea of adapting Edison's moving pictures to the magic lantern or stereopticon was so simple and straightforward that it undoubtedly occurred to hundreds, probably thousands, of people who peered into the kinetoscope. Fewer individuals, but still a surprisingly large number, tried to turn this idea into a reality. Projecting machines were invented independently and more or less simultaneously in four major industrialized countries: France, England, Germany, and the United States. While each inventor gave his machine a different name, their projectors all shared the same basic principles. In France, Auguste and Louis Lumière developed the cinématographe at their Lyons factory, showed it privately in March 1895, and opened commercially in Paris at the Grand Café on the Boulevard des Capucines on 28 December 1895. Robert Paul, who was making films and kinetoscopes in England, realized his own idea for a projector after hearing of a Lumière cinématographe performance. He called it the theatrograph and demonstrated it to the public on 20 February 1896, at Finsbury Technical College. Max Skladanowsky's bioscope, which was shown at Berlin's Wintergarten in November 1895, was the most eccentric and commercially unimportant of the European inventions but is indicative of the many attempts to show projected motion pictures.[1]

In the United States the development of a successful projector took a more circuitous path. Although Edison always gave lip service to the idea of projection, the sales of peephole machines were at first so profitable that he was not at all eager to disrupt his lucrative market. Even if a "screen machine" proved more popular, the inventor believed—with considerable reason—that it would hurt him financially. Correspondingly it was commercial opportunity that beckoned a band of determined exhibitors to build the first American machine for projecting motion pictures. They would call it the eidoloscope.

The Lathams Build a Projector

While showing fight films in their oversized kinetoscopes, the Lathams became convinced that projection would enhance their exhibition business. Soon they were actively pursuing the idea. The impetus, according to Woodville Latham, a former chemistry professor, came from his sons Otway and Gray:

> Two of my sons were engaged at 83 Nassau street in the business of exhibiting pictures by the use of the Edison Kinetoscope. A day or so after

they began the exhibitions, one of my sons came to me and asked if I could not devise a machine for projecting pictures upon a screen. He said that a number of spectators in his hearing had expressed a wish that something of that sort might be done, and subsequently I heard from spectators myself, similar expressions. I said to my son that I had not the slightest doubt of my ability to do what he had suggested, and I immediately began to consider plans for the construction of such apparatus (Woodville Latham, testimony, 4 December 1897).[2]

His sons, however, gave credit to their father: "We were unable to accommodate the crowds we had, as only one at a time could view the pictures exhibited by the kinetoscope, and my father suggested making a machine that would enlarge pictures of this character so that more than one could view them at the same time."[3]

From a showman's perspective, the commercial advantages of projection were obvious. It was a much more efficient method of exhibition that would reduce start-up costs, since each parlor would need only one machine instead of six. Maintenance would be easier and wear reduced. With more people seeing a film at one time, revenues could increase. An exhibitor's mobility would also be enhanced, thus expanding the territory where films could be shown profitably. Moreover, spectators wanted a life-size image that would enable them to see the subject matter more clearly and comfortably. As part of an audience rather than isolated viewers, they could more readily share the experience with their friends. The Lathams' undertaking even opened up the possibility of exhibiting an entire regulation-length boxing match, which was impossible with the peephole kinetoscope's limited capacity. The Lathams, who had no prior connections with the phonograph industry, were quick to see that motion pictures and recorded sound presented quite different commercial realities.

Woodville Latham and his sons did not pursue the invention of a projector within the Kinetoscope Exhibition Company but as a separate undertaking. A group of collaborators soon joined them. W. K. L. Dickson, increasingly dissatisfied with his situation at the Edison laboratory, provided the needed experience with motion pictures. He had met Otway Latham in the process of handling the kinetoscope business and was open to new opportunities. Eugène Lauste, a Frenchman who had worked for Edison from 1886 until April 1892, was close friends with Dickson. Introduced to the Lathams by Dickson, Lauste was promptly hired as chief mechanic at twenty-one dollars a week. The Lathams' activities thus illustrate one way that technological expertise left the Edison laboratory when former associates and employees set up rival firms.

The Lathams planned the creation of the eidoloscope projector (if not a whole new motion-picture system which included that projector), raised the financing, and oversaw the actual execution. Dickson made it unnecessary for the group to start from scratch: even though his ideas about projection were not ultimately utilized, his expertise with printers and other aspects of film production greatly facilitated the process of developing a motion-picture system. Lauste, a mechanical expert of uncommon dexterity, did most of the actual designing and construction.[4] As with other inventive accomplishments, however, the collaborators later disagreed about their relative contributions, with each tending to claim the bulk of the credit for himself.

At first, Dickson's assistance was friendly, informal, and clandestine. The motion-picture expert, still working for Edison and enjoying substantial royalties for his contribution to the kinetograph and kinetoscope, knew that his role in the Latham enterprise was unethical and constantly worried that it would be discovered at the West Orange laboratory. Nonetheless Dickson soon reached a verbal understanding and possibly even a contractual relationship with the Lathams. When the Lambda Company was formed (named after the Greek letter for *L*, the first letter of the Lathams' name) late in 1894, it was agreed that he would receive 25 percent of the stock, provided his assistance resulted in the construction of a satisfactory apparatus for photographing, printing, developing, and projecting films. Because of his relations with Edison, Dickson's share (valued at $125,000) was assigned to his attorney, Edmond Congar Brown.[5] Lauste also received a 4 percent share, valued at $20,000. The remainder was mostly controlled by the Lathams.

The Lathams' projection system, like the kinetoscope, relied on a constantly moving band of film rather than the "intermittent" mechanism that momentarily stopped each frame of film in front of the condensor lens (the basis for all modern projection). According to Woodville Latham's patent interference testimony, September and October 1894 were spent in preliminary experiments "to determine the intensity of light the projection of pictures of movement required and what were the best forms of condenser to be employed, as well as what objective [i.e. lens] would be most suitable for the purpose in view." Tests were conducted at Columbia College in Manhattan, where Dickson brought an old-model kinetoscope and films. By October or November, the Lathams had found financing for the undertaking and set up a machine shop and offices downtown at 35 Frankfort Street. Dickson came to the

The Lathams' Frankfort Street workshop (1895). Otway Latham at right foreground, Eugène Lauste with elbow on apparatus, and Gray Latham between them; Woodville Latham looks out window, second from left.

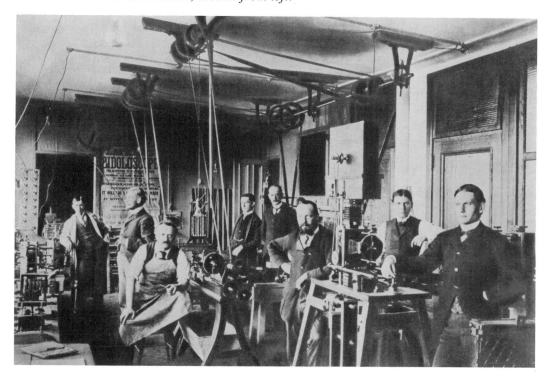

Frankfort Street shop as often as once a week to offer advice and sometimes to participate in the undertaking. By December, Lauste had completed a 1½-inch (about 35-mm) gauge projecting machine. Despite the lack of an intermittent mechanism, the machine was considered fundamentally successful. It was decided, however, to use a wider, two-inch film that would allow more light to pass through the larger image surface.[6] Perhaps to make their system more distinctive, the Lathams had their film move in the reverse direction from Edison's. The necessary motion-picture camera was constructed and then tried out on the night of 26–27 February, with Otway Latham and Dickson filming a swinging light. When this experiment proved successful, the group filmed a simple home movie on the roof of the Frankfort Street building: Woodville Latham smoked a pipe while others, including Lauste's son, shuffled and cavorted (see illustration on page 96).

The new camera was briefly tried out as a projecting apparatus. According to Woodville Latham, it worked but was abandoned because "the life of a film used in a machine where the film is moved continuously is greatly longer than in a machine where the movement is intermittent." Lauste remarked that the film shrank during the process of developing and was too small for the machine's sprockets. Blinded by the precedent of constantly moving filmstrips, they continued to pursue a projecting machine that lacked an intermittent mechanism.[7] In this respect, the eidoloscope relied on principles similar to Muybridge's zoopraxiscope (or the zoetrope).

In January 1895, while Lauste concentrated on the "taking machine," parts were ordered and received for five projectors. Once the camera was operating, work shifted to constructing a projector that could use the two-inch film. The inventors made further improvements over the projection experiments of the preceding fall. A clear-base film stock, purchased from Eastman Kodak, replaced the frosted celluloid appropriate for the peephole kinetoscope. In March, Woodville Latham also located a lens that allowed more light to reach the screen than those previously acquired from J. B. Colt and Company.[8] The eidoloscope projector was soon completed and a demonstration arranged at the Frankfort Street office on the afternoon of 21 April. An article on their "Magic Lantern Kinetoscope" appeared the following day:

> The pictures shown yesterday portrayed the antics of some boys at play in a park [sic]. They wrestled, jumped, fought, and tumbled over one another. Near where the boys were romping a man sat reading a paper and smoking a pipe. Even the puffs of smoke could be plainly seen, as could also a man's movements when he took a handkerchief from his pocket. The whole picture on the screen yesterday was about the size of a window sash, but the size is a matter of expense and adjustment (*New York Sun*, 22 April 1895, p. 2).

Although Edison belittled the event in the same news item, it was the first public demonstration of projected motion pictures in the United States.

With its motion-picture system functioning, the Lambda Company commenced serious production. Arrangements were made to film a fight between Young Griffo (Albert Griffiths) and Charles Barnett on the rooftop of Madison Square Garden. The 4 May encounter involved four rounds of a minute and a half each, with half a minute rest between rounds. The eight minutes of action, however, were filmed without interruption. Previously, the amount of film that could be shot at one time had been

The eidoloscope projector. The film moved from bottom to top.

Screening the new Latham machine for the press. Illustration from the New York Sun.

ENLARGED KINETOSCOPE PICTURES THROWN ON A SCREEN.

The Latham film shown to the press on 21 April 1895. Woodville Latham is seated at far right.

limited to about 140 feet—more than that and the film would tear—but Lauste or Dickson now added a loop to their camera so that the intermittent mechanism would not pull directly on the unexposed film. With what became known as the "Latham loop," the capacity for continuous shooting was limited only by the amount of available film and the size of the film magazine. The improved camera did not stop during the fighters' short rest periods—as with THE CORBETT–COURTNEY FIGHT—but continued to operate. The result, according to the *Brooklyn Eagle* of 8 May 1895, was "Continuous Pictures of the Griffo–Barnett Encounter." The filming of the event generated considerable publicity for the company and its still unnamed machine.[9]

With new fight pictures, the Lathams opened a small storefront theatre at 156 Broadway in New York City on 20 May.[10] Since no relevant ads appear in the newspapers, we know that they spent little on promotion. Nonetheless, the *New York World* ran an enthusiastic article on the newly named eidoloscope and its show, remarking:

> Life size presentations they are and will be, and you won't have to squint into a little hole to see them. You'll sit comfortably and see fighters hammering each other, circuses, suicides, hangings, electrocutions, shipwrecks, scenes on the exchanges, street scenes, horse-races, football games, almost anything, in fact, in which there is action, just as if you were on the spot during the actual events. And you won't see marionettes. You'll see people and things as they are. If they wink their other eye, even though not so expressively as Miss Cissy Fitzgerald winks hers, or Thomas C. Platt winks his, you will see the lid on its way down and up. If their hair raises in fright, or grows gray in a half hour, you'll see all the details of the change (*New York World*, 28 May 1895, p. 30).

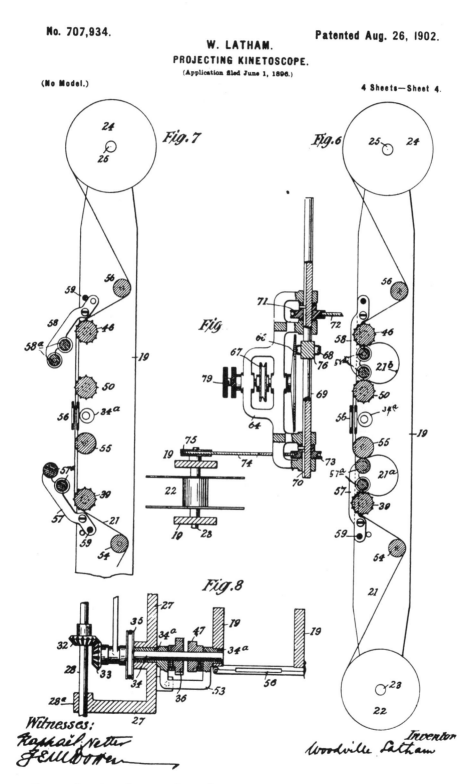

No. 707,934.

W. LATHAM.
PROJECTING KINETOSCOPE.
(Application filed June 1, 1896.)

Patented Aug. 26, 1902.

(No Model.)

4 Sheets—Sheet 4.

Patent drawing showing the Latham equipment and the "Latham loop."

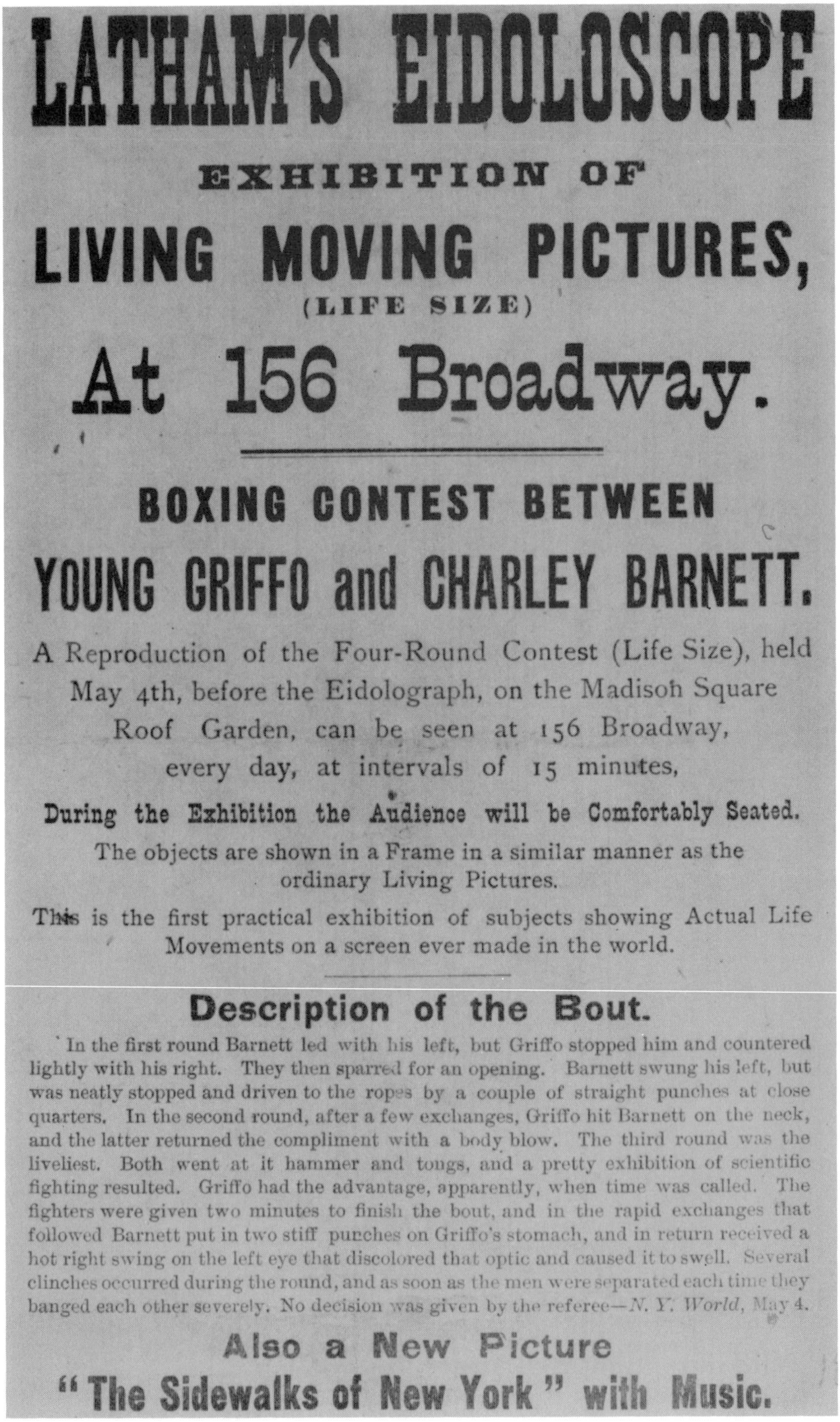

LATHAM'S EIDOLOSCOPE

EXHIBITION OF
LIVING MOVING PICTURES,
(LIFE SIZE)
At 156 Broadway.

BOXING CONTEST BETWEEN
YOUNG GRIFFO and CHARLEY BARNETT.

A Reproduction of the Four-Round Contest (Life Size), held May 4th, before the Eidolograph, on the Madison Square Roof Garden, can be seen at 156 Broadway, every day, at intervals of 15 minutes,

During the Exhibition the Audience will be Comfortably Seated.

The objects are shown in a Frame in a similar manner as the ordinary Living Pictures.

This is the first practical exhibition of subjects showing Actual Life Movements on a screen ever made in the world.

Description of the Bout.

In the first round Barnett led with his left, but Griffo stopped him and countered lightly with his right. They then sparred for an opening. Barnett swung his left, but was neatly stopped and driven to the ropes by a couple of straight punches at close quarters. In the second round, after a few exchanges, Griffo hit Barnett on the neck, and the latter returned the compliment with a body blow. The third round was the liveliest. Both went at it hammer and tongs, and a pretty exhibition of scientific fighting resulted. Griffo had the advantage, apparently, when time was called. The fighters were given two minutes to finish the bout, and in the rapid exchanges that followed Barnett put in two stiff punches on Griffo's stomach, and in return received a hot right swing on the left eye that discolored that optic and caused it to swell. Several clinches occurred during the round, and as soon as the men were separated each time they banged each other severely. No decision was given by the referee—*N. Y. World*, May 4.

Also a New Picture
"The Sidewalks of New York" with Music.

A broadside promoting Latham's eidoloscope.

The shift from peephole to projection was much appreciated by the sporting crowd, many of whom acted just as if they were ringside. "It is all realistic, so realistic, indeed," reported the *World* in the same article, "that excitable spectators have forgot themselves and cried 'Mix up there!' 'Look out, Charlie, you'll get a punch,' 'Oh! What do you think of that Mr. Barnett?' and other expressions of like character."

The Lambda Company went on to film a wide range of subjects, including a horse race at the Sheepshead Bay track, dancing girls, and several wrestling bouts on the roof of the *Police Gazette* building.[11] Unlike the Edison camera, which was confined to the Black Maria or the laboratory grounds, the Latham machine was sufficiently portable to take views at diverse locales, even Niagara Falls. Two additional cameras were built late in 1895 with the hope of filming the Corbett–Fitzsimmons fight, but the event did not materialize owing to protests from reformers and restrictions by state and local governments.

Although the Lathams had only one completed eidoloscope projector during most or all of 1895, they exhibited in several types of venues employed for motion-picture showings over the next ten years. From the storefront theater on Broadway, Lambda moved farther downtown to another storefront theater on Park Row. In late August the company presented films for one week at Chicago's Olympic Theater, a vaudeville house. The eidoloscope was then shifted to Kohl & Middleton's Clark Street Dime Museum, remaining for three weeks as part of the variety show (along with the Irish talkers Cloud and Keshaw and Professor Sherman's school of educated goats).[12] Shortly thereafter, they went to the Cotton States Exposition in Atlanta.

Despite these efforts, however, the eidoloscope was not very successful; the Lathams found themselves running out of money, and the Lambda Company had accumulated considerable debt. Perhaps in an effort to escape this financial crisis, the

Eidoloscope film of a wrestling match.

Lathams sold exhibition rights (accompanied by newly completed projectors) for various territories. The first sale, for the state of Virginia, was made to Woodville Latham's nephew, LeRoy Latham, who opened in Norfolk. An eidoloscope controlled by Vandergrift opened at Keith's Bijou Theater in Philadelphia for one week in late December. D. C. Porter apparently purchased the rights for New York State and played Rochester's vaudeville theater for two weeks in mid January 1896.[13] According to the *Rochester Democrat and Chronicle*:

> There is an eidoloscope among the attractions at Wonderland this week and the exhibition given by it, though the device is as yet very far from perfect, is extremely interesting. Eidoloscope pictures, like magic lantern pictures, increase in size in proportion to the distance of the lens from the screen and the stage of the Wonderland is so shallow that the moving figures in eidoloscope pictures shown there cannot be made more than a foot or so in height. Sometimes, too, slight alternations in the focal distance momentarily dim the image. Nevertheless, the exhibition is most remarkable and to those who have never seen a kinetoscope must be a really startling novelty (*Rochester Democrat and Chronicle*, 21 January 1896, p. 15).

In late March, Porter opened his eidoloscope in Syracuse for two weeks at a storefront on Salina Street.

In fact, "states rights" sales did not solve the Lambda Company's problems, and in January or February the enterprise was reorganized as the Eidoloscope Company, which absorbed Lambda and assumed many of the Lathams' debts. The eidoloscope, however, was about to face competition from technically superior projectors.

Jenkins and Armat Invent the Phantoscope

C. Francis Jenkins, an aspiring but impoverished inventor, had been working on "new methods of, and apparatus for, the recording and reproduction of action" by the beginning of 1893. His tentative efforts were soon preempted by Edison's motion-picture system. Jenkins then turned to devising a peephole machine similar to the kinetoscope but operating on sufficiently different principles to avoid Edison's patents. This "cabinet phantoscope" premiered at the Pure Food Exposition in Washington, D.C., in mid November 1894.[14] Whether or not the machine was actually operational is unknown, but it enjoyed little subsequent commercial success.

That fall, Jenkins met Thomas Armat, a real-estate entrepreneur, at the Bliss School of Electricity. After frequently discussing the possibilities of projected moving pictures, the two formed a partnership and signed a vaguely worded agreement on 25 March 1895. Jenkins contributed his patent application for a "stereopticon phantoscope," while Armat was responsible for "immediate construction and subsequent public exhibition and proper promotion . . . of a stereopticon phantoscope, built in accordance with the principles set forth in the patent application." This projecting machine, which used rotating mirrors, was completed in April 1895 but proved to be a failure. Lacking an intermittent mechanism, it was conceptually similar to the Lathams' eidoloscope. Practically, it was even less viable.[15]

Jenkins' phantoscope on display at the Pure Food Exposition.

By the end of July 1895 Jenkins and Armat were pursuing the idea of an intermittent mechanism. They were aided by Edward F. Murphy, who worked for the Columbia Phonograph Company and gave them ready access to films. "I am very sorry to say that I have not received those intermittent gears from Boston for the lantern although I ordered them more than a week ago," Jenkins wrote to Murphy on 8 August. "The elliptical gears give the desired results but are entirely too noisy. . . . If the gears come today or even tomorrow, we will be on the Jersey coast ready for business Monday evening." Success did not come quite so quickly. It was not until 28 August that Jenkins and Armat submitted a patent application to the U.S. Patent Office—only a week ahead of the Lumières. At the end of August, Jenkins was again writing Murphy:

> The lantern gears were a grand success, with the exception of the terrible noise, as long as they lasted, but the necessity for starting and stopping the sprocket and driven gear so fast, generated so much work that a one-eighth H.P. motor could not drive them above 1000 or 1200 revolu-

Drawings for one of the key Jenkins–Armat phantoscope patents.

(No Model.)   2 Sheets—Sheet 1.

C. F. JENKINS & T. ARMAT.
PHANTOSCOPE.

No. 586,953.   Patented July 20, 1897.

tions per minute. This is too slow, as you know, for all films except dancing girls and similar ones. Fights were a dismal failure; it would take half a minute for a man to fall. Well pretty soon the terrible pounding battered down the locking part of the gears and the whole thing went wrong and we had to abandon it. . . . I anticipate good results from tonight's experiments. We are doing our best to prepare for Atlanta immediately it opens, and we will want you to go with us, of course.

Finally, on 7 September 1895, Jenkins informed Murphy, "The lantern is simplicity itself, Ed, and I know you'll be pleased with it. It is the grandest success you could imagine. I am blessed glad it's finished, too, for I'm dreadfully tired living with it day and night."[16]

Initial Commercial Exploitation

To finance the phantoscope's exhibition, Armat quickly arranged a business deal with his brothers. They promised to provide up to $1,500 "to be applied to the expenses of exhibiting the Phantoscope at Atlanta, Ga., New Orleans, La., and at the Mexican Exposition," with Armat and Jenkins agreeing to pay them "one-half of the net profits of exhibiting said Armat–Jenkins Phantoscope." Later, Armat claimed that they had invested over $2,000 in this enterprise.[17]

In late September, Jenkins and Armat took their projector to Atlanta, where they arranged to exhibit pictures at the Cotton States Exposition. The partners secured one of the last concessions on the eastern edge of the midway for five hundred dollars, and erected a building to house their show. Meanwhile, Jenkins returned to Washington, D.C., for two additional machines that were being built at the shop of John Shultzbach.[18] While in Washington, he promoted the endeavor and garnered a prominent news article:

> The last concession of space made by the Atlanta Exposition management before the opening of the big Cotton States show will be occupied by the machine that Edison has been working years to perfect. There is no Edison in this, however. The Wizard of Menlo Park has been beaten at his own game by two young Washingtonians, and they left this city last week for Atlanta, where they will put up a $5,000 building to display their new device. It is known as the phantoscope and is a combination of the kinetoscope principles with those of the stereopticon (*Baltimore Sun*, 3 October 1895, p. 2).

Jenkins returned to the exposition with the additional machines and helped to install them in the newly constructed theater. According to Armat, "The exhibition place was divided into two rooms with a gallery at the end so arranged that we could point one of the machines at the screen in one room and the other at the screen in the adjoining room so that as we were giving exhibitions in one room the public could be entering the other. We had an extra third machine to take the place of either of the two that were in use in case of a breakdown."[19] This was the first instance of modern commercial cinema—projected moving pictures using an intermittent mechanism—in the United States.

The films shown by Jenkins and Armat had been made by the Edison Manufacturing Company for its peephole kinetoscopes, and their semi-opaque celluloid base was not well suited to projection. Despite this impediment, the *Atlanta Journal* gave the phantoscope favorable if minor notice:

THE MARVELOUS ELECTRIC PHANTOSCOPE

This is unquestionably the most wonderful electric invention of the age. It is the first public exhibition and nothing like it has ever been seen before, consequently is difficult to describe.

By means of this wonderful invention you see a perfect reproduction, full life size, of the living originals, every act and motion absolutely perfect, even to the wink of an eye.

Repertoire includes two acts from Trilby; one act from 1492; Carmencita, Sousa's Band; dances, fist fight; Annabelle in the Sun and Serpentine dances; a cock fight and numerous other interesting subjects.

It is located at the extreme east end of the Midway and everyone should see it (21 October 1895).

Jenkins and Armat were ready for crowds, which never came. According to Jenkins, "The exhibition, itself, was a very successful one," but there were few patrons.[20]

The problem was primarily one of promotion. The Cotton States Exposition attracted other people in the moving-picture field, and the phantoscope's significance may well have been lost on the casual fairgoer. Gray Latham was there with the eidoloscope, and Frank Harrison represented Raff & Gammon's Kinetoscope Company with its peephole machines. Latham saw screenings of the Armat–Jenkins projector and vice versa. While Jenkins and Latham privately discussed the possibility of working together in the future, Armat conversed with Harrison. As Armat recalled, "He was very much impressed with the exhibition, and stated to me that Messers. Raff and Gammon were exceedingly anxious to secure such an apparatus as that I was exhibiting."[21]

Jenkins eventually left the Exposition and took one of the three phantoscopes to his brother's wedding in Richmond, Indiana. Films were then shown at his father's jewelry store, and according to the *Richmond Daily Times*, "Those fortunate enough to see them were enraptured at the wonderful and beautiful effects seen." In Atlanta Armat experienced unexpected difficulties, however: on 15 October 1895 a fire was started in the adjacent "Old Plantation Show" and badly damaged the partners' theater.[22] Discouraged by this and the poor box-office receipts, Armat soon left.

After they returned to Washington, Armat and Jenkins had a falling-out. Once again, a collaboration that had produced valuable results broke down as the invention began to be exploited for financial gain. Each man then acted independently and sought to maximize his claims and commercial opportunities. On 25 November, Jenkins filed a patent application, maintaining that the phantoscope was his own exclusive invention. He also arranged a screening at the Franklin Institute in Philadelphia on 18 December, just prior to the opening of the eidoloscope at Keith's Bijou Theater. Meanwhile, Armat arranged an exhibition for Raff & Gammon. According to Armat:

In the month of December 1895, Mr. Gammon came over to my office on F street to see an exhibition. I had the machine in the basement of the office. Mr. Gammon stated to me in the office, before he went down to see the exhibition in the basement, that he did not believe that I had a successful apparatus for projecting pictures, as his firm had been endeavoring for months to have Mr. Edison produce for them a successful machine for this work. He stated that he had not been able to produce such a machine, and that he did not believe that anyone else could. When he saw the exhibition he was very much astonished, and the result of our interview on that occasion was the contract under which his firm undertook to exploit the invention (*Animated Projecting Co.* v. *American Mutoscope Co.*, p. 87).

Just as Raff & Gammon were contemplating the abandonment of their moving-picture business, Armat's machine offered them new hope. For Armat and his relatives, it was a way to exploit the invention without risking additional capital.

The preceding chapters have traced the history of projected images as a cultural practice originating in the mid seventeenth century. From this early date the screen developed dynamically, its practitioners incorporating technological advances in a timely fashion (chapter 1). A second line of pre-cinema development occurred with the invention and exploitation of communication technologies—telegraph, telephone, phonograph, and so forth—and was centered to an unusual degree at Thomas Edison's New Jersey laboratories in the last quarter of the nineteenth century. For Edison and his competitors, these successive breakthroughs reached a culmination of sorts with the kinetograph. This achievement confirmed a shift from pragmatic, business-oriented technologies to consumer-oriented ones (chapter 2). By adapting Edison's motion pictures to the magic lantern, American inventors and entrepreneurs brought about a conjunction of these two lines of development. This synthesis had been achieved by the end of 1895, but its effects had not yet been felt in the social and cultural life of the nation (chapter 3). That would occur in the "novelty year" of 1896–1897, which is the focus of the following chapters.

PART 2

The Novelty of Cinema:
1896–1897

4

The Vitascope

The vitascope effectively launched projected motion pictures as a screen novelty in the United States. In late April 1896 the vitascope was showing films in only one American theater, Koster & Bial's Music Hall in New York City, but the subsequent pace of diffusion was remarkable. By May 1897, only one year later, several hundred projectors were in use across the country. Honolulu had its first picture show in early February 1897, while Phoenix, in Arizona Territory, followed that May.[1] In the Northeast and Midwest, villages of a few thousand inhabitants had been visited by showmen with motion pictures not once but two or three times. The vast majority of Americans had the opportunity to see motion pictures on a screen, and many took it. Their responses were not unlike those that greeted the magic lantern in the 1650s or the stereopticon in the 1860s—astonishment at the lifelike quality of the images. It was during this brief thirteen- or fourteen-month period that most of the future owners of film-production companies associated with the Motion Picture Patents Company entered the field. A new industry was established and staffed. New practices were introduced and old ones reasserted. It was a period of ferment and rapid change. By its close, a framework for the development of subsequent motion-picture practice had come into being.

Controversy surrounds the history of "Edison's vitascope." For some historians, notably Terry Ramsaye, it is a history of heroic accomplishment that allowed American cinema to achieve meaningful expression. For others, such as Gordon Hendricks and Robert C. Allen, it is a history of greed, dishonesty, and ineptitude.[2] Both views have some validity. Despite its fresh name, the machine was a phantoscope that had been slightly refined by Thomas Armat. Although Edison, Armat, and others reaped ample financial rewards from the machine during its brief commercial life, a group of small-time and often naive investors lost substantial amounts of cash. The only thing these hopeful entrepreneurs made for themselves was a place in film history, insofar as they introduced Americans to projected motion pictures, almost always in the face of severe technical difficulties. Moralizing tales of heroism and villainy have their appeal, but they can easily obscure other issues vital to our understanding of the cinema's beginnings.

The Phantoscope Is Commercialized as the Vitascope

The commercial exploitation of the Jenkins–Armat phantoscope required effective organization, financing, and promotion, which Raff & Gammon were capable of providing. Reaching a contractual agreement was the first step. More than a month of negotiations followed Armat's December screening for Frank Gammon before a final understanding was reached. Armat hoped to manage the business with Raff & Gammon, but the partners refused. "We cannot agree to divide the responsibility and policy of the business with you," they insisted. "As it is our money alone which is to be at stake, and the entire risk is ours, and as we have had long experience in business of a similar nature, we think it right and proper that the management of the business should remain in our hands." Differences over the division of income also had to be negotiated. While Armat bowed to the demands of the kinetoscope dealers, he wanted to retain the exclusive exhibition rights for Washington, D.C., and Atlantic City. Raff & Gammon were agreeable but asked in return, "the right to establish and exhibit in New York for our own exclusive benefit," thus deftly acquiring the rights to the smallest but most lucrative piece of territory in the United States.[3]

The final contract gave Raff & Gammon "the sole and exclusive right to manufacture rent or lease or otherwise handle (as may be agreed upon in this contract or by future agreement) in any and all countries of the world the aforesaid machine or device called the 'Phantoscope.' " Armat received 25 percent of the monies gained by selling exhibition rights and 50 percent of the gross receipts (minus the cost of manufacture) for other areas of the business up to $7,500—above which he was to assume half the general expenses of running the business. Such income would come from the rental of machines, the sale of films, and other miscellaneous services, since the owners of states rights would be obliged to deal exclusively with Raff & Gammon. Projecting machines, moreover, were to be leased—not sold—and were to remain Armat's property.[4]

Once Raff & Gammon reached an agreement with Armat, they did not immediately send him the contract. Rather, they nervously approached Thomas Edison and his chief business executive, William Gilmore, whose reactions to the adoption of a non-Edison screen machine were considered unpredictable. Less than a year before, the Lathams had exhibited their machine to the press and encountered Edison's wrath. A somewhat similar reaction to this new machine seemed possible if not probable. In the interim, however, Edison's motion-picture business had fallen off and commercial rivals had multiplied. While Armat's machine posed yet another threat, it could also help to revive Edison's kinetograph enterprise. For these reasons, the "Wizard" was predisposed to bring the phantoscope into his circle. Meeting with Gilmore and Edison on 15 January 1896, Raff & Gammon obtained an agreement by which the Edison Manufacturing Company was to supply the necessary films and manufacture the projectors. Delighted to have Edison's cooperation, Raff & Gammon informed Armat of their successful arrangements. "We feel like congratulating ourselves over the results of our efforts in this direction and we now have no further doubts as to getting the business promptly into operation and upon a successful and profitable basis, as soon as you furnish us with the machines called for in the contract." These new activities did not continue the old Kinetoscope Company, which Raff & Gammon would liquidate when the appropriate opportunity arose, but formed a new enterprise.[5]

Soon after signing the contract, Raff & Gammon learned of Jenkins' independent activities. The precise moment is uncertain, but by early February all parties recognized that their machine required its own trade name. Raff & Gammon suggested "vitascope"—from the Latin *vita*, "life," and the Greek *scope*, "to see." Armat countered with "zoescope," which he argued, "means the same as 'Vitascope,' but it has the advantage of having both roots derived from the Greek." "Zoescope" was rejected, however. "While we have no special preference for the name 'Vitascope' yet we do not like the name 'Zoescope' as it is too much like 'Zoetrope,' which was brought out by a German here some years since, and was a total failure," explained Raff & Gammon. "We do not like to have the new machine called by a name or similar to that borne by a machine which was a failure." Once the name was settled, Raff & Gammon raised a more delicate question, that of marketing and profit maximization. Potential investors as well as potential audiences were waiting for the screen machine that Edison had promised them many times before. Commercial exhibitions of projected motion pictures by non-Edison showmen had already been given but without notable success. Armat, of course, had some personal experience in this regard. Raff & Gammon, therefore, wanted to attach Edison's name to the machine. Armat and Edison agreed. Henceforth, the machine was known as "Edison's vitascope."[6]

The vitascope group confronted several technical issues during the winter months. Armat was anxious to improve the quality of the projected image by using a clear-base film stock, like that already being used by the Lathams, rather than the frosted or translucent surface best for kinetoscopes. The Blair Company, however, had difficulties providing a serviceable product of this kind, and it was many months before the Edison Company turned out films suited for projection. Raff & Gammon also wanted to switch to a larger-gauge film. As they explained to Armat, "The object in making it wider is not to show scenery, but simply to enable us to make a picture of proper width to exhibit on a theatrical stage. As you yourself heard while here, the criticism made by all the theatrical people is that the picture is too narrow in its width." This change would have been quite easy because the Edison Company had already constructed two kinetographs that used a two-inch format. In the end it was Armat who wisely pushed the idea aside: "Notwithstanding the fact that I think it is a very simple matter to use the wide films, difficulties may arise that it will take experiments to overcome, and experiments take time, and time is a most important factor, so I would certainly rush the machines just as they stand, and they can be modified afterward if desired, for the wide films, with very little expense." Armat spent much of the winter making minor alterations on the vitascope and constructing a new model for the Edison laboratory. Raff & Gammon found it to be "a great improvement over any we have yet seen."[7]

Marketing the Vitascope

The commercial exploitation of the vitascope was affected by the imminent appearance of rival machines. If not for that impinging reality, Raff & Gammon would have orchestrated a more gradual and effective marketing approach. By early March, C. Francis Jenkins had emerged as a disruptive force that could scare away investors. Although he seemed to have held few exhibitions after the Franklin Institute screening, Jenkins frequently boasted that his phantoscope's capabilities were equal or superior to those of the vitascope. When rumors reached the vitascope group that Jenkins had rented a storefront for exhibitions and was making additional machines, Raff & Gammon were deeply concerned. By mid March, they were on the verge of a commercial coup: down payments had been made on territory that would yield more than sixteen thousand dollars when the purchases were completed. Total sales of states rights were expected to exceed twenty-five thousand dollars. Once all the territory had been sold and the money paid in, the enterprise could survive such disruption. "But while we are in the midst of the work of disposing of territory, we must be free from these annoying conditions and dangers which threaten to completely counteract our efforts, and not only prevent future sales, but even upset the sales we have made already," they wrote to Armat. Concluding that "incalculable injury and immense loss to us may be occasioned in a day," they insisted that Armat bring Jenkins' activities to a halt even if it meant "making Jenkins a good, stiff payment, rather than take chances of his going further." Instead Armat instituted a replevin suit and took possession of Jenkins' machine. Temporarily thwarted, Jenkins and his business associates nonetheless publicized their plans to market a projector in the near future.[8]

Although the Lumière cinématographe had been exhibited in Paris since late December 1895 and had opened in London on 20 February, definitive reports of projected motion pictures in Europe only reached Raff & Gammon in mid March. While initially unsure of their rivals' capabilities, Raff & Gammon soon learned that the cinématographe was "creating a sensation" in London. On 25 March several New York theatrical managers received cables offering them the opportunity to book the Lumière machine. In an effort to delay its entrance into the American market, Raff & Gammon arranged for one of these managers (presumably Albert Bial of Koster & Bial's Music Hall) to reply that he already had the Edison machine.[9] The likelihood of foreign and domestic competition undoubtedly discouraged some knowledgeable amusement managers from investing in the vitascope.

Raff & Gammon marketed the vitascope by selling exclusive exhibition rights for specific territories, as they had just done with the kinetoscope and the North American Phonograph Company had done with the phonograph. This approach not only provided the group with a windfall profit but bound a large number of investors to their undertaking. In seeking to recoup their money, "states rights" owners would pursue their activities with zeal, often reselling the rights to cities and counties to others, who would, in turn, lease additional machines and maintain the business on a large scale. As Raff & Gammon explained to Armat in convincing terms, "The maintenance of this territorial plan is of vital consequence to our business."[10]

The "States Rights" Owners

Raff & Gammon began to market the vitascope by looking for purchasers of exhibition rights among their established customers. In early February they offered to sell the California rights to Peter Bacigalupi, owner of a San Francisco phonograph and kinetoscope parlor, but he declined. Interested customers included Thomas L. Tally, who wanted to feature the vitascope in his Los Angeles kinetoscope parlor, and Lyman H. Howe, who hoped to purchase the rights to Pennsylvania and incorporate moving pictures into his phonograph concerts.[11] For both the price proved too high.

Among those who did actually become vitascope rights owners, many entered the field because of a previous interest in the phonograph and/or kinetoscope:[12]

- Robert Fischer, a locksmith with a bicycle repair shop in Great Falls, Montana, owned a kinetoscope and two nickel-in-the slot phonographs. He and J. B. Mau-

THE LATEST MARVEL

✄✄✄ THE "Vitascope"

✄✄✄

A NEW MACHINE is now ready to be exhibited to the public, which is probably the most remarkable and startling in its results of any that the world has ever seen ✄ Several marvels of inventive genius have, in past years, gone forth from the Edison Works, located at Orange, New Jersey ✄ "The Wizard of Menlo Park" has conceived and in due course perfected the Phonograph, the Kinetoscope and the Kinetophone, each of which in turn, has excited the wonder and amazement of the public and, from a practical standpoint, opened up opportunities for exhibition enterprises, many of which are paying handsomely to this day ✄ ✄

A page from the Vitascope Company's promotional brochure.

rer, who ran a general store with his brother, purchased the rights to parts of Colorado (including Denver) and the state of Washington.

- W. R. Miller, a traveling phonograph exhibitor from Stratford, Connecticut, was exhibiting the phonograph throughout the South when he purchased the rights to Tennessee for a thousand dollars in cash and additional deferred payments.
- The Holland Brothers, who were then marketing the phonograph and kinetoscope from their base in Ottawa, Canada, waited patiently through the first months of enthusiasm. They received permission to exhibit the vitascope in Canada gratis and were promised a generous commission if they sold the territorial rights.
- Allen F. Rieser, the first to purchase territory, was also involved with phonograph exhibition. Rieser was president of the American Publishing Association, which

supplied public schools with library books and helped libraries raise the necessary money for their purchases by giving phonograph concerts. He acquired the rights to Pennsylvania, except for Philadelphia and Allegheny County (including Pittsburgh) for $1,500 at the beginning of March and eventually went on to purchase the Ohio rights for another $5,000. A number of his friends and acquaintances also became involved.

Amusement and theatrical entrepreneurs formed another large group of states rights owners:

- Thomas J. Ryan, an amusement entrepreneur with phonograph interests, purchased the rights to Pittsburgh and Philadelphia.
- C. O. Richardson, who purchased the rights to Maine, had worked for the previous twenty years in theatrical circles.
- Walter J. Wainwright, a tightrope walker and carnival showman, and William T. Rock, who had once been in the circus but was then extricating himself from ownership of an unsuccessful electrical company, waited for the first flurry of enthusiasm to pass and then purchased the Louisiana rights for $1,500.
- William A. McConnell, business manager for Koster & Bial's, acquired the rights to Connecticut for $3,000.
- Eurio Hopkins, Jr., also had some background in the entertainment field. He was part of the consortium of White, Barry & Hopkins, which owned the rights to Rhode Island and Texas. One of his backers, Abraham White, was a financial speculator with offices in downtown Manhattan.

At the same time, investors also included many small businessmen and professionals with little experience in the amusement field:

- Peter W. Kiefaber, a Philadelphia dealer in butter, eggs, and poultry, purchased the rights first to New Jersey (including Atlantic City) and then to Massachusetts, Illinois, and Maryland. He was encouraged by A. F. Rieser, who had also been in the wholesale produce business.
- Four merchants from Connellsville, Pennsylvania—J. R. Balsley, builder and lumber-mill owner; Richard S. Paine, shoe-store owner; F. E. Markell, owner of several drug stores, and Cyrus Echard, who was active in the coal trade—formed a consortium and purchased the rights to Indiana for $4,000. Balsley and Paine went on to buy the rights to California for $3,500.[13]
- M. M. Hixson, a doctor in the small town of Dupont, Ohio, bought the rights to Wisconsin with J. J. Wollam, a mechanical expert.
- In Ottawa, Ohio, bank president W. F. Reed and Frank G. Kahle were induced to purchase the rights to Iowa.
- The express agent in St. John, North Dakota, John C. Ryderman, bought the rights to his home state.
- A merchant, Edmund McLoughlin, sold or closed his business in downtown Manhattan to purchase exhibition rights to most of New York State with Arthur Frothingham.
- George J. Llewellyn, the protonotary for Luzerne County, Pennsylvania, and James M. Norris, chief clerk at the county courthouse, purchased the rights to Michigan. Llewellyn, a Wilkes-Barre law student who had recently sold his hardware business, came from the same town as Lyman H. Howe and was the same age; it appears that the protonotary witnessed the showman's excitement over the

vitascope and took the plunge on his own. Such a web of intersecting relationships was typical among states rights owners.

A final group, closely related to those exploiting the phonograph and kinetoscope, consisted of individuals with backgrounds in electricity. They tended to see themselves as simply working with another Edison-inspired invention. W. G. Brown, for example, owner of the Brown Electric & Machine Company, bought the rights to Arkansas (he also had previously been involved in the kinetoscope business).[14] In several other instances, people with electrical experience supplied the enthusiasm if not the cash. Edwin S. Porter, a twenty-five-year-old telegraph operator and electrician with the U.S. Navy, became aware of the vitascope while working at the Brooklyn Navy Yard and informed his hometown friends of the vitascope "opportunity"; after they bought the rights to California and Indiana, he worked for them as an operator. Robert Fischer, co-owner of the rights to Colorado and Washington state, did "Electrical Work of all kinds," according to his stationery. The latter partner of Hixson & Wollam was likewise an electrical expert. (Exhibition rights to states such as New Hampshire, Kansas, and Nebraska were also sold, though information about their purchase is scanty.)

Raff & Gammon were eager to sell vitascope rights overseas—a logical desire given the Continental Commerce Company's previous accomplishments. Juggler Paul Cinquevalli was ready to purchase the English and French rights for $25,000 each, until he returned to London and saw the Lumière cinématographe and other machines in operation. Still hoping to open up European markets, Raff & Gammon sent Charles Webster and a vitascope to London on 22 April, the day before the projector's New York premiere. On his arrival, Webster saw the Lumière cinématographe in action and was deeply impressed. Writing to his employers, he detailed the various Lumière views while stating that "other machines are sold for $200.00 and that quite a number have been sold in France." Webster toured with the vitascope in various parts of Europe but never realized the large profits that Raff & Gammon had initially anticipated. To fill Webster's position during his trip, Raff & Gammon hired James White, who quickly became a key figure in the new enterprise. When the Vitascope Company was officially incorporated in May, he was given one share of stock and placed on the board of directors.[15]

The New York Debut

Raff & Gammon choreographed an abbreviated but effective promotional campaign to launch the vitascope. From the outset, they had decided to have the premiere in New York City, the nation's entertainment and media capital. "Judging from our experience with the Kinetoscope, we are pretty well satisfied that we can do much better and make more money for both parties by exhibiting the machine at the start exclusively in New York City," they wrote to Armat, explaining that the "reports through the news-papers go out through the country, and we shall do a lot of advertising in the shape of news-paper articles which will excite the curiosity of parties interested in such things."[16]

Edison's name and involvement guaranteed extensive media attention. The degree of his cooperation, however, remained uncertain until the popular hero had actually attended a private screening on 27 March. Not only did the machine receive his complete approval, but the "Wizard of Menlo Park" stood ready to play the role of inventor assigned to him. Participating in a press screening at his laboratory on 3 April, he stole the show; if Armat was present, he stayed discreetly in the background. As the *New York Journal* reported the next day:

> For the first time since Edison had been working on his new invention, the vitascope, persons other than his trusted employes and assistants were allowed last night to see the workings of the wonderful machine. For two hours dancing girls and groups of figures, all of life size, seemed to exist as realities on the big white screen which had been built at one end of the experimenting rooms.

Representatives of the *New York World* and other dailies also attended. As predicted, their reports soon appeared in newspapers nationwide.

On 23 March Raff & Gammon approached Albert Bial and asked him to book the vitascope at his Koster & Bial's Music Hall on Thirty-fourth Street and Broadway for a fee of $800 a week.[17] These negotiations were concluded in early April, and when the entertainment opened on 23 April, according to the *New York Dramatic Mirror*, it "was a success in every way and the large audience testified its approval of the novelty by the heartiest kind of applause."[18] The debut helped to sell additional territory; soon only exhibition rights for the South remained unpurchased.

Although Koster & Bial's program promised as many as twelve views, only six scenes were shown on opening night according to New York newspaper accounts:

> The first view showed two dancers holding between and in front of them an umbrella and dancing the while. The position of the umbrella was constantly changed, and every change was smooth and even, and the steps of the dancing could be perfectly followed. [UMBRELLA DANCE]
>
> Then came the waves, showing a scene at Dover pier after a stiff blow. This was by far the best view shown, and had to be repeated many times. As in the umbrella dance, there was absolutely no hitch. One could look far out to sea and pick out a particular wave swelling and undulating and growing bigger and bigger until it struck the end of the pier. Its edge then would be fringed with foam, and finally, in a cloud of spray, the wave would dash upon the beach. One could imagine the people running away (*New York Mail and Express*, 24 April 1896, p. 12).

> This was followed by a burlesque boxing bout, in which the contestants were a very tall, thin man and a very short, stout one. The little fellow was knocked down several times, and the movements of the boxers were well represented. A scene from "A Milk White Flag" was next shown, in which soldiers and a military band perform some complex evolutions. A group representing Uncle Sam, John Bull, Venezuela and the Monroe doctrine got a good welcome from the patriotic. The last picture was a serpentine dancer. The color effects were used in this, and it was one of the most effective of the series (*New York Daily News*, 24 April 1896).

The Music Hall band accompanied the images with appropriate music. Two of the films were in color, using a hand-tinting process similar to that for stereopticon

The text within the image reads: THE MECHANISM OF THE VITASCOPE · THE VITASCOPE IN THE PROMENADE · EDISON'S NEW WONDER, THE VITASCOPE.

The vitascope at Koster & Bial's Music Hall (April–May 1896). Patrons watch Robert Paul's ROUGH SEA AT DOVER, *taken in England.*

slides. This was almost certainly done by the wife of Edmund Kuhn, an Edison employee in Orange, New Jersey.[19]

Reviewers considered the projection of Edison's peephole figures in stereopticon fashion as a screen novelty. The *New York Mail and Express* explained to its readers, "In the vitascope the figures of the kinetoscope are projected, enlarged to life-size, upon a screen in much the same manner as ordinary, everyday stereopticon images." The exhibition methods that typified later vitascope screenings were already in use at the premiere. As with the kinetoscope, each film was spliced end-to-end to form a continuous band so that a brief twenty-second scene could be shown over and over again. Jump cuts regularly appeared at the splice. With the dancers and the waves rolling onto the beach, this jump was not disruptive; with most other subjects, however, the splice created what the *Mail and Express* called "a few hitches in the changes."[20] Although one exhibitor reported showing each endless band of film only three times before turning off his machine, a subject was usually repeated at least half a dozen times. As was to be the case at some other important showings, Koster & Bial's used two vitascopes, so that while one film was being shown on one machine, the subject on the other could be taken off and replaced by a new one (a process that took approximately two minutes).

By projecting one-shot films in an endless band, the vitascope emphasized movement and lifelike images at the expense of narrative. As Raff & Gammon claimed in their prospectus, "When the machine is started by the operator, the bare canvas before the audience instantly becomes a stage, upon which living beings move about, and go through their respective acts, movements, gestures and changing expressions, surrounded by appropriate settings and accessories—the very counterpart of the stage, the field, the city, the country—yes, more, for these reproductions are in some respects more satisfactory, pleasing and interesting than the originals." The spectators were thus assumed to make a conscious comparison between the projected image and the everyday world as they knew and experienced it directly. It was the unprecedented congruence between the two that was being celebrated. Projected images were conceived as a novelty in which lifelike movement in conjunction with a life-size photographic image provided a sense of heightened realism and intensified interest in the quotidian. This new level of realism dramatically expanded the screen's importance as a source of commercial amusement.

Production for the Vitascope

The Koster & Bial screening in April emphasized a problem that had concerned Raff & Gammon for some time: the need for fresh subjects. Few new negatives had been made because of the declining kinetoscope business, and Raff & Gammon were forced to rely heavily on films of dancing girls and excerpts of plays that had long been available for peephole viewing. The dearth of new films was filled to some extent by importations from abroad. The hit film on opening night at Koster & Bial's was ROUGH SEA AT DOVER, produced in England by Robert Paul. Two other foreign films were listed in the opening-night program but not shown; one, KAISER WILHELM REVIEWING HIS TROOPS, was undoubtedly THE GERMAN EMPEROR REVIEWING HIS TROOPS, taken by Birt Acres in the summer of 1895. The other, VENICE SHOWING GONDOLAS, was a Lumière film that had been acquired surreptitiously overseas by Albert Bial. Even though the latter was not presented on opening night, duplicate copies were shown in the vitascope at least a month before the Lumière cinématographe had its United States debut.[21]

Although the Black Maria had fallen into disrepair and had a poor reputation in the theatrical community, the *New York World* arranged for two prominent actors, May Irwin and John C. Rice, to visit the West Orange studio in mid April, on the eve of the Music Hall premiere. There, they went before the Edison camera to reenact the climax of the musical comedy *The Widow Jones*, when the widow and Billie Bikes kiss. William Heise rehearsed the actors several times to get the prelude and the osculatory high point on film, then shot it only once. The results were a success, and THE MAY IRWIN KISS became the most popular Edison film of the year. Under the headline "The Anatomy of a Kiss," the *Sunday World* of 26 April 1896 devoted almost a full page of text and illustration to the production.

For many reasons, however, the Black Maria was no longer adequate to meet Raff & Gammon's needs. Its distance from New York's theater district was a barrier to regular, inexpensive production. Moreover, as ROUGH SEA AT DOVER dramatically demonstrated, scenes of everyday life were often greeted with much greater enthusiasm than excerpts of plays and vaudeville acts. Anticipating foreign and domestic competition, the Edison Company constructed a portable camera that Heise used to take local pictures around New York City starting on 11 May.[22] The results included HERALD SQUARE, showing streetcars moving along and the elevated train visible at the extreme left, and CENTRAL PARK, with children and elderly people around the fountain.[23] ELEVATED RAILWAY, 23RD STREET, NEW YORK, a view of a train pulling into the station, wrote the *Boston Herald*, was "so realistic as to give those in front seats a genuine start."[24] A head-on collision of two trains was filmed in Canton, Ohio, on 30 May. Views of Niagara Falls were shot in late May or early June.

Inspired by the Lumière view of the Venice canals filmed from a gondola, Heise photographed at least one scene of the Falls from a moving train (Niagara Falls Gorge).[25] These films were photographically flawed, however, and most did not have the spectacular effect on audiences that had been intended. As production continued throughout the summer, subjects shot closer to home were usually realized more successfully.

Edison subjects were generally made under Raff & Gammon's auspices, with James White as producer. Some were taken at the makeshift rooftop studio above the Vitascope Company's new office at 43 West Twenty-eighth Street. The steady supply of films enabled the vitascope to stay in major urban theaters almost indefinitely. After a two-month run at the same Boston theater, the *Boston Herald* reported:

> If there be any let-up in the interest taken in the vitascope, there are
> no signs of it in the only place where it is being exhibited in Boston, for
> the applause that follows every display of a picture at each performance is
> as hearty and admiring as when Edison's wonderful invention first came
> to the city. This is accounted for, of course, by the promptness with which
> the management has secured new views. . . . Each new lot seems more
> admirable than those which preceded them (or at least it appears so), and
> the applause of last week was equally distributed between the Suburban
> handicap horse race, shooting the chutes, the surf scene and the "Widow
> Jones" kiss, the latter having retained its popularity since the outset—just
> like the laugh creating comedy it is taken from (5 July 1896, p. 11).

THE MAY IRWIN KISS

SHOOTING THE CHUTES

Raff & Gammon and the Edison Company were uniquely able to deliver scenes of American life. Among the subjects reported in the newspapers in late June and July were THE SUBURBAN HANDICAP; FERRY BOAT LEAVING DOCK, NEW YORK; SHOOTING THE CHUTES; PARADE OF BICYCLISTS AT BROOKLYN, NEW YORK; PARADE OF NEW YORK CITY CROSSING SWEEPERS; PASSAIC [Paterson] FALLS, NEW JERSEY; several views taken at Atlantic City; RETURN OF THE FISHERMAN; THE BAD BOY AND THE GARDENER; STREET SPRINKLING AND TROLLEY CARS; and two scenes illustrating the movements and drill of a battery of artillery.[26]

New Edison films in August included THE HAYMAKERS AT WORK and THE ARRIVAL OF LI HUNG CHANG. Continuing their friendly association with the *New York World*, Raff & Gammon also arranged for Edison cameras to film THE N.Y. "WORLD" SICK BABY FUND, "showing children of the poor people enjoying themselves in swings and on hobby-horses."[27] Undoubtedly this was seen as useful publicity for the newspaper's charity, which helped poor infants and children survive the summer heat. In late July or early August a young *World* cartoonist, J. Stuart Blackton, also performed for the Edison camera, almost certainly at Raff & Gammon's rooftop studio. Three 150-foot films were made:

No. 1 represents him as drawing a large picture of Mr. Thomas A. Edison.
No. 2 showing the artist drawing pictures of McKinley and President Cleveland.

EDISON DRAWN BY "WORLD" ARTIST

No. 3 is a humorous selection, showing the artist drawing a life-size picture of a female figure, in which the expressions of the countenance are rapidly changed (*Phonoscope*, November 1896, p. 16).

The first of these films, EDISON DRAWN BY "WORLD" ARTIST, became a hit. One publicist concluded his remarks on a vitascope exhibition by observing that "the most curious and interesting of the new views was that showing the rapid sketching of Wizard Edison's portrait by a well-known cartoonist."[28] As a result, Blackton became somewhat of a celebrity and found new opportunities to appear on the vaudeville stage.[29] This success whetted his interest in motion pictures as well and subsequently encouraged him and his partner, Albert E. Smith, to enter the field as exhibitors.

Blackton cartoon from the New York World, *24 June 1896.*

Local Debuts of the Vitascope

While the New York debut created intense demand for "the latest Edison invention," the ability to satisfy this desire was hampered by delays in the manufacturing of vitascope projectors. This was particularly frustrating for states rights owners, who had to watch enticing contracts disappear for lack of machines. The most lucrative commercial arrangements could be made during the regular theatrical season, which drew to a close in most parts of the country sometime during May. Allen F. Rieser, who had been promised a machine in mid March, was impatient and "d—— mad" by the second week in May. "The [Summer] Parks that want to engage the Vitascope that I know of wire us if we cannot show them what we have and conclude our engagement they will drop us," he wrote to Raff & Gammon. "Just now I got a telegram from Cleveland Ohio asking whether I could be there on the 16th with the machine. This is the biggest Park in that section of the country. I have to reject them which may be a matter of a couple of thousand dollars." W. R. Miller likewise wrote that he could have extended his phonograph tour and made another five hundred dollars instead of vainly waiting in Tennessee for a promise to be kept.[30] It was not until mid May that the Edison Manufacturing Company completed the first group of projectors.

The vitascope opened in a dozen major cities and resorts, between mid May and mid June. Many others followed in subsequent weeks:

Boston (18 May)	New London, Ct. (15 June)
Camden, N.J. [?] (21 May)	St. Louis (15 June)
Hartford (21 May)	Portland, Me. (22 June)
Atlantic City (23 May)	Bergen Beach, N.Y. (*ca.* 22 June)
Philadelphia (25 May)	Scranton (22 June)
New Haven (28 May)	New Orleans (28 June)
Providence (4 June)	Wilkes-Barre, Pa. (29 June)
Buffalo (8 June)	Cleveland (1 July)
San Francisco (8 June)	Asbury Park (1 July)
Meriden, Ct. (8 June)	Detroit (1 July)
Nashville (13 June)	Los Angeles (5 July)
Baltimore (15 June)	Chicago (5 July)
Bridgeport, Ct. (15 June)	Milwaukee (26 July)

Vitascope openings occurred throughout the continental United States in any locality large enough to boast an electrical system. The rapid pace of these debuts strained Raff & Gammon's resources beyond the breaking point (Raff even suffered a nervous breakdown), but they were generally well received, and the resulting popularity, publicity, and broad diffusion established "Edison's vitascope" as the first motion-picture projector in the minds of the American public.

The vitascope was presented in various types of entertainment venues, thus extending the eclectic nature of sites already used for motion-picture exhibitions by the Lathams. Vaudeville introduced amusement-goers to projected motion pictures in many major cities:

- The vitascope ran at Benjamin F. Keith's Boston vaudeville house for twelve weeks and at his Philadelphia theater for nine. In each locale, it remained the principal feature on the bill throughout the run.

A vitascope projector.

- The California states rights owners arranged with Gustave Walter to play his Orpheum houses in San Francisco (three weeks) and Los Angeles (two weeks).
- The vitascope had its Chicago premiere at Hopkins' South Side Theater, where it remained on the vaudeville bill for twenty consecutive weeks. "It is not only an interesting and instructive novelty for the regular patrons of the house," manager J. D. Hopkins declared, "but is drawing scores and hundreds of people who never

before attended this popular form of entertainment." He went on to claim that the previous Sunday's business "was the heaviest ever known in the 'ten–twenty–thirty' style of entertainment in this country."[31]

- In Louisville, the vitascope was introduced on 20 September at a newly opened vaudeville house and helped to make it a success.
- In Cleveland, where no vaudeville was presented during the summer, A. F. Rieser engaged a hall and presented the vitascope along with his own small vaudeville company.[32]

Theaters offering other entertainment forms also showed the vitascope. In Connecticut, "Wizard Edison's most marvelous Invention" joined with the touring hypnotist Santanelli. Starting in Hartford and moving next to New Haven's Grand Opera House, Santanelli often received more attention than the vitascope. More commonly, films were shown in conjunction with plays, musicals, and even operas.

Allen F. Rieser advertises his exhibition in the New York Clipper.

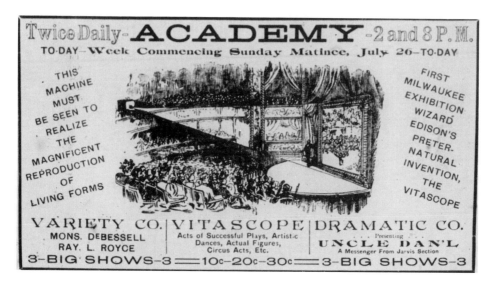

Advertisement for the Academy Theater in the Milwaukee Sentinel, *26 July 1896.*

- In St. Louis, vitascope moving pictures were exhibited immediately after the opera *The Bohemian Girl.* Spectators could either see the films from an outdoor garden or remain inside the theater.
- In Milwaukee, the manager of the Academy of Music engaged Hixson and Wollam's vitascope for an exclusive appearance at his theater, which featured a new play each week and a few specialties between acts. Receiving four hundred dollars a week, the vitascope entrepreneurs played two weeks in late July and early August, then returned for another two weeks in mid September and a single week in early November.
- In Albany, New York, on 17 August, the vitascope debuted between the acts of a play presented by the Corse Payton Company.
- At an opening in Atlanta, Georgia, on 16 November, the Florence Hamilton Company staged a different play each night, with moving pictures concluding each performance. Although Jenkins and Armat had failed to draw audiences of any size at the city's Cotton States Exposition, their invention now became "the reigning fad."[33]

Storefronts were another frequently used outlet for vitascope entrepreneurs. Such premises had often been occupied by phonograph exhibitors and other showmen anxious to avoid the expense and brief runs associated with a regular theater. Once an appropriate space was rented, they could give exhibitions for weeks at a time and pocket all the income above expenses.

- Residents of Providence, Rhode Island—including the mayor and the city's leading citizens—flocked to a storefront show during the first part of June to see ten films for twenty-five cents. Screenings went on twelve hours a day (11 A.M. to 11 P.M.) for four weeks, and according to the *Providence Journal* of 7 June, the "Standing Room Only" sign was often on display in both the afternoons and the evenings.

ALL THE
TOWN IS TALKING!
ABOUT
EDISON'S
ASTONISHING
VITASCOPE!

SO, BY THE WAY, ARE
THE NEWSPAPERS.

PUZZLES THE SCIENTISTS.
BAFFLES ANALYSIS.
CREATES ROUND-EYED WONDER
PROFOUND DELIGHT.
TICKLES THE RISIBILITIES.
EXCITES HEARTY ADMIRATION.
THRILLS THE NERVES.
AND INCIDENTALLY CREATES
WILDAPPLAUSE
SEE IT!

*Your Life is Incom-
plete Without!*

Bring your wives, sweethearts,
cousins and aunts. Not your
mother-in-law! No. Dead! Con-
gratulations!!!

Continuous, 11 a. m. to 11 p. m.
ADMISSION ONLY 25c.
NEW PICTURES,
305 Westminster Street
Talking machine on free exhibi-
tion during change of films on the
Vitascope.
Je4   Ja Bit

Providence Journal, *4 June 1896.*

- After playing for a month at a nearby summer park, Walter Wainwright and William Rock operated a storefront moving-picture show at 623 Canal Street in New Orleans. With a ten-cent admission fee, this profitable effort (one of the few) ran from 26 July through September.
- After earlier turns in nearby summer parks, the New York Vitascope Company opened storefronts in Rochester on 4 September and in Buffalo later in the month. Although the Rochester venue at 64 South Street was "a very fine store in the best location in the city," McLoughlin grossed only one hundred dollars during the first seven days—much less than expenses. Nonetheless, he remained there at least a month. In late December, he opened another storefront in Utica and

stayed for five weeks. Fifteen films were presented at each showing for an admission fee of ten to fifteen cents.[34]

Many of these storefronts were variations on phonograph and kinetoscope parlors.

• In Nashville, Tennessee, the vitascope was featured in the main room, while nickel-in-the-slot phonographs were in the foyer. There, W. R. Miller tried various methods of ballyhooing his films. "I started giving a half hour show for 25¢ but it didn't work, so I put the price [at] 10¢ and run one film and change every fifteen minutes in the evening. In that way many people spend 50¢ or more where they would not spend a quarter."

W. R. Miller's floor plan for storefront.

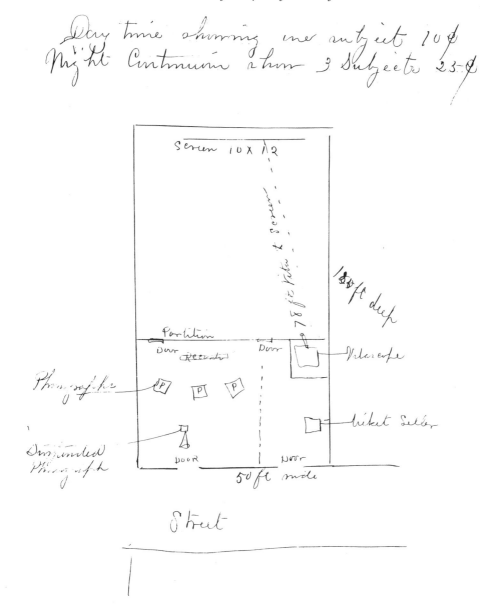

- The California vitascope exhibitors began to show their machine in the rear of T. L. Tally's Los Angeles kinetoscope and phonograph storefront in late July.
- In Asbury Park, Edison's Electrical Casino had the vitascope in its small theater, and kinetoscopes and phonographs in the annex.[35]

Summer parks and resorts provided popular locations for vitascope exhibitions during the warm weather. In most cases these venues were either small theaters that functioned like the urban storefronts or summer theaters adapted for vaudeville.

- The vitascope was presented at three summer parks near Philadelphia, one of which, Willow Grove Park, featured the vitascope, an X-ray machine, kinetoscopes, and phonographs in its newly opened theater.
- At the Casino, a summer vaudeville theater at Baltimore's Arlington Electric Park (run by Ford's Theater manager Charles E. Ford), there was only one projector in operation, and a film was shown after each vaudeville act. By the second week of the vitascope run, 3,500 people attended on a single day, with each paying twenty-five cents. Most were drawn by the screen novelty, and, the *Baltimore Sun* reported, the show became "a favorite point for cyclers out on an evening ride."
- In Atlantic City, which relied heavily on Philadelphia vacationers, Peter Kiefaber exhibited the vitascope at the Scenic Theater, at "the very centre of the 'Boardwalk' and the only room fitted up in theatrical style, finely lit up by electricity and with drop seats." Arthur Hotaling, who saw his first motion pictures there, felt that Kiefaber's lack of showmanship was responsible for his poor box-office receipts. Hotaling, who had previously run a "living picture show" in which performers formed tableaux in imitation of well-known paintings, offered his expertise to the inexperienced showman and was soon managing the theater. Later he recalled:

> As a showman one of my best assets was an ability to handle a brush, and the first thing I did was to plaster the front with banners. The two star films were Cissy Fitzgerald in her dance and the John C. Rice–May Irwin kiss, and I decorated the front with these in vivid color. Then I fixed up the entrance so that the curtain could be drawn back to display the screen. If we saw anyone in the crowd getting interested we would drop the curtain and he would have to pay his dime to see the rest. Generally, though, we would show part of the Fitzgerald picture and I would make a "spiel" about the kiss picture, which was from "The Widow Jones," then a recent Broadway hit. Business picked up (*MPW*, 15 July 1916, p. 380).

In August Kiefaber was running another vitascope in a second Atlantic City location, probably a storefront.

- At Bergen Beach, a resort near Coney Island that was run by Percy Williams, the vitascope played in its own small theater and each day, according to the *Brooklyn Eagle*, delighted "hundreds by its almost perfect simulation of moving scenes in real life."[36]

Problems with the Vitascope

The vitascope entrepreneurs were plagued by a wide range of problems. At first, only a handful of people (Thomas Armat and his brothers, Edward Murphy, James White, and one or two others) knew how to set up and operate the machines; these experts raced from city to city trying to salvage dire situations. Eurio Hopkins' terse telegram from Providence was typical: "Rush Murphy quick. In trouble. Also competent man permanent. Turned five hundred away. Unable to give performance." There were no instructions to send out with the machines; in the best of circumstances, mechanically minded men like Tennessee rights owner W. R. Miller figured out how to assemble the parts and run the machines on their own.[37] Adjustments were often imperfect and sometimes resulted in unnecessary technical difficulties.

The electricity needed to power the vitascopes was one of the entrepreneur's biggest headaches. The machines were designed to run on the direct current favored by Edison, but many locations were wired for alternating current instead. As Robert C. Allen has pointed out, the nation's patchwork of conflicting currents and voltages meant that the projectors frequently had to be adapted to different conditions when moved to a new locale. In some instances, electricity had to be pulled off streetcar lines: when J. Hunter Armat confronted this situation in Baltimore, he declined to present the show, and it was several days before his more experienced brother Christopher arrived and solved the problem. With streetcars using five hundred volts, the vitascope was overloaded and frequently subjected the motion-picture operator to painful shocks. The electrical problem was so severe that theater manager Charles Ford decided not to renew his four-week contract and waited for a more amenable machine to come along. From Halifax, Nova Scotia, meanwhile, Andrew Holland wrote Raff & Gammon that "If I have to get a special motor for every town I go into I may as well drop this country altogether, except in towns large enough to support an electric railway system. In Ottawa the alternating system is 52 volts 1600 frequency; here it is 104 volts. I do not know the frequency, but I thought you had overcome the difficulty of differences in frequency by the adoption of cone pulleys." The Halifax showing was a failure because of electrical problems, and Holland lost two hundred dollars out of pocket.[38]

Solutions were diverse, often ingenious, but rarely satisfactory. In Los Angeles, R. S. Paine, Charles H. Balsley, and Edwin S. Porter relied on batteries to power their machine; after working imperfectly on opening night, the vitascope was soon performing up to standard. But such a solution was not generally practical, since the quantity of batteries needed to project the films would have been prohibitive for someone moving from town to town. Many locales simply did not have electricity. In North Dakota, for example, only four towns could supply electrical power of any kind. In Canada, Andrew Holland tried bicycle power in the hope that "I can make myself entirely independent of electric light and power, and consequently will be able to work the small towns through this country to advantage."[39] This, however, did not give the same steady power and clean light as electricity.

Films were another major expense, costing as much as $12.50 for a new 50-foot (actually 42-foot) subject. To make matters worse, the Edison Company often failed to turn out film prints of acceptable quality. The first exhibitions relied on the semitranslucent strips intended for kinetoscopes. When the Blair Camera Company finally produced a clear-base celluloid film stock, it proved unsatisfactory as the emulsion peeled off the base. Exhibitors despaired at the poor quality of films: some prints lasted only a couple of nights. A. F. Rieser was reduced to sending back those that wore out in less than a week. Edmund McLoughlin complained that his films were very gray and discussed the problem with experts at Eastman Kodak of Rochester, New York, already the country's leading manufacturer of photographic supplies. They suggested that Edison was not using the proper emulsion. McLoughlin also informed them that "the Eastman Co. are shipping very heavily to France. They made a positive and negative emulsion and claim better results than you get." Finally, in mid September the Edison Manufacturing Company shifted its purchases of raw stock to Eastman. From that time on, the photographic manufacturer has been the principal American supplier of motion-picture raw stock.[40]

Individual vitascope entrepreneurs faced still other problems. In more rural areas, the screen novelty was greeted with little enthusiasm or patronage. "After the thing becomes ancient history these Yankees may become interested. But it is a harder task to interest the Maine natives in something new, than it is to preach free silver coinage to Wall Street bankers," declared C. O. Richardson in a letter to the Vitascope Company. W. R. Miller apparently had the same problem with Southerners, as his gross income with the vitascope generally fluctuated between five and thirty-four dollars a day. Far from major urban centers, people were often suspicious of urban popular amusements. In Skowhegan, Maine, Richardson reported, WATERMELON CONTEST was considered "nasty and vulgar because of the spitting and slobbering," and he thus had to ask Raff & Gammon for a replacement. City, county, and state licenses often reflected this hostility. As the owner of the Tennessee rights complained, "The only city where a good business can be done is Memphis where the City license is $22.50 per day. State and county are extra so you see that is prohibitive."[41] Eventually, many of the problems evoked by states rights owners were resolved: electrical difficulties were ameliorated if not completely eliminated; Eastman's satisfactory film stock was adopted; and although vitascope exhibitors complained about the shortage of films, their choice of titles continued to grow.

Despite these improvements, states rights owners rarely recouped their investments. Most did little more than meet expenses, and Wainwright and Rock were the only ones ever to claim a profit. In early September a Holland brother wrote to Raff:

> I am completely disheartened about the Vitascope business in consequence of the wretched films we have been receiving of late. If there is no improvement, it is simply out of the question altogether doing business under present conditions, and I do not wonder at the statements I hear from exhibitors in the United States that they are not making money to warrant paying large bonuses for territory (3 September 1896, MH-BA).

A month later, C. O. Richardson reported to the Vitascope Company:

> The Vitascope business in Maine has been no picnic by any means. Without counting a dollar for services of myself, wife and daughter, who had done all the work, we have since June, profited enough above running expenses to just pay costs of film and rental. After four months work with state two thirds covered I am still out my original $1000 for state (4 October 1896, MH-BA).

The expense and difficulty of introducing a new technology became their burden, allowing others to prosper.

Raff & Gammon, Thomas Armat, and Thomas Edison were the people who chiefly profited from the vitascope. Although the novelty's New York run at Koster & Bial's ended in mid August 1896, Raff & Gammon reopened at Proctor's two New York

WATERMELON CONTEST

vaudeville houses in mid September and remained for almost two months. By the time this run was concluded, Raff & Gammon had made over $10,000 from their exhibition contracts in that city alone.[42] Sales of territory and business dealings with the states rights owners must have roughly tripled that amount. Armat probably accrued more than $10,000. The Edison Company's film-related profits for the 1896

THE LONE FISHERMAN: *one of several Edison comedies made in the summer of 1896.*

EDISON'S MARVELOUS VITASCOPE.

THOS. A. EDISON.

The Greatest Scientific Exhibition Before the Public.

The New York Vitascope Company
Exclusive Owners Edison's Vitascope
State of New York.

EDMUND McLOUGHLAN.
ARTHUR FROTHINGHAM.

1193 BROADWAY,
NEW YORK.
Room 24.

J. H. LAINE,
Business Agent.

Rochester Oct 17/96

The Vitascope Co — Gentlemen:

*The Kinematograph
is being shown here and to day I saw the
machine. It is taken almost wholly from
the Vitascope, using the same gearing device
same pitman, and a face plate. They are also
using your films to-gether with some foreign
ones. It seems to me that your boasted
Patents fail to protect very much against
infringements. Will you kindly let me know
what your Patents cover, if you have any?
The territory will be pretty thoroughly covered
if a few more scopes and graphs get out
in this State and you are unable or unwilling*

E. M. McLaughlin complains to the Vitascope Company about rival projectors invading his territory.

business year were almost $25,000, while the famed inventor received additional compensation from Raff & Gammon in an informal royalty arrangement. Their success was thus in stark contrast to the fate of states rights owners, who never regained the money from their purchase of territory. These local entrepreneurs faced many impediments to success, but only one that could not be overcome: the problem created by competing motion-picture enterprises.

5

Early Motion-Picture Companies

Although "Edison's vitascope" was the first successful screen machine in the American amusement field, competing projectors and enterprises began to appear within a month of its Koster & Bial's debut. Even before this premiere, F. F. Proctor promised the imminent presentation of a mysterious "kintographe"—a promise he did not keep but one that told amusement-goers that the vitascope was not unique.[1] During the spring and summer of 1896, several other companies established themselves as leading enterprises in the field: the Eidoloscope Company, the Lumière firm, and the American Mutoscope Company. While organized somewhat differently, they shared underlying similarities with the Vitascope Company. Each one developed a complete motion-picture system, built its own equipment (cameras as well as projectors), and acted as a self-sufficient entity. All four sought to control the exhibition as well as the production of their films. This was the characteristic structure of film companies in the initial stages of the novelty period.

The Eidoloscope: Its Revival and Demise

In May 1896, before a single vitascope states rights owner had received a machine, the Lathams and their eidoloscope reemerged as a significant competitor. Gray Latham, attending one of the early Koster & Bial screenings, saw the vitascope's inner workings and realized it depended on an intermittent mechanism.[2] Quickly adding intermittent mechanisms to their own projectors, the Lathams opened at Hammerstein's Olympia Music Hall in Manhattan on 11 May. They also exhibited at the St. James Hotel near Herald Square, in a makeshift theater set up while the hotel was awaiting demolition. Later that summer, an eidoloscope was exhibited in a tent at Coney Island. Others appeared in theaters outside New York City. T. L. Diggens, who acquired eidoloscope rights to Michigan, opened at the Detroit Opera House on 28 May and stayed for four weeks. When the vitascope occupied the Opera House on 1 July, Diggens shifted to a summer park for another week and a half. In Boston, theatrical managers hoping to revive the fortunes of their operetta *The Yankee Cruiser* added the new attraction in mid June. The musical was abridged to make it more palatable, and the films were shown after the final curtain. Big crowds attended the eidoloscope's first night, but patronage fell off rapidly and the show closed at week's end. In early July, it moved to Providence and occupied the storefront left vacant by the vitascope. Yet another machine opened in Atlantic City in early July and competed with the vitascope.[3]

Eidoloscope exhibitions were aided by recently filmed subjects. Two were made in Mexico by Gray Latham and Eugène Lauste. BULLFIGHT, shot in Mexico City on 26 March, was the customary headline attraction. Lasting more than ten minutes, it was sometimes billed as a "continuous picture"—one that could play for twenty minutes without having to repeat itself. The Lathams' camera, however, did not pan or tilt on its tripod. As a result, the *New York Dramatic Mirror* reported, "The bull was out of sight a good deal of the time, but one could tell by the actions of the bullfighters that he was making things very hot for them. When he did come into view it was seen that he was a very fierce animal indeed." Among the other recent films on the first program at the Olympia were DRILL OF THE ENGINEER CORPS, also made in Mexico; WHIRLPOOL RAPIDS, NIAGARA FALLS; and FIFTH AVENUE, EASTER SUNDAY MORNING. During their five-week New York run, the Lathams shot a new picture, THE SIDEWALKS OF NEW YORK, borrowing the title from a popular play. "It was taken on Frankfort Street and shows a lot of little urchins dancing to the music of a street organ," according to the *Dramatic Mirror*.[4] All these recent selections were actuality subjects, scenes of daily life that were similar to those being taken by the Lumières but not dependent on them for inspiration.

While BULLFIGHT was sensationalistic enough to pack the theater when the eidoloscope first appeared, the Lathams were hurt by the poor quality of their projection.[5] One reviewer who disapproved of the film, however, found that this sometimes worked to its advantage:

> The whole ended with the incident of a bull fight, set forth in uninterrupted sequence. Here again there were disappointments and imperfect focussing, but there were thrilling moments when the baiting and torture of the luckless animal came out with perfect clearness. The rushes of the bull at its persecutors were vivid in their truth of life, and nothing could be more deceptive than the clouds of dust that it pawed up in the arena as it darted madly on its foes. Fortunately, the scene in which it gores a wretched horse was confused in outline, and the final slaughter of the creature, its spirit cowed and its energies wearied by the cruelties to which it had been subjected, was similarly dim and uncertain (*Boston Herald*, 23 June 1896, p. 9).

The Eidoloscope Company suffered still further from internal squabbling. When the Lathams discovered the secret of the "intermittent" (as it came to be known), Woodville, claiming he had invented such a device early in 1895, applied for a patent to cover it on 1 June 1896.[6] Over the next two months, Eidoloscope shareholders repeatedly demanded that the patent application become company property. Woodville refused and finally he and his sons were expelled from the corporation. They were no longer paid their stipulated salaries; Otway was removed from the board of directors and replaced as secretary.[7] The Eidoloscope Company brought suit against Woodville Latham in the Supreme Court of New York in an unsuccessful attempt to acquire the patent application; a countersuit was also brought though not prosecuted.

With the Lathams' departure, production of new eidoloscope films ceased and exhibitions became less frequent. Finally, in the fall of 1896, the company was sold to Raff & Gammon. One eidoloscope was subsequently attached to a touring theatrical company that performed a dramatic version of *Carmen,* and the bullfight film was incorporated into the fourth act as a feature. Playing in Atlanta, on 23–24 November 1896, the scene "created a great deal of enthusiasm" and the entire performance was described as "a brilliant production." On 11 December *Carmen* provided residents of Austin with one of their first opportunities to see projected motion pictures.[8]

After leaving the Eidoloscope Company, the Lathams did not immediately retire from the motion-picture business. Woodville's patent application, which gave them a chance of controlling important aspects of the industry, attracted E. & H. T. Anthony & Company as an investor. President Richard A. Anthony agreed to manufacture and sell a version of the eidoloscope, renamed the biopticon, which (like the Lumières' cinématographe) was adapted to serve as both a camera and a projector. His company also provided funds to pursue the various patent-interference cases in which Woodville Latham was involved. After the biopticon proved defective and a costly failure, E. & H. T. Anthony & Company eventually gained control of Latham's patents.[9] Occasional eidoloscope exhibitions continued until mid 1897, but the projector did not survive cinema's novelty era.[10]

The Lumière Cinématographe Reaches America

For slightly less than six months, the Lumière enterprise was the most popular motion-picture service in the United States. Early in 1895 Auguste and Louis Lumière came up with a simple, multipurpose machine that could be used as a camera, projector, and printer. Unhampered by the kinds of technological preconceptions that burdened Edison's kinetograph, the Lumières devised a much simpler instrument that relied on hand-cranking rather than electricity for its power. It was far more versatile and portable than the first cameras built in the United States. (Although the cinématographe used 35-mm film, a width almost identical to the 1½-inch gauge introduced by Edison, each frame had single round perforations on the edge of the film. The Lumière and Edison sprocket holes were thus incompatible.) Unlike Thomas Armat and C. Francis Jenkins, their American counterparts in the invention of projection technology, the Lumières had not only a complete motion-picture system (Armat claimed to have a camera, but it did not work) but the financial resources and skills to exploit the invention themselves.[11]

The Lumières gave their first public demonstration of the cinématographe on 22 March 1895, at the Society for the Encouragement of National Industry in Paris. They used the following nine months, prior to their first commercial exhibitions, to create a demand for their new product through judicious screenings at conferences and a coordinated publicity campaign. As Alan Williams has pointed out, the Lumières initially addressed a bourgeois, *sérieux,* technically informed public.[12] They used the lecture circuit to explain their experiments not only in cinematography but also in color photography (with lantern slides). Their subjects and the ways in which they were shot were well suited to these occasions, although audience attention was focused less on the subject of these images than on the apparatus that produced their lifelike quality. The operational aesthetic of earlier technological demonstrations continued.

Shooting a scene with the Lumière cinématographe.

Projecting a film with the Lumière cinématographe.

In France and elsewhere in Europe, the Lumières self-financed their motion-picture enterprise, chiefly through profits from their screenings. This setup gave them control over all commercial decisions but meant a slower start in comparison to that of Raff & Gammon, who, via their association with Edison, quickly raised the necessary financing through the sales of states rights. Self-financing was one of the reasons why the cinématographe was not shown in England until 20 February 1896—the same day the Englishman Robert Paul gave the first public demonstration of his theatrograph/animatographe projector. The cinématographe had its first U.S. screening at Keith's Union Square Theater in New York City on 29 June, more than two months after the vitascope's New York premiere.[13]

In America Benjamin F. Keith not only booked the cinématographe for his vaudeville circuit but acquired U.S. rights to the machine for the first months of its operation. The Frenchmen may have felt ill-prepared to exploit the American market on their own behalf yet recognized the need to act in a timely fashion. Advertised by Keith as "the greatest fashionable and scientific fad of London, Paris, Vienna, Berlin and the entire continent," it was immediately hailed as a sensational hit. "The Cinématographe is worked in the same way as the Vitascope and the Eidoloscope," explained one theatrical journal, "but the pictures are clearer and there is less vibration, so that the pictures are not so trying on the eyes as those produced by the other machines." In fact, patrons at Keith's theaters could make the comparison for

Keith's Union Square Theater, New York City, ca. 1895.

themselves, since Raff & Gammon placed a vitascope in a storefront on Fourteenth Street only a few doors away from the Union Square Theater.[14]

Scenes at the Lumières' American premiere included A DIP IN THE SEA, showing "several little boys running along a plank on stilts, and diving into the waves, which dashed upon the shore in the most natural manner," THE GARDENER AND THE BAD BOY; WASHING DAY IN SWITZERLAND; HYDE PARK, LONDON; THE CASCADE (GENEVA EXPOSITION); and THE MESSERS. LUMIERE AT CARDS. "The best picture was THE ARRIVAL OF THE MAIL TRAIN," claimed one reviewer. "The train came into the station, passengers alighted, met their friends and walked about, and all the bustle incident to affairs of this kind was shown to perfection." Another, who preferred more militaristic displays, argued that "Nothing more realistic or thrilling than the 'Charge of the Seventh Cuirassiers' has been seen on the local stage in many a month." A lecturer, Lew Shaw, explained the pictures as they were shown, "but he was hardly necessary as the views speak for themselves, eloquently." Theatrical sound effects were also employed to heighten the realism.[15]

Four weeks after the New York premiere, a second cinématographe reached the United States and replaced the vitascope at Keith's Bijou Theater in Philadelphia. The appearance of vitascopes at various summer parks in Philadelphia's environs undoubtedly annoyed Keith and encouraged this substitution, but in any case, the French machine entertained audiences with unfamiliar pictures and was soon "creating a genuine sensation." When the third cinématographe to reach the United States replaced the vitascopes at Keith's Boston theater on 10 August, manager E. F. Albee wrote vitascope entrepreneur Peter Kiefaber, "I am sorry to be unable to continue longer, but I have done all I possibly could in giving this feature more

CHARGE OF THE SEVENTH CUIRASSIERS

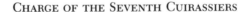

attention than any other branch of our business in order to get good results [but] without success the last four (4) weeks." Notwithstanding Albee's assertion that "it is no more value to me and not at all interesting to patrons," however, the vitascope continued to receive positive press notices even after the cinématographe had been announced.[16] But Keith's commercial interest in the cinématographe, as well as the enthusiastic public reception given the French machine in Philadelphia and New York, doomed its American rival on the Keith circuit.

The first three Lumière machines played Keith's New York theater for twenty-three weeks, his Philadelphia theater for nineteen weeks, and his Boston theater for twenty-two. By early September, new shipments had begun to arrive, and over the next eight months, the Lumières' New York office accumulated 24 machines and more than 1,400 "views." Cinématographes that left the Lyons factory were usually accompanied by an operator who was instructed to keep the machine with him at all times. According to Félix Mesguich, one of the first operators to reach the United States, the employees brought in the machines as personal property, a ruse that avoided immediate difficulties with American customs but eventually created serious problems for the French concern.[17]

In Pittsburgh, amusement entrepreneur Harry Davis opened the cinématographe at his vaudeville house on 7 September even as a rival manager gave the local vitascope premiere in conjunction with a play, *The Sidewalks of New York*. Although both machines were enthusiastically received, the vitascope remained for only three weeks, while the cinématographe lasted three months. On 14 September the French machine opened in Chicago and at New Haven's Wonderland Theater, a vaudeville house run by Sylvester Z. Poli. "Never in all our experience have we seen an attraction draw such crowds as the cinematographe, and never have audiences left a theater with more enthusiasm for the merits of an attraction," remarked the *New Haven Evening Register*. "The cinematographe is, indeed, the fad at this time, and that New Havener is out of fashion who has not seen it." Over a three-week period, Poli's drew 122,607 people—"an average of nearly 6,000 a day, which undoubtedly surpasses any theatrical attendance record in the history of New Haven."[18]

Keith's control over the cinématographe lasted only a few months, until approximately 1 November, when the French company opened the Lumière Agency at 13 East 30th Street in New York City and offered to sell states rights or lease its machines. A month later, a Lumière employee, M. Lafont, arrived from France and took charge of the agency. Knowing neither English nor "the American mentality," Lafont failed to maximize business opportunities—at least in the estimation of Félix Mesguich.[19]

While vaudeville provided an important outlet for the cinématographe, the Lumière machine played other venues as well, especially those with genteel orientations. In Brooklyn, for example, when it opened in a storefront (the old post-office building) on 17 August, publicity appealed to a more sophisticated clientele by emphasizing that the pictures "will be of special interest to those who know something of the artistic side of photography." On 1 November the operation moved to a larger storefront opposite Association Hall, where lectures appealing to lovers of refined culture were regularly given. After announcing that it had leased the premises for one year, the Lumière Agency ceased advertising, thus obscuring the actual length of the run. Another Lumière storefront opened in Philadelphia at Chestnut and 11th streets in December, a few weeks after its run at Keith's nearby Bijou came to an end.[20]

LUMIERE'S Cinematographe.

The greatest attraction of the century. Unapproached in subject, beauty, clearness and natural life movement. A marvel of interest and scientific skill. The unequaled success of the Cinematographe is due to the great care and scientific skill exercised by the Messrs. Lumiere, who engage the highest order of photographic talent in Europe for their immense establishment. New views arrive weekly. By special invitation, private exhibitions are being given before the crowned heads and courts of Europe. Crowds are daily thronging to see it wherever exhibited. Old and young alike are charmed and delighted. The subjoined Keith's Union Square Theatre advertisement appeared in New York papers under date Sunday, Oct. 4, 1896, and tells the story:

Fifth triumphant month of the fascinating and marvelous "LUMIERE'S CINEMATOGRAPHE." The original, the greatest and the only perfect scientific projection of animated photographs in the world. Successful throughout Europe for the past two years, and now universally conceded to be "America's greatest sensation."

THE NEW YORK HERALD, Sunday, Sept. 13, 1896, says: "Frequently, both afternoon and evening, the box office has to be closed. The Cinematographe is considered, by the management, to be largely responsible for the season's success."

For State Rights or Leasing address   LUMIERE'S CINEMATOGRAPHE, 13 East 30th St., New York City.

Lumière advertisement in the New York Clipper, *7 November 1896.*

In some cities the cinématographe appeared in places where refined cultural events such as musical recitals and lectures were usually held. On 3 December 1896 it opened at Hartford's Unity Hall; the appeal to an elite audience was evident in the admission fees, which began at fifty cents for adults and twenty-five cents for children. The Lumière cinématographe opened in Washington, D.C., around 1 January 1897, but ran for only two or three weeks before being replaced by the biograph. In both cases, the programs were devoted exclusively to motion pictures and lantern slides, with "full explanatory lectures, musical accompaniment and all the possible accessories to add to the realism." (In other cities, among them Toronto and Boston, the cinématographe appeared in department stores as a way to attract shoppers.)[21]

The Lumière organization offered types of subject matter that had wide appeal but were generally directed at a more elevated audience than were the exhibitions of their American counterparts, who favored dancing girls, boxing matches, bullfights, and vaudeville acts. Of course, these distinctions were not absolute: Vitascope showmen presented scenes of daily life even before the cinématographe arrived, and the first Lumière exhibitions also included subjects like A FRIENDLY BOXING MATCH. More often, however, as with THE HORSE TROUGH, which resembled Rosa Bonheur's famous painting *The Horse Fair*, they evoked the artistic aspirations of the more refined middle class.[22] Many Lumière films were travel views—scenes of life in foreign countries such as France, Italy, Britain, and Russia. In the course of a twenty-minute turn, operators could transport spectators across Europe with generic views of famous places such as London's Hyde Park, the Paris Botanical Gardens, the Bridge of Sighs in Venice, or the Minerva Baths in Milan.

Other films familiarized audiences with the Lumières, their business, and their family pastimes. Keith patrons often saw EMPLOYEES LEAVING THE LUMIÈRE FACTORY, set in Lyons, France. According to one viewer, "As the whistle blew, the factory doors were thrown open and men, women and children came trooping out. Several of the employes had bicycles which they mounted outside the gate, and rode off. A carryall, which the Lumières keep to transport those who live at a distance from the factory, came dashing out in the most natural manner imaginable." This vignette, in other words, testified to the Lumières' affluence as well as to their

THE HORSE TROUGH

generosity toward their employees—bicycles were still a middle-class luxury item rarely available to the American working class. Almost every program seemed to have at least one film featuring the family, including FEEDING THE BABY, with Lumière parents and child, and M. LUMIÈRE RECEIVING GUESTS.[23] Even the travel views testified to the international nature of the Lumière organization. Many films, therefore, acted as effective publicity for their enterprise.

Genres often overlapped. Some films of the Lumières formed part of a family genre that included CHILDREN AT PLAY, THE CHILDREN'S SEASIDE FROLIC, and THE BA-BIES' QUARREL, "showing two babies sitting in their high chairs having an infantile battle over their bowl of bread and milk." The latter was also described as a "laughable little comedy." There are several versions of another Lumière subject that was often called THE GARDENER AND THE BAD BOY: LE JARDINIER ET LE PETIT ESPIÈGLE (1895) and ARROSEUR ET ARROSÉ (1896). Frames from the latter appear on p. 146. This was another "domestic scene": "A bad boy steps on the hose, causing the water to squirt into the gardener's face. He drops the hose, runs after the boy, and gives him a sound thrashing." This film, or an American remake, had been shown on the vitascope even prior to the cinématographe's American premiere. Considered "the funniest view yet given in any series of this sort," it was frequently imitated by American producers and made a formative contribution to the popular bad-boy genre of early film comedy. Other comic scenes included "a photographer's trouble with a stupid subject"[24] and THE SAUSAGE MACHINE, in which dogs were "transformed" into sausages.

Vaudeville managers and the Lumière Agency heavily promoted military scenes, which were enthusiastically received by audiences. In Philadelphia, "a number of pictures are such phenomenal hits that they are demanded week after week. This is

THE GARDENER AND THE BAD BOY. *The Lumière perforations used only one round hole on each side of a frame.*

especially true of the military pictures, The March of the 96th Regiment of the French Infantry, The Charge of the Cavalry and the Cavalry Sham Battle." It was certainly effective propaganda for the French military; as one reviewer remarked, "That same impetuous dash that in the days of Napoleon earned fame for these troopers is visible and is reproduced on the screen with all the naturalness of life. One sees them charging down the field, urging their excited chargers to renewed efforts as they fly; in their eyes the fierce fire of battle, in their faces the grim, set determination to do or die, and over all an air that betokens victory."[25] At the same time that the army was made heroic, the spectator was placed in the position of the enemy being attacked. Patrons in the forward rows were unnerved by the assault even though the miracle of cinematography allowed them to enjoy the viewpoint and admire the cavalrymen. Indeed, the tension induced by these two conflicting reactions was the secret of these films' appeal. At first, the soldiers were exclusively French, but German, Italian, and Spanish forces were gradually introduced. While the need for variety tempered French nationalism, such scenes introduced a military motif that would continue to play a central role in American cinema.

Lumière films, like their American counterparts, were shot by men and reflected male preoccupations. The military scenes—particularly those of cavalry charging with drawn sabers, threatening to penetrate the spectators' space in the theater— offered a dynamic visual expression of masculinity in the all-male world of the army. This perspective found more complex expression in comedies like THE GARDENER AND THE BAD BOY. On one level, this film functions as what Noël Burch has called a moral tale, warning, "Don't interfere with a person's work or you will be punished." It thus humorously affirms the socialization process of male adolescents in a way that would please Henri Bergson (as would the comic reversal). Yet this comic situation, in which the gardener and the bad boy humiliate each other, reveals a rich latent content from a psychoanalytic perspective. The long nozzle attached to the hose, which practically runs between the gardener's legs, is an allusion to the phallus. The boy's actions in blocking and unblocking the hose suggest masturbatory play with some homosexual references. While the boy's punishment at the end resonates with societal prohibitions against masturbation, it does not fully negate the pleasure involved in the boy's play with the hose. Moreover, an (implicitly assumed) adult male spectator could find nostalgic pleasure in both the transgression and the punishment.

Although every cinématographe could act as a camera and printer, the Lumières did not immediately offer views of the United States to American audiences. Charles Hurd, who ran the concession for Keith, was anxious to have operators film local scenes because "nothing interests Americans as much as Americans," but Lumière films were not shot by just any operator. Keith had to wait for the arrival of one of the Lumières' leading photographers, Alexandre Promio. Disembarking in early September 1896, Promio traveled along the East Coast and as far west as Chicago. On 25 September, after three weeks of shooting, he returned to France with the exposed film. The negatives were developed there and the resulting prints were shipped back to the United States—and the rest of the world. Only in mid November, after failing to fulfill many promises, did the Lumière Agency begin to show American scenes. By then they had resumed control of their machines in U.S. territory.[26]

Contrary to general historical opinion, locally produced scenes did not usually play a key role in Lumière exhibitions.[27] American views appear to have been made with international more than American showings in mind. Scenes taken in New York City

Lumière films taken in America: PASSENGERS DESCENDING FROM THE BROOKLYN BRIDGE *and one of several scenes along Broadway.*

(SKATING IN CENTRAL PARK and BROOKLYN BRIDGE), Chicago (CHICAGO POLICE PARADE), and Boston (ATLANTIC AVENUE, BOSTON), or at Niagara Falls, were similar to those previously taken by American producers. They were, as advertisements claimed, "typical street scenes" and had a generic, nonspecific quality to them.[28] The fact that the Lumière films of McKinley's inauguration (March 1897) were not shown until the following month (four weeks after Biograph showed its version of the ceremony) suggests that the American agency may have never established its own laboratory facilities but rather continued to send negatives back to Lyons for developing and printing. In fact, Lumière production in the United States was much more modest than Mesguich and others have led historians to believe, and it was undoubtedly scenes of foreign lands that provided the cinématographe with its chief attraction for American audiences.

The American Mutoscope Company: A Different Technology

By 1897 the American Mutoscope Company, later renamed the American Mutoscope & Biograph Company and frequently called the Biograph Company after its biograph projector, replaced the Lumière enterprise as the foremost motion picture company in the United States and retained that dominance over the next four years.[29] It resulted from a collaborative venture that brought together the talents of William Kennedy Laurie Dickson, Herman Casler, Harry Norton Marvin, and Elias Bernard Koopman. In 1893 Marvin, Casler, and Dickson together invented the photoret, a detective camera the size and shape of a watch that was subsequently marketed by Koopman's Magic Introduction Company in New York City.[30] The financial rewards from this joint effort were small, but the four felt comfortable working together. Their alliance resumed when they decided to develop and exploit a peephole motion-picture device that would be superior to Edison's then popular and profitable kinetoscope. Dickson, though still working for Edison and surreptitiously helping the Lathams with the eidoloscope, provided the group with the basic idea for the invention. His flip-card device showed a series of photographic images in rapid succession and so created the illusion of movement. Called a mutoscope and designed to run by hand, it would serve the same function as the peephole kinetoscope but work more cheaply and efficiently.

The "K.M.C.D." group, as they called themselves (using the first initials of their last names), set to work. Koopman provided the necessary financing while Casler designed and constructed a mutoscope prototype at the Syracuse, New York, machine shop where he was then employed. The model was completed and a patent application filed in November 1894, when Edison's kinetoscope business was still booming.[31] After Koopman approved the invention, Casler began work on a mutograph camera that would make the necessary series of photographic images. Dickson again supplied crucial advice, and the camera was ready for preliminary testing by late February, when paper was run through it "to determine that the various elements of the mechanism were properly performing their respective functions."[32] Like the kinetograph, the mutograph camera relied on electricity to power its mechanism, but the principles involved were quite different from those of Edison's device. Instead of using sprockets to guide the film through the camera, the mutograph

Biograph Film No. 1, SPARRING CONTEST AT CANASTODA.

relied on a friction feed. In addition, the film stock, 70 mm (2¾ inches) wide, provided more than four times the image surface of a standard 35-mm frame. It was as bulky and complicated as the mutoscope was simple.

In June the camera was successfully tested with actual strips of film, which showed Marvin and Casler sparring. The same month Harry Marvin opened the Marvin Electric Rock Drill Works in Canastoda, New York. Casler joined him as superintendent at ninety dollars a month and brought his motion-picture experiments to this new site. Dickson, who had left Edison's employ in April and distanced himself from the Lathams, stayed with Marvin for part of the summer and fall as work moved forward. On 5 August the first "official" mutoscope film was taken of two more practiced pugilists, Professor Al Leonard and his pupil Bert Hosley—boxing matches were clearly seen as important subject matter in the mutoscope's future. Dickson either was not present or remained discreetly in the background.

While improvements were undoubtedly made between the June test and the August production, the camera probably did not embody all the characteristics detailed in Casler's patent application until shortly before it was filed on 26 February 1896. The mechanism, using a continuously moving friction-feed device, brought the film in front of the aperture, where a pressure plate held it in place while a double punch made holes in it, and the shutter opened and exposed it. Because the resulting frames were not evenly spaced along the negative, the holes provided the necessary registration of images during the printing process.[33]

By the time that work on the mutograph was well advanced, the peephole motion-picture business had fallen on hard times. People in the field were looking toward projection rather than alternatives to Edison's kinetoscope. On 22 September 1895, the K.M.C.D. group met at Marvin's home in Canastoda, posed for a group portrait, and discussed their future. Dickson, who was still in touch with Raff & Gammon and the Lathams, may well have urged the group to develop a projector. Unaware that others had already discovered the secret of projection, they began work and experimentation afresh. One employee at Koopman's Magic Introduction Company later recalled, "We had made several experiments, in which we threw the two arc lights on the Mutoscope [opaque] bromide-paper pictures as they revolved on the reel. We projected them with this reflected light, panopticon method."[34] This approach was not notably successful, and by November 1895 the group had adapted the mutograph camera to work as a projector. Light was directed into the camera and reflected onto a mirror before passing through the film and onto the screen. In a later form, the company's biograph projector dispensed with the mirror, and the light source assumed its now-familiar place behind the film gate and lens. Nonetheless, the pro-

The founders of the American Mutoscope Company in Canastoda, New York (September 1895). Left to right: Harry Marvin, William Kennedy Laurie Dickson, Herman Casler, and Elias Koopman.

jector, like the camera, used not sprockets and perforated film but rather a constantly moving friction-feed device with a clamp to hold the film steady while light passed through it and onto the screen.[35]

The K.M.C.D. group formed the American Mutoscope Company as a New Jersey corporation at the end of December 1895. In mid January the rights to Casler's mutoscope patents and applications were assigned to the company and then offered as security for first-mortgage coupon bonds in the amount of $200,000 by the New York Security and Trust Company. By February 1897, $115,000 from this fund had been subscribed. This money plus the sale of stock to various investors provided American Mutoscope with extensive financial backing, which allowed it to avoid some of the funding pitfalls of both the Vitascope Company and the Lumières. Dun & Company reported that "all identified with the business are considered shrewd and capable and are well known in the commercial world." The company president, George R. Blanchard, was commissioner of the Joint Traffic Association and one of the most prominent railroad executives in the country. First vice-president William H. Kimball was national bank examiner; secretary John T. Easton was a prominent lawyer. The board of directors boasted men such as E. J. Berwind, part owner of the Berwind & White Coal Mining Company, "considered a shrewd and capable merchant, and reputed to be very wealthy." Joseph Jefferson, a famous actor, and Abner McKinley, brother of the future president of the United States, also invested in the enterprise. These investors represented large-scale capital; their background and resources differed markedly from those of the small-time businessmen who bought the vitascope rights. With their support, Dickson and Koopman were installing machinery and other appliances at 841 Broadway in New York City by the end of January. A few months later, a developing and manufacturing plant was being constructed in Hoboken, New Jersey.[36]

The American Mutoscope Company was not prepared to enter the amusement field upon its formation: only six films were available, all of them taken in Canastoda.[37] Four of these were labeled SPARRING CONTEST AT CANASTODA (Nos. 1–4), while two others demonstrated the workings of machinery: THRESHING MACHINE (No. 5) and ENGINE AND PUMP (No. 6). Production for commercial amusement did not really commence until the mutograph camera was moved to New York City. In the spring of 1896 Dickson took charge of the camera and photographed two views of Union Square from the rooftop of 841 Broadway. Six other subjects, among them SKIRT DANCE BY ANNABELLE (No. 9), TAMBOURINE DANCE BY ANNABELLE No. 10), and SANDOW (Nos. 12 and 13), may have been made on the same rooftop. ·They were taken against a black background and bear a strong resemblance to the Black Maria films that Dickson had produced two years earlier. Similar scenes continued to be made against black or white backgrounds throughout the summer as Sandow and Annabelle Whitford [Moore] returned for additional sessions before the mutograph. Other posed subjects with actors included TRILBY AND LITTLE BILLEE (No. 36), an excerpted moment from the popular play *Trilby*, and vignettes of African Americans in "characteristic poses." A HARD WASH (No. 39) shows a black woman scrubbing her child. Spectators were expected to consider the scene humorous since no matter how hard the mother scrubbed, she would never get him "truly clean" (*i.e.*, white). As with WATERMELON FEAST (No. 40) and DANCING DARKIES (No. 41), the plain backgrounds turned these activities, like the images of Sandow flexing his muscles, into exhibits for curious audiences. Even these first motion pictures of African

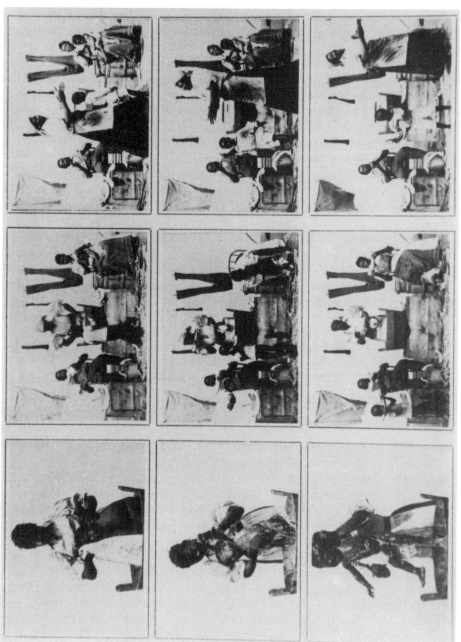

A HARD WASH, WATERMELON FEAST, *and* DANCING DARKIES: *denigrating stereotypes of African Americans that typified an era.*

Americans conformed to degrading, white-imposed stereotypes characteristic of American filmmaking throughout the period covered by this volume.

Despite its immense bulk, the company's only camera was frequently removed from the rooftop and used to film the everyday world. In these efforts, Dickson was often helped by a young employee of the Magic Introduction Company, Johann Gottlob Wilhelm ("Billy") Bitzer. On 6 June, Dickson shot BICYCLE PARADE ON THE BOULEVARD (Nos. 15 and 16) on Broadway north of Columbus Circle. Another large group of films was taken in July at Atlantic City and on the tracks of the Pennsylvania Railroad. PANORAMIC VIEW FROM TROLLEY (No. 22), like an earlier Edison film of Niagara Falls, was photographed from a moving trolley car. Toward the end of August, Dickson visited his friend Joseph Jefferson at his summer home in Buzzard's Bay. There, against natural backgrounds, the actor performed highlights of his famed role in the play *Rip Van Winkle*. Eight scenes were shot, including RIP'S TOAST (No. 45), RIP'S TWENTY YEARS' SLEEP (No. 50), and RIP LEAVING SLEEPY HOLLOW (No. 52). STABLE ON FIRE (No. 44), in which horses are led from a smoking barn, was taken on the same trip. On another expedition, in mid September, Dickson filmed cadets at West Point, took eleven films of Niagara Falls, and shot political demonstrations in Canton, Ohio (MCKINLEY AT HOME, CANTON, O. [No. 72]). From there, Dickson visited Canastoda and took five films of onrushing trains, including EMPIRE STATE EXPRESS (Nos. 77, 78, 81). The camera was placed close to the tracks and pointing toward the train, which came toward and then past the camera. Groups of related films were taken at each location.[38]

Initial Exploitation of the Biograph

The Biograph Company's exhibition efforts began modestly but expanded steadily. During the summer of 1896 Charles B. Jefferson, Joseph Jefferson's son, was organizing a touring vaudeville company that featured Eugene Sandow. Calling it "Sandow's Olympia," Jefferson arranged for the biograph to be one of the acts. It was the only biograph in operation during September and October. Since the vaudeville troupe only stayed in a city for one week, the American Mutoscope Company did not have to worry about changing subjects, which was a desirable arrangement at this stage in the company's development. When "Sandow's Olympia" opened on 14 September in Pittsburgh, Biograph was only one of three exhibition services in the city's theaters. Shown at the conclusion of the program, its presentation was endorsed for its "clear-cut and distinct" images that were nearly twice as large as those shown in other houses. "Sandow's Olympia" moved to Philadelphia and Brooklyn and then concluded its tour at the Grand Opera House in New York City on 10 October. Among the scenes exhibited on this brief tour were TRILBY AND LITTLE BILLEE, three scenes from *Rip Van Winkle*, STABLE ON FIRE, A HARD WASH, views of Sandow, and a timely news subject, LI HUNG CHANG AT GRANT'S TOMB (No. 55), taken on 30 August.[39] These exhibitions generally received favorable notices, although the *Brooklyn Eagle* called one "pretty fair, but not as life like as the cinématographe." With several costly acts, the vaudeville troupe proved "unprofitable financially" and the tour was shorter than originally expected.[40]

Immediately after "Sandow's Olympia" closed, the biograph appeared at Hammerstein's Olympia Theater, advertised under its own name and described in the

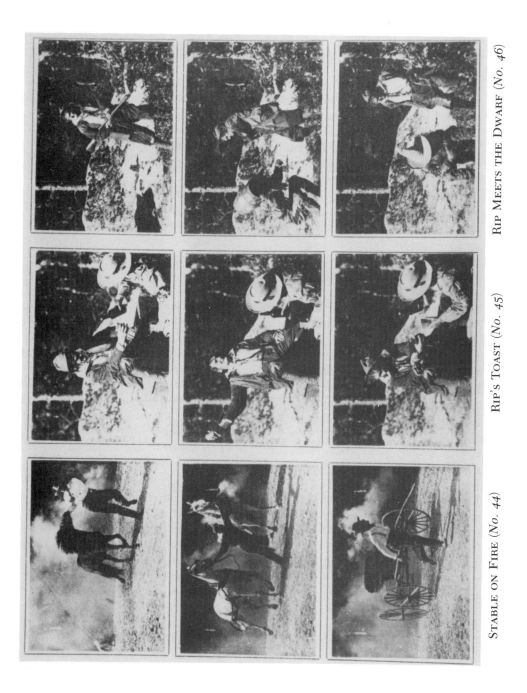

RIP MEETS THE DWARF (*No. 46*)

RIP'S TOAST (*No. 45*)

STABLE ON FIRE (*No. 44*)

program as "the 'dernier cri' in the art of producing light and motion." The official opening on Monday evening, 12 October, was a staged event that served as a political rally for the Republican party. Among the many prominent Republicans present was Garret Hobart, candidate for the office of U.S. vice-president. According to one Republican newspaper:

> The scene of the McKinley and Hobart parade at Canton called forth great applause, but when a few minutes later the audience caught sight of the next President himself, "in the flesh," pandemonium broke loose for five minutes. Men stood up in their seats and yelled with might and main, and flags were waved by dainty hands that would fain cast a vote on November 3, for the good cause. To satisfy the audience the Major was brought forth again with like result. There he stood on his much-betrampled lawn at Canton, talking with his son. Leisurely he read a telegram of congratulations, and then turning he came toward the excited audience, until it seemed as though he were about to step down into their very midst. But at that moment came the edge of the curtain, and he vanished round the corner to address a delegation of workingmen (*New York Mail and Express*, 13 October 1896, p. 5).

The biograph itself was hailed for the absence of flicker and "jump," noticeable in its competitors, and the fortunes of the high-quality machine and the businessman's candidate easily became linked. "No good Republican or upholder of sound money doctrine can afford to miss the lifelike representation of their champion on the lawn of his home at Canton," declared the *Mail and Express*. For the next two weeks, Republicans poured into Hammerstein's Olympia, wanting a glimpse of their candidate "in the flesh"—a rare opportunity since McKinley's front-porch campaign kept him in Canton. In some cases, local Republican clubs bought entire blocks of box seats.

Biograph left Hammerstein's theater after a two-week run and reopened on election eve at Koster & Bial's Music Hall. (During the hiatus, on Saturday, 31 October, Dickson shot SOUND MONEY PARADE [Nos. 89 and 90], showing a huge pro-McKinley rally in New York City.) At the new location, political demonstrations reached a fever pitch. When the biograph showed MCKINLEY AT HOME, a supporter of Democratic candidate William Jennings Bryan booed the image. "Mr. Bryan's friend hissed in his feeble way," reported the *Mail and Express*, "and then there came a sudden thunderclap of cheering which echoed the applause of Saturday's parade, and continued for several minutes. The picture was shown again to the patriotic audience, and the popocrat was observed to escape hurriedly past the box office, where they do not furnish return checks."[41] The following week, after the Republican victory, the biograph showed SOUND MONEY PARADE and NEW YORK FIRE DEPARTMENT (No. 87). Many in the audience may have seen both McKinley and the fire fighters as men coming to the rescue.[42] In any case, these exhibitions provided occasions for the political emotions of the spectators to be collectively expressed.

At the same time, Biograph did more than pander to the political sentiments of its audiences. EMPIRE STATE EXPRESS was a phenomenal hit that thrilled—and momentarily terrorized—unsuspecting viewers. In one instance, "two ladies in one of

Frame enlargements and related information from Biograph photo catalogs.

No. 76
Title *Parade, Canton, Ohio;*
Sound Money Club.
Length *349 ft.*
Code Word *Mollipes.*

No. 77
Title *Empire State Express.*

Length *160 ft.*
Code Word *Molliscomo.*

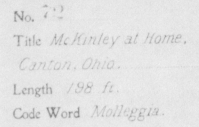

No. 72

Title *McKinley at Home,*
Canton, Ohio.

Length *198 ft.*

Code Word *Molleggia.*

No. 73

Title *Parade, American Club*
of Canton, Ohio.

Length *161 ft.*

Code Word *Mollerada*

the boxes on the left-hand side of the horseshoe, which is just where the flyer vanishes from view, screamed and nearly fainted as it came apparently rushing upon them. They recovered in time to laugh at their needless excitement."[43] Such films attracted their own constituency. Biograph's first night at Hammerstein's, for example, was attended by a large group of men from the New York Central Railroad; on the following Thursday, the railroad bought a block of two hundred seats in the orchestra. The biograph retained its popularity and continued at Koster & Bial's into the new year.

By November, American Mutoscope had additional biographs available for screenings. One machine toured with W. S. Cleveland's Minstrels, opening at Ford's Opera House in Baltimore on 2 November. A third joined Palmer Cox's Brownies, a touring theatrical entertainment also produced by Charles Jefferson, and opened in Chicago on 16 November. Two debuts on 30 November occurred in vaudeville houses: at Poli's Wonderland Theater in New Haven and at Cook's Opera House, in Rochester, New York (the latter may have been a tryout as it lasted a week and only momentarily interrupted a long and successful cinématographe run). The biograph also opened on 14 December in Atlanta in conjunction with plays given by a theatrical stock company. By Christmas week, the biograph was playing in at least six theaters, including J. D. Hopkins' vaudeville houses in Chicago and Pittsburgh.

Biograph's debut at Poli's Wonderland Theater in New Haven was particularly significant because it inaugurated the company's long-standing practice of taking local views. In mid November, Dickson traveled to New Haven and took FIRE DEPARTMENT RUN, NEW HAVEN (No. 91) and WINCHESTER ARMS FACTORY AT NOON (No. 92), which showed employees leaving for dinner. Another street scene, AN ARREST (No. 93), was staged immediately outside the front entrance of Poli's theater. In another film, Dickson on 18 November caught the Yale football team at practice. Although none of these local scenes was unveiled during the biograph's first week at Poli's, reactions to the initial screenings were highly favorable. The *New Haven Evening Register* reported that "the wonderful machine at once established its claims to superiority over all other inventions for the display of moving pictures, and the views shown at once won their way into public favor." For the second week, the biograph showed its views of the Yale football team and "made a vivid impression on the spectator" with its heroic portrayal of the players: "So strikingly has the photographer caught the detail in this picture that the face of every man is recognizable as he stands strained for the rush. There is Captain Murphy at tackle, with taut drawn face and determined air; the powerful Chamberlain at center putting the ball into play and watching for an opening against the opposing team." The remaining local views were shown the following week and "caught on immensely."[44]

Dickson returned to New Haven on 21 and 22 December to make a second group of films, including not only local scenes but three or four comedies acted on a temporary stage behind Poli's theater. Before the end of the year, the new films were being shown at the Wonderland and received hearty praise:

> The local views came in for the liveliest manner of commendation, particularly those of a comedy cast. One very funny view, which was appreciated by many who had been there, was one showing a married couple's misery when awakened after midnight by their crying hopeful and their desperate effort to reduce the fractious infant to terms [WHY

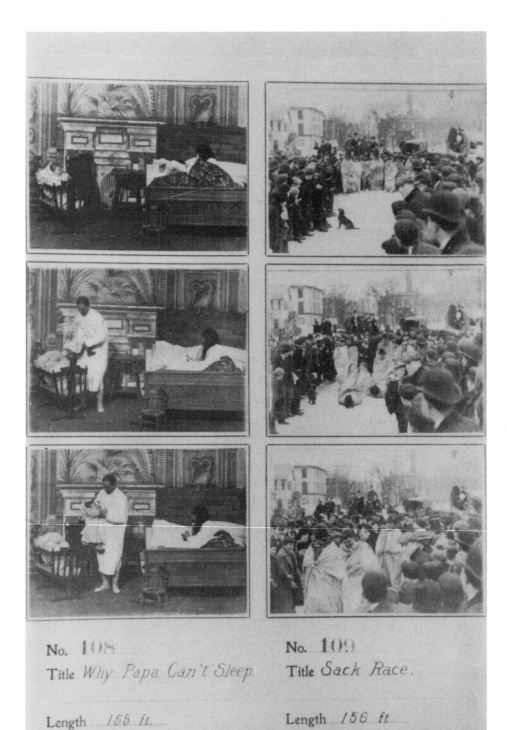

No. 108
Title *Why Papa Can't Sleep.*

Length *155 ft.*
Code Word *Montatigo.*

No. 109
Title *Sack Race.*

Length *156 ft.*
Code Word *Montecitos.*

PAPA CAN'T SLEEP, No. 108]. Still another laughing picture shows a prominent club man returning to his home after midnight in a jolly condition and reveals his trouble when he attempts to find his way into bed [THE PRODIGAL'S RETURN, No. 107] (*New Haven Evening Register*, 29 December 1896, p. 10).

These locally produced comedies became a popular part of the Biograph Company's repertoire even though S. Z. Poli retained the exclusive exhibition rights to Connecticut. The exhibition of local scenes became a specialty service that the Biograph Company offered to theater managers who wanted to enhance the popularity of their bills.

By the end of 1896, the Biograph Company had also established the commercial ties with Benjamin F. Keith that would continue for the next eight and a half years. The biograph opened at Keith's Bijou Theater in Philadelphia on 28 December, at Keith's New Theater in Boston on 11 January, and at Keith's Union Square in New York on 18 January. By then, the American Mutoscope Company was well on its way to supplanting the Lumière cinématographe as the exhibition service favored by first-class theaters.[45] While the demand for moving pictures could have easily accommodated three or more major exhibition companies, even allowing for significant variation in the technical quality of their exhibitions and the attractiveness of subject matter, only the Biograph Company had a significant share of the American market by the end of the 1896–1897 theatrical season. The proliferation of independent exhibitors, who simply purchased 35-mm projectors and films, undermined the Vitascope Company and, to a lesser extent, the Lumière Agency and its cinématographe.

20TH CENTURY PROGRESS

THE WONDERFUL

ANIMATIOGRAPHE

MARVELOUS REPRODUCTIONS!

NOT A MAGIC LANTERN SHOW

Our Pictures do everything but talk; have everything
but life and soul.

THE FIGURES IN THE VIEWS ACTUALLY MOVE!

SEE THE REALISTIC AND ABSOLUTE REPRODUCTION OF THE FOLLOWING SCENES:

FLIGHT OF THE "BLACK DIAMOND" EXPRESS
RESPONSE TO ALARM OF FIRE!
A BURNING STABLE!   A SKIRT DANCE!
WATERMELON CONTEST, and others.

THE LAUGHING, CRYING, SINGING, TALKING, MUSIC-PRODUCING, MIRTH-PROVOKING

PHONOGRAPH

A choice and extensive repertoire of interesting selections, including performances by Gilmore's Band, U. S.
Marine Band, 23d Regiment Band, and other leading organizations.   Sentimental and Comic Songs
by Dan. W. Quinn, Silas Leachman, Len Spencer, and other popular vocalists.   Don't miss
this opportunity of a lifetime to hear and see the latest innovations.

WE APPEAL TO THE EYE, THE EAR, AND INTELLIGENCE!

The Animatiographe engages the first, the Phonograph gratifies the second, and both contribute to the third.

HUTCHINSON BROS., New York City

6

The Proliferation of Motion-Picture Companies and an Assessment of the Novelty Year

*T*he number of motion-picture companies increased rapidly during the 1896–1897 theatrical season. These enterprises no longer tried to develop their own self-contained technological systems but adopted and adapted one already in existence: the 35-mm format with Edison perforations. While an astoundingly large number of firms made projectors that could handle Edison films, only a few actually began to produce their own films. The impetus behind this production of projectors and films came from the many independent exhibitors who began showing motion pictures during the summer of 1896 and whose numbers rapidly proliferated over the course of the new theatrical season. Buying films and machines from one or more manufacturers, they gave entertainments without having to worry about territorial restrictions, royalties, or licensing fees.

The Phantoscope and Other Projectors

The first machine (with an intermittent) sold outright on the American market was Jenkins' phantoscope. On 14 May Edward D. Easton of the Columbia Phonograph Company and the American Graphophone Company came to an agreement with C. Francis Jenkins to manufacture and exploit the phantoscope (which Jenkins was then claiming as his own invention). Because the Columbia Phonograph Company had acquired some expertise in the motion-picture field by running peephole kinetoscopes in its phonograph parlors, this was a logical extension of its business operations. Moreover, Columbia found the competitive opportunity irresistible since Edison had recently tried to destroy its phonograph business. According to Easton, "The American Graphophone Company made a large investment in the business covered by the said agreement with Jenkins." Jenkins conducted the company's motion-picture business, receiving a 10 percent commission on sales and gross receipts from exhibitions. Soon Columbia was selling phantoscopes without territorial

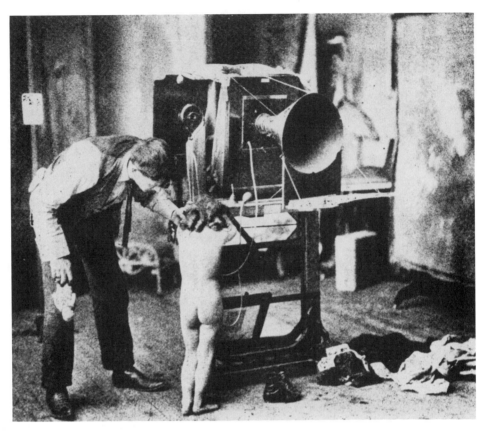

C. Francis Jenkins coaxing a young girl to appear before the camera.

restrictions. Although Armat's associates countered with a lawsuit, their request for a preliminary injunction was denied. Columbia's activities, however, were seriously thwarted that December when Armat and his cousin, T. Cushing Daniel, paid Jenkins $2,500 for withdrawing his exclusive claim to the phantoscope patent and for contractually recognizing Armat's earlier "sale" of the Armat–Jenkins projection patents to Daniel.[1]

A "vidiscope," probably a renamed phantoscope, was in Coney Island in late June, giving the vitascope serious competition. According to the *Brooklyn Eagle*, a barker stood at the front entrance promoting "the genuine and only vidiscope" as "the renowned and successful invention that has captured New York city and attracts more attention than the gold and silver question in politics." For their part, the Long Island vitascope owners sued the exhibitors in Kings County Supreme Court claiming that "the vidoscope [*sic*] exhibition is not genuine and that great damage will come to them if the show goes on." They were fortunate to win a temporary injunction.[2]

In Chicago, vaudeville manager John D. Hopkins faced a difficult situation. Shortly after he added the vitascope to his bill (paying Kiefaber $350 a week for exclusive Chicago rights), a nearby phonograph parlor began to advertise the phantoscope as a vitascope and, even worse, to show it without charging admission. The firm responsible, the Chicago Talking Machine Company, was eventually enjoined from using the name, but exhibitions were allowed to continue. On 11 August, Hopkins' "exclusive" faced further competition when a phantoscope appeared at Chicago's Great Northern Roof Garden. Yet as the *Chicago Tribune* reported, "The apparatus did not work well, and the time apportioned to it was chiefly devoted to cheap kaleidoscopic pictures. It will not be seen again." Hopkins was the first to admit that the episode was not indicative of the phantoscope's true worth: "I had a great deal to do with the failure of the machine," he boasted in a letter to the Vitascope Company, explaining that "one of our electricians was engaged to run it—so you understand the rest." Hopkins sabotaged the phantoscope's Chicago screening, but he was striking a more complicated deal than Raff & Gammon at first realized. At his recently opened St. Louis vaudeville house, Hopkins added the "wonderful phantoscope" to his bill, then supplied the exhibitor there with films purchased from the Vitascope Company for his Chicago house. When Raff & Gammon discovered the ruse, they planned to cut off his supply. By then, however, it was becoming clear that Edison films could be acquired from other sources, notably Maguire & Baucus, and so Raff & Gammon reluctantly accepted the arrangement.[3]

Once projected moving pictures were proven feasible and commercially successful, foreign and American mechanics set to work constructing machines to project Edison-gauge film. The technology was not complicated and many succeeded, with the result that by September, a substantial number of projectors were available to amusement entrepreneurs. A. Curtis Bond, press agent for the Bijou Theater in New York City, acquired the American rights to the kineopticon constructed in England by Birt Acres. After its London premiere on 21 March 1896, the kineopticon ran at

Columbia Phonograph Parlor, Atlantic City (1896). Patrons could peep through a series of small windows and see films projected by the phantoscope.

Tony Pastor's Theater from 24 August until 17 October. Its selection of mostly British views included PRINCE OF WALES'S FAMOUS HORSE and PERSIMMONS WINNING THE DERBY, both shot by Acres. By early September, Bond was offering to sell machines and states rights. That month the zooscope, made in Malden, Massachusetts, was being sold outright for eight hundred dollars. The magniscope was also advertised by Chicago-based Oscar B. and George Kleine, sellers of magic-lantern and stereopticon goods.[4]

The magniscope was built by Edward Hill Amet, whose Amet Talking Machine Company in Waukegan, Illinois, was then turning out high-quality phonographs. George K. Spoor, the local Waukegan theater manager whose principal living came from a newsstand at the Northwestern Railroad station in Chicago, helped finance the development of the projector. "Sold outright, without restrictions and at a reasonable price," the seventy-pound magniscope was portable and designed for work with touring companies. Many itinerant showmen, particularly in the Midwest, eagerly purchased the screen machine and toured the smaller cities and towns. It also found employment in major urban vaudeville houses. Beginning on 9 November 1896, J. D. Hopkins presented the Amet magniscope at his Duquesne Theater in Pittsburgh; a week later, it replaced the vitascope at his Chicago house. Although these runs were fairly brief, other high-profile Chicago theaters engaged the magniscope in subsequent months.[5]

With his projector selling well, Amet moved into film production sometime during March 1897, building his own camera and setting up laboratory facilities in Wauke-gan. Subjects included a street scene outside the offices of the *Chicago Tribune*, which devoted a lengthy article to the new enterprise. Amet's way of developing a 60-foot film was described as follows:

> Two men take the exposed film into the dark room and begin opera-tions. . . . Starting at one end, the film is rapidly fed into the long trough, being run back and forth until it is all placed in layers in the developer. Then, starting again with the same end as at first, it is drawn out of the developing solution at the same rate as it entered, and is run into a jar of water to wash. By that time the proper amount of development is ob-tained and the film next goes into the fixing solution, emerging from that to be soaked in the washing tanks in the drying room.
>
> In the drying room are loops and strings of film sufficient to decorate a theater. The room is fifty feet high, with the ceiling made so that the films may be hung easily from it. Here after the long negatives are washed, they are festooned about until thoroughly dry and ready for printing (*Chicago Tribune*, 4 April 1897, p. 37).

Edward Amet with his camera (1897).

Edison Breaks with Raff & Gammon

As a variety of projectors became available, the leading companies' chief assets were their exclusive ownership of popular subjects. Yet controlling the distribution of standard-gauge films was extremely difficult, perhaps impossible. Edison films from 1894 and 1895 had been sold to a large number of peephole kinetoscope owners. These films could be placed on projecting machines as readily as on kinetoscopes. New films, sold to vitascope exhibitors, were easily resold or traded. Since Edison films were not copyrighted, they could be freely "duped" (*i.e.*, duplicated, usually by someone other than the original owner). The Columbia Phonograph Company found it expedient to "dupe" such films because Jenkins did not have a working camera. The Lumières, as noted in chapter 4, encountered similar difficulties. By August Maguire & Baucus had acquired a large shipment of Lumière films, including SCENE FROM THE CORONATION OF THE CZAR OF RUSSIA (taken in late May), RUSSIAN STREET SCENE, and PLACE DE LA CONCORDE, which they sold for twenty-five dollars per 52-foot film. Some independent exhibitors acquired a selection of both Edison and Lumière films. For example, the kinematographe with Hopkins' Trans Oceanic Star Specialty Company, a touring vaudeville show, was showing the Lumières' SCENE FROM THE CORONATION OF THE CZAR and Edison's HERALD SQUARE.[6]

By October 1896 the Vitascope Company was disintegrating under the pressure of external competition and internal discord. Having made little money from the sale of vitascopes, the Edison Manufacturing Company was dissatisfied with its relationship to Raff & Gammon. Only seventy-three machines had been manufactured, and additional demand was unlikely because other projectors were coming on the market at a lower price and without territorial restriction. Likewise, limiting print sales to vitascope entrepreneurs reduced profits and made little commercial sense. The Edison Manufacturing Company therefore shifted its approach and sold prints to all potential customers, either through Maguire & Baucus or directly from its factory. Over the next eight months, beginning with FEEDING THE DOVES (© 23 October 1896) and several other pictures, films were submitted for copyright to deter if not eliminate unauthorized duplication. James White, hired away from the Vitascope Company, was placed in charge of Edison's kinetograph department, for which he received one hundred dollars a month plus a 5 percent commission on film sales.[7]

White launched an ambitious production schedule. In many instances he shot groups of related films, including several of New York police (MOUNTED POLICE CHARGE and RUNAWAY IN THE PARK—both © 2 November 1896). With the cooperation of the Lackawanna Railroad, which supplied transportation and special cars for filming, White and Heise toured New York and Pennsylvania shooting films. BLACK DIAMOND EXPRESS (© 12 December 1896) was an imitation of Biograph's popular EMPIRE STATE EXPRESS. Going to the Buffalo area, they improved on the scenes of Niagara Falls that Heise had taken earlier in the year; seven views were subsequently copyrighted, including AMERICAN FALLS FROM INCLINE RAILROAD and RAPIDS ABOVE AMERICAN FALLS (both © 24 December 1896). Exhibitors would make selections from these productions and organize them into sequences. Other films imitated popular subjects made by rival producers. A MORNING BATH (© 31 October 1896) remade Biograph's A HARD WASH. Both CLARK'S THREAD MILL (© 31 October 1896), which showed workers leaving a factory, and CHARGE OF WEST POINT CADETS (© 27 November 1896) emulated earlier Lumière successes. A group

Clark's Thread Mill *and* Market Square, Harrisburg, Pa.

of films taken of Barnum and Bailey's Circus in New York City (HORSE DANCING COUCHEE COUCHEE and TRICK ELEPHANTS No. 1—both © 8 May 1897) added to Edison's substantial repertoire of circus-related subjects.

Thomas Edison, having made substantial profits from the sale of peephole kinetoscopes, was likewise eager to sell projecting machines to the general trade. His company soon had its own projector, known as the projectoscope or projecting kinetoscope, which debuted on 30 November at the Bijou Theater in Harrisburg, Pennsylvania, one of the few important cities that had not previously hosted a motion-picture show. The initial morning performance was attended by the mayor, city officials, and the newspaper fraternity, who gave it laudatory front-page reviews. "It is the greatest attraction ever seen in this city, and the crowds will be big all week," wrote one local paper. Although several projectoscopes were in use by early 1897, the machine did not become generally available until late February. Its $100 price tag was affordable for even modest showmen. J. Stuart Blackton and Albert Smith, for example, bought a projecting kinetoscope and presented a group of moving pictures during their Lyceum entertainments. So did D. W. Robertson, a former musician who was then organizing entertainments for church groups through his Brooklyn and New York Entertainment Bureau. The price of films, however, remained quite high. Although discounts were often available, Edison films sold for thirty cents a foot, a price that changed little during the year. Indeed, Edison Manufacturing Company records reveal that films provided its key source of income:

MCKINLEY TAKING THE OATH. *One of a dozen films related to the new president's inauguration on 4 March 1897.*

profits from film sales exceeded $24,000 for both the 1896–1897 and 1897–1898 business years, compared to projector profits of approximately $1,500 and $5,000. This reversed the ratio of equipment sales to film sales that had previously existed.[8]

A Flood of Projecting Machines

Charles H. Webster had left the Vitascope Company by October and was involved with at least two rival motion-picture enterprises. On 21 October he, Charles G. S. Baker, and William C. McGarth incorporated the Cinographoscope Company of New York; two weeks later their cinographoscope projector was being advertised for sale.[9] At about the same time, Webster also formed the International Film Company as a co-partnership with Edmund Kuhn, and by November they were selling "dupes" of Edison films as well as original films. One of their first original films was SOUND MONEY PARADE, taken on 31 October. Once film production was launched, the International Film Company commenced to manufacture its own projector. This projectograph was less expensive than those previously on the market, costing $200 in December and $150 a short time later.[10]

By early 1897 scores of different projectors were available to American showmen. Although little noted by historians, these machines had diverse capabilities and constructions. Some depended on electricity for power, but most were hand-cranked and the operator could use limelight as an illuminant. Many were of European origin, including Robert Paul's highly popular animatographe, one of which toured Pennsylvania with Waite's Comedy Company during much of the 1896–1897 theatrical season. A motograph, probably manufactured by W. Watson & Sons of London, was ballyhooed by Hi Henry's Minstrels, and another was shown by William H. O'Neill at a Boston department store. The kinematographe, first shown at London's Royal Aquarium in April 1896, made several American appearances, including Bradenburgh's Ninth and Arch Museum in Philadelphia and Huber's Museum in New York City.[11]

Many projectors were built in the United States. Little more than pirated vitascopes, centographs were at Miner's Bowery Theater in New York City during early October and toured with Irwin Brothers' Big Specialty Company. By November, J. Whitney Beals, Jr., of Boston was selling his "Wonderful Panoramographe." Lyman H. Howe built his own projector, the animotiscope, and integrated a small selection of Edison films into his phonograph concerts. His first public presentation took place at his hometown YMCA in Wilkes-Barre, Pennsylvania, on 4 December 1896. Thereafter he traveled through Pennsylvania, New York, and New England—one of many traveling exhibitors to present film programs to people living in smaller cities and towns. William Paley was an X-ray exhibitor who had suffered adverse effects from excessive radiation—peeling skin, loss of fingernails, rapidly graying hair, and "a slight buzzing in the ears." The English-born showman had studied electricity in his native country before coming to the United States. Abandoning X-ray exhibition, he built a projector that was similar to the vitascope but with numerous improvements. Paley used the resulting kalatechnoscope (meaning "good technical viewer") to show films with Weber's Olympia Company in March and then began to sell the machine for one hundred dollars.[12]

William Selig, who had been a magician and theatrical-company manager, was trying to build a projector when he discovered that his machinist had surreptitiously made a duplicate cinématographe for a Lumière employee. Using the blueprints accumulated on the project, the machinist built another for Selig and modified it to take Edison-sprocketed film.[13] Charles Urban, who had had a phonograph parlor in Detroit and later toured the Midwest with a projector, had Walter Isaacs manufacture a modified Lumière cinématographe and then sold it as a bioscope.

On the West Coast, William L. Wright of Portland, Oregon, was constructing a projecting machine by early 1896. Later he moved to San Francisco, where he incorporated the United States Animatoscope Company with Gustave Walter, who ran the Orpheum vaudeville circuit, and several other entrepreneurs. Its purpose was "to deal in machines for reproducing photographic films in an enlarged form on canvas." The animatoscope opened at the Chutes, a multi-attraction amusement center in San Francisco, around 9 November. The films were shown outdoors in the evening, with a different film projected every fifteen minutes. The amusement remained at the Chutes on a fairly regular basis for many years. Shortly after his San Francisco opening, Wright returned to Portland, operated a store show for a few days, and then continued up the coast.[14] The animatoscope had wide exposure in the Rocky Mountain area and along the West Coast.

Prominent dealers in magic-lantern goods also built and/or sold motion-picture

Lubin's cineograph projector (June 1897).

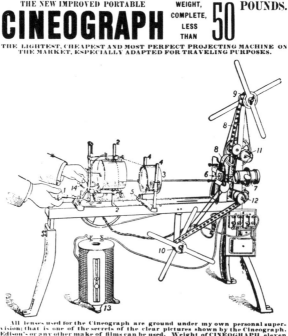

DEWARS SCOTCH WHISKY

Prominent dealers in magic-lantern goods also built and/or sold motion-picture projectors. The Riley brothers sold their kineoptoscope. Sigmund Lubin of Philadelphia enlisted the aid of C. Francis Jenkins and, after some difficulty, constructed the cineograph projector, which he offered for sale in January 1897 at a cost of $150. By the end of February, Lubin had also become an important agent for Edison films. In late March his recently formed cineograph exhibition service gave its first exhibitions in vaudeville, at Bradenburgh's Ninth and Arch Museum, with THE CORBETT–COURTNEY FIGHT providing the theater's main attraction. The optician soon established his own production capabilities, taking UNVEILING OF THE WASHINGTON MONUMENT on 15 May.[15]

During cinema's novelty year, motion pictures found their way into most aspects of American entertainment. By spring 1897, circuses and carnival men were using films, sometimes in light-inhibiting black tents. Leon W. Washburn's Shows, starting out in Passaic, New Jersey, gave free exhibitions every night with the vitascope; the films featured acts that spectators could later see live in big tents and were presumably taken with Peter Kiefaber's own camera by his chief photographer, Jacob (James) Blair Smith. The Curtis & Howard Electric Belt Company, active in Ohio and Indiana, featured a high-wire act, juggler, magician, and magniscope. The Bonheur Brothers, who traveled by wagon through the Plains states, offered a variety of acts. The magic lantern had been an important staple in their amusement repertoire, and by April they boasted an imatoscope which may have been a motion-picture machine. In large cities, exhibitions were given for advertising purposes, projected from rooftops onto large canvases hung at busy intersections such as Herald Square in New York.[16] The International Film Company's DEWARS SCOTCH WHISKY (1897) was made for this kind of outlet. Such screen advertising had been popular in previous years, when exhibitors had shown only slides. Now films were added to their repertoire. This was part of the rich diversity of exhibition circumstances generally provided by independent exhibitors who were not associated with larger organizations.

The Biograph at Home and Abroad

Large-scale organization can provide commercial enterprises with many advantages, and the American Mutoscope Company generally maximized these opportunities of scale. By early 1897 the company was paying expenses and making a profit. "Our machine known as the Biograph is meeting with success and we now have about 25 exhibits throughout the country," Koopman reported on 11 February. "These machines are rented, and we derive a good income therefrom." In many instances, Biograph rented its services to local theatrical entrepreneurs. Thus, its Washington, D.C., exhibitions were known first as Allen's Biograph and then Jay Denham's Biograph.[17] But while most people who hired the Biograph service were amusement professionals, there were also cases like that of the Oneida County Wheelway League, which rented the Biograph service for a week in April and ran it at the Utica Opera House. Not only were free passes given to children from the Utica Orphan Asylum and other groups who could not afford admission but, according to announcements,

> every penny of profits will be devoted to the construction and repair of the cinder paths. Inasmuch as every 'cyclist finds pleasure in riding the cinder paths, it is the duty of every 'cyclist to contribute to their maintenance. The officers of the League have provided the Biograph entertainments for the purpose of tempering the stern sense of duty with an alloy of pleasure, for each patron may have entire confidence that the entertainments will be well worth the cost of seeing them (*Utica Observer*, 9 April 1897, p. 6).

Once success was assured, the American Mutoscope Company constructed a motion-picture studio on the roof of its building at 841 Broadway. As he had with the Black Maria, Dickson insisted on an elaborate setup that could be rotated to face the sun. This outdoor studio was ready for filmmaking early in 1897. SAUSAGE MACHINE (Nos. 132 and 133), an imitation of the Lumières' SAUSAGE MACHINE, may well have been taken on the completed stage in late February. A production still of LOVE'S YOUNG DREAM (No. 154), taken soon after McKinley's March inauguration, indicates that the studio was in full operation by this date. Elaborating on the osculatory motif, the film shows two lovers kissing in the parlor when they are interrupted by the girl's irate father. Several one-shot comedies were quickly filmed on the new rooftop. In A BUNGLING WAITER (No. 156), the waiter spoils a tête-à-tête between a young couple by spilling food on them. A PILLOW FIGHT (No. 158), showing four young girls hitting each other with pillows until the feathers pour out, was extremely well received—in Boston it was encored until shown again—and the Edison Company promptly responded with an imitation called PILLOW FIGHT (© 24 May 1897). THE MISER (No. 160) was a close view of "the familiar character played by Paul Gilmore," giving spectators a much more intimate look at the actor than they normally enjoyed in the theater.[18]

No. 131

Title *Projectile Striking Water, Sandy Hook.*

Length *159 ft*

Code Word *Mordit*

No. 132

Title *Sausage Machine.*

Length *160 ft*

Code Word *Morenuta.*

Filming LOVE'S YOUNG DREAM *on Biograph's rooftop studio.*

Dickson remained in charge of the American Mutoscope Company's single camera throughout this period. One typical filming trip found him in Hartford, Connecticut, on 8 April 1897, ready to photograph local views. Rainy weather delayed filming until four days later, when a clear day provided sufficient light. After a rehearsal in which the city's horseless fire engine, Jumbo, charged down Wyllys Street, the fire run was repeated twice more for Dickson's camera (JUMBO, Nos. 170 and 171). He then shot COLUMBIA BICYCLE FACTORY (No. 172), showing workers leaving the Pope Manu-facturing Company at noon, and A NEWSBOYS' SCRAP (No. 173), featuring paperboys for the *Hartford Times*.[19] After the Hartford filming, Dickson headed north to Fort Ethan Allen near Burlington, Vermont, and took eleven scenes of military drills and maneuvers (MUSICAL DRILL, TROOP A, 3RD CAVALRY, No. 176). Back in New York, he was responsible for ten films of the 27 April parade celebrating the dedication of Grant's Tomb.

The American Mutoscope Company expanded its operations overseas during the first part of 1897. Biograph's London premiere came at the Palace Theater on 18 March. The reception was favorable, and on 12 May, Dickson and Koopman left New York for England, bringing with them at least one camera (increasingly referred to as the "biograph camera" rather than a "mutograph"). Their first subjects in England were Queen Victoria's Diamond Jubilee celebrations on 22 June. Lacking facilities for developing and printing the films, Dickson sent back lantern slides of the jubilee to the American office. "The biograph keeps well up with the times," reported the *New York Mail and Express*, "and yesterday it showed two good views of the in-tercollegiate boat races as well as five stationary views of the Queen's jubilee, the latter being the first in America of that famous celebration." A royal command performance of the biograph and its jubilee pictures for the Prince of Wales on 20

No. 154

Title *Love's Young Dream.*

Length *145 ft.*

Code Word *Mostardal.*

No. 155

Title *A Bowery Cafe.*

Length *141 ft.*

Code Word *Mostearon.*

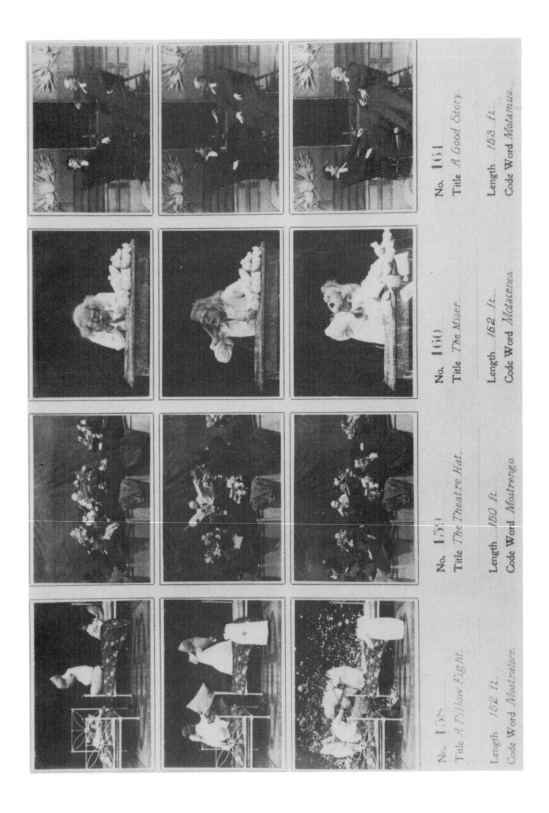

No. 171
Title "Jumbo".

Length 126 ft.
Code Word Moulinames.

No. 172
Title Columbia Bicycle
Factory.
Length 158 ft.
Code Word Moulinames.

July forced the Biograph group, notably Eugène Lauste, to work around the clock to set up the developing system of tanks and wooden reels and then to make the necessary films. The screening was a success and was followed by exhibitions in leading music halls throughout the British Isles. In London they constructed a rotating studio similar to the one at 841 Broadway.[20] After setting up the British Mutoscope Company, Biograph was on its way to becoming an international network of sister companies.

Biograph soon took over the market for peephole motion-picture devices. In 1896 the mutoscope had been of marginal importance. "The first pictures we took were of loom-weaving materials which the traveling salesman could use to show merchants what they were buying," cameraman Billy Bitzer recalled. "We also photographed very large machines, whose working parts could be demonstrated by this method better than they could by chart. All the salesman needed was to carry a lightweight box with a cord to hook into the electric plug. Inside the box was a series of postcard-size flip pictures, which could be stopped at any point for discussion or inspection, and were a great boon to sales." Such limited use was necessary since producing mutoscope reels in large quantities was difficult at first. According to Bitzer, these "were hand-assembled, and it was a Chinese puzzle to squeeze and crowd, say, the last pack of cards around the block and have them all—from one to 999— steady." A solution to this problem was found by punching holes in the cards, running a rubber band through the holes, and tying the ends. These could then be stretched over the large wooden spools and cinched by flanges.[21]

The Biograph Company did not start to exploit its mutoscopes extensively until launching them for amusement purposes early in 1897. On 10 February it was said to be "engaged in manufacturing for early introduction before the public, coin-operated Mutoscopes, the introduction of which will be undertaken by local companies, a number of which have already been organized, and others are organizing in various states." An extensive publicity campaign soon detailed its advantages over the kinetoscope. The mutoscope was attractive to investors, explained the *New York Herald*, because "it is operated by hand and requires no motor battery or attendant; so simple is it that a child can operate it." Likewise, the device was attractive to the viewer because "in the operation of the mutoscope the spectator has the performance entirely under his own control by the turning of the crank. He may make the operation as quick or as slow as fancy dictates, or he may maintain the normal speed at which the original performance took place; and if he so elects the entertainment can be stopped by him at any point in the series and each separate picture inspected at leisure."[22] LITTLE EGYPT (Nos. 136, 140, 141), the first mutoscope hit, showed the famed hoochie-coochie dancer. It was soon followed by subjects such as PARISIENNE GIRLS (No. 165) and A DRESSING ROOM SCENE (No. 228). Subjects like these appealed to male spectators who not only wanted to peep but to control the unfolding of the image, perhaps searching for that frame which most revealed these women's bodies.

The Lumière Cinématographe in Decline

While the American Mutoscope Company expanded overseas, the Lumières faced increasing difficulties within the United States. Initially, although their cinématographe had lost many of its original venues, it found alternate sites in many instances.

Expelled from all of Keith's theaters by early January 1897, the Lumière service soon reopened in New York at Proctor's two theaters, and in Boston at the Grand Opera House—with the result that the French enterprise remained reasonably prosperous during the first months of 1897 and grossed an average of ten thousand dollars a month.[23]

Despite the availability of alternate venues, the cinématographe ceased to be a powerful force in American cinema during the spring of 1897. According to Félix Mesguich, the Lumière Agency suffered setbacks when the American Mutoscope Company, with its powerful political connections to the Republican Party, was rewarded by the new pro-tariff administration. The French enterprise faced legal actions for customs irregularities because the cinématographes had been brought into the country as personal property rather than as commercial goods. Lumière manager Lafont eventually learned that he faced arrest for his company's activities and fled the country, reaching a French liner in the Hudson River by canoe.[24]

The liquidation of the Lumières' American holdings of machines and stock, commencing in April 1897, would seem to support Mesguich, except that the company adopted a similar commercial strategy in England at the same time,[25] which suggests that intervention by the U.S. government was not the only and perhaps not even the principal reason for their withdrawal from the American market. By that date, the cinématographe was becoming technologically outmoded. Its single-hole sprocket system was incompatible with English and American projectors that had adopted Edison's four-sprocket format, which meant that only Lumière films could be shown on Lumière projectors. Since Lumière prints were increasingly available in the four-sprocket format, the French machine was not a wise choice for someone purchasing a projector. Whether the marketing of cinématographes was a desperate attempt to reassert the Lumière format, a retrenchment within the world market, a response to customs problems, or some combination of the three remains unclear. The sale, however, accelerated the decline of the French company on the American market.

The Lumière Agency sold its equipment and films to a variety of small-time exhibitors. Boston's Grand Opera House purchased a cinématographe and then rented a complete change of films each week to keep its selections fresh and attractive. F. F. Proctor chose not to become an owner, and the cinématographes left his theaters after the first week in May. Maguire & Baucus purchased fifteen hundred films of various subjects and soon became the American (and English) agent for Lumière films.[26] While exhibitions on the cinématographe retained some of their popularity into 1898, the Agency's large-scale, effectively coordinated organization had ceased to exist.

By the end of the 1896–1897 season, the American industry was proceeding along two somewhat different lines. On one hand, the Edison Manufacturing Company, the International Film Company, Edward Amet, Sigmund Lubin, and the Lumières (via Maguire & Baucus) were principally concerned with selling films and hardware to anyone who wished to purchase them. On the other hand, the Biograph Company featured a special-size film that other exhibitors could not use. It showed only its own productions, and soon those of its sister companies overseas. With its superior image and high fee, the biograph service tended to play in first-class houses as a leading attraction. Thus, film production and exhibition were unified under one enterprise when it came to 70-mm (or other nonstandard formats) but were commonly performed by independent entities in the 35-mm branch of the industry.

Assessing the Novelty Year: Sound and Image

The first year of projected moving pictures reaffirmed and established screen practices that would be elaborated in ensuing years. Nothwithstanding frequent references to the "silent screen," the cinema had an important audio component from the
outset. At the vitascope's Boston premiere, a pianist was used during the first week.
Soon after, stage effects provided the sounds of hammer blows when THE BLACK-
SMITH SHOP was shown. In New York, the cinématographe was accompanied by "the
flash of sabers, noise of guns, and all the other realistic theatrical effects."[27] After
seeing a performance at Keith's Bijou, one Philadelphia critic remarked:

> No play of the past season has contained a situation more thrilling than the
> reproduction of a parade of the Ninety-sixth Regiment French Cavalry.
> The soldiers march to the stirring tune of the "Marseillaise" and the scene
> stirred the audience to a pitch of enthusiasm that has rarely been equaled
> by any form of entertainment. The playing of the "Marseillaise" aided no
> little in the success of the picture. In the sham battle scene the noise and
> battle din created also added to the wonderful realism of the scene. A
> political argument and a street scene (children dancing to the strains of a
> hand-organ) were also excellent specimens of the work of the cinemato-
> graphe (*Philadelphia Record*, 11 August 1896, p. 2).

This policy continued with the biograph. The same newspaper later reported:

> Not content with showing the living picture, Manager Keith furnishes
> with every view the noises which accompany the scene. Thus is antici-
> pated what will come soon—a device that will be a phonograph as well as
> a reproducer of scenes. At the Bijou the roar of the waves, splashing of
> water, the playing of bands of music, a locomotive whistle, bell, stream,
> etc., are accompaniments that have played no small share in the 48 weeks'
> success of the biograph (*Philadelphia Record*, 23 November 1897, p. 2).

Other exhibitors showed projected images with phonograph recordings. "Music
can be very appropriately and effectively rendered simultaneously with the exhibition of many vitascope subjects," Raff & Gammon told prospective buyers in their
brochure. "The Edison phonograph can thus be utilized to render band and orchestra
selections." But some showmen went beyond this. When Lyman Howe projected
films, many "were accompanied by the phonograph, which reproduced the sounds
suitable to the movements in the pictures." Thus he recorded an approaching train
for BLACK DIAMOND EXPRESS, so that, according to one newspaper account, "it
seemed as if the train were dashing down upon the audience, the rushing of steam,
the ringing of bells and the roar of the wheels making the scene a startlingly realistic
one." After witnessing Edison's Wonderful Magniscope and Concert Phonograph,
one spectator remarked, "Not only could the observer see the moving pictures, but
by some contrivance entirely new here, the sound of the horses' feet while running
upon the pavement and the whistle of the Black Diamond Express could be distinctly
heard."[28]

Modern-day film producers distinguish four basic kinds of sounds: music, narration, effects, and dialogue. Of these, all but the fourth were commonly used during the first year of moving pictures. But even dialogue was employed within a short time as actors or singers were placed in back of the screen. Since sound accompaniment remained the responsibility of the exhibitors—as had been the case with precinematic screen practice—variation was inevitable, and the complete lack of sound accompaniment was one of many possibilities. The introduction of projected motion pictures, which had such a profound effect on image production and exhibition, had very little effect on sound production.

The Arrangement of Scenes

Exhibitors were also responsible for the arrangements of films. At first, they evinced very limited concern with the issue of editing, in the sense of juxtaposing one film to the next. This was particularly true for the early vitascope screenings. Each scene was a completely self-contained, one-shot unit, unrelated to the preceding or following film. Generally, no thematic, narrative, spatial, or temporal relationships existed between scenes. Only a few possible exceptions to this practice were reported in the first months. When showing scenes of Niagara Falls in June and SHOOTING THE CHUTES in July, vitascope exhibitors presented two or more scenes of the main attraction on the same bill.[29] Even then, however, it is not certain that the related films were shown successively to create any kind of continuity.

Rather, exhibitions were initially organized along variety principles that emphasized diversity and contrast even while the selections often built to a climax and ended with a flourish. In this regard, vitascope exhibitions represented only an extreme instance of a general trend: even exhibitions on the Lumière cinématographe, which was technically incapable of showing films as loops, operated within the same conceptual framework. Surviving programs from the period suggest the extent to which exhibitors favored variety over possible spatial, temporal, narrative, or thematic continuities. At Proctor's Twenty-third Street Theater in March 1897, the Lumière cinématographe was listed as showing the following twelve subjects:

1. Lumière Factory.
2. Columbus Statue, Entrance Central Park.
3. A Battle with Snowballs.
4. Niagara Falls.
5. Children Playing.
6. Dragoons of Austrian Army.
7. Brooklyn Bridge.
8. French Cuirassiers.
9. Union Square.
10. The Frolics of Negroes While Bathing.
11. Card Players.
12. Shooting the Chutes.[30]

The four scenes of New York were scattered throughout the program. The military scenes were also separated. CHILDREN PLAYING was far removed from CARD PLAYERS. Clearly, in this instance, discontinuity was preferred to other editorial possibilities, but in the course of the novelty year, a range of editorial techniques emerged to permit the exhibitor to organize shots into sequences.

When Biograph first exhibited at Koster & Bial's, during election week, it offered this program:

- Stable on Fire
- Niagara Upper Rapids
- Union Square at Noontime
- Trilby and Little Billee
- Joseph Jefferson—Toast Scene from *Rip Van Winkle*
- A Hard Wash
- Niagara American Falls
- Empire State Express, 60 Miles an Hour.
- McKinley and Hobart Parade at Canton, O.
- Major McKinley at Home.[31]

Rather than grouping NIAGARA, UPPER RAPIDS (UPPER RAPIDS FROM BRIDGE, NIAGARA FALLS, No. 71) with NIAGARA, AMERICAN FALLS (possibly AMERICAN FALLS, LUNA ISLAND, No. 63), Biograph separated them. MCKINLEY AND HOBART PARADE AT CANTON, O. and MAJOR MCKINLEY AT HOME, however, were shown one after the other. Both dealt with the same subject and were photographed in the same town at approximately the same time. Here, the juxtaposition served to emphasize the McKinley pictures as the headline or feature attraction. But the general organization still suggests a return to "the old-fashioned, spasmodic, hitchy way" of showing images that was described by a lantern exhibitor in the 1870s (see page 38). Now the perfected continuity of successive film frames in each "series of images" or scene allowed for discontinuity to be reasserted on another level.

By the fall of 1896 W. K. L. Dickson at Biograph and James White at Edison were regularly producing groups of subjects that exhibitors could select and sequence. Such production was highly practical since filming different aspects of the same subject was easier and cheaper than filming the same number of unrelated ones. It also anticipated the desires of exhibitors. Lyman Howe's first film program in December 1896 was remarkable for its interweaving of variety techniques with narrative and thematic relationships between shots. Howe grouped his fifteen films into two series. In the first series, two films of police activities in Central Park, MOUNTED POLICE CHARGE and RUNAWAY IN THE PARK, were shown successively—thus maintaining continuities of subject and place. In the next series, three fire-rescue films were shown in succession to create a clear, brief narrative on which Howe later elaborated by adding new scenes. At the same time, this fire sequence was framed by two comedies, both scenes involving water play (TUB RACE and WATERMELON CONTEST). Both "series" ended on high points with two very popular subjects, THE MAY IRWIN KISS and OLD OCEAN OFF MANHATTAN BEACH (probably SURF AT LONG BRANCH, an Edison remake of ROUGH SEA AT DOVER).

To maintain its hold on the public, the Biograph Company increasingly relied on establishing continuities between shots. In early April, it offered the following views in succession: INAUGURAL PARADE, 71ST REGIMENT, NEW YORK (No. 142); THE GOVERNOR OF OHIO AND STAFF (No. 147); and TROOP A OF CLEVELAND AND THE PRESIDENT (No. 143). As was the Biograph custom, each film was preceded by an announcement slide projected by the magic lantern. Since Biograph had only a single, ponderous camera, these scenes were all taken from the same camera position and did not create a spatial world with different perspectives. When Biograph showed scenes of Queen Victoria's jubilee several months later, it was announced that the views—apparently also shot from a single camera position—"are three in number, but will be exhibited as one continuous picture." Editorial contrast, which relies on establishing many similarities to pinpoint specific differences, was also employed. Thus a Biograph series featuring the Chicago electric train was "in two sections, and affords the spectator an opportunity of seeing the contrast between steam and electric power."[32] Editorial technique became increasingly elaborate as the novelty year progressed.

The Motion-Picture Operator

The motion-picture operator (*i.e.*, the projectionist) not only played a crucial creative role but was a highly skilled technician whose job was in many respects comparable to that of the motion-picture photographer. In fact, an experienced projectionist could easily become a cameraman: Charles Webster, James White, Edwin S. Porter, Arthur Hotaling, Oscar Depue, Billy Bitzer, and Albert Smith were among the many American projectionists who later became cinematographers. One of the most compelling passages in Billy Bitzer's memoirs details the complex acrobatics and timing required to show a reel of film. He operated two "lanterns," one for slides and one for film. The biograph projector held approximately ten films spliced together on a reel with leader between each subject. Before each scene, he showed a slide that announced the forthcoming picture, then engaged the motor and quickly brought the machine up to speed:

> I gingerly started the large motor controller, my left hand reaching up to help guide the film. When I got up to speed, my right hand quickly clutched the rod that controlled the picture on the screen. The beater cam movement, which pulled the picture down into position, was uneven and could gain or lose into the aperture frame. The lever which operated a friction drive disk controlled this; when I put my foot down and pushed, the pedal would open the light gate.
>
> I had hung a mirror in a wooden frame on the front drape, at an angle which enabled me to intermittently observe how the film was feeding. If it tried to creep toward the edge of the feeder pulley, I would give it a push back with my forehead or nose. I straightened it out enough to finish the first one-minute picture, all the while keeping my eyes pretty well glued to the screen, otherwise the picture would have started riding up and down (*Billy Bitzer*, pp. 16–17).

At the end of the film, the machine was stopped, a new slide thrown on the screen, and the whole process repeated. Since the first motion-picture cameras did not pan on a tripod, and full sunlight provided the only lighting conditions under which a scene could be filmed (because of the limited sensitivity of the photographic emulsions), the process of making a single-shot film was, in certain respects, easier than showing it afterward.

An operator's failures could be costly. Bitzer mentions the many times he momentarily quit or was fired after something went wrong with an exhibition.[33] One careless moment could blow up an entire machine and produce a raging fire. One of the first

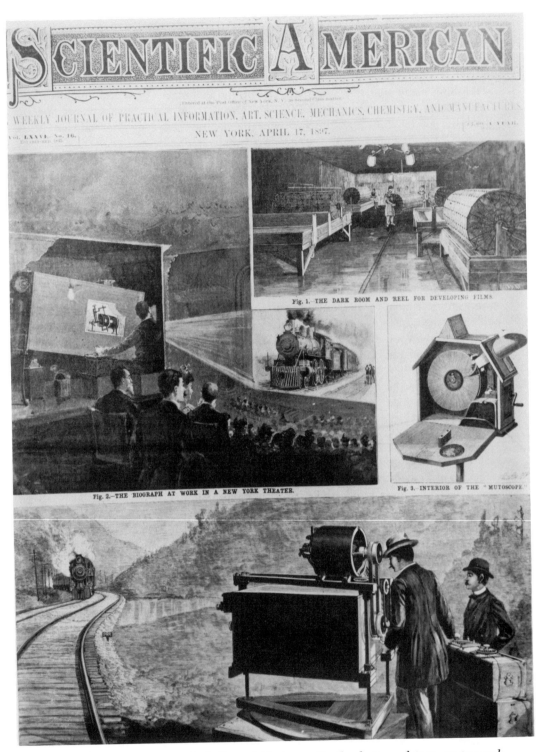

Projecting on the biograph (left) and filming with the battery-driven mutograph camera (bottom). The Model A mutoscope, called the "wooden mutoscope" and used for initial commercialization, is also shown.

film fires occurred on 9 September 1896 at the Pearl Street Theater in Albany, New York. Hopkins' Trans Oceanic Star Specialty Company was just commencing its fall tour with a cinematoscope as its leading attraction. The operator was inexperienced, and the curtain surrounding the machine caught fire during the screening:

> Notwithstanding the efforts of the performers on the stage to quiet the audience, a panic ensued on the cry of fire, and many persons were injured in their endeavors to reach the street. The exits became blocked, men and women rushed for the windows, and from them dropped to the street below. Fortunately, no one was fatally hurt. The fire department responded quickly to the call, and speedily put the fire out. It is said the cinematoscope is ruined but the damage to the theatre is trifling (*Clipper*, 19 September 1896, p. 456).

This was hardly the last such incident. On 14 June 1897 the Eden Musee was almost burned down by Eberhard Schneider's "American cinematograph." A few months later, on 5 September, an independently operated Lumière cinématographe caught fire at the Orpheum Theater in San Francisco. On 29 September at Association Hall in New Brunswick, New Jersey, an electroscope was being shown to a small afternoon audience when the film broke, touched the arc lamp, and burned. The auditorium walls were still decorated with dried grasses and netting from a recent bazaar, and the fire spread quickly, badly burning one member of the audience; had it been an evening performance with good attendance, many deaths would have resulted. When a magniscope burst into flames at the Grand Opera House in New Haven on 22 November 1897, one man broke his leg and a woman was knocked senseless as the crowd rushed to the doors. Nonetheless, while other film fires followed—almost twenty have been documented for the pre-nickelodeon era, and many more undoubtedly occurred—a serious disaster like the charity bazaar fire in France was fortuitously avoided.[34]

Audiences and Cultural Groups

Ascertaining who watched the early motion-picture shows is a difficult task. One major factor was economics, and poorer members of the working class and the underclass rarely if ever saw films within an entertainment context (although in large urban areas they might see them in the form of commercial advertisements). From the outset, however, the cinema drew its audiences from across the working, middle, and elite classes. Vaudeville theaters and local opera houses offered a scale of prices that accommodated people of diverse financial status.[35] While Benjamin F. Keith's theaters had a fee scale that ranged from twenty-five cents to a dollar fifty, Huber's Museum in New York City, Austin & Stone's in Boston, and Bradenburgh's Ninth and Arch Museum in Philadelphia all charged ten cents. In Boston, the Nickelodeon Theater charged only five cents and showed films at least occasionally. In many other cities, as already noted, vaudeville played in "ten–twenty–thirty houses" that charged between ten and thirty cents. Traveling exhibitors visiting more rural areas usually charged between ten and fifty cents.

While motion pictures were still a novelty, they sometimes altered the makeup of a theater's customary audience by attracting an elite clientele. With the cinématographe at Keith's Bijou, "theatre parties and box parties take up almost all of the reserved section of the house," the *Philadelphia Record* reported. "Gentlemen prominent in the professional and business life of the city bring their families to enjoy the clean, wholesome and high-class vaudeville entertainment provided."[36] With dime museums, repertory companies, and storefronts offering motion pictures for as little as ten cents, the more prosperous members of the working class could afford to see the late-nineteenth-century novelty, too. Spectatorship was undoubtedly distributed unevenly through these different economic groups, but economic difference was only one of many factors that determined attendance. Geography, general accessibility to cultural events, age, sex and standing within one's family, ethnic and racial background, religion, and personal tastes all affected the likelihood of seeing films.

Cultural differences weighed heavily in determining the composition of early film audiences. While cultural orientation was influenced by economic status, it remained a far more complex factor than most film historiography has acknowledged. Too often, scholars have seen frequenters of secular, commercial, urban-oriented amusement as *the* audience, but this was not the case. While venues that provided this sort of entertainment had a virtual monopoly on exhibition during the first months of public exhibition and continued to dominate the industry, two other cultural groups were very important: churchgoers (many of whom opposed commercial, secular amusements) and lovers of refined entertainments.

In addition, even commercial, urban amusements consisted of several subgroups with important differences. Keith's and Poli's, for example, emphasized the presentation of clean amusement. Sexual jokes that were too explicit or risqué did not receive the management's approval, and some acts were designed to appeal to children. In contrast, burlesque houses commonly called their film shows the "tabascoscope" or the "cinnimatograph" to suggest that their presentations were "spicy." Some films were suitable only for adults, others only for men. With the press screening of the vitascope featuring films of women dancers, Edison purportedly "clapped his hands, and turning to one of his assistants, said: 'That is good enough to warrant our establishing a bald-head row, and we will do it, too.' "[37] Yet the assumption (conscious or unconscious) of a male audience could lead to unexpected contradictions. While scenes of a scantily clad Sandow were meant for male patrons interested in the manly physique, they must have held considerable erotic interest for women spectators. Thus, the very films that were meant to affirm the masculine, homosocial world of amusement often encouraged its breakdown. The original intent of such films was overturned by the unexpected conditions of their reception. Because of this dynamic quality even more than because of its size, the cinema of commercial amusement was of central concern to all involved with film. Its dynamism was indirectly acknowledged by contending cultural groups, all of which were compelled to situate themselves in relation to it.

During the 1890s, religious groups, particularly Protestant ones, commonly sponsored film programs. While the Methodist-Episcopal Church had reaffirmed its ban on commercial theatrical amusements in May 1896, it offered alternate forms of officially sponsored entertainment to its faithful through the Epworth League. Founded in 1889, the league rapidly grew to include more than eight thousand chapters, and by the late 1890s it was enjoying its greatest success. One of its main purposes was to blunt the threat posed by the urban amusements that were pene-trating into the smaller cities and towns. As the church ceased to be the center of the community's cultural life, the Epworth League embarked on counter-revolution. Other denominations had equivalent organizations, and the nondenominational Young Men's Christian Association served similar goals. Organized sports, meetings, and classes were meant to fill the independent males' leisure time and keep them out of the saloons. Many YMCA's had lecture halls, which they used for their own entertainments or rented out to acceptable religious and civic groups.

The "entertainments" offered by these religious organizations regularly incorpo-rated sanitized elements of popular culture. At the same time, they raised money that could be used for other programs and for building expenses. For the sponsoring groups, who had frequently offered screen entertainments in the past, moving pictures were acceptable and logical extensions of established practices. This phenomenon is evidenced, for example, by Lyman Howe's first two seasons as a motion-picture exhibitor: out of thirty-seven well-documented engagements, twenty-five were sponsored by church groups, including eight Methodist (five being local Epworth chapters), seven Baptist, two Congregational, two Lutheran, and two Pres-byterian. Six others were sponsored by quasi-religious organizations, including four YMCA's. Only the remaining six engagements were sponsored by civic groups, and a third of these exhibitions actually took place in churches.

Exhibitors who addressed audiences under church sponsorship showed many of the same 35-mm films as commercial theaters. Dancing girls and fight films were generally absent—although Lyman Howe did show a hand-tinted film of a serpentine dance by Annabelle, a bullfight scene, and THE MAY IRWIN KISS. Serious opposition rarely arose within a congregation, although older, more conservative members of the Methodist-Episcopal Church did occasionally resent the incursions. Exhibitors had to gauge their sponsors, making their programs as enticing as possible without alienating their constituency. The potentially sinful quality of these pictures was perhaps somewhat mitigated by the obvious financial compensation that such events generated. Whether or not this was a pact with the devil, church members could see a wide selection of films but in a sanctioned setting and presented by exhibitors who knew how to appeal to their sensibilities. Religious, morally conservative groups who saw themselves opposed to commercial amusements were thus leading users of films.

Lovers of refined culture sometimes saw moving pictures as part of lecture series, particularly those focusing on travel. Thus the Lumière cinématographe made an early though limited appearance on the American lecture circuit under the auspices of the Brooklyn Institute of Arts and Science (which, it will be recalled, had provided Edison with the first public forum for his peephole kinetoscope in 1893). In hopes of pursuing its members' long-standing interest in animated photography, a trustee and one of the institute's organizers went to Koster & Bial's Music Hall to look at the vitascope. This pair, neither of whom had previously ventured into a vaudeville theater, were disappointed and soon found themselves at Hammerstein's Olympia, but the eidoloscope was not to their liking, either, and so they eventually secured the French machine for an exhibition on 27 November 1896. The cinématographe, with subjects designed for a similarly sophisticated bourgeois audience in Europe, was conveniently (and not coincidentally) located across the street from the institute's main gathering spot, Association Hall. So the machine was easily moved across the street. Although Alexander Black was scheduled to introduce the opening program,

THE PICTURE PLAY
"A CAPITAL COURTSHIP"
BY
Mr. ALEXANDER BLACK
WITH MANY NEW SCENES
AND INTRODUCING
PRESIDENT McKINLEY, SPEAKER REED,
SIR JULIAN PAUNCEFOTE, AND
THE BATTLESHIP "MAINE,"
AND TEN
NEW CINEMATOGRAPHE VIEWS

ASSOCIATION HALL, Bond and Fulton Sts.

Saturday Evening, April 30th.

Reserved Seats to Members on the presentation of Members' Coupons, at Members' Reduced Rates (25 cents), on and after Wednesday, April 20th, at 8.30 A. M.

The Biological Laboratory
COLD SPRING HARBOR, LONG ISLAND.

COURSES OF INSTRUCTION.

High School Zoology, - - Dr. DAVENPORT
Comparative Anatomy, - - Dr. FERNALD
Invertebrate Embryology, - Dr. SIGERFOOS
Cryptogamic Botany, - - Dr. JOHNSON
Phænogamic Botany, - - - Dr. JOHNSON
Bacteriology, - - - - - Dr. DAVIS
Microscopical Methods, - - Mrs. DAVENPORT

The Season opens Tuesday, July 5th, and closes August 24th. The Regular Class work begins Wednesday, July 6th, and continues for six weeks.

Announcement for A CAPITAL COURTSHIP at the Brooklyn Institute.

he was replaced by the lecturer Franklin W. Hooper, who commented on the films. The evening was filled out with Hooper's lecture on glaciers in Switzerland, which utilized color photographic slides. This combination of color and animated photography thus paralleled the Lumières' early lectures in France, described in chapter 5. Since the color slides were sensitive to heat and could only be shown using gaslight as an illuminant, they proved somewhat of a disappointment. The exhibit as a whole, however, was enthusiastically received.

Many times during 1897 speakers associated with the Brooklyn Institute gave illustrated lectures that incorporated motion pictures. On 13 January Alexander Black presented his well-known talk "Ourselves as Others See Us," which was "illustrated by Cinematographe, Chromograph and Stereopticon."[38] On 11 February Professor Henry Evans Northrop gave the first of several lectures entitled "An Evening with the Cinematographe," which included slides and at least thirty films. By March it had been retitled "A Bicycle Trip Through Europe" and included a collection of his own stills interspersed with Lumière films of various European scenes. This shifting back and forth between slides and film may have been awkwardly handled, for one critic remarked that while the pictures were "excellent" and the cinématographe views "especially interesting," the lecture itself "was not on a par with the pictorial part of the entertainment because Professor Northrop is not, in the sense of the word, a lecturer. He is not cut out for stage work, and should either follow a carefully written text in describing his pictures or engage someone else to do the talking."[39]

As the case of Brooklyn demonstrates, the unified enthusiasm that first greeted motion pictures was disintegrating as exhibitors increasingly appealed to distinct cultural groups with specific kinds of films. With its strong emphasis on cultural refinement, Brooklyn differed from the general pattern of exhibition found in most other large American cities during the first year. The institute lecturers who incorporated films into their lantern-slide programs seemingly had no immediate counterparts elsewhere in the country, and indeed, when Northrop and Black traveled outside their home city, they went without the cinématographe views. Even the Lumière storefront show appealed to the more elite elements of the populace, and if films were also shown in Brooklyn churches, they were rarely shown in theatrical venues. At the same time, Brooklyn was host to one of the most dynamic and controversial sites of commercial popular culture in the nation, Coney Island, which often served as a target for conservative groups. When the Biograph Company scattered its mutoscopes throughout the resort, outrage from religious elements was not far behind. In July 1897 the Reverend Frederick Bruce Russell personally raided a number of Coney Island locales in order to halt the showing of pictures. Those that fell under the ban of the reformer's eye were entitled WHAT THE GIRLS DID WITH WILLIE'S HAT (KICKING WILLIE'S HAT, No. 219) and FUN IN A BOARDING HOUSE (GIRLS' BOARDING SCHOOL, No. 220).[40]

During cinema's first year of success, motion pictures enjoyed the status of a novelty. This very concept or category served to address the problem of managing change within a rapidly industrializing society: novelties typically introduced the public to important technological innovations within a reassuring context that permitted spectators to take pleasure in the discontinuties and dislocations. While technological change created uncertainty and anxiety, "novelty" always embodied significant elements of familiarity, including the very genre of novelty itself. In the

No. 219
Title *Kicking Willie's Hat.*

Length *150 ft*
Code Word *Mulcemus.*

No. 220
Title *Girls' Boarding School*

Length *157 ft*
Code Word *Mulcenda.*

Salacious images that earned the wrath of the Rev. Frederick Bruce Russell.

case of cinema, greater verisimilitude was initially emphasized at the expense of narrative. But if the American public responded positively—typically enjoying their initial experience of projected motion pictures—the dynamic of novelty was such that film companies had to quickly move beyond the simple task of dispersing a technological innovation through large sectors of society. As a result, film practice underwent a radical and extensive reorganization that made it different from other novelties before it, even the peephole kinetoscope. The novelty year soon saw the development of narrative through both the elaboration of brief skits (primarily comedies like LOVE'S YOUNG DREAM) and the sequencing of shots by the exhibitor. Though not totally replaced, the endless-band technique of exhibition, typified by the vitascope, gave way to a more linear, singular unfolding of the film through the projector.

During this year-long period cinema's industrial organization changed as well, moving from self-sufficient and closely held companies, each with its own distinctive technological system, to an industry where the technology or hardware was readily available at an affordable price. The initial potpourri of formats thinned, and 35-mm-gauge film with Edison-type perforations came to be widely used, while the Lathams' format and the Lumières' perforations had reached their zenith and were being phased out. Only the Biograph Company, which sponsored the last of the four major formats to appear, retained the vertically integrated organizational structure that characterized these initial efforts. The use and even the development of unique formats were not ending, but they now occurred within the technological framework of a widely accepted 35-mm standard. Likewise, equipment had improved to the point where exhibitors had much greater flexibility. Finally, within the 35-mm branch of the industry, producers generally sold films and equipment to anyone who wished to buy, without restrictions on their use (other than that of copyright). Thus the novelty period involved dispersion outward from the motion-picture industry's centers (New York City and to a lesser extent Chicago and Philadelphia) and transformation within these centers.

PART 3

The Exhibitor
Plays a Creative Role:
1897 – 1900

7

Full-Length Programs: Fights, Passion Plays, and Travel

*I*n the post-novelty period, exhibitors played a key creative role in the motion-picture field. Their claims to authorship were indeed often merited as they expanded and explored the wide-ranging possibilities for expression under their control. These showmen were responsible for the rich panoply of sound accompaniment that included voice, music, and effects. Perhaps even more fundamentally, they were responsible for either the construction of elaborate narratives or the shape and character of the variety programming. This potential for creativity was no more evident than in the evening-length, single-subject screen entertainments that became common during 1897–1898. These programs fell into three distinct genres, each of which was directed at a different cultural group. They thus underscored another significant aspect of the post-novelty era: the reassertion of social and cultural differences within the realm of reception or spectatorship.

A few travel lecturers, operating within the well-established expectations of refined culture, added motion pictures to their stereopticon exhibitions. Here the integration of motion pictures into conventional screen entertainment was particularly straightforward. Two other genres involved more complex issues that deserve particular scrutiny. These revolved around the passion play and boxing matches. Although at opposite ends of the cultural spectrum, both depended on the cinematic medium for their success in somewhat analogous ways. In each instance, their subject matter lacked societal approval when presented as live performances, yet came to enjoy wide acceptance when mediated by cinematography.

Prizefighting had an impassioned following among those enjoying blood sports and other male-oriented amusements, not withstanding the strong opposition of religious groups and cultural elites. Although bouts were technically illegal in every state of the Union, they continued to be fought, often under the guise of "boxing exhibitions" or "sparring contests." The police, however, often stopped these "performances," as when they abruptly ended a "Boxing and Bag Punching Entertainment" at New York's Academy of Music with the arrest of the two contenders, Mike Leonard and George Dixon, in August 1895.[1] Even fights in out-of-the-way places were not entirely safe from interruption, but the more prominent the match, the greater the likelihood of government intervention. As the grand-jury investigation of THE CORBETT–COURTNEY FIGHT demonstrated, filming such matches only added to the difficulties. Motion-picture photography of bona fide bouts required elaborate preparation and extensive publicity to maximize the public's interest and assure a profitable return on investment.[2] These requirements encouraged civic protest and made state intervention almost inevitable.

Because the Lathams had already demonstrated the popularity of fight films, many amusement entrepreneurs were eager to capitalize on this commercial opportunity even as they tried to avoid controversy. Harry Davis, a Pittsburgh theatrical magnate, produced THE MAHER–CHOYNSKI FIGHT in a way that avoided many production problems—including the uncertain legality of fistic encounters. Peter Maher and Joe Choynski fought a contest that was slated to go twenty rounds at New York's Broadway Athletic Club on Monday evening, 16 November 1896; in the sixth round, Maher knocked out his opponent. Since Maher spent much of his time in Pittsburgh, Davis arranged for the fight to be reenacted there, apparently using both boxers and local Pittsburgh "sports" as audience members. As shown on the "zinematographe," the six-round MAHER–CHOYNSKI FIGHT opened at Davis' Eden Musee in Pittsburgh on 1 February and received a favorable response.[3] Less than twenty minutes long, The MAHER–CHOYNSKI FIGHT was subsequently displayed at Bradenburgh's 9th and Arch Dime Museum in Philadelphia, Huber's Museum in New York, and other big-city venues that appealed to frequenters of inexpensive, sensationalistic amusement.

The Corbett–Fitzsimmons Fight

Films of championship bouts promised to generate the greatest financial rewards. Following the success of THE CORBETT–COURTNEY FIGHT, the Kinetoscope Exhibition Company sought a similar subject for its large-capacity peephole kinetoscopes but encountered many obstacles. Samuel Tilden, Jr., and Enoch Rector arranged with fight promoter Dan Stuart to film a heavyweight bout between Corbett and Robert Fitzsimmons in Texas. The Edison factory even constructed new, wide-format cameras to photograph the event. When Texas chief justice James M. Hunt ruled on 17 September 1895 that no law in that state prohibited pugilistic exhibitions, Stuart's plans seemed almost certain to reach fruition. A few weeks later, however, the governor requested and the Texas legislature enacted a bill that outlawed prizefighting.[4] Subsequent attempts to stage the bout in Arkansas likewise ended in disappointment.

By November, Stuart was trying to hold the fight in Mexico, just across the border from El Paso, Texas. When Corbett announced that he had retired and turned his championship over to Pete Maher, Fitzsimmons angrily accepted the new matchup against Maher. On 21 February 1896, two hundred dedicated boxing aficionados took a train from El Paso to Langtry, Texas, tramped through a half mile of deep sand mixed with mud, crossed a pontoon bridge, and eventually reached a crude ring. The heavily overcast sky precluded cinematography, but delay was impossible lest the authorities disrupt the proceedings. Maher, still recovering from an eye infection, was routed in one minute and thirty-three seconds. Rector then offered a five-thousand-dollar purse for the two to fight for the kinetograph on the following day, but Fitzsimmons demanded ten thousand dollars and 50 percent of the profits. His price was too high, and the match failed to materialize.[5] After six months of almost continual preparation and expense, the kinetoscope group still lacked a fresh subject to place in its peephole machines.

Projection came before further boxing matches could be arranged. Finally, on 4 January 1897, Robert Fitzsimmons and James Corbett signed an agreement to fight for a ten-thousand-dollar purse offered by Dan Stuart. The kinetoscope figured prominently in the negotiations. Fitzsimmons demanded and eventually received an equal share of the revenues, 15 percent of the profits going to each of the fighters.[6] Stuart's task was to find a place to hold the prizefight legally: only then could he attract a large number of ringside spectators and sufficient press to publicize the bout, and only then would it be possible to organize the filming. While all states forbade prizefighting, they did not prohibit the exhibition of prizefight films. Thus the participants planned to make money not from the fight itself but from the films. Motion pictures suddenly made boxing a profitable sport *per se*. Previously, fighters like John L. Sullivan and James Corbett had made their living on the stage—by giving exhibitions and appearing in plays. The heavyweight championship had turned these boxers into celebrities, but fighting had not in itself been enormously profitable. Motion pictures changed this.

Stuart convinced Nevada officials that the Corbett–Fitzsimmons fight would help the state's struggling economy. Despite protests from state governors and religious leaders, prizefighting was legalized on 26 January. Stuart selected Carson City as the site and 17 March as the date. Corbett, then appearing in *A Naval Cadet*, disbanded his theatrical company in Kansas City on 6 February and headed west to train for the bout. Meanwhile, Enoch Rector built new cameras especially for the event. These used a 2³⁄₁₆-inch-gauge film stock with a wide-screen format ideally suited for photographing a boxing ring.[7]

The reaction from Protestant groups and moralistic legislators was predictably angry. Congressman William F. Aldrich, at the request of the Reverend Wilbur F. Crafts of the National Reform League, submitted a bill providing that "no picture or description of any prize fight or encounter of pugilists or any proposal or record of betting on the same shall be transmitted by the mails of the United States or by inter-state commerce, whether in a newspaper or telegram."[8] Clergy gave countless well-publicized sermons attacking this form of amusement. In a typical sermon, "Nevada's Shame and Disgrace," the Reverend Levi Gilbert of the First Methodist Church of Cleveland declared:

> This state, this deserted mining camp, revives brutality by an exhibition that must make its Indians and Chinamen wonder at Christianity. Corbett is called a gentleman, yet acted like an infuriated animal in his last fight. He is dissipated as is John Sullivan, who clubs his wife, and both of these are shining lights of the theater, and Christian people are lampooned for non-attendance.
>
> Such exhibitions promote criminality by feeding the bestial in man. They debauch the public ideal. Such men sell their bodies for merchandise as surely as the harlots of the street. They show pluck, yes, but no better than the bulldog or the tiger (*New Haven Register*, 9 March 1897, p. 12).

Yet even those newspapers that condemned the bout devoted large amounts of space to its preparations as the fight became a national event. Gunfighter Wyatt Earp

Watching the Corbett–Fitzsimmons fight in Carson City.

was a special reporter for the *New York World.* Bat Masterson attended. And, as the *Boston Herald* announced in a front-page headline, "The Kinetoscope will Dominate Wholly the Arrangements for the Holding of the Battle." The battery of cameras, grouped together in a wooden shed, were given the best seats in the house while paying customers were forced to look into the sun. Stuart arranged for several lesser bouts so that the big fight could be postponed and the spectators placated, if the day was cloudy. On the night before the battle, Stuart even had the ring cut down from the regulation twenty-four feet square to twenty-two feet so the cameras would be certain to capture all the action. Only in this last instance was he unsuccessful, for the referee noticed the difference and insisted that the original size be restored.[9]

As the fight unfolded, round-by-round descriptions were telegraphed to the nation's theaters and read from the stage. In large cities, it was reenacted by experts—at Proctor's Pleasure Palace, for example, in a simultaneous exhibition billed as "a purely scientific illustration of the blows and ring tactics used at Carson," Fitzsimmons was played by Professor Mike Donovan, the New York Athletic Club's boxing instructor, while the role of Corbett was assumed by Professor Alfred Austin, an ex–middleweight champion of England. In Massachusetts, legislators left a debate on a women's-suffrage bill to follow its progress. For once, the bout went off as scheduled, and Fitzsimmons defeated Corbett with a blow to the heart in the fourteenth round. The fray equaled everyone's highest expectations. "I consider that I have witnessed today the greatest fight with gloves that was ever held in this or any other country," declared Wyatt Earp.[10] But some spectators claimed that Fitzsimmons fouled his opponent with a smashing blow to the jaw as Corbett collapsed from the jab to the heart. If the punch had been late, partisans argued that Fitzsimmons should have lost. Many were anxious to see the films and judge the timing of the blow for themselves.

While the *New Haven Evening Register* believed that legality would tear the veil of romance from prizefighting and leave it "exposed in all its hideousness and depravity," most opponents of pugilism rejected a laissez-faire approach. Bills to prohibit the exhibition of fight films were introduced in Massachusetts, Pennsylvania, Illinois, as well as other state legislatures, although in most instances they were defeated. Probably to reduce similar efforts, Rector announced that the Corbett–Fitzsimmons negatives had been ruined and that no exhibitions would take place. In some cases Dan Stuart's generous distribution of funds to lawmakers may have made a significant difference. In Massachusetts, the legislative calendar was drawing to a close and introduction of new bills needed approval by four-fifths of the legislature. This did not happen, for many of the legislators were themselves anxious to see the films. Only in Iowa and perhaps a few other states was the exhibition of fight films banned. A few localities, such as Pueblo, Colorado, also prohibited them.[11]

THE CORBETT–FITZSIMMONS FIGHT, shown by the Veriscope Company, had its debut on 22 May 1897 at the Academy of Music in New York City. Developing and printing the films as well as building the necessary apparatus for projection had taken over two months. The opening was heavily promoted, particularly by the *New York*

THE CORBETT–FITZSIMMONS FIGHT: *Corbett is down after the blow to the heart.*

World, which published a two-page spread showing drawings of the fight derived from key frames of the films. According to this pro-Corbett perspective, the term "veriscope" or "truth-viewer" was appropriate because it emphasized one of the selling points of the pictures: the camera recorded the foul that had eluded the referee. In the words of the *World*, it illustrated "a triumph of science over the poor, imperfect instrument, the human eye, and proves that the veriscope camera is far superior." Spectators could judge for themselves whether or not Fitzsimmons had fouled Corbett. The average man did not have to accept the authoritative word of the referee or the sportswriter but could reach his own conclusions. But were the *World*'s drawings faithful to the film? "I do not believe there is single picture in the veriscope that will substantiate those published in The World," replied Fitzsimmons. "Those purporting to be scenes from the fight are manufactured."[12]

The war of fists had become a war of words, and the Academy of Music was jammed on opening night. The program lasted for approximately a hundred minutes and was one of the first full-length performances devoted exclusively to motion pictures. The projected images, according to the *New York Tribune*, "were larger than any that have been seen hitherto, but the flickering and vibration were most troublesome to the view and extremely trying to the eyes." Nonetheless, for the first time in almost everyone's experience, they could see a regulation championship fight, if not live, then recorded mechanically. Theater seats became seats at ringside as patrons saw this ritualized sport unfold from a single camera perspective in realistic time. As was to become the custom when exhibiting fight films, an expert stood to the side of the screen and offered a running commentary: the sports announcer had arrived.

> In the sixth round, when Fitzsimmons was brought low for a few seconds, the crowd became so much excited that the lecturer who was explaining incidents had to give it up and let the spectators understand the rather complicated situation the best they could. He managed to get in just a word of explanation when it was nearly over.
>
> Although the fight seemed to be pretty familiar to most of the persons present, the final blow of Fitzsimmons was unexpected, and few, if any, were prepared to say afterwards that they saw it. Corbett was seen suddenly to go down on one knee and crawl away, while the house rang with shouts of "Where's the foul? Where's the foul?" Corbett's attempt to get at Fitzsimmons after the fight was over was shown with great clearness, and was one of the most interesting incidents of the exhibition. At the end there were loud requests for the last round to be shown over again, but the operators seemed to think that they had done enough (*New York Tribune*, 23 May 1897, p. 8).

While the single-camera perspective (perhaps with some jump cuts as one camera stopped and the next began) encouraged a sense of theatrical space, and indeed, the whole event had been engineered as a display for the camera, the presentational elements of THE CORBETT–FITZSIMMONS FIGHT were most evident in the use of a commentator beside the screen. The details and significant moments that would one day be brought out by close-ups were now emphasized by the narration.

During the summer months Coney Island patrons might take in "Corbett's Last Fight."

The veriscope played at the 2,100-seat Academy of Music for just over five weeks and then moved to Brooklyn for two more. It opened a four-week stand in Boston on 31 May and one of nine weeks in Chicago on 6 June. According to the *Chicago Tribune*, the attraction drew "immense audiences at the Grand Opera House both at the evening and daily matinees, and the receipts for this reproduction have broken all records of the theater since its existence." Admission ranged from twenty-five cents for a gallery seat to one dollar in the orchestra. Generally, there were breaks of three to five minutes every fourth round while the operator changed reels of film on his single projector. In Boston, at least, these intermissions were considered a desirable means of saving the spectators' eyes. Efforts were quickly undertaken to solve some of the exhibition's technical problems: improvements were made in the printing and developing as new prints replaced the first positives, and the projecting machines may have also been modified. Additional openings soon followed: Buffalo for four weeks on 7 June, Philadelphia for three weeks on 26 June, and Pittsburgh for two weeks on 3 July.[13] A West Coast company opened in San Francisco on 13 July for three weeks and then moved up to Portland. Also widely exhibited overseas, the veriscope opened in London on 27 September.

The program was seen by enormous numbers of Americans, not only in large cities but smaller towns. Distribution was frequently handled by sales of territory on a states rights basis. By fall, approximately eleven companies were touring the United States with THE CORBETT–FITZSIMMONS FIGHT, usually performing in crowded theaters. The program also returned to many cities. For its two-week Boston reengagement in April 1898, admission was lower, the technical quality had improved, and 1,400 feet of film showing the ring after the fight had been added. This program sparked interest in the Bob Fitzsimmons Vaudeville Company, which played immediately afterward at the same theater. A Veriscope and Vaudeville Company toured other major cities for one-week stands during the 1897–1898 season. In remote parts of the country, veriscope exhibitions continued to be given, albeit with decreasing frequency and attendance, until 1900. With profits said to exceed $120,000 (apparently after the fighters received their percentages), Rector was forced to sue Dan Stuart for an accounting and his share of the proceeds.[14]

Although men of sporting blood were the veriscope's intended audience, the fight films drew from an unexpectedly broad cross section of the population. Many attendees had never previously seen a boxing match of any kind. Not only members of New York's four hundred families (who symbolized refined culture) but members of "the fairer sex" visited the Academy of Music. In Boston, women were reported to form "a considerable portion of the audience," and according to at least one source, women constituted fully 60 percent of Chicago's patronage. In many other cities and towns, a similar pattern emerged. To male reporters, it was a puzzle. Perhaps the absence of noise, blood, and the sounds of distress made the fight acceptable to women's more refined sensibilities, the *Boston Herald* suggested, or perhaps many of them attended "with the expectation of being shocked and horrified." Today other explanations seem more credible. By attending, women asserted their independence and loosened a code of conduct that narrowly circumscribed their public sphere. Many middle-class women took this opportunity to see a part of the male world from which they were normally excluded. The theaters housing the veriscope were those that women regularly visited, and many of the "fairer sex" felt free to go on their own, at least to the matinees. Suddenly they had access to the forbidden and could peruse the semi-naked, perfectly trained bodies of the male contestants. For women of the leisure class, the *Herald* noted, it had "become quite the proper thing to drop in and see a round or two of the pictures."[15]

The fact that THE CORBETT–FITZSIMMONS FIGHT was an "illustration" of a fight rather than a fight itself made the attraction not only legally but socially acceptable viewing material. The moralistic, conservative Protestant groups who condemned the sport as barbaric were at least temporarily routed, defeated by proponents of popular culture who had managed to win over or neutralize the cultural elites as well. Opponents of pugilism were put on the defensive. Fighting was legalized in New York State, at least for a time, and several championship bouts would be fought there in the late 1890s. Although the death of a fighter later set back the cause of legal boxing in New York, never again did championship fighters lack an American location where they could hold a contest.

Lubin and Facsimile Reproductions

The Corbett–Fitzsimmons fight raised other questions about filmic representation. When live bouts had been so hard to see, urban "sports" often had to be satisfied with staged reenactments that either coincided with the event (like the one at Proctor's Pleasure Palace mentioned above) or were restaged by the reigning champion as he toured the country's theaters. During the 1897–1898 theatrical season, for example, Fitzsimmons toured with his vaudeville company and gave a sparring exhibition with Yank Kenny, who "wears his hair in a pompadour and greatly resembles Jim Corbett in style and action." Sigmund Lubin took advantage of the reenactment tradition to produce his own fight films "in imitation of Corbett and Fitzsimmons." The performers, two freight handlers from the Pennsylvania Railroad, were made up to look like the champions and acted out the drama on a makeshift rooftop studio.[16] By condensing the action and decreasing the camera speed (the number of frames exposed per second), Lubin filmed each round on fifty feet of 35-mm stock.

Lubin advertised his REPRODUCTION OF THE CORBETT AND FITZSIMMONS FIGHT a week before the Veriscope's premiere and sent several exhibition units on the road. The Veriscope Company threatened to sue, but nothing legally prohibited the practice. Audience reaction was less easily ignored, however. In Chicago, the " 'fake' veriscope" opened in a storefront. According to one published account,

> the fighters maul each other in unscientific fashion and the supposititious knockout in the fourteenth round is a palpable burlesque. Several patrons of the performance protested yesterday and were informed by the gentleman in charge that they were "lobsters." "We advertise a facsimile of the fight," he declared, "and that's what we give. What do you expect for 10 cents, anyhow?" (*Phonoscope*, June 1897, p. 12).

In many locales, hoodwinked patrons proved less complacent. When the Arkansas Vitascope Company showed the films in Little Rock, five hundred people attended opening night, including ex-governor Clarke and many members of the state legislature. According to one published account:

> The audience was entitled to a kick before the exhibition was five minutes old. The views were decidedly on the fake order, being unrecognizable by people who are familiar with the ring and who know pictures of Corbett and Fitz. The first round was so tame that the lovers of the manly art could not restrain the disgust they felt at the palpable fakeness of the alleged representation.
> "Fake!" "Cheat!" "Give us our money back!" and various other cries rang out in all parts of the theatre. Dozens of people picked up their hats and started out. Some left the theatre and others lingered in the entrance lobby around the box office. Some others remained in their seats hoping that the succeeding views would be better; but they were doomed to disappointment. At the conclusion of the third round, the indignation of the duped spectators knew no bounds. A rush was made for the box office and the cries of "Give us our money back!" were deafening. The "fight" came to an abrupt termination at the end of the third "round" for lack of an audience. Scores of indignant men joined the clamorous crowd in the lobby and declared that they would not budge an inch until their money was refunded. Several policemen were on hand but they could no more restrain the impatient and thoroughly exasperated crowd from rushing pell-mell at the box office than human hands could push back the Johnstown flood (*Little Rock Gazette*, in *Phonoscope*, June 1897, p. 12).

At Ringling Brothers Circus, amusement-goers could see Lubin's REPRODUCTION OF
THE CORBETT AND FITZSIMMONS FIGHT *(1897).*

The opera-house manager, fearing a riot, turned over receipts of $253 to a state
senator who, after a brief deliberation, refunded the patrons' money. Members of the
crowd fought their way to the box office. "The fellow with a 25 cent check ran the risk
of having his limbs broken, his face smashed and his clothes torn off, but it seemed
to make no difference. The satisfaction of getting the money back after being duped
was worth a great deal." Similar "misunderstandings" occurred elsewhere. In Elizabeth, New Jersey, when people with fifty-cent seats learned the meaning of the
word "facsimile," the theater management also felt fooled and, anxious not to alienate
its regular customers, offered a refund.[17]

In urban settings, where the conventions of fight reenactments were well known,
spectators came to accept facsimile reproductions as a legitimate form of amusement.
Over the next ten years Lubin produced at least a score of such subjects, which found
regular outlets in places like Bradenburgh's Ninth and Arch Museum in Philadelphia
and Huber's Fourteenth Street Museum in New York. One clever manager even
made moralistic arguments in favor of the reproductions, claiming that the ring's
"objectionable environment" had been eliminated.[18] Generally shown where admission fees were lower, these films were usually part of a larger variety entertainment.
Lubin's facsimile reproductions became the poor man's way to see the fight.

Although THE CORBETT–FITZSIMMONS FIGHT was immensely profitable and the
pictures served as a long-standing model for future amusement entrepreneurs, these
epigones often encountered misfortune. On 9 June 1899, the American Vitagraph
Company photographed the next heavyweight championship bout, between Fitzsimmons and Jeffries, at night under the intense illumination and heat of seventy-five arc
lights. When the lights overheated and burned out, filming came to an abrupt halt.

A Lubin "facsimile reproduction" of round ten of SHARKEY–MCCOY FIGHT REPRO-
DUCED IN 10 ROUNDS (*February 1899*).

Nonetheless the bout continued, with Jeffries the victor in eleven rounds. Lubin's
reproductions with counterparts filled the resulting void and enjoyed wide circulation; even Vitagraph used them for a time. Somewhat belatedly, Vitagraph and the
Edison Manufacturing Company filmed their own reenactment with the actual fighters. The Palmer–McGovern fight encountered somewhat different adversity. Filmed
by the American Sportagraph Company on 12 September 1899, the bout was expected to be a vicious, closely fought battle, and interest was high. Modeling themselves on the Veriscope Company, the group built their own special-gauge cameras,
printers, and projectors, but when Terry McGovern knocked out "Pedlar" Palmer in
the first round, American Sportagraph folded.[19]

The most successful set of fight pictures after the Veriscope effort was THE
JEFFRIES–SHARKEY FIGHT, taken on 3 November 1899 at the Coney Island Sporting
Club. This twenty-five-round fight went the distance, with the decision given to
Jeffries. Biograph shot the entire bout with 70-mm film, and some 350 miniature arc
lights to illuminate the nighttime scene. The 10,050 spectators were not permitted to
smoke lest it harm the quality of the pictures. Although Lubin produced his usual
reenactment and American Vitagraph smuggled a camera into the club and filmed
some of the rounds, Biograph enjoyed marked success after opening its program in
New York on 20 November, less than three weeks after the event. This initial
program interspersed vaudeville acts between films of each round—a practice that
was generally not continued in other venues. Publicity once again emphasized that
spectators could decide for themselves whether the referee's decision was just. In
Philadelphia at least, the theater manager distributed ballots to his patrons "so that
every spectator may vote on the question."[20] Biograph soon had at least six companies on the road, first playing major cities for a few weeks and subsequently touring
the smaller population centers for the remainder of the 1899–1900 season.

Although fight films continued to be a prominent if financially risky genre throughout the period covered by this volume, they never enjoyed the broad-based success
of THE CORBETT–FITZSIMMONS FIGHT. After their initial glimpse of the exclusively

Biograph's production team for THE JEFFRIES–SHARKEY FIGHT. *The four camera-men are (left to right) Frederick S. Armitage, G. W. Bitzer, Arthur Marvin, and possibly Wallace McCutcheon. Harry Marvin stands in left foreground.*

THE BATTLE OF JEFFRIES AND SHARKEY FOR CHAMPIONSHIP OF THE WORLD, *shot by Vitagraph, copyrighted by James White on 4 November 1899, and subsequently marketed by the Edison Manufacturing Company.*

DON'T BE FOOLED BY FAKE PICTURES OF THE

SHARKEY-JEFFRIES BATTLE.

WHEN YOU CAN GET THE REAL THING AT A REASONABLE FIGURE.

Our Special Photographers

were at the Coney Island Sporting Club on the night of November 3, and photographed the great fight between Sharkey and Jeffries, under the special direction of MESSRS. HOWARD AND EMERSON. Our pictures are copyrighted and fully protected at the Library of Congress at Washington, D. C.

WE WILL PROTECT OUR RIGHTS AGAINST ALL FAKE EXHIBITIONS OF THESE FILMS.

The copyright laws of the United States make it a felony to exhibit illegitimate copies of a copyrighted article. We will vigorously prosecute infringements on these films. Don't discourage the public by shoddy exhibitions when you can give them something good for the same money.

FOR TERMS FOR EXHIBITION OF THE SHARKEY-JEFFRIES FILMS APPLY TO

Edison Manufacturing Company,

ORANGE, N. J., AND 135 FIFTH AVENUE, NEW YORK.

The advertising battle for The Jeffries–Sharkey Fight *was three-sided: Edison versus Lubin versus Biograph.*

804   THE NEW YORK CLIPPER.   NOVEMBER 18

$5,000
TO THE
EDISON MANUFACTURING CO.

If it can successfully dispute the fact that its scattering pictures of the

Jeffries=Sharkey
FIGHT

Are anything more than fragmentary snap shots of a few rounds, taken by cameras surreptitiously smuggled into the Coney Island Sporting Club and worked secretly, the view of the ring being often obscured entirely by the movements of the spectators, and interrupted by fear of detection, and the results being wholly without completeness or continuity.

It was this exhibition that closed after **ONE NIGHT** at Sam T. Jack's. It was made to last 15 minutes by repeating films. The authentic representation of fight and preliminaries occupies 2¼ hours.

THE PUBLIC WELL UNDERSTANDS
THAT THE
ONLY COMPLETE AND ACCURATE PICTURES
OF THE GREAT
JEFFRIES=SHARKEY FIGHT
WERE TAKEN BY THE
American Mutoscope
and Biograph Co.

837-847 BROADWAY, NEW YORK.
Any Infringement upon its Copyright will be
Vigorously Prosecuted to a Finish.

HOW THE
AMERICAN MUTOSCOPE
AND BIOGRAPH
TOOK THE REAL PICTURES WITHOUT A BREAK

The current was conveyed by two special feed wires from the central station at Coney Island to the Club House, direct from the dynamos to the 400 specially built arc lights.

The reflectors over the ring are lights were so arranged that a correct lighting could only be had from the position occupied by the four cameras of the American Mutoscope and Biograph Co.

There was a total candle power of 800,000.

There was light enough to illuminate a city of 50,000 inhabitants concentrated beneath the reflectors over a 24 foot ring.

To operate the lights eleven electricians were stationed over the ring.

To work the four cameras 12 skilled operators were kept on the lighting, one camera taking up the pictures as another left off.

The daily expenditures included : $3,200 for 400 arc lights, $1,200 for wiring, $80 for reparators, $800 for current, $200 for reflectors. Thus, at a total cost of $10,300 were taken

7¼ MILES OF FILM,
From which have been developed

216,000 DISTINCT PICTURES

Vividly representing every move in the 25 round contest, rendering recognizable the faces of well known men who were at the ring side, and requiring in reproduction 2 hours.

THESE FILMS ARE THE LARGEST EVER MADE

and the result is the most marvelous ever known in the history of moving photography.

$5,000
TO
S. LUBIN, OF PHILADELPHIA,

If he can demonstrate that his alleged reproduction of the

Jeffries=Sharkey
FIGHT

Is anything more than a series of views posed for by boxers masquerading in a make believe contest for the real fighters.

THE FAKE PICTURE SCHEME

Was fully exposed when dummy boxers, made up as the real contestants, were exhibited in a bogus representation of the recent Jeffries-Fitzsimmons battle, **OF WHICH NO PICTURES WERE TAKEN**, owing to a failure to secure satisfactory results by electric light.

THE PEOPLE KNOW THIS.

FOR SALE,
TERRITORIAL and FOREIGN RIGHTS
To this Marvelous Moving Portrayal of the
JEFFRIES=SHARKEY FIGHT
THE ONLY COMPLETE AND ACCURATE PICTURES.
APPLY TO THE
American Mutoscope
and Biograph Co.,
837-847 BROADWAY, NEW YORK.

DO NOT BE DECEIVED
OR WASTE MONEY, AND
DO NOT INVEST IN FAKES,
WHEN
THE ONLY REAL PICTURES
Covering every instant of the GREATEST FISTIC BATTLE OF THE CENTURY, are those of the
AMERICAN MUTOSCOPE
AND BIOGRAPH CO.,
WHICH ARE FULLY PROTECTED BY COPYRIGHT AT WASHINGTON and will receive their
First Public Exhibition
AT THE
NEW YORK THEATRE
Formerly Olympia, Broadway and 44th St., New York City.
On MONDAY, NOV. 20

Wm. A. Brady   **FOR**   James J. Jeffries
Thomas O'Rourke   Tom. Sharkey

male sporting world, women ceased attending these amusements in significant numbers. Having satisfied their curiosity and asserted their right to see such events, they withdrew. The faddish aspects of fight films passed away, and the all-male world of blood sports reasserted its homosocial identity.

Fight films focused attention on representational issues. Before cinema, an event could not really be re-presented. It could be recounted, recreated, or reperformed but the results always involved the subjective reinterpretation of the performers or reporter. Now a view of an event could be captured on film and shown again and again. Promoters and spectators recognized the possibility of, and the demand for, what is now called "observational cinema."[21] The filmmaker's role was to record an event and then re-present it with as little intervention as possible, so that the audience was in a position to judge the outcome for themselves. The kinds of re-enactments or even jump-cut ellipses commonly found in turn-of-the-century documentary material had the opposite effect. Although fight films utilized performances of a kind as their raw material, they implicitly challenged certain theatrical conventions that had been carried over to film, for instance the indicating of unfolding time (through manipulation of the mise-en-scène) rather than a credible rendition of its actual unfolding. Fight pictures thus worked against crucial aspects of the presentational approach that dominated early cinema, even as they retained or reinforced other aspects, such as the lecture.

Passion Plays

The passion play has had a tumultuous history in the United States. On 3 March 1879, a dramatic version by Salmi Morse was performed in San Francisco amid much controversy. The play opened despite vehement protests, but the manager deemed it wise not to perform the last scenes of the Crucifixion and Resurrection, and the performance ended with Christ (played by James O'Neill) being turned over to Pontius Pilate.[22]

Salmi Morse found a new backer for his play in Henry E. Abbey, a leading New York impresario who later explained, "I was so impressed by the subject and treatment by him that I signed a contract for its production at Booth's under his personal supervision." This New York City debut was scheduled for 7 December 1880. Opposition from religious groups and the press intensified, however, as the board of aldermen voted, with only one dissenter, to do everything possible to ban the production. The Baptist Ministers' Conference, noting the general outcry among Protestant leaders, condemned the "sacrilegious use of the most sacred things of our religion." In the face of such pressure, Abbey withdrew the play the Sunday before it was to open. Ministers quickly altered their sermons to fit the new situation. The Reverend John P. Newman of the Central Methodist Church noted "the impossibility of an actor projecting himself into the character of Christ according to the requirements of his art." He predicted such a play would increase infidelity since it represented only the weakness of Christ without a counteracting view of his divinity. Newman praised the many newspapers, community leaders, and even the the "best" theatrical managers and actors whose opposition prevented the play from being produced. In a desperate and final effort, Morse gave a reading of his play. The New York Times reprinted portions of the text, praised the music, found the playwright to be of reverential spirit, and then called it a "painful burlesque of sacred mysteries."[23] The fiasco was indelibly imprinted on the memory of every amusement entrepreneur.

Cultural activities, nonetheless, often embody contradictions. The passion play had just been performed at Oberammergau, Bavaria, that summer, an event occurring once every decade. On 11 December 1880, only four days after the abortive premiere of the Morse drama, travel lecturer John L. Stoddard presented his illustrated lecture "Ober-Ammergau's Passion Play" in New York. Taking his audience on a tour of the village and introducing the principal actors going about their everyday lives, Stoddard argued that these villagers were not rude peasants but artists whose rendition retained "all the simplicity and reverence of ancient days." Having established the milieu from which the play sprang, Stoddard showed fifty stereopticon slides of the performance. At the drama's high point, as Christ dies on the cross, Stoddard dissolved from one lantern slide to the next. Otherwise identical, the two slides gave an illusion of movement as Christ's head dropped to his breast.[24] At this moment Stoddard was saying:

> Finally it is evident that the end draws near. With a loud voice he cries at last:
> "Father, into thy hands I commend my spirit." The head drops wearily upon the breast. It is finished (John Stoddard, *Red Letter Days Abroad* [1884], p. 98).

Stoddard's lecture, attended by people who had objected so strenuously to the Salmi Morse play, was widely praised and enhanced his reputation. After the 1890 performance at Oberammergau, many itinerant lecturers gave screen presentations that closely followed Stoddard's. The possibilities of using motion pictures to present a similar program were obvious to everyone. While preparing for the vitascope's commercial debut, Thomas Armat imagined such an undertaking. So, apparently, did the Lumières. Although a twelve-scene passion play was filmed by a Frenchman named Lear in the spring of 1897, THE HORITZ PASSION PLAY, filmed in an Austrian Village (now Hořice, Czechoslovakia), was much more ambitious and apparently was the first to be shown in the United States.[25]

The Horitz Passion Play

The Horitz villagers had performed miracle plays for centuries, and their passion play, first mounted in 1816, had become an elaborate production by the early 1890s. A major tourist attraction attended by royalty, the play still used local actors but had a professional staff. Zdenek Stabla reports that the Lumières' American representative, Charles Smith Hurd, had returned to Europe in 1896, visited Horitz, and saw a performance of their passion play.[26] He immediately approached the theater group about making a film and negotiated a contract which called for the actors to be paid 1,500 Austrian florins and the company to receive 2,000 florins per year for five years. Exhibitions were also limited to non-German-speaking countries. With permission in hand, Hurd looked for a producer to finance the production, exhibit the films, and share the profits.

Hurd's search for financing ended when his proposition was accepted by the theatrical producers Marc Klaw and Abraham L. Erlanger. They placed Dr. Walter W. Freeman in charge of the project and hired Charles Webster and the International Film Company to do the cinematography and lab work. Although the "Lumière process" was said to be used, the cinématographe had become readily available and the undertaking had no formal ties to the Lumière organization. The group spent much of the following spring and summer in Horitz as Freeman supervised the taking of slides and films. Once again the earlier Stoddard lecture was used as a model, and the leading performers were introduced with lantern-slide portraits. Some of the play's opening tableaux, among them one of Adam and Eve being expelled from the Garden of Eden, were also presented as lantern slides.[27] The Horitz rendition traveled quickly through the Old Testament and Christ's early years, before focusing on the traditional events leading up to the Crucifixion. The final program of thirty negatives totaled 2,400 feet of film. Unfortunately, neither prints nor frame enlargements exist to tell us any more about this ambitious project.

THE HORITZ PASSION PLAY was presented in an hour-and-a-half exhibition that also included projected slides, a lecture, organ music, and sacred hymns.[28] Klaw and Erlanger, acquainted with New York's reaction to the Salmi Morse production, chose to tour other cities before arriving in the nation's theatrical capital. The American

A drawing taken from THE HORITZ PASSION PLAY (Philadelphia Record, *23 November 1897*).

premiere occurred on 22 November 1897 at the Philadelphia Academy of Music and received a highly favorable response, with local clergy making up a substantial portion of the appreciative audience. Calling it the "most notable, and certainly the most noble use to which that marvelous invention, the cinematograph, has yet been put," the *Philadelphia Record* observed:

> Endless lectures on Ober-Ammergau have not been able to give so vivid an idea of that more famous Passion Play as last night's spectators at the Academy gained as they sat in silent and all-absorbed attention before these scenes. The Horitz drama is much more marked by primitive simplicity than that of Ober-Ammergau. There is a decidedly more naive and child-like treatment of these great sacred themes and episodes. Without the life-like movement of these views it would have been impossible to have appreciated anywhere near to the full the unquestioning, credulous simplicity of this theatrical representation. In these pictures, however, we actually see the half-naked Adam and Eve running about in a quaint little Garden of Eden, with invading devils lurking under the Tree of Life, and an odd-looking Serpent of Evil leaning its flat head out of the boughs. Cain kills the kneeling Abel, but one sees how the pretense of realism is not so necessitous but that the bad brother brings his club down unmistakably far away from Abel's head. The Flood scene, with its swimmers in the immovable scenic waves, affords also a queer spectacle (23 November 1897, p. 6).

Various technical imperfections (blurred images and flickering) were noted but were played down. After the first week, THE HORITZ PASSION PLAY moved to Horticultural Hall, where it remained for an additional two weeks. The exhibition was gradually polished. While organ music accompanied the lecture from the outset, the producers soon added three singers, including baritone N. Dushane Cloward.[29]

The producers, assuming they had an exclusive attraction, opened next in Boston on 3 January and remained for two weeks. The program provoked little controversy, in part because of the careful way it was promoted. Initial publicity distinguished the exhibition from a regular theatrical performance. "There will be no 'real' actors, no living personages in the presentation of this most sacred and sublime of the world's tragedies," the *Boston Herald* assured its readers, "and yet it will seem to be instinct with life and physical movement but with an entire absence of flesh and blood and vocal concomitants, that will relieve it from all trace of irreverence and make the conception seem sublime." The newspapers also ran an interview with Professor Ernest Lacy, who delivered the descriptive lecture. Lacy, a Philadelphia high-school teacher, was described as a "brilliant young scholar, poet and playwright." Alluding to his previous appearance in Philadelphia, the *Herald* told Bostonians that "a finer or more reverent piece of word-painting has seldom been heard."[30] Lacy's reputation was a guarantee of high quality.

Because past lectures on the passion play had celebrated the Oberammergau performance as something special and unique, focusing on Horitz posed potential hazards. To avoid these dangers the Klaw and Erlanger group astutely situated their exhibition in relation to the Oberammergau play. On one hand, they promoted the

Horitz actors as the "Austrian Oberammergau Company" and imposed a format on THE HORITZ PASSION PLAY that inevitably recalled Stoddard's famous lecture. On the other, Lacy defused the danger of seeing the Horitz play as a cheap imitation by arguing:

> The Horitz production is nearer to nature, in that the players who perform the various parts are untutored, unread peasants, with nothing but their faith to guide them.
> . . . The Oberammergau production is more up-to-date as it were, and the effect of sincerity is not so deeply impressed on the mind as in the Horitz production (*Boston Herald*, 2 January 1898, p. 32).

The Horitz rendition, it was asserted, was preferable to the better-known performance. A brief history of the Horitz passion play was provided to authenticate this choice.

Publicity had the desired results. Boston's opening night was attended by what the *Boston Herald* called "a splendid audience, including in its numbers not only regular theatregoers but a considerable contingent of people who are much oftener to be found at church than attending a play." For the paper's reviewer, the exhibition had all the power of a theatrical performance yet none of its drawbacks. At first aware that the images were only representations of a representation, the critic soon felt in the presence of the actors themselves. "Then the players begin to depict the birth and life of Christ, and with this change of subject there comes a new change of mental attitude. So absorbing becomes the interest of the pictures that the onlooker, from merely regarding the figures of the real, live people who acted the play in Bohemia, begins to forget all about what was done in Bohemia and henceforth is lost in the thought that the faces and forms before him are the real people who lived in Palestine 2000 years ago, and with their own eyes witnessed the crucifixion of Christ."[31]

As late as April 1898 only a single set of Horitz films was available for exhibition. After Boston, these were shown for two weeks in Baltimore, where Cardinal Gibbons attended and endorsed the pictures as "wonderfully realistic and deeply religious." A Rochester, New York, opening followed. By the time that THE HORITZ PASSION PLAY opened in New York City on 14 March as a Lenten lecture at Daly's Theater, any possibility of controversy had been dissipated, not merely because of the positive reactions generated in other cities but because a similar type of exhibition had already opened at New York's Eden Musee.[32]

The Passion Play of Oberammergau

New York City's Eden Musee was on Twenty-third Street, west of Madison Square. Opened in late March 1884, it appealed primarily to a well-to-do clientele by cannily mixing an "educational" approach with sensationalism. Waxworks and musical concerts were its key programming elements until 18 December 1896, when films were first projected in the Musee's Winter Garden. Popular with patrons, moving pictures quickly became a major commitment.[33]

Richard Hollaman, the Musee's president, had been anxious to acquire the film rights for the Horitz passion play and felt betrayed when Hurd gave the contract to Klaw & Erlanger. Nevertheless, Hollaman and an associate, Frank Russell, attended

Advertisement in The New York Clipper, *26 February 1898.*

the Philadelphia premiere and were sufficiently impressed to embark on their own production, which, for promotional purposes, was said to be based on the Bavarian staging. In reality, while photographs and drawings from that famous rendition may have provided some guidelines, the Salmi Morse play was dusted off and generally performed the role of scenario—as one informed critic later noted, nearly one-third of the scenes in Hollaman's version did not even exist in the Oberammergau passion play. Albert Eaves became involved in the Hollaman effort and provided the costumes that he had acquired from the Abbey production. The well-known stage director Henry C. Vincent supervised the production, painted the scenery, made the properties, and selected the actors. Frank Russell played Christ, while William Paley, who had given exhibitions with his kalatechnoscope projector, photographed the scenes with his camera on the roof of the Grand Central Palace.[34] With cinematography possible only on sunny days and even then only for a few hours, it took six weeks to accumulate twenty-three scenes totaling approximately 2,000 feet. Shot at about thirty frames per second, they produced some nineteen minutes of screen time. The resulting scenes, with their sparse sets and simple, frontal compositions, evoked the long, powerful tradition of religious paintings.

The films were made in great secrecy. Just as putting on a boxing match was illegal but showing films of such a match was fine, the discovery that an actor was playing Christ for money might have created a public outcry even though the exhibition of

Scenes from THE PASSION PLAY OF OBERAMMERGAU. SALOMÉ'S DANCE BEFORE HEROD, THE MESSIAH'S ENTRY INTO JERUSALEM, CARRYING THE CROSS, THE CRUCIFIXION.

such films would not. And it would surely have alerted Klaw & Erlanger, who might well have preempted the Musee's New York debut. Hollaman was also uncertain how to publicize the resulting PASSION PLAY OF OBERAMMERGAU. THE HORITZ PASSION PLAY had gained public acceptance in part because it was performed by simple Bohemian peasants. The reaction to Hollaman's project, if its actual production circumstances were known, could not be fully predicted. Ties to the Oberammergau passion play were thus maximized and the re-enactment aspect downplayed. It was hinted, if not clearly stated, that the filming involved the Oberammergau villagers.

Following a press screening on 28 January, it became clear that journalists were less concerned about the potential for religious sacrilege than about misrepresentation. "All the preliminary announcements of this exhibition have tended to convey the impression that this is a genuine reproduction of the celebrated passion play at Oberammergau," the *New York Herald* protested in its February review. In the face of such skepticism, Hollaman made a strategic retreat, and subsequent advertisements and publicity emphasized the reenactment aspects of the production—although the debt to the Morse play went largely unmentioned.

By 1898 the screen presentation of religious subjects was sufficiently familiar that the Musee's awkward handling of the press failed to harm the program's popularity, and the show did even better than Hollaman had expected. Among the many visitors were ministers and church people, many of whom enthused about the moral benefits of the passion-play pictures. "The 'Passion Play' might well be said to give those who see it a personal and loving acquaintance with the Divine One. After the exhibition was over I left feeling like living a better life, becoming a better man, trying to follow the teachings of One whom I now know as I never knew before," a prominent lawyer told the Musee manager.[35] A short time later, the Reverend R. F. Putnam wrote the editor of one prominent magazine:

> The performance of this play in New York by living actors and actresses was prohibited by the conscientious sentiment of the people, the influence of the press and the action of the authorities. But to the rendition of it by these pictures there can be no objection. One might as well object to the illustrations of Doré and other artists in the large quarto Bibles. Intensely realistic they are, and it is this feature which gives them truthfulness and makes them instructive. Painful they are necessarily to sensitive and sympathetic souls, and so are many of the pictures which surmount some of the altars of our churches. . . . I cannot conceive of a more impressive object-lesson for Sunday school scholars (*Home Journal*, 15 February 1898, reprinted in *Motion Picture World*, 22 February 1908, p. 133).

Other ministers, including Madison C. Peters of the Bloomingdale Reformed Church, attended and offered their endorsements.[36] The devout saw THE PASSION PLAY OF OBERAMMERGAU as an effective way to convert those who were not religious and to inspire the faithful. At times, the Musee seemed like a church.

THE PASSION PLAY OF OBERAMMERGAU had no fixed form. Because reviews usually focused on the films, the full diversity among programs is difficult to establish fully. At the Musee, a well-known lecturer, Professor Powell, stood beside the screen and accompanied the films with a narration. The extent to which lantern slides were

THE NEW YORK CLIPPER.

FEBRUARY 19.

PASSION PLAY
OF OBERAMMERGAU
IN ANIMATED PICTURES.

F. Z. MAGUIRE & CO. offer to Theatrical Managers and Owners of Animated Picture Apparatus the most sublime of all subjects, THE PASSION PLAY. Playing to crowded houses at the EDEN MUSEE, New York. Endorsed by press, public and clergy.

READ SOME OF THE PRESS COMMENTS:

"Follows quite faithfully the dramatic representation at Oberammergau."—NEW YORK HERALD.

"The exhibition made a decidedly favorable impression, and will doubtless attract many visitors to this popular place of amusement."—WORLD.

"However it was done it was well done; the pictures are artistic and interesting."—EVENING JOURNAL.

"The pictures are life size, and all the action is brought out in detail."—DAILY NEWS.

"The display was in every respect interesting and held the attention of the spectators from beginning to end."—NEW YORK TIMES.

"One would prophesy that those 'who came to scoff' will 'remain to pray.'"—BROOKLYN CITIZEN

"The tableaux, in their entirety, bring the Saviour's mission on earth, and His sufferings, more vividly before the spectator than any prominent lawyer of this city, after having witnessed the representation, expressed himself to the management of the Musee as follows: The lesson taught by the representation strikes vividly to my mind, much more than ever before, the teachings of Scripture. The Passion Play might well be said to give those who see it a personal and loving acquaintance with the Divine One. After the exhibition was over I left feeling like living a better life, becoming a better man, trying to follow the teaching of One whom I now know as I never knew before."—MAIL AND EXPRESS.

ABOUT 2,200 FEET IN 23 SUBJECTS, AVERAGING 100 FEET IN LENGTH.

SPECIAL NOTICE.

These films ARE TAKEN UNDER LICENSE OF THOMAS A. EDISON, whose patents cover moving photographic films. Any other production of this subject is unauthorized by him, and parties so attempting will be vigorously prosecuted.

LECTURE FURNISHED FOR EXHIBITORS.

As Lent is rapidly approaching, a special opportunity is afforded Managers and Exhibitors, who can easily reap large profit during this sacred season by utilizing THE PASSION PLAY for Lenten Matinees, etc. This production has cost a vast sum of money to produce. For particulars apply to

F. Z. MAGUIRE & CO., SOLE SELLING AGENTS,
LORD'S COURT BUILDING, Williams Street and Exchange Place, New York.

Selling Agents for THOS. A. EDISON.

WRITE FOR NEW CATALOGUE OF FILMS AND PROJECTING APPARATUS.

THE PASSION PLAY OF OBERAMMERGAU *went on the market in February 1898.*

integrated into these initial programs in order to create a full-length entertainment is uncertain. The immense popularity of these exhibitions, however, meant that the Musee was soon sending out traveling companies to present two-hour passion-play entertainments. One of the first units traveled through the Northeast, opening at the Hyperion Theater in New Haven on 14 March. This full evening's entertainment, narrated by the Reverend N. B. Thompson of New York, used slides and film and began "by showing a map of the Holy Land and then [took] the listener on an imaginary journey detailing the many events in the life of Christ and the most important of which were illustrated by the cinematograph."[37]

Thompson's Musee-sponsored exhibition, however, immediately found itself in competition with a rival showing identical films. For reasons discussed in the following chapter, films from the Eden Musee's production were quickly sold on the open market. Professor Wallace, a Boston-based exhibitor of lantern slides and films, opened a passion-play program at Sylvester Z. Poli's Wonderland vaudeville theater in New Haven one week before Rev. Thompson's Hyperion run. Poli charged ten and twenty cents for admission, much less than the Hyperion had intended. But the show not only appealed to Poli's regular, often working-class, clientele: according to local press reports, the theater was crowded with "audiences representing the best people of the city." Church people entered a vaudeville house! "Some beautiful sacred music is introduced, and while the audiences are coming and going a fine set of stereopticon views of semi-sacred subjects are shown," one reviewer noted. "During the performance of the play no passing to and fro will be permitted, and the doors will be closed against newcomers."[38] THE PASSION PLAY OF OBERAMMERGAU had an appeal beyond the specific audience of evangelical Christians to include frequenters of more refined and popular commercial culture.

After its commercial runs, THE PASSION PLAY OF OBERAMMERGAU was shown increasingly in churches and for religious purposes. Colonel Henry H. Hadley, a noted Methodist evangelist, also bought a set of these films, which he showed in a tent at Asbury Park, New Jersey, during the summer of 1898 and then at evangelistic meetings during the fall. Hadley's program had two parts: first, a lantern lecture on missionary rescue work delivered by the English evangelist Sara Wray and then a nineteen-scene presentation of THE PASSION PLAY. Hadley's program appears to have included individual scenes from several productions including those by Hollaman–Eaves and Klaw & Erlanger.[39]

Early cinema's presentational elements were powerfully articulated in these passion-play programs. The images were designed as moving illustrations of "the greatest story ever told." Yet the narratives were actually constructed both in the spectators' responses to familiar iconography and through the lecturers' narrations. The programs' dominant presentationalism was not only in their old-style theatrical indicating of space, time, and place but also in their consistent reliance on lecturers who linked and interpreted the images.

Other Passion Plays and Religious Subjects

Other versions of the passion play were made and/or shown in the United States. The Lear passion-play scenes appear to have had their American debut in February 1898, when the Reverend Thomas Dixon, Jr., future author of *The Clansman* (the basis for

D. W. Griffith's THE BIRTH OF A NATION), gave an illustrated lecture on "The Story of Jesus" in New York. Fifty stereopticon slides were also used, and music was provided by an organ and choir. Sigmund Lubin made his own version of THE PASSION PLAY OF OBERAMMERGAU in the spring of 1898.[40] Although the Horitz and Eden Musee passion-play films were initially offered to exhibitors only in complete sets, they were soon sold on a scene-by-scene basis so that exhibitors could purchase and then organize individual scenes into any combination that they desired. In some cases, an exhibitor used films made by more than one producer, purchasing the scenes he liked best or adding to his collection when finances permitted. Many exhibitors showed passion-play films, but no two programs were exactly alike. Showmen exercised a fundamental, creative role. They each selected their own moving pictures and stereopticon scenes, placed them in a particular order, wrote and delivered a narration, and provided incidental music. They had to know the audience to which they were appealing in order to avoid offending religious sensibilities. In short, their exhibitions revealed a strong continuity with earlier screen traditions.

Religious subjects in general were an important genre for the early film industry. Early in 1898, W. K. L. Dickson arrived in Rome with references from an array of prominent prelates and spent the next four months trying to obtain permission to film at the Vatican. He won Pope Leo XIII's cooperation after explaining that "in this way the pontifical blessing could be conveyed to his many thousands of subjects in Amer-

W. K. L. Dickson filming Pope Leo XIII.

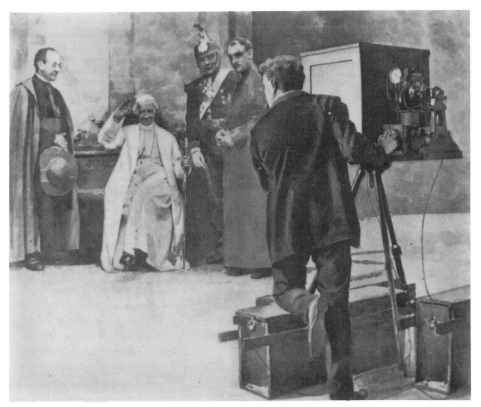

POPE LEO XIII IN CARRIAGE. *The pope bestows his blessing on the camera.*

ica." That April and May, Dickson photographed twelve scenes of the pope. Leo XIII, who saw at least one of the films on a mutoscope before giving his consent to having them shown, was reportedly delighted with the results. These had their New York premiere at Carnegie Hall on 14 December 1898 and were enthusiastically received. "In all the pictures the face of the Pope came out with extraordinary distinctness, while his white robes contrasted strongly with the dark color of his attendants and guards, and made him the most prominent object in every picture," the *New York Tribune* reported. "The Pope was seen being carried in his sedan chair through the chamber of the Vatican, walking in the grounds, on his way to an audience, driving in his carriage, and sitting on his bench in the grounds." According to the same source, the high point for the audience came when "His Holiness blessed the instrument which had recorded his movements, and through it . . . those who would see the pictures afterwards." As with the passion-play exhibitions, an accompanying lecture was given by a church official, in this instance the Reverend Thomas N. Malone; the Catholic clergy were now in heavy attendance.[41]

By the end of 1898, a program of Pope Leo films was being shown in Boston with its heavily Irish Catholic population. Playing at Keith's Theater on Sundays and at the vaudeville magnate's smaller, underutilized Bijou Opera House during the week, the films were preceded by a stereopticon lecture, "Ancient and Modern Rome." M. T. H. Cummings, who had lived for several years in Rome, narrated both parts of the program.[42] The well-publicized show enjoyed an eight-week run.

Watching inspirational religious subjects was usually seen as a desirable Sunday afternoon activity. The Reverend Thomas Dixon, Jr., gave his passion-play lecture on that day, and the Reverend N. B. Thompson also performed regularly on the holy day. "Sunday concerts" featuring Pope Leo films were given at a Rochester vaudeville house and at New York City's 14th Street Theater. Other films in these Biograph programs, however, were less serious. In Rochester, scenes of football games were projected in reverse, producing a ludicrous effect and much hilarity. (Even in the original Pope Leo exhibition at Carnegie Hall, scenes of the pontiff, too brief to constitute an entire program, were supplemented by coronation views of Queen Wilhelmina of Holland as well as other American and European scenes.) For many showmen, religious subjects simply became a way to evade Sunday blue laws. While Waite's Comic Opera Company showed regular films between the acts of its musical comedies during the week, it presented THE PASSION PLAY OF OBERAMMERGAU on Sundays, when the troupe could not otherwise perform.[43] A strong argument could be made that in the end amusement entrepreneurs exploited religious subject matter for their own commercial purposes and ultimately absorbed it within their own cultural framework. Religious subjects did not necessarily oppose the flourishing world of popular amusement but rather were often subsumed by it.

Travel Lectures

Films of religious subjects and boxing matches often attracted more than their intended audiences of devoted churchgoers and fight aficionados. This was less true for illustrated travel programs, which embodied principles of America's refined culture. While Henry Northrop and Alexander Black gave combined motion-picture and stereopticon programs during 1897–1898, both eventually lost interest in motion pictures and returned to their earlier, exclusively lantern-slide formats. However, two prominent travel lecturers made long-term commitments to using films: E. Burton Holmes and Dwight L. Elmendorf.

Many believed that E. Burton Holmes was the first to show moving pictures as part of the illustrated travel lecture, perhaps because Holmes laid claim to this "first" in his programs. While this is not strictly true, he appears to have been the first to make films specifically for his own lectures and to use films regularly in conjunction with a course of such refined presentations. During the summer of 1897, Holmes's lantern operator, Oscar Depue, purchased a 60-mm motion-picture camera from Léon Gaumont in Paris and with his new acquisition, took films of Rome, Venice, Milan, and France. The exposed stock was then turned over to Gaumont for developing and printing. When Depue returned to the United States, he became self-sufficient by building his own printer and turning the camera into a projector. This accomplished, the cameraman filmed an onrushing express, Fort Sheridan, and various sights in Yellowstone National Park. At the conclusion of each lecture, Holmes showed seven to nine films, with selections usually focusing on a few locales.[44]

The year 1897 was a momentous one for Holmes. John Stoddard retired from lecturing after the 1896–1897 season and designated the young man as his successor. Holmes thus stood out from his competitors and was given many new opportunities. For the first time, he presented lectures in New York City, Brooklyn, and Boston. As Stoddard had done, Holmes gave "courses" of five lectures that generally met once or twice a week, in either the afternoon or evening. A course ticket cost $5, with single tickets selling for 50¢ to $1.50, thus excluding all but the well-to-do. Holmes's first New York lecture, "The Wonders of Thessaly," won over a large majority of his audience, and critics praised the lecturer, who took his own photographs, for his ability "to recognize just what would make an interesting, an instructive, a characteristic or an amusing picture." According to the *Brooklyn Eagle*, "New Yorkers will agree that however he may differ from John L. Stoddard in looks, manners and platform methods he is every way worthy to fill the latter's place."[45]

Critical popularity was reflected at the box office. Holmes's 4 March afternoon lecture, "The Yellowstone National Park," grossed $578, of which he kept half. On other days he did less well but usually grossed from three to four hundred dollars a performance—enough to guarantee his return the following year. Films helped to give his presentations their own distinctive appeal. At his Manhattan lectures, a critic noted with surprise that "motion pictures seemed to be an entire novelty to a large part of the audience, in spite of the fact that such pictures have been on constant exhibition for the last year and half and more in the music halls and continuous performance theatres and have been used for advertising purposes in the streets."[46] Holmes, like other travel lecturers, appealed to an elitist group that was little concerned with novelty outside its own select world. Since films had often been shown at Brooklyn Institute functions, Holmes's moving pictures aroused little comment at that location.

During the 1898–1899 season, Dwight L. Elmendorf used films in his programs and enjoyed increased attention as a result. To prepare his exhibitions, the New Yorker traveled to Mexico and throughout the West Indies, and spent time with a military unit in Cuba. He not only accumulated 160 slides for his program, "The Santiago Campaign," but purchased pertinent standard-gauge films from producers and interspersed them throughout his presentation. One enthusiastic critic devoted almost a full column to his review, remarking:

> Mr. Elmendorf was with the Ninth Regular Infantry. Their marches and evolutions, the routine of camp life and the amusements indulged in by the soldiers while waiting to go aboard the transports were deftly and wittily described as the successive scenes were actualized on the canvas. Stationary and cinematograph pictures of cavalry and artillery evolutions followed, with a good word for the black cavalry, especially the famous Tenth, whom the lecturer alluded to as "the black rough riders." Portraits of Colonel Adna R. Chafee, of General Wheeler and the familiar figures of Colonel Wood's and Lieutenant Colonel Roosevelt's command came in such a way as to arouse a demonstration (*Brooklyn Eagle*, 4 April 1899, p. 3).

Elmendorf's lecture "Old Mexico and Her Pageants" also interwove slides and films, including motion pictures of a Mexican bullfight.

Holmes, meanwhile, continued to show films only at the conclusion of his lectures. During the summer of 1898, he had visited Arizona and America's newly annexed Hawaiian Islands, where he took still photographs and Depue shot the motion pictures. For programs on these subjects, the films focused on the same topic as the main exhibition. Holmes's remaining programs, however, repeated earlier lectures and lacked films that paralleled the principal topics. It was not until the following season (1899–1900) that he integrated films into his lantern-slide programs, using material he and Depue had gathered while in Hawaii, the Philippines, and Japan. The lecture on Hawaii, reworked from the previous year, emphasized the local populace's enthusiasm for annexation and focused on the warm reception given U.S. soldiers on their way to the Philippines. His lecture "Manila and the Philippines" emphasized the primitive conditions of life on the islands as well as the heroic actions of American soldiers fighting the local guerrillas.[47]

To dismiss these programs as mere travel lectures is too simplistic. They were elaborate, sophisticated documentary presentations. Some were political, focusing on the Spanish-American War and the United States' expansionist policies in the Pacific. Others, like Holmes's study of Mokiland, were ethnographic in orientation. While they appealed primarily to aficionados of refined entertainment, they were considered sufficiently enlightening and informative to have the support of moralistic Protestant religious groups. Thus, when Association Hall was booked, the Brooklyn Institute often held its illustrated lectures in a local church. The long-standing alliance of church moralism and polite culture continued to operate. Travel lectures, however, did not generate broad patronage comparable to the veriscope and THE PASSION PLAY OF OBERAMMERGAU. In a few cases, these were condensed and appeared on the vaudeville stage. Early in 1899 J. C. Bowker gave "an entertaining number" entitled "Travelogue on Hawaii" in Keith theaters.[48] His stereopticon program was one of Keith's many attempts to provide vaudeville with a more refined image.

Travel programs were limited in their commercial success partly because they were not designed for exhibition by multiple units. An Elmendorf lecture required Elmendorf to accompany the images with his thoughts and voice: it was his perceptions and analyses that were presented. Holmes was one of the rare lecturers ever to use stand-ins, but even so in an extremely limited way. In contrast, THE CORBETT–FITZSIMMONS FIGHT and the various passion-play programs simply relied on an appropriate individual to narrate them. Travel lectures not only addressed a different audience but involved distinctively different methods of exhibition from other feature-length film programs.

For all their differences, these three kinds of full-length programs functioned within an already extensive practice of nonfiction screen presentations. They looked backward to the stereopticon lecture and forward to what became known as the documentary.[49] Reviews and other information about these evening-long programs testify to the ambitious scope of motion pictures in the wake of the novelty era. In contrast, the smattering of surviving films, frequently of poor quality, offers only the slightest idea of what it was like to witness those exhibitions. Unless today's viewers recognize that these brief pictures were frequently the building blocks for much larger shows, they will fail to understand some of the most basic characteristics of 1890s cinema, for on these occasions the exhibitor was typically the creator—or at least the arbiter—of narrative, the author of the show. Showmen integrated moving pictures into established screen practice and so transformed it.

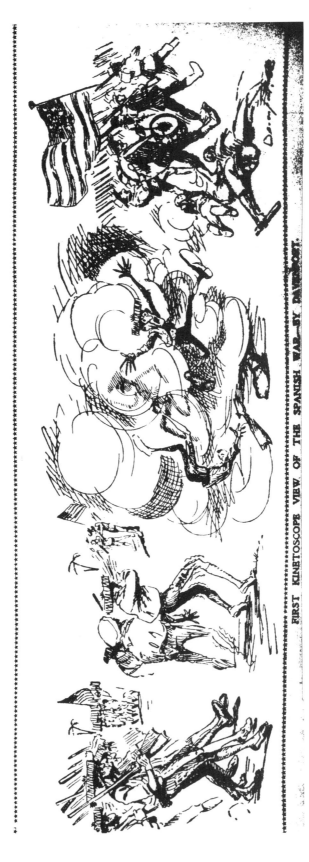

FIRST KINETOSCOPE VIEW OF THE SPANISH WAR—BY DAVENPORT.

A political cartoon, New York Journal, 28 April 1898.

8

Commercial Warfare and the Spanish-American War: 1897–1898

With the onset of the Spanish-American War the motion-picture industry discovered a new role and exploited it, gaining in confidence and size as a result. The cinema's capacity as a visual newspaper was extended as exhibitors unspooled scene after scene related to the struggle. Even more impressively, however, motion-picture showmen evoked powerful patriotic sentiments in their audiences, revealing the new medium's ideological and propagandistic force in the post-novelty era. Across the country, exhibitors found ways to tell the story of the war with slides and motion pictures. While special evening-length productions, like those discussed in the previous chapter, expanded the boundaries of cinema practice, they operated at the periphery of the small and vulnerable industry. It was the ongoing production of a few firms that provided the commercial foundation for the American industry, and it was the war that gave this sector new life.

The established companies generally ran into difficulties at the end of the 1896–1897 novelty season, as moving pictures showed signs of fading, at least when exhibitors did not appeal to specific audiences with the passion play or THE CORBETT–FITZSIMMONS FIGHT. The small town of Owego, New York, was not unusual: while projected motion pictures drew crowded houses when first shown in March 1897, interest faded with familiarity. Two months later, another showman booked films for three nights at the local opera house. "Although it was a good exhibition, there was less than half a house the first night," reported the *Phonoscope*. "The second night the attendance was not sufficient to pay for the gas and subsequent exhibitions were 'declared off.' "[1] Although the number of exhibitions in the nation's opera houses increased slightly during the fall of 1897, the vast majority (approximately 85 percent) were given by the Veriscope Company. The number of independent exhibitors showing regular 35-mm productions in these venues had declined precipitously.

Contraction was palpable in the large cities. While Boston newspapers had advertised as many as seven concurrent motion-picture exhibitions in May 1897 (including two storefronts), by fall this number never exceeded four and for many weeks fell to one (a biograph at Keith's). In New York City, the number fluctuated between five and one (the Eden Musee) during the fall and early winter. In Philadelphia and Chicago weeks went by without films being shown in commercial theaters. Adversity battered many small-time exhibitors, encouraging them to look elsewhere for profits and employment.

Nonetheless, the industry bounced back in early 1898 as events leading up to the Spanish-American War revived interest in moving pictures. Indeed, warfare not only provided American producers with their key subject matter but served as an apt metaphor for commercial competition within the industry itself. Both conflicts involved issues of markets and dominance of their respective realms. Within the film world, Edison used his patents and the legal system as weapons to vanquish rival producers. Yet ironically, the Spanish-American War created such a demand for films that other producers soon appeared. Throughout it all, the major companies—Biograph and Edison—were locked in a multilevel struggle.

Biograph Continues to Prosper and Expand

During the course of 1897 and 1898, the American Mutoscope Company (*i.e.*, Biograph) expanded rapidly and solidified its commercial position. Its rate of production steadily increased, from approximately two hundred subjects for the year ending 31 May 1897 to roughly 350 new negatives during the year ending 31 May 1898 and nearly five hundred new negatives during the year ending 31 May 1899. After W. K. L. Dickson and Elias Bernard Koopman departed for England in the spring of 1897, Wallace McCutcheon assumed charge of production. That June the company established a second production unit. One camera usually stayed in the New York area and was often used at the rooftop studio. A second machine operated in diverse locations but spent much of its time in the Boston environs. Few of the new films were meant exclusively for local audiences. THROWING OVER A WALL (No. 231, photographed 12 June 1897), for example, imitated a popular Lumière subject (FALLING WALL) but on a grander scale. The photographers also returned to Buzzard's Bay and filmed the Jefferson family of actors in a group of one-shot comedies. THE TRAMP AND THE BATHER (No. 242) was one of the first tramp comedies, a genre that remained popular throughout the period covered by this volume. After a tramp steals a bather's clothes, the victim swims to the shallows, squirms into a barrel to conceal his nakedness, and gives chase. In THE BIGGEST FISH HE EVER CAUGHT (No. 250), Charles Jefferson hooks a fish but tumbles into the water going after it. In STILL WATERS RUN DEEP (No. 243) "a nephew is deposited in the stream through the breaking of a plank over which he is following a young lady into a boat."[2] Such scenes relied on a simple gag that had the narrative complexity of a newspaper cartoon, from which many were undoubtedly derived.

Biograph embraced the world of journalism, and its programs often acted as a visual newspaper. If the short comedies were like comic strips, many scenes showed front-page news events. The Harvard-Yale-Cornell boat races, photographed by Biograph's other camera in Poughkeepsie, New York, on 25 June, were a sports-page equivalent. Another newspaper–film connection was made when the camera crew visited the *New York Journal*'s summer camp for young urchins in New City (Rockland County), New York. In TRIAL SCENE (No. 260) the campers learned about the operations of the American judicial system—a way to make them law-abiding citizens. For Hearst and the *Journal*, this effort at Americanizing recent immigrant groups demonstrated their good works and sense of responsibility. For Biograph, the film built good relations with a news organization that could give it assistance as well as publicity.

No. 242
Title *The Tramp and the Bather.*
Length *158 ft.*
Code Word *Mundinova.*

No. 243
Title *Still Waters Run Deep.*
Length *143 ft.*
Code Word *Munequeria.*

During the summer of 1897, Biograph's itinerant cameramen returned to Atlantic City, where the company was showing films on Steel Pier. They took various scenes of happy vacationers (No. 275, A JOLLY CROWD OF BATHERS)—until the camera was destroyed and the operators seriously injured while photographing ATLANTIC CITY FIRE DEPARTMENT (No. 278). "It is a turnout of the fire department at Atlantic City," reported the *Boston Herald*, "and the driver of the chemical engine had to take choice between running down a hand engine or the biograph apparatus and chose the latter. One of the funny results is that the horses seem to be about to jump into the auditorium of the theater."[3] The unfortunate mishap only temporarily disrupted the company's production schedule.

Perhaps the most popular Biograph film was THE HAVERSTRAW TUNNEL (No. 301), taken on the West Shore Railroad along the Hudson River. While cameras had been placed on moving trains for more than a year, in this novel film the camera was mounted on the cowcatcher and sent through a tunnel. When shown in the theater, this "attraction" (to use Tom Gunning's term) demonstrated that moving pictures could still elicit a strong visceral response. As described by the *Boston Herald*, "One first has a view of track and surrounding country, then the entrance to the tunnel looms up ahead, draws nearer and is finally entered. There is momentary darkness, such as one experiences when suddenly plunged into such a tunnel, and then the opening at the other end appears and finally the train emerges into the light once more, and the beautiful panorama of scenery is continued." And, the *Herald* noted, "The applause which followed was the heartiest accorded any picture since the Empire State [Express] was first shown." According to one New York critic, "The shadows, the rush of the invisible force and the uncertainty of the issues made one instinctively hold his breath as when on the edge of a crisis that might become a catastrophe. If there had been a collision in that tunnel half of the women in the audience would have been carried off in a collapse."[4]

Acted films, which included such diverse genres as comedies and scenes of dancers and vaudeville performers, constituted a large percentage of Biograph's output and distinguished the company from Edison and other American competitors. Of the ninety-seven titles listed between production No. 200 (CAUGHT NAPPING) and No. 300 (SOAP BUBBLES), fifty-nine fell into this general category. Most were studio productions, and many continued to present women as objects of sexual desire. AN AFFAIR OF HONOR (No. 238), for example, based on a popular painting, shows two women who strip off their outer garments and engage in a sword fight until one is seriously wounded. In ONE GIRL SWINGING (No. 246), two coquettes push a woman on a swing. She is facing the camera, and at the top of each arc her undergarments are revealed. The back-and-forth motion directed at the camera is equally suggestive. PEEPING TOM (No. 245) employed a reflexive strategy: the male spectator inside the frame acts as a surrogate voyeur in relation to the film spectator. Perhaps the first such scene made in the United States, this archetypal situation had already been employed by the French; it proved very popular and would be reworked many times. (Biograph eventually remade the subject in 1905 as PEEPING TOM IN THE DRESSING ROOM.) These sexually enticing scenes continued to be made primarily for the mutoscopes and were clearly directed at a male audience, even though women might glimpse these forbidden pleasures as they had done with fight films.

Less sexually suggestive genres were deemed more appropriate for vaudeville audiences that included women and children. BAD BOY AND POOR OLD GRANDPA

No. 300

Title *Soap Bubbles.*

Length *129 ft.*

Code Word *Tesserula.*

No. 301

Title *The Haverstraw Tunnel*

Length *348 ft.*

Code Word *Tessitrice.*

No. 241

Title *Two Girls Swinging.*

Length   152 ft.
Code Word *Munerabo.*

No. 245

Title *Peeping Tom.*

Length   153 ft.
Code Word *Mungimos.*

(No. 269), in which a naughty boy creeps up behind an old man reading the newspaper and sets it on fire, was part of the bad-boy genre. THE VANISHING LADY (No. 271) was modeled on a well-known magic trick, though an early Méliès subject served as a more direct antecedent. Most of these acted films were self-contained one-shot units that could be used in either a simple variety program or a mutoscope. In November 1897, however, Biograph took a three-part series of Christmas films (Nos. 372–374) that was remade into an expanded, four-part series shortly thereafter: THE NIGHT BEFORE CHRISTMAS (© HANGING STOCKINGS CHRISTMAS EVE), SANTA CLAUS FILLING STOCKINGS (© SANTA FILLING STOCKINGS), CHRISTMAS MORNING, and CHRISTMAS TREE PARTY (Nos. 380–383). All four pictures used the same set and were photographed from the same camera position. Title slides specified the unfolding of the narrative and bridged ellipses (as previously done with multiple parade scenes taken from the same camera position). "The series of Christmas pictures, designed especially for the little folks, are pleasing their elders just as much," *Boston Herald* readers were informed, "and are no doubt serving as a reminder to many how happiness can be given at this season by the bestowal of a small present upon a child."[5]

With its increased level of production, Biograph needed story ideas and began to advertise that it would pay five dollars "for any suggestion of a good scene adopted and used by the Mutoscope Company for their Biograph or Mutoscope." The ad led to over fifteen hundred suggestions from interested spectators in the course of one week—almost all of which were impractical. One New York newspaperman, Roy L. McCardell, found this offer to be a profitable way to make extra money and regularly contributed ideas. Soon he was hired on a permanent basis not only to provide sketches but to handle advertising and promotion. He may have also been responsible for placing a long-running series of promotional articles and photographs on the Biograph company in the *New York Mail and Express*.[6]

Biograph further augmented its repertoire of films with subjects received from the British Mutoscope & Biograph Company, commencing with W. K. L. Dickson's moving pictures of Queen Victoria's jubilee, three scenes of which were finally shown "as one continuous picture" in early August.[7] The steady flow of European subjects included scenes of royalty, displays of military pomp, and news films (such as Queen Victoria reviewing the Coldstream Guards at Aldershot). Once production facilities were established in London, Dickson made periodic filming trips to the Continent, shooting Kaiser Wilhelm of Germany and Emperor Franz Josef of Austria in Budapest, and the coronation of Queen Wilhelmina of Holland at The Hague. These European activities provided invaluable diversity of subject matter for Biograph's American exhibition service.

Biograph had established a nationwide exhibition network by the fall of 1897, when its activities reached the West Coast. Bypassing the United States Animatoscope Company, in which he had invested, Gustave Walter hired Biograph for his Orpheum vaudeville circuit. When a biograph opened at his San Francisco theater on 25 October, it was called "the best of all the projectoscope machines yet seen." After a six-week run, it moved to Walter's Los Angeles theater for several weeks in December. Overseas exhibitions likewise proliferated, with the German premiere in Berlin during late August, the French debut in Paris the following month, and an opening in Australia.[8] All were successful and led to long runs, allowing Biograph to develop an international network of production and exhibition that recalled the Lumières' efforts of the previous year.

James H. White and Edison Production Activities

The Edison Manufacturing Company, like other 35-mm producers, faced strikingly different circumstances. Edison was not engaged in exhibition but manufactured films and projectors that were marketed to exhibitors. While distribution was nationwide, Thomas Edison did not establish sister companies or branches overseas. His company's film output was roughly the same as Biograph's during 1896–1897, and while it increased slightly the following year, this growth did not keep pace with that of the American Mutoscope Company. And while the Edison Company still enjoyed robust film sales, it was increasingly challenged not only by Biograph but by rival 35-mm producers. When its output fell during 1899, Edison's production was only about 20 percent that of its chief rival:

1 May 1896–31 May 1897	*ca.* 160 films produced
1 June 1897–31 May 1898	*ca.* 200 films copyrighted
1 June 1898–31 May 1899	*ca.* 80 films copyrighted[9]

The Edison Company rarely used the Black Maria studio and, in contrast to Biograph, favored less-expensive actualities. No more than 15 of the 67 Edison films copyrighted in the last six months of 1897 were "acted" (involving fictional narratives or vaudeville performers), and only a handful of these were shot at the West Orange facility. The ratio was even lower during the first six months of 1898, when only 5 of 136 films fitted into this category (all five, however, were shot in the studio). The Edison Company had clearly departed from its earlier, pre-projection and pre-Lumière production practices.

During the summer of 1897, kinetograph department manager James H. White and cameraman William Heise filmed a diversity of outdoor scenes, including WATERFALL IN THE CATSKILLS; BUFFALO POLICE ON PARADE; and SHEEP RUN, CHICAGO STOCKYARDS (all © 31 July 1897). Most films showed only a single scene. Some were taken from a single camera position but consisted of more than one "take," or subshot. PHILADELPHIA EXPRESS, JERSEY CENTRAL RAILWAY first showed a train racing toward and past the camera. The cameraman then turned off his machine and waited until a second train approached on another track to resume filming. These two takes were joined together in an almost invisible fashion. The results undercut the depiction of real time: the time taken for the action to unfold is indicated rather than actually depicted, offering a filmic equivalent to the presentational methods of condensing time through unrealistically rapid exits and entrances.

The Edison crew photographed several horse races, including the Suburban Handicap run at Sheepshead Bay, New York, on 22 June. SUBURBAN HANDICAP, the resulting 150-foot film, was an exception to the general practice of equating one film with a single camera setup. It consisted of four shots and showed the horses passing on parade before the race, the start, the finish, and the weighing out. While Biograph would have treated each shot as a separate film (thus retaining maximum flexibility in the arrangement of its programs), the Edison Company found that it made more commercial sense to combine these scenes and sell them as a single unit. The camera frame, however, remained static, since Edison personnel still lacked the technology needed to pan their camera on its tripod.

Later that summer, White departed on an ambitious filming trip that took him halfway around the world. Heise was left behind at the West Orange laboratory, where he supervised the development of negatives, the manufacture of positive prints, and the production of local films. White traveled and collaborated with photographer Frederick W. Blechynden. They reached San Francisco by late August, on a tour that lasted approximately ten months and yielded over 120 copyrighted subjects. Among their resources was a tripod that enabled an operator to pan his camera. While incapable of smooth movement, this rather crude device could keep a moving subject within the camera frame. Filming of RETURN OF THE LIFEBOAT was interrupted at several points as White re-aimed the camera at the boat pulling toward shore. As the boat approached the beach, the camera followed: the rough movement emphasized the intensity of the action and the unpredictable nature of the event.

RETURN OF THE LIFEBOAT. *White turns the camera to keep the action in frame.*

White's trip was facilitated and often subsidized by transportation companies interested in promoting tourism, including the Denver and Rio Grande Railroad, the Atchison, Topeka & Santa Fe Railroad, and the Mexican International Railroad. These commercial arrangements repeated those already established with important railroad companies in the East. Many of the resulting films featured the railroads themselves in their most heroic settings (SOUTHERN PACIFIC OVERLAND MAIL and GOING THROUGH THE TUNNEL). While some presented hotel accommodations (HOTEL DEL MONTE), most featured natural beauty or tourist sights (LICK OBSERVATORY, MT. HAMILTON, CAL.). CALIFORNIA ORANGE GROVES, PANORAMIC VIEW was taken from the front end of a train passing through endless expanses of orange trees. With travel expenses paid, White and Blechynden toured the Far West, stopping in Denver and sweeping south into Mexico, where they photographed a bullfight.

Back in San Francisco, the photographers arranged passage with a shipping firm, and in early February 1898 they embarked for Hong Kong via Yokohama on the SS *Coptic*. On their way, they filmed the ship as it was buffeted by a monsoon (S.S. "COPTIC" RUNNING AGAINST THE STORM). A group of films were taken in China and Japan, including HONG KONG WHARF SCENE, SHANGHAI POLICE, and THEATRE ROAD, YOKOHAMA. Returning home on 10 May, White and Blechynden stopped in the recently acquired U.S. possession of Hawaii (WHARF SCENE, HONOLULU). By then, the United States was at war with Spain. A week later White reached the West Coast, took a few scenes relevant to the war (TROOP SHIPS FOR PHILIPPINES), and headed East, seriously ill from his travels. The trip, which reflected White's adventurous spirit, found him on the wrong side of the world when war was declared.

During White's absence, William Heise's output included scenes of winter sports (HOCKEY MATCH ON THE ICE) and a baseball game. At the Black Maria he filmed dance scenes such as CHARITY BALL and a handful of one-shot comedies. WHAT DEMORALIZED THE BARBERSHOP, perhaps Heise's most ambitious studio production, may have been made about this time.[10] In this elaboration on THE BARBERSHOP (1894), the all-male world of a cellar barbershop is disrupted by the unexpected display of the legs of two women. The customer receives a mouthful of shaving cream from the distracted barber. The women, apparently prostitutes, are trying to drum up business. Their legs, centered in the upper part of the frame, invited film spectators to look up the women's skirts along with the men in the barbershop. Once again, surrogate male spectators were placed in the scene. Remaining in the Newark area, Heise made little effort to take newsworthy, war-related events.

Lubin and the International Film Company

Other American producers of 35-mm films emphasized actualities much as the Edison Manufacturing Company did. In July 1897 Lubin offered a series of films that included SHOOTING THE CHUTES AT ATLANTIC CITY; only LIFE RESCUE AT ATLANTIC CITY, in which a drowning person is saved by lifeguards, could be described as an acted subject. Lubin exhibited these and many local views at Bradenburgh's Ninth and Arch Dime Museum when it reopened in September; THE PHILADELPHIA CITY HALL, SCENE ON THE DELAWARE RIVER, and others competed with the local scenes that Biograph was then presenting at Keith's Philadelphia theater. In No-

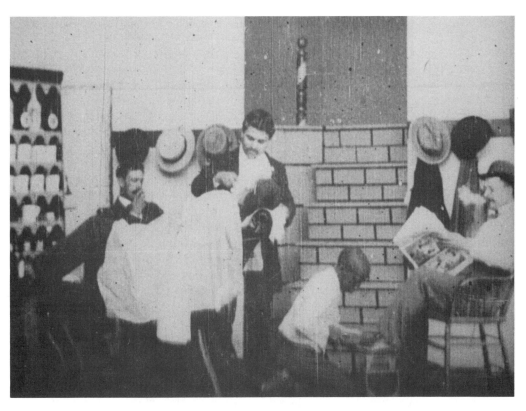

WHAT DEMORALIZED THE BARBERSHOP

vember, after a brief hiatus, Lubin's cineograph returned to Bradenburgh's museum with new local views, including recent parades by the police and fire departments and the departure of two cyclists starting on a fifteen-thousand-mile trip. Lubin also sold these films to other exhibitors, sometimes making them more attractive by selective tinting. Advertisements for SIXTY MINUTE FLYER announced that "the signal can be seen changing color."[11]

During the fall, Lubin established a working relationship with C. A. Bradenburgh. His Dime Museum not only became a reliable customer for Lubin's exhibition service, but he allowed Lubin to build an open-air studio on its rooftop. Indulging in some customary exaggeration, the "manufacturing optician" claimed that he had spent $100,000 building a complete film plant. Earlier he announced that he had hired experts previously associated with the Edison and Lumière companies. In fact, these two new employees were probably Jacob (James) Blair Smith and Arthur D. Hotaling, who had previously been connected with Peter Kiefaber, the former vitascope states rights owner. They worked under John J. Frawley, who headed Lubin's filmmaking activities. Among the fall productions were such fiction films as BURGLAR CAUGHT IN THE ACT and LOVER IN A BROKER'S OFFICE, which Lubin's cineograph service showed not only in Philadelphia but in New York City and Louisville, Kentucky.[12] Lubin's business was becoming one of regional importance.

Webster and Kuhn's International Film Company produced numerous actuality subjects, including a series made at New York's summer resort of Glen Island and another shot on a farm. The firm offered its clients a variety of dance scenes, train scenes, and comic vignettes. In FARMER'S FIRST TRIP TO BERGEN BEACH, a rube character runs after a street car and stumbles, whereupon his bag splits open, allowing a live duck to escape. According to the *Phonoscope,* "The struggle of Reuben to regain possession of his duck is most comical and laughable." Many films—for example, LOVING AGAINST PAPA'S WISHES and PASSAIC FALLS—were remakes of rival companies' hits.[13]

Little is known about the activities of Edward Amet of Waukegan, Illinois. His films and magniscope continued to be available to exhibitors through the Kleine Optical Company in Chicago and McAllister in New York, but since their trade advertisements rarely specified titles, characterizations of Amet's work remain speculative. Modestly produced, they would appear to be consistent with the practices pursued by Lubin and the Edison Company. The heavy emphasis on actualities was particularly obvious in the case of Lumière films. Available to American showmen via Maguire & Baucus, these were almost exclusively travel scenes and foreign views of daily life.[14] In contrast to the American Mutoscope Company, 35-mm producers heavily favored the making of actuality subjects.

Legal Battles

For most producers, competition among rival firms was a reality of commercial life. For Thomas Edison, once the world's sole producer of motion pictures, competition often seemed the work of upstarts who were pirating his invention. As he and other inventors had done in the past, he sought recourse through the courts. Indeed, in the early motion-picture industry, commercial warfare involved a crucial legal dimension. Thomas Edison, Thomas Armat, and Woodville Latham generally sought to

C. A. Bradenburgh's Dime Museum, Philadelphia.

Charles Webster and Edmund Kuhn filming ROYAL BLUE, LIMITED (*1897*).

have their patents recognized in the broadest possible terms so they could use them to control key parts of the industry. Since the Lathams' eidoloscope and Armat's vitascope enterprises were commercial failures, their principal recourse was through the courts. Biograph, in contrast, sought not only to have its own patents recognized but to invalidate or restrict those patents that threatened to curtail important parts of its business; only the company's mutoscope was safe from prior patent claims. Edison, however, was in a unique position because he headed a viable motion-picture company, the Edison Manufacturing Company, and had strong patent claims as well. Moreover, he could afford the legal costs better than most, while his mythic position in American culture gave him a psychological edge in these confrontations.

As mentioned in chapter 2, Edison's patent applications encountered difficulties in the U.S. Patent Office. All claims for application No. 403,534, which covered his method of taking and showing pictures, were rejected, first on 2 January 1892 and again on 15 October 1895. Waiting until 18 April 1896, the last day he could appeal and less than a week before the vitascope's debut at Koster & Bial's, the inventor's lawyers appealed and offered a new set of specifications. These were accepted on 28 December and created a patent-interference case, *Casler et al.* v. *Edison*, which was decided in Edison's favor on 26 March 1897. Shortly after the interference was dissolved, Biograph's Harry Marvin petitioned the commissioner of patents seeking authorization "to take depositions of witnesses to prove that the apparatus described and claimed in the application of Thomas A. Edison, filed August 24, 1891, Serial No. 403,534, was in use for more than two years prior to the date of making any claim for said apparatus in this application." Marvin maintained that the new specifications were for an entirely different invention from the one Edison had originally submitted. In his ruling of 31 July 1897, however, Commissioner Benjamin Butterworth threw out the petition on a technicality. Edison's patent for a motion-picture camera, No. 589,168, was issued a month later, on 31 August. Marvin later insisted that fraud was involved.[15]

With a broad patent, Edison's lawyers prepared to bring suit against the inventor's commercial rivals on both the new patent, No. 589,168, and kinetoscope patent No. 493,426, granted 14 March 1893. On 7 December 1897 Edison filed two suits against Charles H. Webster and Edmund Kuhn individually and as members of the International Film Company. On that same day, he also brought suit against Maguire & Baucus Limited, the principal selling agent for International and Lumière films and the bioscope projector. The following month he sued Sigmund Lubin in the Eastern District of Pennsylvania and Edward H. Amet in the Northern District of Illinois. The International Film Company hesitated, uncertain whether it should fight the case or retire from the field. In February, after suffering a serious fire, Webster and Kuhn decided not to contest the suit and agreed to close their film plant. Deterred by the enormous expense involved in litigation, they chose "to rest on their oars (with two years' handsome profit) and let the larger fish foot the bill of litigation." Maguire & Baucus also declined to contest the suits and arranged with Edison to sell Lumière films under special license. They stopped selling the Urban bioscope in the United States and concentrated most of their energies on business opportunities in England. Lubin and Amet, however, contested the suits. Because Edison lawyers were not eager to pursue cases outside the New York area, these two cases were not brought to a hearing.[16]

Edison brought further actions in the Southern District of New York instead. The Eden Musee and its president, Richard Hollaman, producer of THE PASSION PLAY OF OBERAMMERGAU, were served with a warrant on 8 February; the makers of the rival HORITZ PASSION PLAY were sued a short time later. Rather than contest the suit, Richard Hollaman became an Edison licensee, and prints of THE PASSION PLAY OF OBERAMMERGAU were sold through the newly licensed F. Z. Maguire and Company. When Klaw & Erlanger hesitated in settling the Edison suit, the inventor announced his intention to prosecute anyone showing an "unauthorized version" of the passion play and backed it up by suing Augustin C. Daly, whose New York theater was showing the Horitz films. The latter case was quickly discontinued after Klaw, Erlanger, and Freeman came to a licensing agreement with Edison. This involved the outright sale of film prints, with Edison receiving a 7¢-per-foot royalty or $168 per complete 2,400-foot set for the first four sets. For subsequent sets the Edison Company would receive 16¢ per foot or $384 per set, though it was also responsible for manufacturing the films.[17] Klaw & Erlanger thus encountered heavy additional expenses on top of the royalties already owed the Horitz performers.

Outright sales, moreover, undermined a policy of retaining exclusive exhibition rights.

Edison also sued Walter S. Isaacs, manufacturer of the Urban bioscope as well as his own cinematograph projector. Like others, Isaacs was unwilling to challenge the famous inventor. When the Veriscope Company was sued and proved ready to defend its interests, Edison lawyers found it a difficult target, since its films of the Corbett–Fitzsimmons fight were made prior to the issuance of Edison's patent.[18]

After intimidating most New York–based 35-mm film producers and equipment manufacturers, Edison sued the American Mutoscope Company and Benjamin F. Keith on 13 May 1898.[19] Biograph was not only a large, profitable concern but one that used its own unique system of motion-picture technology, and the company undertook a spirited defense: even a preliminary ruling would be more than three years away. Nonetheless, Edison had greatly strengthened his company's commercial position. Some competitors had gone out of business, while others were operating under an Edison license.

Legal complexities also occurred with projection patents. Once Patent Interference No. 18,032, *Jenkins v. Jenkins and Armat*, had been dismissed on 24 February 1897, and their phantoscope patent, No. 586,953, had been granted on 20 July 1897, Armat and T. Cushing Daniel brought suit against the American Mutoscope Company and Benjamin Keith. Yet this case was discontinued, as Herman Casler—with the backing of the American Mutoscope Company—challenged the patent's validity in two other patent-interference cases. In *Casler v. Armat*, Patent Interference No. 18,460, Casler successfully argued that certain fundamental aspects of the Jenkins-Armat patents had been anticipated by Étienne-Jules Marey, who had intended to use his camera as a projector. Projection of motion-picture film was not something Jenkins and Armat could claim to have invented *per se*.[20] Patent Interference No. 18,461, *Edward H. Amet, Woodville Latham, and Herman Casler v. Thomas Armat*, was undertaken as Casler and Latham unsuccessfully—and from different perspectives—tried to have the Jenkins-Armat patent thrown out. Latham, of course, wanted his claim for prior projection to be accepted, while Casler continued to seek rulings that would limit the patent's commercial impact and value. Biograph was confident of its ability to prosper in an American market where patents did not play an important role. In contrast, Edison and Armat each wanted to use their respective patents to regain a dominant position in the industry. The courts would not rule on the merits of these cases until the beginning of the new century.

The Spanish-American War

As commercial warfare within the film industry was reaching new levels of intensity, the United States found itself involved in a real war. On 15 February 1898, the day Edison brought suit against Klaw & Erlanger, the USS *Maine* blew up in Havana Harbor. Although the cause of the explosion was never definitively established, commentators suggested that a Spanish mine or torpedo was responsible. Anti-Spanish, pro-Cuban sentiment in the United States was strong, and many Americans wanted their country to assert its power and even begin to build an overseas empire. However, proponents of American imperialism were matched by strong isolationist supporters. Newspaper magnate William Randolph Hearst wanted war and filled his newspapers with lurid accounts of Spanish atrocities, but President William Mc-Kinley was initially reluctant to start such a conflict.

The Cuban crisis and the Spanish-American War revived the film industry after a brief period of commercial difficulty. Even Biograph had been struggling; although its year-long run continued in Keith's Boston house, Keith's Philadelphia and New York theaters terminated their biograph engagements early in 1898. This was an ominous sign, although many leading vaudeville theaters still employed the service. In Chicago, where films had not been shown—or at least advertised—for eight weeks during the fall and early winter of 1897–1898, Hopkins' Theater added the Biograph service beginning Monday, 7 February. J. Austin Fynes, former manager of Keith's Union Square Theater and recently made head of the rival Proctor organization, hired a biograph for the Pleasure Palace on East Fifty-eighth Street, where it opened on 14 February. From these theaters came the patriotic wave that tossed Biograph to new heights.

Although Hearst and other newspaper editors sought to fan American outrage over the *Maine*, reading their inflamed rhetoric remained a private act. It was in the theater that their readers' emotions found public expression. According to the *New York Tribune:*

> There is no other place where it is so easy to get the people of New York together as in a theatre. . . . So it is naturally to the theatres that one turns to find public sentiment expressed. As far as there is any record it was Daly's Theatre that began it. About the second night after the Maine was sunk the orchestra at Daly's played "The Star Spangled Banner" and "Yankee Doodle" between the acts and the audience showed its approval of the tunes in no uncertain manner.
>
> The next night half the theatres in town were doing things of the same sort or were announcing what they were going to do as soon as they could make the necessary elaborate preparations. And they all did it. The determination seems to have been to stir the audience with the sight of a flag or the sound of a tune at every possible or impossible opportunity (25 February 1898, p. 3).

If an American flag touched off a demonstration, imagine the effect of a lifelike image of the *Maine* in all its glory. Biograph did not have such an image, but it was easily created. A few months earlier, Biograph had fortuitously filmed BATTLESHIPS "IOWA" AND "MASSACHUSETTS;" now the film was relabeled BATTLESHIPS "MAINE" AND "IOWA" (No. 367), put into the theaters, and prominently advertised. It became an instant hit. In Chicago, the *New York World* reported, "there was fifteen minutes of terrific shouting . . . when the battleships Maine and Iowa were shown in the biograph manoeuvering off Fortress Monroe. The audience arose, cheered and cheered again, and the climax was reached when a picture of Uncle Sam under the flag was thrown on the canvas." These pictures were quickly augmented by other "patriotic subjects"; scenes of Grant Day and of American cavalry charging the camera were "cheered to the echo."[21]

Looking for new subjects to enrich its exhibitions, Biograph filmed SPANISH BAT-TLESHIP "VIZCAYA" (No. 443) on 28 February, while the vessel was paying a visit to New York. Unable to film Captain Charles Sigsbee, commander of the *Maine*, or

No. 367

Title *Battleships "Maine" and "Iowa".*

Length *317 ft.*

Code Word *Titansame.*

No. 368

Title *Warships "Marblehead" and "Miantonomah".*

Length *156 ft.*

Code Word *Titerista.*

No. 443
Title *Spanish Battleship*
"*Viscaya*".
Length *152 ft.*
Code Word *Tortillage.*

No. 441
Title *Spanish Battleship*
"*Viscaya*".
Length *141 ft.*
Code Word *Tortolette.*

Consul General Fitzhugh Lee, who was responsible for investigating its sinking, Biograph filmed them "in counterpart." First exhibited during the second week in March, even this "counterfeit presentment" was deemed "highly instructive" by the press.[22]

The political demonstrations that had greeted scenes of presidential candidate McKinley were being revived, but images of McKinley, the reluctant warrior, now received as many boos as cheers. An extensive report of one exhibition at Proctor's Pleasure Palace suggests how the skillful manipulation of images and text (via the magic lantern) could affect the audience:

> Loud applause followed the production on canvas of life-like pictures of the Thirteenth Regiment on parade, a cavalry charge and sailors marching in review before Grant's Tomb.
>
> The Spanish ship Vizcaya was exhibited crossing the bar. But no demonstration was made until a huge illuminated sign was shown bearing this inscription:
> "No hidden mines here."
> This brought men and women to their feet, and for several minutes the place was in a tumble.
>
> But the most remarkable demonstration was to come near the close of the performance. The pictures of Capt. Sigsbee and Consul General Lee had been loudly cheered. Next came an excellent likeness of President McKinley. For a moment there was silence, followed by some hand clapping and an equal amount of jeers and hisses.
>
> The operator of the biograph was equal to the emergency, and quickly flashed on the canvas the Stars and Stripes. Then the good humor of the crowd was restored, and as the curtain went down they shrieked their approval (*New York World*, 8 March 1898, p. 4).

The situation varied from city to city. In Rochester, where the biograph opened in late March, a film of the *Vizcaya* had to be eliminated from the program. According to the *Rochester Post Express*, "At first the audience hissed and with every performance there were indications of an approaching storm. Finally the gallery gods showed their disapproval with potatoes and other garden truck, and as the management did not care to start a grocery, the obnoxious picture has been permanently removed." In Boston, where war fever and patriotic display were less pronounced, the biograph was given little prominence; likewise, the biograph and its war views were not brought back to Keith's Philadelphia theater until April.[23]

Biograph and Edison Cameramen Travel to Cuba

Harry Marvin, Wallace McCutcheon, and other Biograph executives quickly recognized the production opportunities offered by the Cuban crisis. By early 1898, they had three camera units in almost constant operation: one in Boston, another in New York, and a third in New Orleans filming THE MARDI GRAS CARNIVAL (No. 452) and other scenes. Shortly after the *Maine* was sunk, cameramen G. W. Bitzer and Arthur Marvin (Harry Marvin's brother) headed south to Cuba. Despite the high cost of the trip (subsequently estimated at one thousand dollars), Biograph executives were

Biograph man Arthur Marvin filming from aboard Hearst's news yacht, Anita.

determined to acquire pictures of the sunken *Maine* and events occurring on Cuban soil.[24] Once in Tampa, the photographers were forced to wait, impatiently filling their time by shooting FIGHTING ROOSTERS IN FLORIDA (No. 459) and other scenes. Finally, they reached Havana and filmed DIVERS AT WORK ON THE WRECK OF THE "MAINE" (No. 476), and THE WRECK OF THE "MAINE" (No. 477) from a circling tugboat. Landing in Cuba, the crew took THE CHRISTIAN HERALD'S RELIEF STATION, HAVANA (No. 475), A RUN OF THE HAVANA FIRE DEPARTMENT (No. 479), and CUBAN RECONCENTRADOS (No. 484). In the meantime another camera crew headed to the Washington, D.C.–Virginia area and filmed LAUNCHING THE BATTLESHIP "KENTUCKY" (No. 483) at Newport News, Virginia, BAREBACK RIDING, SIXTH U.S.

No. 476
Title *Divers at Work on the Wreck of the "Maine."*
Length 169 ft.
Code Word *Tracotiamo.*

No. 477
Title *The Wreck of the "Maine."*
Length 88 ft.
Code Word *Tradecaba.*

CAVALRY (No. 486) at Fort Myers, Virginia, and THEODORE ROOSEVELT (No. 490), which showed the assistant secretary of the navy outside the White House. In the words of the *New York Clipper*, these films, which reached American screens during the last week of March as peace and war hung in the balance, guaranteed that "the patriotic feelings of the audience invariably get plenty of fresh and sterling material for frequent outbursts." Advertisements read, "Peace at Any Price! Do We Want It? Read the Answer in the Wonderful Biograph." It was excellent business. With the biograph in demand, the company charged several hundred dollars for a week-long exhibition.[25]

In mid May, the American Mutoscope Company listed seventeen American cities where the biograph was enjoying extensive runs.[26] Rival managers competed for its services. Fynes's acquisition of the biograph for Proctor's vaudeville circuit distressed and embarrassed the Keith organization and may well have encouraged the circuit's reorganization. While each local manager had formerly been responsible for hiring acts in his own theater, all acts were now booked under the direct supervision of E. F. Albee.[27] Albee used his leverage to reacquire the biograph for Keith's Union Square Theater—taking it away from Proctor's—beginning 25 April, a few days after Spain declared war on the United States. In large cities several theater managers wanted the Biograph service, but the company's contracts were customarily made on an exclusive basis for a given locality. Satisfying the demand for war films thus opened up opportunities for exhibitors using 35-mm films.

The sinking of the battleship *Maine* occurred at a time when the 35-mm portion of the film industry was in disarray. The International Film Company photographed a sister ship of the *Maine* and passed it off as an authentic film of the *Maine* taken in Havana Harbor before the disaster, but the company itself was going out of business.[28] At Edison, James White, manager of the kinetograph department, was on his way to the Far East, leaving behind William Heise, who was incapable of responding to the demands and opportunities created by the war. In addition, Edison's general manager, William Gilmore, had many responsibilities and little expertise when it came to production. Since Edison's new licensees—particularly sales agents Maguire & Baucus and the Eden Musee—needed films pertinent to the Cuban crisis if they were to compete successfully with Biograph, they were forced to fill in for the absent White. F. Z. Maguire arranged for William Paley, the Eden Musee's cinematographer, to become an Edison licensee and cover the Cuban crisis. The Edison Manufacturing Company agreed to provide Paley with negative stock and to pay him fifteen dollars for every 50-foot negative they accepted, plus a royalty of thirty cents for each print that was sold (with double and triple the amounts for 100-foot and 150-foot subjects).[29] Maguire also arranged for the *New York Journal* to provide Paley with transportation to Cuba, a position on one of its news yachts, and a collaborator—reporter Karl C. Decker. The Hearst organization, recognizing the propaganda value of these films, happily cooperated with Edison as well as Biograph.

Paley arrived in Key West in time to film BURIAL OF THE "MAINE" VICTIMS on 27 March. This 150-foot subject showed a procession of nine hearses, each draped with an American flag. Other films taken at that locale included WAR CORRESPONDENTS, a staged scene in which correspondents race to the cable office to telegraph news to their newspapers, and U.S. MONITOR "TERROR," showing one of the warships coaling at the nearby wharf. Putting out to sea on a *Journal* yacht, Paley was able to photograph CRUISER "DETROIT," U.S. BATTLESHIP "IOWA," and other scenes of

Edison's BURIAL OF THE "MAINE" VICTIMS.

warships in the Dry Tortugas, the open water west of Key West. Although Paley's camera lacked a panning mechanism, Hearst's boat was a convenient moving platform; from it the cameraman also took sweeping traveling shots for WRECK OF THE BATTLESHIP "MAINE" and "MORRO CASTLE," HAVANA HARBOR. The films were shown for the first time at the Eden Musee on 18 April, copyrighted by Edison the next week, and quickly offered for sale by Maguire.

In mid April, as war became increasingly likely, Biograph and Edison cameramen returned to Florida and Cuba. While Biograph photographed a captured Spanish ship (No. 523, CAPTURE OF THE "PANAMA") in the opening days of the war, most of its films were taken at military camps where soldiers trained and awaited orders. In ROOSEVELT ROUGH RIDERS (No. 642), shot at Tampa Bay, the horse soldiers of Theodore Roosevelt's popular military unit were filmed in two takes from a single camera position. First they charged the camera, and then they galloped across the frame, offering a side view; the troops were shown from two perspectives but without any attempt to construct a spatially or temporally continuous world. Among Biograph's other noteworthy titles were ADMIRAL CERVERA AND SPANISH OFFICERS LEAVING "ST. LOUIS" (No. 703), made of war prisoners at Annapolis, Maryland, on 16 July, and THE WRECK OF THE "VIZCAYA" (No. 707), shot off the coast of Santiago on 3 July:[30] both suggest Biograph's willingness to expend considerable resources for an attention-grabbing picture. In early September, once the war had ended, its cameramen made additional films at Camp Wikoff on Montauk Point, Long Island (PRESIDENT MCKINLEY'S INSPECTION OF CAMP WIKOFF, No. 783), and Camp Meade, Pennsylvania (22ND REGIMENT, KANSAS VOLUNTEERS, No. 785). Later that month, they staged and filmed numerous battle scenes at Camp Meade, including THE LAST STAND (No. 799), IN THE TRENCHES (No. 802), and DEFENSE OF THE

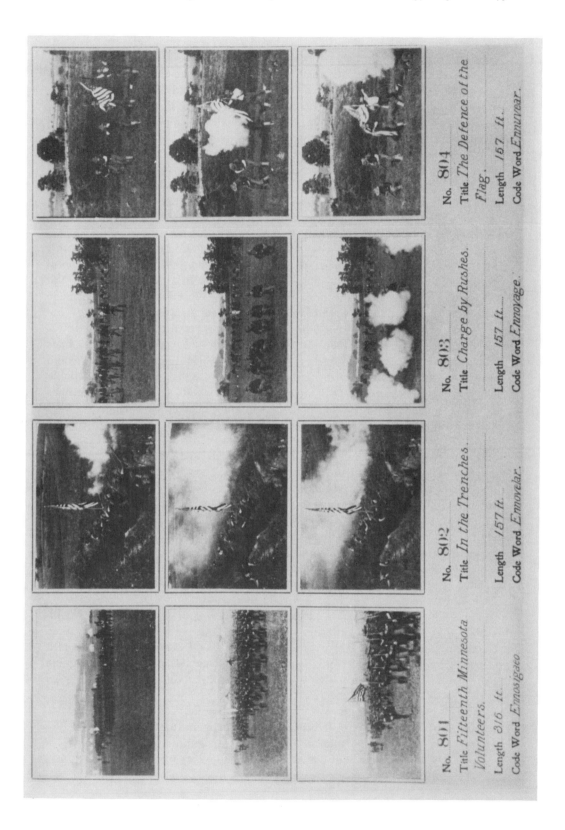

No. 804
Title *The Defence of the Flag.*
Length *157 ft.*
Code Word *Ennovrear.*

No. 803
Title *Charge by Rushes.*
Length *157 ft.*
Code Word *Ennovyage.*

No. 802
Title *In the Trenches.*
Length *157 ft.*
Code Word *Ennovelar.*

No. 801
Title *Fifteenth Minnesota Volunteers.*
Length *316 ft.*
Code Word *Ennosigaeo*

FLAG (No. 804), but long after Lubin had produced re-enactment films of this kind.

Despite its deep commitment to war-related actualities, Biograph continued to produce a wide range of comedies and acted films. Of the one hundred productions between Nos. 600 and 699 (roughly from early June to early July 1898), seventy-seven were photographed in the studio, and seventy-nine could be called acted, fiction films. Although this sampling overrepresents Biograph's output of fiction material, it was not a fluke. Of the ninety-seven productions listed from Nos. 700 to 799, forty were fictional in nature. In many cases, the rooftop stage was dressed as either an army camp or the deck of a ship. Thus, in UNCLE RUBE'S VISIT TO A MAN O' WAR (No. 588), sailors play a practical joke: they lead a farmer to a soap-covered deck area where he loses his balance and falls. In HE WANTED TOO MUCH FOR HIS PIES (No. 584), a farmer visits an army camp and, after demanding high prices for his pies, has them pushed in his face.

Other studio productions, such as TRYING TO SKIN THE CAT (No. 634) and DOING HER BIG BROTHER'S TRICKS ON THE BAR (No. 635), offered the customary scenes of women doing acrobatics that reveal their underclothing. In A WINDY CORNER (No. 643), a girl crosses a grate and her dress blows up. Within a framework of male voyeurism established by the filmmakers, women spectators were allowed to revel in the pleasures of exhibitionism via their screen counterparts. Although the intent was to elicit a certain "naughty" pleasure from both men and women, other reactions from spectators were possible, either separately or in combination. Women could share in the voyeuristic pleasure, partaking of the male gaze in a way that polite society found disconcerting. Of course, members of both sexes were sometimes shocked by the suggestive nature of the images and peephole viewing.

Short Biograph comedies often presented sexuality as a source of social disruption and personal embarrassment. In HOW THE BALLET GIRL WAS SMUGGLED INTO CAMP (No. 592), military discipline is breached as two soldiers sneak a woman into camp in a large barrel, while in A TIME AND A PLACE FOR EVERYTHING (No. 702), a man kisses a maid and she drops the dishes as a result. Authority is frequently challenged, outwitted, or lampooned. In HOW THE ATHLETIC LOVER OUTWITTED THE OLD MAN (No. 608, also listed as THE ATHLETIC LOVER), the father spies on his daughter's "lovemaking" by climbing onto a chair and looking through the transom. Preparing to shoot her lover with a rifle, he makes some noise that alerts the couple. When the young man races out the door to see the source of the sound, he knocks the father to the ground. This comic defeat of the oedipal father lends itself to a psychoanalytic reading.

Figures who represent the law often use this power to their own ends. In MILITARY DISCIPLINE (No. 593), a sentry is wooing an attractive woman when his superior officer appears, orders the private back to work, and walks away with the girl. Women without men are frequently ridiculed, as can be seen in this Biograph description of THE OLD MAID AND THE BURGLAR (No. 700):

> This old maid has been looking under her bed for years for a man. At last she finds one, as our picture shows, who happens to be a burglar; but that makes no difference to the old maid, and she promptly falls on his neck and gives him an effusive welcome, much to his surprise and disgust (*Picture Catalogue*, November 1902, p. 17).

No. 608

Title *How the Athletic Lover Outwitted the Old Man.*

Length *155 ft.*

Code Word *Venulus.*

No. 609

Title *A Romp in Camp.*

Length *156 ft.*

Code Word *Venusium.*

The burglar pays for his transgressions by receiving the undesired attentions of a desperate old maid. Some comedies, such as How Bridget Served the Salad Undressed (No. 539, copyrighted as No Salad Dressing Wanted), were made at the expense of ethnic groups, in this case the "thick-headed" Irish. Bridget is asked to serve the salad "undressed," so she takes off her clothes before entering the dining room. (As Patrick Loughney has shown, this joke had been presented earlier as a comic photograph.[31])

The Edison Company's percentage of acted, fiction films was much lower than Biograph's. Of the fifty-nine subjects Edison copyrighted in June, July, and August 1898, only five could be comfortably placed in this category, and two of these had been previously copyrighted in May. Fake Beggar, shot on the street, shows a legless, blind beggar who is given alms by passersby. When a coin misses his cup, the beggar picks it up, exposing his charade to a nearby policeman. To escape, he stands up and runs away. Cuban Ambush and Shooting Captured Insurgents were staged battle scenes probably shot in New Jersey.

The Edison films in greatest demand were made by William Paley, who returned to Florida just before the declaration of war. Because he was transported and housed by the *New York Journal*, the trip was expected to cost Edison and Maguire & Baucus almost nothing. In Tampa, Paley filmed American troops preparing for the invasion of Cuba (U.S. Cavalry Supplies Unloading at Tampa, Florida; Roosevelt's Rough Riders Embarking for Santiago; etc.). Many of these scenes suffered from poor frame registration on Paley's Gaumont camera (see, for example, Colored Troops Disembarking). Paley accompanied reporters covering the Cuba invasion (Mules Swimming Ashore at Daiquiri) and filmed various scenes behind American lines (Troops Making Military Road in Front of Santiago). Finally, the intrepid cameraman found a wagon to take his bulky camera from Siboney on the coast to El Caney, where General William Shafter's headquarters were located. The cart broke down en route, however, and Paley spent a rainy night in the open with his camera. While the cart was fixed the next morning, his camera no longer worked, and Paley soon came down with a fever. He returned to Siboney with the help of Charles H. Hand, a correspondent for the *London Daily Mail*, and reached New York seriously ill. Bitzer of Biograph likewise suffered serious illness from his Cuba sojourn and was unable to work for several months thereafter.[32]

Even before Paley's films were marketed in April, the Cuban crisis enabled many 35-mm exhibitors to find new venues or to return to old ones. Lubin's cineograph was reengaged as the headline attraction at Bradenburgh's museum in late March with "an Extensive Series of Genuine and Realistic Views of Scenes and Incidents Relating to the *Maine*." In Jersey City, New Jersey, a Lumière cinematographe that featured war films opened in a storefront at the beginning of April and drew large crowds. New York City theaters also added a group of films to their programs. At Huber's Museum, Minnie Schult sang patriotic tunes illustrated with moving pictures, including "The Battleship *Maine* Song." By May, motion pictures were being shown in at least seven New York theaters—an all-time high. In most cases, these exhibition services were labeled "the wargraph" or "warscope," generic titles that often make identification of the specific showman extremely difficult.[33]

New York exhibitors enjoyed unique advantages during the war. In no other city did chauvinistic feelings produce a comparable demand for films. In Boston, for example, only two or three theaters had motion pictures on their bill. Since each

Eberhard Schneider's business card.

New York theater manager generally demanded an exclusive arrangement with the exhibition service that he hired, a strong need existed for additional showmen. Eberhard Schneider, the German immigrant who had shown films at the Eden Musee in the early part of 1897 (until the fire noted in chapter 6), prospered in part because of his development of a reframing device. Since the beginning of projection, exhibitors had been plagued by films jumping out of the projector sprockets so that the frame line ran across the middle of the screen. The operator then had to stop his machine and rethread the film before the screening could resume. With the technological improvement of a reframing device, an operator could make a quick adjustment while continuing his projection. Any exhibitor who could assure theater managers that their programs would avoid these embarrassing interruptions had a clear advantage. Schneider's service thus filled the void at Proctor's Pleasure Palace when the biograph returned to Keith's. Schneider also found a number of opportunities outside New York City.[34]

Blackton and Smith Move into Production, Form American Vitagraph, and Become Edison Licensees

J. Stuart Blackton and Albert E. Smith owed much to the Spanish-American War. Seeking out new ways to make a living, the partners started the Commercial Advertising Bureau and rented a small office at 140 Nassau Street, New York City, in late December 1897. By spring they owned two outdoor "branches" where advertising slides and films were being projected onto canvas. Shortly after selling one branch for $250 in mid April, they bought a group of Paley war films for $87 and broke into vaudeville exhibition at the Central Opera House at Sixty-seventh Street and Third Avenue, in New York City. For this new enterprise, which they called American

Vitagraph, the partners received $47.50 a week for two weeks. That month Blackton and Smith made two important steps that brought them to the forefront as an exhibition service: first, they modified their projectors by adding a reframing device, thus improving the quality of their exhibitions; they also purchased another Edison projecting kinetoscope and turned it into a camera.[35] Entries in the Commercial Advertising Bureau's account books for 19 May indicate that the firm bought two naval books, gunpowder, and sensitized film. These were undoubtedly for BATTLE OF MANILA BAY, a miniaturized reenactment of Dewey's great naval victory, which had occurred two weeks earlier. This and other productions helped them to break into first-class vaudeville at Proctor's. After Blackton performed his chalk act at Proctor's New York vaudeville houses for two weeks in June, manager J. Austin Fynes hired the vitagraph service for his Twenty-third Street house.

Blackton and Smith soon encountered Thomas Edison's legal arm in a situation that was precipitated by their desperate shortage of cash. Unwilling to sell their own films—their exclusive control of these films made vitagraph exhibitions attractive to theatrical managers—they chose to generate additional income by selling duplicates of Paley's copyrighted films for seven dollars each. Among the visitors to Blackton and Smith's Nassau Street office on 2 June were Eugene Elmore, who was in charge of film exhibitions at the Eden Musee; Edwin S. Porter, now Elmore's assistant; and a salesman for Maguire & Baucus. They acquired the necessary evidence, and in mid July Edison filed three suits, two for patent infringement and one for copyright violation.[36] Blackton and Smith panicked. The two young men had no money to fight the cases; moreover, they were challenged by one of America's great popular heroes and felt certain to lose. The next day, both men visited Edison's general manager, William Gilmore, and worked out a deal. If they did not contest the lawsuits, they would be allowed to work as Edison licensees, to take films for their own exhibitions, and to sell prints of their original subjects through the Edison Manufacturing Company under an arrangement similar to William Paley's. Blackton and Smith's talents as performers were valuable assets that helped them win such an agreement, since White, Heise, and Paley had little experience in making the acted films that were an important component of Biograph's output. The young partners were also willing to turn over their reframing device, allowing it to be incorporated into Edison's projecting kinetoscope. The result of the Edison-Vitagraph confrontation was a new working relationship that benefited all concerned, at least for the short term.

Exhibitor William Rock noted Blackton and Smith's rapid settlement of the lawsuits and made some rapid calculations. Rock, one of the few vitascope states rights owners still in the film business, had moved his base of operations to New York City, where he was running a small film exchange. The showman remained on friendly terms with Thomas Armat, who authorized him to sue "Proctor, of Proctor's Theatre, and the party or parties who have the animated picture apparatus at said theatre, which said apparatus is an infringement upon my U.S. patent No. 578,185, if they refuse to pay a royalty."[37] Rock threatened Proctor, Blackton, and Smith with a lawsuit. Perhaps he was hoping to supplant Vitagraph at Proctor's Theater or to receive a percentage of Armat's royalty. From Proctor's perspective, the Vitagraph service, with its exclusive subjects and reframing device, was not easily discarded. Instead of litigation, the parties formed a new alliance, with Rock joining American Vitagraph as a third partner—without in any way compromising his own independent motion picture business. As part of this peace agreement, Vitagraph may have received a contract to exhibit films at Proctor's Pleasure Palace, beginning on Labor Day, 5 September. Profits had to be divided another way, but the two young men had gained an older, more experienced partner, whom they came to call "Pop."

Selig, Lubin, and Others

Chicago was another center of war-related motion-picture activity. A magniscope opened at the Clark Street Museum with war scenes on 2 May and remained into the fall. As was the case with most exhibition services, the machine became known as the "wargraph." Whether it was run by George Spoor is not known. A cinematograph that showed films at the Schiller Theater for one week in mid May, however, was apparently owned by William Selig. The demand for Spanish-American War films had encouraged Selig to move into production, and he shot a series of pictures depicting life at Camp Tanner in Springfield, Illinois. According to the *Chicago Inter-Ocean,* the "Cinematographe Views," including SOLDIERS AT PLAY, WASH DAY IN CAMP, and FIRST REGIMENT MARCHING, were "a feature which caught the crowds . . . and were cheered to the echo."[38]

Edward Amet also continued to make films for sale during the war. Although he took scenes of military camp life, his most successful and elaborate productions featured naval battles done with miniatures. Advertisements strongly implied that

William Selig's SOLDIERS AT PLAY.

these were photographed accounts of actual battles. Thus, according to a description of BOMBARDMENT OF MATANZAS:

> The new TELESCOPIC LENS is a triumph of modern photography. It is possible to obtain accurate pictures at very long range. This is a most marvelous picture; in the distance can be seen the mountains and shore line where are located the Spanish batteries. The flag ship New York and monitor Puritan are in full action pouring tons of iron and steel at the masked batteries on the shore. Volumes of smoke burst from the monster guns, while shot and shell fall thick and fast. Some shells are seen to burst in the air, scattering their deadly missiles in all directions, while others explode in the sea, throwing volumes of water in the air. A final shot from one of the thirteen inch guns of the Puritan lands exactly in the centre of the main battery, completely blowing it out of existence. 600 feet of this engagement was taken and it has been cut down to 100 feet, using only the best and most interesting parts. Price of this film only $30 (*Clipper*, 2 July 1898, p. 302).

Flickering and other flaws in the 35-mm projection system were still severe enough to help obscure at least some of the fake qualities.[39] Other films of this type included FLAGSHIP "NEW YORK" UNDER WAY, FIRING BROADSIDE AT CABANAS, DYNAMITE CRUISER "VESUVIUS," and SPANISH FLEET DESTROYED, which, according to one

Edward Amet's BOMBARDMENT OF MATANZAS.

Edward Amet's Freedom of Cuba.

advertisement, showed "Cruiser Vizcaya under heavy fire, beached and burned."[40] In addition to scenes of military activities, Amet filmed allegorical tableaux such as Freedom of Cuba.

Sigmund Lubin's business boomed as he produced and exhibited war-related subjects. At the outset of the war, he acquired a new, more mobile camera and used it to film The Big Monitor "Miantonomah" as the vessel left the Cramps Navy Yard in Philadelphia on 22 April. Other actualities were taken in the Philadelphia area over the next months and shown at the local Woodside Park. When President McKinley visited Camp Alger, near Falls Church, Virginia, a Lubin cameraman photographed 15,000 Soldiers Reviewed by the Pres. at Camp Alger, May 28 and related scenes. Other Lubin views were taken at Camp Chickamauga, in the northwest corner of Georgia. By May, he was offering to sell the films for fifteen cents per foot, considerably less than Edison's twenty-cent-a-foot sale price.[41]

Lubin, perhaps encouraged by the success of his fight films taken with "counterparts," soon began to stage battle scenes. In late June he was selling "Four New Battle Films of the Spanish American War Just Received from the Battlefield": Capture of a Spanish Fort near Santiago, Battle of Guantanamo, Hoisting the American Flag at Cavite, and Fighting near Santiago. "In these films can be seen the dead and wounded, and the dismantled cannon lying on the battlefield," Lubin ads announced. "The men are seen struggling for their lives, and the American flag proudly floats over them and can be plainly seen through the dense smoke."[42] Others such as Execution of the Spanish Spy and Spanish

INFANTRY ATTACKING AMERICAN SOLDIERS IN CAMP quickly followed. These were only 50 to 100 feet in length, but AFTER THE BATTLE, which showed priests and nuns administering the last rites, was 200 feet long and yielded over three minutes of screen time. In every case, however, an exhibitor could purchase the length that he desired in 50-foot segments; AFTER THE BATTLE was thus sold in 50-, 100-, and 200-foot lengths.

The war boom extended to other forms of projected images as well. Special sets of war-related lantern slides were placed on the market, and many illustrated lectures on the subject were offered. Lubin claimed to be selling over one thousand different slides on Cuba and the war plus twenty-two illustrated songs. With Biograph and other urban exhibition services offering a visual newspaper of up-to-date news films, several prominent vaudeville managers introduced the stereopticon to their vaudeville theaters on a similar basis. In early February 1898 Keith's Boston theater "introduced the idea of picturing current events by means of stereopticon slides, starting with scenes in and around Boston during the recent blizzard, pictures of men who were lost in the Merrimac street fire and reproductions of the *Herald*'s picture of Señor Lomé and the cartoon that accompanied it." A few weeks later, Keith's ads declared that Professor George H. Gies's stereopticon album was "commanding as much applause as any feature in the show." At Keith's Philadelphia theater, Professor Mapes's stereopticon showed local and patriotic views for many weeks prior to the biograph's return.[43] During the summer, Keith's large Sunday advertisements often devoted over half their space to listing the stereopticon views being shown. These and the biograph were clearly the featured acts on the program. The stereopticon thus acquired a permanent place at Keith's theaters.

Slides and films were commonly interwoven to produce unified programs, not just by a few travel lecturers but within the larger world of amusement. By November 1897, William B. Moore of the Stereopticon and Film Exchange in Chicago was offering a "Stereoptigraph, a Combination Moving Picture Machine and Stereopticon. Something radically new." While British dealers had offered this combination at an earlier date, Moore's machine was an American innovation that was promptly and widely imitated by almost every domestic manufacturer. As Lubin's advertisements for his "Cineograph and Stereopticon Combined" explained, exhibitors wanted to be capable of interspersing slides and film in the course of a single program. The general shortage of films as well as their expense encouraged Maguire & Baucus and many other sales agents to sell slides of Cuba and the *Maine* along with their films.[44]

The Role of the Exhibitors

All exhibitors, not just those creating evening-length single-subject programs, held important creative responsibilities. As already noted in chapter 6, the initial approach to organizing slides and films was largely based on principles of variety. The survival—and mastery—of this "noncontinuous program" is well exemplified by the presentations of Eberhard Schneider. In his opening show at Fox's Pleasure Palace in Reading, Pennsylvania, the sixteen-film program included six war-related subjects, from a cavalry charge and a view of the USS *Iowa* to a patriotic finale with "Old Glory," but these war images were always separated from one another by vastly different subjects from the repertoire of comedy, travel, dance, melodrama, boxing, and the like:

1. The Gardener
2. Cavalry Charge
3. The Alarm
4. Cubans Firing Dynamite Gun
5. Annabelle Butterfly Dance
6. USS Iowa
7. Panorama Scene from a Moving Train
8. Negroes Eating Water Melon
9. Barracks in Havana
10. A Warm Reception
11. Storm at Sea
12. Boxing Match
13. Fun in Camp
14. Old Glory[45]

This emphasized variety but also encouraged spectators mentally to reorder scenes so as to form other kinds of connections.

By 1898, however, programs that offered a much higher degree of continuity were very common. Biograph, for example, often presented complete sets of war views:

> Now that we are going to have war sure New Haven people wish to realize what it is all about and what we have to do it with. The great American biograph at Poli's Wonderland theater gives the answer in the most important series of views ever shown by the machine. There is the case of the Maine, shown both before and after her destruction, not a mere picture but a view on all sides, for the machine was carried around the vessel and wreck in each instance, giving the view such as one could obtain while in a boat sailing around the object biographed. This by no means ends the series of views. Another shows the divers at work on the wreck, and still more show the Spanish cruiser Vizcaya, under full headway, General Lee leaving his hotel, when he started to make that memorable farewell call to Blanco, a rattling cavalry charge, a review of marines, President McKinley, Captain Sigsbee, who now commands the Yale, Cuba's flag, "Old Glory," all the Yankee cruisers, gunboats and torpedo boats and the crew of the Maine (*New Haven Journal-Courier*, 21 April 1898, p. 3).

This series utilized some phenomenological continuity, for the first group of films were all taken on board ship, causing at least one susceptible spectator to fear seasickness. This and other Biograph programs also offered couplets of contrasting shots. Thus the *Maine* was shown before and after the explosion. For a later couplet entitled "Before and After Taking Uncle Sam's Medicine," the *Vizcaya* was first shown leaving New York Harbor and then wrecked off Santiago Bay. Lubin's programs, which used both slides and films, were usually grouped by subject matter and at least in some instances were accompanied by "A Brilliant Descriptive Lecture." New York's Eden Musee made a regular practice of focusing each program on a single subject. Some groupings merely consisted of scenes that were thematically related, as in late May, when Musee employees Eugene Elmore and Edwin Porter showed "scenes in and about Key West and Tampa, Florida." Other programs, however, had a clear narrative line. Once the war was over, the Musee showmen offered "a panorama of the whole war." According to their announcements: "The moving picture scenes begin with the arrival of the soldiers at Tampa, and it includes the various

Broadside for Vitagraph exhibition (1898).

important movements that followed up to the surrender of Santiago. Over twenty views are shown."[46]

Lyman H. Howe's program for the fall of 1898 also focused on the war. Although it was introduced by a selection of miscellaneous views, the veteran exhibitor followed these with several series of war films. The first began with THE 71ST REGIMENT OF NEW YORK, showing the unit on parade before it left for the front, and then shifted to Tampa with the arrival of troops and the subsequent embarkation for Cuba. It culminated with THRILLING WAR SCENE, depicting the defense of the American flag. After an interval of stereopticon slides, Howe shifted his focus from the army to the navy, retelling the history of the war, but this time exclusively with naval scenes.

Amet's traveling picture show featured war films (1898).

These began with BATTLESHIP "MAINE" before the vessel left New York harbor and included a faked picture showing the explosion of the *Maine,* a few scenes of American warships, and then Amet's battle reenactments, culminating with THE BOMBARDMENT OF MATANZAS.[47] Howe's audience experienced the joys of victory not once but twice in the course of the evening.

J. Stuart Blackton and Albert E. Smith also devoted one of two evening programs they gave while on vacation in Martha's Vineyard to an illustrated war lecture, "With Dewey at Manilla," for which Blackton posed as an eyewitness. Similar, though more authentic, eyewitness accounts were offered by travel lecturers such as Dwight Elmendorf. Many other exhibitors toured the country with their wargraphs and warscopes during the 1898–1899 theatrical season, each one offering his own distinctive selection and organization of motion-picture and stereopticon views.

In the wake of the novelty era, the American industry struggled to find its direction. The commencement of the motion-picture patent wars in late 1897 (which would not be fully resolved for another fifteen years) only added to the demoralization. But before this malaise reached crisis proportions, the Spanish-American War gave the industry new hope and new opportunities. Its more hardy, astute members filled the screen with emotionally charged images and enjoyed renewed prosperity. On an unprecedented and previously unimagined scale, they demonstrated cinema's value as a visual newspaper and as propaganda. Moving pictures had a tangible effect on the way Americans experienced a distant war. Much has been written about the yellow journalism and jingoistic press of Hearst and Pulitzer, but cinema complemented these efforts in a way that made them much more powerful and effective. Moving pictures projected a sense of national glory and outrage. It would be a gross exaggeration to say that the cinema launched a new era of American imperialism. But cinema had found a role beyond narrow amusement, and this sudden prominence coincided with a new era of overseas expansion and military intervention. Who can say what fantasies of power audiences experienced in those darkened halls, and how these emotions continued to resonate outside the theater?

The Model D mutoscope, called the "Clamshell" (January 1899), used for the popular mutoscope parlors. Actress Anna Held takes a peek.

9

The Film Industry Achieves
Modest Stability: 1898–1901

Biograph at Its Zenith

*I*n the years immediately following the Spanish-American War, the motion-picture industry gained a modicum of stability as exhibitors found permanent venues for their services, primarily in vaudeville houses. Since dependable outlets in turn required a larger and more regular supply of films, all aspects of the industry were affected. Biograph, in particular, prospered. By October 1898, Biograph's service was employed at twenty different locations. After the war, biographs remained at Keith's four vaudeville theaters on a permanent, year-round basis. Across the country, most other first-class vaudeville managers booked the biograph for at least one extended run per theatrical season, a policy that continued for the next two to three years. At Cook's Opera House in Rochester, New York, it played for twenty-one consecutive weeks during the 1898–1899 season, fifteen weeks over two runs during 1899–1900, and nine consecutive weeks during 1900–1901. The Orpheum theaters in San Francisco and Los Angeles shared a biograph during the same three seasons.[1]

Biograph's mutoscope business also thrived. The machines were initially placed in saloons, amusement resorts, and railway stations and on steamers, where each earned between 75¢ and $1.80 per day. At bicycle races, sportsmen's exhibits, and dog shows, groups of three to fourteen mutoscopes earned as much as $5 per machine per day. Early in 1898, Biograph began to build a network of mutoscope parlors. The first opened at 1193 Broadway, New York City, where seventeen machines brought in $236.05 over seven days—an average of $2.32 per day per machine. Three additional Manhattan parlors soon appeared, with machines averaging between 92¢ and $1.98 per day. A parlor with twenty mutoscopes was established in Boston. When another opened in Philadelphia early the following year, it was received as something "entirely new to this city" but quickly "established itself with the amusement-loving public, including the women and children." Biograph estimated that mutoscopes would gross approximately $1.00 a day or $300 a year. With expenses (maintenance, commissions, and rental of new subjects) and a 15 percent ($45) royalty, investors could expect to earn $135 per year per machine. Regional subcompanies like the

New England Mutoscope Company and the Ohio Mutoscope Company, formed in 1899, not only boosted the parent company's sales as they acquired mutoscopes and reels of cards but continued to pay substantial royalties.[2]

By mid 1899, when it had officially changed its name to the American Mutoscope & Biograph Company, Biograph was part of an international organization that included eight sister companies: the British Mutoscope and Biograph Company (for which Dickson remained chief producer and cameraman), the Biograph and Mutoscope Company for France, Ltd., and the Deutsche Mutoskop and Biograph Gesellschaft in Berlin, as well as companies in the Netherlands, Belgium, South Africa, Italy, and India.[3] The viability of these organizations varied, as did their actual contributions of films to the parent company. Biograph's "remarkable series of panoramic views of Venice," for example, were taken by W. K. L. Dickson, not by the Italian organization. In early September 1899, Dickson also went to Gibraltar, at the entrance to the Mediterranean, and took a series of views of Admiral Dewey and his fleet on their way to the United States.[4] These were shot for the American company and sent directly to the New York office, where they arrived prior to Dewey. As the war hero's return stirred the nation, ADMIRAL DEWEY RECEIVING HIS MAIL (No. 1234), OFFICERS OF THE "OLYMPIA" (No. 1238) and "SAGASTA," ADMIRAL DEWEY'S PET PIG (No. 1240) were shown to enthusiastic audiences. Assuring an international selection of films and an added market for the American product, Biograph's network of sister companies reached its apex at about this time.

The American Mutoscope Company's production levels remained high:

1 June 1898–31 May 1899	486 views
1 June 1899–31 May 1900	437 views
1 June 1900–31 May 1901	412 views

By mid April 1899, when Biograph records become more detailed, the company had four main cameramen: Frederick S. Armitage, "Billy" Bitzer, Arthur Marvin, and C. Fred Ackerman. In addition, head producer Wallace McCutcheon occasionally acted as cameraman, primarily for studio productions. (Eugène Lauste also made a series of short films in New Haven in May 1899.) These cinematographers periodically shifted assignments, either as individuals rose and fell in the esteem of executives or to ensure that no one was constantly on the road. F. S. Armitage shot the vast majority of studio films from April 1899 to May 1900, when Arthur Marvin took over and Armitage was sent out on location. After a few months, Armitage returned and they shared the duties. Despite what he suggests in his memoirs, Bitzer would not photograph a significant number of studio or acted films until 1903.

Biograph was the only American company to send a cameraman to the Philippines, where the U.S. military was fighting a dirty guerrilla war against the native independence movement. There, from November 1899 until early March 1900, C. Fred Ackerman took scenes of America's newest territorial acquisition and U.S. troops fighting to secure it: CO. "L" THIRTY-THIRD INFANTRY GOING TO FIRING LINE (No. 1350), REPELLING THE ENEMY (No. 1383), and MAKING MANILA ROPE (No. 1384). This ambitious undertaking was matched by Biograph's English sister company, which sent W. K. L. Dickson to South Africa to film the Boer War. Ackerman returned to the Far East in September 1900 and shot films in China during the Boxer Rebellion (SIXTH CAVALRY ASSAULTING SOUTH GATE OF PEKIN, No. 1763; IN THE FORBIDDEN CITY, No. 1766). Home from his Far East assignment, Ackerman assumed the role of projectionist and teamed up with war correspondent Thomas F. Millard. Together they toured the United States presenting the illustrated lecture "War in China" which included Ackerman's own lantern slides as well as his biograph films. In Boston their lecture was "classed among the most interesting of the season's entertainments," and some of the pictures were said to be "thrilling enough to arouse the patriotism of the most apathetic soul."[5] Biograph's propagandistic stance continued.

As Ackerman's activities suggest, the line between photographer and projector operator was a thin one at Biograph. Bitzer had started out as a projectionist (and Dickson's camera assistant) before becoming a cinematographer. F. A. Dobson, who ran a biograph at the Lyceum Theater in Memphis, Tennessee, for eight weeks late in 1898, would work as a Biograph cameraman from June 1904 to June 1907. Cameramen often had more than one job. Bitzer not only made films but was a trouble-shooter, responsible for keeping projectors in running order.[6] Avoiding narrow specialization, many of Biograph's personnel thus familiarized themselves with different phases of cinema practice.

Biograph organized production along different lines depending on the choice of subject matter and the circumstances under which it was to be filmed. What has been termed the cameraman system was frequently used for shooting actualities.[7] Here a cameraman, usually part of a team, was responsible for production. Bitzer, for example, headed a three-man unit while taking local views in Boston. As the equipment became easier to handle, a cinematographer (like Ackerman) may have occasionally functioned on his own. Yet cameramen frequently worked closely with Wallace McCutcheon, who, as general manager, assumed the role of producer. He arranged the filming of actualities even when he was not directly responsible for the camera. As the *New York Clipper* remarked more than once, "Wallace McCutcheon keeps that machine in the front rank of animated picture machines." When the New York Naval Parade steamed up the Hudson on 20 August 1898, "McCutcheon was on hand with a tug and secured a striking reproduction of the seven battle scarred victors in parade, and the biograph added another link to its chain of success."[8] Important news events, such as New York's Dewey celebration in late September 1899 and the America's Cup races that immediately followed, involved complex logistics and extensive filming with multiple cameras. The results justified the expense: these films became the featured act at Keith's and other theaters.

In its dual role as production entity and exhibition service, Biograph was in a unique position to meet the demands of amusement managers by making films of particular interest to a specific theater's patrons. Biograph's methods for delivering these scenes took two principal forms. In some instances, the cameraman would visit a gathering of fraternal organizations or military units and selectively photograph groups hailing from cities where Biograph was showing or would soon be showing its films. During the Spanish-American War, for example, cameramen filmed pertinent regiments at various army camps. After the war, a Biograph cameraman shot at least a dozen views of the Knights Templar parade in Pittsburgh on 11 October 1898, including ST. BERNARD COMMANDERY, CHICAGO (No. 813), BOSTON COMMANDERY

Billy Bitzer and other Biograph personnel outfitted to take local views in the Boston area (summer 1899). According to a clipping accompanying the photograph, "The total weight of the outfit is over 1700 pounds and it comprises a large camera and electric motor, weighing about 265 pounds, five storage batteries weighing 200 pounds each, and a large trunk containing films, lenses, cable and other paraphernalia."

(No. 821), and THE GRAND COMMANDERY OF NEW YORK STATE (No. 822). When BOSTON COMMANDERY was shown at Keith's Boston vaudeville house, "the new pictures made the biggest hit of the program."[9]

In other instances, a cameraman traveled to a specific city and took various local views for use on the contracting theater's bill. Thus, in early April 1899, an unknown cameraman (probably Billy Bitzer) went to Providence and shot PROVIDENCE FIRE DEPARTMENT (No. 917), MARKET SQUARE, PROVIDENCE, RHODE ISLAND (No. 920), and other scenes. In late August F. S. Armitage took eight views of Rochester, New York. That fall, during its eleven-week run, Biograph showed a new local view each week except for the first and last weeks (with many of these views reprised for the finale). On occasion, a special trip might yield only a single subject, as when Arthur Marvin photographed HEROES OF LUZON (No. 1199), a scene of President McKinley reviewing troops in Pittsburgh on 28 August 1899. At the other extreme, Bitzer stayed in the Boston area for most of 1899 (since he had grown up in nearby Roxbury, he was a logical choice). By this stage the resulting pictures were intended primarily for Keith's Boston house.

Meanwhile the Biograph camera itself was undergoing significant modifications. By early 1899, its tripod had a panning head that turned smoothly and quickly, yielding results far superior to any achieved by the Edison group. The new head was employed for IN THE GRIP OF THE BLIZZARD (No. 875) in mid February and then PANORAMIC VIEW OF NIAGARA FALLS IN WINTER (No. 878, copyrighted as NIAGARA FALLS, WINTER), which contains a sweeping panorama of about ninety degrees moving from left to right and then reversing itself. Biograph employed the same apparatus several times during the next months, but it was not applied to fictional film until September 1900, when Bitzer shot LOVE IN THE SUBURBS (No. 1632), a one-shot comedy. By this time, Bitzer was using an experimental, hand-cranked camera that had been developed and tested by Marvin and Casler earlier that year. Much more portable than earlier models, it also was used by him while he was photographing the Galveston disaster that same month.[10]

Studio productions were made by collaborative teams and not, as Bitzer's memoirs suggest, spontaneously created by individual cameramen. Even simple gags required scenarios, sets, and careful planning, and the potential expense in wasted stock alone was high enough to concern Biograph executives. Most studio comedies consisted of about 132 feet of 70-mm film. Since Biograph's camera and projectors consumed roughly 4 feet of film per second, a 132-foot subject lasted less than 35 seconds.[11] Although the length was sometimes doubled in 1899 and 1900, Biograph productions developed a reputation for being short and rarely very complex.

A production still from THE X-RAY MIRROR (No. 1179), taken 17 July 1899, documents the personnel involved in such productions: five men off-camera and three women and a man performing. One man (McCutcheon) is clearly giving directions, since a second (Frank J. Marion?) stands by his right shoulder, timing the scene. Three stagehands also watch the proceedings. In addition, a camera operator may be in the booth with the camera.[12] Carefully rehearsed comic timing is evident in A GOOD SHOT (No. 1024), which Armitage filmed on the rooftop. The set is the backyard of a house, where a girl holds a target attached to a broom while a boy shoots at it with his rifle. The first time everything works well, but then Bridget (the Irish maid, played by a hefty man in drag) comes out and does some laundry. The children, enjoying their activity, repeat it: this time Bridget feels the charge in her behind. The gag is thus set up by the successful trial, allowing the audience to anticipate and enjoy the denouement.

Careful planning was particularly evident in a few multi-shot fiction narratives that Biograph made in 1900, by which time the company was lagging behind many domestic and foreign rivals in this area.[13] That May, Arthur Marvin shot and McCutcheon produced THE DOWNWARD PATH (Nos. 1471–1475) with each scene listed separately in the catalog. The series, according to the catalog, was "intended to convey a moral lesson in the career of a young country girl who succumbs to temptations, and becomes involved in the wickedness of a big city." The country lass is seduced by a book agent who "pictures to her the fascinations of the city" (THE CHEEKY BOOK AGENT). She flees from her family and elopes with the book agent (SHE RAN AWAY WITH THE CITY MAN). In the city, she becomes a streetwalker, and the book agent prevents her from being rescued by her aged parents (THE GIRL WHO WENT ASTRAY). She takes a job in a Bowery concert hall as a dancer and prostitute (THE NEW SOUBRETTE). Finally, the fallen woman is deserted by the book agent and despairingly commits suicide with carbolic acid (IN SUICIDE HALL). One month later, Marvin photographed the five-part A CAREER OF CRIME, which showed the ruin of a young man. Although he nabs a thief at his new job, the youth is soon

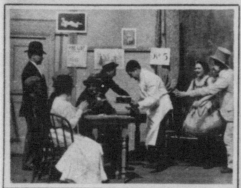

No. 1471

Title *The Downward Path.*
The New Soubrette.
Length 167 ft.
Code Word *Gaethacke.*

No. 1472

Title *The Downward Path.*
The Cheeky Book Agent.
Length 164 ft.
Code Word *Gaetone.*

The proper sequence for THE DOWNWARD PATH: *Nos. 1472, 1475, 1473, 1471, and 1474.*

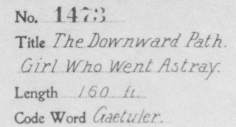

No. 1473

Title *The Downward Path.*
Girl Who Went Astray.

Length *160 ft.*

Code Word *Gaetuler.*

No. 1474

Title *The Downward Path.*
In Suicide Hall.

Length *169 ft.*

Code Word *Gaetuliam.*

No. 1475

Title *The Downward Path.*
She Ran Away with the City Man.
Length *164* ft.
Code Word *Gaetulicus.*

No. 1476

Title *Gatling Gun Drill.*

Length *434* ft.
Code Word *Gaetulorum.*

on the downward path as well. Losing his hard-earned money at the horse races, he turns to a life of crime. While robbing a safe, the young man kills a banker and afterward indulges his wanton desires in a disreputable saloon, only to be captured by the police. He finally pays for the crime in the electric chair. Here again, the tale recalls a Briggs lantern-slide series, "Story of a Country Boy."

In both multi-shot subjects, key moments of conflict are represented in a rudimentary fashion; the woman's seduction by the agent, for example, is stated rather than shown. The characters lack any psychology or individuality: why and how the young man ends up at the racetrack is never explained. Yet these brief scenes, which appropriated situations if not complete narratives from popular melodramas, laid out many themes found in subsequent American dramatic films. THE DOWNWARD PATH already emphasizes the central role of the family; the parents' failed attempts to rescue their daughter and their grief over her death intensify the moral lesson. The family is the principal obstacle to corruption, the key social institution in the struggle against evil. By contrast, the policeman, a representative of the law and the state, is indifferent to the woman's plight in scene 3 and shrugs off her death at the denouement. The evil of the large, impersonal city is contrasted to the innocence of the countryside. The city slicker corrupts an unsuspecting country girl, and the upright country boy, ruined by the racetrack, eventually turns to murder. At the same time, the countryside is threatened by the city, thus evoking not only an economic reality but the social counterpart of industrialization: the massive migration of rural Americans into urban areas, where they encountered a harsh and impersonal world.

Nonetheless, when these "dramas" (actually listed under "Miscellaneous Views" in Biograph's 1902 catalog) are compared to Biograph's many comedies and sexually suggestive scenes, certain contradictions emerge. The gay young women who display their bodies before the camera are meant to be savored and enjoyed. Their "downward path" is not emphasized lest it interfere with the pleasure of viewing. The wisdom of authority (the father, who throws out the book agent) is venerated in the dramas but lampooned in the comedies. Tramps and burglars are distanced from the viewer through burlesque. The male spectator does not pause to think that he could enter such a downward spiral. Film comedy and film melodrama both confront urbanization and industrialization, just as both articulate progressive and conservative values—but in inverted relation to each other. In fact, the moralizing dramas were atypical of most Biograph productions, which epitomized the freedom, excitement, and opportunity of city life. They played with and/or appealed to people's desires—sexual desire; the desire for sophistication; the desire to belong, to succeed, to consume.[14]

35-mm Exhibitors Experience an Interim Period of Difficulty

The 35-mm section of the industry did not achieve commercial stability as readily as Biograph. Although the Spanish-American War had rescued these exhibitors from commercial difficulty, unsettling conditions returned at its end. The number of theaters showing films in New York City again declined; by late September 1898, there were only four prominent ones: Keith's, the Eden Musee, Proctor's Pleasure Palace, and Proctor's Twenty-third Street Theater. At Proctor's houses, Vitagraph supplemented war-related scenes with its own version of VANISHING LADY in Sep-

Albert E. Smith in VANISHING LADY.

tember and a short comedy, THE BURGLAR ON THE ROOF, in early October. The press commended the exhibition service for its efforts; nonetheless, its run at the Pleasure Palace was terminated in early November, "much to the relief of the regular patrons."[15] A month later, Vitagraph's presentations at the Twenty-third Street Theater ended as well, leaving the function of a visual newspaper to be continued by Tobey's views on the stereopticon. By the end of the year, the Eden Musee was the only New York theater regularly showing 35-mm films. Exhibitors had to scramble for short-term opportunities in order to survive.

The stability of the 35-mm industry was made even more uncertain as Edison continued to sue competitors, often with the encouragement of its licensee, American Vitagraph, which tried to replace the unlucky defendants in the theaters. Although Eberhard Schneider attempted to join the Edison group, his efforts were not successful, and he was served with a subpoena just before Christmas. When he failed to appear in court, an injunction, widely publicized by the Edison Company, was issued against him. Schneider claimed, however, that he had been tricked into going to the company's offices on the court date after being promised a license. Whatever the cause, he was required to show only Edison films on his programs. George Huber, manager of Huber's Museum, was also sued for patent infringement after he hired several unlicensed exhibitors, culminating with d'Hauterives's historiographe in April 1899. In response, Huber simply removed all films from his bill.[16]

With biographs in the top vaudeville theaters, 35-mm exhibitors generally depended on outlets in second- or third-class houses for the 1898–1899 season. In Boston, Austin & Stone's Museum offered films during most of that period (though often switching services). In San Francisco, 35-mm films were shown regularly at the Chutes (a mostly outdoor entertainment center) and later also at A. W. Furst's small Cineograph Theater, which opened sometime in 1899 and offered a picture show for

ten cents. Venues of any kind were scarce. In St. Louis, only after Biograph concluded a three-month stay did 35-mm showmen win a few brief contracts over the
remainder of the theatrical season. In Chicago, the biograph was at two theaters
during the fall of 1898, while 35-mm films were rarely shown (or at least advertised).
For many weeks during the winter and spring of 1899, Chicago's commercial theaters
were not showing films of any kind. Yet this retreat was a brief pause while vaudeville
managers absorbed the lessons of the Spanish-American War. The war had taught
them that under the proper circumstances motion pictures could act as a headline
attraction on the bill. Yet to benefit fully from such circumstances, vaudeville managers had to nurture the exhibition services they called upon.

35-mm Moving Pictures Become a Permanent Vaudeville Attraction

The bleak situation endured by 35-mm exhibitors changed dramatically during the
course of 1899 as vaudeville theaters established permanent relations with exhibition
services. Lubin's cineograph was first: returning to Bradenburgh's museum in Philadelphia on 30 January, it henceforth remained on the bill whenever the amusement
center was open (it closed during the summer). American Vitagraph was next: the
vitagraph opened at Tony Pastor's Theater in New York City on 19 June and provided
what the *New York Clipper* called "an entertaining part of the programme."[17] With
their own production capabilities, the Vitagraph partners offered an effective, timely
service that rivaled the biograph at Keith's. Continued enthusiasm gave it a permanent place on Pastor's vaudeville bill for the next nine years.

Pastor's decision to hire Vitagraph for an indefinite run paid rich dividends when
Admiral Dewey arrived in New York City on 26 September to celebrate his victory
over the Spanish fleet in Manila Bay. As a theatrical journal subsequently reported:
"The American Vitagraph has been excelling in enterprise during the past week.
Several views were taken at the Olympia [the Admiral's flagship] and projected here
the evening of the same day, and the Dewey land parade was seen on Saturday
evening, five hours after the views were taken. The vitagraph is a popular fixture
here and continually gains in favor."[18] Vitagraph cameramen then followed Dewey to
Washington and filmed his reception there on 3 October. The views were shown the
following day at Pastor's matinee. Following a rough chronological order, Vitagraph's
programs offered a narrative account of "Dewey's Doings":

- A panoramic view of the Olympia
- Receiving of Mayor Van Wyck and the reception committee by Admiral Dewey
- Departure of Mayor Van Wyck and the committee
- Arrival of Dewey at the city hall
- Presentation of the loving cup to Dewey by Mayor Van Wyck at the city hall
- Start of the Dewey parade from Grant's Tomb, led by Sousa's band
- The West Point Cadets
- Dewey reviewing the parade at the Dewey Arch
- Parade from the White House, Washington, led by Dewey and President
  McKinley
- Presentation of the sword to Dewey by Secretary Long and President McKinley[19]

J. Stuart Blackton waits to film the Dewey Celebration at City Hall, New York.

Proctor's theaters did not show films of the Dewey celebration, although the Twenty-third Street house celebrated the admiral's arrival by exhibiting a cycloramic oil painting of the Manila bombardment. Stereopticon slides of Dewey's reception were also projected, but moving pictures shown at other houses received much more favorable comment in the press. Proctor's was outdone again the following week on the occasion of the America's Cup yacht races. While Vitagraph received applause for showing pictures of the events at Pastor's and Koster & Bial's Music Hall only a few hours after their occurrence, Proctor's opted for a cumbersome and ultimately less interesting presentation: the positions of the boats on the race course were reported to the theater by Marconi's wireless and their progress charted on an immense map between acts.[20] Since the races occurred during the day such a map was useless during the evening, when most patrons attended the theater—and on off-racing days as well.

When manager J. Austin Fynes and owner F. F. Proctor saw the error of their ways, they quickly formalized a relationship with William Paley, famed for his films of the Spanish-American War. His kalatechnoscope opened on 9 October at Proctor's Twenty-third Street Theater and two weeks later at the Pleasure Palace, where Paley soon had an office and lab facilities that enabled him to put films on the screen with maximum speed. Paley filmed a vessel that caught fire in Long Island Sound off Rye, New York, on 14 October and then showed the results, THE BURNING OF THE "NUTMEG STATE," that same evening. He filmed AUTOMOBILE PARADE and DICK

CROCKER LEAVING TAMMANY HALL in November and quickly put them on the screen.[21] In the trade papers, Fynes declared:

> The secret of Moving Pictures consists in the TIMELINESS. Without that feature such an Exhibition must inevitably fail. I regard the Kalatech-noscope as incontestibly the most perfect and most thoroughly Up-to-date Machine in existence. It has proved its superior qualities in these Houses and I have booked it for an indefinite run (*Clipper*, 4 November 1899, p. 756).

The kalatechnoscope was soon at Proctor's house in Albany, New York, as well, and once the vaudeville impresario took over the Fifth Avenue Theater in May 1900 and the 125th Street Theater in August, Paley had his service in five Proctor houses on a full-time basis. The opening of Proctor's Montreal theater in March 1901 provided Paley with a sixth permanent outlet. Although Paley exhibited in other venues, these contracts were of brief duration; Proctor was to remain his key customer in the years ahead.

The general popularity of moving pictures at this time is underscored by Paley-related evidence. A photograph of Proctor's Twenty-third Street Theater in 1900 shows that over the marquee there was a sign in bright lights announcing "Moving Pictures." The kalatechnoscope was also given a prominent role in Charles Frohman's theatrical production of *Hearts Are Trumps*, which opened at New York's Garden Theater on 21 February 1900. According to Cecil Raleigh's script, a music-hall girl lures a lecherous, evil earl to a studio and has him surreptitiously filmed as they do a dance. Later, after the nobleman's perfidious nature is revealed, he is humiliated—and the music hall is saved from bankruptcy—when the films are shown to delighted crowds.[22] For the play's story to be believable, film exhibitions had to be seen as having drawing power, particularly when they could offer a popular subject.

Another exhibition service that established a permanent outlet in New York City was the newly formed Kinetograph Company. This enterprise had two silent partners: James White, head of Edison's kinetograph department, and John Schermerhorn, assistant general manager of the Edison Manufacturing Company and also William Gilmore's brother-in-law. The third, public partner was Percival Waters, a small, New York-based jobber of Edison films and former Vitascope Company employee. Since the Edison Company—unlike its principal licensees and rivals—did not have its own exhibition service, this newly formed partnership partially filled the void. Although Waters ran the enterprise, White and Schermerhorn sent business to him, extended him several thousand dollars worth of credit, and made films that would help their joint enterprise.[23] In November 1899, Waters' kinetograph service opened at Huber's Fourteenth Street Museum, where it remained for many years.

By the end of 1900, eight New York theaters—seven of them vaudeville houses—were showing moving pictures on a permanent basis. These managers had come to conceive of films quite differently from other vaudeville turns. They were permanent fixtures, not acts booked for a few weeks or months at a time. (Not coincidentally the widespread diffusion of the reframing device at this time, improved exhibitions and made a permanent service more attractive.) Vaudeville managers had come to provide film companies with steady commercial outlets that enabled them to retain the necessary staff and resources to cover important news events and provide a reliable service.

The White Rats Strike

According to one contemporary observer, Robert Grau, film exhibition in vaudeville houses assumed special prominence and reached a quantitative peak with the White Rats vaudeville strike of 1901. While this claim has been alternately accepted and contested, historians have generally shied away from the extensive research necessary for even a preliminary assessment.[24] On 21 February, the White Rats of America, an organization of vaudeville performers, walked out of the theaters controlled by the Eastern members of the Association of Vaudeville Managers, which included Benjamin F. Keith, F. F. Proctor, P. B. Chase in Washington, and Hyde & Behman and Percy Williams in Brooklyn. For Grau, who was then a theatrical agent, "the situation proved not only an opportunity but a harvest," reported the *New York Dramatic Mirror* on 2 March. "He met the difficulty thoroughly and didn't sleep for seventy-two hours." Scouring New York's metropolitan area for acts to place in these short-handed houses, Grau experienced the crisis firsthand.

The strike appears to have had little impact on the number of machines used in Manhattan, Boston, and several other cities, since the houses that were struck already exhibited motion pictures on a regular basis. In these places, however, films often assumed a more important role insofar as they filled in for missing acts.[25] Not surprisingly, evidence for such activities is sketchy, since the newspapers generally played down the troubles of managers who advertised prominently in their pages.

The situation was quite different in Brooklyn, where not a single vaudeville house showed films on a permanent basis prior to the strike. Although Percy Williams had occasionally placed the vitagraph in his three theaters since January 1899, many weeks went by when films were not shown in any Brooklyn house. As the strike began, one Williams venue happened to be showing films (THE McGOVERN–GANS FIGHT), but it belonged to a touring vaudeville company. By the following week, however, the vitagraph was playing in all three of Williams' locations, and the biograph became a last-minute addition at Hyde & Behman's. Thus, as the strike went into its first full week, four Brooklyn vaudeville houses had added films.

Managers were clearly ready to use films to fight the strike and fill out their bills. Just as clearly, the motion-picture companies were pleased to accommodate them. It is worth noting, moreover, that those houses supporting the White Rats, such as Koster & Bial's, did not have any motion pictures on their bills during the strike. Vaudevillians generally evinced negative attitudes toward motion pictures, seeing them as a money-saving device for management. Although Brooklyn was an extreme example, the Biograph Company reported that "there are more Biographs playing in the leading vaudeville theatres of the United States than have been in any week since moving pictures were invented."[26] In Washington, P. B. Chase hired the biograph to fill out his strike-battered bill and kept it there for almost four months. Generally, the boom was short-lived. In Brooklyn, Hyde & Behman quickly dropped the biograph, and Williams soon retained the services of only one vitagraph, which he rotated among his theaters. Nonetheless, Vitagraph had won a new, permanent outlet and cemented relations with an important manager.

The impact of motion pictures on the White Rats strike, and vice versa, was thus real if modest. Films provided only one of several ways to flesh out bills depleted by striking performers. In some cases, the pictures made a difference in the managers' ability to operate their houses, but they were not in themselves decisive. Nevertheless, the exhibition services had proved that they were the managers' allies, bringing the two groups closer together. Perhaps this saved some outlets for films during the "chaser period" that would follow. (See chapter 10.) Grau therefore seems a credible chronicler of events, but with an important proviso: generalizing from his own experiences with the Brooklyn houses, where the situation was the most serious, he overstated the nationwide significance of this incident.[27]

Steady outlets and relative prosperity required new organizational structures. The heads of successful 35-mm exhibition services became less involved in actually presenting the films and focused more on management. At Vitagraph, Blackton and Smith were responsible for keeping accounts as well as acquiring and making new films, while Rock booked theaters and handled commercial relations. Others were hired to serve as projectionists. (Nonetheless, all three partners continued to pursue outside interests: magic work for Smith, chalk acts for Blackton, and slot machines for Rock.) The activities of traveling exhibitor Lyman Howe also reflected this separation of planning and execution. Beginning with the 1899–1900 theatrical season, he stopped traveling with his company and instead established a base in his hometown of Wilkes-Barre, Pennsylvania, to devote himself to planning and administration. Freed from actual performances, Howe cultivated his contacts with New York producers, enriched his selection of films, and improved the quality of his exhibitions.

As they sought to change programs each week at their permanent venues (a goal not always attained), American exhibition services benefited from a growing diversity of films from foreign sources. Walter Wainwright, William Rock's original partner in the Louisiana Vitascope enterprise, acted as Vitagraph's special London agent, thus assuring an attractive supply of European subjects. In 1900 American Vitagraph had 246 non-Edison films in its collection, 117 of which were made in England and 66 in France. Méliès's trick films in particular were reported to have "created no end of merriment" among American spectators and proved an invaluable antidote to a year of war topicals; by 1899 Lubin boasted two such trick films, both of which he called A TRIP TO THE MOON (one was undoubtedly LA LUNE À UN MÈTRE, otherwise known in English as THE ASTRONOMER'S DREAM).[28] The most popular and influential Méliès's film was CINDERELLA, which first appeared in the United States during the 1899 Christmas holidays. Its use of dissolves when shifting from scene to scene was soon emulated by Blackton and Smith (CONGRESS OF NATIONS © 16 November 1900) and then others, but the unprecedented spectacle of CINDERELLA exceeded any American accomplishment for some time. Over the next few years the film was a featured attraction wherever it played, underscoring both the importance of international contacts and the popularity of more ambitious films. American production, weakened by Edison's patent suits, was increasingly supplemented by overseas productions.

Edison and His Licensees

The symbiotic relationship between the Edison Manufacturing Company and its licensed affiliates functioned effectively in many situations. To cover the Dewey celebration, Edison manager James White organized and coordinated eight camera crews, many composed of licensed filmmakers. By relying on its licensees, the Edison group covered more locations than Biograph. Arrangements among the licensees were handled equitably as prints simultaneously reached all the license-affiliated theaters. The subjects were then quickly copyrighted and offered for sale to other exhibitors, enabling Edison to achieve a profit. Edison also depended on Vitagraph for developing and duping uncopyrighted Lubin and Amet films, which it then marketed.

Perhaps half of the films sold by the Edison Company in the period between 1898 and 1900 were made by its licensees, while the other half were made by White and Heise. By the end of the century, acted films had become a larger part of the Edison Company's repertoire: approximately 40 percent in 1899 (32 of Edison's 77 copyrighted subjects) and in 1900 (27 of 69). Vitagraph supplied many popular comedies (MAUDE'S NAUGHTY LITTLE BROTHER copyrighted by Edison 16 November 1900) and various trick films (THE CLOWN AND THE ALCHEMIST copyrighted by Edison 16 November 1900). Blackton and Smith combined the mysterious and comic in A VISIT TO THE SPIRITUALIST, which, according to the Edison catalog of March 1900, was "acknowledged by exhibitors to be the funniest of all moving magical films." Using double exposures and stop-action techniques, the film showed a country rube who is mesmerized by a spiritualist and "sees funny things." A handkerchief turns into a ghost. The rube tries to shed his clothes, but they jump back onto his body. The naive farmer is once again a victim of the sophisticated city and modern technology, in this case the motion-picture camera.

After James White recovered from an illness contracted in the Far East, he assumed multiple roles: producer, salesman, department executive, cameraman, and actor. Blessed with a sparkling personality, the kinetograph department manager used his position to enjoy life to its fullest. He not only made the ADVENTURES OF JONES series, a group of nine short comedies that were shot intermittently during 1899 and 1900, but sometimes played the title role. In these brief vignettes, Jones is a clubman, a well-to-do businessman (the catalog description suggests a broker) who indulges in alcohol and extramarital sex, and must often pay for his excesses. In JONES' RETURN FROM THE CLUB, a fight ensues after the drunkard insults and abuses a helpful policeman. In WHY MRS. JONES GOT A DIVORCE, Jones seduces the pretty cook, only to be discovered by his wife. White also produced reenactments of military battles taking place in the Philippines (ADVANCE OF KANSAS VOLUNTEERS AT CALOOCAN and FILIPINOS RETREAT FROM TRENCHES) and South Africa (BATTLE OF MAFEKING). Like McCutcheon, this manager performed many functions that would later be assigned to different individuals and whole departments.

James White may have been a problematic executive, but he understood what many exhibitors wanted: groups of related films that could be sequenced into larger units. During the summer of 1900, he visited the Paris Exposition, enjoyed the sights, and shot at least sixteen films (PANORAMA OF PARIS EXPOSITION, FROM THE SEINE). On his trip, he may also have picked up a new piece of camera equipment—a panning head for the tripod—since the camera now swiveled with much greater ease than in earlier Edison productions. The photographer indulged the camera's new-found freedom in PANORAMA OF PLACE DE L'OPÉRA, where his framing follows one carriage, then picks up and follows a bus, and finally assumes a static position as the frantic vehicles move on- and off-screen. For PANORAMA OF EIFFEL TOWER, White moved the camera vertically, first showing the base of the tower, then tilting up to its top, and finally returning to eye level. Edison camera pans, however, still lacked the evenness and precision found in Biograph's camera movements from this period.

A VISIT TO THE SPIRITUALIST (1899)

James White used sweeping camera moves when filming PANORAMA OF PLACE DE L'OPÉRA.

The vast majority of films at this time still consisted of one shot, but in the latter part of 1899 White made several multi-shot films. As with the 1897 SUBURBAN HANDICAP, he was ready to impose his editorial ideas when the situation seemed appropriate. SHOOT THE CHUTES SERIES showed that familiar pastime from three different vantage points. The camera was placed first at the bottom of the chutes, then at the top looking down the ramp, and finally in a boat as it went down the ramp and into the basin. With two or more takes made from each camera position, the film totaled 275 feet. White made two multi-shot acted films late in 1899 as well, both of which were "picture songs," an application of the song-slide idea to motion pictures. As described in the March 1900 Edison catalog, the more elaborate was the six-shot LOVE AND WAR, in which a soldier is promoted to the rank of captain for bravery, meets and marries a Red Cross girl, and returns home to his parents. The Edison Company also supplied the necessary words and music. The illustrated-song idea allowed the production company to assume responsibility for the complete organization of picture and sound. Since these appropriations of editorial control remained infrequent, however, they did not challenge the exhibitor's dominant responsibility for the arrangement of scenes.

Although Edison's licensing arrangements provided his company with a diversity of film subjects for its customers, the licensor-licensee relationship did not work as well as the inventor must have initially expected. Four of the five New York–based exhibition services with permanent outlets were licensees, yet the Edison Company did not prosper. Its profits from film sales fell from more than $24,000 a year for the 1896–1897 and 1897–1898 business years to sums fluctuating between approximately $13,000 and $20,000 for each of the following three years. Gross income from such sales was also considerably reduced. While the sale price of films had been driven down during the course of 1898 to fifteen cents a foot, the number of feet sold either remained steady or decreased slightly.

The licensing arrangement often benefited the licensees more than the licensor. Since licensed exhibitors made their own films, their demand for Edison's product was much lower than if they had been without this capability. In addition, many licensee activities were such that Edison could not make a profit. Frequently, news films were not turned over to Edison until their economic value had faded. Vitagraph sometimes serviced its clients by giving them special films that would have been of no interest to anyone else. When the First American Vaudeville Excursion, which toured with a vitagraph, went to Cuba early in 1899, a film was made of the members' departure, developed on board ship, and shown in a Havana theater on their arrival. Likewise, when Paley's kalatechnoscope presented local views in Worcester, Massachusetts, in the spring of 1900, the trade press reported that they "drew very heavily." But while Paley received substantial remuneration from this undertaking, the films were of no economic value to Edison (they were neither copyrighted nor offered for sale).[29] Since Paley's and Vitagraph's incomes were derived chiefly from their exhibitions, they considered film sales of little importance. Yet such sales were the keystone of Edison's motion-picture business.

Edison, frustrated by his licensing arrangements, tried to shift the commercial balance in his favor when he contracted with the Klondike Exposition Company in March 1899. Organized by Thomas Crahan of Montana, the Klondike Exposition Company acquired two large-format motion-picture cameras that the Edison Company had built the previous year, in clear emulation of Biograph. That summer,

For BOSTON HORSELESS FIRE DEPARTMENT (1899), *White juxtaposed the new fire truck with old horse-drawn apparatus. Despite innovative editing technique, the film suffered from poor image quality caused by water spots left during developing and inadequate focusing. These were common problems in the 1890s (particularly at the Edison Company) and were further compounded by projection flicker.*

accompanied by Edison's motion-picture expert Robert K. Bonine, Crahan went to Alaska to make films for possible display at the 1900 Paris Exposition. From the exhibition of these films, Edison was to receive 20 percent of the net receipts, but the cameras failed to operate properly, and the company exhausted its cash long before any films were ready. Thus this attempt to establish a new kind of licensing arrangement failed.

The symbiosis between Edison and his licensees became increasingly tense. Perhaps attempting to redefine the relationship, Edison failed to acknowledge (through either cash or credits) Vitagraph's royalties on print sales. Finally, "Pop" Rock threatened to sue for an accounting. As a result, Edison terminated Vitagraph's license on 20 January 1900 and forbade any activities that did not use Edison films and machines. Since such restrictions were certain to ruin Vitagraph's business, the Vitagraph partners responded by turning their company over to a new corporation of the same name that was owned by George S. W. Arthur, Albert Smith's father-in-law, and Ronald Reader, an earlier associate of Blackton and Smith from their days on the Lyceum circuit. This "new" management then rehired the "old" partners as employees. Forbidden to violate Edison's patents, Blackton and Smith simply had someone else turn the camera crank. While this bold ruse allowed Vitagraph to continue its operations for a time, Edison challenged the evasion in court. Judge E. Henry Lacombe believed that Blackton and Smith had conspired to disobey the court's earlier injunction and was ready to punish them with imprisonment. He insisted, however, that Edison first pay for a close examination of the new corporation and its stockholders.

In the fall of 1900, before further action was taken, the Edison Company reconciled its differences with Vitagraph. White was eager to market the HAPPY HOOLIGAN SERIES, a group of comedies that Blackton and Smith had made over the summer. When a hurricane struck Galveston, Texas, in September 1900, Albert Smith traveled to the devasted town and photographed the aftermath. Using the new tripod head, he filmed the ruins in long, sweeping panoramas. Eight subjects, including SEARCHING RUINS ON BROADWAY, GALVESTON, FOR DEAD BODIES, were copyrighted, and between seventeen and thirty-five positive prints of each subject were sold. In resuming a licensee relationship with Edison, the new American Vitagraph Company acknowledged Edison's patents (making future attempts to avoid court injunctions impossible) and agreed to pay Edison a 10 percent royalty on its exhibition income. This seemed certain to provide Edison with a new source of profits from his licensee. Similar arrangements also may have been made with Paley.

Edison faced many difficulties in the motion-picture field: not only were profits low, and licensees recalcitrant, but Biograph was posing very serious competition. Biograph's profits for the first two months of 1900 were more than Edison's total film-related profits for that entire year. Its spirited legal defense against Edison's patent-infringement suit stood a strong possibility of success, and if it won, Edison's licensees were certain to join the ranks of its competitors. Discouraged, Thomas Edison contemplated selling his business to Biograph. On 12 April, Biograph executive Harry Marvin paid Edison $2,500 as an option for the right to purchase Edison's motion-picture interests for $500,000.[30] When the financing fell through, however, Edison withdrew from the arrangement and began to restructure and expand his business—even as Biograph was finding itself in a less favorable commercial position.

Lubin rooftop studio (ca. *1899*).

The Industry Outside New York

The 35-mm motion-picture industry functioned on two different levels in the late 1890s. Film sales were commonly international in scope even as exhibitions were executed by regionally based companies. New York was clearly the industry's heart, but Chicago and Philadelphia were active centers too. In Philadelphia, Lubin prospered as his cineograph service became a permanent attraction at Bradenburgh's Museum and toured with traveling vaudeville and burlesque companies like Sam Devere's Own Company. Other exhibition outlets included a small, portable theater that opened in October 1899, on the esplanade of Philadelphia's National Export Exposition and remained for a month.[31] Lubin even began to penetrate the New York market early in 1899, when the cineograph played at Huber's Museum. Yet the threat (and reality) of legal action against theaters employing his service prevented Lubin from establishing a strong presence in New York.

The scale of Lubin's film production may well have rivaled Edison's during this period. Although the Philadelphia producer relied heavily on fight-film reenactments, he made many comedies and actualities (even if they were less prominently advertised). His photographers shot many newsworthy subjects in the Philadelphia area, including the G.A.R. (Grand Army of the Republic) parade on 4 September 1899 and the Republican National Convention in mid June of the following year. A fire in Hoboken, New Jersey, involving three ocean liners and the loss of three hundred lives was filmed on 30 June 1900. Lubin, like Biograph and Edison, sent a cameraman to film the Galveston disaster with sweeping panoramas. For TAKING OUT THE DEAD AND WOUNDED and SCENES OF THE WRECKAGE FROM THE WATER FRONT, the photographer introduced large signs that clearly named the ruined busi-

Lubin's Cineograph Theater (1899).

Lubin's SCENES OF THE WRECKAGE FROM THE WATER FRONT (*1900*).

CHINESE MASSACRING CHRISTIANS

nesses and buildings. Some distant news events, such as the Boxer uprising in China, were reenacted on Lubin's rooftop studio, as with the one-shot CHINESE MASSA-CRING [*sic*] CHRISTIANS and BEHEADING A CHINESE PRISONER (both June 1900).

THE TRAMP'S DREAM is a remarkable three-shot subject made late in 1899.[32] The opening shot, showing a tramp asleep on the grass, is followed by that of the dream—the tramp graciously received in a parlor by members of well-to-do society. He charms an attractive young lady and enjoys a delicious lunch. The final shot returns to the sleeping tramp as he wakes up and disappointedly realizes that the preceding scene was only a dream. The film's title assisted the spectator in understanding the relationship between shots. This and other films suggest that Lubin's filmmaking activities were much more vital in this period than has been generally recognized.

The situation in Chicago was different from that on the East Coast. For one thing, vaudeville managers had not developed comparable relationships with exhibitors. Kohl, Castle, and Middleton, who controlled many of the major vaudeville houses in Chicago, almost never placed films on their programs. From early 1899 to mid 1901, the average number of advertised exhibitions in Chicago had declined 30 percent from the novelty era, averaging less than two sites per week. Nor was the concept of cinema as a visual newspaper so fully developed, in part because Chicago was not comparable to New York as a news center.[33] The Dewey celebration in New York City, for example, occurred in September 1899, while its Chicago equivalent was not held until 1 May 1900, by which time commemorating Dewey's victory had become a somewhat tiresome ritual. Boat races and visits by foreign dignitaries occurred earlier or more frequently on the East Coast than in the Midwest. Finally, the rivalry between Chicago and New York was particularly strong in the areas of culture and entertainment, and not surprisingly, East Coast exhibitors—with their emphasis on East Coast news—were avoided by Midwestern managers.

William Selig and George Spoor emerged as the principal Chicago-based exhibitors in the period after the Spanish-American War. Like their East Coast counterparts, they abandoned the generic term "wargraph" in late 1898 or early 1899 and took distinctive names for their services. Selig's service was known as the polyscope, Spoor's as the kinodrome. Spoor's kinodrome appeared at two Kohl & Castle's theaters for a week each in September and October 1899. From February to May 1900, it enjoyed almost steady employment at one of four Chicago houses as it showed Méliès's CINDERELLA.

Most kinodrome screenings occurred outside the city, in the Midwest and the Mississippi Valley. The service briefly appeared on vaudeville programs in New Orleans and St. Louis during February and March 1899, and that October it became a permanent vaudeville attraction at St. Louis' Columbia Theater. Except for the 1901–1902 theatrical season, it remained there into the nickelodeon era, corresponding to the long-term contracts enjoyed by East Coast exhibition services. Spoor's kinodrome appeared at Kansas City's Orpheum Theater in the fall of 1899; a year

Lubin's THE TRAMP'S DREAM.

later the Orpheum hired it as a permanent attraction. In time the Orpheum circuit would become one of Spoor's key customers. After the 1899–1900 season, the kinodrome was supplanted by the polyscope at many theaters. The precise reasons remain unclear, but Edward Amet ceased his filmmaking activities at about this time, leaving Spoor at a disadvantage because he had no production capability.[34]

William Selig's Polyscope Company, with its own production capacity, dominated 35-mm exhibition in Chicago and much of the Midwest during the 1900–1901 season and the first part of the 1901–1902 season. Selig's largest customer was J. D. Hopkins, who employed the polyscope at his Chicago vaudeville house in August 1900 and kept it there until late January 1901. Hopkins also hired it for his Grand Opera House in Memphis, Tennessee, where it ran from September through January. To maintain interest toward the end of the run, local views were filmed of Main Street, the riverfront, and the Memphis Bridge. According to the *Memphis Commercial Appeal*, they made the polyscope "one of the very popular features of this season's attractions." As was often the case, a film of the local fire department drew the most comment.[35] The cameraman then moved on to Louisville, Kentucky, where he filmed LOUISVILLE FIRE DEPARTMENT, L & N'S NEW FLORIDA TRAIN, and FOURTH AVENUE, LOUISVILLE in January. The polyscope had opened at that city's Temple Theater in mid December, when the local manager supplemented his plays with vaudeville acts provided through J. D. Hopkins; it remained through the end of March. Selig was also active in Milwaukee and the Great Lakes region.

By November 1900, Selig's operations were sufficiently large for him to incorporate the Selig Polyscope Company. His visibility was also such that he attracted Edison's attention and on 5 December 1900 was sued for patent infringement. Selig, who had no intention of being intimidated, acquired the services of the law firm of Banning & Banning. His recent incorporation facilitated this process, and Ephraim and Thomas A. Banning agreed to defend the new corporation until 1 January 1903, in exchange for stock estimated at $12,500. Of a total of 500 shares of stock, they at one point held 100 shares to Selig's 373. The lawyers not only succeeded in deflecting Edison's suits but assumed an influential role in the company.[36]

The size and scope of Selig's film business is suggested by information relevant to its incorporation. The business, based at 43 Peck Court in Chicago, was generously valued at $50,000, with net profits averaging $350 to $400 a month. Equipment worth $5945 included three regular cameras and six projectors as well as perforators, developing drums, lenses, rheostats, and four hundred lantern-slide negatives. Over a hundred film negatives were valued at $33,065. Two of Selig's trusted employees were John J. Byrnes, who was vice president of the new corporation until the spring of 1901, when he was replaced by William Rattray, and Thomas Nash, who helped evaluate Selig's business in late 1900 and finally replaced Rattray as vice president early in 1903.[37] Even at this early date, Nash was probably responsible for the production of many Selig films.

Financial information for December 1900 through June 1901 outlines the economics of Selig's activities:

Month	Receipts	Disbursements	Net Profits
December 1900	$5,142.01	$4,998.21	$143.83
January 1901			684.37
February 1901			84.41
March 1901			408.84

For the following quarter, finances were noted in a manner that lacks obvious consistency but suggests a surge that made Selig almost the equal of Edison or Lubin:

Month	Disbursements	Earnings
April 1901	$2,315.30	$1,655.70
May 1901	1,929.70	2,204.89
June 1901	2,307.58	1,952.24

During the following quarter, Selig claimed an actual net gain of $2,032.72, including $1285 for an increase in materials and $600 for purchase of stock. The cash gain for the quarter, however, was given as only $147.70.[38] As with Lubin, virtually all his assets were tied up in the business.

Although Selig's productions from this period have not survived, catalog descriptions and a list of negatives available at the time of incorporation are illuminating. His most important subject was LIFE OF A FIREMAN, a 450-foot film that was valued at $2500. Designed "to illustrate the entire workings of a model fire department," it consisted of at least three shots:

> This picture, in its complete form, shows the firemen sitting in front of a fire house, when suddenly an alarm is sounded. You see the rush and break for the inside of the fire house, to get to their respective places on the apparatus before going to the fire. The next picture shows them leaving the engine house; the mad dash out of doors, and the most realistic fire run ever shown on canvas. Twenty-eight pieces of fire fighting machines madly rushing and plunging down a thoroughfare on the way to the fire (Selig Polyscope Company, *1903 Complete Catalogue of Films and Moving Pictures*, p. 11).

Once again, an American producer assumed editorial control to make a more ambitious production with a simple narrative. It was in fact one of the first multi-shot films on this popular subject, antedating James Williamson's FIRE! by many months. As was the case with other producers, however, Selig's assumption of editorial responsibility was limited. Other fire subjects on his list (CHICAGO FIRE RUN, FIRE ENGINES AT WORK, and THE FIRE RUN) were apparently only a single shot. In these instances, exhibitors remained free to construct their own narratives, by combining individual films, if they so wished. With all these pictures, the image of the heroic firefighter offered an alternative to the often bitter class conflicts of American life: daring workingmen risk their lives to save innocent children, the property of the wealthy, and society as a whole. With the Chicago fire still a living memory for some, such films must have inspired strong emotions.

Selig also valued his "Stockyards set, complete" at $2500. This was apparently the STOCK YARDS SERIES he made for the large meat-packing corporation Armour & Company. This group of approximately sixty individual films, the 1903 catalog indicates, was "made with a POLYSCOPE CAMERA with the aid of powerful electric lights." Copyrighted by Armour & Company on 3 June 1901, these were sold both in sets and individually. One such set, entitled "Cattle Department," included ENTRANCE TO UNION STOCK YARDS, ARRIVAL OF TRAIN OF CATTLE, BRIDGE OF SIGHS, STUNNING CATTLE, DUMPING AND LIFTING CATTLE, STICKING CATTLE, KOSHERING CATTLE, DRESSING BEEF, and CUTTING BEEF. Selig's extensive production capabilities were confirmed by his filming of THE GANS–MCGOVERN FIGHT on 13 December 1900, for which the ring was lit by six hundred arc lamps. But once again, filmmakers had bad luck, and Terry McGovern knocked out Joe Gans after two minutes of the second round.[39]

Selig, like other prominent 35-mm exhibitors at this time, supplied his customers with images of local interest. Several news films were taken of well-publicized ceremonies in Chicago: PRESIDENT MCKINLEY LAYING CORNER STONE, shot on 9 October 1899; DEWEY PARADE, taken on 1 May 1900; and SCENES AND INCIDENTS IN THE G.A.R. ENCAMPMENT, taken in the last week of August 1900. Other scenes taken in the Midwestern city included PANORAMIC VIEW OF STATE STREET, CHICAGO POLICE PARADE, and WINTER SPORTS ON THE LAKE. COOK COUNTY DEMOCRACY PARADE, BRYAN AT HOME (shot in Lincoln, Nebraska), and ROOSEVELT IN MINNEAPOLIS (taken 17 July 1900) captured politicians and political events that were pertinent to the 1900 election. FLORAL PARADE and FOOLS PARADE, taken at the Milwaukee Carnival, were essentially local views.

Selig, who had been a magician and manager of a minstrel show, made films that revealed his theatrical background. SHOOTING CRAPS, WHO SAID WATERMELON?, PRIZEFIGHT IN COONTOWN, and A NIGHT IN BLACKVILLE are examples of the minstrel humor that Selig adapted to film. The last-named

> shows a "coon" dance in full swing; all the boys have their best babies; the old fiddler and orchestra are shown seated upon a raised platform; the dance is on. Six coons are shown. A bad coon starts a fight. Razor drawn, girls faint, coon with razor starts to do some fearful execution, when little coon lets fly with a large 45 gun; finale, coon seen jumping through window; big bass viola broken and dance ends in general row. The picture is simply great; one continued round of laughter (*1903 Complete Catalogue*, p. 4).

These burlesque comedies portrayed African Americans as childlike beings—unsocialized, opportunistic, and easily frightened—and ultimately, as comic counterparts to the white world: SOMETHING GOOD—NEGRO KISS was simply labeled "Burlesque on the John Rice and May Irwin Kiss."[40] Selig magic films were frankly unexceptional. In HERMANN LOOKED LIKE ME, a magician dressed to look like the Great Hermann makes a litter of rabbits disappear. Rather than work extensively in this genre, Selig acquired a large supply of Méliès subjects. In these and many other instances, he made duplicate negatives and sold prints to independent exhibitors.

Though weak in production, Chicago was already a major supplier of motion-picture goods. Indeed, the role that Chicago assumed in the film industry was not unlike the one it played in the general economic life of the United States: the major distribution center in the Midwest. Thus the Kleine Optical Company, after being threatened with an Edison lawsuit for patent infringement, became a selling agent for Edison films and projectors in June 1899. Sears, Roebuck & Company did a substantial mail-order business in motion-picture equipment and prints. The manager of this department, E. E. Wade, had close ties with William Selig and sold many of his films.[41] John Hardin managed a similar department for the Montgomery Ward Company. In addition, several companies catered exclusively to the "optical trade"—magic-lantern and moving-picture exhibitors (often semiprofessionals). All featured the optigraph projector, manufactured by the Chicago-based Enterprise Optical Company and depending on two improvements patented by Frank McMillan and Alvah C. Roebuck.[42] These firms also sold Selig films to exhibitors, and many of them were sued by Edison: Sears, Roebuck in April 1900, the Stereopticon and Film Exchange managed by William B. Moore in February 1901, the Chicago Projecting Company and Enterprise Optical Company that September. Unlike many of their New York counterparts, all resisted the suits—the latter two, in fact, used Selig's law firm, Banning & Banning, for their defense.[43]

To appreciate the importance of the 1898–1899 period for the formation of the early motion-picture industry, one has only to recall that the movie moguls of the studio era would be drawn from those exhibitors and distributors who best exploited the opportunities of the nickelodeon era. Then consider an earlier parallel: those motion-picture entrepreneurs who located permanent venues in vaudeville between 1898 and 1900 would generally go on to own the major production companies of the next ten years. These theaters, which usually wanted new pictures each week, encouraged production and fostered a certain level of filmmaking expertise. Through their weekly exhibition fees, they provided producers with the crucial financial capital that allowed them to expand. Perhaps only the Edison Manufacturing Company (where the affiliated Kinetograph Company played the same role) could have survived without this support. For William Selig, George Spoor, Sigmund Lubin, William Paley, American Vitagraph, and even Biograph, such resources were critical. Despite the diversity of exhibition outlets that existed at the turn of the century, vaudeville clearly had a unique impact on the film industry. In effect, a handful of vaudeville managers, by hiring exhibition firms on a long-term basis, chose the emerging generation of industry leaders.[44] They ended the turmoil of the mid 1890s, when film companies appeared, achieved prominence, and then disappeared, all within extremely short periods. Uncertain and difficult times were still ahead for all these producer-exhibitors, particularly as the Edison-initiated litigation progressed. But the figures whose activities dominate the remainder of this volume had already come to the fore.

PART 4

The Production Company Assumes Creative Dominance: 1900 – 1905

Penny arcade at Rocky Point, Providence, Rhode Island, runs the "Clamshell" mutoscope across the back wall (ca. 1901).

10

A Period of Commercial Crisis: 1900–1903

*B*y 1900, producers were assuming occasional though still infrequent control over editing and the construction of multi-shot narratives. This slight shift, however, became much more pronounced over the next several years as the production companies appropriated more of the responsibilities that had previously been shared with or determined by the exhibitor. This was particularly pronounced in fiction film-making, where centralization of control allowed producers to explore new representational techniques that proved popular among audiences. Although resistance to such a shift occurred with the illustrated lecture or travelogue, exhibitors were generally more and more restricted to supplying the sound accompaniment and acting as programmers. To be sure, these residual responsibilities still merit close attention, since the aggressive use of innovative sound could strongly shape the spectators' experience of the narrative and of the screening more generally. Nevertheless, during the 1900–1903 period, the production company became the principal site for cinematic creativity. This radical reorganization of cinematic practice had many underlying causes, but the rapidity of such change was clearly sparked by a period of sustained commercial crisis.

The American motion-picture industry experienced severe difficulties in the early 1900s on account of numerous factors: problems with technological standardization, patent and copyright problems, audience boredom with predictable subject matter, stagnant demand, and cutthroat competition. Sometimes old formulas still worked. In many localities film exhibition even enjoyed brief booms, but sustaining interest proved to be more difficult. Vaudeville theaters in cities such as Washington, D.C. (Chase's Theater), Philadelphia (Keith's), and Rochester, New York (Cook's Opera House), dropped motion pictures from their bills.[1] During most of the 1902–1903 season, Keith's Bijou was the only theater in Boston advertising motion pictures; similarly, there were many weeks in Philadelphia during both the 1901–1902 and 1902–1903 seasons when either Bradenburgh's or Keith's was the only theater showing films. In Pittsburgh, films were shown for only a few weeks during the course of

1901. Although moving pictures enjoyed a local revival early in 1902, they eventually moved to the bottom of the bill and assumed the role of "chasers."[2]

"Chaser" was a vaudeville term that referred to the concluding act of a program, during which large portions of the audience left the theater. It sometimes had a more pejorative sense, as when managers purposely put a bad act on the bill to "chase" patrons out of the theater so that new customers could be seated, but generally, it was analogous to the chaser of beer that followed a shot of whiskey (the star act of the show). Thus, "medium" or inexpensive acts were usually placed in this end position. As Keith's Boston manager remarked, "It seems a shame to waste [a good act] down in this part of the bill, for that is practically what it means as people keep going out all through the act. Personally, I believe it would be better to close the show . . . with a medium act, as not more than half the audience will remain to see a good one, no matter what it is."[3] By 1900 a "turn" (*ca.* fifteen minutes) of 35-mm films had become an inexpensive act. In Cincinnati, one long-standing critic later remarked:

> When pictures first came out people said it was only a craze—that it would not last—that the people would soon tire of it and after a few years it did seem that the public was really getting tired of moving pictures. One illustration of this seeming indifference was the habit the people got into of walking out of the vaudeville theatre as soon as the moving pictures, which closed the show, would be put on. . . . It did seem for a while that moving pictures would go out of fashion (*Billboard*, 27 June 1908, p. 8).

Many vaudeville houses billed their shows as "continuous," so that inexpensive acts were routinely used at slack times, and films in particular were shown more than once in the course of the day. "Chasers" often signaled the end of the leading acts and the beginning of the "supper show." Such was the case at Harry Davis' Avenue Theater in Pittsburgh when the nitrate films caught fire at the beginning of a screening in November 1903. As one reporter described the incident:

> When the film exploded a great portion of the audience was leaving the theater. The cinematographe is used as a sort of interval between the feature acts of the programme and what is termed the "supper show." At the conclusion of the regular acts many of the people in the house leave, and it is the late comers, those who drop in for a few minutes, who stay. The audience was wending its way leisurely to the exits when the explosion occurred (*Pittsburgh Dispatch*, 26 November 1903, p. 1).

Even during this period motion pictures seem to have had a small band of devotees, which is perhaps one reason they remained on the bill. Retrospective comments from the early nickelodeon era (1906–1908) suggest that the film-chaser phenomenon remained common at least through 1903.[4] Verification of this habit is difficult, however, since moving pictures then received very little critical attention. Yet the general indifference to film programs—in reviews, promotional blurbs, and advertising— seems to confirm these retrospective statements.

Storefront Theaters Struggle

Other kinds of exhibition also encountered difficulties. Storefront picture shows continued to operate, particularly in the Far West, generally for short periods. The Miles brothers operated in a vacant Seattle storefront for four months, beginning in November 1901. The capacity (seating and standing) was 160 people. Admission was ten cents and receipts were said to be as high as $160 a day. More typically these specialized houses suffered from a shortage of films and often failed in the face of competition from vaudeville. In Washington, D.C., for example, the Armat Moving- Picture Company turned the Halls of the Ancients into a picture house that opened on 10 September 1902. With six shows a day and a twenty-five-cent admission, it soon became a fairly popular entertainment center, showing such subjects as A TRIP THROUGH CHINA and THROUGH SWITZERLAND for several weeks at a time. (Many of the films were supplied by Burton Holmes as part of a licensing arrangement.) The city's principal vaudeville house, however, responded to this competition by adding the vitagraph to its bill in late November. Starting with A TRIP TO THE MOON, Vitagraph presented a new headline attraction each week, and within a month, the Halls of the Ancients had closed.[5]

Perhaps the best-known storefront from this period is Thomas L. Tally's Electric Theater, which debuted in Los Angeles on 16 April 1902. Open each evening from 7:30 to 10:30 P.M., it featured CAPTURE OF THE BIDDLE BROTHERS, NEW YORK CITY IN A BLIZZARD, and other views that Tally had apparently purchased. After a month, a new headline attraction was presented: THE GREAT BULL FIGHT. This was followed by films of the Martinique disaster and King Edward's coronation, each of which headed the bill for more than a month. Tally, faced with competition from a growing number of ten-cent vaudeville houses, may have closed his theater for several months (in any event, he stopped advertising) and toured as a traveling exhibitor. When he reopened in January, he had a new selection of films and a new feature—A TRIP TO THE MOON. Nevertheless, six months later Tally turned the Electric Theater into a ten-cent vaudeville house renamed the Lyric. That October, he announced his newest discovery, Méliès's FAIRYLAND; OR, THE KINGDOM OF THE FAIRIES, which he billed as "Better Than a Trip to the Moon." In a lengthy column the *Los Angeles Times* called it "an interesting exhibit of the limits to which moving picture making can be carried in the hands of experts equipped with time and money to carry out their devices." Nonetheless, after playing the picture for two weeks, Tally closed his theater and took to the road. He found that traveling exhibition was more profitable—at least until the nickelodeon era got under way.[6]

One ambitious effort to make storefront exhibition viable was launched by James MacConahey, who ran a chain of four or five such theaters from his base in Seattle. Besides the flagship house at $1305\frac{1}{2}$ Second Avenue in Seattle, there were houses in Spokane and Tacoma, Washington, as well as Victoria and Vancouver, British Columbia. The most detailed records exist for the storefront in the Donnelly Hotel at 744 Pacific Avenue in Tacoma. It was run by Mrs. Sally C. Sloan, a widow and one of the few women involved in motion-picture exhibition in the pre-nickelodeon era. Her picture house opened in mid November 1900 and ran through 1 June 1902. During the last eight weeks of 1900, gross income varied from $101.10 to $160.00 per week. During the first nine months of 1901, receipts usually fluctuated between $123.00 and $61.30, with $90 being about average. For three atypical weeks (holidays, convention weeks), however, the gross went as high as $299.30. The Searchlight Theater suffered a declining gate from late 1901, when films related to the McKinley assassination were shown, until it closed (see table 1). Not only did attendance decline in general, but repeated programs almost always drew fewer

TABLE 1. SEARCHLIGHT THEATER RECEIPTS

Week	Featured Subject	Receipts
13–19 Oct.	McKinley Funeral	$ 99.25
20–26 Oct.	McKinley Funeral	99.10
27 Oct.–2 Nov.	—	80.85
3–9 Nov.	—	81.60
10–16 Nov.	Transformations/Egypt	75.40
17–23 Nov.	Corbett and Fitzsimmons	89.00
24–30 Nov.	Bullfight	88.35
1–7 Dec.	War Scenes	70.15
8–14 Dec.	McKinley Funeral	83.85
15–21 Dec.	Tarrant Fire	82.45
22–28 Dec.	Execution of Czolgosz	148.95
29 Dec.–4 Jan.	Carnival Program	109.80
5–11 Jan.	Carnival Program	61.10
12–18 Jan.	Bulldog Tramp	73.10
19–25 Jan.	Bulldog Tramp	56.40
26 Jan.–1 Feb.	Eiffel Tower	30.90
2–8 Feb.	Eiffel Tower	57.85
9–15 Feb.	McKinley Speech	58.50
16–22 Feb.	Czolgosz Execution	80.35
23 Feb.–1 Mar.	Red Riding Hood	70.35
2–8 Mar.	Cinderella	75.05
9–15 Mar.	Trip Through Egypt	62.50
16–22 Mar.	Rough Riders	71.90
23–29 Mar.	[illegible]	86.00
31 Mar.–6 April	[illegible]	86.30
7–13 April	—	57.05
14–20 April	Boer War	59.70
21–27 April	Bullfight	60.25
28 April–4 May	Carnival Program	48.00
5–11 May	N.Y. Police Parade	40.40
13–18 May	Queen's Funeral	35.80
19–25 May	Red Riding Hood	35.70
26 May–1 June	—	29.55

SOURCE: Searchlight Theater, account book, 1900–1902.

The Searchlight Theater in Seattle, Washington.

Mrs. Sally C. Sloan of the Searchlight Theater in Tacoma.

"SEARCHLIGHT"

CONTINUOUS ENTERTAINMENT

EDISON'S

...Moving Pictures...

1 to 5, 6:30 to 10

744 PACIFIC AVE

DONNELLY HOTEL.

THIS WEEK'S PROGRAM

Volunteers Returning Home from the Phillipines

The Henley Boat Race

A Pillow Fight.

Santa Claus' Visit on Xmas Eve.

A Cold Trick on a Cold Night—Very Funny

May Pole Dance and Unthreading the May Pole

DRAGON RAILWAY AT PARIS

THE OLD TIME MINUET DANCE

Snow Scene—A French Hollowene Night

Panoramic View of Auburn State Prison

Where **LEON CZOLGOSZ** was taken after his sentence, and kept until the day of his **EXECUTION.** The door leading to the **DEATH CELL.** Taking Czolgosz to the **EXECUTION ROOM.** Testing electric chair with lamps. Arrival of Czolgosz. He stumbles as he comes to the chair. This was his only faulter. Received **3 SHOCKS OF 18,000 VOLTS** and is pronounced dead by the doctors.

The Mysterious Mirror Illusion

744 Pacific Ave.

(DONNELLY HOTEL)

1 to 5; 6:30 to 10.

ADMISSION 10 CTS.

Searchlight Theater program, Christmas week 1901.

customers the second and third time. Lacking new and exciting films, the Searchlight Theater closed its doors.[7] Storefront theaters like this one proved to be an exhibition form of limited viability in the early 1900s.

Traveling exhibition experienced a similar crisis, with the number of full-scale motion-picture exhibitions given by traveling showman in commercial venues reaching unprecedented lows from fall 1900 to fall 1902. The exhibitors who survived, men such as D. W. Robertson and J. P. Dibble, usually played in churches, schools, and YMCA's, where the audience's expectations were different from those of theatrical outlets, and sponsors could deliver patrons. Lyman H. Howe was the only traveling motion-picture showman who regularly played in commercial theaters and prospered.

If this decline is examined from the other end of the industry, namely from the point of view of raw-stock manufacturing, sales figures suggest an industry-wide crisis. Thus, Eastman Kodak's sales of cinematograph films reached a high in 1899 and then began to fall:

1897	$129,383
1898	72,546
1899	134,654
1900	104,425
1901	85,317
1902	89,153[8]

The crisis of this period may be best understood by examining the major American producers and exhibition services.

Biograph Struggles

While virtually every American producer and exhibitor encountered serious problems during the early 1900s, none faced greater difficulties than Biograph. Despite its unprecedented number of projectors in vaudeville houses during the White Rats strike of February–March 1901, many established customers either had abandoned the service or were soon to do so. In New Haven, S. Z. Poli stopped using Biograph's service after the 1898–1899 season and subsequently relied on various 35-mm exhibition services, particularly the vitagraph. In Rochester, Cook's Opera House avoided the biograph after a nine-week run from January to March 1901. In Chicago, Kohl & Castle tried the biograph in their vaudeville houses for May and June 1901 but then switched to a 35-mm service; Biograph's presence in that market was supplanted by Selig's polyscope and Spoor's kinodrome.

In part, the decline stemmed from the fact that Biograph's collage of short comedies, news films, and travel scenes had become familiar to audiences and no longer merited the service's high cost. With standard-gauge exhibitors offering similar programs at much lower fees, Biograph had to reduce its fees to remain competitive; by May 1901, the company was renting a biograph and twenty mutoscopes to summer parks for only $135 a week. This made Biograph competitive but devastated company profits. Barely two months after the White Rats strike, Biograph's exhibition service was losing money. Since the company was reluctant to cut expenses by reducing its

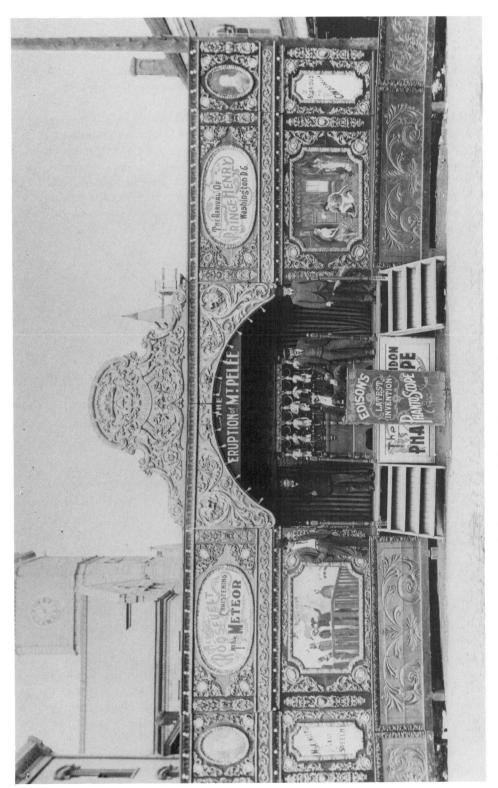

A European-style fairground front for an unidentified traveling showman (1902).

rate of production (as the previous chapter showed, its output remained essentially unchanged), profits turned into losses.[9]

Biograph's deteriorating financial situation was documented in a series of monthly reports, shown in table 2. Soon Keith's vaudeville circuit and the Orpheum houses in San Francisco and Los Angeles were among the company's few remaining customers.

Biograph's downward spiral was exacerbated by developments in the courts. Edison's patent-infringement suit against Biograph was decided in the U.S. Circuit Court for the Southern District of New York on 15 July 1901. Judge Hoyt Henry Wheeler ruled that Biograph "appears to have taken the substance of the invention covered by these claims, and the plaintiff, therefore, appears to be entitled to a decree."[10] Although his opinion was expressed in tentative terms, Wheeler was prepared to issue an injunction. Desperate Biograph executives sought a stay while they appealed the ruling to a higher court. In a deposition accompanying the motion for a stay, Harry Marvin declared:

> An injunction against us at this time would not only stop the production and reproduction of new films, but would render valueless most of the large stock of films on hand, for even should we ultimately succeed in the suit, those films which are in present demand because of their novelty and public interest, would have become obsolete and uncalled for, because of the distraction of the public mind by intervening events. Besides this, such an injunction would, of course, necessitate the immediate breaking of every contract we have with users of mutoscopes and biographs, for it would mean the withdrawal from the latter of all the films which they now have, and would stop the supply of mutoscope reels to users of the mu-

TABLE 2. MONTHLY EARNINGS OF THE AMERICAN MUTOSCOPE & BIOGRAPH COMPANY

1900		1901	
Net Earnings		*Biograph Earnings*	*Net Earnings*
Jan.	$ 23,501.04	Jan.	$1,788.54	$5,371.10
Feb.	12,783.88	Feb.	3,007.06	5,189.63
Mar.	9,315.08	Mar.	2,278.62	4,130.62
Apr.	10,986.23	Apr.	1,953.82	4,954.41
May	14,025.66	May	Loss 926.41	Loss 499.31
June	14,822.29	June	Loss 1,261.27	98.44
July	5,832.90	TOTAL	$6,840.36	$19,245.69[11]
Aug.	8,817.93			
Sept.	14,361.42			
Oct.	5,070.68			
Nov.	9,094.96			
Dec.	6,220.25			
TOTAL	$134,892.02			

toscope. I have every reason to believe that this would result in such a multiplicity of damage suits against us by our licensees as would bankrupt and utterly ruin our Company (23 July 1901, *Edison* v. *American Mutoscope Company*).

The stay was granted, subject to certain conditions, including a careful financial accounting. Biograph continued the production of news and actualities but not of studio or acted productions. It was also unable to alter its commercial methods: when Biograph attempted to sell 35-mm films supplied by the British-based Warwick Trading Company, the new enterprise was quickly blocked by the threat, if not the fact, of judicial action.[12]

During the eight-month appeal process, from 17 July 1901 (production No. 1950) to 14 March 1902 (production No. 2120), Biograph entered 171 films into its catalog, all of which were actualities. Robert K. Bonine, a cameraman who had previously worked for Edison, toured the Far East. Leaving San Francisco in June, he took almost seventy films in Hawaii (CUTTING SUGAR CANE, HONOLULU, No. 1968), the Far East (STREET SCENE, TOKIO, JAPAN, No. 2014; CHIEN-MEN GATE, PEKIN, No. 2052), and across the United States (COACHING PARTY, YOSEMITE VALLEY, No. 2063). Other cameramen photographed President McKinley's funeral ceremonies in September (almost twenty films) and the America's Cup race in late September and October (twelve films). Additional subjects included horse races, groundbreaking ceremonies for the forthcoming St. Louis World's Fair, and some local views in Cleveland, where the biograph was being featured. Based on court-mandated monthly financial reports providing the gross income of its biograph service plus the cost of negatives and prints, it is almost certain that the Biograph Company continued to lose money on its exhibition service given other business expenses (table 3).

The American Mutoscope & Biograph Company won a major legal victory on 10 March 1902, when the circuit court of appeals reversed the lower court's decision and dismissed Edison's case. Judge William J. Wallace found the inventor's patent claims to be fatally flawed because "the functional limitations which are inserted in the claims do not restrict the patent to the scope of Mr. Edison's real invention."[13] Edison's key motion-picture patents were declared invalid, terminating all of Edison's lawsuits for patent infringement. Biograph was thus free to pursue its motion-picture activities without restriction and immediately sought ways to bolster its faltering finances and revitalize its commercial activities. The company started to sell

TABLE 3. BIOGRAPH REPORTS, 1901–1902

Month	Gross Income	Film Costs
Aug.	$4565.66	$ 710.00
Sept.	4357.78	1621.73
Oct.	5110.13	1402.04
Nov.	4173.50	792.22
Dec.	4824.00	1594.10
Jan.	4074.79	954.87
Feb.	4373.25	818.98[14]

THE

UNITED STATES CIRCUIT COURT OF APPEALS
Second Circuit.

EDISON,
Appellee,
--- vs. ---
THE AMERICAN MUTOSCOPE COMPANY,
Appellant.

WALLACE, Circuit Judge.
"We conclude that the Court below erred in sustaining the validity of the claims in controversy, and that the decree should be reversed with costs, and with instructions to the court below to dismiss the bill."

BIOGRAPH

OUR NEW SPROCKET FILM
PROJECTING MACHINE,
THE
"BIOGRAPHET."
Superior to All Other Machines.   Film Runs Continuously.   No Shutter,
No Flicker. $65.00 Per Week, Machine and Operator,
With All the Film You Want.

WINS

By virtue of the above **FINAL DECISION,** we now offer for sale standard size sprocket film made from the ORIGINAL BIOGRAPH NEGATIVES, the FAMOUS MELIES STAR FILMS, and the celebrated films of the WARWICK TRADING CO. We have a large stock on hand, which can be delivered at once.

AMERICAN MUTOSCOPE & BIOGRAPH CO., No. 841 BROADWAY, N. Y.

35-mm "reduction" prints of its earlier large-format films. These were printed optically, usually dropping every other frame to reduce the "proper" projection speed from thirty frames per second to a more typical fifteen.[15] It also became the American agent for the Warwick Trading Company. Yet the company's jaunty advertisements, declaring "The Biograph Wins," masked the fact that this shift in policy took time and money to implement. Biograph's first sales catalog was not distributed until November, and copyright records suggest that the process of making its full repertoire of films available in 35-mm may have taken over a year, from mid 1902 to mid 1903. Biograph also continued to push its old-style 70-mm-gauge exhibition service for $105 a week along with the standard 35-mm format (first known as the biographet, then the bioscope) for $65 a week.[16] With Robert K. Bonine acting as principal cameraman, production activities were expanded. The first production was WHEN THE CAT'S AWAY, THE MICE WILL PLAY (No. 2122), a simple studio film of rats in silhouette, which may have been intended to comment on Edison's defeat. Although feline Edison was at least temporarily incapacitated, the Biograph mice did not resume studio production of acted films until mid May. Meanwhile, Biograph used cameras of two different gauges to complement its different services. In some cases, both types were at the same events. Two films entitled INSTALLATION CEREMONIES OF PRESIDENT BUTLER, COLUMBIA COLLEGE (Nos. 2132 and 2133) were photographed on 19 April 1902, one in each gauge.

Of the approximately 110 Biograph films taken between mid May and mid September, about 45 (40 percent) used actors. Most comedies were in 70-mm, including A POET'S REVENGE (No. 2142) and A PIPE STORY OF THE FOURTH (No. 2183, also known as UNCLE PETE'S PIPE: A TRAGEDY OF THE GLORIOUS FOURTH). Frederick Burr Opper's well-known comic-strip characters Alphonse and Gaston were presented in ALPHONSE AND GASTON HELPING IRISHMAN (No. 2169), THE POLITE FRENCHMEN (No. 2171), and THE SMOKING LAMP (No. 2187), all of which were shot on 70-mm stock. Wallace McCutcheon, however, chose 35-mm negative for the eight-part FOXY GRANDPA SERIES (Nos. 2141, 2145–2151), which, according to the catalog, "illustrates scenes and incidents from Wm. A. Brady's musical production *Foxy Grandpa*." The films used the actors and sets of the musical that was then (mid May) concluding a four-month run at the nearby Fourteenth Street Theater. The musical was based, in turn, on a well-known comic strip created by Carl E. ("Bunny") Schultz. One scene, THE CREATORS OF FOXY GRANDPA, introduced Schultz and the principal performers—Joseph Hart (Foxy Grandpa), Carrie DeMar (Polly), and the two actors playing mischievous boys. The others were comic vignettes, similar in complexity to a newspaper comic. While the scenes were often shown as individual subjects, exhibitors also grouped them in more elaborate combinations.

Multi-shot acted films were still rare at Biograph. A PIPE STORY OF THE FOURTH, filmed by Bitzer, was composed of two shots: the first shows an old gentleman entering a store and buying fireworks; in the second he is walking home and smoking a pipe when the fireworks catch fire and explode. CAUGHT IN THE UNDERTOW (No. 2210) begins with a broad establishing shot taken from a pier: a swimmer tires, and the lifeguards launch their boat and rescue the stricken vacationer. The next scene, a much closer view that was taken on the beach, shows the victim being resuscitated. (The subject recalls the two-shot LIFE RESCUE AT ATLANTIC CITY [© as LIFE RESCUE AT LONG BRANCH], taken by the Edison Company a year earlier.) GRAND-

No. **2121**
Title *B.F.Keith's New Theatre, Philadelphia.*
Length *276 ft.*
Code Word *Garangan.*

No. **2122**
Title *"When the Cat's Away, the Mice will Play."*
Length *67 ft.*
Code Word *Garanhao.*

No. 2149 S.

Title *"Foxy Grandpa" Shows Boys He is a Magician.*

Length 112 ft.

Code Word *Garatura*

No. 2150 S.

Title *Boys Take Grandpa's Cigars with Distressing Results*

Length 50 ft.

Code Word *Garauna*

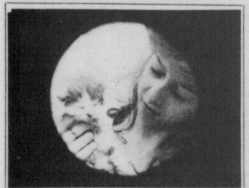

No. 2197
Title *Grandpa's Reading Glass.*
Length *525 ft.*
Code Word *Garenklos.*

No. 2198
Title *Sweethearts.*
Length *246 ft.*
Code Word *Garenmolen.*

PA'S READING GLASS (No. 2197) reworked a popular film made by the Englishman G. A. Smith, GRANDMA'S READING GLASS. Biograph's fourteen-shot film intercuts scenes of a little girl looking through a magnifying glass with views of the objects at which she is looking. This second group of shots does not show the objects from her perspective but rather, isolates them against a black background and further concentrates the spectator's attention with a circular matte that is meant to suggest the reading glass. The objects, in other words, are presented to the audience rather than being integrated into a verisimilar spatial world.

Biograph's many problems did not end with its March victory over Edison. On 30 September 1902, the Wizard of Menlo Park obtained two patent reissues based on more refined claims, Nos. 12,037 and 12,038. In November, Edison once again sued the American Mutoscope & Biograph Company for patent infringement.[17] Even before the suit, Biograph was making few films for its vaudeville service, which suggests that this area remained unprofitable and that cost cutting was necessary. Instead, the company turned to industrial films for clients such as the National Cash Register Company. Early in 1903, Bonine took approximately thirty standard-gauge films in Dayton, Ohio, including GIRLS IN PHYSICAL CULTURE, N.C.R. CO. (No. 2270), TESTING JACKS (No. 2280), and many scenes of company executives. These films were used for illustrated lectures promoting innovative company activities. In March, Biograph also acquired some forty 35-mm films made by the Miles brothers in the Klondike and California and was soon marketing their BLASTING IN TREADWELL GOLD MINE (No. 2305) and DOG BAITING AND FIGHTING (No. 2326) to interested exhibitors.[18]

Biograph's limited production and its uneasy split between two film gauges adversely affected its exhibition service. Although the price of its 70-mm service was reduced to eighty dollars a week plus transportation (and its 35-mm bioscope service to forty dollars), even Benjamin F. Keith grew unhappy, and when the vaudeville magnate opened his new Philadelphia theater in late November 1902, the biograph was not on the bill. At his other houses, Biograph offered a "very ordinary selection of pictures this week, there not being one of exceptional interest." Dissatisfied patrons often left in large numbers before the program was over. "Personally, it is always attractive for me," reported Boston manager M. J. Keating, "and I cannot see why it does not interest others." Keith's managers tried to revive interest by moving the biograph from its final "chaser" position to one that was earlier on the bill. There, it "seemed to catch a class of people to whom it was comparatively new," but their initial interest faded with greater familiarity.[19]

A typical Biograph program relied on a variety format of short actualities with a few trick films and comedies thrown in for relief. One "fairly good selection of views" from late March, according to New York manager S. K. Hodgdon, ran thirteen minutes and included the following:

THE AMERICAN BIOGRAPH

The Most Perfect of All Picture-Moving Machines

THE FOUR MADCAPS (New)
Acrobatic dance by a famous troupe from the Winter Garden, Berlin.

"TWO'S COMPANY"
An animated reproduction of the famous painting by Vergillio Tojetti.

A QUIET HOOKAH (New)
A vivid and characteristic bit of local color from Constantinople.

AN OCEAN FLYER
SS *St. Paul* of the American Line, at full speed in the Narrows, New York Harbor, as she appears on her way to Southampton.

AN ATTACK BY TORPEDO BOAT
Splendid work by a German flotilla in their famous wedge formation. Taken at Kiel.

A LITTLE RAY OF SUNSHINE
Comedy scene.

THE GALETEA BRIDGE (New)
The only bridge to Stamboul. A remarkable picture of Turkish life.

THE GRAND FOUNTAIN
Longchamps Palace, Marseilles, France.

IN THE REDWOODS OF CALIFORNIA (New)
A tourist coaching party on the road to the Yosemite.

THE BLACK SEA (New)
A beautiful panorama.

DIVERSE DIVES
Bathing scene at Bath Beach, L.I.

A MODERN MIRACLE
The law of gravitation overcome by the expert swimmers at Bath Beach, L.I. Backward leaps from the water to the pier.

All but one new picture came from Biograph's sister companies in Europe. No news films or multi-shot productions were included on the program. The travel scenes of Turkey were scattered throughout rather than consolidated into a single headline attraction as Vitagraph was then doing. The following week, Keith's managers expressed their universal disappointment, and beginning with the week of 6 April, Biograph was supplanted by Vitagraph in Keith's Boston and New York theaters.[20]

Manager Hodgdon in New York was enthusiastic about the vitagraph:

> This is the first day of the new moving picture machine, which is evidently going to be a big success, judging from the way it was received by the audience this afternoon. There is no question that when it comes to steadiness the Biograph is the nearest mechanically perfect of any of the motion picture machines, but so far as interesting subjects are concerned, the people who control this instrument have them badly beaten (*Keith Reports*, week of 6 April 1903).

Similar relief was expressed throughout the circuit as Vitagraph offered Méliès's ROBINSON CRUSOE and A TRIP TO THE MOON. Biograph's 70-mm service made its last appearance at San Francisco's Orpheum Theater in September 1903, and even during its final year, the Orpheum increasingly "rested" the service (*i.e.*, dropped it from the bill for a week or two at a time). Meanwhile Biograph's 35-mm bioscope service found outlets in a number of second-class theaters, including Grauman's small-time vaudeville house in San Francisco.[21] Not until the fall of 1903 did Biograph complete its transition to the 35-mm standard format. Until then, its ability to act as an effective exhibition service was severely limited, thus giving credence to the argument that film exhibition in the 1901–1903 era commonly functioned as "chasers."

Edison and His Licensees

Thomas Edison's actions affected the 35-mm sector of the industry as well. By 1900 the inventor's reliance on licensees was a failure, not only curtailing his potential profits but leaving him vulnerable if the courts did not sustain his motion-picture patents. In response to this undesirable situation, the Edison Manufacturing Company inaugurated several important changes. That November, general manager William Gilmore and kinetograph department head James White hired Edwin S. Porter to improve their technical system. Porter had previously built highly regarded cameras, printers, and projectors, but his workshop had suffered a devastating fire. Now he agreed to work on the projecting kinetoscope for fifteen dollars a week. The resulting 1901 model was "a complete revolution in projecting machines" and the first to take up 1,000 feet of film on a single reel.[22] The Edison Company also constructed a new motion-picture studio to replace the Black Maria. Located at 41 East Twenty-first Street, it was in the heart of New York's entertainment district, where all the material and personnel needed for production were readily at hand. Although the rooftop studio depended on sunlight for illumination, it was glass-enclosed and could operate year-round. Construction began in October, cost $2,800, and was completed by January 1901. A month later, the studio was in operation, outclassing the open-air stages of Biograph, Lubin, and others.

Even as the Twenty-first Street studio was being finished, Edison's relationship with his most important licensee changed drastically. On 10 January, after American Vitagraph failed to pay its 10 percent royalty on exhibition income, Gilmore and White terminated the company's license, forcing Blackton and Smith to stop making films. Although Vitagraph henceforth suffered under Edison's onerous restrictions, the company still managed to extend its exhibition circuit. When a vaudeville theater opened in Utica, New York, on 19 January 1901, a vitagraph was regularly featured on its bill. In Brooklyn, Percy Williams offered Vitagraph steady employment after the White Rats strike. In New Haven, Vitagraph became Poli's exhibition service of choice during the 1901–1902 and 1902–1903 seasons. Though legally required to show only Edison films, Vitagraph increased its reliance on European pictures to fill the void left by its own curtailed production. In fact, this halt in filmmaking may not have been absolute. To retain its newly acquired New Haven outlet, Vitagraph may have filmed President Roosevelt's visit to New Haven for Yale University's two-hundredth anniversary on 23 October 1901.[23] If so, such activities were rare and much too risky to undertake in the immediate New York area.

While William Paley with his kalatechnoscope continued as an Edison licensee (apparently paying a substantial royalty), his productions were of only minor importance to the Edison enterprise. Much of Paley's energies went to servicing Proctor's growing chain of theaters with local views. Several were taken for the opening of Proctor's Montreal theater in March 1901, but only one of these, MONTREAL FIRE DEPARTMENT ON RUNNERS, was copyrighted by Edison and sold to independent exhibitors.[24] Another group of Canadian subjects, including ARRIVAL OF GOVERNOR GENERAL, LORD MINTO, AT QUEBEC, were taken for the Montreal theater in February 1902 and likewise copyrighted by Thomas Edison. The need for new subjects, however, was primarily filled by the kinetograph department's own productions.

MONTREAL FIRE DEPARTMENT ON RUNNERS

Production at the New Edison Studio

Between early 1901 and early 1903 film production at the new Edison studio was clearly the most important in America. There, filmmaking personnel assumed un-precedented (by American standards) control over motion-picture storytelling, and as a result, the production company, rather than the exhibitor, began to create the program. Edison's filmmakers, along with those in other countries, began to elabo-rate a system of representation, of spatial and temporal relations between shots, that typified the cinema for the remaining years covered by this volume. An understand-ing of this development requires careful scrutiny of the films because the process took place over the course of many pictures, and with frequent interruptions and digressions.

The collaborative team undertaking this important shift consisted of George S. Fleming, an actor and scenic designer, and Edwin S. Porter. The Edison Company hired Fleming for twenty dollars a week and placed him in charge of its new studio, while Porter was shifted from the Edison laboratory to serve as cameraman. Although Porter was the junior member of this collaborative team, he quickly emerged as its key contributor: his expertise as an electrician and mechanic help to maintain the studio in operating order, and at the same time, his work as a motion-picture oper-ator and exhibitor made him familiar with the kinds of films that pleased audiences.

Working under White's supervision, Fleming and Porter soon established their worth with films like KANSAS SALOON SMASHERS (© 23 February 1901), which reenacted and burlesqued a recent news event—Carrie Nation's saloon-smashing spree in Wichita, Kansas. For the one-shot film, men in drag played many of the female roles, making the women sexually unappealing. The women's invasion of a male refuge is seemingly attributed to sexual frustration and the concomitant need for revenge. With imitation a sure indication of a film's commercial value, it was notable that Lubin was selling MRS. NATION AND HER HATCHET BRIGADE by early March, and Biograph made CARRIE NATION SMASHING A SALOON (No. 1845) for its exhibition service and mutoscopes in early April. Porter and Fleming had quickly produced a hit.

The new studio resulted in a burst of activity; Edison copyrighted sixty films in the six months following its completion, and many more pictures were made. Thirty-five (58 percent) used actors of some kind. Among the vaudeville performers who frequented the studio were the Gordon Sisters with their boxing act, the Lukens brothers, who were novel gymnasts, and the Faust family of acrobats. Laura Comstock and her dog, Mannie, appeared in LAURA COMSTOCK'S BAG-PUNCHING DOG, a two-shot film in which Porter asserted editorial control by following a portrait-like view of the attractive Comstock and her dog with a shot of Mannie punching a suspended bag with his nose. In the late 1890s, as we have seen, exhibitors often showed portraits of prominent persons in their programs using lantern slides. Portraits of admirals were followed by scenes of their ships. Porter, the veteran exhibitor, recognized that the film producer could adeptly appropriate this practice, and thus LAURA COMSTOCK'S BAG-PUNCHING DOG introduced what Tom Gunning calls the "emblematic close-up." This technique became popular with other American producers and remained in frequent use throughout the period.[25]

The Edison Manufacturing Company produced an abundance of comedies. Some, such as HAPPY HOOLIGAN APRIL-FOOLED and HAPPY HOOLIGAN SURPRISED, consisted of one shot and were quite similar to those made in the 1890s. Often Porter added a brief tag or punch line at the conclusion of a typical one-shot scene. In THE FINISH OF BRIDGET MCKEEN, made that February, the Irish cook has difficulty lighting the stove and adds kerosine. With Porter substituting a dummy for the actor by using stop-action techniques, an explosion sends the cook flying up into the air. After an extended period, pieces of her body fall back to earth. (Here time is stretched rather than condensed, as with most pro-filmic manipulations of time in early films.) The picture then dissolves to the last scene, a painted backdrop of a grave on which is written "Here Lies the Remains of Bridget McKeen, Who Started a Fire with Kerosine." This additional shot did not make any sense when shown on its own and so was sold with the first scene. In this regard, the output of two-shot pictures did not directly challenge the editorial prerogatives of the exhibitor. Yet these films reveal a filmmaking team eager to juxtapose shots to produce a more effective picture.

Beginning with THE FINISH OF BRIDGET MCKEEN, the dissolve from one scene to the next became a common procedure at the Edison Manufacturing Company. Executed during the printing process rather than in the camera, it enabled the producer to exert editorial control in a manner that enhanced exhibition. In most high-class lantern programs, exhibitors dissolved from slide to slide; some exhibitors even dissolved from slides to film or from film to film. To execute such techniques in the projection booth with films was difficult and required extra personnel. Thus Porter and Fleming found ways to give potential purchasers something extra.

LAURA COMSTOCK'S BAG-PUNCHING DOG

Groups of actualities, filmed under White's supervision, complemented Fleming and Porter's comedies. In addition to President McKinley's second inauguration, particular emphasis was placed on the Pan-American Exposition at Buffalo, New York. OPENING, PAN-AMERICAN EXPOSITION was photographed on 20 May 1901, and at least another twenty films followed shortly thereafter.[26] One of the most popular of these was A TRIP AROUND THE PAN-AMERICAN EXPOSITION, a 625-foot, ten-minute film taken from the front of a launch that toured the canal winding through the exposition grounds. Exhibitors could purchase the film in shorter lengths of 200, 300, 400, or 500 feet. PAN-AMERICAN EXPOSITION BY NIGHT, photographed by Porter, was a technical tour de force that began with a smooth, sweeping pan-

An Edison advertisement in The New York Clipper.

A TRIP AROUND THE PAN-AMERICAN EXPOSITION *utilized a common technique and turned the spectator into an armchair tourist.*

orama of the electric tower during the day and continued at night in the same direction and at the same pace, with the lights of the tower providing a decorative image. Only a new and highly sophisticated panning mechanism made this film possible. The time change was modeled on a popular stereopticon convention—day-to-night dissolving views.

In early September, James White and several kinetograph department employees filmed William McKinley's visit to the Pan-American Exposition on President's Day, 5 September (PRESIDENT MCKINLEY'S SPEECH AT THE PAN-AMERICAN EXPOSITION and PRESIDENT MCKINLEY REVIEWING THE TROOPS AT THE PAN-AMERICAN EXPOSITION). On the following day, the camera crew waited outside the Temple of Music while McKinley was inside shaking hands with well-wishers. Suddenly the President was gunned down by the anarchist Leon Czolgosz, and the camera crew filmed the stunned and angry crowd. These scenes were an Edison exclusive. After McKinley's death, Edison cameramen, like their Biograph rivals, filmed the funeral ceremonies. PRESIDENT MCKINLEY'S FUNERAL CORTEGE AT BUFFALO, NEW YORK; PRESIDENT MCKINLEY'S FUNERAL CORTEGE AT WASHINGTON, D.C., and a half-dozen films of the funeral at Canton, Ohio, fulfilled cinema's promise as a visual newspaper. Films such as FUNERAL LEAVING THE PRESIDENT'S HOUSE AND CHURCH AT CANTON, OHIO consisted of many brief shots as the cameramen struggled to capture glimpses of the casket on the way to the cemetery. Camera movement and improvised shooting convey a sense of immediacy and urgency.

The Edison Company assumed greater editorial control than before. PRESIDENT MCKINLEY'S FUNERAL CORTEGE AT BUFFALO, NEW YORK was a 400-foot "series" consisting of four separate films held together by dissolves introduced in the printing stage. COMPLETE FUNERAL CORTEGE AT CANTON, OHIO was another series, consisting of six different subjects. A similar approach was used for the America's Cup races, which Edison cameramen filmed in early October. In these several instances, editorial responsibility had become a contested arena. If the exhibitor did not like the sequence of subjects or only wanted some of the films and not the whole series, Edison was happy to sell them on an individual basis. Programs and reviews indicate that most prominent exhibitors were not yet willing to relinquish control over this area of practice.

Editorial control remained ambiguous in the four-shot EXECUTION OF CZOLGOSZ WITH PANORAMA OF AUBURN PRISON, Porter and Fleming's most ambitious undertaking during 1901. Exhibitors could purchase the picture either with or without the opening two shots, which were sweeping panoramas of Auburn State Prison taken on the morning that McKinley's assassin, Czolgosz, was executed. Porter then dissolved to two studio scenes that reenacted the execution. Shot 3 shows Czolgosz in his cell. The wardens enter, open the cell door, and escort him off-camera. Shot 4 shows the testing of the electric chair, Czolgosz's entrance, his being strapped to the chair, and the actual execution. Its strong frontal composition leaves the spectator with a head-on view of the assassin's death. Not only is the operational aesthetic at work in this display, but the spectator is turned into a witness (with the reenacted nature of this event suppressed).

EXECUTION OF CZOLGOSZ focuses attention on the filmic representation of space and time. In its longer form, at least, the film offers a well-developed spatial world. Its relationship between outside and inside, while just beginning to be utilized by American and European producers, was hardly novel, for it had been commonly used in stereopticon shows. Temporality was more puzzling and complex. Czolgosz's cell was right next to the execution chamber, and in the actual sequence of events, the wardens tested the chair before removing the condemned man from his cell. The film did not present the scenes along a simple, linear time line. First, all actions in Czolgosz's cell are shown, then everything of interest that took place in the execution chamber. Time does not move steadily forward as the scene shifts from scene 3 to scene 4. Portions of the two scenes occur simultaneously as Porter offers two different perspectives on the same event. Film thus allowed the spectator to be in two places simultaneously or see an event from two perspectives. It was this insight that underlay many of the innovations in cinematic representation that followed.

Edison's July 1901 court victory over Biograph, although later overturned, meant that his company was virtually the only American film manufacturer providing exhibitors with films (the setbacks suffered by 35-mm competitors are discussed below). Pressure to reduce prices was eliminated as film sales rose 65 percent (from $49,756.22 in 1900–1901 to $82,107.82 in 1901–1902) and film profits rose 85 percent (from $20,278.26 to $37,433.90). The McKinley films provided the Edison Manufacturing Company with a rare opportunity to derive maximum commercial benefit from its legal monopoly, and it sold more than $45,000 worth of films in the last four months of 1901—practically equal to the whole of the previous business year.

The Edison Manufacturing Company adequately met its new responsibility as sole domestic supplier of films to American exhibitors throughout the summer and early

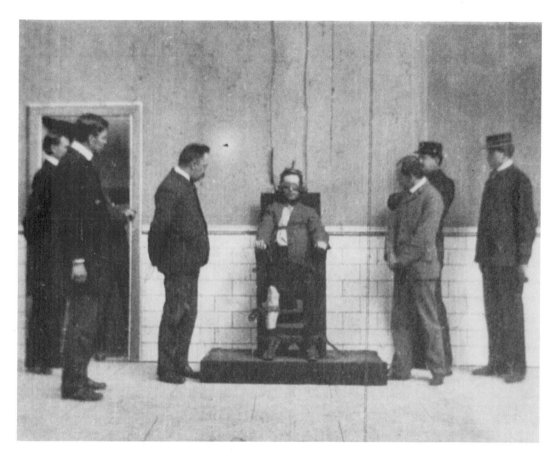

Execution of Czolgosz (*scene 4*) *uses presentational staging to reenact the electrocution.*

fall of 1901. However, the absence of competition was soon felt, and by November, studio production had declined and then almost ceased. Only fourteen of the ninety-seven films copyrighted by Edison between mid November 1901 and mid April 1902 relied on actors, and many of these were acquired from Vitagraph. Much energy was devoted to Jeffries and Ruhlin Sparring Contest at San Francisco, Cal., November 15, 1901. Since the disappointing fight had lasted only five rounds (barely twenty minutes), the picture could be shown only as one act in a variety program. New scenes were taken along the West Coast (Panoramic View Near Mt. Golden on the Canadian Pacific R.R. and Ostrich Farms at Pasadena) and in Mexico City, where James White photographed a bullfight on 2 February.

During White's absence, production on the East Coast practically ceased. Porter and Fleming returned to the studio in early 1902 with a few productions, but nothing compared to the first months of 1901. One clever effort was Uncle Josh at the Moving Picture Show, which lampoons a rube farmer who confuses what he sees on the screen with real life and becomes more and more involved with the images. He climbs on stage and mimics an attractive female dancer in the first film but jumps back into his seat as the onrushing Black Diamond Express approaches in the next. The denouement comes when he tries to break up a kissing scene and stops the show

UNCLE JOSH AT THE MOVING PICTURE SHOW. *A title slide introduces the films. Rear-screen projection, although featured in this film, was unusual (but not unknown).*

instead. An imitation of Robert Paul's THE COUNTRYMAN'S FIRST SIGHT OF THE ANIMATED PICTURES (1901), Edison's version was redone to feature its own films and titles, advertising the projecting kinetoscope.

Duping of European fiction films effectively substituted for studio production, although the Edison staff still found it necessary to shoot American news events and scenes of local interest. With White's return from Mexico, the kinetograph department resumed its treatment of cinema as a visual newspaper. Films were taken of

important news events such as the Paterson, New Jersey, fire of 9 February 1902. Multicamera coverage was used for the visit of Prince Henry of Prussia to the United States in late February and early March. A kinetograph record of Theodore Roosevelt's appearance at the Charleston (South Carolina) Exposition on President's Day, 9 April, demonstrated the chief executive's courage in emulating McKinley's fateful visit to the Buffalo Exposition six months earlier (PRESIDENT ROOSEVELT REVIEWING THE TROOPS AT CHARLESTON EXPOSITION).

If cinema was typically seen as a visual newspaper in 1902, newspapers sometimes borrowed from the cinema. A Sunday comic strip from The New York Journal.

Edison Story Films

The dismissal of Thomas Edison's patent suit in March 1902 dramatically altered his company's commercial standing. As Biograph and other producers resumed business, the inventor's firm was compelled to undertake more ambitious projects. With Fleming increasingly in the background, Porter began work on a series of story films, including the three-shot APPOINTMENT BY TELEPHONE (April 1902), the ten-shot JACK AND THE BEANSTALK (June 1902), the three-shot HOW THEY DO THINGS ON THE BOWERY (October 1902), and the nine-shot LIFE OF AN AMERICAN FIREMAN (November 1902–January 1903). With these works he asserted clear control over the editing process, explored the possibilities of fictional storytelling, and further developed the possibilities of spatial and temporal relations between shots. This small group of films is among the most innovative in American cinema

APPOINTMENT BY TELEPHONE was a preliminary application of principles that Porter used for JACK AND THE BEANSTALK, a 625-foot fairy-tale film that took six weeks to make and cost almost one thousand dollars. In both cases, the narrative was distributed among the various shots, a marked innovation over previous Edison fiction films. JACK AND THE BEANSTALK was modeled on several Georges Méliès productions, particularly BLUEBEARD (1901), and followed the well-known, bowdlerized version of the fairy tale, in which a fairy tells Jack that the bags of gold, magical harp, and hen once belonged to his father (the giant took them after killing him) and that Jack must slay the giant and regain his rightful possessions.[27] In the course of telling this story, Porter created visions using "object animation" superimposed against black backgrounds. While temporality remains nonspecific, if generally linear, the spatial world is meticulously constructed, often by effective use of entrances and exits. In shot 5, for example, Jack exits by climbing the beanstalk and moving out of the frame. In shot 6 he is still climbing the beanstalk, then looks downward and waves as if to his mother and playmates beneath him. Such glances reinforce the spatial relationships between shots.

Temporality became a central concern in Porter's next two story films. Once again, Méliès provided a picture to emulate—A TRIP TO THE MOON (LE VOYAGE DANS LA LUNE). In one juxtaposition of shots, a scene ends with the rocket hitting the man in the moon in the eye, and the next scene begins with the rocket landing on the moon's surface and its travelers disembarking. The landing of the space vehicle is thus shown twice in rapid succession. Porter applied this brief temporal overlap to a problem that he had previously explored: the depiction of simultaneous actions and the representation of an event from multiple points of view. The results can be seen in HOW THEY DO THINGS ON THE BOWERY. The first shot takes place on a city street as the rube is picked up by a prostitute and they go inside a saloon. In scene 2, they enter the saloon and sit down. The woman drugs the farmer's drink, and when he feels its ill effects, she takes his valuables and leaves. The waiter, discovering that he cannot pay the bill, ejects him and his suitcase. The final scene takes place outside: a paddy wagon comes down the street, parks, and waits for the rube and his suitcase, which are soon thrown in the gutter. Actions unfold in staccato form, with the passage of time manipulated for comic effect. Events that happen simultaneously are shown in successive views. The repeated ejection of the rube and his suitcase at the end of shots 2 and 3 specifies the temporal and spatial relationship between the two shots that would have previously remained imprecise or dependent on extra-textual clar-

Porter's JACK AND THE BEANSTALK. *The fairy shows Jack the giant's castle magic-lantern style (shot 7). Jack steals the gold from the giant's home, which is furnished with a real table and a pasteboard cauldron (shot 8). In the closing tableau, the fairy leads Jack and his mother to their new home.*

ification. This was also the first Edison fiction film with a panning camera, a technique that not only conveyed the immediacy of actualities but emphasized the existence of a spatial world beyond the confines of the camera frame.

Porter systematically applied these techniques to LIFE OF AN AMERICAN FIRE-MAN, which he made with James White. As already noted, almost every producer had a selection of fire films, and several were multi-shot films, such as Selig's LIFE OF A FIREMAN, Lubin's GOING TO THE FIRE AND RESCUE, and James Williamson's FIRE! The plethora of such subjects encouraged innovation, however, as James White and Porter emphasized spectacle, introduced novel scenes, and utilized new strategies of representation.

It is hard to give a precise narrative account of LIFE OF AN AMERICAN FIREMAN. The Edison Manufacturing Company, for example, offered two quite different descriptions. In the often-reprinted catalog version, the opening scene shows a fire chief dreaming of his wife and child, whom he subsequently rescues, while another description, offered in the *New York Clipper*, emphasizes the film's documentary qualities over the elements of fictional narrative.[28] Thus it becomes clear that exhibitors could shape the spectators' understanding of the screen narrative along divergent lines through their live narration and advance publicity (newspaper promotions, posters, etc.).

LIFE OF AN AMERICAN FIREMAN is one of the most extreme expressions of early cinema's distinctive nonlinear continuity, one that was so unfamiliar to later spectators and scholars that a modernized, reedited version of the film was long accepted as the original, "logical" ordering of shots. In fact, the authenticated version relies on overlapping action and extreme forms of narrative repetition. Overlapping action is evident in shots 3 and 4, where a long line of firemen jump out of their beds and slide

LIFE OF AN AMERICAN FIREMAN. *Two frames each from eight of the nine shots (shot 5 is shown once, shot 7 is missing).*

down the fire pole, and then come down the pole again and harness their horses inside the firehouse. At the next cut, the horse-drawn engines dash off twice, in interior and exterior views. The last two shots show the rescue from two different perspectives. Shot 8 shows an interior of the burning bedroom, where the woman struggles to the window, cries for help, and collapses. The fireman enters and breaks the window (at which a ladder promptly appears); he then carries her out through the window and returns via the ladder for the child hidden in the bed covers. In shot 9, the same actions are shown from the exterior, yet these two concluding scenes are complementary rather than redundant. The same event unfurls twice, but time is severely condensed whenever something happens offscreen. In the interior scene, for example, the time allowed for the fireman to go down or up the ladder is very brief. Together, these final shots provide a "complete" idea of what is actually taking place, demonstrating how indicational rather than verisimilar temporality within scenes complements the relationship between scenes. Porter thus offered a concept of continuity (indeed, scenes such as these were often referred to as "continuous") that is radically different from the linear continuity of the classical Hollywood cinema. In early cinema, time rather than space could be easily manipulated both within scenes and in the relation between scenes. These sequences also encouraged spectators to mentally reorder and synthesize the actions depicted in different shots. Such reorganization is not unlike that required of the variety-program spectator, who needed to mentally integrate related scenes that had been separated for purposes of diversity (see programs, pp. 259, 312–313). Variety programs and story films thus demanded surprisingly similar methods of interpretation and reception.

This burst of innovative filmmaking might suggest that the industry was fully capable of supplying exhibitors and spectators with new, attractive films. Yet the output of such subjects was very limited. Edison was the sole American producer of elaborate story films during 1902 and even its ambitious undertakings came to an abrupt end after LIFE OF AN AMERICAN FIREMAN. A virtual ban on production at Edison lasted for almost four months. Once again, these disruptions were caused by events in the courts. Two quite different types of cases were involved. The first and most important (at least in terms of production) dealt with copyright infringement and was precipitated by Sigmund Lubin, while the second involved Edison's infringement of Thomas Armat's projection patents. To understand these problems, Lubin's activities during this period need to be considered.

Sigmund Lubin

Production and exhibition continued at Lubin's company during the first half of 1901. Some of his films were remakes of popular subjects made by competitors, such as AN AFFAIR OF HONOR, which mimicked the popular Biograph film of the same name. Others elaborated on the original: MRS. NATION AND HER HATCHET BRIGADE, for example, inspired by Porter's one-shot KANSAS SALOON SMASHERS, became a two-shot film billed as "Direct from Kansas."[29]

> Mrs. Nation addressing a large number of her followers after which she leads them into the Senate Saloon and proceeds to demolish the interior. Bottles are seen flying through the air, and beer kegs are rolled into the

street and emptied. The picture concludes when a policeman arrests Mrs. Nation followed by hundreds of persons hooting and yelling (*New York Clipper*, 9 March 1901, p. 44).

This precocious film almost certainly confronted the crucial conceptual problem of depicting spatial and temporal relationships between outside and inside—several months before EXECUTION OF CZOLGOSZ—and for this reason, it is particularly unfortunate that a print does not survive. But imitation was not practiced only by Lubin. He produced PHOTOGRAPHER'S MISHAPS and TWO RUBES AT THE THEATRE in March 1901 and saw them remade by the Edison Company later in the year.

Although Edison claimed "special photographic concessions" for the Pan-American Exposition, Lubin took many films there, including PANORAMA OF THE EXPOSITION, COUCHE DANCE ON THE MIDWAY, and WEDDING PROCESSION IN CAIRO. He was also granted the only concession on the midway as a moving-picture exhibitor, which Edison lawyers attempted to end by threatening legal action against the Pan-American Exposition Company. The company, however, declined to terminate Lubin's contract, remarking that "no matter what concern we might grant a concession to for the exhibition of moving pictures we would, in all probability, be sued or at least be threatened with suit by a number of other concerns manufacturing similar apparatus. Mr. Lubin happened to offer us the best terms for a concession."[30]

Edison curtailed Lubin's business with greater success after his court victory against Biograph. One of Lubin's leading cameramen, J. Blair Smith, joined Edison's staff in July 1901 and was in a position to testify to Lubin's infringing activities. The Philadelphia filmmaker then stopped advertising films in the United States (though small ads for his cineograph projector occasionally appeared in the *New York Clipper*) and fled the country; he continued to sell films, but through offices in Berlin.[31] When Bradenburgh's museum reopened that September, Lubin's cineograph was no longer on the bill. Although it returned to the museum in December, Lubin's service was unable to offer the local views that had previously made it such a popular attraction.

Biograph's court victory was also a victory for Lubin. Edison's suit against him was dismissed, and the Philadelphia optician immediately reopened for business. He quickly published advertisements in the *New York Clipper*, declaring:

Lubin Is Victorious
The United States declares that we are legitimate Manufacturers of "Films" and Moving Picture Machines. There will be no more bluffs made about infringements on patents. The Bluff has been called. Now, buy your Films where you get the most for your money (22 March 1902, p. 88).

Edison's temporary legal victory had left Lubin's business in serious disarray. Claiming to have invested $150,000 to $200,000 in his film enterprise, Lubin conceded that it was no longer worth more than $10,000, while he had liabilities of $2,000 to $3,000. He owned no real estate or other holdings outside the business. It was many months (perhaps years) before the fifty-six-year-old Jewish immigrant fully recovered. Moreover, he was sued again in November 1902 for infringement of Edison's patent reissues.[32]

Lubin was never someone who passively deflected Edison's legal assaults. He too went on the commercial and legal offensive. Reopening for business, Lubin openly sold films of Prince Henry's well-publicized visit to the United States early in 1902— Edison-copyrighted films that he had duped. Edison, refusing to tolerate this disregard for his ownership, again sued Lubin, this time for copyright infringement.[33] Lubin defended himself by claiming that Edison's method of copyrighting films was inadequate. According to Lubin, each frame, rather than each film, had to be submitted separately. In fact, Edison's submitted copyrighting practice had never been tested in court. When, on 25 June, the inventor's lawyers asked Judge George Mifflin Dallas to grant a preliminary injunction against Lubin's activities, their request was denied, and the following January Dallas handed down a decision favoring Lubin. He ruled that each image had to be copyrighted separately in order to be protected and that Congress would have to legislate new copyright methods before Edison could find the kind of protection he envisioned. As a result of this decision, it became imprudent for an American producer to invest substantial sums of money in a film's negative, and the copyright issue disrupted American production for several months, until the court of appeals found in Edison's favor.

As part of his commercial offensive, Lubin challenged Edison's price structure by selling films for eleven cents a foot. Ultimately this move forced the Edison Company to reduce the sale price for its dupes and older or less-expensive subjects from fifteen to twelve cents a foot. Selig and Biograph likewise came down to twelve cents a foot and so reduced their profit margin.[34] The duping of European imports, including Pathé's THE PRODIGAL SON, Méliès's ROBINSON CRUSOE, and others, became the principal means for American producers to meet the growing demand for story films.

Lubin and his chief photographer, John J. Frawley, resumed production after Biograph's court victory, but hardly a single film from the 1902–1903 period seems to have survived. In late April, a Lubin cameraman filmed the Forepaugh-Sells Circus on its Philadelphia visit (CAKE WALKING HORSE, BURLESQUE COCK FIGHT, FEEDING THE RHINOCEROUS, etc.). Fight-film reenactments resumed with REPRODUCTION OF THE JEFFRIES–FITZSIMMONS FIGHT in 1902. By September, Lubin's company had taken RUBE WADDELL AND THE CHAMPIONS PLAYING BALL WITH THE BOSTON TEAM and a large number of comedies, including SERVING POTATOES, UNDRESSED (a remake of Biograph's HOW BRIDGET SERVED THE SALAD UNDRESSED). For WHO SAID WATERMELON? the catalog explained that "the demand for a new watermelon picture has induced us to pose two colored women in which they are portrayed, ravenously getting on the outside of a number of melons, much to the amusement of the onlookers."[35]

Like his contemporaries, Lubin pursued the notion of cinema as a visual newspaper. In the fall, the coal strike in eastern Pennsylvania was front-page news and was covered by one of his photographers, probably Frawley. Films included TRAIN LEAVING PHILADELPHIA WITH TROOPS FOR THE COAL MINES and NON-UNION MINERS AT WORK UNDER GUARD OF THE TROOPS. On 29 October, the cameraman took MITCHELL DAY AT WILKES-BARRE, PA. (100 feet), showing "a parade which took place on the day the great coal strike was settled," and PRESIDENT MITCHELL'S SPEECH, showing the union president addressing the miners and their supporters. To exhibitors, Lubin promotional material suggested, "If you want an effective and striking picture, buy the strike parade and join it on the front end of the Mitchell's Speech Film."[36] Here, as elsewhere, such editorial recommendations may have already been tested by his own exhibition service.

Lubin's THE HOLY CITY.

At the beginning of December 1902, Lubin released THE HOLY CITY, a 350-foot subject designed to be accompanied by the singing of that well-known hymn. He advertised it as a three-thousand-dollar production with eighteen scenes. While the first figure was certainly exaggerated and the second one may have been as well, two surviving stills suggest it was of a spectacular nature.[37]

After his own January 1903 court victory invalidated any viable copyright practice, Lubin virtually ceased making original productions. Thus, a Lubin advertisement in February listed THE ROYAL LEVEE IN INDIA (then also being sold by Edison and Biograph), James Williamson's THE SOLDIER'S RETURN, and other subjects made by foreign manufacturers. Since Lubin and Edison had mutually agreed that the loser of their court case would not be fined and the victor would not use the decision for publicity purposes (the goal being merely to establish a verdict that would have the force of law), the final vindication of Edison's practical methods of copyright may have been as desirable for Lubin as Edison.[38] After Lubin's initial victory, the case was brought to the court of appeals and reversed in April 1903. The court declared that the frame-by-frame method of copyrighting was impractical, and so the lower court's ruling violated the intent of Congress. Rather each film could be covered in its entirety by one copyright submission.

Thomas Armat Goes to Court Too

Thomas Armat contributed to the disruptive nature of the 1900–1903 period as he sought to establish the commercial value of his projection patents. The Armat Moving-Picture Company, which owned the Armat-Jenkins patents, pursued its suit against the American Mutoscope & Biograph Company, seeking a judgment of $150,000 in damages. On 21 October 1902, Armat won a favorable decision from Judge John R. Hazel. With Biograph prepared to appeal, both sides acknowledged the uncertainties continued litigation would involve for them and thus reached an agreement whereby, in exchange for accepting the lower-court ruling, Biograph did not have to pay a penalty and would not have to pay licensing fees until the Edison Company did so. The Armat Moving-Picture Company, therefore, promptly filed suit against the Edison Manufacturing Company for infringement of Patent No. 585,953, and Edison was enjoined on 8 January, though the injunction was suspended later that month.[39] At that point, Armat, still reluctant to test his patent in higher court, ceased to pursue his infringement cases with much vigor.

Throughout this period Armat pressed for a combination of Armat, Biograph, and Edison patents that would withstand any court challenge and remunerate him (and the others) financially. As he wrote to Edison late in 1901:

> This combined action would establish a real monopoly, as no infringer would stand against a combination of all these strong elements. The way things are now the woods are full of small infringers who are reaping that which belongs to yourself and ourselves. Prices have sunk in vaudeville until now the top-notch price, I understand, is about $40 a week, while free shows of motion pictures are becoming more and more common. These small incompetent exhibitors are getting the business into such disrepute that it will require great effort to raise it to a really profitable

plane. There is big money in *all ends* of this business if properly conducted and little otherwise. For instance the number of films you sell in Washington is but a small percent of the number that could be used under the close organization of the trust (15 November 1901).

Armat envisioned a centralized office in charge of production and exhibition throughout the United States. In actual practice he tried to intimidate smaller exhibitors into paying a licensing fee. Thus, at the end of 1900, Burton Holmes acquired a license that ran for three years at a cost of twenty-five dollars a week. During the next two years Armat freely distributed flyers and circulars threatening costly patent suits; these informed showmen that they were "liable to summary injunction, to damages (as much as three times the actual damage), and for past profits." He also brought suits against leading exhibitors, including Vitagraph at Chase's Theater in Washington, Sigmund Lubin in Philadelphia and at the Pan-American Exposition, Lyman Howe, and the Eden Musee. The Edison Manufacturing Company was forced to announce its intention "to vigorously resist any and all encroachments upon our rights and to protect all customers using moving picture apparatus and films of our manufacture."[40] These threats and lawsuits merely added to the commercial uncertainties that characterized the "chaser period."

Chicago and the Selig Polyscope Company

While the East Coast was thrown into turmoil by Edison's court victory over Biograph in 1901, the Chicago area was not so directly affected. The Selig Polyscope Company continued to make films, often relying on local views to maintain interest in its programs. Nonetheless, the company suffered a major setback involving the Chicago-based theatrical manager J. D. Hopkins, who was then using the polyscope service in his several theaters. In late August 1901, Selig's photographer filmed KNIGHTS TEMPLARS PARADE AT LOUISVILLE, KY. and several related subjects for presentation at the Hopkins-run Temple Theater in Louisville. Shown between the acts of plays performed by the theater's stock company, these local views were hits. Then, on the afternoon of 22 October, the polyscope exploded and the frightened spectators ran for the exits. Fourteen people were seriously injured in the stampede, and Selig's exhibition service was promptly banished from the Hopkins circuit (Louisville, Chicago, etc.), to be replaced in some instances by the biograph.[41] Having lost its largest customer, the Selig Company's receipts and earnings plummeted. Selig enjoyed few exhibition opportunities after the Louisville fire, and the disaster permanently hurt his service.

As soon as Biograph's March 1902 victory over Edison made it safe, Selig advertised his goods in the *New York Clipper*, thus suggesting that the patent-infringement case also may have limited his opportunities for film sales. The copyright issue hurt as well. Although Selig's fiction-film production at this time is hard to ascertain, the available evidence indicates that those fiction films his company did produce were not offered for sale during the period of copyright uncertainty. Selig's *New York Clipper* ads from mid 1902 list dupes of European films and then ceased altogether. Otherwise Selig limited himself to producing actualities subsidized by railroad companies. By fall 1902, he was selling two dozen subjects taken in Colorado. Mostly scenery photographed from railway cars, these films were designed for lectures promoting the state as a tourist attraction. A second catalog issued in February of the following year listed more of the same. Selig's "Western representative," H. H. Buckwalter, was based in Denver and involved in organizing the shooting. Since the goal for these films was broad distribution, and since the railroads had absorbed most or all of the costs, sales policy was not affected by the copyright issue. Only after the question of copyright was resolved did the Selig Polyscope Company offer its own original, acted films for sale. Moreover, Selig was among those sued by Thomas Edison for infringement of the inventor's reissued patents in November 1902.[42]

In contrast to Selig, Spoor's kinodrome service enjoyed relative prosperity as it became a permanent attraction in key Chicago theaters. In July 1901—at the very moment that Edison won his patent victory in Federal Circuit Court—a group of Western vaudeville managers who included Kohl & Castle, J. D. Hopkins, and the Orpheum Theater Company formed a "vaudeville trust" to oppose Eastern vaudeville interests then threatening to enter the Chicago market.[43] Preparing for a possible commercial confrontation, Kohl & Castle solidified a relationship with Spoor's exhibition service. The kinodrome was regularly rotated among their Haymarket, Chicago Opera House, and Olympic theaters after 21 July 1901. Starting in October, Kohl & Castle rotated two projectors among the theaters. Perhaps the appearance of films related to McKinley's assassination encouraged this expansion and underscored the value of having a film service. In May 1902, when the Olympic and Haymarket theaters closed for the summer, Spoor's service remained as a permanent feature at the Chicago Opera House. When the two other houses reopened in late August, the kinodrome had a permanent position on all three bills. Selig's misfortunes gave Spoor a clear field. Although his kinodrome lacked production capabilities, it not only won over the three Kohl & Castle vaudeville houses in Chicago but had secured the eastern portion of the Orpheum vaudeville circuit, notably its houses in Denver, Omaha, Kansas City, and New Orleans, by the early part of 1903. It soon achieved a commanding presence throughout the Midwest, the Far West, and much of the South.

American Vitagraph Builds Its Exhibition Circuit

In the Eastern United States, American Vitagraph returned to more active production after Biograph's victory. Blackton and Smith took films of local news events such as the trial trip of the yacht *Meteor* in May 1902. They also filmed an excerpt from the stage play *A Gentleman of France,* starring Kyrle Bellew; completed in late 1902, THE GREAT SWORD COMBAT ON THE STAIRS ran five minutes and showed the high point of the drama.[44] These films were not sold on the open market but were used almost exclusively for Vitagraph's own exhibitions. Nonetheless, the partners placed less emphasis on filmmaking during 1902–1905 than in the 1890s. Vitagraph's ability to acquire European subjects from overseas in a timely fashion and its promotion of "headline attractions"—subjects of either a fictional or documentary nature that lasted between six and twenty minutes—enabled its exhibition circuit to expand without resorting to expenses associated with the making of ambitious story films.

By March 1903 Vitagraph was showing films at Pastor's, Hurtig & Seamon's Music Hall, and Percy Williams' Circle Theater in New York; at the Orpheum in Brooklyn;

at Poli's in New Haven; and in Detroit, Toledo, and Washington, D.C. That April, as mentioned above, it took over the Keith circuit from Biograph, losing at least one customer in the process. (S. Z. Poli switched to the electrograph service rather than share the same service with Keith.) Its success was qualified, however. Although A TRIP TO THE MOON and other Méliès story films created an immediate sensation on the Keith circuit, after only a few weeks, Keith managers commented that the films "were not as productive of laughter or applause as those of the first or second week."[45] A backlog of popular 35-mm films that had never been shown in Keith theaters assured Vitagraph's success for some time, but local managers occasionally questioned the film selections and complained about the technical quality. In situations where Vitagraph had long runs, the same subjects were often repeated for several weeks or replaced by less-interesting scenes that did not sustain everyone's interest.

To label the early 1900s the "chaser period" is somewhat reductive, and the term can, for that reason, be problematic. The role of motion pictures as "chasers" in vaudeville houses was only symptomatic of the complex crisis that gripped the film industry. It was easily the most severe and extended of the four contractions that the motion-picture industry experienced from its start in 1894.[46] This was due in large part to its multiple determinants: patent wars, copyright chaos, technological incompatibility, fee reductions, and too-familiar subject matter that resulted in audience boredom. For many veterans, recurrent commercial instability seemed to be a fact of life in the moving-picture world. Some, like Edwin Porter, contemplated leaving the business.

The crisis—in its immediate and cyclical forms—was gradually overcome as these interlocking causes were resolved. Important problems such as copyright and technological standardization were ultimately worked out, placing the American industry in a stronger position that justified more adequate investment for film production. Likewise, Edison's eventual setback in the courts gave his rivals greater confidence and unleashed their productive and creative energies. When Edison sued them again, they were not so quick to fold. Most important, however, the problem of subject matter was resolved by a new conception of cinema as a storytelling form. With this development came new techniques that made the storytelling itself more compelling. Nevertheless, as we have seen, these solutions were neither obvious nor easily instituted on a wide basis in a period of commercial uncertainty and economic contraction.

11

The Transition to Story Films: 1903–1904

*T*he American film industry was entering a new phase of rapid expansion by mid-to-late 1903, and a key factor in this revival was the popularity of story films. If such subjects had yet to become the dominant product for American manufacturers, they had at least become the kind of cinema emphasized at urban theaters. In their Sunday newspaper advertising, Kohl & Castle announced the featured pictures at their three Chicago theaters where Spoor's kinodrome service was used. An analysis of these announcements in terms of actuality or documentary-like subjects on the one hand and acted or fiction subjects on the other yields the progress charted in the graph on page 338. As discussed in the previous chapter, a similar shift had taken place at Keith theaters only a few months earlier, when Vitagraph was hired. By mid 1903 successful exhibition companies and the theater managers who hired them recognized the enthusiasm with which audiences greeted story films. Although making story films required a substantial investment, American producers felt ready to meet this demand with original subjects now that they were clearly protected by copyright law.

Biograph and Its New Fourteenth Street Studio

Biograph was in the forefront of this revival. Production had slowed to a virtual standstill during late 1902 and early 1903 while personnel devoted much of their energies to building a new indoor studio at 11 East Fourteenth Street. This ambitious and expensive undertaking was the first motion-picture studio in the world to rely exclusively on artificial light, depending on banks of long, tubular lights, supplied by Cooper-Hewitt, to illuminate the stage.[1] These powerful lights had a greenish cast that made them highly desirable for photography and cinematography since film emulsion was orthochromatic and insensitive to the red end of the light spectrum. As one trade journal subsequently described this new technology:

> The very quality of eliminating the red rays is what makes the Cooper-Hewitt lights so valuable in photography. Pictures made . . . [with them]

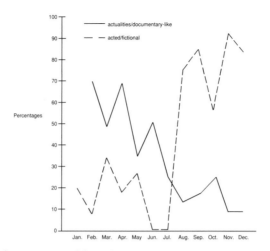

Top: *Fictional vs. documentary-like subjects shown in three Chicago theaters in 1903.* Bottom: *Pages from Vitagraph's summer 1903 catalog showing the importance of story films and European productions.*

3

<u>NORTH, SOUTH, EAST and WEST.</u>

THE AMERICAN VITAGRAPH

IS UNIVERSALLY USED AT ALL

LEADING ÷ THEATRES ÷ AND ÷ SUMMER ÷ PARKS.

MANAGERS ARE REALIZING THAT WE FURNISH

MORE NEW SUBJECTS!

MORE UP-TO-DATE FILMS!

MORE HEADLINE ATTRACTIONS!

THAN ALL THE OTHER EXHIBITORS IN

THE FIELD PUT TOGETHER. - - - - - - -

That is the Reason we control the Largest Exhibition Business in the World.

SPECTACULAR.

GULLIVER'S TRAVELS.

A Journey to Lilliput (among the dwarfs). A Voyage to Brobdingnag (with the giants). Based on the great story by Dean Swift. 8 minutes.

SLEEPING BEAUTY AND THE BEAST.

This magnificent spectacular production,. which created such a sensation recently, can now be seen in a gorgeous series of vitagraph tableaux. 20 minutes.

4

MARY JANE'S MISHAP.

The hired girl question is herein settled in a highly amusing manner. Mary Jane is "settled" also. A great laugh from start to finish   6 minutes.

ROBINSON CRUSOE.

Daniel Defoe's wonderful masterpiece of literature, illustrated in twenty-five marvelous scenes. 20 minutes.

THE LITTLE MATCH SELLER.

Picturing the pathetic fairy tale by Hans Anderson. 6 minutes.

THE BABY FARM;

or, the Fairy Cabbage Garden Where Babies Grow. An entirely new and enchanting pantomime. 10 minutes.

A JOURNEY TO LUNA

in thirty stupendous dissolving scenes. The most wonderful motion picture creation ever conceived. Based on the story by Jules Verne, "From the Earth to the Moon Direct." 20 minutes.

THE FAIRY GODMOTHER.

Pleasing to old and young alike. 5 minutes.

THE LIFE OF AN AMERICAN FIREMAN.

An entirely new and thrilling series of five pictures. illustrating the duties and dangers of our fire-fighters' lives. 10 minutes.

THE LIFE OF A LONDON FIREMAN.

This series forms a striking contrast to the above and allows of a good comparison between English and American methods of fighting fire. 15 minutes.

AFTER DARK;

or, the Life of a London Policeman. An extremely humorous and entertaining illustration of a London "Bobby's" adventures." 6 minutes.

MOTHER GOOSE NURSURY RHYMES.

All the old familiar children's stories reproduced in motion. 15 minutes.

No. **2342**.

Title *For the Upper Crust*

Length **159** ft

Code Word *Garrisco*.

No. **2355 S**.

Title *A Shocking Incident*.

Length **78** ft

Code Word *Garrochada*

Biograph's first pictures using Cooper-Hewitt lights. The "S" appearing after the pro-
duction number means that the film was shot on standard or 35-mm film.

stand out as clear and sharp as any daylight pictures ever made (*Film Index*, 15 December 1906, p. 4).

The lighting, however, tended to be flatter and more diffuse than sunlight.

The first tests were made in late March with FOR THE UPPER CRUST (No. 2342) and SPILT MILK (No. 2343), but it was not until May that the studio went into full operation, perhaps with A SHOCKING INCIDENT (No. 2355), a one-shot, 85-foot film in the bad-boy genre. According to the *Biograph Bulletin*, "Willie attaches the wires of an electric battery to the legs of a turkey which Bridget is preparing for dinner. Bridget takes hold of the legs with disastrous results." Many ensuing comedies dealt with risqué subjects; THE PAJAMA GIRL (No. 2366), for example, presented "a young and shapely girl in pajamas taking her morning bath." But at the other end of the spectrum, "I WANT MY DINNER" (No. 2362) showed Wallace McCutcheon's two-year-old son Ross "first crying for his dinner and then devouring a big bowl of bread and milk with the utmost satisfaction." The film was a hit. According to one manager, it was "scoring as much laughter and receiving as much applause, proportionately, as any act on the bill."[2]

Once Biograph had its new studio in working order, its production output easily exceeded that of the Edison Company. Between 1 May 1903, and 1 May 1904, Biograph listed 653 new subjects in its production records (Nos. 2351–2904). These were not only more numerous than at the turn of the century but in many cases much longer and more ambitious: during the same period, Edison copyrighted only 129 films.[3] Although Robert K. Bonine left the Biograph Company when the new studio was being put in working order, Biograph retained a large staff of photographers. Its two principal cameramen, G. W. Bitzer and A. E. Weed, not only worked extensively in the studio but also took actualities and other films on location. At times Wallace McCutcheon assumed control of the camera, perhaps when these two were otherwise occupied. In addition, Fred Armitage and Arthur Marvin were sent afield for special projects, and Herbert J. Miles continued to provide Biograph with a few films taken on the West Coast.

A remarkable burst of creativity came out of the Biograph studio in the year and a half following its opening. This flowering was the responsibility of a collaborative team, with Wallace McCutcheon and Frank Marion, his friend and one-time housemate, playing crucial roles in the production process.[4] McCutcheon sometimes wrote (with or without Marion), usually directed the actors, and occasionally even did the camera work. Marion wrote and frequently produced. Bitzer, now an experienced electrician, and Weed undoubtedly contributed as well. Freed from the restrictions of a large-format film and the conception of cinema as a visual newspaper, Biograph quickly regained its reputation for quality productions.

While the first films made under electric light were primarily short comedies, Biograph was eager to sell more ambitious "headliners," which an exhibitor could use to promote his show. This was evident in the release of RIP VAN WINKLE in mid May. This 200-foot, eight-shot subject featuring Joseph Jefferson was a collection of scenes taken in 1896. When first made, they were shown separately on vaudeville bills, but now Biograph released them as a single package. The first fiction headliner to be made in the new studio was THE HAYMARKET (No. 2400), shot on 20 June. According to the *Biograph Bulletin*, "It depicts in six scenes, six lively hours at New York City's famous Tenderloin dance hall." The spatial and temporal relations between the shots

No. **2400** S.
Title The Haymarket.

Length 303 ft.
Code Word Gartenrose.

remain imprecise; even though they clearly exist as action moves from one location to another, these relationships lack the kind of obvious continuities that Porter and Méliès had laid out. Beginning with the opening of the dance hall and ending with a police raid, THE HAYMARKET emphasizes daily life and the re-creation of a real world rather than melodramatic narrative.[5]

Other multi-shot dramatic films quickly followed, though the company did not always assume control over the editorial process. THE DIVORCE, shot 2 July 1903, was a three-part narrative in which each scene was listed and sold individually. In the opening "DETECTED" (No. 2410), the husband bids his wife and child good-bye but drops a compromising letter that she reads. In "ON THE TRAIL" (No. 2411), the wife visits a detective agency and makes the necessary arrangements. In "EVIDENCE SECURED" (No. 2412), the detective is in a hotel corridor and peeks through a keyhole. Calling the wife to the scene, the sleuth bursts into a bedroom, exposing the husband and his lover. These scenes were sold separately, in part, so that the exhibitor could introduce each one with a lantern-slide title, as Biograph had been doing since its inception. These title slides, which could be made up inexpensively by the exhibitor, were used like intertitles in later silent films. THE UNFAITHFUL WIFE (Nos. 2427–2429) was a similar three-part subject that focused on a wayward woman. Both films conveyed a strong moral message.

THE AMERICAN SOLDIER IN LOVE AND WAR (Nos. 2418, 1575, 516, 2419, 2420) consisted of three newly filmed studio scenes that were "used in connection with two war views to make a complete story in one film for projection."[6] During the United States' war in the Philippines, a soldier bids farewell to his sweetheart as he goes off to fight. The recycled second scene (FIFTEENTH INFANTRY, USA, No. 1575) shows troops at Governor's Island as they march off to war, while the third (PRACTICE WARFARE, No. 516) is realistically staged battle footage. These segments provided a credible milieu for the story, especially in contrast to the following studio-created jungle scene in which the wounded soldier is saved from certain death by a Filipino woman who intercedes with his captors. In the last scene, two native women are caring for the convalescing soldier when his sweetheart arrives. After learning that one of the women saved his life, the American woman gives her a necklace. As at Lubin and Edison, the filmmakers displayed little interest in trying to create a consistent mimetic world. The picture's system of representation thus relied on disparate, syncretic elements and was rooted in the practices of exhibitor-dominated cinema.

In all three of the films discussed above, continuity operates almost exclusively on the level of narrative and performance. Although this continued to be the case with other multi-part subjects, such as THE KIDNAPPER (Nos. 2442–2444) and THE WAGES OF SIN (Nos. 2445–2446), Biograph placed increasing emphasis on constructing a spatial/temporal world through the organization of shots, as Porter, Méliès, G. A. Smith, and others were already doing. The two-shot A DISCORDANT NOTE (No. 2404), which was taken by Bitzer on 26 June, uses a temporal overlap to show the climactic moment from two different perspectives. It begins with the interior of a private house where a pleasant party is interrupted by an amateur singer. After a frustrated listener throws the singer out, through the window, the film cuts to an exterior view of the house, where the singer again crashes through the window and lands in the street. A similar construction is used in NEXT! (No. 2678), a live-action comedy that was shot in early November. Cartoon characters Alphonse and Gaston are in a barbershop. When each repeatedly defers to the other rather than exiting through

No. 2419 S.
Title The American
Soldier in Love and War.
Length 47 ft.
Code Word Garzatura.

No. 2420 S.
Title The American
Soldier in Love and War.
Length 53 ft.
Code Word Garzava.

Two studio scenes from THE AMERICAN SOLDIER IN LOVE AND WAR.

Next!

the door, the barbershop patrons throw both through the window, one after the other. An exterior view of the shop shows them again crashing through the window in the same fashion.[7] THE BURGLAR (No. 2491), taken by A. E. Weed in August, was described by Biograph as "a very humorous picture in two continuous scenes."[8] The burglar sneaks from the bedroom to the adjoining room. Again there is a temporal overlap, although this is apparent to spectators only if they assume that the two rooms are contiguous spaces, as the catalog specifies.

A SEARCH FOR EVIDENCE (No. 2433) used a visual device similar to the looking glass in GRANDPA'S READING GLASS, in this case a keyhole. Elaborating on the scene "EVIDENCE SECURED" from THE DIVORCE, a detective and a woman search a hotel corridor for her husband. Each time she looks through a keyhole, the scene cuts to a new view with a keyhole mask. From her point of view, the spectator sees a young man taking care of a baby, a rube trying to light a match on an electric lightbulb, and so forth. The same set and shot-setup and are repeated (with only the numbers on the door changing) as the wife and detective move down the hall. Finally, at room 13, she discovers what she is looking for—her husband. Point-of-view motivation is used twice as the wife and then the detective peer through the keyhole. The final shot, from inside the bedroom as the wife and detective confront the husband and his lover, is from an angle perpendicular to the previous scene of the hallway. The temporal relationship between the shots is not precisely delineated (it could be a match-cut with linear continuity but it also could involve some overlap of time).

Biograph's commercial situation was affected by the fate of its sister companies overseas. The British Mutoscope & Biograph Company made little effort to adopt the 35-mm format and continued to supply the parent American company with 70-mm films well into 1903. When American Biograph made a complete switch to standard gauge, the British company rapidly faded. In 1904, the rights to its films were taken over by Gaumont, and Dickson returned to inventing.[9] Biograph retained good contacts in Britain, however, particularly with the American Charles Urban, who left the Warwick Trading Company to start his own enterprise, the Charles Urban Trading Company, early in 1903.

As Biograph switched to a 35-mm format, it introduced a three-blade shutter that greatly improved projection quality. Previous shutters had blocked the projected light whenever the film in the gate was moving, so that the alternation of image and its absence coincided with the number of frames per second. As the number of frames per second became fewer, the flicker effect became worse. With the three-blade shutter, the picture was blocked for fractions of a second even when the film strip was not being moved. This tripled the alternation of image and non-image, and since the eye synthesized this rapid alternation more readily, the flicker effect was considerably reduced. The device was developed by John Pross, working with Marvin and Casler in Canastota, New York; Biograph submitted a patent application on 19 January 1903, and it was granted on 10 March 1903. Biograph, though not making its own 35-mm projectors, adapted the shutter to its Urban bioscopes.[10] The use of a three-blade shutter in conjunction with its new and often exclusive productions soon gave the company an opportunity to revive its exhibition service.

By mid July, Biograph had won a new contract with Keith and returned to his circuit's Boston and New York theaters on 27 July; the following week, it was in Keith's Philadelphia theater as well. The reaction from the managers was initially mixed. In Boston, M. J. Keating complained:

No. 2433 S.

Title *A Search for Evidence*

Length *217 ft.*

Code Word *Garzuolo.*

Biograph's catalog shows the keyhole shots, concluding with a view of the philandering husband.

The show was greatly hurt by the inability of the Biograph people to perform this work. For two weeks I have been at them anticipating some trouble, and felt that I had forestalled any possible accident but after promising me that they would be ready to give a performance today, at the last moment they failed. As a consequence the entire show was delayed twenty or twenty-five minutes (*Keith Reports*, week of 27 July 1903).

The New York manager, meanwhile, stated, "While there is no question but that the biograph machine pictures are very fine from a mechanical standpoint, the list of views that they sent us this afternoon is rather ordinary." But the following week, the Philadelphia manager reported, "Pictures are smaller than Vitagraph; pictures are clearer. Views this week were good," and the New York manager announced, "The selection of views they have furnished us this week is a great improvement over that of last week, nearly all of them are new and all are good."[11] After two years of disruption and declining prospects, Biograph's commercial position was once again on the rise.

The Edison Company Resumes Production

The Edison Manufacturing Company resumed production activities in the United States in late April 1903, shortly after the copyright issue was resolved. In the meantime, James White had left for Europe to represent Edison's phonograph and film interests. William Markgraf, brother-in-law of Edison general manager William Gilmore, assumed White's title if not his role. Markgraf, who had little motion-picture experience, could not offer the know-how and experience that White had provided. By this time the Edison Manufacturing Company had three cameramen: Edwin S. Porter, Alfred C. Abadie, and James Blair Smith. Fleming had left and been replaced by William Martinetti, a scenic designer, but Porter was now in full charge of the studio, and the only one to photograph subjects made within its confines. Outside the studio, he usually worked only in the New York City area. Abadie, who had been responsible for Edison's motion-picture interests in Europe, was freed from these obligations with White's arrival. After filming in the Middle East and Europe from mid March to mid May 1903, he returned to the United States. In June, he was sent to Wilmington Springs, Delaware, to take local scenes for the exhibitor N. Dushane Cloward, who had a summer motion-picture theater at the local park. Abadie subsequently devoted most of his efforts to taking news films and actualities, including a flood in Paterson, New Jersey, the ruins of a fire in Coney Island, and the Princeton-Yale football game. Smith filmed a few news films and actualities but spent most of his time supervising the development of negatives and the production of prints at Edison's factory in Orange.

When Edwin S. Porter returned to filmmaking in late April 1903, he collaborated with J. Blair Smith on a series of actualities showing the "other half" of city life with views such as NEW YORK CITY DUMPING WHARF; SORTING REFUSE AT INCINERATING PLANT, NEW YORK CITY; and NEW YORK CITY "GHETTO" FISH MARKET. Studio production resumed on 16 July with Porter filming a young vaudeville performer for LITTLE LILLIAN, TOE DANSEUSE. Short comedies, including THE GAY SHOE CLERK, followed. In this three-shot film, a shoe clerk helps a young woman try

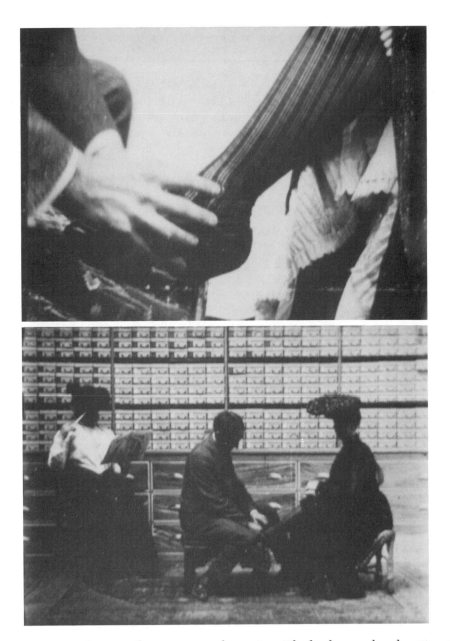

THE GAY SHOE CLERK. *The cut-in to a closer view. The background and petticoats change with the cut as well.*

on some shoes, while her chaperone settles in a chair and reads the paper. This is followed by a close view of the woman's leg as she discreetly raises her skirt and the shoe clerk's hands slowly move up her calf. In a return to the establishing shot, the two kiss, but osculatory pleasure is interrupted as the chaperone hits the shoe clerk over the head with her umbrella. Presentational elements occur on several levels as the woman displays her ankle to the shoe clerk and, in turn, to the spectator. The close view takes place against a white background rather than the set, further focusing the spectator's attention.

THE GAY SHOE CLERK is the site of two intersecting genres typified by WHAT DEMORALIZED THE BARBERSHOP and THE MAY IRWIN KISS. On one hand, the comedy makes use of the voyeurism of a hypothetical male spectator. Unlike the shoe clerk, who can touch and even kiss the girl but gets punished, the male viewer can see but runs no risk of chastisement. He can enjoy the shoe clerk's fate in contrast to his own safety. THE GAY SHOE CLERK thus savors the spectatorial position of the male cinematic voyeur. The position of the female spectator is harder to construct (unless the woman assumes the role of a mock male self), for the camera's point of view is male oriented. The film suggests the woman's pleasure at being seen (at least the young woman in the picture seems to enjoy displaying her leg) and perhaps a slight sadistic satisfaction as she entices the young man toward his defeat. At the same time, THE GAY SHOE CLERK can be seen as a kiss film that places the young couple in opposition to the chaperone and Victorian norms of propriety. In this sense the camera exalts this intimacy taken on the sly.

None of these short studio productions was released for distribution as Porter and the Edison staff prepared for the making of UNCLE TOM'S CABIN, completed in late July. Like Biograph's RIP VAN WINKLE, Edison's UNCLE TOM'S CABIN was an example of filmed theater. Even more than RIP VAN WINKLE, this fourteen-shot "feature," or principal film, evoked a story that native-born Americans outside the South knew intimately. The play was regularly presented in the nation's small-town opera houses by touring companies, and it was just such a company that was hired to perform in the Edison studio. Porter's skill came in adding a few special effects (such as Eva's spirit ascending to heaven) and most important, in reducing the evening-length performance to approximately fifteen minutes. Taken at twenty frames per second, this yielded 1,100 feet of film, which was longer than any studio subject Porter had yet produced and too large for the standard 1,000-foot reel that equipped most projectors. Despite its length, the sets had already been built and the play staged, so it undoubtedly cost significantly less than JACK AND THE BEANSTALK. While production decisions made it difficult to create a spatial/temporal world as Porter had done in several earlier films, this was not a notable failing since audiences, like the producer, recognized that the film was operating in a different genre from either LIFE OF AN AMERICAN FIREMAN or THE GAY SHOE CLERK—that of filmed theater.

UNCLE TOM'S CABIN did inaugurate one important innovation in American production by borrowing a representational technique from the English fairy-tale film DOROTHY'S DREAM, made by G. A. Smith. Each scene was prefaced by a title on film, which helped the audience follow the story by identifying the scene and some of the principal characters. While films and scenes within multi-shot films had been previously announced by titles, they were the responsibility of exhibitors, who either purchased the necessary title slides or made their own. (Some exhibitors, of course, had simply provided an on-the-spot commentary to identify films and add needed information.) With UNCLE TOM'S CABIN and many subsequent films, the producer assumed control over the titles. This was not the case with every film (short comedies from this period still generally lacked main titles), but for the most ambitious ones, producers soon followed the lead of G. A. Smith and Porter.

Porter was responsible for two other notable multi-shot "features" during that summer, RUBE AND MANDY AT CONEY ISLAND and A ROMANCE OF THE RAIL. Both used actors and tentative stories yet remained tied to the travelogue and its repertoire of techniques (for instance, the frequently panning camera). RUBE AND MANDY AT CONEY ISLAND was designed to show off the famed New York amusement park,

RUBE AND MANDY AT CONEY ISLAND. *In one scene the couple are barely noticeable as they tour the amusement park (they are going down the steps near the right edge of the frame), allowing the panning camera to caress the spectacular locale. In a later scene the couple themselves become spectacle, not only for the camera but for the amusement seekers in the background.*

which fascinated Americans. Like Biograph's THE HAYMARKET, it emphasized everyday events at one of New York's famous "resorts." A ROMANCE OF THE RAIL worked within the popular railway subgenre of the travelogue. Exhibitors frequently assembled programs of passing scenery, viewed from the front end of a train, with vignettes of actions taking place at the station or in the trains. Many of the vignettes were, of course, comic in nature. Whether or not a showman intercut A ROMANCE OF THE RAIL with railroad-travel films, the conventions would have been immediately recognized by audiences. Yet the picture differs from other such comedies because of its cultural specificity. This 275-foot, six-shot travel film lightheartedly spoofed the Lackawanna Railroad's extensive advertising campaign, in which Phoebe Snow rode the company's trains in a white gown. Despite the fact that the Lackawanna was known as a major coal carrier, her clothing never became soiled. Porter created a male counterpart, also dressed in white, who appears at the station and meets Phoebe Snow. They board and the train pulls out. Traveling through the Delaware Water Gap, the couple watch the scenery from the observation platform at the rear of the train: the camera is framed to present the passing scenery as much as their interaction. Romance blossoms and a minister—also in white—promptly marries them from the rear platform. Here a documentary genre is reoriented around the emerging story film.

Fiction "Features" at Biograph and Edison

The three Edison "features" discussed above were specifically American in their subject matter and depended heavily on the domestic market for sales. Although the UNCLE TOM'S CABIN narrative was known overseas in book and even play form, its audience was much more limited there than in the United States. Since familiarity greatly facilitated the spectators' understanding of the film, many foreigners must have considered the film a puzzling American curiosity. A ROMANCE OF THE RAIL would have been even more puzzling, since it depended on familiarity with an advertising campaign that only Americans could be expected to have seen. Biograph often took a similar U.S.-oriented approach. The ten-shot KIT CARSON (Nos. 2538–2547) and the six-shot THE PIONEERS (Nos. 2555, 2557–2561)—both made by Mc-Cutcheon in early September—revolved around heroic actions of the famed American scout, who was the subject of various plays and many dime novels that were particularly popular in the United States.

In KIT CARSON, the scout and his companion are trapping in the woods and are attacked by Indians. Carson is captured and escapes, then is recaptured. Tied to a tree in the Indian village, he is rescued by an Indian maiden who cuts him loose. In the last scene, he is reunited with his family. In THE PIONEERS, Indians kill a family of settlers except for one girl who is taken captive and eventually freed by Carson and his band of scouts. All the scenes were photographed in the Adirondack Mountains in an effort to provide appropriate scenery. Nonetheless, their mise-en-scène is highly theatrical: the performances are frontal, the camera is at eye level, and the landscape is often treated as a stage. As a result, the potentially dramatic impact of the scenery is largely lost, revealing the limitations of McCutcheon's camerawork. While there is one camera pan, the scenes are disconnected spatially and temporally. Though later Biograph brochures offer introductory titles for each of the scenes, they were not copyrighted with the images. For almost a year, Biograph's exhibition service retained exclusive use of these pictures and continued to use slides for titles rather than switching to filmed intertitles as Edison had done.

In November, Biograph and Edison each made a picture that synthesized many of the advances apparent in their previous film practice: THE ESCAPED LUNATIC (No. 2693) and THE GREAT TRAIN ROBBERY. Both films were strongly influenced by a group of English imports—story films of violent crime in which burglars, thieves, and poachers are pursued by representatives of the law. In Biograph's ten-shot THE ESCAPED LUNATIC, these elements are employed for comic purposes. Photographed by Weed, but also the responsibility of Wallace McCutcheon and Frank Marion, the film was the first American production to be structured around the chase. In addition, it displays continuities of space, time, and action at opportune moments. In the opening, interior scene, the title character, who believes himself to be Napoleon, breaks his cell window and climbs through it. The action overlaps slightly with the following exterior shot as he climbs out of the window, drops to the ground, and makes good his escape—with the guards in close pursuit. Several chase scenes follow as the lunatic eludes his pursuers. The lunatic loves the chase: when he discovers the guards asleep on the grass, he wakes them up so their "game" can be continued. Internal cuts often occur within shots. A "take" photographed in reverse motion and another using regular forward motion are incorporated into a single shot using an "invisible" cut. This allows the lunatic to climb quickly and easily up a rope, creating a crazy world that distorts normal expectations.

THE ESCAPED LUNATIC contains one particularly notable scene in which a guard grapples with the patient on a bridge. Here, the filmmakers cut to a distant shot of the two combatants taken from a different angle, with a dummy substituted for the guard. The cut, recently experimented with in OFF HIS BEAT (No. 2679) and A GUARDIAN OF THE PEACE (No. 2680), is a perfect match. The change of angle functions within the trick-film repertoire and conceals the substitution more effectively than if executed using a single camera position. After the guard is thrown off the bridge and into a rocky stream, a conventional stop-action substitution (executed from one camera position) replaces the dummy with the actor, who continues on his way. Eventually the lunatic returns to his cell, where the exhausted guards find him reading a newspaper. The chase, violence, a simple but effective narrative as well as a coherent spatial and temporal world: all these mark the film as a significant breakthrough.

Edison's THE GREAT TRAIN ROBBERY was—and still is—the best known and most commercially successful film of the pre-Griffith era. Edwin S. Porter was responsible for producing and photographing it in November 1903, but the young actor G. M. Anderson probably helped him with the staging. Anderson, who had just appeared as the man trying to steal a kiss in WHAT HAPPENED IN THE TUNNEL, played several small roles (the passenger who is shot trying to escape, the tenderfoot dancing to the sound of six-shooters, and an outlaw). Another actor, Justus D. Barnes, played the bandit chieftain Barnes, while many of the passengers were employees at Edison's factory. Professional and nonprofessional actors were used, and Porter, as he had done earlier with Fleming, worked collaboratively.

The film had a plethora of antecedents. The title and basic story were inspired by Scott Marble's play *The Great Train Robbery* (1896). Some scenes, such as the fight on the tender in scene 4, were modeled on train robberies in the Far West.[12] The film carefully analyzes the robbery and the bandits' getaway in the first nine scenes, starting with the false message that the outlaws force the telegraph operator to hand the engineer. The outlaws board the train at the water tank (scene 2) and overpower

THE GREAT TRAIN ROBBERY. *Outlaw Barnes shoots at the spectator as passenger; in the mail car of the train, passing scenery is shown with a matte shot.*

The camera follows the escaping outlaws in scene 7 of THE GREAT TRAIN ROB-BERY.

the messenger in the express car (scene 3). Another bandit hurls the fireman off the tender (scene 4); the engine is uncoupled from the rest of the train (scene 5); passengers are forced onto the tracks and relieved of their valuables (scene 6). The bandits escape on the engine (scene 7), scramble down the embankment (scene 8), and race across a stream to their horses (scene 9). An operational aesthetic, with its emphasis on process, was at work.

Although THE GREAT TRAIN ROBBERY lacks repeated actions that signal temporal overlaps, the film nevertheless returns to earlier points in time. The catalog description indicates that scenes 3 and 4 occurred simultaneously. As André Gaudreault has pointed out, a second line of action developed in scenes 10 and 11 (the freeing of the telegraph operator by his daughter and the raising of the posse at the dance hall) is unfolding while the robbery takes place.[13] These two lines of action come together in scene 12 as the posse chases the bandits on horseback. The opportunity for chase, maximized in Biograph's THE ESCAPED LUNATIC, is limited to this single shot. The final scene is the shootout, in which the posse is victorious.

In making his famous film, Porter included one emblematic shot of the outlaw leader Barnes shooting his gun directly at the camera and audience. Labeled "Realism" in the catalog, this extra shot could be placed at either the beginning or end of the film. At the beginning, it introduced the leading character just like the opening shot in Edison's earlier LAURA COMSTOCK'S BAG-PUNCHING DOG. Shown at the end as an "apotheosis," it abstracted a single moment from the narrative as had been done with RUBE AND MANDY AT CONEY ISLAND. In either position (but more effectively at the beginning) the shot added realism to the film by intensifying the spectators' identification with the victimized travelers. It reiterated and intensified the viewer-as-passenger convention of the railroad subgenre.

The term "realism" can also be applied to the entire film, reflecting the ways in which the filmmaker integrated common cinematic practices into an effective whole. Although the opening scene was filmed at the studio, a view of the train pulling into the station was matted into a window frame. This striking ability to show outside activities through the window set the tone for later scenes. As David Levy has pointed out, camera movement, particularly in scene 7, where the cinematographer struggled to keep the outlaws in frame by panning and tilting simultaneously, provided a cinematic technique that was already associated with the urgency of news films.[14] The careful attention to the details of robbing a train, the emphasis on process as narrative, almost takes THE GREAT TRAIN ROBBERY out of the realm of fiction and suggests a documentary intent.

While the Edison Company was working on THE GREAT TRAIN ROBBERY, Biograph made yet another story film, THE STORY THE BIOGRAPH TOLD (No. 2705). As with Porter's epic, Biograph confronted the problem of depicting actions occurring simultaneously in two distant locations. The film was loosely inspired by a vaudeville skit, *In the Biograph* (© 29 May 1901 by Wilfred Clarke). In this nineteen-minute playlet performed by Wilfred Clarke and his acting troupe, a motion-picture camera catches a doctor in a compromising situation:

> "In the Biograph" is full of action and calls for a new laugh each moment. It deals with the adventure of a prominent physician who, seated on a bench by the seaside, suddenly has an infant thrust into his arms, the mother of the child hastening away. It develops that the incident has been photographed for biograph reproduction. The physician's wife, who is jealous, and the father of the child, said father being a professional strong man, chance to see the picture reproduced and recognize the principals. Stormy scenes follow, but, of course, all ends happily (*Washington Star*, 28 January 1902, p. 10).

The act "goes briskly and creates a great deal of laughter," reported one vaudeville manager.

In THE STORY THE BIOGRAPH TOLD, the office boy at a film company is shown how to use the camera. When the boss and his pretty "typewriter" (*i.e.*, secretary) arrive, work is forgotten as she sits in his lap and they kiss passionately. Meanwhile, the proprietor's wife calls on the phone, and the naughty office boy surreptitiously uses his new talents to grind away with the camera. In the next shot, the husband and wife are in box seats at the theater and a card onstage announces the biograph. The third shot shows the close-up of the screen: the kissing scene taken by the "bad boy." In shot 4, the outraged wife beats her husband and leaves the theater. In the fifth and final shot, the wife enters the husband's office and replaces the "typewriter" with a young man.

In the first shot, the producers were faced with the problem of showing the husband and the wife in two locations as they spoke to each other on the phone. Neither a split-screen effect nor a narrative repetition seemed suitable, and cross-cutting between the two scenes, which would be the logical procedure at Biograph within another five years, was not yet possible. Instead, the two scenes were shown simultaneously by double exposure: the image of the wife begins when the husband pick up the phone and ends when it is placed on the hook. In certain respects, this

THE STORY THE BIOGRAPH TOLD. *The first two stills are from the opening, as the office boy films the illicit lovers. The second still, a double exposure of two simultaneously unfolding scenes, is muddy and extremely difficult to decipher. The third still is the office boy's "film" as it is shown in the theater.*

solution is more "advanced" than the one offered by Porter in THE GREAT TRAIN ROBBERY, where viewers had to infer the temporal relations between shots. Here the temporal relationship between the two shots is made explicit. Yet, what Biograph gained in specificity it lost in clarity; the image became muddied and hard to decipher. For this reason, Biograph's experiment was discarded, and overlapping action and temporal repetition remained the dominant means of spatial/temporal and narrative construction through 1907.

Both Edison and Biograph made fewer "headline" fiction films during the winter and spring of 1904. In this respect, Edison output was particularly meager, and one factor may have been the dismissal of kinetograph department head William Markgraf after he had gone on a drunken binge in late December. It was not until March that a replacement, Alex T. Moore, was found, and he lacked any previous film-related experience. The commercial success of THE GREAT TRAIN ROBBERY also may have kept the Edison factory operating at full capacity to produce positive prints, thus allowing several months to pass before the need for new negatives was felt. At any event, it was not until early March that Porter completed BUSTER BROWN AND HIS DOG TIGE (copyrighted as THE BUSTER BROWN SERIES), a 710-foot, seven-shot film that was based on the well-known *Buster Brown* cartoon strip. The opening scene showed the strip's creator, Richard F. Outcault, making a charcoal sketch of Buster and Tige. Remaining scenes were live-action vignettes of Buster creating his comic mayhem. It was sold "in one length only," a departure from the marketing of earlier comedy series on an individual-scene basis. A common character thus provided the production company with sufficient justification to assume editorial control, suggesting that the centralization of production and postproduction under one roof was rapidly advancing, at least when fiction filmmaking was involved.

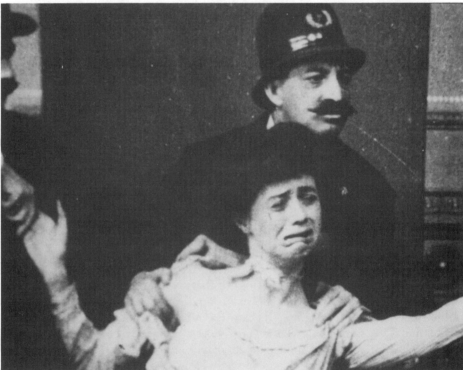

In PHOTOGRAPHING A FEMALE CROOK (*No. 2781, January 1904*) *the camera dollies in to a close-up. The woman contorts her face, seeking to hide her identity in the mug shot.*

Biograph, meanwhile, moved most of its production activities into the studio for the winter and likewise curtailed its efforts to create ambitious fiction films. A modest exception was OUT IN THE STREETS (No. 2864, copyrighted as THE WAIF), the story of a desperate, impoverished woman who is unable to feed her children, and abandons the youngest on the doorstep of a rich but childless couple. Four studio sets—two interiors and two exteriors—depict the woman's garret apartment and the house of the wealthy family. The abandonment and subsequent discovery of the infant at the mansion occur simultaneously with the eviction of the woman's older child in the middle of a snowstorm. A policeman befriends the child and takes him home.[15] Discovering this second loss, the bereft mother collapses on the wealthy couple's doorstep, is brought inside, and is reunited with her baby. At the end, the rich couple take the mother to her dwelling, the policeman returns the child, and all is well. THE WAIF is filled with the characteristic elements of nineteenth-century melodrama: contrasts, extremes of emotion, coincidence, and a moral ending. The causes of the woman's impoverishment and the couple's wealth are never suggested, and class barriers are easily bridged, though only in a charitable, paternalistic fashion.

While Weed and McCutcheon worked in the studio, Bitzer filmed scenes of daily life at St. John's Military Academy in Syracuse, New York. During his stay there, he also made THE BATTLE OF THE YALU (Nos. 2846–2848, 2855), in which the military cadets reenacted a battle in the recently begun Russo-Japanese War. Costumes were credibly authentic, and its four scenes trace the ebb and flow of battle with attack and counterattack. The film received extensive publicity, including a full-page article in the Hearst newspapers, and was a featured presentation in Keith theaters.[16] Rather than keep it as an exclusive for the exhibition circuit, Biograph quickly put it on the market in both 400-foot and 623-foot lengths. The Edison Company quickly responded by making SKIRMISH BETWEEN RUSSIAN AND JAPANESE ADVANCE GUARDS (565 feet), which was virtually identical.

Production records testify to the diversity and scope of Biograph's other filmmaking ventures. Of the 653 films made from 1 May 1903 to 1 May 1904, more than 120 were sponsored by large corporations or the United States government. In late July, Weed was sent to Washington, D.C., to film United States Post Office Department employees sorting letters, loading cars, and delivering mail. Other agencies of the federal government soon wanted to promote their services. Extensive series were made for the United States Navy, showing recruitment, training, the administration of first aid, and the auctioning of personal property left behind by deserters. The Department of the Interior commissioned films of its Indian schools (FIRE DRILL, ALBUQUERQUE INDIAN SCHOOL, No. 2654) and daily life on the reservation (NAVAJO SQUAW WEAVING BLANKETS, No. 2659), as well as views of the Grand Canyon and Yosemite National Park. Films taken for the Missouri Commission showed students from various schools across the state; these were probably made for exhibition at the forthcoming St. Louis World's Fair (Louisiana Purchase Exposition).

Bitzer photographed the Westinghouse works in East Pittsburgh, Wilmerding, and Trafford, Pennsylvania, in April and May 1904. Many of these films show factory interiors with women punching their time cards and winding wire on armatures for generators (GIRLS TAKING TIME CHECKS, No. 2887 and COIL WINDING, SECTION E, No. 2889). Several stunning traveling shots were taken from overhead cranes that moved the length of these huge buildings. Today they offer some of the earliest film documentation of the American workplace. Designed for lecture formats rather than amusement, the pictures then enjoyed significant sales overseas. Frank Marion reported:

> Among all the nations of the world the Japanese are among our best customers. They are intensely keen in regard to everything that shows the interior workings of American establishments, the factory, the hotel, the store, the municipal and Government buildings. We sent a portrayal of the postoffice department and that vied in popularity with the Westinghouse factories (*Pittsburgh Post*, 11 November 1906, p. 66).

Biograph also made a small number of advertising films for Shredded Wheat Biscuits, Mellin's Baby Food, and the Gold Dust Twins. More than a dozen films taken in October and November 1903 were for "thumb books"—"riffle" or "flip" books of still photographs that are transformed into a moving image when the viewer bends back and then releases the pages in rapid succession. Made for the *New York Journal*, these featured its leading comic-strip characters: Foxy Grandpa, Alphonse and Gaston, Toodles, Happy Hooligan, and the Katzenjammer Kids.

Biograph's diverse output thus included many sponsored films, mutoscope subjects, and pictures for Biograph's own exhibitions or outright sale to independent showmen. But with this impressive array of films, it is worth considering why the Edison Manufacturing Company and Porter retained a higher profile both at the time and in subsequent histories. The most important reason would seem to be that Edison sold its films as soon as they were completed. By Christmas week of 1903, all the major exhibition services in New York City owned copies of THE GREAT TRAIN ROBBERY and were showing them in eleven Manhattan and Brooklyn theaters. Throughout the country exhibitors quickly acquired the film.[17] In contrast, Biograph retained its most attractive productions for its own exhibition circuit, and even at these limited outlets, the films were not displayed immediately. Rather, the company waited until the winter months, when weather conditions created a shortage of new products, before unveiling its exclusive story films. KIT CARSON, for example, was not shown at Keith's Boston theater until late January, four months after it was produced and well after THE GREAT TRAIN ROBBERY was seen in Boston. And although the hand-tinted print was hailed as the star feature on the bill—"It is splendidly worked out, much of the photography is almost stereoscopic and the coloring is the work of the artist"—Keith's patrons were warned, "It will not be seen elsewhere in New England."[18] Likewise, THE ESCAPED LUNATIC was shown at Keith's in late March. Since neither film was sold to exhibitors, their distribution was primarily limited to vaudeville. Both Edison and Biograph found effective ways of achieving profits, but the Edison policy assured more immediate impact and greater diffusion.

Other American Producers Revive Production

The affirmation of viable copyright practices in April 1903 encouraged other American producers to embark on more ambitious projects, particularly the making of longer story films. While few of these productions, unfortunately, have survived, they reflect the industry's general revival. Lubin found still more ways to challenge Edison's commercial base. A week after Edison marketed UNCLE TOM'S CABIN at a cost of $165, Lubin announced the imminent release of his own 700-foot version for $77.[19] It was shot at fewer frames per second and eliminated a cakewalk dance but was remarkably similar in other respects. This film was followed by TEN NIGHTS IN A BARROOM, also 700 feet, in mid October. Lubin's advertisements suggest that this, too, was an example of filmed theater.

In mid December, the producer offered three new "song films": DEAR OLD STARS AND STRIPES GOOD-BYE (340 feet), ONLY A SOLDIER BOY (215 feet), and EVERY DAY IS SUNSHINE WHEN THE HEART BEATS TRUE (255 feet).[20] Illustrating senti-mental and patriotic ballads, these elaborate productions contained at least four shots each and ran three and a half to five minutes. EVERY DAY IS SUNSHINE WHEN THE

ACROSS THE RIVER ON THE FLOATING ICE.

THE AUCTION OF ST. CLAIR'S SLAVES.

Two scenes from Lubin's UNCLE TOM'S CABIN *catalog. In "The Auction of St. Clair's Slaves" Sigmund Lubin (third from left in the front row) plays the auctioneer.*

ONLY A SOLDIER BOY

215 feet.   Price, $23.65.

Now the hour has come at last, Soldier Boy,
Don't you hear the bugle blast, Soldier Boy?
Surely you have heard the news,
There's no time for you to lose,
Love or duty you must choose, Soldier Boy.

She'll be waiting at the gate, Soldier Boy,
Waiting there to know your fate, Soldier Boy;
And her heart will break, that's all,
If in battle you should fall,
Yet you'll answer to the call, Soldier Boy.

Images and words for part of Lubin's ONLY A SOLDIER BOY.

HEART BEATS TRUE was written from the perspective of a man who has lost his beloved wife and recalls their happiness together. The chorus of ONLY A SOLDIER BOY, which was intended to be sung as pertinent sections of the film were projected, went:

> *You are a soldier boy, that's all you know,*
> *When duty calls you're always first to go*
> *You're not supposed to have a heart,*
> *Let others play the lover's part,*
> *So brush off your sweetheart's tears and say "good-bye."*
> *Don't let her hear your parting sigh.*
> *When the band begins to play, fall in line*
> *And march away, for you're only a Soldier Boy.*

Lubin also sold sets of lantern slides for a long list of illustrated songs (including ONLY A SOLDIER BOY and EVERY DAY IS SUNSHINE WHEN THE HEART BEATS TRUE).[21]

Lubin also continued to make short comedies, such as STREET CAR CHIVALRY, where men willingly offer their seats to a pretty woman but not to an ugly one. Although news films, such as one of the Iroquois Theater fire in Chicago, and fight reenactments remained commercially viable, longer acted films became increasingly important for the Philadelphia producer. Perhaps these signs of prosperity encouraged Lubin's chief sales manager, Lewis M. Swaab, to leave the producer's employ and open his own business—as agent for many of Lubin's competitors in the Philadelphia market—in April 1904.[22]

Since Selig advertised only irregularly and without listing most of his films, his productions are harder to trace. By the time he printed his complete catalog sometime late in 1903, he was selling two original productions based on well-known fairy tales: PIED PIPER OF HAMELIN and SCENES FROM HUMPTY DUMPTY. PIED PIPER OF HAMELIN (350 feet) was indebted to Robert Browning's poem of that name, and according to the Selig catalog, "Even those who fancy the great poet to be as intelligible read backwards as forward, are constrained to make an exception in favor of the charming ballad which sets forth, in fantastic fashion, the danger of leaving one's debt unpaid." The film thus acted as a moral tale for children and adults. SCENES FROM HUMPTY DUMPTY, meanwhile, "were made from the great pantomime Humpty Dumpty and were posed for by one of the greatest European Pantomimists." This 675-foot film had eight scenes, each of which was sold separately at thirteen cents a foot, and the catalog assured potential exhibitors that "these films are without doubt the finest ever made and will create no end of amusement to the little folks as well as the old folks, who in these films will recognize the familiar scenes of their childhood when they witnessed Humpty Dumpty."[23] Such fairy tale films were designed for adult nostalgia as much as for children, linking them in significant ways to the bad-boy comedy genre.

Selig continued to produce numerous actualities. In the spring of 1903, one of his cameramen toured with President Roosevelt and took scenes at the dedication ceremonies for the Louisiana Purchase Exposition in St. Louis on 30 April. The cinematographer then journeyed to Oregon and Washington for the president's May tour (PRESIDENT ROOSEVELT AT WALLA WALLA) and also took a series of films along the Columbia River (PANORAMIC VIEW OF MULTNOMAH FALLS). A 600-foot scene of a

Mexican bullfight was shot sometime in 1903, though the locale may have actually been a Chicago stockyard.[24]

Vitagraph's production activities were modest, and its original subjects were principally for use on the company's exhibition circuit. Acted films played a modest role. Like its competitors, Vitagraph produced an example of filmed theater, EAST LYNNE. Condensing the well-known melodrama into fifteen minutes of screen time, Vitagraph claimed to offer "the entire play acted by well-known members of the theatrical profession."[25] A news film of a devasting fire in Rochester was prominently advertised in that city and attracted patrons to the Baker Theater, where Vitagraph was giving a Sunday program. As with Biograph, Blackton, Smith, and Rock used these exclusive subjects to win and retain venues. Perhaps more importantly, Vitagraph rushed its European purchases to the United States and projected them ahead of their rivals.

By the end of 1903, Vitagraph, Lubin, and Selig all made longer narrative films with clear theatrical antecedents, coinciding with the fairy-tale or filmed-theater orientation previously explored by Méliès, Porter, and G. A. Smith. However, they failed to move quickly into the production of chase and crime films as did Edison and Biograph. This failure meant that, in the realm of commercially successful filmmaking at least, they could not challenge their larger, better-established rivals. They made up the second tier of American production companies.

The Impact of the European Industry on the United States

The European industry continued to play a major role in shaping American cinema even though French and English producers had had little direct access to American markets since 1896–1897. While they sold a certain number of prints to American exhibitors with overseas connections, their films generally reached American screens as dupes marketed by U.S. companies. Undoubtedly the world's leading filmmaker during the first years of the new century was the Parisian Georges Méliès, whose pictures had been duped by every major American producer. Dissatisfied with this state of affairs, he sent his brother, Gaston Méliès, to the United States to represent his interests. Gaston arrived in March 1903—while the copyright case was still unresolved—and discovered, for example, that Biograph had been paying Charles Urban one-cent-per-foot royalties for prints of Méliès subjects. The money, of course, had never reached the original artist.[26]

To secure the economic benefits of these films for their creator, Gaston opened a New York office and factory in June. Georges Méliès began to make two negatives of each subject and ship one to New York, so that his brother could not only distribute but also print his Star-brand films. (Gaston, as agent, received a salary plus 25 to 40 percent of the profits, the percentage growing as the size of the profits increased.) In his first catalog, Gaston chided American manufacturers, who "are searching for novelties but lack the ingenuity necessary to produce them" and "found it easier and more economical fraudulently to copy the Star Films and to advertise their poor copies as their own original conceptions." In opening the New York branch, he announced, "we are prepared and determined energetically to pursue all counterfeiters and pirates. We will not speak twice, we will act." To make the threat real,

Gaston took the precaution of registering his films with the Library of Congress, commencing with THE ENCHANTED WELL (© 25 June 1903). This forestalled the duping of most subsequent Star films.[27]

Notwithstanding Méliès's actions, American companies still had a wide choice of European films to dupe. Among their favorites were those of Pathé Frères, such as SLEEPING BEAUTY (January 1903), DON QUIXOTE (August 1903), and CHRISTOPHER COLUMBUS (March 1904). Several English story films that reached the United States during the summer of 1903 were also duped, including the Sheffield Photo Company's A DARING DAYLIGHT BURGLARY, Robert Paul's TRAILED BY BLOODHOUNDS, and Walter Haggar's A DESPERATE POACHING AFFRAY. While Edison sold only dupes it had acquired surreptitiously through James White, Biograph usually made arrangements with the original producers. In some cases the latter offered to sell either prints made from the original negative (for fifteen cents a foot) or duplicates made from prints (twelve cents a foot).[28]

The three British films mentioned above offered two important innovations. First, and in sharp contrast to the earlier fairy-tale films, they were films of violent crime. In A DARING DAYLIGHT BURGLARY, for example, a burglar looting a house is discovered by police, makes his escape, and is finally captured after a prolonged chase, while in DESPERATE POACHING AFFRAY, two poachers are chased by game wardens, with resulting shootings and hand-to-hand fights. Second, these films used the chase as a central narrative element. As a result, the British conveyed a sensationalistic energy that American and French producers soon emulated.

Despite their innovative subject matter, however, British firms did not establish a solid base in the United States. Most producers were small and sold their films through larger distributors, particularly the Charles Urban Trading Company or British Gaumont. Similarly, during the period covered by this volume, not a single British film company opened an American agency, but rather sold films through American sales agents. While Gaumont sold Biograph films in England, Biograph served as the American agent for Gaumont and several other British companies, including Hepworth and Robert Paul.[29] The American company was soon protecting these rights by copyrighting such pictures as British Gaumont's AN ELOPEMENT A LA MODE (© 1 December 1903 as RUNAWAY MATCH) and THE CHILD STEALERS (© 9 June 1904).

Exhibition and Distribution

The rise of the story film coincided with other important changes in the film industry, including increased production and improved projection: all contributed to cinema's revived and increasing popularity. The number of theaters showing films as a permanent feature as well as the number of traveling exhibitors rose rapidly. During October and early November 1903, approximately eleven prominent New York theaters were showing films, a figure that had changed little in three years. By April 1904, the number had increased to seventeen. Keith's had been the only Boston theater to show films on a regular basis during the 1902–1903 season, but by fall 1903, films were appearing at four theaters. Two of these also gave Sunday concerts that included films. Although still shown at the end of the bill, these films, wrote the

Boston Herald, "caused many persons to forget that there were such things as railway schedules."[30] The "chaser period" was coming to an end.

In Rochester, moving-picture exhibitions reappeared on a sporadic basis at commercial theaters in March 1903. Their increasing frequency in the fall coincided with the programming of story films. The Kinetograph Company's screening of THE GREAT TRAIN ROBBERY created tumultuous excitement in January 1904 and reportedly "scored the biggest moving picture hit ever made in Rochester."[31] The following Sunday it was shown at another theater, where crowds packed the house from gallery to orchestra and a great many people were turned away. Two weeks later, in response to many requests, a return engagement was arranged. Soon the Kinetograph Company was exhibiting at Cook's Opera House on a permanent basis, while Sunday film shows were given at a rival theater.

A similar boom began among traveling exhibitors in the nation's opera houses. A survey of records documenting these showmen's activities suggests that the number of exhibitions given in the spring of 1903 was almost double that of the previous two years. These numbers increased another 50 percent in the fall, and more than 50 percent again in the spring of 1904. Lyman Howe started a second exhibition company to travel through the Midwest in early 1903. That summer, an employee, Edwin Hadley, left and started his own company. Archie Shepard, who had shown films between play acts for the Maude Hillman Stock Company, started his own traveling motion-picture show in the fall of 1903; he added a second unit in January and a third in February 1904. Other exhibitors were either getting started or moving into commercial venues at about the same time. Morgan & Hoyt's Moving Picture Company may have been operating during the first years of the new century, but in the fall of 1903, they added a ladies' orchestra, a whistling soloist, and two singers to present illustrated songs. They were thus assured of successful exhibitions in commercial theaters.[32]

Perhaps the only form of exhibition that did not prosper during this period was, ironically, the storefront theater, which, for reasons discussed in the previous chapter, suffered as existing vaudeville theaters added motion pictures to their bill. Moreover, new vaudeville houses opened in many middle-size cities, such as Hartford, Connecticut, where S. Z. Poli added a theater in September 1903; here as elsewhere on the Poli circuit, the electrograph had become a permanent attraction. The proliferation of inexpensive vaudeville was particularly characteristic of the Far West (Portland, Los Angeles, etc.). Known as small-time vaudeville, these places had between six and eight acts on their bill—much fewer than at Keith's—and the admission charge was correspondingly less, usually a dime. Motion pictures had a prominent role in these houses, but potential patrons received more for their money in these situations than at specialized storefront picture shows.

During 1903–1904, fundamental changes in the method of distribution became widespread. Until this period, distribution had been only one of several functions performed by exhibitors. Now, some established companies began to rent a reel of film to the theater for less money (about twenty-five dollars a week) and let its management be responsible for the actual projection. The theater thus became the exhibitor, while the old exhibition service retained the more limited role of distributor. This development was not some belated "discovery" but a practical response to recent changes in the industry. The exhibitor's role had become simpler and easier. With titles usually incorporated into the films rather than on separate slides, the mechanics of the editorial process were no longer performed in the projection booth, at least in vaudeville houses where a single reel of film was being shown. With projectors easier and safer to operate, astute exhibition services shifted projection responsibilities onto the theater's electrician (often selling a projector to the theater in the process).

While films had been rented occasionally in the past, the practice now became much more common. In August 1903 Lubin announced that "A Million Feet of Film of all the latest and Up-to-date Subjects will be rented."[33] Yet this offer did not have the commercial impact of similar moves made by others, particularly the Miles Brothers and Percival Waters' Kinetograph Company. In December, several months after making the shift to story films, Biograph sought to dispose of many of its old actuality subjects by offering them for sale at eight cents a foot. The Miles Brothers, who had located their New York office first in Biograph's new building on Fourteenth Street and then across the street, saw a commercial opportunity in the sale. According to Albert Smith, "They bought a number of these old copies of films, and went across the country to San Francisco, stopping at the small towns en route, and making arrangements with the managers of theaters in these small towns to supply them with programs from week to week on a circuit basis."[34] Because they had purchased the film at a low price, the Miles Brothers could offer theater managers an attractive bargain. Many of their customers were in the Far West, where small-time vaudeville managers found films an effective way to keep within their budgets.

Even though it was inaugurated with actuality footage, the Miles Brothers' venture was made possible by the shift toward story films. As this contradiction suggests, advances within the film industry were rarely instituted uniformly. A company making advances in one area, in fact, usually did not make comparable advances in others. The Miles Brothers' picture circuit indirectly challenged the business practices of exhibition services by simply renting a reel of films rather than a service that also included projector and operator. Perhaps because the theaters supplied by the Miles Brothers were small and removed from New York City, and the films were secondhand and nonfiction, the implications of this commercial strategy were not immediately apparent. The separation of distribution from exhibition and the treatment of a reel of film as a standardized interchangeable commodity had commercially revolutionary implications for the film industry.

Percival Waters' Kinetograph Company made the move to renting a reel of film at about the same time as the Miles Brothers. The precise date is uncertain, but the results were obvious. Four Boston theaters were showing films at the beginning of December 1903: Keith's with the biograph, the Boston and Majestic with the vitagraph, and Howard's with the cineograph. A month later, five theaters were showing films: Waters' kinetograph or kinetoscope service was at the Howard, Majestic, and Music Hall, while the biograph remained at Keith's and the vitagraph at the Majestic. In Rochester, where the biograph, vitagraph, and kinetograph were all contending for a place on the local vaudeville bill, the Kinetograph Company probably won the competition because of its lower cost. Nor is it surprising that the Kinetograph Company was the first to make such a move toward rentals. Unlike Biograph or even Vitagraph, Waters could rarely offer exclusive programs. He was thus forced to experiment with innovations in other areas to challenge his leading competitors.

The policy of renting films was quickly adopted by others. In Chicago, Eugene Cline and Company was advertising "Film for Rent" by the beginning of January

1904. In New York City, Alfred Harstn & Company followed in March, and William Paley by April. By that month George Spoor, whose kinodrome was the leading exhibition service in the Midwest, was also renting films through his National Film Renting Bureau.[35]

High-Class Moving Pictures

The rise of the story film and the decline of film as a visual newspaper meant that moving pictures were assuming more and more clearly the role of commercial amusement. Not surprisingly, more genteel motion-picture exhibitions did not experience the same dramatic expansion. Burton Holmes and Dwight Elmendorf remained among the few to show films in their travel lectures. Holmes had switched from 60-mm to regular 35-mm film stock in 1902. Although his original productions (still taken by Oscar Depue) remained central, the lecturer would now include films taken by other producers in his programs. For the 1903–1904 season, Holmes delivered a series of lectures on America, "having chosen them with the patriotic intention of extolling the beauties of our own country."[36] These included "The Yellowstone National Park: The Wonderland of America," in which, according to one critic:

> By means of motion pictures and stationary projections, accompanied by almost sublime word painting, the speaker carried the audience from Livingston, Mont., through the Gate of the Wonderland, indicating as he proceeded the changes wrought in the last seven years, taking the observer to the very crater of the famous geysers, skirting the various falls and rushing down through the canyons and gorges. Not for a minute did interest lag. Among the most interesting and thrilling of the many motion pictures were those showing the mammoth buffalo herd, the minute man in action, the great fountain, the Black Warrior geyser, brink of the upper fall, the great fall of the Yellowstone and the upper falls from the right bank (*Pittsburgh Post*, 28 November 1903, p. 4).

By late February 1904, Holmes had added "St. Petersburg and the Russian Army," which, reported the *New York World*, was based on a trip he had taken to Russia three years earlier, during which "he made a close study of the Czar's military system."[37] Thus a simple travelogue became a timely documentary program on a country engaged in war.

During the 1903–1904 season, Elmendorf gave his own illustrated lecture "The Yellowstone Park: The Wonderland of the World." One critic wrote:

> Moving pictures constituted more than half the views shown on Saturday and included the majority of the geysers in the park first pictured in the gorgeous coloring of their surroundings and then shown in action. There were also many comical pictures of bears, one of an old bear and her cub, being immediately suggestive of "Mrs. Grumpy" and "Little Johnny" of Mr. [Ernest Thompson] Seton's tales of the animals of the Yellowstone (*Brooklyn Eagle*, 16 November 1903, p. 5).

Elmendorf and Holmes thus offered their overlapping audiences different views of the same subject. The following year, Elmendorf became a cause célèbre with "Old and New Castile." As originally announced, the illustrated lecture at the Brooklyn Institute was to include "the only moving pictures of a complete bull fight from start to finish," and announcements of the event jammed Association Hall with 1,500 eager patrons, two-thirds of whom were women. Elmendorf's intentions were thwarted by Professor Franklin W. Hooper and officers of the institute, who forbade the film. Elmendorf protested but reluctantly accepted the censorship. At the exhibition, however, there were vehement calls for the banned subject. "The audience was made up of the very best people in Brooklyn, and there was nothing rowdyish or threatening in the demonstration, but it was certainly carried to the extreme limit of expression which well-bred people permit their emphatic and earnest disapproval to take."[38] Despite these protests, the film was not shown.

Illustrated lectures had a strong following by 1903–1904, yet few joined Holmes and Elmendorf in appealing to patrons of refined culture with motion pictures. Likewise, American producers made little effort to cultivate religious groups with films on sacred subjects. Although exhibitions in noncommercial venues are particularly difficult to document, church-sponsored exhibitions do not appear to have grown with the same rapidity as those located in theatrical amusement centers. But even the exhibitors who appealed to religious groups were sometimes attracted to films of violence and crime. Lyman H. Howe, who retained important ties to Protestant groups, included A DESPERATE POACHING AFFRAY in his repertoire—and this must have dismayed conservative churchgoers. Film practice thrived when it catered to one particular cultural group, lovers of commercial amusement, and it was here that virtually all the innovations in production, representation, and industrial organization were made in the early 1900s.

12

Cinema Flourishes Within Its Existing Commercial Framework: 1904–1905

During 1904–1905, the number of exhibition venues increased rapidly and soon reached a saturation point as the industry secured reliable but limited outlets for exhibition. As *Views and Film Index* later recalled, "Scores of picture companies toured the country with brass bands, lady orchestras, widespread billing and newspaper puffing that threatened to put the circus out of business. Swell advance agents swaggered about the theatre lobbies and hotel corridors, boasting of how their picture shows were 'packing them in.' Managers of theatres were given the alternative of conceding a fat percentage or suffer a dark house while the coin rolled into the opposition theatre." By September 1905 George Kleine could say that "We know of no vaudeville house in the United States which does not fill one number of its programme with motion pictures."[1]

Arcades with phonographs, mutoscopes, and other film-showing devices (sometimes including a small room for projection at the rear or on the second floor) steadily gained in popularity. Mitchell Mark of Buffalo and two partners had a small arcade on 125th Street in New York City. The trio wanted to open a bigger arcade on 14th Street, in the heart of the city's entertainment district, but lacked the finances. One partner, Max Goldstein, convinced his cousin, Adolph Zukor, a furrier, and Zukor's partner, Morris Kohn, to invest in the operation. In March 1904, the Automatic Vaudeville Company was formed, with Mitchell H. Mark of Buffalo and Adolph Zukor of New York City acting as president and secretary respectively. When their Automatic One-Cent Vaudeville enterprise opened on Fourteenth Street east of Broadway and proved popular, other arcades followed. In November 1905, Zukor visited Pittsburgh, leased a building, and planned a "sumptuously furnished" arcade where, according to the local press, "attendants will all be uniformed and all attractions will be of the highest order."[2] By then the group had more than a dozen arcades in Buffalo, Boston, and the New York area.

Because motion pictures were, in many respects, simply part of a diverse amusement industry, the extensive nature of some types of showings has been obscured.

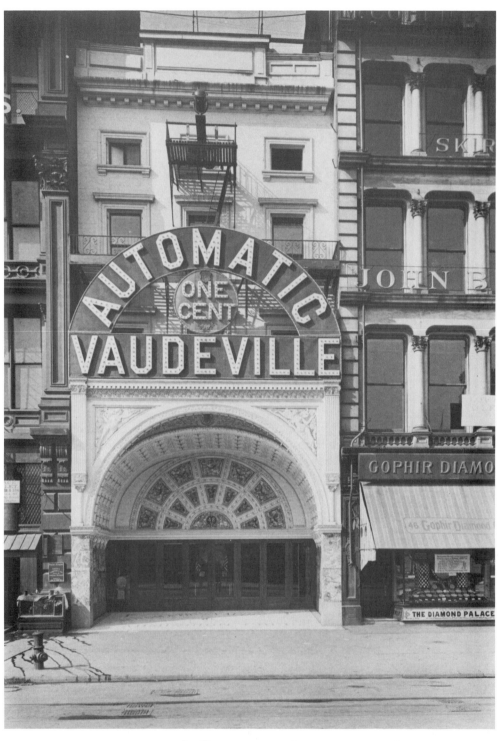

Automatic One-Cent Vaudeville on Fourteenth Street, New York City (interior on following page). Adolph Zukor was one of the owners.

Films were often screened in cafés, for example, particularly around amusement parks such as Coney Island:

> Of the hundred [Coney Island] halls of beer and smoke with stage performances half are run this season with motion pictures, yet not so very cheaply either. A boy or a woman with a strong voice to sing ballads for illustration, an operator for the projectoscope, a barker outside to tell folks that it costs nothing to get in, and a force of waiters to convince them that they can't stay in without buying drinks, make up the pay roll (*Kansas City Star*, 28 May 1905, p. 7B).

Likewise, regular Sunday motion-picture shows were given in many Eastern cities and towns: by late 1905 Archie Shepard was supplying twenty-two regular theaters on Sundays. These houses, including the West End, Third Avenue, and Fourteenth Street theaters in New York, showed motion pictures "to evade any contact with the authorities," who were busy enforcing the Sunday blue laws that prohibited most regular theatrical entertainments.

Coney Island in 1903: a Lubin fight film is featured at one arcade. Two years later, half the resort's beer halls would be showing films as well.

The proliferation of exhibition outlets further increased the demand for new story films. Although these were generally more difficult and expensive to produce, their popularity encouraged and finally necessitated a further shift in the production practices of major American producers. A statistical analysis of Edison production records for 1904–1905 shows that staged or acted films sold approximately three and a half times as well as actualities, a ratio that remained constant for the following two years of this survey and was probably typical of the wider industry. Furthermore, producers recognized that the quantity of actuality footage that they could sell was limited and tied to important news events. As a result, American producers came to rely on longer fictional narratives for the bulk of their revenues—and the bulk of their production expenses—by the second half of 1904.

Biograph Makes Story Films Its Dominant Product

The Biograph Company was the first in the United States, if not the world, to make the decisive shift toward fiction "feature" films—headline attractions that filled at least half of a thousand-foot reel. Beginning with PERSONAL (No. 2934), shot in early June 1904, the company's creative team averaged more than one new story film a month over the next year. The next story film, THE MOONSHINER (No. 2939, June–July), was copyrighted with film intertitles, a policy that became standard with subsequent pictures, including THE WIDOW AND THE ONLY MAN (No 2964, August), THE HERO OF LIAO-YANG (No. 2968, September), THE LOST CHILD (No 2974, October), THE SUBURBANITE (No. 2975, October), THE CHICKEN THIEF (No. 2977, November), THE GENTLEMAN HIGHWAYMAN (No. 2980, January 1905), TOM, TOM, THE PIPER'S SON (No. 2987, February), THE NIHILISTS (No. 2992, February), and WANTED: A DOG (No. 2997, March 1905).

By means of complex spatial and temporal constructions, camera movement, and interpolated close-ups, these Biograph films yield accomplished examples of the representational system established in the pre-nickelodeon era. In THE SUBURBANITE, for example, a coherent spatial world is created as different camera angles show overlapping spaces in successive shots (*e.g.*, the front of the house in shots 2 and 3). However, specific temporal continuities are rarely established between scenes: the film is structured by a series of imprecise ellipses, with two exceptions (shots 12 through 14) where overlapping actions are used to show activity moving back and forth between two contiguous rooms. While subservient to a narrative, each shot is still discretely organized.

Similarly, a presentational approach is evident in the use of emblematic shots at the beginning of THE CHICKEN THIEF and THE WIDOW AND THE ONLY MAN. These individual close-ups of principal characters were shot against plain backgrounds as a way of clearly showing their facial features. Interpolated close-ups sometimes freeze the narrative, allowing the spectator to savor the moment or a single action outside of the normal advance of pro-filmic time. In THE WIDOW AND THE ONLY MAN, for example, a close-up simply focuses on the widow smelling a bouquet of flowers, while in THE LOST CHILD, the filmmakers cut-in to a medium shot of the supposed kidnapper and hold a tableau-like moment in which the baby is revealed to be a guinea pig. Chase films such as PERSONAL and THE LOST CHILD, in which the performers run almost directly at the camera, continue a convention of confrontation

Two scenes from THE LOST CHILD. *The outraged, if eccentric, populace gives chase. After they capture the culprit, a medium shot features their facial expressions as they react to the unexpected discovery.*

that dates back to THE EMPIRE STATE EXPRESS. Thus, although Biograph had brought the editorial process firmly under its control in these films, there are residual traces of a still-recent period when the shot, rather than the larger narrative, was the "basic unit" of film production. Even in 1904–1905, the transitions across shots are not completely integrated into a consistent fictional world.

In their content, these Biograph films stand as a remarkable articulation of a self-confident, urban popular culture aligned with the new American middle class. This self-assurance is apparent in a film such as PERSONAL, which lampooned the tendency of American girls from wealthy families to marry impoverished foreign aristocrats, thus refinancing noble titles in exchange for international social standing. For this relatively sophisticated sexual comedy, much is made explicit in the catalog description (a possible source for live narration) or implied through specific cultural references. The French gentleman is named Alphonse and owes something to the comic-strip character who appears in previous Biograph films such as NEXT! The film takes its title from the fact that the gentleman has placed an ad in the *New York Herald*'s personal column indicating his desire for matrimony and requesting a meeting with interested parties at Grant's Tomb. Since it is summer, the wealthy women he seeks are out of town, and instead, he is greeted at the advertised rendezvous by a rapidly growing crowd of enthusiastic widows, old maids, fat girls, and working-class women. Panicked by the sheer numbers, he runs off, and the women follow. At this point, PERSONAL turns into a chase film: each of the next eight scenes begins with Alphonse entering in the distance and running toward and past the camera pursued by the women, and ends with the last of the women exiting in the foreground. As the women encounter one geographic barrier after another (a stream, an embankment, a rail fence), they expose enticing portions of their anatomy. "A neat little lady with white stockings also attracts attention as she lifts her fluffy skirts and

PERSONAL

chases the Frenchman," noted the Biograph catalog. Finally, in the last scene, "one fleet-footed Diana discovers him, and drawing a revolver from her shopping bag she holds him up and claims him as her own."[3] Here feminine and masculine are cleverly reversed, with the woman drawing on the phallic power of the gun and thus subverting the usual position of man as aggressor and suitor. This burlesque would have held particular appeal for a male American audience, and all the more so because the Frenchman suffers considerable humiliation. Along with working-class women, upper-class foreigners are parodied and marked as socially déclassé.

Brash self-confidence took another form with THE LOST CHILD, which played on a popular genre originating in Europe—the kidnapping film. Like British Gaumont's THE CHILD STEALERS, most films in this genre were simple dramas in which the family's only child is stolen by Gypsies or some other type of ne'er-do-well. After the parents suffer anguish and guilt, the child is finally restored to them through good fortune and police intervention. In THE LOST CHILD, a mother believes her child is kidnapped and dashes after a passerby with a basket, who flees as she approaches. The chase is joined by a policeman and various onlookers. Finally the suspect is caught, but when the contents of his basket are inspected, a guinea pig is discovered, and the man is freed. Society's insecurity and paranoia are gently spoofed when the woman returns home and finds her child hiding in the doghouse.

Those seeking refuge from the dynamism of the city receive similarly good-natured ridicule in THE SUBURBANITE. As Pat Loughney has pointed out, the film's title derived from a newsletter of that name which was passed out on the New Jersey Central Railroad, a line the Biograph team often took when traveling to more rural locations.[4] The handout described suburban life in glowing terms that were similar

In THE SUBURBANITE, one disaster follows another. The movers destroy the furniture, the mother-in-law arrives, and then the cook annihilates the kitchen.

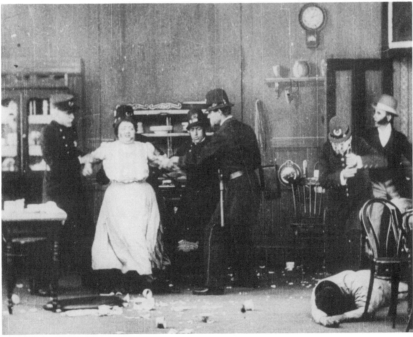

to THE SUBURBANITE's first intertitles: "A Sweet Little Home in the Country" and "Such a Nice Place for the Children." These homilies are quickly lampooned by the succeeding images: the home may be "sweet," but the movers destroy every piece of furniture the poor family owns. The children, meanwhile, cover themselves with suburban mud, to the distress of their mother. In subsequent scenes the reality behind this heavily promoted paradise becomes even more unpleasant. The third title reads, "Plenty of Good Help" but then adds, "The Sixth Girl in Three Weeks." This cook, a man dressed as a middle-aged Irish maid, is bigger and tougher than the family head. By the last title, "Mother-in-law Arrives," the idyllic claims are fully exposed. Utter disaster looms as the mother-in-law's taxi wheels down the street, following the path earlier established by the nightmarish moving van. When she challenges the intoxicated cook, only the police can restore order. In the final scene, the father puts out a sign, "To Let Furnished," and leads his (suddenly much larger) family back to their original home, presumably in the city.

Other films offer comedies of manners. THE WIDOW AND THE ONLY MAN was loosely based on the O. Henry short story "Transients in Arcadia," published three weeks earlier in the *New York Sunday World*.[5] At a summer resort, a horde of women wait impatiently for available men to arrive. When "the only man" finally appears, he has a wide choice from the eager group but settles on an attractive young widow. They go for a canoe ride, the craft capsizes, and he saves her from drowning. He courts the temporary invalid with flowers, which she nuzzles appreciatively. She has been won. The film has an unexpected dénouement, however, as the widow visits the ribbon counter in a fashionable department store, finds herself waited on by her "only man," and faints. The unconventionality of resort life had made possible the meeting of strangers of disparate backgrounds and the man's misrepresentations. But here the dangers of city life are a source of comedy, not of crisis and melodrama, as is the case in Edwin S. Porter's THE EX-CONVICT (1904) or THE MILLER'S DAUGHTER (1905).

In contrast to the foibles of city living, existence in rural communities is depicted as impoverished and violent. THE MOONSHINER, though filmed in Scarsdale, New York, portrays the primitive life of mountain folk in Kentucky. The desperate confrontation between moonshiners and revenuers ends in a shootout and tragedy as the head mountaineer is killed. His death is immediately avenged by his wife, who shoots the deputy, thus continuing a cycle of senseless violence. The film treats the story in a realistic, reportorial manner as it seeks to reenact typical incidents of rural life. The characters are never named. The operational aesthetic described by Neil Harris remains evident as the process of exchanging corn for liquor, of readying the concealed still, and of making the whisky are carefully shown for their own sake. Such documentary-like elements were also employed in popular theatrical melodramas of the day such as *The Kentucky Feud* by James R. Garey and William T. Koegh. Claiming to lift the veil on a way of life that few had seen, it featured "The Haunts of the Moonshiners, an Illicit Distillery in Full Blast, True Pictures of the Blue Grass State."[6] Although incorporating melodramatic elements, the film lacks a strong moral message. The last title ("The Law Vindicated") is a sop to moralizing sensibilities that has no place in the logic of the story, which actually builds considerable sympathy for the moonshiner, a good family man with a devoted wife and children. Rural poverty and backwardness appear to be the underlying causes of the meaningless carnage.

Violence is again linked with rural poverty in THE CHICKEN THIEF, one of several Biograph "comedies" using racial stereotypes. "From the opening of the picture where the coon with the grinning face is seen devouring fried chicken, to the end where he hangs head down from the ceiling, caught by a bear trap on his leg, the film is one of continuous laughter," the catalog insists.[7] In fact, the film elaborates on A NIGGER IN THE WOODPILE (No. 2866), shot less than six months earlier, and in both cases, African Americans are portrayed as lazy, petty thieves stealing wood for their fire or chickens for their dinner. The "comedy" comes after whites retaliate, by either placing a stick of dynamite in a log so that a black parson's home is blown apart or setting a bear trap in a chicken coop so that the thief can be trapped like an animal

THE MOONSHINER

and successfully tracked by a group of white farmers. As the enthusiasm of the catalog suggests, the filmmakers' own racism has clearly been displaced onto the rural "Sunny South."

The opposition between city and country life portrayed in this group of Biograph films departs significantly from earlier productions like THE DOWNWARD PATH and, as we shall see, many films made by Edwin Porter at Edison. The country is no longer an idyllic refuge from the corrupting influences of the city; rather, the city becomes the site of leisure, wealth, opportunity, and pleasure. In this respect, such films act as an affirmation of the filmmakers' own life-style as well as of the socio-economic and cultural conditions that made cinema possible.

Biograph's endorsement of modern life can be seen in two films dealing directly and indirectly with the Russo-Japanese War. THE HERO OF LIAO-YANG treats the

Japanese in sympathetic terms. A young Japanese army officer is "interrupted from the quiet pleasures of his home life" and soon finds himself at the front, where he is called upon to carry a message.[8] Wounded and captured by the Russians, he nonetheless makes his escape and reaches company headquarters with his message in the midst of a decisive battle. Biograph's shift from the expected Eurocentric viewpoint might best be explained by distaste for Russia's backwardness coupled with admiration for the Japanese efforts at industrial and military modernization. The NIHILISTS, by contrast, focuses on the Russians and strongly condemns the tsarist state. As is often the case in films from this era, the protagonist is shown to be sympathetic because he is surrounded by a loving family. In this instance, a happy family of the

THE CHICKEN THIEF *elaborates on earlier degrading stereotypes of African Americans, unifying them around a narrative.*

Polish nobility is shattered when the elderly father is accused of revolutionary acts and arrested.

While all these films played on popular stereotypes, many continued to rely on well-known antecedents to provide audiences with a framework to understand—and even more important, to enhance the enjoyment of—the narratives. Tom, Tom, the Piper's Son, which operated within the bad-boy genre even as it was given a historical dimension, took its simple premise from a nursery rhyme:

> *Tom, Tom, the Piper's Son*
> *Stole a pig and away he run.*

Costumes, scenery, and the film's opening scene at the fair were based on a print by William Hogarth, *Southwark Fair* (1733). This quoting of a work of art is particularly noteworthy because historians have generally seen the initial shot as an extreme if characteristic example of early cinema's compositional naïveté. Inspired by experimental filmmaker Ken Jacobs' Tom, Tom, the Piper's Son (1967), which reworked the Biograph film using an optical printer, they argue that early filmmakers had not yet learned how to organize pro-filmic elements within the frame (as Griffith and others would do) and therefore important action was not clear to the spectator.[9] In fact, the reference to the Hogarth print suggests a sophisticated if not totally successful principle of organization, whereby references to the poem and engraving provided some spectators with a basis for deciphering the film's complex, busy opening scene. Admittedly, those unaware of this antecedent were dependent on whatever clarification the exhibitor supplied, but the other shots in this film have clearly "readable" compositions. Although useful for comprehension and appreciation of the preliminary shot, an intertextual framework is unnecessary for the subsequent seven scenes, in which Tom is pursued, caught, and chastised for his transgression.

During 1904–1905, Biograph continued to take numerous actualities. Among the most elaborate were The Slocum Disaster (No. 2932), Fighting the Flames—Dreamland (No. 2950), Launching of the USS Battleship "Connecticut" (No. 2973), and Midwinter Bathing (February 1905, No. 2993). The launching of

Hogarth's Southwark Fair *served as a model for the opening scene of* TOM, TOM, THE PIPER'S SON.

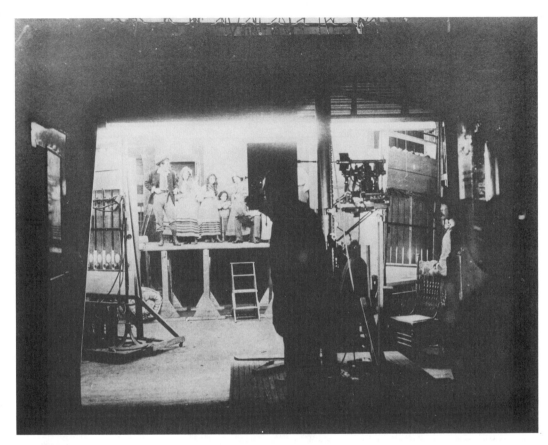

Filming an unidentified subject at Biograph's Fourteenth Street studio (ca. 1905).

the *Connecticut* is particularly noteworthy. Photographed by the company's full staff of cameramen (McCutcheon, Weed, and Bitzer) on 29 September, the film was featured at Keith's Union Square Theater during the following week. According to manager Hodgdon, it was "a new idea and a good picture" with "five views, each from a different position."[10] In fact, the surviving copyrighted version shows the launch from only three positions but still utilizes temporal and narrative repetitions that were consistent with the methods employed for the concluding scene of LIFE OF AN AMERICAN FIREMAN. This multi-camera approach enabled spectators to see the launching from several vantage points and reflected a preoccupation with sight and point of view that was manifest in many different areas of American culture, including amusements like baseball, where the need for multiple umpires was being strongly felt.[11]

With its ambitious output of story and news films, Biograph reestablished its position as the leading American film company and soon threatened to create difficulties for rival firms through its policy of retaining key films exclusively for its exhibition service. Percival Waters found that the theaters his Kinetograph Company was supplying desperately wanted PERSONAL. After he tried to acquire a print but failed, Waters suggested that the Edison Manufacturing Company make an imitation and place it on the market, of course allocating the first prints to himself. Porter's remake, HOW A FRENCH NOBLEMAN GOT A WIFE THROUGH THE NEW YORK "HER-ALD" PERSONAL COLUMNS, sold seventy-one copies over the next six months, making it the most popular Edison subject of that business year. Although Biograph responded by selling prints of its original version, the Edison Company probably enjoyed the bulk of the sales.

In an effort to recoup its loses, Biograph sued the Edison Company for copyright infringement but failed to gain an injunction and lost its case both in the lower courts and on appeal.[12] Biograph had copyrighted the film as photographs, but the judges ruled that this measure only prevented duplication of the actual image and did not protect the subject matter or story. For many months afterward, Biograph copyrighted its story films as both dramatic productions and photographs. In the meantime, the Edison Company remade Biograph's popular THE ESCAPED LUNATIC, called it MANIAC CHASE, and sold it on the open market as well. The systematic employment of this policy forced Biograph to sell its films shortly after they were made rather than keep them as exclusives for its exhibition service.

In the spring of 1905 the Edison Manufacturing Company challenged Biograph's dominance on the level of its production staff as well. Early in the year, Edison hired former Biograph employee Robert K. Bonine; soon after, a talent raid enticed away Wallace McCutcheon and cameraman A. E. Weed. Cinematographer Frederick S. Armitage also left Biograph at this time (his last recorded filming was in April). The creative team that had worked together over the previous years was broken up, leaving only Marion as producer and Bitzer as cameraman, with projectionist F. A. Dobson now assuming responsibility for much of the camerawork. McCutcheon's departure was a particularly severe blow, since neither Marion nor Bitzer had much aptitude for directing actors.[13]

This talent raid seriously disrupted Biograph production. THE WEDDING (No. 3005), a 484-foot film released in late May, did little more than reenact the typical wedding day of many middle-class Americans. Using actors in a documentary-like, process-oriented portrayal, it was recommended for "those exhibitors who cater to church entertainments." A month later, Biograph advertisements featured THE DEADWOOD SLEEPER (No. 3029), a 230-foot, one-shot subject that shows a plethora of events unfolding inside a Pullman car (the protests of a finicky old maid, the wedding night of a rube couple, a robbery). Like WHAT HAPPENED IN THE TUNNEL, it was well suited for exhibitors looking for comic moments to cut into railway-travel scenes. REUBEN IN THE SUBWAY (No. 3034) was copyrighted in several parts, perhaps because Edison's lawyers were then arguing in court that each shot had to be registered independently if a film was to be properly copyrighted. One brief shot, copyrighted under this release title, shows an entrance to the Fourteenth Street subway and the rube heading underground. This was followed by the first section of a film copyrighted as INTERIOR NEW YORK SUBWAY, 14TH STREET TO 42ND STREET, for which Biograph mounted its electric lights on an open subway car and filmed another train moving through the tunnel. When the scene reaches the Twenty-third Street stop, the film cuts to another studio scene, copyrighted as A RUBE IN THE SUBWAY. The country bumpkin gets out of the car, is pickpocketed, misses the departing train, tries to jump on the back platform, ends up on the electrified third rail, and is finally rescued in "a badly shocked condition."[14] The film then concludes with the train arriving at the Forty-second Street station. These films not only were

INTERIOR NEW YORK SUBWAY, 14TH STREET TO 42ND STREET

Production still showing Biograph's Cooper-Hewitt lights mounted on open subway cars (1904).

short but lacked the clever narratives and representational techniques that characterized McCutcheon's efforts.

Biograph was hurt again in July 1905 by its loss of the Keith circuit to Percival Waters' Kinetograph Company, the Edison-associated film exchange—a shift that may have been facilitated by McCutcheon's recent affiliation with Edison. This time Biograph did not regain the lucrative contract. Decimating if not immediately destroying Biograph's distribution/exhibition business, this loss put greater emphasis on the company's ability to sell prints to exchanges and exhibitors. Under Frank Marion's leadership, production returned to some semblance of order in late July with THE FIREBUG (No. 3055), and from this point on, Biograph's rate of production was increased to roughly two story films per month. Many films imitated earlier Biograph successes, while others were based on well-known songs, comic strips, or other antecedents in American popular and mass culture—strategies Biograph had employed since its inception.

The Edison Manufacturing Company Reluctantly Makes a Commitment to Story Films

In mid 1904, the Edison Company concentrated on producing news and human-interest films such as ANNUAL PARADE, NEW YORK FIRE DEPARTMENT; INTER-COLLEGIATE ATHLETIC ASSOCIATION CHAMPIONSHIPS, 1904; OPENING CEREMONIES, NEW YORK SUBWAY, OCTOBER 27, 1904; ELEPHANTS SHOOTING THE CHUTES AT LUNA PARK and BOXING HORSES—LUNA PARK, CONEY ISLAND.

Edison's peripatetic cameraman Alfred Abadie also shot a series of Western scenes in Bliss, Oklahoma Territory. The absence of new Edison story films may have been due to commercial decisions by company executives as they pursued an effective cost-reducing policy of duping European films and selling them through the Kleine Optical Company and other sales agents. Following THE BUSTER BROWN SERIES (March 1904), Porter did not complete another feature story film until HOW A FRENCH NOBLEMAN GOT A WIFE THROUGH THE NEW YORK "HERALD" PERSONAL COLUMNS in late August. Since Biograph films were at least partially protected by copyright, Edison's various remakes were the ethical equivalent of duplicating foreign subjects. CAPTURE OF "YEGG" BANK BURGLARS, which Porter made in August and early September, bore a strong resemblance to Lubin's newly advertised THE BOLD BANK ROBBERY. It may have been seen as a way of undercutting the Philadelphia producer, but in addition to being first in the field, Lubin offered lower prices.

During the later part of 1904 the Edison Company produced several longer films, but all were made inexpensively. EUROPEAN REST CURE burlesqued the travel genre as a vacation becomes an ordeal for an American tourist—he has a disastrous fall while leaning over to kiss the Blarney Stone, is robbed, suffers through a mud bath, and so on. Pasteboard sets of the pyramids and Roman ruins are syncretically combined with four previously released actuality films that exhibitors had often used for their travelogues. The actualities helped to specify the genre and hold down costs by reducing the amount of new footage. PARSIFAL, shot in early October, was based on the Wagner opera, which was enjoying great popularity at the time. Despite its 1,975-foot length, the film was also relatively cheap to produce, since the Edison Company had been approached by theatrical producer Harley Merry, who had already obtained the motion-picture rights to a dramatic production as well as the actors' cooperation in staging the play for the camera. Although extensively advertised, the film sold only a small number of copies, and Merry almost certainly lost a substantial portion of his $1,800 investment.

Edison's failure to create its own original story films, coupled with the growing popularity of its competitors' productions, undercut the company's commercial position. George Kleine, for instance, who had dealt exclusively in Edison films, began to sell Biograph and Pathé pictures to many of his customers. Angered by this move, Edison general manager William Gilmore ended the corporation's close association with Kleine and opened a Chicago office to market its own films in October 1904. Kleine subsequently became a selling agent for several American and European producers, including Biograph, Paley & Steiner, Pathé, and Méliès.[15]

Pressure from foreign and American competitors finally forced Edison to alter its production policies. While often continuing to rely on established genres and well-known antecedents in popular culture, Porter and his colleagues began to make story films that were no longer strict imitations of competitors' hits. This shift coincided with the hiring of W. J. Gilroy as Porter's full-time assistant and was enhanced by the addition of Wallace McCutcheon to the staff in May 1905.[16] Beginning with THE EX-CONVICT, produced in November 1904, Porter made approximately twenty feature story films over the next year. While he retained responsibility for the making of actualities both in the New York area (CONEY ISLAND AT NIGHT, June 1905) and elsewhere along the East Coast (SCENES AND INCIDENTS, RUSSO-JAPANESE PEACE CONFERENCE, PORTSMOUTH N.H., August 1905), fiction films had become a priority.

For these, Porter and his collaborators generally selected the story or subject and shaped the narrative. The shooting ratio (the amount of film shot compared to the length of the final film) varied from approximately 1.2 to 1 (THE MILLER'S DAUGHTER, 1,147 feet reduced to 974 feet) to 2.1 to 1 (THE NIGHT BEFORE CHRISTMAS, 1,670 feet reduced to 798 feet). Although some of these films were clearly influenced by Wallace McCutcheon's presence and others were clever though straightforward adaptations of hit songs and cultural crazes, many offered an elaborate view of American life that was distinctly different from the one presented in the Biograph films of the same period. While Biograph articulated the attitudes and beliefs of a self-confident new urban middle class that prospered with the rise of large-scale capital, Porter tended to express the outlook of an old middle class that often felt under siege. These two perspectives had many attitudes in common, but they also had significant differences.

THE MILLER'S DAUGHTER (September 1905), made by Porter and McCutcheon in Scarsdale, New York, and New York City, used some of the same locations as THE MOONSHINER, but this free adaptation of a well-known melodrama, Steele Mackaye's *Hazel Kirke* (1880), viewed the city/country opposition in terms virtually the reverse of Biograph's. Hazel, the miller's daughter, is courted by two men: Aaron Rodney, an honest country farmer, and Arthur Carringford, a sophisticated city-bred artiste. The miller favors Rodney, but Hazel is fooled by Carringford's worldly ways and elopes with him. As they are about to marry, Carringford's wife appears and stops the ceremony. Hazel returns home but is banished by her angry father. Expelled from the Eden of the countryside, she enters the hell of city life and works on a sewing machine to earn her living. When Hazel's machine is repossessed, she again returns home and once again is rejected by her father. In despair, Hazel jumps into the swirling waters of the mill stream but is rescued by Rodney, the faithful farmer. Rodney and Hazel are reunited and have a child, who becomes the vehicle for reconciliation between Hazel and her father.

Through Porter's camera's eye, the city is anonymous and uncaring. Family values have no chance there. Underneath the suave sophistication and wealth of city life lurk corruption and degradation. Its surface appeal threatens country life, drawing innocent youths into its destructive vortex. Left behind are the elderly—the miller and his wife—and the values of family, decency, and greater economic equality. It is Rodney's courage that saves Hazel and this way of life. These are the angry yet nostalgic themes of much late-nineteenth-century melodrama, themes that Biograph had only sketched briefly and obligatorily in THE DOWNWARD PATH. In fact, they coincided with Porter's own youthful experiences, for he had moved to the city after his small, hometown tailoring business had been forced into bankruptcy by the popularity of ready-to-wear clothing (made in cities like New York) and the 1893 depression.

Porter's view of the city is elaborated in films such as THE EX-CONVICT, THE KLEPTOMANIAC, and LIFE OF AN AMERICAN POLICEMAN. THE EX-CONVICT was an adaptation of a well-known vaudeville sketch by Robert Hilliard, *Number 973*, which previewed in March 1903, but once again Porter added many new elements and reshaped the narrative. The ex-convict is a happy family man until a policeman informs his employer of his past and he is discharged from his job. Reduced to poverty, he is forced to return to a life of crime in order to feed his sick child. A wealthy homeowner catches the ex-convict stealing but befriends him after learning that the thief had saved his daughter's life by pulling her from the path of a speeding automobile. Here, family ties become a mechanism for transcending class conflict.

THE MILLER'S DAUGHTER. *Having disobeyed her father, Hazel is forced into urban poverty and eventually attempts suicide by jumping into the patriarchal mill stream.*

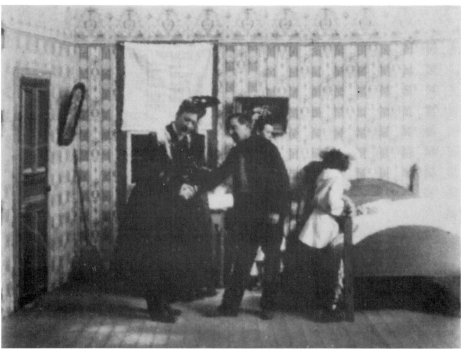

In THE EX-CONVICT *the two fathers ultimately act on each other's behalf. The well-to-do homeowner and the out-of-work ex-convict are bound together by a recognition of familial responsibilities, implied by the representations of their respective homes.*

The ex-convict's decision to return to a life of crime is viewed empathetically, while a society that destroys a man's life after he has already paid for past mistakes is condemned. Thus many of the criticisms being raised by Progressive reformers of the period were expressed in motion-picture form.[17]

Like Biograph's output, Edison films often pitted established society against its outcasts—the tramps, thieves, Gypsies, or other evildoers who threaten the social fabric. In THE BURGLAR'S SLIDE FOR LIFE (April 1905), the message takes a comic form. The slide for life was a madcap feat often performed at amusement parks: the daredevil held onto a pulley-like attachment that moved along a descending wire, and at the proper moment, he had to leap from his rapidly moving attachment or risk death. In THE BURGLAR'S SLIDE FOR LIFE, the tramp flees an urban apartment that he is burglarizing, using the clothes line as a "slide for life." He is hotly pursued by the Edison dog, Mannie, who finally catches up with him and bites into his pants. Here, "man's best friend" punishes a threat to society. THE TRAIN WRECKERS (December 1905), the most popular Edison film made that year, used melodrama to demonstrate the need for social cohesion. A romance between the engineer and the switchman's daughter is threatened by a group of train wreckers seeking to derail a train. The girl overhears their plans, is captured, escapes, and successfully warns her lover. Ready to try again, the train wreckers knock her out and leave her on the tracks to be run over. After the heroic engineer courageously positions himself on the train's cowcatcher and rescues her from certain death, railroad personnel and passengers chase and kill the desperados: society unites to protect itself.

Among Porter's most successful cinematic innovations of this period were "jumble announcements," animated intertitles whose letters and shapes swirled around the black background, finally forming words and silhouettes.[18] These were used extensively in several comedies, starting with HOW JONES LOST HIS ROLL (March 1905) and continuing with THE WHOLE DAM FAMILY AND THE DAM DOG (May 1905) and EVERYBODY WORKS BUT FATHER (November 1905). Many of the most successful Edison films were comedies, and these often adapted popular crazes to the screen. EVERYBODY WORKS BUT FATHER and ON A GOOD OLD 5¢ TROLLEY RIDE were based on lyrics from popular songs, while THE WHOLE DAM FAMILY AND THE DAM DOG, which sold 136 copies during the next year and a half, adapted images from a picture postcard that was then enjoying wide circulation. Comedies and simple films of violent crime typically commanded much larger sales than more serious films like THE MILLER'S DAUGHTER (thirty-eight copies during 1905–1906) or THE KLEPTOMANIAC (forty-three copies during the same period).

Sigmund Lubin Prospers

During 1904, smaller American producers increasingly emphasized the production of story films as they abandoned fairy tales and moralistic plays to concentrate on comedies and crime. By the fall, Sigmund Lubin was producing approximately one fiction "feature" a month, with a marked emphasis on the two popular genres. Lubin remade Edison's THE GREAT TRAIN ROBBERY in June 1904; as he had done earlier with UNCLE TOM'S CABIN, the Philadelphian made his version significantly shorter than the Edison original—600 feet as opposed to 740 feet. Because the number of frames per second was lower, Lubin could add a new scene of the robbery being planned and additional shots of the chase between posse and bandits, and still offer a shorter film. Instead of attempting the complicated matte shots in the station scene à la Porter, Lubin's filmmaker, apparently John J. Frawley, built a set by the railroad tracks and had a train pull in. With Lubin's picture selling for $66—versus $110 for the Edison original—it was bought by small-time traveling showmen whose modest income had precluded purchase of the Edison film.

In early November, Lubin offered THE LOST CHILD and A NEW VERSION OF "PERSONAL," both remakes of Biograph hits. Scenes in the latter, a 400-foot comedy, were connected by dissolves. While Lubin appropriated Biograph's premise of a desperate French gentleman (Count Hardup) seeking an American bride through the personal columns of a New York newspaper (in this instance, said to be the *Journal*), his Philadelphia locations created a distinctive flavor. Gilbert Saroni, a female impersonator, played the ultimately successful old maid who goes to great lengths to capture a husband. Two weeks after the film's release, seventy-five feet of new footage were added, including an emblematic shot of the count at the beginning that complemented a kissing scene in close-up of "the victor and the victim" at the end. The longer version of the film was then retitled MEET ME AT THE FOUNTAIN to avoid a legal confrontation with Biograph. (In fact, Edison's remake copied the original subject more closely even though it did not use the same title.) Saroni also played the mother in THE LOST CHILD, which was soon retitled THE KIDNAPPED CHILD (despite the fact that the child only hid in the doghouse and was never kidnapped).[19] Both were attractive buys to exhibitors with limited budgets.

TRAMP'S REVENGE and A DOG LOST, STRAYED, OR STOLEN (June 1905) were both indebted to Biograph's WANTED: A DOG, and though selling them separately, Lubin urged exhibitors to show them together. In TRAMP'S REVENGE, three tramps visit a suburban house in rapid succession, looking for handouts. The first two tramps are successful, but the frustrated homeowner (Mrs. Brown) sics her dog on the third, who captures the canine and takes it away, thus creating a premise for the WANTED: A DOG narrative that was lacking in the Biograph original. A DOG LOST, STRAYED, OR STOLEN, however, simply follows the Biograph story line as Mrs. Brown offers twenty-five dollars for her missing dog but fails to describe it; huge numbers of reward seekers appear and a chase ensues. I. B. DAM AND THE WHOLE DAM FAMILY (July) imitated Edison's THE WHOLE DAM FAMILY AND THE DAM DOG but was shorter (150 feet versus 300 feet), while its $16.50 price tag made it a good buy compared with Edison's $45.

Lubin did more than imitate his rivals' successes. In September 1904 he produced LIFE OF AN AMERICAN SOLDIER, a 600-foot film of approximately eighteen scenes. Like Biograph's THE AMERICAN SOLDIER IN LOVE AND WAR, the film combined newly shot fictional scenes with actuality footage, but here, the narrative focuses on a family man who answers the president's call for volunteers. His enlistment and farewell to his aged mother, wife, and baby, are followed by scenes of military life, probably shot at the time of the Spanish-American War; these not only provided the film with a sense of spectacle but reduced negative costs. The film then cuts away to the hero's home, where his sick child struggles for life. The soldier receives a letter and later dreams (via a dream balloon) of his wife and child. Eventually he is reunited with his family, and the picture concludes with a medium shot of him saluting the camera/audience, clearly associating spectators (many of whom would have been immigrants) with the nation.

Lubin's MEET ME AT THE FOUNTAIN. *The women chase Count Hardup around Philadelphia. The winner, played by female impersonator Gilbert Saroni, shows off her prize.*

The following month Lubin released THE BOLD BANK ROBBERY, a 600-foot, twenty-four-scene picture that opens with an emblematic shot of three well-dressed men who plan and execute a robbery and concludes with a similar portrait of the trio, this time in prison stripes. The film's motifs were drawn from earlier American and European crime films. Among his 1905 offerings were SAVED FROM A WATERY GRAVE (January), made with the cooperation of the U.S. Life Saving Service; THE COUNTERFEITERS (February); THE SIGN OF THE CROSS (April), "a Soul Stirring Drama of the Christian Persecution"; and THE FAKE BLIND MAN (May). The few news and actuality films that Lubin was producing by this time included THE LIBERTY BELL ON ITS WAY TO THE EXPOSITION (July 1904) and SHAD FISHING, which detailed the process of catching shad on the Delaware River during the spring of 1905. Crime subjects such as HIGHWAY ROBBERY (July) and comedies such as THROUGH THE MATRIMONIAL AGENCY (October), a reworking of the PERSONAL narrative, were more typical of Lubin's productions in this period.

Many subjects were taken at Lubin's recently acquired forty-acre farm, located a short distance from Philadelphia, including FUN ON THE FARM (November 1905), which shows rural folk enjoying themselves at harvest time. Farmers claim free kisses at every opportunity from women (whose reactions vary) in the midst of washing and milking, on hay rides, or at corn huskings. Another source of merriment for these white farmers is provided by chasing the local "chicken thief," a "darky" who is tarred and feathered after being caught stealing chickens and . . . pumpkins. While appropriating elements from Biograph's THE CHICKEN THIEF and Edison's WATERMELON PATCH, the German-born producer and his staff failed to master the correct cultural references; among other things, the substitution of pumpkins for watermelons implicitly exposes the racist conventions and becomes anarchic. This is the kind of film that the surrealists would later celebrate as unintentionally subversive.[20]

Lubin's success was based on a combination of elements. While retaining particularly close ties to hit films or genres already established by his competitors, his films consistently offered larger doses of sex, violence, and sensationalism than those of the other American companies. They were designed to appeal to immigrant, working-class, and lower-middle-class audiences and were consonant with his pricing structure, which placed them in venues with lower admission fees. This appeal is apparent in such short comedies as A POLICEMAN'S LOVE AFFAIR (May 1905), in which a policeman is wooed by a cook with free meals and kisses—until the mistress of the wealthy household discovers the couple together. (For the kissing scene, the filmmakers cut-in to a closer view of the lovemaking.) The cop, knowing he has violated the code of social order that he is supposed to defend, tries to escape, but his efforts prove futile when the upper-class woman douses him with a pail of milk as he jumps out the window. Working-class audiences obviously found amusement in seeing the economic elite at odds with law enforcers who were designated to serve their interests. In THE POLICEMAN'S PAL (120 feet), a policeman chases a purse snatcher, but after the two men jump over a wall they abandon appearances and prepare to divide the spoils, only to discover that the stolen satchel is empty. Lubin films often portray the police as hypocritical and undermine their moral authority. His deep-seated skepticism about the existing social order, formed in part by the anti-Semitism he encountered, is evident in these anarchic constructions.

Lubin's commercial interests remained diverse. Well known for the excellent photographic quality of his films, the Philadelphia producer continued duping Pathé

A POLICEMAN'S LOVE AFFAIR. *There is a cut from establishing shot to two shot. However, continuity remains problematic as the maid pours an unfamiliar bottle of wine in the closer view.*

and other foreign films throughout this period—long after Pathé had opened a branch office in New York and appointed a former Lubin employee as its local agent in Philadelphia. His cineograph continued to be a widely used projector; the Exposition model sold for seventy-five dollars, complete with an electric lamp, adjustable rheostat, and calcium light.[21] The company also offered its customers a wide array of song slides, many made by Lubin photographers. During this period, Lubin also helped to introduce at least one technical innovation, "mono-tinting." Hand-tinting individual frames had been a common if expensive practice from the beginning of cinema; in April 1904, however, Lubin announced that he was offering subjects in several tints at no extra charge. Interested parties soon discovered that Lubin was playing on a confusion of words and that each shot was chemically dyed a single color. In fact, even this effect was not entirely novel, since exhibitors had occasionally placed tinted glass over their lenses when projecting black-and-white images, but the shift in responsibility from exhibitor to producer made the use of toned images much more practical. This innovation, which may not have originated with Lubin, gradually became widespread; more than a year later it was still considered "new."[22]

Lubin experimented not only with color but with sound, and in August 1904 marketed the cinephone, which, his advertisements announced,

> is the Combination of Instrumental Music, Song and Speech with Life Motion Pictures. You see the Black Face Comedian in Life-motion Pictures on the screen, and you hear him talk and sing at the same time. You see the Cornet Soloist playing and at the same time you hear the melody he plays (*New York Clipper*, 27 August 1904, p. 613).

With the exception of one song, the 100-foot films were instrumental solos; they were meant to be projected with Victor Monarch disk records not specifically made for this purpose. The process of synchronization was very primitive: showmen were told to "use your own machine" and had to retain approximate synchronization by increasing or decreasing the projection speed. Extensive utilization was thus impractical.[23]

Lubin's expansion in many areas of production paralleled his continued success with distribution that had been enhanced by his early adoption of the rental system. Distribution guaranteed an outlet for films and provided an incentive for novelties that might attract new customers.

Selig's Exhibition Service Fades

William Selig, based in Chicago, did not enjoy the same degree of prosperity as Lubin. A key factor was the failure of his atrophied exhibition service to survive the transition to a rental system; as a result, he concentrated more and more on selling the polyscope projector and prints made from his original negatives. By July 1904 Selig had joined other producers in exploiting the popularity of violent crime films by making TRACKED BY BLOODHOUNDS; OR, A LYNCHING AT CRIPPLE CREEK, a 450-foot subject shot in Colorado with crucial assistance from Selig's western agent, H. H. Buckwalter.[24] Promoted as "the most sensational picture ever made," this twelve-scene melodrama depicts the killing of a generous woman by a ruthless tramp, the husband's vow of vengeance, and the pursuit, capture, and lynching of the tramp.

At the beginning of October, Selig and Buckwalter produced THE HOLD-UP OF THE LEADVILLE STAGE, which was photographed near Colorado Springs and directed by Selig. According to promotional literature, the film reenacted incidents that had occurred twenty-five years earlier and used the stagecoach and driver who had actually made these dangerous journeys and been robbed many times. Typically, the film showed the planning and execution of the holdup, the killing of a fleeing child (recalling the shooting of a fleeing passenger in THE GREAT TRAIN ROBBERY but displaying even greater brutality), and a chase in which all but two of the robbers are captured or killed. The two remaining bandits fight over the loot and one dies. As the survivor is about to escape, he is overpowered by the posse and "the picture ends with the triumph of right over wrong and the supremacy of law over the bandits and their evil ways." Despite this strong narrative, the filmmakers allowed themselves a digression to show Colorado's magnificent countryside:

> A dozen different views are given of the stage climbing the mountain trails toward the cloud city of silver and gold. In each case the background includes some famous spot of deep significance or absorbing interest to those who have journeyed over the route. Ute Pass, North Cheyenne canyon, Garden of the gods, Pike's Peak, Cheyenne mountain, Cameron's Cone and a hundred other points are easily recognized (Selig Polyscope Company, *The Hold-up of the Leadville Stage*).

The display of Colorado's scenery, which had been the prime purpose of earlier Selig travel films taken in the area, remained strong enough to dominate the narrative impulse for part of the film.

THE HOLD-UP OF THE LEADVILLE STAGE generated considerable publicity, and in a local report of the filming, Selig emphasized the indirect advertising benefits for the area: "We are asking no subscriptions or contributions of any sort for this work for the pictures themselves are a strong attraction for our circuits," Selig informed the reporter but added, "The amount of good advertising the state will get can hardly be estimated."[25] As if to confirm this statement, a national publicity stunt soon appeared in the Hearst papers. According to the Hearst story, titled "The Joke Was on the Bandits," tourist Mr. Fred C. Aickens (*i.e.*, Fred C. Aikens) stumbled innocently across Selig's crew filming the holdup. Upon witnessing the innocent child being gunned down:

> "By gum! This is too much!" exclaimed Mr. Aickens, and blazed away at the bandits.
> The driver, equally indignant, let his revolver speak and the cartridges in these revolvers were not blank. Colonel Selig, who had come out of the coach with the other terror stricken passengers, uttered a yell, and his arm dropped to his side, shot through the fleshy part. Another bullet went through a bold bandit's hat, neatly shaving his hair (*San Francisco Examiner*, 30 October 1904, magazine section).

This story ended with the outraged local citizenry setting fire to the coach. Aikens, however, was not an innocent passerby but co-founder of the Amusement Supply Company, a Chicago-based mail-order house for motion-picture goods (including Selig films) that was started in October 1903 with Alvah C. Roebuck.[26]

In October 1904, Selig began to sell THE GIRLS IN OVERALLS, a six-minute picture also taken during the Colorado trip. Shot at the Vidal ranch near Gunnison, the film shows seven sisters performing traditionally masculine farming tasks, as they did each summer in order to pay off a loan that threatened to put the family property into the hands of a moneylender. Cavorting for the camera, they defend their father's legacy.[27]

Selig produced only two longer fiction films in 1905, both of which were comedies. THE SERENADE was based on a four-scene dramatic composition that Selig wrote and then copyrighted on 1 May 1905, although the film itself, elaborated to twelve scenes, was not offered for sale until September. Freddie, a "Romeo," serenades Fannie, his "Juliet," until the girl's father sets the dog on him. The young man flees but too late, for the dog grabs his pants. A chase follows, with the father and daughter both in pursuit, but for different purposes. Finally the girl rescues Freddie, and the couple leaves the exhausted father behind. THE GAY DECEIVERS, "a somewhat different comedy" of 775 feet, dealt with the delicate issue of marital infidelity. Two husbands concoct a story and leave their unsuspecting wives at home while they rendezvous with two attractive women. The wives discover their plans and, aided by binoculars and a camera, document their activities. When the men return home, they receive a firm thrashing.[28] As was the case with other American producers, Selig relied heavily on sex and violence to sell his products.

Nonfiction filmmaking continued to be a significant part of Selig's production efforts. A Selig cameraman visited the South Pacific during the winter of 1904–1905 and returned with more than 700 feet of film depicting Samoa and the Fiji Islands; several scenes held out the exotic and even erotic possibilities of semi-naked native dancers. Exhibitors and exchanges could purchase either individual scenes (to construct their own programs) or a single 600-foot subject, A TRIP THROUGH SAMOA AND THE FIJI ISLANDS.[29] Overall, Selig made far fewer important subjects than Edison, Biograph, or Lubin.

Paley Moves into Fiction-Film Production

The expansion of the industry, the increasing emphasis on longer story films, and the more limited responsibilities of exhibition-services-turned-exchanges encouraged two leading firms to move extensively into fiction-film production and sell their products on the open market: William Paley and American Vitagraph. By mid 1904 Paley, whose kalatechnoscope remained in all the Proctor theaters, had formed a partnership, Paley & Steiner, with William F. Steiner. While the origins of this collaboration are unknown, Steiner had probably been working with or for Paley in previous years. Whatever the case, Paley & Steiner copyrighted a group of their Crescent films at the end of October and placed them on the market. Six of the seven films that they advertised were short comedies. JUST LIKE A GIRL contained one shot: a man jumps in a pond to escape a woman, and rather than jump after him, she stays at the water's edge desperately waving her hands. TRAMP ON THE FARM lasted less than three minutes but had at least six shots: a farmer leaps off a moving streetcar and is saved from serious injury by landing on a tramp; in gratitude, the rube befriends the vagabond, who happily wallows in a pigsty, sleeps in a doghouse, and finally ends up sharing a drink with the dog. THE TRIALS AND TROUBLES OF AN AUTOMOBILIST, a chase film,

TRAMP ON THE FARM. *The unsocialized tramp takes advantage of his benefactor's hospitality and enjoys the life of a domesticated animal.*

was the most ambitious of this group: an auto knocks over an apple cart and is pursued by the vendor and police; the driver is beaten up and escapes but is finally captured.[30]

The partners continued to release Crescent films at frequent intervals over the following months; by late January 1905 they had more than twenty films for sale. Their most sensational was AVENGING A CRIME; OR, BURNED AT THE STAKE (© 19 November 1904), the story of an African American (played by a white in blackface) who loses at gambling, kills a woman, and flees. After a chase, the killer is caught, tied to a stake, and burned alive; as in Edison's later THE "WHITE CAPS," vigilante justice is portrayed as effective and reliable. AROUND NEW YORK IN 15 MINUTES (© 31 January 1905), a travelogue showing various street scenes in Manhattan and Brooklyn, was a compilation of shots that Paley & Steiner also offered as short films. The last scene, "Flat Iron Building on a Windy Day," shows women's skirts blowing up to reveal their underwear.[31]

The production methods that Paley & Steiner used in making these films are not known in any detail. Both individuals, however, were competent cameramen and trained in all phases of filmmaking. As partners they had approximately equal input, an arrangement suggesting that a collaborative method of production was being practiced at their firm. Seemingly on their way to success, they suddenly encountered difficulties and hesitated. The reasons are not fully known, but Thomas Edison sued Paley & Steiner (along with Méliès, Pathé, and Eberhard Schneider) on 23 November 1904. Rather than confront Edison in the courts, the partners may have reached an agreement whereby they ceased producing fiction films, which competed

In AVENGING A CRIME, *a black kills a woman. He is then pursued and lynched by a vigilante squad (following page).*

The growth in motion-picture business is suggested by a page filled with relevant advertisements in The New York Clipper, *19 November 1904.*

with Edison's own efforts, but were allowed to continue making local views and actualities, perhaps under some kind of licensing arrangement. In August 1905, Biograph announced its acquisition of the Crescent negatives, including the previously unreleased THE LUCKY WISHBONE (820 feet), and its sale of prints to the trade.[32] By this time, the Paley-Steiner partnership was being dissolved.

After Paley & Steiner closed, Paley continued his exchange and exhibition service. When Proctor opened his vaudeville theater in Troy, New York, in the fall of 1905, the veteran cameraman took local views of the police and fire department. The films brought huge crowds to the theater and were held over for a second week.[33] Steiner started the Imperial Motion Picture Company, focused much energy on Connecticut, and established his presence as an exhibitor by offering local views. In Meriden, Steiner was called an Edison operator; his visit received front-page coverage:

> The first pictures were taken at the corner of Colony and Main streets [this] afternoon, just as the crowds came from the factories, offices and schools. Hundreds and hundreds of men, women and children as they came to the principal crossing of the city stepped in front of the camera, unconscious that they were being photographed, then manager W. D. Reed, of the [Meriden] theatre, threw handfuls of pennies into the air, and the boys and girls scrambled for them in delight, while the picture machine recorded their actions on the films (*Meriden Daily Journal*, 15 November 1905, p. 1).

Steiner also supplied Connecticut theaters with films for Sunday shows. Seeking to avoid risk, these two men retreated into the backwaters of actuality filmmaking at a time when fiction film was on the ascendant. It was a decision they would soon regret.

Vitagraph Becomes an Important Production Company

The American Vitagraph Company was one of the last old-line exhibition services to begin offering film rentals to its clients. As the company's half-page ad announced in April 1905, "We Don't Rent Films. We Don't Have To! When our subjects become scratched, worn out and passé we sell them to the concerns who do rent films." Despite this boast, Blackton, Smith, and Rock lost some vaudeville customers to renters and assumed a less prominent role in this area than they had in the recent past. By the fall of 1904, however, they also had four exhibition companies touring opera houses in various sections of the United States. A cameraman preceded at least some of these units by approximately ten days and took local views for the forthcoming shows. Films were taken of local fire departments, employees leaving nearby factories, and children at school. Townspeople were informed, "You can see pictures of your very own town, your very own fire department, and what is more, you can see yourself." The entire community was encouraged to participate in the process of making as well as seeing the films. Newspaper announcements urged townspeople to make suggestions for possible subjects or to appear at certain places for the filming.[34] The results drew huge crowds to the theaters and assured return dates, when the same local views were shown again but with a full complement of new pictures.

During this period, Blackton and Smith continued to film current events such as the opening ceremonies for the New York subway system on 27 October 1904 and President Roosevelt's inauguration on 4 March 1905. (Their filming of these events provided Edison with some of the evidence he needed to initiate a new suit for patent infringement.)[35] If story films were produced, they were used only on Vitagraph's circuit. The changing role of exhibition must have helped to convince Blackton, Smith, and Rock that it was time to inaugurate full-scale commercial production and then sell the films on the open market. In August 1905, construction was begun on a studio on Locust Avenue in the Flatbush section of Brooklyn at the same time that production was started on the rooftop of their Manhattan office building.[36] As we shall see in the next chapter, these events coincided with the beginnings of the nickelodeon boom.

After incorporating its production entity as Vitagraph Company of America, Vitagraph formally introduced its new commercial policy in September 1905, by selling the vitagraph projector as well as films. Pictures, however, were first distributed by the company's rental operation several weeks before being sold outright. RAFFLES, THE AMATEUR CRACKSMAN (© 23 August 1905) was thus exhibited in Washington, D.C., for the week beginning Monday, 10 September, yet it was not advertised for sale until 23 September (at 12¢ per foot or $126 for 1,050 feet). The film was inspired by E. W. Hornung's stories of a society burglar and the stage adaptation starring Kyrle Bellew (the actor who appeared in Vitagraph's THE GREAT SWORD COMBAT ON THE STAIRS, 1902). By this time, a comic strip based on the Raffles character had also appeared, as had the Edison comedy-drama RAFFLES—THE DOG. Rather than produce a film version without arranging permission from the owner, as most companies then did when making such adaptations, Vitagraph acquired the exclusive picture rights from Bellew and Liebler & Company, a policy it pursued in several other instances, notably with ADVENTURES OF SHERLOCK HOLMES; OR, HELD FOR A RANSOM (McClure, Phillips & Company), MONSIEUR BEAUCAIRE (Booth Tarkington), and later, A CURIOUS DREAM (Mark Twain).[37]

On the basis of the brief fragments that survive (the paper prints submitted for copyright), RAFFLES, THE AMATEUR CRACKSMAN appears to have consisted of long establishing shots that retained the distant, frontal spatial relationship typical of theater with a proscenium stage. Familiarity with the play and short stories helped audiences follow the narrative of Raffles' secret life as pickpocket, robber, and gang leader. The picture was notable for its depiction of criminal activities by a respectable member of high society who is not a conventional villain and is never caught. Such portrayals might have been acceptable in books or plays directed at the middle class, but when they were presented to working-class audiences in nickelodeons, many community leaders soon voiced their opposition.

Vitagraph's biweekly releases retained close ties to specific cultural works as well as established genres. MONSIEUR BEAUCAIRE—THE ADVENTURES OF A GENTLEMAN OF FRANCE (© 13 November 1905) was based on the play and novel by Booth Tarkington. BURGLAR BILL (© 9 November 1905) took its title and main character from a well-known comic strip. ESCAPE FROM SING SING (© 30 September 1905) and THE GREEN GOODS MEN; OR, JOSIAH AND SAMANTHY'S EXPERIENCES WITH THE ORIGINAL "AMERICAN CONFIDENCE GAME" (© 4 December 1905) borrowed titles from well-known melodramas but were not indebted to their plots. Both chase films survive, the latter in somewhat truncated form. In THE GREEN GOODS MEN, scenes

RAFFLES, THE AMATEUR CRACKSMAN. *The police are baffled and Raffles plays the cop.*

THE GREEN GOODS MEN. *After demonstrating their scam, the con artists approach their victims.*

are introduced by intertitles, which, like the main title itself, clarify the action. Country folks, easily fooled by a letter from "Green Goods Men" (*i.e.*, con artists), come to the city with their life savings. The process whereby they are relieved of their money is carefully detailed. Following the title "Setting the Trap," the second scene gives a demonstration of an "original trick table borrowed from the criminal collection at Police Headquarters." The ruse is pulled off, but the police come to the rescue, and a rooftop chase ends as "the Green Goods Men crawl down the wrong chimney and land in a POLICE STATION."[38] Throughout the film, the Vitagraph Company used a distant camera without the editorial elaboration of interpolated close-ups or intercutting. Nonetheless, both THE GREEN GOODS MEN and ESCAPE FROM SING SING convey a manic energy that made them popular with audiences.

At the core of Vitagraph's films is the vital, often humorous, quality of city life: dynamism, not morality, is the issue. The city offers opportunity, as in THE NEWS-BOY, a Horatio Alger–type story that follows the hero's upward path from poor boy to Supreme Court justice. MOVING DAY; OR, NO CHILDREN ALLOWED (© 20 September 1905) applauds ingenuity in skirting the rules: parents pack their numerous offspring into trunks and move into new quarters where children are prohibited. Once again these films were made by men and usually addressed masculine aspirations, fantasies, and fears. THE SERVANT GIRL PROBLEM (© 1 September 1905), for example, begins with close-ups of two different women labeled, "His Choice" and "His Wife's Choice." The first is a beautiful woman, the second a vacuous matron played by a man. In the course of the narrative "His Wife's Choice" wins the "servant girl" opening, and the film ends with the husband doing the dishes.

Of all the symbols of urban life, Vitagraph was most enchanted by the automobile, which was still a vehicle for the well-to-do. THE VANDERBILT AUTO RACE, shot on 14 October with as many as ten different cameras, was the only actuality film that Vitagraph offered for sale in 1905.[39] Another film, LICENSE NO. 13; OR, THE HOO-DOO AUTOMOBILE, used various camera tricks as well as titles in comic verse before each scene:

> *Charlie and Molly go out for a spin,*
> *In Charlie's new automobile*
> *But the number's thirteen and as soon will be seen*
> *It bothers them quite a good deal.*
> (*New York Clipper*, 14 October 1905, p. 880)

Information about Vitagraph's production practices during 1905 and early 1906 is minimal. In later biographical sketches, G. M. Anderson (then known as George, and later as Gilbert, Maxwell Anderson) claimed directing credit for RAFFLES, THE AMATEUR CRACKSMAN. He directed and acted in many Vitagraph films produced from August 1905 to early 1906. Vitagraph projectionist Max Hollander later recalled, "When we were idle, G. M. Anderson (Broncho Billy) would use us as extras in his pictures. Anderson was directing and acting in Vitagraph pictures which were soon to make his name famous throughout the country." After William Ranous was hired as a second director, two production units were active. One was headed by Blackton and the other by Smith. With the two partners acting as cameramen for their respective units, they adopted the collaborative model of production previously employed when working on a more intimate scale.[40]

THE SERVANT GIRL PROBLEM

Moving into fiction filmmaking during the later part of 1905, Vitagraph promptly established itself as a major American producer. Its pictures tapped into many of the playful, liberating possibilities of commercial entertainment. As exhibitors, their prolonged exposure to the tastes of urban pleasure seekers as well as their protracted struggles with Edison and other powers within the industry armed these filmmakers with a strong irreverence.[41] This sensibility found an eager reception in vaudeville and in the nickelodeon theaters that were just beginning to proliferate. The company's heavy commitment to story films, moreover, underscores the extent to which this type of production had become the mainstay of the American industry. The five major production companies—Edison, Biograph, Lubin, Selig, and Vitagraph—all depended on them for their commercial vitality.

Pathé and the Europeans

By 1904, Pathé, with a strong commercial base in the French motion-picture and phonograph industries, was rapidly setting up sales offices in countries throughout the world, from Germany and England to Japan and South America. The French concern had an agent in the United States during the first part of that year and finally opened a full-scale branch in late August at 42 East Twenty-third Street.[42] Rather than copyright its films as Méliès did, Pathé pursued a commercial solution to the duping problem: it began to market pictures in the United States before selling them in Europe.[43] This move undercut Edison and other producers who bought Pathé films in London and then shipped them back to the United States for duping. Yet ultimately, Pathé's output was so popular, and the company had so much difficulty satisfying the American demand, that Edison and Lubin bought popular films from Pathé's New York office and sold duplicate copies to meet the demand.

By the time the New York office opened, Pathé's rate of production at least equaled that of any American production company and was increasing rapidly. Among its many popular films were ANNIE'S LOVE STORY (May 1904), which traces the fall of a young woman in a manner that recalls Biograph's THE DOWNWARD PATH (1900); COWBOYS AND INDIANS (August 1904), a Western shot in France; and BARNUM'S TRUNK (1904), one of the company's many popular trick films. By May 1905 Pathé was advertising "Something New Every Week."[44]

Widely seen on American screens, Pathé films covered a diverse range of subjects. Many, like THE FAITHLESS LOVER (1905) and A FATHER'S HONOR (1905), are melodramas of love, betrayal, and revenge. Sensationalism, combined with a detailing of process similar in style and approach to Biograph's THE MOONSHINER, is evident in SCENES OF A CONVICT'S LIFE (1905). The film's emotional impact is heightened by the matter-of-fact way in which it traces the fate of a prisoner from his incarceration through his failed escape and death by firing squad to the disposal of his body in the sea. Some films, such as MODERN BRIGANDAGE (1905), operate within the crime genre; others, such as A PASTRY COOK'S PRACTICAL JOKES (1905), are comedies. In the case of CINDERELLA (1905?), Pathé was among the few companies still producing fairy-tale films.

Pathé often portrayed working-class life and class conflict, but, more frequently than American films, did so by showing events occurring in the workplace. THE MINING DISTRICT (1905) shows a man and his son toiling in a coal mine when an explosion occurs, killing the son. It concludes with the weeping father standing over the body of his dead child. Location and studio filming are syncretically combined. In THE STRIKE (July 1904), the just demands of the striking factory workers are ignored by the owner, and a confrontation occurs in which several workers are shot dead. A woman then avenges her husband's death by killing the owner, but when she is brought to trial, the owner's son, knowing that his father was wrong, asks that the woman be acquitted, and she is freed. A concluding apotheosis shows labor and capital reconciled. This sympathetic portrayal of striking, even violent, workers occurred within a framework that sustained existing social relations, albeit in a more enlightened form: a liberal and more insightful son takes over from his father.

Méliès pictures, in contrast to Pathé films, faded in popularity as the Parisian filmmaker failed to adopt the crime and comedy-chase genres. Longer films such as AN IMPOSSIBLE VOYAGE (1905) and THE PALACE OF THE ARABIAN NIGHTS (1905), though executed on a grander scale, were fairy-tale films similar to earlier efforts. THE BARBER OF SEVILLA (1904) and RIP'S DREAM (1905) were versions of well-known plays or operas, and recalled previous efforts such as Biograph's RIP VAN WINKLE. Most Star productions were shorter (100–300 feet) trick films similar to those made in earlier years. Méliès's "artistic integrity," his determination to make films within prestidigitator traditions, may have been admirable, but it cost him his central role in the industry. It was the Pathé approach—a wide range of subject matter, a hierarchical organization with various departments, and international branch offices—that was proving successful.

Moving pictures as a popular form of amusement boomed during 1904–1905. Within the existing framework of possibilities, exhibition outlets proliferated, and the demand for new films was such that print sales per picture increased dramatically. This surge in demand, however, was limited primarily to story films, which became the key product of all the major producers. Profits increased, providing the incentive for further investment as well as the necessary funds. The years of commercial troubles had been left behind. Making an analogy that evokes the Wright brothers' startling 1903 invention, the airplane, we can say that the film industry was taking off and would soon soar upward to unimagined heights.

PART 5

The Beginnings
of the Nickelodeon Era:
1905–1907

Biograph's Model E "New Style" mutoscope, nicknamed "The Eagle."

13

Nickels Count:
Storefront Theaters,
1905–1907

*T*he rapid proliferation of specialized storefront moving-picture theaters—
commonly known as "nickelodeons" (a reference to the customary admission
charge of five cents), "electric theaters," and "theatoriums"—created a revolution in
screen entertainment.[1] They would alter the nature of spectatorship and precipitate
fundamental shifts in representation. Their explosive demand for product would not
only increase film production but force its reorganization. It is not too much to say
that modern cinema began with the nickelodeons.

In retrospect, the period between 1895 and 1905 witnessed the establishment and
finally the saturation of cinema within preexisting venues. By the fall of 1905, nickelodeons were becoming recognized as important outlets for films. Commenting on
this new development, George Kleine noted that "many circuits of so-called ten-cent
houses are springing up, some of them of pretentious construction and heavy investment. These make motion pictures and illustrated songs the chief, sometimes the
only numbers on their program." Nickelodeons transformed and superseded earlier
methods of film exhibition. Saloons, particularly around amusement parks, had shown
films to customers; now picture houses as inexpensive sources of entertainment
and socializing began putting many of them out of business.[2] Theaters presenting
melodramas had shown films between acts; suddenly they saw a falling off of business, and some would eventually be converted into picture houses. Burlesque, penny
arcades, vaudeville: each found its circumstances challenged by the nickelodeon
craze.

The storefront theater, a minor venue for picture shows since 1895, rapidly became the dominant site of exhibition because changes in motion-picture practice had
created new conditions that made it immensely profitable. These new elements
included a large and growing audience base, a minimal level of "feature" production,
a rental system of exchanges, the conception of the film program as an interchangeable commodity (the reel of film), frequent program changes, a continuous-exhibition
format, and cinema's relative independence from more traditional forms of entertainment (except illustrated songs). While such changes were gradual and cumulative, a turning point of sorts was reached after the Miles Brothers began to advertise
a semiweekly change of films for their customers in July 1905, and George Spoor's
National Film Renting Bureau followed in September.[3] This move pointed toward

new patterns of exhibition since the previously standard once-a-week program change had been based on vaudeville's weekly rotation of acts. By summer 1905 something new was in the making: the nickelodeon era was getting under way.

Although New York City was the center of the American film industry and the source of many innovative commercial practices, nickelodeons did not appear there first. Rather, the nickelodeon phenomenon began in urban, industrial cities of the Midwest like Pittsburgh and Chicago. (Not only was Harry Davis' picture house in Pittsburgh often called the first nickelodeon, but, according to at least one nearly contemporary source, Eugene Cline's Chicago storefront was the second of its kind in the United States.) As one trade journal remarked in May 1906, "Smaller places could boast of these moving picture shows long before it was ever thought that New York would ever have one." Why Pittsburgh and Chicago as opposed to New York or Boston? The different structures of the entertainment industries in these cities was one key determinant. Sunday was the only full day of the week that working-class people had leisure. In New York and Boston, exhibitors gave "Sunday concerts" in theaters banned from providing their customary forms of entertainment on "God's day." Since there were no blue laws in Chicago, vaudeville and other types of theaters showed the same programs all week long; as a result, they could not respond to the post-1903 rise in the popularity of films by showing them on Sundays. In Pittsburgh, blue laws were so strict that there were no Sunday concerts at all.[4] Thus, in Chicago and Pittsburgh, the fact that traditional structures were less open to the incorporation of motion pictures and alternate exhibition practices encouraged the early appearance of storefront theaters.

Harry Davis and the "Pittsburgh Idea"

While favorable conditions existed for the appearance of nickelodeons in many Midwestern cities, the nickelodeon boom began in Pittsburgh in June 1905, when Harry Davis opened a storefront theater on Smithfield Street. The significance of this theater is not that it was some official "first" but that it was to some degree responsible for the rapid proliferation of theaters across the United States. But who was this Harry Davis? As we have seen, he was Pittsburgh's leading vaudeville magnate, whose Grand Opera House included a group of films (supplied by the Kinetograph Company) on its vaudeville bill during the 1904–1905 season. By the later part of 1904 the Grand provided Davis with clear evidence of the cinema's popularity. As one reporter noted, "The bill is closed by the realistic bank robbery portrayed by the kinetograph, and very few people left their seats until it was concluded." Even more important, Davis was Pittsburgh's leading purveyor of popular amusements. At his Avenue Theater, the Harry Davis Stock Company offered a different play each week. In October 1904, he opened a third theater, the Gayety, with the Harry Davis Travesty Company. The experiment was not successful but illustrates how Davis operated as a local entrepreneur who was willing to try out a wide range of new entertainments on local citizens.[5]

Davis also faced challenges from potential competitors. The most serious was B. F. Keith, who acquired a downtown theater site and threatened to open a rival vaudeville house. Keith was bought off, but in October 1904 a small-time vaudeville house opened with motion pictures. Clearly, Davis had to rely on his knowledge of the

Exterior and interior view of Harry Davis' original Nickelodeon.

Pittsburgh market to retain his position. The previous April, he had opened an amusement arcade; by fall, he was using part of it to exhibit films. Located on Diamond Street, just below the Grand Opera House, this arcade theater was run by Howard Royer, a Davis employee. According to Royer, who claimed credit for its introduction:

> An idea of the size of the space can be imagined when it is stated that the room only accommodated 32 people standing. If chairs had been installed, there would have been room for only about 15. A picture about 2 × 4 feet was projected from an Edison machine and a reel of film 300 to 400 feet in length was a complete show, lasting four or five minutes. After each show the house was cleared and filled up again while the operator was rewinding (*Pittsburgh Moving Picture Bulletin*, 23 April 1914, p. 4).

This practice, which was common in other cities, suggests one way in which the penny-arcade business pointed toward the nickelodeon era. In Pittsburgh, this small room was "an instant hit." When a fire burned down the Avenue Theater and destroyed the arcade in June 1905, Davis moved his motion-picture show to a larger storefront on Smithfield Street. He called it the Nickelodeon, a title that had been used for other amusement ventures that cost only a nickel. When Davis' brother-in-law, John P. Harris, was named manager, Royer went into the nickelodeon business on his own.[6]

Two additional factors help to explain the early appearance of nickelodeons in Pittsburgh. First, the Pittsburgh area was enjoying unprecedented prosperity. Men in the steel mills were earning record pay, giving them disposable income that they could spend on cheap amusements. The second factor again involved Davis: like others in that city, he was speculating extensively in real estate. In June 1905 he made a $25,000 profit from the sale of two buildings. At the time one observer of the real-estate market noted, "He has been setting the pace in the downtown realty market this year, and since January he has been the principal in purchases and sales of fully $2,500,000 worth of downtown property, on which he has made many thousands of dollars and he is still the leading factor in the market." In July he was offered $525,000 for property on Fifth Avenue and Olive Street but declined, explaining that the property was worth at least $600,000 and that he planned to put an amusement hall on the first floor. When offered $600,000 a few months later, he again declined. "Davis says the property is not on the market," one journalist reported. "He is spending money liberally in remodeling the first floor of the building into an amusement hall and is going to put the entire building in good condition."[7] Davis' commercial property, some of it temporarily vacant storefronts, gave him space to try out the nickelodeon idea. When it succeeded, he had the ability to increase quickly the number of picture houses.

The success of his first nickelodeon theater not only led to Davis opening similar theaters but was emulated by other Pittsburghers, many of whom had no experience in the field. On 18 November, the Grand Moving Picture Machine Company opened a theater on Penn Avenue. When owner Sol Leight sent the regular operator out for dinner and tried to run the projector himself, the film caught fire; it quickly spread, injuring thirty people. This was one of the first fires in the new nickelodeons and sparked a formal inspection of several downtown picture houses by city officials. According to the press account, the inspectors "made many recommendations and ordered changes in the buildings. All places were ordered to use magazine boxes and take-off reels instead of allowing the celluloid films to fall upon the floor, and oil lamps kept lighted near the door, so that people might see to get out in case the electric lights failed." Once the officers made their reports, regulations were to be issued for the conduct of these places, which the news report generically called nickelodeons after Davis' Smithfield Street house.[8]

By the new year, the proliferating nickelodeons were causing complaints in the business district. According to one local paper,

> Brokers and property owners in the downtown district especially are complaining because so many places are springing up where moving pictures are on exhibition at an admission of five cents. The places are becoming so numerous as to be nuisances. Of themselves they are not objectionable except that each is equipped with a noisy phonograph that annoys everybody within hearing of it. The latest place of the kind to open is at 409 Fourth Avenue. The rooms used were formerly occupied by a real estate firm and are certainly not well suited as a place of amusement. Offices in the vicinity lose much of their desirability by the constant noise. An amusement place such as the one next to the Park building on Fifth Avenue is legitimate, but if landlords and property owners keep up the agitation recently started the makeshift amusement parlors will not last long (*Pittsburgh Dispatch*, 5 January 1906, p. 8).

In fact the agitation was not successful, and the nickelodeons continued to multiply, increasing at the rate of five to eight a month during the first six months of 1906. By June of that year, forty-two nickelodeons were paying a two-dollar-per-month license fee to the city.[9]

Davis understood how he could combine motion pictures and real-estate speculation to make a fortune: they were two sides of the same coin. He also took the "Pittsburgh idea" to other cities. Late in 1905 he opened the first motion-picture theater in Philadelphia and had four in that city by 1907. Another Bijou Dream (while his first theater was called the Nickelodeon, most Davis houses were named Bijou Dream) was the first such theater in Rochester, New York, opening during the early part of 1906. Other Davis theaters appeared in Toledo, Buffalo, and Cleveland, and by the later part of 1907, he had a total of fifteen in Pittsburgh alone. His strategy for rapid expansion depended on leveraging his theaters. In Philadelphia, *Moving Picture World* reported, "he made $35,000 within a few weeks on the property at the southeast corner of Eighth and Market streets. The store and basement had been bringing $6,000 a year rental. Davis bought the building for one of his Bijou Dreams. After executing a lease to himself for the store and basement at $15,000 a year, he sold the property at a profit of $35,000."[10] When a sharp depression hit toward the later part of 1907, the danger of this aggressive activity came back to haunt him as a drop in patronage made it impossible to pay costly leases. Nonetheless, this method of financing enabled Davis to build a large chain of theaters speedily.

His nickelodeons were quickly copied by other entrepreneurs. In Philadelphia, moving pictures accompanied by illustrated songs had become "a big fad" by January

1906. By mid 1908 over two hundred Philadelphia nickelodeons were in operation. Moving pictures also did well in Rochester; by August 1907, the Bijou Dream had been joined by eight others, with two more in the course of construction.[11] In a number of instances, fellow Pittsburghers moved to new cities and became the first to open a storefront picture house:

- Josiah Pearce and his sons, J. Eugene and Frederick W., moved to New Orleans in late 1905 and opened the 250-seat Electric Theater. Their 125-seat Theatorium opened in Birmingham, Alabama, in January 1906. Within the year, "the Pittsburgh of the South," had eight to ten houses.[12]
- W. C. Quimby left Pittsburgh for Zanesville, Ohio, and opened the Pictorium on 1 February. "Shortly after the advent of the original place," *Billboard* reported, "it could not accommodate the crowds, so another one, known as the Electric Theatre, was opened in the Signal Building on Main Street. Added interest and larger crowds encouraged a third one, known as the Nickelodeon in the Merrick Block, all under one management." Quimby had several other motion-picture theaters in neighboring towns.[13]
- The first nickelodeon in Wilkes-Barre, Pennsylvania, was opened by C. R. Jones of Pittsburgh in March 1906.[14]

Apostles of "the Pittsburgh Idea" did not always have to travel to other cities to spread the moving-picture craze, for the news of quick money spread in other ways. When Chicago's second nickelodeon opened on State Street on 26 November 1905, *Billboard* credited Pittsburgh, explaining,

> As a matter of record, it is but fair to state that nearly all of the films used in Pittsburgh are rented by a certain leading Chicago firm. They call these shows "Nickelodeons"—by reason of the fact that five cents is the price of admission. Continuous shows are given from early in the morning to late at night. Now we are to have them in Chicago, and soon they will be sprinkled all over our business districts wherever suitable locations can be secured" ("Adopts Pittsburgh Idea," *Billboard*, 2 December 1905, p. 30).

Eugene Cline, who was almost certainly the person renting films to the Pittsburgh theaters, probably opened the first nickelodeon in Chicago. The next theater, referred to above, was called the Electric and was owned by either Davis or his protégés, the Riley brothers.[15]

By the time Carl Laemmle visited Chicago in January 1906, a handful of small five-cent theaters were in operation. Laemmle paid his nickel and entered a small converted storefront on State and Polk streets, where, he later recalled, "Not only was every seat occupied, but the right and left sides were jammed with standing patrons. The rear was also filled and after waiting ten minutes, the duration of the performance, at which time people trickled out, I was finally able to secure a seat." Laemmle, the future president of the Universal Film Company, quickly convinced himself that starting his own moving-picture theater was preferable to the five-and-ten-cent store he had originally planned. (With a background in mass-market retailing, Laemmle is the appropriate symbol of this new era of exhibition.) He opened the 214-seat White Front Theater in Chicago on Saturday, 24 February 1906, and followed it with a second two months later.[16]

The Chicago Theater on South State Street between Harrison and Polk, opened by Gustav Hollenberg in early 1906.

In April 1906, the proliferation of storefront theaters had advanced sufficiently to be noted by the *Chicago Sunday Tribune*:

NICKEL THEATRE PAYS WELL; SMALL COST AND BIG PROFIT.

Nickels count. They have to, if the so-called vaudeville theaters where the entertainment provided consists of moving pictures, with sometimes an illustrated song or two thrown in, are to pay. That the ventures are profitable is evidenced by their multiplication, and there hardly is a section of the city that is without this class of show houses. From the theater in the heart of the shopping district on State street, where the rental is $2100 a month and the daily expenses $110, to the more modest establishment well up North Clark street, where $200 satisfies the land-lord and other expenses are proportionately lower, is a far cry, but all along the line comes the cheering note that nickels count, and profits are regular.

. . . [At the shopping-district theater], they must gather 2,200 5 cent coins before profit begins. The house seats 399 people, and two shows an hour are given, except Saturday and Sundays when the crowds are largest and an extra performance is wedged into every sixty minutes.

The hours are from 10 a.m. to 10 p.m., and during this time there is no cessation. It is the genuine continuous. The rush hours of the theater's day are from 12 to 2, and from 6 to 8 p.m., when the capacity of the house is taxed as a rule (8 April 1906, p. 3).

The nickelodeon boom produced its own trade paper, *Views and Film Index*, which was first published on 25 April 1906. It was owned by Vitagraph and Pathé—the two production companies that took best advantage of the initial nickelodeon craze.

By this time, the boom was also under way in New York. *Views and Film Index* remarked, "These enterprises are practically new to this city but are now springing up in all the boroughs." Six months later, New York was assumed to have more shows than any city in the nation. The Miles Brothers and J. Austin Fynes, who had left Proctor's in November 1905, were among the first to open moving-picture houses in Manhattan.[17] The largest concentration was on Park Row and the Bowery, where at least two dozen picture shows and as many arcades were scattered along a mile-long strip. Reporting on the burgeoning phenomenon, *Views and Film Index* commented:

They all do business. This is evident at any hour during the day and up to 12 o'clock at night. Places are continually opening. East of the Bowery lies the great East Side section of New York, with its great tenements and the countless humanity living in it. The character of the people who use the Bowery as a thoroughfare and who may be classed as transient is not of such a nature that they would attend these shows: therefore the logical conclusion, and what is now the established fact, is that these moving picture shows and arcades are supported by the residents of the vicinity, the great Italian settlement on the one side and the great Jewish settle-ment on the other. Proof of this is that on Saturdays, which is the Jewish Sabbath, great holiday crowds from the East Side throng the Bowery, peeking into the slot machines, looking at the pictures and testing their powers on other devices, and this is the best day of the week (6 October 1906, p. 3).

While Jewish, Italian, and other working-class groups were hard-core filmgoers, middle-class shoppers from the Upper East Side and Upper West Side helped support the theaters along Fourteenth Street and Sixth Avenue. The attendance of this wealthier clientele was incidental to the main purpose of their daily trips, however; when New York's middle classes went to an amusement in the evening, it was to a play or a vaudeville show, not to motion pictures.[18]

The "nickel madness" of motion pictures spread outward from its Midwestern, urban base in an uneven pattern; almost two years passed before all areas of the United States experienced its presence. Although the five-cent theater had "at last gotten into Kansas" by May 1906, Topeka's first picture house, the Oddity, did not open until early December. (Two more were opened by March 1907.) Likewise, Dallas, Texas, did not have its first picture house until that fall. By October 1906, the "gold rush" was on. As *Billboard* informed its readers, many of whom worked for carnivals or in summer parks, "Excellent opportunities are presented to the summer show people who are about to retire without definite plans for the investment of small capital for the winter. There is an abundance of new territory to be opened up for the five-cent theater, or nickelodeon, and the vogue of this institution promises a great future."[19]

Cities and towns in New England and upstate New York generally did not begin to have specialized motion-picture theaters until the later part of 1906:

- The Theater Comique, owned by Mitchell H. Mark, was Boston's first motion-picture house, opening 30 August with a ten-cent admission. Mark and the Automatic Vaudeville Company added the city's second picture house, the 400-seat Theater Premier, on 2 April 1907.[20]
- In Worcester, the Palace Museum was reopened as a film house, the 890-seat Nickel, on 24 September 1906.[21]
- In Haverhill, Massachusetts, Archie L. Shepard opened the town's first nickelodeon on 19 January 1907. Later that year, his Bijou Theater was transformed from a simple storefront into an ornate 500-seat house. Competition came from the Orpheum, which had opened by early December. Owned and managed by twenty-four-year-old Louis Burt Mayer, it featured Miles Brothers Moving Pictures.
- In Middletown, Connecticut, the first picture house did not appear until 25 February 1907, when the McDonough Opera House reopened as the 850-seat Nickel Theater.[22]
- Oswego, New York, had a regular Sunday motion-picture show during 1906, and a grocery store was converted into a nickelodeon by 3 December.[23]
- In Troy, New York, a small penny arcade reopened as the Nickolet Theater on 20 December. Two other Troy picture houses were opened the following March.[24]

Typically, the first picture show in a large town or small city lost its local monopoly within a few months.

The Keith organization, under E. F. Albee's guidance, became an important operator of motion-picture theaters in New England and Canada. Most were called the Nickel and charged five cents admission. Keith's first picture house was also the first in Providence, Rhode Island, opening on 19 April 1906. From opening day, the

Amusement advertisements in the Lewiston (*Me.*) Evening Journal *on Saturday, 2 February 1907.*

thousand-seat former Park Theater was well attended, clearing eight hundred to one thousand dollars a week. When Keith's nearby Pawtucket Theater ended its regular season, motion pictures took over for the summer on 28 May and, according to the local press, "caught the fancy of Pawtucket people like Wild Fire." On 20 August, when the theater prepared to reopen with a stock company of actors, Keith executives shifted their moving-picture enterprise to the nearby music hall.[25]

The success of motion pictures gave the Keith organization greater flexibility. In Lewiston, Maine, for example, it acquired and revamped a 1,254-seat theater during November 1906 and reopened with vaudeville and a turn of films. When the theater lost money, management switched to motion pictures and illustrated songs for the week before Christmas. After another week of vaudeville, Keith switched perma-

Keith's Nickel Theater in Bangor, Maine, opened 12 August 1907.

nently to motion pictures, renaming its Lewiston theater the Nickel. The "Lewiston policy" was also instituted in Manchester, New Hampshire, where vaudeville had been marginally profitable at best, even prior to the opening of the 250-seat Orpheum picture house in November 1906. On 1 April 1907, Keith's 1,700-seat Manchester theater became the Nickel, with moving pictures and illustrated songs.[26] Motion pictures, it was said, turned unprofitable theaters into veritable "klondikes" (*i.e.*, gold mines).

In December 1906, *Billboard* published a list of 313 nickelodeons in thirty-five states (including Oklahoma, which was then "Indian Territory") and three Canadian provinces. The thirteen unrepresented states included Virginia, North and South Carolina, and Arkansas in the South; Connecticut and Vermont in the Northeast; and the Rocky Mountain states of Idaho, Montana, Wyoming, Arizona, Nevada, Colorado, and Nebraska, but at least one state, Connecticut, had motion-picture theaters by this date. Denver did not have its first nickelodeons until mid 1907; Gastonia, North Carolina, acquired its first on 13 June. Many middle-sized towns in the South and Northwest did not have a picture house until 1908.[27] In many parts of the country, however, the number of nickelodeons had saturated the market by the first part of 1907:

- By 1 February 1907, Chicago had 158 theaters showing films.[28]
- Seven new theatoriums opened in Akron, Ohio, during one ten-day period in February.
- Austin, Texas, had at least four electric theaters in early March; by May it had nine.
- Youngstown, Ohio, had twenty nickelodeons by April.
- Downtown Nashville, Tennessee, had sixteen picture shows in June.
- According to Police Commissioner Theodore Alfred Bingham, New York City had over four hundred picture houses and arcades by June.[29]

Diverse patterns of early motion-picture exhibition emerged. New England, with its many large converted theaters, differed from the Midwest with its small storefronts. The Northwest, with its numerous small-time vaudeville houses, did not experience a rapid boom of specialized motion-picture theaters like the Midwest or Northeast. San Francisco did not have its seventh nickelodeon until June 1907. The South also differed, for vaudeville was a comparative rarity and economic underdevelopment often delayed the appearance of picture houses.

Exhibition Practices in the Early Nickelodeons

The 1906 storefront theaters were generally small: rarely more, but often less, than two hundred seats. The number of seats, however, did not indicate a nickelodeon's true capacity since the shows were short enough for patrons to stand.

- Nine Pittsburgh nickelodeons listed in *Billboard* ranged in size from 70 to 200 seats. Four had 100 seats, three had 200, and the other two 70 and 90 seats. These Pittsburgh venues gave between fifteen and forty shows a day, although twenty-five was the standard.
- Five Baltimore theaters reported having 60, 75, 84, 108, and 110 seats, respectively, and giving between forty and fifty-two shows a day, with fifty the mean.

- In Birmingham, Alabama, Pearce's 125-seat Theatorium gave forty-five shows a day, while a rival nickelodeon, one block away, seated 100 and gave sixty shows. A third seated 200 and turned the house over forty times a day.
- Rochester's Bijou Dream seated 250 and gave twenty shows a day.
- In Chicago, Laemmle allowed ten minutes for the film to be projected and another ten minutes for customers to enter and exit. On his second day, the former clothing store manager took in $200 (5¢ × 20 shows × 200 seats), thus coming within $20 of his weekly expenses. Box office receipts usually ran about $180 a day. Laemmle subsequently claimed to have made $15,000 at his first theater during its first year of operation.[31]

Not all theaters were so small or so rapid in their turnover, however.

- Four Jersey City theaters reported seating capacity/shows per day as 425/12, 200/10, 200/14, and 450/?
- Six Iowa houses reported 200/2, 200/3, 300/continuous, 500/15, 400/8, and 400/3.
- Sigmund Lubin's Bon Ton Theater in Philadelphia had 1,000 seats and thirty-five shows a day.
- Two houses in Newark, New Jersey, seated 500 each.[32]

The New England houses, with seating capacities already mentioned, were even larger.

Another form of specialized motion-picture exhibition that developed simultaneously with the nickelodeons took the viewer-as-passenger convention characterizing many travel programs to its logical conclusion.[33] Hale's Tours and Scenes of the World initiated the craze with a theater that looked like a railway car from the outside. Spectators boarded the "train," paid their dime to a "conductor," and sat in a theater that resembled the interior of a carriage. With rear-screen projection, the film was projected onto a screen at the front of the space—the equivalent of an observation car. In some of the more elaborate shows, the pictures were accompanied by the rocking of the car and the sound of railway clatter. The novelty was simply a refinement of efforts made by previous showmen: "Le Ballon Cineorama," for example, had used film in a similar way at the 1900 Paris Exposition, where Hale had presented his exhibition of American firefighting.[34] In another popular nineteenth-century entertainment, the spectator sat in a mock railway carriage and watched the scenery—painted on a moving canvas—pass by; this technique was subsequently used in the production of such films as Lubin's THE GREAT TRAIN ROBBERY and Biograph's HOLDUP OF THE ROCKY MOUNTAIN EXPRESS.

George C. Hale, a former Kansas City fire chief, opened his first touring cars at Kansas City's Electric Park on 28 May 1905, showing films from a train going over a rocky gorge and another going down Broadway. Even as it opened, entrepreneurs in other summer parks sought a Hale concession for themselves. That summer the craze was introduced at Coney Island. When the annual exposition opened in Pittsburgh on 30 August, it included "In and Around New York," a variation of Hale's Tour. By early September, Hale had joined forces with Fred W. Gifford and sold licenses and territory. The Brady-Grossman Company, incorporated by William A. Brady of New York and Edward B. Grossman of Chicago on 26 January 1906, owned rights to ten Eastern states. Their Hale's Tour on Fourteenth Street east of Union Square included among its offerings Biograph's HOLDUP OF THE ROCKY MOUNTAIN EXPRESS,

Chief Hale's New Concession at Electric Park.

One of the new concessions and one in which the people of Kansas City may take a justifiable pride is the "Tours and Scenes of the World," an invention of George C. Hale, ex-chief of the fire department. He has been working on this for a year, and as a panoramic effect it is probably without an equal. The person wishing to make the tour enters what has every appearance of a regular coach. A colored porter is at the door and the seats are arranged inside the same as in a regular tourist car.

Two views are shown. By a splendid arrangement which is an elaboration on the moving picture scheme the passengers can without effort imagine that they are traveling on a train and viewing the scenery. There is a slight rocking to the car as it takes the curves, and in addition there is the shrill whistle of the locomotive and the ringing bell at intervals to carry out further the illusion. One of the scenes shown is over a rocky gorge and is most realistic. The other is a trip over Brooklyn bridge and down Broadway in New York. Compliments are showered upon Mr. Hale, and already the "car" is in demand at various resorts in this country.

An advertisement announcing the first opening of a Hale's Tours, at Electric Park, Kansas City.

a trip to California where "passengers" saw the devastating effects of the San Francisco earthquake, and THE GREAT TRAIN ROBBERY.[35]

By the following summer, Hale's Tours and its many imitators were popular features at the nation's amusement parks. Claude L. Hagen's "Le Voyage en l'Air," which simulated a balloon voyage, was shown at Coney Island and Happyland on Staten Island, while Tim Hurst's Auto Tours had three cars at Coney Island. Other imitators included the Trolley Car Tours Company and the Trip to California Amusement Company.[36] Such specialized theaters proved to be a fad in the way that the nickelodeons were not. After the 1906 summer season, their impact on film practice receded, although in at least a few situations they continued to operate into the 1910s.

Electric theaters, theatoriums, and nickelodeons created a new kind of specialized spectator, the moviegoer, who did not view films within the variety format of vaudeville, as part of a visit to a summer amusement park, or as one of an opera house's diverse offerings over the course of a theatrical season. Over several years, this transformation would stimulate the evolution of new methods of cinematic represen-

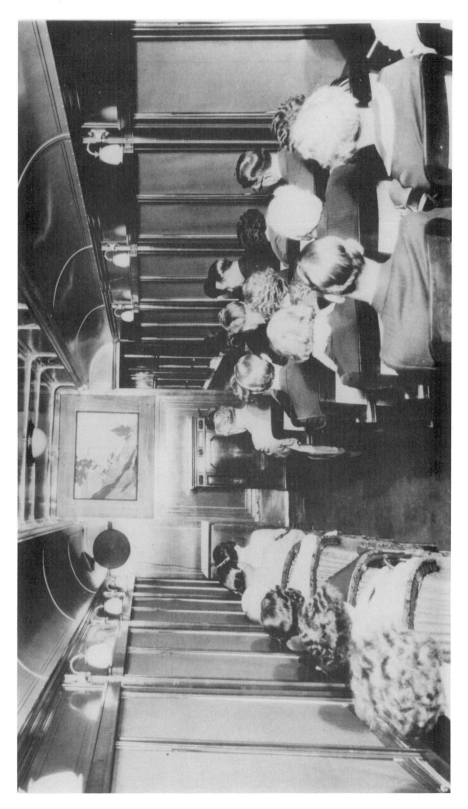

The interior view of a later version of Hale's Tours.

tation and audience reception. Nickelodeons often integrated theatrical amusement into people's daily lives (particularly the daily lives of the working class) in ways that previously had not been possible. Going to vaudeville or the theater took an entire evening and commonly cost ten to twenty-five cents. Summer parks were a day's outing, a special occasion. But picture houses were almost everywhere: on the major thoroughfares, in shopping districts, and in many working-class neighborhoods. Shows lasted from ten minutes to an hour; they could be taken in during lunch, on the way home from work, or in the evening, without constituting a major expenditure.

Moviegoing was generally seen as a working-class activity. In this respect it was different from other theatrical forms of entertainment. Scaled admission fees gave most classes access to vaudeville and melodrama, but once inside, the classes were segregated by ticket price. The single price at nickelodeons not only gave the working class ready access to the theater but, once they were inside, annihilated class distinctions on that class's terms. Those who had known only the gallery suddenly sat in the orchestra. Such economic democracy had social and political implications that the custodians of conservative middle-class values found unsettling. Members of the upper-middle and upper classes (the cultivated or leisure classes, often called the "better" classes) generally were not part of the moviegoing public, at least in large cities. Although the "better" classes saw films, they did so at illustrated lectures like those given by Burton Holmes or at vaudeville performances, not in dingy storefronts. As newspaper editorials soon made clear, these classes usually viewed the nickelodeons with condescension, if not alarm.

In smaller locales where there was a more homogeneous population, nickelodeons were not always seen as the preserve of the working class. Yet even there, cultural distinctions remained in effect. Conservative religious leaders, whose churches might sponsor film exhibitions in their halls under proper supervision, continued to oppose popular culture in general and focused their strongest condemnations on this emerging form of mass entertainment in particular. In large cities or small towns, this opprobrium surely discouraged committed Methodists and other religious conservatives from attending.

The nickelodeons offered not only a kind of economic democracy but greater sexual egalitarianism, as women were encouraged to attend and did so in large numbers. Kathy Peiss has observed that immigrant parents were more willing to let their daughters attend the picture show than any other form of amusement, and the price also was low enough so that working-class women, with their lower wages, could scrape together the admission fee. Even many married women were able to integrate moviegoing into their constant round of household responsibilities. As the nickelodeons opened, almost every one emphasized that it catered "especially to the ladies and children." In Dallas, women and children established themselves as loyal customers before men began to attend in significant numbers. Promotional material for Keith's Lewiston house emphasized that "Everything is clean and neat, the attendants are polite and the best of order is maintained, and the ladies and children can enjoy the pictures in comfort and peace." At the rival Bijou, the manager was soon dispensing Teddy Bear souvenirs to female patrons, in acknowledgment of women's increasingly important role as consumers. When a third Lewiston theater opened in June, it announced that "baby carriages will be taken care of while parents are seeing the show." The emphasis was not only on women patrons but on cultivating mixed-sex patterns of social interaction.[37]

Picture houses also provided children with unprecedented access to popular

The Wonderland Theater in Troy, New York. Women and children were an important audience.

amusements. Over two-thirds of the people seriously injured in Pittsburgh's first nickelodeon fire were children between the ages of seven and sixteen (with twelve being the average age). Keith's Lewiston Nickel encouraged parents to send their children after school; unaccompanied children were seated in the balcony so they would not disrupt the adults' enjoyment.[38] This type of encouragement often turned theaters into centers around which local communities built much of their socializing. Perhaps not seeing these community ties so clearly, reformers would soon find this easy access for children and unaccompanied young women deeply disturbing.

Moviegoing was a casual activity that made frequent viewing practical and seductive. Sigmund Lubin was one of many who recognized that moving pictures were becoming part of everyday life and would soon be as common as the ice cream parlor or soda fountain. Extrapolating on this trend, he predicted that "the time will come when the life moving picture machine will be part and parcel of every up-to-date home" and "the moving picture will be delivered at home as is the morning newspaper of today." To attract the avid moviegoer, nickelodeons found it profitable to change their offerings with increasing frequency. While new programs were being offered twice a week in July 1905, three changes a week were becoming common by November 1906. By May 1907, nickelodeons were beginning to change programs every day but Sunday.[39] The cinema was rapidly becoming a site of mass entertainment and mass consumption. Although this process was not complete, the lateral expansion of motion-picture houses across the country and the vertical increase of program change caused a tremendous demand for films.

A New Generation of Film Exchanges

Nickelodeons created immense opportunities not only for exhibitors and producers but for film renters, who operated at the interface of production and exhibition. Chicago became the first and largest center for these new film exchanges. The early

"Unique" was a common name for the many picture theaters that opened around the United States.

and rapid proliferation of nickelodeons in the Midwest and the city's traditional role as a distribution center helped this group to dominate the field. By March 1907 approximately fifteen Chicago exchanges controlled as much as 80 percent of the rental business in the United States. George K. Spoor's National Film Renting Company, Eugene Cline & Company, Max Lewis' Chicago Film Exchange, and Robert Bachman's 20th Century Optiscope were all active film renters by 1905. Cline, who had been earning a $6 a week salary in 1900, claimed to be making in excess of $100,000 a year by 1907, when he was twenty-five years old. Max Lewis was the same age. He had come to the United States from Russia in 1901, entered the carnival business, and had two hundred customers and thirty employees by July 1907. They were joined by the Inter-Ocean Film Exchange, which first advertised in April 1906. William Swanson became a renter in the spring of 1906. Swanson, who had been a traveling exhibitor showing Lubin's filmed reenactment of the Britt–

Nelson fight in late 1905, settled in Chicago, where he worked briefly as an operator/ projectionist in one of the city's first nickelodeons (the Electric). Aided by William Selig, who did not enter the rental business himself, and a partner, James H. Maher, Swanson started William H. Swanson & Company. It prospered and by November had purchased half a dozen storefront theaters.[40] The Temple Film Company began to offer films for rent in June.

Renting films for his two Chicago theaters during mid 1906, Carl Laemmle felt dissatisfied with the high-handed treatment he received. The exchanges, he later recalled, were "enthroned as 'czars.'" Pictures were promised but not always delivered; sometimes an exchange would take back a film and rent it to a nearby competitor who offered to pay a higher fee:

> You paid your money and you had no choice. More often than not, the prints were fit for the scrap heap. It must be explained that the distributor owned these prints outright, having purchased them from the manufacturer at an average price of ten cents per linear foot, and his only interest was to squeeze as much revenue as possible out of its rental. For example, a subject of eight hundred feet cost eighty dollars and would be rented and rerented until the characters became blurred to the naked eye (Laemmle, "The Business of Motion Pictures," p. 41).

The only way that Laemmle was assured of good-quality prints and fresh subjects was by renting new pictures for $35 a week, compared with an earlier $27.50 a week for one reel and a semiweekly change. He soon discovered that nearby nickelodeons were doing the same. Such problems were severe enough, and the commercial opportunities large enough, for Laemmle to start his own exchange rather than develop a chain of theaters.

Setting out to attract customers by offering them "service" as well as a reel of film, Laemmle found an office, bought some secondhand films from George Spoor, contracted for films with two local film agents, and began to advertise. He was fortunate to have ties to a local advertising firm, the Cochrane Advertising Agency. The ads, which changed each week, were folksy in style and contributed significantly to his success. His first advertisement, appearing in *Billboard* on 6 October, announced:

> Absolutely disgusted with our inability in recent months to rent good, clean, clear, lively and strikingly new films, we have gone into business ourselves with the grim determination to supply ourselves and a few select others with
>
> ### THE BEST FILM SERVICE THAT
> ### CAN POSSIBLY BE MAINTAINED
> Not a single old or time-worn subject on our list!
> Not a single film that is disappointing!
> Not a single film that blurs or skips or dazzles!
> Everything you want and nothing you don't want! (p. 22).

A few weeks later, Laemmle further individualized his service with ads in the first person. He assured potential customers that "I know your film troubles. I've had them myself. . . . During the brief time I have been advertising my film service and furnishing managers with the kind of film service they want, I've received dozens and scores of letters—AND NOT A COMPLAINT IN THE LOT." Emphasizing his identification with fellow exhibitors and encouraging the same exhibitors to identify with him, Laemmle's advertisements soon featured the exchange man's portrait. Many of these methods would be used again in 1909–1910, when he promoted his films by featuring their leading actors. Certainly his promotional techniques hit a responsive chord in 1906. Three years later, the Laemmle Film Service would be known as "the largest in the world."[41]

Fred C. Aiken and Alvah C. Roebuck, partners in the Amusement Supply Company, were operating the Theater Film Service Company with Samuel S. Hutchinson by the end of 1906. The resources required to start such an enterprise are suggested by the exchange's January 1907 incorporation papers, whereby the three equal partners each received stock valued at $4,000. This stock was given in exchange for:

86 reels of motion-picture film	$8,600.00
30 sets of song slides or transparencies	240.00
1 desk and revolving chair	50.00
2 plain tables	15.00
2 chairs	2.00
1 film cabinet with 85 compartments	75.00
1 film reeling mechanism on inspector's table	10.00
1 letter file cabinet	15.00
95 reels	60.00
sundries, printing, printed matter, stationery, and advertising	3,000.00
	$12,067.00[42]

Though the trio were equal partners, Hutchinson and Aiken were to become major figures in the industry.

By March 1907 other Chicago film exchanges included the Globe Film Exchange, American Film Company, General Film Exchange, New Era Film Exchange, United States Film Exchange, Grand Film Rental Bureau, and Mutual Film Exchange. Competition intensified. As one Chicago correspondent remarked, "Some people in the trade here, who are very humorous, say, 'there will soon be more renters than store shows.' This remark, although a little exaggerated, should, however, be given serious consideration. Some people in the trade predict that a number of new renters will eventually come to a survival of the fittest." Laemmle revealed that many of these exchanges were part of a "Film Trust" operating under different names but controlled by the same person, Eugene Cline. The number of Chicago-based film exchanges continued to increase through 1907 and 1908, although their control over national distribution gradually waned.[43]

The New York film rental business was at least six months behind Chicago's. Although Eberhard Schneider had started a rental business by November 1906, and L. Hertz by February, neither they nor Harstn & Company and Paley became important renters. William Fox, who operated a group of theaters in Brooklyn, did not open his Greater New York Film Rental Company until March 1907. To William Selig he wrote, "You can put my name on your books for one print of every subject you make in the future and if my business grows, which we trust it will, we will increase our order accordingly." Soon he was advertising in *Moving Picture World*.

"I'm Not Running a Bargain Counter."

Spending my good money liberally for the best ideas, the best facilities and the best films is what makes : : : :

The Laemmle Film-Service

better than any you've tried. I wouldn't pay a cent for the cheap and rotten clap-trap that has been flooding the market. If you want what I wanted for so long and couldn't get until I bought my own films outright—**The Best, Newest, Liveliest, Finest stuff that human brains can conceive and human facilities execute**—I say, if you want that, then you're willing to pay for it If you're looking for clap-trap and stale stuff—if "any old thing will do"—then don't waste your time on me. I'm not running a bargain counter. Nor am I gouging my customers with higher prices than a legitimate business calls for. I'm simply running the best film service in the world. If you want it in your territory, you know how to get it.

CARL LAEMMLE, Pres.,

LAEMMLE-FILM-SERVICE,

167 Dearborn St., Chicago.

Dealers in Machines, Films and all Accessories.

An early advertisement for Laemmle's film exchange in Billboard.

Charles Dressler and Isaac W. Ullman formed the Consolidated Film Company of New York at about the same time.[44]

Increasingly exchanges appeared in cities outside the traditional centers: New York, Chicago, and Philadelphia. Many were started by exhibitors who wanted to be guaranteed a steady supply of films for their theaters. Some were agents for film producers and found their customers wanting to rent films rather than buy them; others had previously supplied exhibitors with equipment and supplies.

- In Pittsburgh, the owner of the Pittsburgh Calcium Light Company died and was succeeded by his son, Richard A. Rowland, who formed a partnership with James B. Clark. In April 1906 the company was renamed the Pittsburgh Calcium Light and Film Company and became a prominent exchange.
- Harry Davis had entered the rental business by March 1907, by which time he controlled "twenty-five of the largest and most successful picture shows in America."
- Harry Warner, who operated a circuit of nickelodeons with his brothers in western Pennsylvania, began to buy films for his Pittsburgh-based Duquesne Amusement Supply Company in April 1907.
- In St. Louis, O. T. Crawford, manager of the Gaiety Burlesque House and owner of ten nickelodeons, opened an exchange at the end of 1906. Initially he kept a small supply of films (fifteen or twenty reels) that he used and rented to others. "We just went into Crawford's place and looked over his subjects and took what we wanted," recalled one nickelodeon manager. By mid February 1907, however, his exchange was renting to twenty-five of twenty-seven motion-picture venues in St. Louis and one hundred in all.
- In Kansas City, A. D. Plimton and several partners operated two small-time vaudeville houses. Tired of renting films from Eugene Cline in Chicago, they opened the Yale Film Exchange sometime in 1906.
- Josiah Pearce and Sons, owners of a circuit of nickelodeons in the South, started an exchange in Birmingham, Alabama, by March 1907.
- Marcus Loew, owner of several theaters in Cincinnati and New York, placed a standing order with William Selig at about the same time. Loew was apologetic, yet confident: "It is impossible for us to buy two of a copy at the present time but we are branching very extensively in this business and no doubt by next fall we may be able to buy ten of a copy."[45]

Similar moves into distribution were made by entrepreneurs in other cities.

Implications of the Nickelodeon Era
for Those Involved in Exhibition

The nickelodeons transformed exhibition practices. With theaters changing programs between three and six times a week, the relationship between the exhibitor and what he showed became more and more attenuated. The theater manager, however, continued to exercise control over the sound component of the audiovisual screen experience, even though the economics of the nickelodeon restricted the range of possibilities. Musical accompaniment of some sort was standard, with options including a phonograph, player piano, piano player, or small orchestra. In larger theaters a sound-effects person was often employed. In August 1907 Lyman H. Howe began to promote his use of actors behind the screen as "Moving Pictures That Talk."[46] The dialogue dubbed synchronously with the image was not only enjoyed but soon imitated. It became extremely popular in 1908–1909, although the expense generally made it impractical for small nickelodeons. The lecture also enjoyed a revival as an accompaniment to films in amusement venues.

Nickelodeon exhibitors did not simply cease to play an editorial role, as had many of their predecessors: even their opportunities to act as film programmers were circumscribed. During the early nickelodeon era, there was a general shortage of product. One of the chief criteria for a desirable exchange was its ability to supply films not previously shown in that town or neighborhood or, at the very least, to avoid "repeaters"—films that had already been shown in the same theater. Through early 1908 nickelodeons that changed films three or more times a week showed virtually everything made by the major American and European producers. Some managers urged their exchange to satisfy patrons' interest in actualities, while others pleaded for sensational melodramas, but the range of possibilities was severely limited. Keith's circuit of theaters was one of the few customers with sufficient economic clout to receive individual attention. To keep them satisfied, Percival Waters' Kinetograph Company periodically arranged for the Edison Company to make special news films (*e.g.*, AUTO CLIMBING CONTEST, which showed a race at Crawford Notch, New Hampshire, on 31 July 1906). Since most nickelodeon owners and managers were new to the film business, they were relatively unaware of this loss of creative responsibility, considering their theaters instead simply another business venture.

To be sure, exhibitors hired singers and were involved in the selection of illustrated songs, but in 1906–1907 their programming choices were circumscribed.[47] Showmanship of a more entrepreneurial kind offered these exhibitors increasing opportunities for individual activity. As early as March 1907 the owner and manager of a Philadelphia nickelodeon "had souvenir postal cards made of the beautiful snow white front of their theatre and the cards are in all the novelty stores. It has helped popularize the place." A California proprietor gave a watch away to a lucky ticket bearer. To gain maximum return on the gimmick, the promotion was spread over several screenings.[48]

Exchanges, while specializing in distribution, continued to practice residual activities that reflected their earlier role as old-line exhibition services. They still acted as programmers, usually by adding a few shorts to a longer story film in order to fill out a thousand-foot reel. They also determined the range and mix of films available to an exhibitor via their purchases. Exchanges associated with certain producers predictably favored their works, though here again the shortage of pictures meant that most large exchanges acquired at least one print of virtually every available fiction film. A few exchanges (again usually those associated with producers) had the capability to take films of some news events, which they could supply as specials to their customers. Some, notably the Miles Brothers, arranged to acquire exclusive films from European sources.[49] A few also created their own "head titles" to place on films, a residual strategy for claiming authorship. Thus the main title on a surviving print of Vitagraph's AUTOMOBILE THIEVES (1906) reads "Bold Bank Robbery" and displays the logo of J. W. Morgan, a film renter in Kansas City.[50]

At the Star, customers were encouraged to save their ticket stubs for a Thursday drawing, when the holder of the lucky number would receive a free gift.

The Projection Booth Becomes a Sweatshop

The individuals whose work, status, and economic opportunities suffered the greatest damage as a result of the nickelodeon era were the motion-picture operators, who ran the projectors. Once they had handled complicated machines that required dexterity, wide-ranging mechanical expertise, and experience. In the late 1890s and early 1900s many operators (including Edwin Hadley and Ben Huntley) headed their own exhibition companies. Others (G. W. Bitzer and C. Fred Ackerman) doubled as cameramen. A few (Edwin S. Porter and Nicholas Power) were equipment manufacturers. Many were skilled mechanics. The early 1900s saw not only a shift in creative and editorial responsibilities to the production company but a simplification of the projection process. Much less skill was required of the operators to give a minimally competent show.

The rapid proliferation of nickelodeons put downward pressure on operators' wages; novices were frequently hired at ten to twelve dollars a week, and by early 1907 many veterans accustomed to salaries ranging from twenty to twenty-five dollars a week found themselves looking for jobs.[51] Many of them complained loudly about their new circumstances. J. A. Shackelford, an experienced but unhappy operator in Florida, wrote in a letter to the editor of *Moving Picture World*:

> I have operated machines for eleven years and know my business; can give a good show, know what light I can get, how to wire my machines, and take care of films.
>
> A lot of dissatisfaction is caused by not having [films] properly spliced and in running order. I believe that if the film-renting agencies would take the matter up, and require a registered operator, and one who knows how to handle a film properly, half the damage now caused could be avoided and a longer lease given to the life of the films. They could then reduce the cost of renting to about one-third and be a large saving to the theater people. I shall be pleased to give my views on the requirements of an operator to give a good exhibition (6 April 1907, p. 73).

In a letter to the same publication, an Indiana operator remarked, "The managers in this locality are inclined to hire some boy to handle the machine, at a salary that no one but a boy can exist on."[52]

Working conditions deteriorated for operators. Most nickelodeons had only one operator and were in active operation twelve hours a day, six and often seven days a week. The same reel or two of film was screened on hand-cranked projectors over and over again at the many houses with continuous shows. While rewinding, the projectionist was showing illustrated songs. The pace was so unrelenting for one poor operator that "the habit had grown upon him so that it is said he often while asleep goes through the motions of turning a crank." The manager or someone else might spell the operator briefly on his breaks, but these people had their own responsibilities and lunch or dinner time must have been brief. As if this was not enough, operators often had to sweep out the theater and put up advertisements before their real task began. Some were even expected to explain the pictures and turn the crank at the same time.[53]

Nickelodeon operators faced not only unprecedented tedium and long hours but physically uncomfortable, sometimes dangerous, and finally unhealthy working conditions. The projection booth became a furnace from the immense heat generated by the arc light and rheostat. City and state legislatures frequently passed fire laws requiring operating booths made of steel, with very limited openings for ventilation. Temperatures of 113 degrees Fahrenheit were typical. "The effect of the continuous high temperature in which the operator is compelled to work will be the general weakening of the entire system," remarked Willis Elliot Reynolds of Philadelphia. The carbon dust from the arc lamps used for projection also filled the booth and with it, the operator's lungs. "It may not matter for a few months; perhaps a year, but in time the tiny particles of dust will produce irritation of the mucous membrane. It is therefore highly injurious to the lungs, throat and membrane of the nose," warned Reynolds. "From this irritation may result pneumonia, pleurisy, tonsillitis and chronic catarrh of the nose. It also produces weakness of the brain, excites the nervous system and impoverishes the blood." A further health hazard unknown to Reynolds was created by the asbestos that lined many projection booths, often at the insistence of fire marshals and insurance underwriters. Furthermore fires in the projection booth posed the risk of serious burns, injury, or in a few cases, death.[54]

The projection booths in nickelodeons became small, individualized sweatshops. "What is an operator?" asked one experienced projectionist. "A machine, a slave, a dog to be kicked or a man to whom some consideration should be shown?" Suffering a falling wage scale, loss of status, and deteriorating working conditions, operators began to organize by early 1907. Some attempts were made to limit the labor pool through an operators' league and certification of operators by the state, but this tactic proved cumbersome and ultimately ineffective since it depended on local and state governments to take action. At the same time, operators were being organized by established unions. In Philadelphia, a series of preliminary meetings in late 1906 led to the formation of the Moving Picture Operators Union on 6 January 1907 with thirty-five members. The group met each week on Sunday afternoons. In New York City the International Brotherhood of Electrical Workers organized a local in February with almost seventy-five members after its first month of meetings. By August the American Federation of Labor and the International Association of Theatrical and Stage Employees (IATSE) were fighting over who should organize and represent the picture operators.[55]

Although unions often set some standards for accepting new members, their main goal was to organize operators whatever their skill and experience and then form them into a cohesive body. As F. H. Richardson, who would subsequently become *Moving Picture World*'s correspondent on projection, argued in a letter to that publication:

> What is needed is a bona fide union of operators, affiliated with the electrical workers' union, whose avowed and only purpose is to protect the operator. There is one thing and one thing only [that] will ever eliminate the incompetent man, and that is establishment of a uniform wage scale. When the employer has to pay the same for the incompetent as for the good man he will naturally employ the latter, but so long as he is allowed to put on an incompetent because he can get him cheap the incompetent will be with us. You may attempt his elimination by means of "examining boards." That would probably help some, but only in a very

measurable degree. An operators' union by itself would be able to accomplish little, but by the aid of the electrical workers it could do much. An operator should receive 50 cents per hour on long hauls with time and a half for "evening only" shows but he will never again get that wage except through a fight (11 January 1908, pp. 25–26).

The diversity of the operators' backgrounds, the low level of skill needed to present some kind of image on the screen, the elitism of some veterans, and the tenuousness of unionism in the United States prevented these efforts at organization from being immediately effective.

Film Fires in the Nickelodeon Era

Film fires were a highly controversial subject in the motion-picture, theatrical, and amusement industries. *Views and Film Index* had a policy of not reporting them, considering this kind of publicity bad for business. While *Billboard* provided occasional mentions, *Moving Picture World* was the only trade journal to cover the issue extensively. As we have seen, such fires had been a problem since the beginning of cinema, but the nickelodeon boom turned it into a crisis. (Nitrate film has a combustion point of only 284 degrees Fahrenheit.) Theater owners often lacked the expertise or financial resources to make their theaters safe, and the large number of inexperienced operators created by the rapid spread of nickelodeons further increased the likelihood of disaster. By the summer of 1907 two to three film fires were occurring each week in the state of Ohio, where the press reported "75 disastrous fires within the past year." Although Akron had only three picture houses in December 1906, it suffered two minor film fires in a single week. By the following August, Birmingham, Alabama, had experienced three fires in its picture houses.[56] The total by late 1907 was perhaps a thousand. And although the vast majority were minor, were confined to the projection booth, and frequently involved only the loss of a reel of film, the possibility of something much more serious—the death of a large number of moviegoers—always existed.

This risk to society quickly led to the intervention of state and local governments. In early 1905, even prior to the nickelodeon boom, the Massachusetts legislature passed a law requiring certain safety standards for motion-picture projection. Film reels had to be mounted in enclosed metal cases, a rail placed around the machine, and the machines inspected by the district police; the operator, meanwhile, was required to have at least six months of experience or show sufficient evidence of his abilities. More often, however, local ordinances and police inspectors came in the wake of a fire in a local nickelodeon. Although Akron's mayor and fire chief closed all three picture houses after its two fires, these theaters were quickly reopened once the owners made small changes. Following the fires in Birmingham, electricity was cut off in all but one of the city's nickelodeons until they conformed to newly adopted fire laws. In some cases, the regulations were severe and even unreasonable. Thus, after repeatedly complying with a series of escalating demands—the final one required the use of asbestos wiring that was manufactured only by a French firm—Houston's nickelodeon owners had to sue the city to get an injunction that would allow them to reopen their houses. The rash of fires also proved of great concern to insurance underwriters, who often encouraged draconian measures in an attempt to reduce the risks. In many cases, they raised their premiums $1 per $100 of insurance on buildings that housed picture theaters, with some reductions for those that conformed to the rules of the National Board of Fire Underwriters and the National Electric Code. Problems involved not only standards for machines and licensing of operators but fire exits, wiring, and even locations (in New York, nickelodeons were not allowed in tenement buildings).[57] Fires and the issues surrounding their prevention continued to be of great concern through the first five years of the nickelodeon era.

Traveling Exhibition as the Nickelodeon Era Begins

The growing popularity of motion pictures, which made the nickelodeon system of exhibition possible, at first benefited the traveling exhibitors. Lyman Howe not only added a third company in the fall of 1904 but purchased a camera and began to take some local views for inclusion in his programs. By early 1906 D. W. Robertson had five units, one based in New York City and four traveling around the country and playing primarily to religious groups.[58] For many traveling picture men, however, prosperity soon gave way to poverty as the nickelodeons destroyed their business wherever these new venues were established.

It would be wrong to say that traveling exhibition was more expensive for patrons. Nickelodeons' ten-to-thirty-minute shows for five cents were no less costly per minute than the traveling exhibitors' two-hour entertainments for ten to twenty-five cents. Yet, unlike the traveling shows, nickelodeons targeted their local audiences on a daily basis. Sometimes they arranged to screen the same films as the itinerant showman but before his arrival. And because they operated continuously, the storefronts were also more convenient. As the spread of nickelodeons increasingly restricted the territory within which traveling exhibitors could profitably operate, they were forced to rely on smaller and smaller communities—those that did not yet boast their own picture show.

If by mid 1908 a whole generation of traveling showmen had lost their calling as a result of the nickelodeons, many had already made a successful transition into this new exhibition era. Archie Shepard, for example, opened the first picture house in Meriden, Connecticut, on 20 October 1906. Then, after a competing theater appeared by the following April, the showman opened a second theater in the same town. By the end of April, the former projectionist had picture houses in New York and a number of other cities, including Lewiston, Maine, where his traveling companies had provided regular doses of motion-picture entertainment between 1904 and 1906. Elsewhere Shepard continued to ply his specialty of Sunday concerts, and during the summer of 1907 he enjoyed substantial profits giving regular picture shows at legitimate theaters in various Eastern cities. Thomas L. Tally was another traveling exhibitor who shifted easily to nickelodeon exhibition. He opened the five-hundred-seat New Broadway Theater at 554 South Broadway in Los Angeles on 3 March 1906 and by November was operating a film exchange. J. A. Le Roy, meanwhile, who would later make a bogus claim to have been the first to project motion pictures, shifted from traveling exhibition to equipment manufacture (the acmegraph projector) and operated a modest film exchange.[59]

Tally's New Broadway Theater (as photographed in 1910).

Many showmen, however, suffered the fate of Max Hollander, who toured a circuit of small towns in northern New York and gave picture shows during the summer of 1906. By the following year, he found that the same localities were supporting nickelodeons. As a result, he became a projectionist for one of the very few individuals who continued to prosper as a traveling showman in the nickelodeon era: Lyman Howe.[60]

Howe and his general manager, Samuel Maxwell Walkinshaw, took advantage of cinema's growing popularity by making their first tentative moves into the big cities— Detroit and Cleveland—during the spring of 1905 and added Baltimore, Milwaukee, and Boston the following theatrical season. Howe's picture shows offered an alternative to the type of film entertainment presented in either the new picture houses or vaudeville. For the 1905–1906 season, films of the Russo-Japanese War provided him with an unusual headline attraction. They were acquired on a semi-exclusive basis from Charles Urban, whose cameraman Joseph Rosenthal had been at Port Arthur during the siege. With President Roosevelt sponsoring a peace conference that brought the war to a close in August 1905, Americans found these films of tremendous interest. In addition, Howe filmed Roosevelt's visit to his hometown of Wilkes-Barre immediately after the successful conclusion of the president's diplomatic mission. These subjects enabled one Howe company to gross almost six thousand dollars in eight consecutive play dates. He also enjoyed a highly successful week-long engagement at Ford's Opera House in Baltimore during May 1906. (Before this, Howe's companies stayed in a theater for a few days at most.) The following May, Howe returned and generated 21,477 paid admissions—more than seven thousand dollars—in six days. This was so successful that one of his companies revisited Baltimore in August 1907 to play a four-week summer season with program changes at the beginning of each week. For the next twelve years, Howe's companies were to present summer seasons of motion pictures in prominent, big-city theaters.

Howe's shows appealed to people who often felt out of place in the nickelodeons. Admission fees of twenty-five, thirty-five, and fifty cents (fifteen cents for children at matinees) as well as his mixture of actualities (rarely shown in the nickelodeons) and sanitized comedy distinguished these exhibitions from the storefronts. The showman drew audiences from middle-class amusement goers (or those aspiring to the middle class), from conservative Protestants who wanted to be entertained even though they needed to feel they were receiving some instruction, and from consumers of refined entertainment. As a Howe employee would later explain to a prominent theater manager, "Each of the programs is so assembled to appeal to all classes. In subject matter they are just heavy enough to attract the serious minded and yet light enough for those seeking amusement only."[61]

In many respects, Howe had continued to refine and rework the types of subject matter evident in the earlier Lumière programs, though from a pro-British perspective. Military subjects were always an important part of his show (ENGLAND'S NAVAL DISPLAY, SERVIA AND ITS ARMY, etc.), with England favorably portrayed as the dominant world power and the military buildup that led to World War I glorified. Many films, such as TEAK FOREST IN INDIA and PICTURESQUE JAVA, showed the exoticism and economic value of distant colonies. Such display of foreign military and colonial spectacle supported the interventionist, imperialist policies of President Roosevelt. Other scenes showed royalty and the wealthy enjoying leisure activities. These programs, like Howe's earlier exhibitions, lacked a critical stance toward their subject matter. They offered a cinema of reassurance, albeit by excluding large areas of reality from their view. A few other exhibitors, such as Edwin Hadley, survived by following Howe's programming lead.

The growing popularity of motion pictures finally affected the illustrated lecturers. With the 1906–1907 season, a number of these men joined Burton Holmes and Dwight Elmendorf in incorporating films into their programs. Frederick Monsen's four lectures on California and the Southwest, including "The San Francisco Earthquake" and "Arizona: The Egypt of the New World," used slides tinted by the speaker and motion pictures he acquired from commercial sources. Edward Howe, editor of the *Atchison* (Kansas) *Globe*, gave a travel lecture, "Around the World," featuring stereopticon slides taken by himself and his daughter with a Kodak. The evening concluded, however, with moving pictures of the 1906 Atchison Corn Carnival, shot by William Selig especially for Howe. Edward S. Curtis, who had earlier given illustrated lectures on the American Indian, added motion pictures to his talks by 1907, the year that his first volume of *The North American Indian* (1907–1930) appeared. Topics included "The Apaches and the Navahoes," "The Northwestern Plains Tribes," and "The Alaskan People and Eskimo Life," with photographs and films taken by Curtis and his assistants.[62] During 1906 and 1907 Robert K. Bonine, the Edison cameraman, traveled to Hawaii, Yellowstone Park, and the Panama Canal to take both stills (which he owned) and films (which were the property of the Edison Company). He then used some of the slides and films to give his own illustrated talks on Hawaii. All the films were placed on the market, however, and purchased by a variety of lecturers for their own programs.

The growing popularity of motion pictures meant that Americans of all classes and cultural backgrounds were likely to see more and more of them. This expansion, however, was not uniform, nor did it have the same impact on all groups or types of film practice. Elites saw motion pictures within the illustrated-lecture format that had been well established by the 1870s and 1880s. If D. W. Robertson's success is any indication, church-sponsored film entertainment continued to be popular and may even have expanded. But it was the nickelodeons that spread like wildfire. When people thought of picture shows they increasingly thought of storefront theaters. These offered amusement and a regular theatrical experience to many working-class people who never before could afford it. It was something new in American life. Outside of the large cities, theaters had traditionally been built and controlled by local elites. Now they were started by an ex-saloon keeper, the owner of a dry-goods store, a furrier, car dealer, or someone who had recently left the carnival. Nickelodeon managers were often immigrants, often Jewish, and often from out of town. Established community leaders didn't know what to think about the change except to know that they did not control it. Some thought it should be abolished, others were more laissez-faire. A few embraced it, but many thought it needed to be reformed. Film fires proved they were dangerous, but there was even more concern with the way the collective though intimate experience of the screen could change—and from a certain viewpoint corrupt—the consciousness of its devotees. The nickelodeons inaugurated an era in which the "movies," as they came to be called, were seen in a new light.

Power's Cameragraph projector (1906) sold for $140 without fireproof magazines or take-up device, and $175 with them.

14

Production as the Nickelodeon Era Begins: 1905–1907

*T*he proliferation of nickelodeon theaters created a huge demand for films and film equipment. Projector sales boomed for the chief hardware manufacturers: Edison (projecting kinetoscope), Lubin (cineograph), Selig (polyscope), Nicholas Power (cameragraph), the Enterprise Optical Company (optigraph), and Charles Dressler (American projectograph). Vitagraph meanwhile ceased manufacturing its projector and concentrated on film production, and the Urban bioscope, imported from England, no longer held an important share of the market. A number of small concerns also entered the field in 1906–1907, including the Viascope Manufacturing Company (viascope) and Eberhard Schneider with his Miror-Vitae projector. By mid 1906, Nicholas Power had forty employees and was turning out approximately two machines a day, or seven hundred a year. By September 1907, Lubin had eighty-six employees whose time was devoted solely to the manufacture of projectors.[1]

The skyrocketing demand for these machines is suggested by figures available for the Edison Manufacturing Company. Edison projectors, generally selling for $135, generated $182,134.52 in sales during the 1906 business year, an increase of 131 percent over 1905, and then jumped another 130 percent in 1907 to $418,893.33. Accounting for discounts to agents, Edison probably sold more than 1,500 projectors in 1906 and more than 3,500 in 1907. With the cameragraph and projecting kineto-scope enjoying the best reputations, Edison may have commanded 30 percent of the market. Although some projectors went into vaudeville houses and others replaced damaged or worn-out machines, a large majority were purchased to open nickelode-ons at a time when virtually every theater relied on a single projector.

Film supply likewise responded to the intense demand. New subjects coming on the market in January and February 1906 totaled approximately 7,000 feet a month.[2] If one ignores the substantial backlog of subjects available to newly opened nickel-odeons and assumes a theater was showing 1,000 feet of film and changing its pro-gram twice a week, the rate of film production was insufficient to avoid repeaters. If several theaters were located close together, the lack of variety inevitably created serious problems. Demand was far greater than supply. *Moving Picture World* subsequently estimated that the following amounts of new subjects were available to the nickelodeons:[3]

November 1906	10,000 ft	February 1907	14,000 ft
December 1906	10,800 ft	March 1907	28,000 ft
January 1907	12,200 ft	August 1907	30,000 ft

These figures suggest that the increasing rate of program change, from two to three times a week in November 1906 and from three times to six times a week in the spring of 1907, became practical only when output had reached sufficient levels. Production practices undoubtedly acted as an impediment to the rapid transformation of exhibition. Correspondingly, this new form of exhibition created pressures on film producers that forced and encouraged them to change.

The big March increase resulted from the greater availability of foreign films, primarily through George Kleine, and not from a sudden expansion in domestic production (which only rose dramatically much later in the year). While foreign manufacturers moved successfully into this new market, American producers had difficulty increasing their supply. Some even had periods when their production dipped or suffered temporary disruption. Of the established American producers, Vitagraph and Lubin took most effective advantage of the new opportunities created by the nickelodeon era. Biograph, Edison, and Selig, however, encountered difficulties or failed to expand their film output rapidly.

Various factors kept American production in disarray. Ironically, one was the vigor of the nickelodeon expansion and the immense profitability of picture theaters and rental exchanges. Opening nickelodeons and exchanges could be done more quickly and involved much lower cost than establishing production facilities. The expertise needed to operate a profitable picture house was simpler and took less time to acquire than the skills needed for successful film production. Industry entrepreneurs therefore focused initially on expansion in exhibition and distribution rather than production. Even so, new opportunities in production created short-term disruptions as experienced personnel left long-standing companies like Biograph and Selig to form their own enterprises such as Kalem and Essanay. Output at the affected concerns was curtailed as new personnel established themselves. The building of new studios, while essential for long-term expansion, took energy away from immediate production. In some instances, notably at Edison, the strong demand for films actually reinforced the status quo, since larger print sales per picture meant that facilities for positive-print production ran at full capacity and the company could boast much higher profitability. Finally, established methods of film production and representation were not amenable to a rapid increase in the output of new negatives. While the transformation of these practices was necessary if expansion was to occur efficiently, many production personnel either resisted or failed to recognize the underlying pressure for change and the direction it would take.

The status of Edison's patents was another factor that deterred a rapid increase of domestic production capabilities. Edison, as detailed earlier, had once again sued all the leading American producers and foreign importers between late 1902 and 1905. On 26 March 1906, Judge George W. Ray handed down a decision that narrowly interpreted Edison's camera patent and would have allowed film producers to operate without fear of infringement. Yet, Edison's lawyers promptly appealed the case to a higher court, and intense uncertainty still reigned within the industry. There was little incentive for substantial investment in a studio and plant that might easily prove worthless. On 5 March 1907 the court of appeals rendered a new decision that reversed part of the lower court's ruling. The case, in fact, involved two types of cameras: the Warwick camera, a standard 35-mm camera made by the Warwick Trading Company in England and used by many producers, and the old Biograph camera with its unusual method of moving the film forward and punching holes in the film just before each exposure. According to the judges, Alfred C. Coxe, E. Henry Lacombe, and William J. Wallace, the device that moved the film through the Warwick camera was "the fair equivalent" of the mechanism patented by Edison and so infringed on Edison's invention. They declared, however, that the Biograph camera was not an infringement since it operated on a different principle. This decision allowed Biograph to function without further legal interference as long as the company used 35-mm equivalents of its old 70-mm cameras. But while freeing Biograph, the opinion offered strong support for Edison's legal position in his many other suits. Both parties were, therefore, sufficiently content that neither appealed the case to the Supreme Court. Legal developments became even more ominous as Edison's lawyers reactivated the inventor's infringement case against William Selig. Thus, the climate for investment in American film production grew steadily worse as the nickelodeon era began.[4]

The shortage of domestic films was also due to specific shortcomings at Biograph and Edison. Neither company effectively exploited the opportunities presented by the nickelodeon boom, even though they alone were spared the many legal uncertainties facing their American competitors. One might expect that they would increase their supply of new pictures to meet the increased demand, but this did not happen. In fact, for extended periods of time, each company actually decreased its rate of production, albeit for opposing reasons. Biograph became less and less profitable and, incredibly, was on the verge of being closed by mid 1907.

Biograph Fails to Expand Production

Francis J. Marion had chief responsibility for Biograph films from the second half of 1905 until his departure at the end of 1906. During this period, the rate of production remained at two major releases per month. For THE CRUISE OF THE "GLADYS" (No. 3217, August 1906) and lesser productions, Marion directed. For more ambitious efforts Marion usually hired a stage director: THE PAYMASTER (No. 3203, June 1906), for example, was directed by a Mr. Harrington. Marion often felt more comfortable working within a modified collaborative framework.[5]

From THE FIREBUG (No. 3055, August 1905) to TRIAL MARRIAGES (No. 3268, December 1906), comedies and melodramas were the core of Biograph's output, with the former outnumbering the latter by a 3:2 ratio. In addition, there were a smattering of comedy-dramas (A FRIEND IN NEED IS A FRIEND INDEED, No. 3138, January 1906) and novelty subjects. Among the latter, "LOOKING FOR JOHN SMITH" (No. 3212, July 1906) utilized the cartoon tradition as "the characters are made to speak their lines by means of words that appear to flow mysteriously from their mouths."[6] Actualities continued to be made, including a few news films (DEPARTURE OF PEARY FOR THE NORTH POLE, No. 3062) and human-interest subjects (SOCIETY

BALLOONING, PITTSFIELD, MASS., No. 3159). A group of Hale's Tours pictures were also produced in the spring to meet demand for this type of film (IN THE HAUNTS OF RIP VAN WINKLE, No. 3152, April 1906). Through the end of 1906, Biograph also continued to sell films made by Gaumont of London and Paris, including THE OLYMPIAN GAMES, RESCUED IN MIDAIR, THE DOG DETECTIVE, and THE LIFE OF CHRIST. From Biograph's advertising, it is evident that the company's energies were focused on fiction films.

Many Biograph comedies reworked ideas underlying the company's earlier hits. THE SUMMER BOARDERS (No. 3068), in which a city family goes to the country for a week of vacation, bears a marked resemblance to THE SUBURBANITE. WANTED: A NURSE (No. 3230, September 1906) and MARRIED FOR MILLIONS (No. 3260) are indebted to PERSONAL. Other films retained strong ties to American culture. EVERYBODY WORKS BUT FATHER (Nos. 3100–3101, October 1905), acted straight and in blackface, was meant to be accompanied by the singing of Lew Dockstader's hit song of the same name. MR. BUTT-IN (No. 3139) was based on the well-known cartoon strip of that name then appearing in the *New York World*. It has an episodic, comic-strip structure as the character interferes in a variety of situations, each time with disastrous results. Dr. Dippy of DR. DIPPY'S SANITARIUM (No. 3237) was also "made famous by the comic supplements." DREAM OF THE RACE-TRACK FIEND (No. 3091, September 1905) evoked Winsor McCay's famed cartoon strip *Dream of the Rarebit Fiend* in its structure and use of dream.

The newspaper, the dominant form of mass communication, continued to provide spectators with a central frame of reference for many Biograph films. TRIAL MARRIAGES (No. 3268, December 1906) evokes a scandal that was widely publicized in the Hearst press when Mrs. Elsie Clews Parsons, wife of Congressman Herbert Parsons, published a book in which she advocated temporary or "trial" marriages. "Mrs. Parson Recommends Marriages 'On Trial' " was a front-page headline in the *New York American*, and it was followed by additional coverage on the subject. The Biograph film cites the initial article as a frame of reference when its opening medium shot of a man reading the newspaper is followed by a close-up of the *New York American* headline. The impressionable young man then tries a series of "trial marriages" with "the crying girl," "the jealous girl," etc. Each situation proves unappealing, and he finally gives up on the idea of marriage altogether.[7] THE SUBPOENA SERVER (No. 3160, April 1906) was a chase film in which "the hero" tries to serve a millionaire with a subpoena. It followed "the recent experience of the Standard Oil magnate," John D. Rockefeller, which had received wide coverage in the newspapers.

Biograph also combined theatrical and newspaper antecedents to generate stories and provide a context for publicity and audience appreciation. Dalan Ale, the main character in THE CRITIC (No. 3140), witnesses several horrendous vaudeville acts, criticizes them in the press, and is later assaulted by those he roasted—a burlesque of the fate of Alan Dale, a caustic theater critic for the *New York American*. In THE BARNSTORMERS (No. 3109, November 1905), a fourth-rate *Uncle Tom's Cabin* theatrical troupe arrives in Rahway, New Jersey, and performs its specialty. The staging burlesques the most famous scenes from the play. With a solitary puppy standing in for a pack of bloodhounds and three white squares representing the ice floe, the actors are bombarded with food and forced to make their escape. The manager absconds with the funds and the film ends with the company walking the tracks back to New York. Assuming audience knowledge of the play, the *Biograph Bulletin* described the film's story with a news report clipped from the *Rahway Times*.

The crime genre and melodrama were virtually synonymous during Marion's reign. Although A KENTUCKY FEUD (No. 3106) took its title and some plot elements from a popular melodrama that had earlier inspired Biograph's THE MOONSHINER, it depicted the well-publicized feud between the Hatfields and the McCoys.[9] The feud finally destroys the love between Sally McCoy and Jim Hatfield as Sally witnesses a knife fight between her brother and her lover. Paralyzed by indecision, she watches them kill each other. Once again the primitive, violent nature of country life was emphasized. Lengthy intertitles were necessary to assist the audience in following the story line and identifying characters, but much of the film's commercial value and audience enjoyment came from their prior knowledge of the feud.

Most crime films, at Biograph and elsewhere, show family and society confronted with a group of evil outlaws. THE RIVER PIRATES (No. 3071), shot by Bitzer in September 1905, was loosely based on the robbing of Paul Bonner's summer residence in Sound Beach, Connecticut, near Frank Marion's home, the month before.[10] Marion retained key elements, such as the removal of the safe by boat, but superimposed a melodramatic plot. The robbers murder the wealthy landowner after their leader has been jilted by his daughter. Eventually, they are caught and the ringleader is killed. Even though the real thieves escaped undetected, the filmmakers added a "crime-doesn't-pay" ending. Supposedly based on another unsolved crime in which a strongbox of jewelry mysteriously disappeared in transit, THE GREAT JEWEL MYSTERY (No. 3093) was more indebted to the play *The Great Diamond Mystery*. Two other 1906 Biograph films were also said to be based on recent events in the New York underworld: THE SILVER WEDDING (No. 3148) and THE BLACK HAND (No. 3150). All four crime pictures end with the capture and/or death of the evildoers, but what is most convincingly detailed is the execution of their plans, while their seizure appears arbitrary and often unbelievable. The lack of credible moral endings and the emphasis on criminal violence were not unusual. In the face of a rapidly growing audience for these cheap amusements, many influential Americans greeted the tawdry nature of such melodramas with mounting concern.[11]

During 1906 Marion produced three pictures set in the workplace, an unusual locale for American films of this era. THE PAYMASTER (No. 3203, June), shot at a factory in Mianus (near Greenwich), Connecticut, opens with a scene of a mill girl (Gene Gauntier in her first screen role) working at a power loom—one of the first filmed interiors to rely exclusively on natural light. The paymaster is the girl's lover, but the superintendent uses his power to force his unwelcome attentions on her. Killing two birds with one stone, the superintendent steals the payroll and frames the paymaster for the deed. When a dog finds the hidden money and the superintendent is confronted by the mill girl, the villain throws her into the pond, thus revealing his true perfidious nature.

Both THE TUNNEL WORKERS (No. 3251, October) and SKYSCRAPERS (No. 3258, November) involve similarly melodramatic confrontations between men from different levels of management, and both were shot on locations that received significant news coverage. In THE TUNNEL WORKERS, the superintendent's secret relationship with the foreman's wife is discovered as the film begins.[12] This studio scene is followed by a series of actuality shots showing the building of the tunnel between Manhattan and Long Island, according to one title, "the greatest engineering feat the world has ever known." Next, in the bowels of the earth, the two men enter an air lock and fight over the woman. As the foreman is about to brain the superintendent, there is an explosion. After this fortuitous (or divine) intervention, the foreman comes to his senses and rescues his rival. A tentative reconciliation occurs at the end as the superintendent visits his rescuer's bedside and asks forgiveness. A film rich with interpretive possibilities, THE TUNNEL WORKERS explores the tensions between the all-male workplace and the domestic life of the family.

SKYSCRAPERS was filmed at a construction site for the tallest office building in New York City. A worker, "Dago Pete," robs the contractor but pins the blame on the foreman. In a fight on the unfinished skyscraper, the foreman throws the contractor off the platform, but the loser luckily grabs hold of a girder and stops his fall. At the foreman's trial, however, Dago Pete is exposed by the foreman's daughter and the two levels of management—contractor and foreman—are reconciled. The plot is inconsistent and sometimes illogical, but the titles preserve a minimal coherence. The film itself reveals an anti-immigrant (particularly anti-Italian) prejudice, with ethnic background providing the sole motivation for reprehensible actions and the immigrant himself fostering misunderstandings between native-born whites. All three workplace films present the lower-level manager (often with a working-class background) as a character who is falsely accused or otherwise betrayed and struggles to redeem himself. On one hand, the focus is on someone with whom many male nickelodeon spectators could comfortably identify, someone a notch or two above them in social or economic standing. On the other hand, the last film was insensitive to the heavily immigrant composition of the new audiences. Italian moviegoers, living only a few blocks from the Biograph studio, were likely to be offended.

The system of representation used for these films, moreover, changed little from Biograph efforts of the previous two years. Narratives were generally made understandable through intertitles used in a title/scene/title/scene format. With A FRIEND IN NEED IS A FRIEND INDEED, the story of a man and his faithful dog (performed by Mannie) is virtually told through titles, with the images carrying little of the narrative burden. By contrast, the intertitles of THE LONE HIGHWAYMAN (No. 3223) are brief, if frequent, naming a scene rather than explaining the story (continuing a convention of theatrical melodrama). Generally, title cards were a way to provide spectators with necessary "special knowledge" just before they saw the relevant scene. This was essential because, for the most part, the narratives were neither clearly nor effectively depicted within the scenes. In this respect, Biograph films regressed in McCutcheon's absence.

The depiction of temporality had not changed either. In THE TUNNEL WORKERS, for example, there is still overlapping action as the rivals move back and forth between tunnel and air lock. Editing structures were generally simpler compared to previous efforts involving McCutcheon. There were few close-ups. While Biograph continued to use three-dimensional sets (as it had done consistently since 1904–1905), this realistic touch was easily accommodated by a more general syncretic framework. Thus, SKYSCRAPERS juxtaposes actuality material with scenes displaying a wide range of presentational elements (conventionalized acting gestures, melodramatically contrived plots) with the result that an informal, spontaneous, catch-as-catch-can style of filming suddenly shifts to old-style theatrical conventions as quotidian space is transformed turned into a stage. While individual elements of a later proto-Hollywood system may be present, they are structured within the system of early cinema.

In May 1906, Biograph opened a Los Angeles office under G. E. Van Guysling, who had previously increased the standing and profitability of its mutoscope business. This Pacific Coast branch briefly served as a second production center as Otis M. Gove shot A DARING HOLD-UP IN SOUTHERN CALIFORNIA (No. 3209), which depicted the robbery of a trolley car and the ensuing pursuit and capture of the bandits. Other films were taken of such well-known local sites as the mammoth ostrich farm in Pasadena. By October the branch had moved to a larger office at 116 North Broadway, where films were sold and mutoscope reels rented.[13]

Biograph suffered another upheaval at the beginning of 1907 as Marion left to form a new production company, Kalem, with fellow Biograph employee Samuel Long, manager of the Hoboken factory where prints and mutoscope reels were made. TRIAL MARRIAGES and MR. HURRY-UP (No. 3262) were among Marion's last productions; these were already perfunctorily executed and suffered in comparison to those made by rival producers. After seeing MR. HURRY-UP at Pastor's vaudeville house, Sime Silverman, founder of *Variety*, complained, "Other than being considerably too long, this picture contains little fun, and that only at long intervals." Even the parts that were suppose to be funny had "no humorous effect to speak of."[14]

Van Guysling replaced Marion as vice-president and general manager in early 1907.[15] Although attempts were made to continue releasing subjects at the same pace, the company lacked experienced production personnel. Indeed, the search for a new creative head did not fully end until Griffith assumed the role of director in 1908. For THE FENCING MASTER (No. 3279, February 1907), Biograph enlisted the assistance of two Frenchman to tell a story of love and remorse that was supposedly set in Paris. In addition to his camera responsibilities, Billy Bitzer may have been given the chief creative role in such productions as IF YOU HAD A WIFE LIKE THIS (No. 3278), a comedy farce about a Mr. Peck who is henpecked by his wife. If so, the surviving pictures explain why he was not made producer-director on a more permanent basis.

At least from April (HYPNOTIST'S REVENGE, No. 3300) through June (TERRIBLE TED, No. 3320), Joseph A. Golden, an experienced stage director and stock-company manager, wrote and mounted many of the company's productions.[16] Among them were several clever comedies, including TERRIBLE TED, which gives an unusual twist to the bad-boy genre. A boy reads a dime Western, *Terrible Ted*, and imagines that he is an invincible gunslinger who sends cops running through the streets, shoots a band of outlaws, and saves an Indian girl from a bear that he kills with a knife. He also eliminates a tribe of Indian warriors and subsequently displays their scalps to the camera and audience. His reveries end, however, when his mother enters and gives him a sharp slap. The evil influence that popular culture was said to have on young minds is spoofed, but the filmmakers displace its supposed immorality from the movies onto cheap literature.

Golden's production team employed extensive object animation—something already popularized by Vitagraph—for three Biograph films: DOLLS IN DREAMLAND (No. 3294), CRAYONO (No. 3295), and THE TIRED TAILOR'S DREAM (No. 3313). In the last of these, the technique was used for a dream sequence where a tailor, obliged to finish a suit in one hour, falls asleep and dreams that his almost impossible task is accomplished without any human labor. When the customer returns, the new clothes

TERRIBLE TED

THE TIRED TAILOR'S DREAM

dress him without his assistance, again through object animation. This reverie of production without anxiety or labor may have had considerable appeal for working-class audiences, whose experience of the workplace was radically different. The film itself must have been very time-consuming to photograph, although Biograph's studio lighting made the task much easier than if sunlight had been used. The results, while impressive, are also quite lengthy and slow-moving.

By mid 1907 Biograph had fallen into a state of profound crisis. After Marion's departure, its operations were disorganized: films ceased to be copyrighted, and old subjects had to be dusted off for release. When the corporation's board of directors met on 17 July, Jeremiah J. Kennedy was elected company president. According to Terry Ramsaye, he was assigned the task of liquidating the company, since interest payments on its $200,000 loan/investment from the New York Security and Trust Company were long overdue. Instead, Kennedy decided to restructure the company and began by firing Van Guysling, who departed in a state of nervous prostration. Golden left at the same time. By October, Wallace McCutcheon had rejoined Biograph and was making WIFE WANTED (No. 3377), another variation on the PERSONAL idea. His return was not an immediate cure-all, however: the financial panic of October 1907 resulted in the laying off of many Biograph employees.[17] Biograph thus struggled to survive at the very moment that the industry was booming.

Production at Edison Declines

While the Edison Manufacturing Company prospered, its rate of negative production (of new subjects) was significantly lower from the end of 1905 through the first seven months of 1907 than it had been over the course of the previous year. During this twenty-month period, Porter produced only fifteen fiction "features" for sale and distribution by the Edison organization.[18] Sales on a per-film basis, however, increased dramatically with DREAM OF A RAREBIT FIEND (February 1906), which sold 192 copies during its first year of release, twice the number sold by the most popular Edison subject of the previous year. Even at the low end, WAITING AT THE CHURCH (July 1906) managed to sell fifty-two prints. While sales per film roughly doubled from 1905 to 1906, fewer new subjects meant that total sales increased only 64 percent from one business year to the next. Yet increased sales allowed for more time to be spent on individual subjects. With the Edison factory working at full capacity in an effort to fill its print orders, the production team led by Porter and McCutcheon was under no pressure to increase output. DREAM OF A RAREBIT FIEND, while only 470 feet, took almost two months to make.

The production of actualities continued at Edison through the first months of 1907. News films were seldom made and rarely for general release; rather, most were travel scenes taken by Robert K. Bonine. These sold far fewer copies than the acted films, and some failed to sell at all. Bonine, who felt that the Edison Company was only interested in fiction subjects, left in May and was not replaced. Thereafter, virtually all attention was focused on satisfying the nickelodeons' voracious appetite for story films.

Porter's involvement in all phases of Edison film activities also made it difficult for negative production to increase. The filmmaker not only spent time refining the projecting kinetoscope but helped to supervise the building of Edison's new Bronx

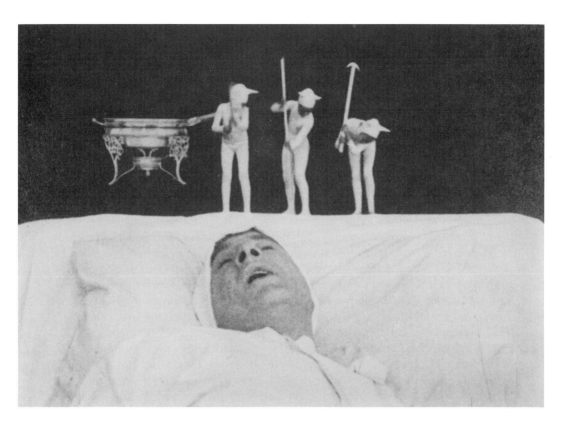

Dream of a Rarebit Fiend

film studio. Construction began in early 1906 and cost $39,556.97 (not including the purchase of land). Even after the studio officially opened on 11 July 1907, putting the facility in working order required large amounts of Porter's energy. Despite such time-consuming responsibilities, Porter never assigned Wallace McCutcheon to his own film projects—an option that could have increased the output of new subjects. At Edison, McCutcheon worked collaboratively with Porter, much as he had worked with Marion during his previous stint at Biograph. In making a film, Porter not only produced but worked on scripts, served as cameraman, did lab work on the exposed negative, and "trimmed" the negative (apparently without making a positive print). McCutcheon worked on scripts and was responsible for the actors. It was perhaps because of tensions around their collaboration that McCutcheon left in May 1907 (and as we have seen, he returned to Biograph). In any case, his role was filled by James Searle Dawley, a dramatist and stage manager who had been working for the Brooklyn-based Spooner Stock Company. It took Porter and Dawley time to evolve a smooth working relationship and put the studio in full operation. Only in August did Edison begin to turn out two story films a month. By then the nickelodeon era had been under way for roughly two years.

Of the twenty films Porter made for Edison distribution between December 1905 (THE NIGHT BEFORE CHRISTMAS) and September 1907 (JACK THE KISSER), several, such as LIFE OF A COWBOY, were 1,000 feet (sixteen minutes), while the great majority were between 755 feet and 975 feet, with shooting ratios still varying between 1.2:1 and 2.1:1. Half were comedies, a fourth melodramas, and the remainder fell into miscellaneous categories. These Edison films had much in common with their Biograph counterparts (the ratio of comedies to melodramas, for example, was quite similar); but while the companies operated within the same system of representation, their products had distinctive styles. Edison pictures were not as closely tied to the newspaper nor were its melodramas in the contemporary-crime genre. Although the heroine is kidnapped in KATHLEEN MAVOURNEEN (May 1906), the action is set in Ireland during an earlier era. Based on an immensely popular play of the same name, the results were promoted as a "new style of film" and helped lead to the adaptation of theatrical material that became common in later years.[19] DANIEL BOONE; OR, PIONEER DAYS IN AMERICA (December 1906) was also based on a well-known historical drama and thus set in a previous century. The violence in LIFE OF A COWBOY occurred on the distant frontier, where civilization had yet to penetrate fully.[20] Perhaps for this reason, in comparison with the pictures of other producers, Edison films were rarely considered "off-color."[21]

As with Biograph's output, almost every Edison film focused on some well-known story or incident in American popular culture. Edison comedies included WAITING AT THE CHURCH (July 1906), which played off the song of the same title. THE RIVALS (August 1907) was based on a T. E. Powers comic strip, often called *Chollie and George*, that ran intermittently in the *New York American*; here, the title characters compete for the affections of a young woman until she finally leaves both for a third. THE TERRIBLE KIDS (April 1906) was part of the popular bad-boy genre. After disrupting a community with their pranks, the boys are finally captured by the police; at the end, however, they escape punishment with the aid of their faithful dog (played by Mannie). THE NINE LIVES OF A CAT (July 1907) was inspired by the well-known saying in the title: a man repeatedly tries to kill a cat, but each time it survives. In these last three examples, the films are constructed out of "linked

Edison's new Bronx studio as it appeared in its finished state (taken March 1908).

vignettes." Built around a single premise, these variations on a gag do not portray a complicated story. In all Edison films, the main title performs a key naming function and provides a framework for audience response.

DREAM OF A RAREBIT FIEND was a trick film that took its title from Winsor McCay's comic strip, *Dream of the Rarebit Fiend;* nonetheless, it was a close imitation of Pathé's popular RÊVE À LA LUNE (1905). THE NIGHT BEFORE CHRISTMAS was a special holiday subject that closely followed Clement Clarke Moore's well-known story and introduced scenes with lines of the poem, appealing both to children and

THE "TEDDY" BEARS. *Goldilocks looks through a peephole at the animated teddy bears. Rescued from the bears by paternalistic President Theodore Roosevelt, she saves the baby bear from further carnage.*

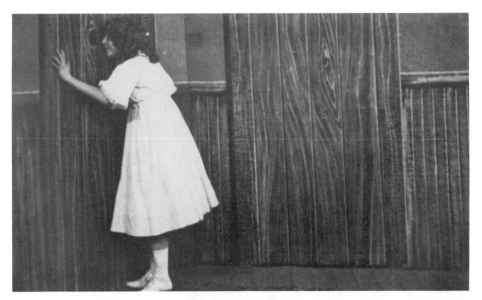

to adult nostalgia. THE "TEDDY" BEARS (February 1907) was based on *Goldilocks and the Three Bears* but also referred to Teddy Roosevelt's killing of a mother bear and his capture of her cub, said to be at the origin of the teddy bear craze then at its height. The penultimate scene reworks the 1902 political cartoon that made this incident famous: instead of nobly refusing to shoot the bear cub as in the cartoon, Roosevelt is deterred from his carnage only by the pleadings of Goldilocks. These adult references are crucial for a full appreciation of the picture, although one critic of the time chose to ignore them and thus viewed the picture as a macabre children's

One version of the 1902 political cartoon showing Roosevelt sparing the bear cub.

film.[22] THREE AMERICAN BEAUTIES was a one-minute subject intended to close an evening performance with its hand-tinted images of a rose, a young woman, and the American flag. Expanding upon a well-established genre (shots of the American flag often brought an exhibition to a close), the picture was so popular that the negative wore out and the film had to be remade.

The 1906–1907 Edison films continued to operate within the representational framework that Porter and his associates had already established. Relying on well-known stories, songs, and anecdotes, they avoided intertitles almost completely. The audience's special knowledge, however, sometimes proved inadequate, and films such as DANIEL BOONE, with its complicated narrative, were considered best suited for a lecture. Sets routinely combining pasteboard props with three-dimensional elements retained a strong syncretic approach, and temporal repetitions were common. Although studio head Edwin S. Porter would later resist any move away from early cinema's system of representation, such resistance was not yet a problem, and Edison films remained popular. Their timely and often ambitious narratives, the cleverness with which the ideas were executed, and the care often taken in the actual production all served to distinguish them from their Biograph counterparts and at least partially account for the increasing profitability of the Edison Manufacturing Company.

Continued dependence on the specifics of American culture—key to Edison films and, to a lesser degree, those made by Biograph—meant that transatlantic sales, particularly on the Continent, were necessarily limited. WAITING AT THE CHURCH must have seemed bizarre to people unfamiliar with the song; likewise, KATHLEEN MAVOURNEEN was hardly an attractive purchase in a country where the play was unknown, and TRIAL MARRIAGES obviously lost some of its effectiveness when audiences did not know the humorous context within which it was made. Edison had European offices for its phonograph business, and these did make some motion-

One scene from THREE AMERICAN BEAUTIES. *The woman smells a rose known as an American Beauty.*

picture sales, but attempts to turn Europe into an important market did not succeed during this period. Biograph found that "the humorous and tragic scenes of American life are probably what they want and appreciate best," and Marion's contemporary crime films must have enjoyed some popularity overseas.[23] Yet Biograph's foreign sales declined as the quality of its films deteriorated, and its reciprocal agreement with Gaumont ended in early 1907. The domestic market was the principal one for both Edison and Biograph.

Vitagraph Becomes the Leading American Producer

By the end of the period covered in this volume, Vitagraph had emerged as the leading American producer with a repertoire of films conveying a dynamism that was closely associated with urban life. In THE 100 TO ONE SHOT; OR, A RUN OF LUCK (July 1906), a farmer facing foreclosure on his home goes to the city, where he pawns his remaining possessions and looks for last-minute salvation. Deciding to risk everything at the horse races, he plays a hot tip and wins. With some of his new wealth, he hires an automobile and races home to prevent the landlord from expelling his aged parents. The city provides new opportunities, just as it had for Blackton and Smith, who had found a hot tip in moving pictures, bet on their future, and won. In this film, the "evil" of gambling serves a positive function, violating the moralistic messages of conservative religious groups. In THE JAIL BIRD AND HOW HE FLEW (June 1906), an escaped prisoner outwits the prison wardens by assuming different disguises. Finally they catch an innocent bystander (a man in a white suit who sits down on a newly painted park bench) as the escapee waves at the departing guards. Once again, cleverness, luck, and the unexpected are valued more than conventional morality.

AUTOMOBILE THIEVES

Vitagraph's fast-paced, energetic style drew the attention of a *Brooklyn Eagle* reporter who visited the company's offices in the summer of 1906 and wrote that the scenario writer (probably J. Stuart Blackton) "must have something happening every minute, allowing for no padding with word-painting, following climax with climax, and developing all kinds of intricate situations so that the interest of the onlookers will never sag from the picture on the canvas."[25] THE AUTOMOBILE THIEVES (September 1906), in preparation at the time the article was published, is exemplary of this approach. During the course of the 985-foot, twenty-three-shot drama, the

thieves—an attractive young couple—commit a string of holdups and robberies. They are indifferent to the fate of their victims, who are often beaten or shot. They manage to escape a police trap, largely because of the fearless intervention of the woman, but the ensuing chase ends in a shootout and the death of the couple. At the conclusion, the dying man staggers to his beloved, kisses her, and dies. (In fact, his actions throughout appear based on sexual obsession, and his periodic sense of guilt is assuaged by alcohol.) Romance, traditionally the domain of the hero and heroine (THE TRAIN WRECKERS, etc.), is shifted to those outside the law. The thieves become the protagonists and the police the antagonists in this explosive mix of sex and violence.

Vitagraph comedies contained important slapstick elements and often lampooned authority. OH! THAT LIMBURGER: THE STORY OF A PIECE OF CHEESE (April 1906) is a bad-boy comedy in which mischievous youngsters hide some smelly cheese in their father's suit pocket. Putting on his coat and going to work, the father alienates all acquaintances and receives various beatings in a series of linked vignettes. The jokesters are ultimately discovered and receive a thrashing in kind. In PLEASE HELP THE BLIND; OR, A GAME OF GRAFT (May 1906), a cop emulates undersocialized boys and a tramp by using a "Please Help the Blind" sign to beg from passersby. Soon this figure of authority must flee from a squad of fellow policemen seeking his arrest. He ultimately escapes by hanging the sign (and the responsibility) on an unsuspecting housepainter. In THE SNAPSHOT FIEND; OR, WILLIE'S NEW CAMERA (July 1906), the boy uses his new camera to take portraits. This activity serves as an excuse for a variety of facial-expression shots, including one of a preacher in the arms of an old maid.

Most scenes for these 1906 films were filmed outdoors in Brooklyn or Manhattan. The few interiors were shot on the open-air stage above Vitagraph's New York office. The schematic sets were photographed in ways that generally reproduced the frontality and framing of theatrical space. In AUTOMOBILE THIEVES, the opening scene includes a fake-looking bookcase constructed of pasteboard, an actual writing table (which is reused in a later, unrelated scene), and a convincing safe. Police headquarters is an almost barren stage with handcuffs and nightsticks painted on the back wall running perpendicular to the camera. Spatial and temporal relations between shots are frequent though inconsistently handled, with overlaps in some instances and a strong linearity across cuts in others.

The company's new Brooklyn studio, started in 1905, was designed to provide facilities for increased, more efficient filmmaking and to improve production values, thus silencing the criticism that was sometimes directed at the slapdash quality of Vitagraph releases.[26] Completed in November of the following year, the studio cost approximately twenty-five thousand dollars:

> The building which is made of concrete blocks is supplied with a 100 horse-power engine which will operate dynamo to furnish electric light, heat and power for the machine shop and dark room. There will be a complete outfit of Cooper-Hewitt lights in the studio.
>
> Special apparatus and stage have been made for taking novel pictures with special scenic effects. The entire roof and upper part of the building is covered with a specially designed prismatic glass. This construction of glass diffuses and intensifies the rays of light so that shadows are not perceptible (*Film Index*, 25 August 1906, p. 6).

Vitagraph's new Brooklyn studio as it neared completion (1906).

Vitagraph thus opened the first American studio of the nickelodeon era, beating Edison, Selig, and Lubin by almost a year.[27] As Jon Gartenberg has noted, the studio allowed for a big jump in production quality. The studio sets were so large that in a film like FOUL PLAY (December 1906), the camera panned across one room and (relying on an absent fourth wall) followed the characters into the next. In other scenes, the framing became closer and more intimate, reducing the sense of stagelike compositions. The combination of artificial and diffused natural light resulted in superior images and a heavier reliance on sets.

During late 1906 and early 1907 Vitagraph frequently produced accomplished dramas and comedies. FOUL PLAY, for example, is an effectively told tale of a bank clerk who steals money and frames a fellow employee for the crime. The victim's wife subsequently tracks the clerk, drugs his drink, steals incriminating evidence, and soon has the real crook exposed and arrested. Justice triumphs though the victory is achieved by underhanded means. AND THE VILLAIN STILL PURSUED HER; OR, THE AUTHOR'S DREAM (November 1906) and ON THE STAGE; OR, MELODRAMA FROM THE BOWERY (April 1907) burlesque the conventions of melodramatic theater and cheap literature. In the first, an impoverished playwright works in a garret where the signatures of William Shakespeare and melodramatist Charles E. Blaney— presumably two of his role models—comically coexist on the back wall. He falls asleep and dreams of a story in which a dastardly villain pursues a beautiful young

ON THE STAGE; OR, MELODRAMA FROM THE BOWERY

J. Stuart Blackton in LIGHTNING SKETCHES.

woman. The dream ends with the author—who casts himself as the hero to the rescue—leaping from a cliff and crashing into his own bed. He then wakes up and begins to write. A MID-WINTER NIGHT'S DREAM; OR, LITTLE JOE'S LUCK (December 1906) was a Christmas story in which a street urchin falls asleep and dreams of being taken in by a wealthy family. Although his dream proves a mirage, he is befriended by a kind policeman who rescues him from the snowy cold.

Vitagraph became a pioneer in various animation techniques. HUMOROUS PHASES OF FUNNY FACES (April 1906) elaborated on earlier films of Blackton executing "lightning sketches" on an easel. Through the use of object-animation techniques and various stop-motion substitutions, Blackton extended the form while keeping many presentational elements intact from his days as a vaudeville performer. LIGHTNING SKETCHES (July 1907) further elaborated on many of these achievements: the execution of still more complicated animation techniques was aided by the new studio with its electric lights. Object animation using toy animals was introduced in A MID-WINTER NIGHT'S DREAM. Similar techniques were employed for other Vitagraph subjects during 1907, including THE HAUNTED HOTEL (February 1907) and possibly THE DISINTEGRATED CONVICT (September 1907). These films were closely related to trick subjects such as the immensely popular LIQUID ELECTRICITY; OR, THE INVENTOR'S GALVANIC FLUID (September 1907), where an old professor sprays

THE BOY, THE BUST, AND THE BATH

people with galvanizing fluid and, through accelerated action (*i.e.*, undercranking the camera), unleashes hidden reservoirs of energy.

Although Vitagraph pictures were closely bound to American popular culture, they rarely focused or depended upon specific antecedents. Typically, the producers worked within a wide range of previously established genres, from the fire rescue (MAN WITH THE LADDER AND THE HOSE, February 1906) to the Western ("THE BAD MAN"—A TALE OF THE WEST, January 1907). More than Biograph and Edison, they managed to steer a middle course between very simple, minimal stories and those so complex that they were difficult to follow without special assistance. In fact, surviving Vitagraph films from 1906–1907 consistently avoided intertitles until FRANCESCA DI RIMINI; OR, THE TWO BROTHERS (September 1907), which used titles to clarify otherwise elusive narratives. Only thereafter does it seem to have become a regular practice.

These Vitagraph films incorporated a rich array of well-executed representational techniques. The filmmakers used a panning camera for both interior and exteriors. Cutting in to closer views or cutting back to establishing shots was quite common (particularly in A MID-WINTER NIGHT'S DREAM). The company's production increasingly adopted a linear time line. In THE BOY, THE BUST, AND THE BATH (August 1907), for example, there is a whole series of match-cuts as the characters move between the hallway and bathroom. Yet later conventions of screen direction involving exits and entrances are not employed between the opening two shots. Some scenes also rely on frontal compositions, and a presentational approach remains evident as the male characters communicate extensively with the camera/spectator. Nonetheless, the unsuspecting female housekeeper (played by Florence Lawrence) is unaware of the camera's presence, a mixed convention that was continued in the comedies of the 1910s. Its genre (the omnipresent bad-boy genre) and many narrative elements (the infantile sexuality and voyeurism of the male boarders) are squarely within the parameters of early cinema, but the elaboration of a single prank over the course of the film points toward a later era.

Vitagraph subjects were so popular that the company found itself sixty days behind on print orders even though its developing rooms operated night and day. This strong demand was due not only to domestic consumption but to the company's international activities. At first, Charles Urban sold Vitagraph films in Europe (just as Vitagraph sold Urban films in the United States). But by February 1907 the company had opened its own sales offices in London and Paris. The Vitagraph partners, all of European birth, paid particular attention to these markets and soon were the one American company with large foreign sales. By the end of March, Vitagraph was expanding its Flatbush facilities, adding a new and much larger building.[28] In May, the company began to release one new fiction film a week (often more when short [*ca.* 250 feet] subjects were involved). By August the company was selling at least two new pictures each week, though most were half reels of approximately 500 feet.

Vitagraph's methods of production underwent a profound reorganization during this period. Between October 1906 and early 1907, there were three production units, headed by cameramen J. Stuart Blackton, Albert E. Smith, and their senior and most trusted employee, James Bernard French (Vitagraph's first-hired projectionist). Working with each was an "artist and general assistant" who was responsible for the "posing and arranging of scenes." These included G. M. Anderson (until spring 1906), William Ranous, and George E. Stevens (between October 1906 and March 1907). Clearly it would be inaccurate to consider these stage directors/stage managers to be "film directors" in the somewhat later sense of the word. They worked collaboratively with the cameramen, who were, in two of the three cases, the producers and company owners. Each unit was largely autonomous, functioning independently under the protection of a key figure. At the same time, almost everyone had multiple responsibilities. French was also in charge of the production department, which hired operators. Stevens was occasionally responsible for camerawork on exterior scenes. Out-of-work operators often served as extras.[29] Lack of specialization and broad expertise thus characterized production at Vitagraph, the most successful American producer, into early 1907.

Things began to change when Albert Smith left for Europe to establish Vitagraph's European branch offices at the beginning of 1907. With his departure, French assumed responsibility for managing the increasingly large studio, and Blackton remained as producer to oversee all three units, each headed by a director. While Blackton and even Smith remained actively involved in production, less experienced cameramen, among them perhaps operators who took local views for Vitagraph's now-disbanded traveling exhibition units, were hired to work under these directors.[30] The cameramen, however, reported not only to the new directors but also to the producer and the studio manager. Nevertheless, a new hierarchical organization of production, fundamentally different from the previous horizontal one, was emerging.

BARGAIN FIEND; OR, SHOPPING À LA MODE

The increasing level of production likewise encouraged Vitagraph to establish a stock company of actors, and by 1907, many leading players and stars of later films were working for the studio in some capacity. Leo Delaney appeared in FOUL PLAY (1906) and THE WRONG FLAT (June 1907). William J. Shea, who later appeared with John Bunny in such comedies as DAVY JONES IN THE SOUTH SEAS (January 1910), had a role in AMATEUR NIGHT; OR, GET OUT THE HOOK (April 1907). Florence Turner teamed up with Florence Lawrence in ATHLETIC AMERICAN GIRLS (July 1907) and BARGAIN FIEND; OR, SHOPPING À LA MODE (July 1907). Elements of the studio system were beginning to emerge in the second half of 1907.

Paley's Fortunes Fade
as Selig Enjoys Good Luck

William Paley was forced out of business as an independent producer and renter sometime in late 1906 or early 1907. The merging of the Proctor and Keith circuits in June 1906 led Proctor to switch his film rental account from Paley's Kalatechnoscope Exchange to the Edison-affiliated Kinetograph Company. The veteran producer and cameraman felt betrayed and particularly bitter, for he, more than any other figure in the industry, had been willing to acknowledge Edison's patents. This loss of the Proctor account undermined the basis of Paley's business, and he soon found himself looking for work as a free-lance cameraman.[31]

Making BARGAIN FIEND *(August 1907) in Vitagraph's new studio. The director is probably William Ranous.*

The Selig Polyscope Company was on the edge of bankruptcy by late 1905. Changes in film practice and legal expenses from fighting Edison's patent suit had undermined Selig's business, and his advertisements ceased to appear in trade journals. Then in February 1906 Upton Sinclair's *The Jungle* was published and caused a furor with its revelations of conditions in the meat-packing industry. According to Terry Ramsaye, Armour & Company turned to Selig, whose films of its stockyards and slaughterhouses, made with an eye toward promotion, presented the company's activities in a more favorable light. Armour not only arranged for these to be exhibited but provided Selig with legal support and a badly needed infusion of capital.[32]

Armour's support enabled Selig to return to production after a long hiatus, and he resumed with THE TOMBOYS, a 535-foot comedy released in the middle of August. At about this time, Selig hired the actor/director G. M. Anderson, who had previously worked for Edison, Vitagraph, and Harry Davis (discussed later in this chapter). Anderson was not given the partnership he wanted but worked on a commission basis. After the completion of TRAPPED BY PINKERTONS (October 1906) and a half-dozen other fiction films, Selig sent Anderson to Colorado, where his Western agent, H. H. Buckwalter, helped the director make several Westerns, including THE GIRL FROM MONTANA (March 1907), THE BANDIT KING, and WESTERN JUSTICE (released June 1907).[33] Returning to Chicago from Colorado, Anderson continued to direct for Selig and was soon recognized by *Show World* as "one of the most prominent moving-picture producers in the country."[34] During July, the company released four story films, including THE MATINEE IDOL, another takeoff on the PERSONAL idea, in which a theater star is pursued by a bevy of overly enthusiastic female fans. Sometime during that month, Anderson left Selig to start up his own motion-picture company.

Selig's output was lower for August and September, not only because of Anderson's departure but because his company was deeply involved in the construction of a new Chicago studio that was in full operation by the end of the year. Until then, Selig relied heavily on exterior locations: the rare interior scenes, in ALL'S WELL THAT ENDS WELL (August 1907), for example, reveal lighting by harsh direct sun. The new studio would make more diffuse lighting possible, as seen in films like WHAT A PIPE DID (November 1907).[35] Selig quickly found replacements for Anderson, among them Otis Turner, Francis Boggs, and John M. Bradlet, and began an ambitious process of expansion.[36] By November he was releasing a new film every week. While suffering serious difficulties at the outset of the nickelodeon era, the Selig Polyscope Company regrouped and finally expanded with the boom.

Although fiction filmmaking was paramount, Selig continued to make some actualities: the 600-foot WORLD SERIES BASEBALL GAME of the 1906 White Sox–Cubs championship, a series of scenes of the G.A.R. encampment in Minneapolis, and a November flood in Seattle. In 1907 William Selig himself took views of tarpon fishing off Padre Island in South Texas.[37] As at Edison, actuality production had become quite separate from production of story films.

None of Selig's 1906–1907 films survive except for a few brief paper fragments submitted for copyright purposes. This is particularly unfortunate because catalog descriptions and reviews suggest that they displayed noteworthy vitality. With THE GRAFTERS, *Variety* reported, the filmmakers had "managed to extract a considerable amount of active fun out of the subject based upon nature's desire to secure 'something' for nothing," and it was "exhibited to large, interested audiences in a number

Pansy Perry in THE GIRL FROM MONTANA.

of Chicago theaters." Some Selig subjects employed advanced editorial constructions. In WHEN WE WERE BOYS (January 1907), two old men are shown conversing about their childhoods and the many pranks they pulled. The film cuts back and forth between the old men and scenes of their youth. In an elaborate flashback construction that predated regular use of alternating scenes, the film makes explicit the nostalgic nature of this pre-nickelodeon genre that was then coming under attack.[38] WOOING AND WEDDING A COON (November 1907) and THE MASHER (June 1907) indicate that the depiction of African Americans at Selig had not changed from the owner's minstrel-show days.

A number of Selig pictures show women assuming active roles often associated with masculine behavior. In THE TOMBOYS, young girls act like their bad-boy counterparts by skipping school and playing pranks on adults. The protagonist of THE FEMALE HIGHWAYMAN (November 1906) is a clever thief who executes her crimes with daring and nerve. The catalog description suggests that her detection and final capture was an unconvincing, obligatory ending. Likewise the heroine in THE GIRL FROM MONTANA (March 1907), played by Pansy Perry, saves her lover from death and several times keeps angry mobs at bay with her revolver.[39] In many respects, the Western with its cow*boys* supplanted the bad-boy genre. The personal nostalgia of the male filmmakers and spectators was replaced by a more mythic conception of the recent but still-fading past. In these Westerns, codes of civilized conduct were not yet fully asserted, so men and women alike were freer to assume nontraditional roles and responsibilities. It thus provided a place where women might forge new, more active identities.

Lubin Is Involved in All Phases of the Industry

Lubin's business expanded with alacrity as the nickelodeon boom gathered speed. During the first half of 1906, however, he barely produced one new subject a month, and some of these, such as IMPERSONATION OF NELSON–MCGOVERN FIGHT (March 1906) and THE SAN FRANCISCO DISASTER (May 1906), were still fight reenactments or news films. Others were remakes of rivals' popular hits, continuing the policy discussed in chapter 12. THE WRECKERS OF THE LIMITED EXPRESS (January 1906, 800 feet) closely followed Edison's THE TRAIN WRECKERS; RESCUED BY CARLO (April 1906) mimicked Cecil Hepworth's RESCUED BY ROVER; A NIGHT OFF (July 1906, 800 feet) was heavily indebted to Edison's DREAM OF A RAREBIT FIEND (February 1906); and even GOOD NIGHT (November 1906, 65 feet) was similar to Edison's THREE AMERICAN BEAUTIES. With A NIGHT OFF Lubin used a somewhat different commercial strategy. While immensely popular, DREAM OF A RAREBIT FIEND was only 470 feet long and very compact in its use of cinematic tricks. Lubin's trick comedy followed the same story and often used similar sets and tricks but added several flourishes, notably a chase that almost doubled the length.

As the pace of Lubin production increased by mid 1906, new personnel were hired and films of greater originality were produced. THE SECRET OF DEATH VALLEY (September 1906) was a story of murder and revenge. The picture's power derives from a series of visions attributed to the principal characters. In the final scene, the wife, whose vision reveals how her husband was killed, avenges his death by killing the murderer, who has himself just guiltily recalled his dastardly act.

Although THE BANK DEFAULTER (November 1906, 1,000 feet) had an obvious antecedent in Edison's THE KLEPTOMANIAC, it was a free and extremely interesting reworking. In the Edison drama, the wealthy kleptomaniac is called Mrs. Banker, indirectly linking her thievery with the banking activities of her husband. (Such identification, however, appears only in the catalog description—for use in the exhibitor's lecture—and not in the film itself.) This implied allusion became the new film's focal point, with the banker serving as the film's central character. In the opening scenes, he attends church and dotes on his family, evincing all the outward trappings of social responsibility. A second line of action is then established as working-class congregation members deposit their savings at his bank. Subsequently, the banker's double life is revealed by a visit to his mistress, the theft of a large sum of money, and eventual flight. The film returns to the second line of action with one of the depositors, an older woman, working at a scrub tub presumably after losing all her savings. It cuts to the banker being arrested and then shifts to a courtroom where the old woman is convicted of stealing bread. The banker is brought before the judge as well but is acquitted of his crime. An allegorical apotheosis of "Justice Ashamed" concludes the subject. The stories of the banker and the depositors are interwoven throughout the course of the film, whereas the Porter-Edison film presents Mrs. Banker and the poor, desperate mother in separate stories that are not united until the final scene. The Lubin film's explicitly subversive view of society is intensified by this alternation between different lines of action.

The sensationalism of THE BANK DEFAULTER, with its revelation that the rich were unprincipled and had secret lives, may have suggested the making of the most controversial American film produced prior to the establishment of the Board of Censorship in 1909: THE UNWRITTEN LAW: A THRILLING DRAMA BASED ON THE THAW-WHITE TRAGEDY (March 1907). Still well known today, the "tragedy" was a front-page news item for many months. On 25 June 1906, millionaire Harry K. Thaw shot and killed famed architect Stanford White at the Madison Square Roof Garden. Thaw's wife, Evelyn Nesbitt, had been White's mistress prior to (and perhaps even after) her marriage. Thaw went on trial for murder and was ultimately judged insane. The trial, however, was still under way when Lubin's film appeared, taking a pro-Thaw position with the argument that the killing was condoned by "unwritten law." To make its point, the film shows Evelyn's visit to White's "room with the velvet swing," his drugging of her wine, and her rape/seduction. The film's integration of sex and violence, its revelation of decadence and corruption among the rich, fascinated many and scandalized others. It was banned in Houston, Texas, and many other locales, but in others it was the biggest hit of the year. Six months later Lubin scathingly burlesqued oil king John D. Rockefeller with JOHN D. ——— AND THE REPORTER (September 1907), in which the president of Rancid Oil tries to escape the reach of the law, but an ambitious reporter finally serves him with a summons. In the last scene the tycoon pays a $29 million fine, "which is squeezed out of the poor consumers' pockets and poor John D. is happy again."[40]

While many of these Lubin films articulate a viewpoint that resonated with working-class audiences, they were frequently misogynist and, as we have already seen, relied on demeaning racial stereotypes. In TOO MUCH MOTHER-IN-LAW (May 1907), newlyweds find it impossible to escape the wife's mother. In despair, the husband commits suicide, and in like manner, the bride follows her husband to Hades. The mother-in-law won't give up, however, and kills herself so she can join

The heroine and her husband's killer share the same vision over the course of THE SECRET OF DEATH VALLEY.

them there. In WHEN WOMEN VOTE (June 1907, 700 feet), Mr. O'Brien takes care of the baby while Mrs. O'Brien prepares and delivers her campaign speech. During the election, women vote but men are arrested when they approach the polls. After Mrs. O'Brien wins a judgeship, she sends one man to prison for twenty years when he tries to kiss his wife. Her own husband is stuck with the housework and wants a divorce, but, according to Lubin's promotional material, "such cannot be obtained when women vote."[41] While the film creates an absurd exaggeration to articulate its anti-suffrage position, it unintentionally exposes the excesses of patriarchy in ways that provide a double-edged message. In this respect, it recalls Lubin's earlier FUN ON THE FARM.

Those films which were clearly aimed at female spectators placed them in a passive position and indulged their most masochistic fantasies. In MOTHER'S DREAM (June 1907), for example, the mother puts her children to bed, and then falls asleep on the couch. Dreaming of her own death and the difficulties facing her orphaned children, she finally awakens in a state of joyful disbelief. The narrative's ideological implications obviously differed from the Anderson-Selig films, with their dynamic, self-assured female protagonists.

Lubin enjoyed a booming business during 1907, releasing one film a week by May and producing three a week by September. As fall began, he was about to open a new indoor studio at 926 Market Street, complete with electric lights, *Billboard* reported,

THE UNWRITTEN LAW. *Stanford White prepares a drug for the unsuspecting Evelyn Nesbitt, Harry K. Thaw kills White on the Madison Square Garden rooftop; the resulting trial.*

"so that the pictures may be taken in any kind of weather." Meanwhile, the Philadelphia entrepreneur was expanding his involvement in other phases of the picture business as well. He not only had a successful film rental exchange but had moved into exhibition. According to Lubin, he became a theater operator when a local theatorium closed and assumption of ownership was the only way to gain payment. Appreciating the nickelodeon's profitability, he began to build a chain of picture houses in Philadelphia and elsewhere. His thousand-seat Bon Ton Theater was operating in Philadelphia by late 1906. He opened a multi-unit vaudeville/motion-picture theater in Baltimore on 1 April 1907, with local scenes taken especially for the occasion. Vaudeville was upstairs for ten cents admission (five cents in the balcony), while the basement was devoted exclusively to motion pictures and illustrated songs. The first floor of his new five-story headquarters at 926 Market Street was opened as a motion-picture theater on 4 July. By September he had another Philadelphia theater at 217 North Eighth Street, three more about to open in the same city, and other picture houses in Wilmington, Delaware, and Reading, Pennsylvania.[42] Lubin was thus the only established producer in the motion-picture business to be building a vertically integrated business.

New Production Companies

The demand for films also encouraged the formation of new production companies. Capital acquired from other areas of the industry usually provided the means as successful entrepreneurs in distribution and exhibition moved into production. Early in 1906, the Miles brothers became seriously committed to making story films and constructed an elaborate studio in San Francisco. They might have become major producers if the earthquake and fire had not destroyed their facilities. Although the financial setback stymied their attempts, they continued to make actualities (SHRINERS' CONCLAVE AT LOS ANGELES, CAL., MAY 1907), and they established a reputation for filming important boxing matches. When THE GANS–NELSON CONTEST, GOLDFIELD, NEVADA, SEPTEMBER 3, 1906 was shot in Nevada, it was announced during the preliminaries that President Roosevelt's son (Theodore, Jr.) was at ringside; according to a press account, as the fans cheered, "Some one stood up in the crowd and yelled: 'Show yourself and turn your face toward the moving pictures.'" On 26 November 1906 the Miles brothers shot THE O'BRIEN–BURNS CONTEST, LOS ANGELES, CAL., NOV. 26TH, 1906 under Cooper-Hewitt lights, which turned blood to a sickening green. By mid 1907, they had engaged Fred A. (George) Dobson, a former Biograph cameraman, to take actualities in the New York City area.[43]

Harry Davis moved into film production on 22 May 1906, when his new Pittsburgh-based company shot a local Knights Templar parade.[44] A Decoration Day baseball game between Pittsburgh and the Cincinnati Reds was next shot, and both films were shown at Davis' Grand Opera House in early June. Company offices were located above the Dreamland penny arcade and across the street from the Grand Opera House. Davis employed James Blair Smith, formerly in the Edison Company, as a cameraman and technical expert. G. M. Anderson came from Vitagraph to write and stage pictures for forty dollars a week. Only a few films were made, including one chase comedy, before Anderson moved on to Selig. By the following year Davis had withdrawn from the production field.[45] The exchanges did not purchase his films in

THE O'BRIEN–BURNS CONTEST, LOS ANGELES, CAL., NOV. 26TH, 1906.

large quantities, and playing these original subjects as "specials" in his various theaters may not have markedly increased box-office receipts, at least once the initial
novelty had passed. The costs and effort of production proved too high, causing Davis
to shift his expansionary energies into setting up film exchanges to service nickelodeons, particularly his own.

It was not until 1907 that businessmen in the motion-picture field moved into
production in substantial numbers. The Kalem Company began operations on 12
April and was incorporated on 2 May. Fifty shares of stock were issued: twenty-nine
went to Frank Marion, ten to Samuel Long, and ten to George Kleine (with a single
share going to employee Walter Hatt). Kalem (the company's appellation was an
acronym derived from the initials of these owners' last names) had offices at 131 West
Twenty-fourth Street in New York City and production facilities at Marion's home in
Sound Beach (near Greenwich), Connecticut. Its first picture was THE RUNAWAY
SLEIGHBELLE.[46] When the company started actively selling films in June, it already
had a half-dozen completed subjects to offer. With stock company and repertory
theaters closed for the summer, an array of experienced players joined the enterprise, including Gene Gauntier (whose real name was Genevieve Liggett), Joseph
and Fred Santley, Ed Boulden, Joe Sullivan, and Gus Carney. As Gauntier later
recalled,

Mr. Marion had been compelled to give up directing because of increasing duties in the business end. It was a lucky contingency and made the difference between success and failure for the infant project. Mr. Olcott accepted the position of director for the summer at the munificent remuneration of ten dollars a picture. He gathered about him a score of actors who were personal friends and threw himself whole heartedly into the work ("Blazing the Trail," unpublished MS, n.d.).

Sidney Olcott (actually John Sidney Allcott) became the company's regular director and was soon producing almost one new subject a week, with Gauntier writing many of the film scripts. The films, most of which were comedies, were noted for their elaborate intertitles, which included cartoons as well as text (and continued the emphasis on intertitles evident in earlier Biograph films made under Marion's supervision). In the fall, however, Gauntier left to assume the title role in the stage play *Texas*.[47] A firmly established stock company of actors had yet to be introduced.

Essanay Film Manufacturing Company, which began its existence as the Peerless Film Manufacturing Company, was formed in Chicago by Gilbert Maxwell Anderson and George K. Spoor, who filed incorporation papers in late April. Anderson, who continued working for Selig even after their plans were well advanced, had finally accomplished his goal: ownership in a film company. Spoor, however, retained the controlling interest, owning fifty-one of one hundred shares of stock, with forty-eight going to Anderson and one to a third board member. Gilbert P. Hamilton, who began his motion-picture career as a projectionist for the Eidoloscope Company and eventually worked for Spoor's Kinodrome firm as an operator, was promoted to cameraman and worked closely with Anderson. By the end of July, their developing and printing facilities were set up and Essanay advertised its first film, AN AWFUL SKATE, a 612-foot comedy that took advantage of the roller-skating craze to show a tramp on rollers. Anderson's experience enabled Essanay to turn out popular films, and according to *Billboard*, "Its first productions were grabbed up so quickly that the factory was run night and day."[48]

By August the Filmograph Company had completed and was selling several comedies working within well-established genres, including YOUNG AMERICANS, about mischievous boys playing pranks on a variety of adults, and WORK FOR YOUR GRUB, a tramp comedy. This new Philadelphia concern hired Fred Balshofer, a former Lubin cameraman, to photograph the films. The firm was short-lived, however, and when Balshofer visited New York, he found a job with the Actograph Company, which had been recently formed by Norman Mosher, Edward M. Harrington, and Fred L. Beck (who was later bought out by A. C. Hayman). By late August, Balshofer was taking films from the front end of a train going through Sacandaga Park, a summer amusement center with a Hale's Tour car that subsequently showed the local view. The Actograph Company's first official release, SPORTS OF THE ADIRONDACKS, appeared in early September. By 1 December they were preparing to make fiction films starring Mosher's dog, Mannie, who had appeared in many Edison and Biograph films.[49]

In Detroit, William H. Goodfellow, owner of the successful Detroit Film Exchange, started the Goodfellow Manufacturing Company, which was turning out long story films by September 1907. The month before, the St. Louis–based O. T. Crawford organization, which owned many theaters and several exchanges, had announced

Kalem Films

(THE NEW LINE)

THE TENDERFOOT

A Merry Western Comedy Full of Laughs and Ginger

LENGTH, 850 FEET   READY JULY 31

THE TENDERFOOT is a callow Eastern youth who goes West with an ambition to become a cow puncher. Of course he is an easy mark from the moment he strikes the ranch, and the cowboys have no end of fun with him until one fine day they enveigle him into a game of poker. Then the deal suddenly changes, and the tenderfoot wins the game and the girl.

6 Great Scenes With Cartoon Titles

1. HEAP BAD INJUN.
2. He Would Be a Cowboy.
3. Love a la Carte.
4. The Bear Hunt.
5. Captured by Redskins.
6. Stung.

RECENT KALEM SUCCESSES

THE HOBO HERO, 760 Ft. Bowser's Housecleaning, 675 Ft.
Pony Express,   880 " Dog Snatcher   -   595 "
New Hired Man, 575 " Gentleman Farmer - 720 "
Runaway Sleighbelle, 535 Feet

KALEM COMPANY, Inc.

31 W. 24th STREET (Telephone 4510 Madison) NEW YORK CITY
Selling Agents, Kleine Optical Co. 52 State St., Chicago

A New One in America

ESSANAY FILMS

now ready for delivery

A SURE HIT

tremendous laugh-making picture that will make a warm weather audience wilt.

"AN AWFUL SKATE"

or

The Hobo on Rollers

(Copyright, 1907, by Essanay Film Mfg. Co.)

Length, 614 feet

Originated by G. M. Anderson, responsible for "His First Ride," "Girl from Montana," and a long list of best American films.

GET THIS ONE!
It will show you a new standard of photographic quality has been attained by new American makers.

P. S. "An Awful Skate" has been copied by a rival concern who employed spies to follow our camera. Our picture is the original and best value for your money. Don't let anyone convince you otherwise

ORDER AT ONCE

ESSANAY FILM MFG. CO.

(Incorporated)

501 Wells Street, CHICAGO, ILL.

Advertisements from two new companies, Kalem and Essanay, 27 July 1907.

its intentions of going into production. Its first film was taken at the International Balloon Races in St. Louis on 21 October; Crawford, however, was constructing a studio and planned to make "clean comedy and thrilling dramatic subjects" under the name American Films.[50] By fall 1907, a rapidly increasing number of industry personnel were starting their own production companies, and threatening the dominance of established producers, particularly Edison and Biograph.

Foreign Productions Flood the American Market

The shortage of American pictures in 1906 and early 1907 opened up tremendous opportunities for foreign producers. Lawrence Karr has found that only one-third of the films released in the United States during 1907 were American-made. The other two-thirds were European. Of this group, Pathé Frères was easily the most important, being responsible for over a third of the films shown on American screens. Its films enjoyed a certain mystique: as one Coney Island exhibitor remarked in May 1906, "We rather prefer the foreign films ourselves, especially the Pathé. They're fine." Pathé was known for a wide variety of subjects: elaborately hand-colored scenes, outrageous chase comedies like THE POLICEMAN'S LITTLE RUN (January 1907), violent stories of crime like THE FEMALE SPY (December 1906), historical dramas like VENETIAN TRAGEDY (December 1906), and some social dramas and actualities. (With a few exceptions, these films were between 200 feet and 600 feet long with 400 feet being typical.)[51]

Pathé was operating on a much larger scale than any contemporary American concern, and the level of organization and planning was commensurate. Thus the Coney Island showman justified his admiration for Pathé films by explaining:

> That company you know is big. They have a capacity of 2,500,000 francs. Over in France they have no less than four theatres to pose their shows for filmmaking, and a huge open-air amphitheatre besides. They keep permanently a regular company of professionals to rehearse the shows they get up (*Film Index*, 19 May 1906, p. 6).

Thus by mid 1906 the French company had already introduced such key aspects of the studio system as a stock company of actors and multiple production units, both of which did not become common in the United States for at least another two years. Pathé had offices in London, Berlin, Vienna, Milan, Moscow, Barcelona, and Shanghai, as well as New York. By October 1906 it was exporting as many as twelve pictures a week and seventy-five copies of each film to the United States. By year's end it released at least one new film each day. Pathé's position as a foreign company with international markets made it less dependent upon the outcome of litigation in the United States. Nonetheless, this country was a crucial outlet for its goods. As Charles Pathé recalled, "The American market by itself amortised the costs, however modest, of our negatives. We sold at least as many in the rest of our offices. There were then fourteen. The columns of American receipts represented a net profit or nearly so."[52]

Méliès retained its American offices but, in contrast to Pathé, faced increasing difficulties. Problems with anachronistic subject matter were augmented by the theft of many original negatives, including JOAN OF ARC and A TRIP TO THE MOON, from his New York office on 19 May 1907.[53]

George Kleine emerged as the leading American agent for European producers. After severing ties with Biograph at the end of 1906, Gaumont immediately associated itself with Kleine, and when the Vitagraph-Urban alliance broke down in early 1907, he began representing both the Charles Urban Trading Company and Urban-Eclipse. Representing Théo Pathé as well, Kleine could list 117 new subjects, totaling more than 45,000 feet, for the first four months of 1907. After enjoying successful European buying trips, the Miles brothers opened London and Paris offices in the spring of 1907 "to handle the exclusive American trade—for leading Foreign Makers." Herbert Miles, meanwhile, claimed to have secured the agencies for roughly eighteen foreign companies, among them the Danish firm Nordisk; their representation of these firms, however, was of short duration. Lubin, Charles Dressler & Company, and Williams, Brown & Earle likewise became American agents for one or more European concerns, but with the exception of Kleine's ties to Gaumont and Urban, the match of American agents with European producers usually proved unsatisfactory for one or both parties, and alliances shifted frequently.[54]

European producers were generally much more dependent on international markets than their American counterparts—not just the United States but Europe and to a lesser extent South America and the Far East. Since cinema enjoyed increasing popularity in Europe but lacked the dynamic expansion and the reorganization of exhibition practices that characterized the American nickelodeon boom, production may have offered European entrepreneurs more desirable opportunities for expansion than in the United States. Because of this dependence on foreign markets, however, European producers had to take a more cautious approach toward the ephemera of their local national culture than did most of their American counterparts. Imports generally avoided titles or reduced them to a bare minimum. Pathé films occasionally had intertitles, which the French concern was equipped to provide in most European languages. Like Vitagraph in the United States, the Europeans looked toward creating a more international, nonspecific popular culture that relied on genres much more than on particular antecedents.

During the first two years of the nickelodeon boom, several well-established American producers found it difficult to exploit the intense demand for new pictures by significantly expanding their output. Taking advantage of this failure, their European counterparts found the United States to be a ready market for foreign films. Nevertheless, American filmmakers, working within the framework of a firmly developed representational system, turned out an impressive array of pictures. Vitagraph's AUTOMOBILE THIEVES, Edison's THE "TEDDY" BEARS, Biograph's TERRIBLE TED, and Lubin's THE SECRET OF DEATH VALLEY make us regret the loss of so many films from this period all the more.

15

Concluding Remarks

*B*y the fall of 1907, American companies were beginning the rapid expansion of film production that would continue throughout the period covered by Eileen Bowser in volume 2 of this series. Yet to be successful, or even possible, this increase required a radical reorganization of film production based on hierarchy and specialization—something that Pathé and Vitagraph were just beginning to institute. These changes quickly annihilated existing methods of representation and transformed established ways of audience reception. As Bowser shows in *The Transformation of Cinema,* this process of reorganization was not simple. Only hints of such innovations can be seen at the very end of this period, in such films as Vitagraph's THE BOY, THE BUST, AND THE BATH and Pathé's THE DOINGS OF A POODLE (1907). Their linear organization of shots, once well established, would provide audiences with a new framework for understanding and appreciation at the same time as it created opportunities for new cinematic techniques such as parallel editing. The changes in quantity and quality of production thus brought to a close the period in film history that has been labeled "early cinema" and soon pushed many prominent pre-1907 filmmakers, such as Wallace McCutcheon and Georges Méliès, to the periphery of the industry. The next volume shows how the presentationalism and syncretism of early cinema were curtailed and dominated by new assumptions about the "well-made" film. In the process a new, proto-Hollywood system of representation emerged.

The early years of American cinema have often been treated as a romance in which a few people with keen insight saw the future of motion pictures, struggled for a time, and finally prospered. In an industry that enjoyed extraordinary growth, such a perception is not without basis. Nonetheless, the industry's growth was erratic and unpredictable; many shared the same vision of cinema's future, yet some of them failed. In this respect, Woodville Latham, William Paley, and a few others whose careers have been chronicled in these pages can stand for the many who were less talented, less well situated, or less lucky and as a result faced continual struggles simply to survive. Nor should it be forgotten that a whole class of people working in the industry, the motion-picture operators, experienced the debasing of their work and the daily grind of sweltering nickelodeon projection booths.

Yet the history of cinema should not be recounted as a tragedy either. As Miriam Hansen notes, a whole series of changes, dislocations, and contradictions within cinema created new opportunities to affirm or to challenge the dominant ideology and power relations within the nation's social, political, and cultural realms.[1] Creative personnel who had been marginalized (and in some respects radicalized) by other cultural practices found new freedom in this quickly transforming domain. Those who entered the motion-picture industry often did so because they were stuck at the periphery of related fields or because they had failed outright in some other business. G. M. Anderson, an actor relegated to minor theatrical troupes touring the nation's small-town opera houses, saw films as an alternative to life at the margins. Sigmund Lubin, a modestly successful optician and supplier of photographic goods who had suffered bankruptcy, was also ready to exploit an innovative product in his field. Edwin S. Porter, who had gone bankrupt in the early 1890s and so had abandoned the hope of owning his own small-town business, entered the navy and eventually moved to New York to find work in the field of electricity. For them, cinema represented a break from the status quo. And while this break did not occur systematically in all areas of their thought and action, neither was it an isolated phenomenon. A few, such as Lyman H. Howe, D. W. Robertson, Dwight Elmendorf, and Burton Holmes, projected relatively conservative public personas in their efforts to woo particular groups. But the vast majority of the motion-picture industry's first generation looked elsewhere for patrons and eagerly contributed to the dynamism of America's popular culture in all its contradictory convictions.

The motion-picture industry exemplified a general trend toward larger commercial units and a hierarchical structure. Yet such conservative trends were often contradicted or reversed, at least in the near term. Despite all his efforts in the courts and through commercial means, Thomas Edison was never able to completely rout the independents who sprang up around him. By the late 1910s, the Edison and Biograph companies would be out of the motion-picture business altogether. Ironically, the very dynamics of change that favored consolidation and rationalization frequently worked against those in a dominant position. Change was commonly introduced by those companies or individuals who were at a competitive disadvantage. Lubin was the first 35-mm producer to find a permanent outlet in vaudeville, while the Edison organization, via the Kinetograph Company, was the last. Vitagraph, with its reputation as an exhibitor, was the last to become a renter, while these older rental firms generally gave way to a new group of Young Turks. Opportunities to succeed or fail abounded: many individuals and firms did one, and then the other. The rapid reorganization of cinema's methods of production was part of a profound transformation of American life in which the positive and negative aspects were inextricably intertwined.

Although the period surveyed here concludes just as motion pictures were becoming a new form of mass communication, it should be clear that screen practice even during this early era profoundly altered American life. Even though cinema continued a presentational framework evident in screen and related cultural practices, it also strengthened contradicting impulses that eventually found expression in the seamless realism of Griffith. Projected motion pictures redefined the horizon of expectations for realism and eventually for intimacy and spectacle. They had not only an immediate impact but a cumulative one that echoed throughout Western culture, affecting a wide range of forms and representational systems.

By 1897 the moving image was already transforming the world of sport, turning it into a big business. Yet instead of simply expanding and affirming male homosocial amusement, fight films sometimes (but not always) had the opposite effect, giving women access to many aspects of that world. Likewise, while many films assumed and overtly supported a male-privileged society, their intent was frequently subverted by unexpected conditions of production or reception. The influx of theatrical personnel toward the end of the period, as well as the new audience created by the nickelodeons, thus set the stage for a pro-suffrage cinema in the 1910s. The filmmakers may have intended to bolster the privileged world of white, middle-class males, but in seeking to secure their own place within that world, they actually changed it.

Early cinema in America displayed surprising ideological diversity, even though the worldviews it expressed were centered around clusters of middle-class belief. Actualities and documentary programs often offered an overtly conservative agenda, with Lyman Howe's cinema of reassurance exemplary in this respect. During the Spanish-American War, cinema demonstrated its effectiveness as a vehicle for political and wartime propaganda. Here, perhaps more than anywhere else, the immediate results unambiguously championed the extension of American power overseas and emphasized the responsibility of Nordic Americans to protect and then rule those seen as less skilled in (and less suited for) self-government. Certainly the marginalization of these traditionally dominant forms of screen entertainment by 1904 was seen (and properly so) as a defeat for the efforts of traditional cultural arbiters to dictate cultural and ideological tastes. The ascendency of fiction films meant that ideological domination would have to be less direct and less predictable. The methods and consequences were more mysterious and often puzzling. Yet if this new cinema worked less directly, it also worked more pervasively with the arrival of cheap film theaters—and perhaps more deeply as well. Comedies, in particular, favored more relaxed attitudes toward sex and contributed to the breakdown of Victorian values. They might have appeared to be simple moral tales wherein transgressors received just punishment, yet images and actions could have quite different effects: the shoe clerk who steals a kiss under the eyes of the chaperone may suffer a beating in THE GAY SHOE CLERK, but the pleasure of the kiss is not entirely eradicated. This 1903 film, set appropriately in a shoe store, looked toward a consumer society of mass-produced goods and greater leisure. Did it liberate the spectator from the constricting norms of the past or did it more firmly and more insidiously bring the spectator under industrial society's domination? These contradictory movements occurred simultaneously and functioned in a way that even today remains familiar.

Early cinema embraced contradictory qualities. Its technological sophistication, its initial appearance as a novelty and early association with the newspaper and vaudeville, its frequent rejection of the genteel values of nineteenth-century America, its raucous commercial life, and its rapid development as an entertainment form all associated moving pictures with the new, the modern, and the dynamic. Yet the cinema also looked back longingly at a receding, idealized past. The bad-boy and fairy-tale genres nostalgically remembered a less-regimented world. The plethora of family-centered dramas that focused on separation and reunion, at a time when migration from country to city and from Europe to the United States split up many families, reveals a cinema compensating for loss. Films such as THE MILLER'S

DAUGHTER romanticized rural life and condemned the alienation and impersonality of the city; others such as THE 100 TO ONE SHOT did the reverse. Truly, American early cinema was, as Noël Burch has said about the work of Edwin S. Porter, a two-headed Janus looking backward toward the past and forward into the future. It is the intensity and the intimacy of these contradictory phenomena that are so striking. Every backward look seemed to be accompanied by slippages and dislocations that propelled cinema forward.

New forms of communication emerging in the 1890s, notably the phonograph and moving pictures, provided Americans with unexpected sources of pleasure. This tentative shift toward a consumer culture was greatly extended with the proliferation of storefront theaters, which only a year or two before had suffered a seemingly irreversible setback owing to the success of vaudeville. The unexpected success of nickelodeons posed new challenges and offered new possibilities. Filmmakers had tended to assume that their audiences matched their own backgrounds in terms of class and culture. Before the nickelodeon era, this assumption was not literally true, but it was not inappropriate either. From the filmmakers' perspective the bad-boy films were a return to carefree days, and these comedies do seem to have been accepted on those terms. But with the nickelodeons these pictures were seen very differently—as schools of crime for American youth. Vestigial memories suddenly posed a powerful threat against the existing order when appropriated by those who had previously been all but excluded from theatrical-style entertainments.

Many American films of the early period, for instance COHEN'S FIRE SALE (Edison, 1907), often treated European ethnic groups in a demeaning fashion. Yet other films reflected the inter-ethnic nature of much film production. In 1904 the Edison motion-picture studio, operating under the WASP Edwin S. Porter, employed two Jews, a Lebanese Arab, and an Italian. This basis for production suggests a more sympathetic interpretation of some pictures than they have generally received. For example, in the short comedy COHEN'S ADVERTISING SCHEME (Edison, 1904) a Jewish businessman combines charity with shrewd business in a way that need not be seen as anti-Semitic. The differences between such films, moreover, may be productively understood if we realize that Edison's two Jewish employees had moved on to new opportunities in the intervening three years and had not been replaced. Anglo-Saxon exclusivity and nativism vied with Anglo-Saxon inclusivity and interracial collaboration for dominance. Although the polyglot nature of many motion-picture companies can sensitize us to the potential ambiguity and contradiction in their representations of diverse European ethnic groups, there can be no equivocation or excuse for the demeaning racial stereotyping of African Americans and others outside the European pale.

With the advent of the nickelodeons, moving pictures became a democratic art, at least by the standards of the day. Inside the new movie houses, particularly in the downtown areas, an Italian carpenter in need of a bath might sit in an orchestra seat next to a native-born white-collar salesman or a Jewish immigrant housewife—in short, next to anyone who shared with him a sometimes secret passion for what might flicker across the screen. The working class had unprecedented and frequent access to the pleasures of theatrical entertainment, often to the kinds of stories that had previously been available only to more well-to-do citizens. This access brought a new degree of equality, but it also brought screen narratives with middle-class and even elitest assumptions. And yet the fantasies of sex, violence, success, and death that found intensely graphic depiction on the screen seemed to take on new meaning, a different resonance, when watched by people subjected to long hours of exploitative labor, tedium, and even danger in the course of their workweek. What all this meant was just beginning to be debated, as it is debated today in more sophisticated but also sometimes more arcane form.

This study has explored the many continuities and affinities that allow us to consider pre-1907 cinema a unified period. Yet it has also emphasized the enormous changes that occurred within that time frame. Ironically, these changes were so fundamental that they have often gone unrecognized. They raise troubling issues that call for seeing motion-picture history not as the history of a product (the films) or of an industry (Hollywood and its precursors) but of a practice. Fitting the film product or the producers into this larger practice has required extensive research and a new approach. As a result, however, we can begin to understand how a simple one-shot film with no obvious narrative component can, by being placed next to another film and perhaps accompanied by narration, become part of a narrative. Something that appears to today's viewer as one thing was often, but not necessarily, seen as its opposite in its original context. This explains why the history of early cinema cannot be a history of its films alone. For it is during this early period that the gap between the surviving product and the largely forgotten practice is greatest and the most fundamental transformations of screen practice occurred. By exploring the many distinctive qualities of early motion pictures, I have sought to lay the basis of a new historical perspective for looking at subsequent cinema and even today's moving-image practices in film and video. We may even gain a greater freedom to imagine how we as filmmakers, exhibitors, teachers, students, archivists, producers, and spectators might make our cinema, our culture, and our society more open, and more constructive as we live our lives.

List of Abbreviations

FREQUENTLY CITED PERIODICALS

Clipper   *New York Clipper*
Film Index   *Views and Film Index*
Mail and Express   *New York Mail and Express*
MPW   *Moving Picture World*
NYDM   *New York Dramatic Mirror*

ARCHIVAL COLLECTIONS

CLAc	Academy of Motion Picture Arts and Sciences, Margaret Herrick Library, Los Angeles
CBevA	American Film Institute, Center for Advanced Film Studies, Los Angeles
CLCM	Los Angeles County Museum of Natural History
CLU	University of California at Los Angeles
CU-BANC	University of California at Berkeley, Bancroft Library
DLC	Library of Congress, Washington, D.C.
DNA	National Archives, Washington, D.C.
ICFAR	Federal Archive and Record Center, Chicago, Ill.
ICHi	Chicago Historical Society
ICC	Cook County Clerk's Office, Chicago
IaU	University of Iowa Library, Iowa City, Ia.
MdSuFR	Washington National Record Center, Suitland, Md.
MH-BA	Harvard Business School, Baker Library, Boston
MH-TT	Harvard Theater Collection, Harvard University
NN	New York Public Library
NNHi	New-York Historical Society
NNMOMA	Museum of Modern Art, New York City
NNMus	Museum of the City of New York
NNNCC-Ar	New York County Clerk Archives, Division of Old Records
NR-GE	George Eastman House, Rochester, N.Y.
NjBaFAR	Federal Archive and Record Center, Bayonne, N.J.
NjWOE	Edison National Historic Site, West Orange, N.J.

PP	Free Library of Philadelphia
PPFAR	Federal Archive and Record Center, Philadelphia
PPS	Franklin Institute of Arts and Sciences, Philadelphia
PW-bH	Wyoming Historical and Geological Society, Wilkes-Barre, Pa.

Notes

INTRODUCTION

1. Judith Mayne, "Uncovering the Female Body," in Jay Leyda and Charles Musser, eds., *Before Hollywood: Turn-of-the-Century Films from American Archives* (New York: American Federation of the Arts, 1986), pp. 63–67.
2. Since very few women acted as exhibitors, cameramen, projectionists, and producers during this period, masculine pronouns will be applied to these categories.
3. Tom Gunning, "The Cinema of Attraction[s]," *Wide Angle* 8, no. 3–4 (1986), pp. 63–70.
4. Georges Sadoul, *Histoire générale du cinéma* (Paris: Éditions Denoël, 1948), vol. 1, p. 304.
5. Eileen Bowser, "Preparation for Brighton: The American Contribution," in Roger Holman, comp., *Cinema 1900–1906* (Brussels: Federation Internationale des Archives du Film, 1982), vol. 1, pp. 3–29.
6. Noël Burch, "Porter, or Ambivalence," *Screen* 19 (Winter 1978/1979), pp. 91–105.
7. Janet Staiger, "The Eyes Are Really the Focus," *Wide Angle* 6, no. 4 (1985), p. 15.
8. Roberta Pearson, "The Modesty of Nature: Performance in Griffith's Biographs" (Ph.D. diss., New York University, 1986).
9. Daniel Gerould, "Russian Formalist Theories of Melodrama," *Journal of American Culture* 1 (Spring 1978), p. 160.
10. *Ibid.*
11. David Bordwell, Janet Staiger, and Kristin Thompson, *The Classical Hollywood Cinema: Film Style and Mode of Production to 1960* (New York: Columbia University Press, 1985), p. 117.
12. Kathy Peiss, *Cheap Amusements: Working Women and Leisure in Turn-of-the-Century New York* (Philadelphia: Temple University Press, 1986).
13. Interested readers may consult other writings by the author for a more detailed treatment of these issues, particularly *Before the Nickelodeon: Edwin S. Porter and the Edison Manufacturing Company* (Berkeley: University of California Press, 1991).
14. Book-length treatments include Terry Ramsaye, *A Million and One Nights* (New York: Simon and Schuster, 1926); Gordon Hendricks, *The Edison Motion Picture Myth* (Berkeley: University of California Press, 1961), and *The Kinetoscope: America's First Commercially Successful Motion Picture Exhibitor* (New York: Beginnings of the American Film, 1966); David Levy, "Edwin S. Porter and the Origins of the American Narrative Film, 1894–1907" (Ph.D. diss., McGill University, 1983); Musser, *Before the Nickelodeon.*
15. Gordon Hendricks, *Beginnings of the Biograph* (New York: Beginnings of the American Film, 1964); Paul Spehr, "Filmmaking at the American Mutoscope and Biograph Company, 1900–1906," *Quarterly Journal of the Library of Congress* 37 (Summer–Fall 1980), pp. 413–421.
16. Albert E. Smith with Phil A. Koury, *Two Reels and a Crank* (Garden City, N.Y.: Doubleday, 1952); Anthony Slide, *The Big V: A History of the Vitagraph Company* (Metuchen, N.J.: Scarecrow Press, 1976); Charles Musser, "American Vitagraph: 1897–1901," *Cinema Journal* 22 (Spring 1983), pp. 4–46; Jon Gartenberg, "Vitagraph Before Griffith: Forging Ahead in the Nickelodeon Era," *Studies in Visual Communication* 10 (Fall 1984), pp. 7–23; Kalton C. Lahue, ed., *Motion Picture Pioneer: The Selig Polyscope Company* (South Brunswick, N.J.: A. S. Barnes, 1973); Joseph P. Eckhardt and Linda Kowall, *Peddler of Dreams: Siegmund Lubin and the Creation of the Motion Picture Industry, 1896–1916* (Philadelphia: National Museum of American Jewish History, 1984). Lubin usually simplified his first name to "Sigmund," the spelling that will be used here.

17. Robert Sklar, *Movie-Made America* (New York: Random House, 1975), p. 18.

18. Robert C. Allen, "Contra the Chaser Theory," in John Fell, ed., *Film Before Griffith* (Berkeley: University of California Press, 1983), pp. 162–175.

19. Musser, *Before the Nickelodeon;* "American Vitagraph, 1897–1901"; and, with Carol Nelson, *High-Class Moving Pictures: Lyman H. Howe and the Forgotten Era of Traveling Exhibition* (Princeton: Princeton University Press, 1991).

CHAPTER 1. Toward a History of Screen Practice

1. Jean-Louis Comolli, "Technique and Ideology: Camera, Perspective, Depth of Field," in *Film Reader* 2 (Evanston, Ill.: Northwestern University Press, 1977), pp. 128–140.

2. Cecil M. Hepworth, "The Electric Light in the Optical Lantern," *Optical Magic Lantern Journal,* 7 November 1896, p. 184; C. Francis Jenkins, *Animated Pictures* (Washington, D.C.: By the author, 1898), p. 100; Henry V. Hopwood, *Living Pictures: Their History, Photoduplication, and Practical Working* (London: Optician and Photographic Traces Review, 1899), p. 188.

3. Jacques Deslandes, with the collaboration of Jacques Richard, *Histoire comparée du cinéma,* 2 vols. (Brussels: Casterman, 1966–1968); Kenneth Macgowan, *Behind the Screen* (New York: Delacorte Press, 1965).

4. Robert Grau, *Theatre of Science* (New York: Broadway, 1914); A. Nicholas Vardac, *Stage to Screen: Theatrical Methods from Garrick to Griffith* (Cambridge: Harvard University Press, 1949); John Fell, *Film and the Narrative Tradition* (Norman: University of Oklahoma Press, 1974); Erwin Panofsky, "Style and Medium in the Moving Pictures," in Daniel Talbot, ed., *Film: An Anthology* (New York: Simon and Schuster, 1959), pp. 15–32; Robert C. Allen, *Vaudeville and Film, 1895–1915: A Study in Media Interaction* (New York: Arno Press Dissertation Series, 1980).

5. Michael Chanan, *The Dream That Kicks: The Prehistory and Early Years of Cinema in Britain* (London: Routledge and Kegan Paul, 1980).

6. Olive Cook, *Movement in Two Dimensions* (London: Hutchinson, 1963), p. 82.

7. Athanasius Kircher, *Ars magna lucis et umbrae* (Rome, 1646; 2d rev. ed, Amsterdam, 1671). All translations are made from the revised edition of 1671, which included new sections with the old ones. Translations are by Barbara Hurwitz.

8. Christopher Hill, *The Pelican Economic History of England: Reformation to Industrial Revolution* (London: Weidenfeld and Nicolson, 1967; reprint, Harmondsworth and Baltimore, Penguin Books, 1969), pp. 190–210.

9. H. Mark Gosser, "Kircher and the Lanterna Magica—A Re-examination," *Journal of the Society of Motion Picture and Television Engineers* 90 (October 1981), pp. 972–978.

10. Kircher, *Ars magna,* pp. 768–770; Gosser, "Kircher and the Lanterna Magica," p. 972.

11. Kircher's illustrations of the magic lantern in his 1671 edition have the lens incorrectly placed between the light source and the glass slides; in addition, the slides are not flipped. Such shortcomings suggest that his firsthand knowledge was extremely limited and perhaps nonexistent. Given that this edition was printed in Amsterdam, not Rome (where Kircher lived), however, the errors may be mistakes of the engraver.

12. Deslandes and Richard, *Histoire comparée du cinéma,* vol. 2, pp. 101–211.

13. Cook, *Movement in Two Dimensions,* p. 82; William Hone, *Ancient Mysteries Described* (London, 1823), pp. 230–231 quoted in Richard D. Altick, *The Shows of London* (Cambridge: Harvard University Press, 1978), p. 233. Xenophon Theodore Barber, "Evenings of Wonders: A History of the Magic Lantern Show in America" (Ph.D. diss., New York University, 1992), chap. 1.

14. É[tienne] G[aspar] [Robert] Robertson, *Mémoires récréatifs, scientifiques et anecdotiques,* vol. 1 (Paris: Chez l'auteur et Librarie de Wurtz, 1831), pp. 278–279.

15. Robertson thus prefigured many of Christian Metz's observations on "the reality effect." See Christian Metz, "On the Impression of Reality in Cinema," in *Film Language* (New York: Oxford University Press, 1974), pp. 3–15.

16. Their claim about London was probably true, for the first half of this audacious partnership must have been Jack Bologna, who provided Londoners with a variety of entertainments (Altick, *The Shows of London,* pp. 79–80, 217–219).

17. Charles Joseph Pecor, *The Magician and the American Stage* (Washington, D.C.: Emerson and West, 1977), pp. 167–168. Pecor's excellent work on early phantasmagoria exhibitions provides the basis for this section.

18. *Boston Gazette,* 22 December 1806, p. 3; 29 December 1806, p. 3.

19. *Boston Gazette,* 1 January 1807, p. 2.

20. *Boston Gazette*, 15 December 1806, p. 3; "Fire!" *ibid.*, 19 January 1807, p. 2.

21. Franz Paul Liesegang, *Dates and Sources: A Contribution to the History of the Art of Projection and of Cinematography* (London: The Magic Lantern Society of Great Britain, 1986), p. 20. Richard Altick (*The Shows of London*, p. 219) dates this development between 1807 and 1818.

22. *New York Evening Post*, 15 March 1826.

23. *New York Evening Post*, 7 July 1825; 6 September 1826; 9 October 1826; "E. Robertson's Exhibition," programme, courtesy of Françoise Levie.

24. Patent No. 7,458, improvement in producing photographic pictures upon transparent media, issued 25 June 1850; Louis Walton Sipley, "The Magic Lantern," *Pennsylvania Arts and Sciences* 4 (December 1939), pp. 39–43; Louis Walton Sipley, "W. and F. Langenheim—Photographers," *Pennsylvania Arts and Sciences* (193_) pp. 25–31; William Welling, *Photography in America: The Formative Years, 1839–1900* (New York: Thomas Y. Crowell, 1978), pp. 43–79.

25. F. Langenheim, broadside, 27 June 1852, cited in Sipley, "The Magic Lantern," p. 42.

26. L. J. Marcy, *The Sciopticon Manual: Explaining Marcy's New Magic Lantern and Light, Including Lantern Optics, Experiments, Photographing and Coloring Slides, Etc.*, 5th ed. (Philadelphia: Sherman, 1874), p. 52. Some other commentators suggested that the term "stereopticon" referred to the use of two lanterns so that the exhibitor could dissolve from one slide to the next. The introduction and wide acceptance of the name may well have involved multiple sources.

27. Barber, "Evenings of Wonders," chap. 2; Mayor M. B. Kalbfleisch *et al.* to John Fallon, 25 April 1863, reprinted in *Brooklyn Eagle*, 4 May 1863, p. 17; "The Stereopticon at the Atheneum," *ibid.*, 15 April 1863, p. 3; "Modern Miracles," *ibid.*, 15 April 1863, p. 3; 29 April 1863, p. 1; 15 May 1863, p. 1; 7 May 1863, p. 3.

28. *New York Daily Tribune*, 4 May 1863, p. 7.

29. *New York Daily Tribune*, 17 May 1864, p. 3; 30 May 1864, p. 3.

30. "Professor Morton's Lantern Lectures," *Magic Lantern*, August 1875, p. 14.

31. T. H. McAllister, *Catalogue and Price List of Stereopticons* (New York, 1885).

32. Sipley, "The Magic Lantern," p. 40; Terry Borton, "The Magic of America: Joseph Boggs Beale" (report on a work in progress, presented at the 1987 conference of the Magic Lantern Society of the United States and Canada, Museum of Our National Heritage, Lexington, Mass.).

33. Patent No. 77,800, improvements in magic lanterns, issued 28 April 1868, and Patent No. 92,330, improvements in magic lanterns, issued 6 July 1869; L. J. Marcy, *The Sciopticon Manual* (Philadelphia, 1871); "Sigmund Lubin," Dun and Co., Pennsylvania, vol. 163, p. 56, MH-BA.

34. "Wilson's Lantern Journeys," *The Magic Lantern*, December 1874, p. 5; "$100—Our $100 Outfit— $100," *ibid.*, October 1874, p. 14; November 1874, p. 24.

35. "C. B. Kleine Retires," *Moving Picture World*, 4 November 1910, p. 371; George Kleine, "Progress in Optical Projection in the Last Fifty Years," *Film Index* 28, May 1910, p. 10.

36. William Despard Hemphill, *Stereoscopic Illustrations of Clonmel and the Surrounding Countryside* (Dublin: William Curry, 1860).

37. See Edward Wilson, "How They Live in Egypt," *Wilson's Lantern Journeys*, vol. 3 (Philadelphia: By the author, 1874–1886), p. 215; John L. Stoddard, *John L. Stoddard's Lectures*, vol. 7 (Boston: Balch Brothers, 1897–1898), pp. 226–268.

38. Stoddard, vol. 3, pp. 120–138.

39. "Stoddard on Napoleon," *Philadelphia Record*, 25 April 1896; "The Lecture Platform," *New York Daily Tribune*, 12 December 1880, p. 2; Daniel Crane Taylor, *John L. Stoddard: Traveler, Lecturer, Litterateur* (New York: P. J. Kennedy, 1935), p. 126.

40. Genoa Caldwell, *The Man Who Photographed the World. Burton Holmes: Travelogues, 1886–1938* (New York: Harry N. Abrams, 1977); Oscar A. Depue, "My First 50 Years in Motion Pictures," *American Cinematographer*, April 1948, pp. 124–127; E. Burton Holmes, programs, 1890–1896, courtesy Burton Holmes International (BHI).

41. "Land of the Eskimos," *Brooklyn Eagle*, 14 April 1894, p. 7; "The Society of Amateur Photographers of New York," *Photographic Times*, 3 February 1888, pp. 58–59; "Flashes from the Slums," *New York Sun*, 12 February 1888, p. 10; "How the Other Half Lives: Studies Among the Tenements," *Scribner's Magazine* 6 (December 1889), pp. 643–662. Two years later Jacob Riis adapted and expanded his illustrated lectures to produce the classic *How the Other Half Lives* (New York: Charles Scribner's Sons, 1890). See also Ferenc M. Szasz and Ralph F. Bogardus, "The Camera and the American Social Conscience: The Documentary Photography of Jacob Riis," *New York History* 60 (October 1974), pp. 409–436; and Peter Hales, *Silver Cities: The Photography of American Urbanization, 1839–1915* (Philadelphia: Temple University Press, 1984).

42. Ramsaye, *A Million and One Nights*, pp. 91–103.

43. Alan Trachtenberg, *The Incorporation of America: Culture and Society in the Gilded Age* (New York: Hill and Wang, 1982), pp. 107–112.

44. *Orange* (N.J.) *Chronicle*, 27 October 1894, p. 6.

45. "Harry Knapp's Excellent Collection of Old Theatre Programs," *Billboard*, 1 June 1907, p. 20; *Boston Herald*, 9 October 1894, p. 9; 29 October 1895, p. 7; "The Illustrated Song Is Now the Latest Novelty of the Stage," *San Francisco Examiner*, 7 June 1896, p. 33. Joseph E. Howard and Ida Emerson were soon considered "the best in the business" of giving "illustrated songs" and then went on to become "the first artists to apply motion pictures to the illustration of popular songs" ("Bijou Theatre," *Washington Evening Star*, 22 December 1900, p. 22).

46. L. J. Marcy, *Priced Catalogue of Sciopticon Apparatus and Magic Lantern Slides*, 6th ed. (Philadelphia, *ca.* 1878), p. 32.

47. C. W. Ceram, *Archeology of the Cinema* (New York: Harcourt, Brace, and World, 1965), p. 71.

48. Thomas Coulson, "Philadelphia and the Development of the Motion Picture," *Journal of the Franklin Institute* 262 (July 1956), pp. 1–16.

49. Welling, *Photography in America*, p. 151. In fact, Sir Charles Wheatstone had already sought to integrate the illusions of depth and movement with a kine-viewing device in 1852.

50. Patent No. 93,594, optical instrument, issued 10 August 1869; Academy of Music program, 5 February 1870, Merritt Crawford Collection, NNMOMA; Heyl Papers, Franklin Institute, quoted in Coulson, "Philadelphia and the Development of the Motion Picture," p. 8. The Heyl papers were unfortunately unavailable for study while this volume was being written.

51. Ceram, *Archeology of the Cinema*, p. 118.

52. Full-scale studies on Muybridge include: Robert Bartlett Haas, *Muybridge, Man in Motion* (Berkeley: University of California Press, 1976); Gordon Hendricks, *Eadweard Muybridge: The Father of the Motion Picture* (New York: Grossman, 1975); Anita V. Mozley, *Eadweard Muybridge: The Stanford Years* (Palo Alto: Stanford University, Department of Art, 1972). See also Thom Andersen's documentary film *Eadweard Muybridge, Zoopraxographer* (1975).

53. Patent No. 212,865, improvement in the method and apparatus for photographing objects in motion, filed 27 June 1878, issued 4 March 1879. Whatever Isaacs' contribution, it was Muybridge who took out the patent.

54. Geoffrey Bell, *The Golden Gate and the Silver Screen* (Cranbury, N.J.: Associated University Presses, 1984), pp. 17–37.

55. "Muybridge's Photographs," *Daily Alta California*, 9 July 1878, p. 2.

56. "Moving Shadows," *San Francisco Chronicle*, 5 May 1880, p. 3; "Muybridge's Magic Lantern Zoetrope," *San Francisco Alta*, 5 May 1880, p. 2. The basic text for these lectures is reprinted as an appendix in Hendricks, *Eadweard Muybridge*, pp. 234–242.

57. *Orange* (N.J.) *Chronicle*, 3 March 1888, p. 5.

CHAPTER 2. Thomas Edison and the Amusement World

1. Matthew Josephson, *Edison* (New York: McGraw-Hill, 1959), pp. 131–155; Robert Conot, *A Streak of Luck* (New York: Seaview Books, 1979). The Thomas A. Edison Papers and scholars associated with that organization are currently embarked on a far-reaching reevaluation of Edison's life, inventions, and business practices. The early results of this include Thomas E. Jeffreys *et al.*, *Thomas A. Edison Papers: A Selective Microfilm Edition*, part I, *1850–1878*, and part II *1878–1886* (Frederick, Md.: Unversity Publications of America, 1985); and Reese Jenkins *et al.*, *The Papers of Thomas A. Edison*, vol. 1, *The Making of an Inventor, February 1847–June 1873* (Baltimore: Johns Hopkins University Press, 1989).

2. "Grand Exhibition of Nature & Art," broadside [mid to late 1840s], Ohio Historical Society; "Church Entertainments," 22 July 1879, *Thomas A. Edison Papers: A Selective Microfilm Edition* (hereafter *TAEM*), 25:294. See also Daniel J. Czitrom, *Media and the American Mind: From Morse to McLuhan* (Chapel Hill: University of North Carolina Press, 1982), pp. 6–7.

3. Neil Harris, *Humbug: The Art of P. T. Barnum* (Boston: Little Brown, 1973), pp. 57, 72–89, 108, 213, 290.

4. Reese V. Jenkins, "Words, Images, Artifacts, and Sound: Documents for the History of Technology," *British Journal of History and Science* 20 (January 1987), pp. 39–56.

5. "The Talking Phonograph," *Scientific American*, 22 December 1877, p. 384.

6. Thomas Edison, Gardner [*sic*] G. Hubbard, G. L. Bradley *et al.*, contract, 30 January 1878, *TAEM*,

19:2–16; Edison Speaking Phonograph, certificate of incorporation, 24 April 1878, *TAEM*, 19:62; Gardiner G. Hubbard to Thomas Edison, 16 April 1878, *TAEM*, 19:56; James Redpath to Thomas Edison, 6 June 1878, *TAEM*, 19:81; *Cape Ann Advertiser*, 24 May 1878, *TAEM*, 25:214; see also Roland Gelatt, *The Fabulous Phonograph, 1877–1977*, 2d, rev. ed. (New York: Collier Books, 1977), pp. 17–32.

7. Conot, *A Streak of Luck*, pp. 264–265.

8. Contract, Thomas A. Edison and Jesse Lippincott, 28 June 1888, NjWOE; *Ottawa* (Ontario) *Journal*, 19 October 1891, clipping, NjWOE.

9. "The Phonograph," *Ottawa* (Ontario) *Journal*, 19 October 1891, clipping, NjWOE; See also Edward Thompson to Thomas Edison, 11 January 1889, NjWOE. Thompson estimated that the phonograph would save him at least $3 per day.

10. *Boston Transcript*, 1 February 1889, and other clippings, NjWOE; James B. Metcalf, chairman of the Metropolitan Phonograph Company, to Jesse Lippincott, 1 August 1889; *Proceedings of the 1890 Convention of Local Phonograph Companies of the United States Held at Chicago, May 28 and 29, 1890* (Milwaukee: Phonograph Printing Company, 1890); L. Halsley Williams to Thomas Edison, 18 June 1889, NjWOE; *Proceedings of the Second Annual Convention of Local Phonograph Companies of the United States*, 16–18 June 1891, pp. 53, 60.

11. *Allentown Daily City Item*, 2 April 1890, HPS.

12. *Orange Chronicle*, 23 February 1889, p. 4; M. C. Sullivan, "How to Give Concert Exhibitions of the Phonograph," *Phonogram*, February 1893, pp. 324–325; *Allentown Chronicle and News*, 27 November 1891, Howe Phonograph Scrapbook, courtesy of Lyman Howe III.

13. "A Nickel Brings the Phonograph," *New York Times*, 9 February 1890, p. 2; *Richmond* (Va.) *State*, 29 August 1890, clipping, NjWOE; *Proceedings of Second Annual Convention*, p. 56.

14. "The Exhibition Parlors of the Ohio Phonograph Company," *Phonogram*, November–December 1891, p. 248; *Proceedings of Second Annual Convention*, pp. 52–53.

15. *Lansing* (Mich.) *Journal*, 18 January 1895, NjWOE.

16. Lyman H. Howe, contract form, early 1890s, PW-bH; *Proceedings of Second Annual Convention*, p. 53.

17. Gordon Hendricks, *The Edison Motion Picture Myth*, p. 12.

18. Thomas Edison, Caveat 110, 8 October 1888, filed 17 October 1888, patent records, NjWOE; Reese V. Jenkins, "Elements of Style: Continuities in Edison's Thinking," *Annals of the New York Academy of Sciences*, 424 (1984), pp. 149–162; Thomas Edison, Caveat 114, 3 February 1889, filed 25 March 1889; Caveat 116, 20 May 1889, filed 5 August 1889, patent records, NjWOE. These caveats, of course, may have reflected suggestions made by Edison's associates and employees, including W. K. L. Dickson. Edison's four motion-picture caveats are transcribed in Hendricks, *The Edison Motion Picture Myth*, pp. 158–163, but without the accompanying illustrations.

19. Edison Laboratory, General Ledger No. 5, January 1888–June 1890, p. 806, Edison Caveat 114; Complainant's Exhibit, "Work on Kinetoscope Experiment from February 1, 1889 to February 1, 1890," *Thomas Edison* v. *American Mutoscope Company and Benjamin Franklin Keith*, No. 6928, Circuit Court, Southern District of New York, filed 13 May 1898, NjBAR.

20. Antonia and W. K. L. Dickson, *The Life and Inventions of Thomas Alva Edison* (New York: Thomas Y. Crowell, 1894), pp. 303–304.

21. Complainant's exhibit, "Work on Photograph Building," *Edison* v. *American Mutoscope Co.* This was authorized by Charles Batchelor, a trusted Edison associate who ran the laboratory in Edison's absence.

22. Here Hendricks' anti-Edison skepticism leads him to dismiss almost all Edison motion-picture experiments prior to late 1890 in a way that is hard to justify.

23. Hendricks convincingly dates the photographic sheets from November 1890, when the likely subject, G. Sacco Albanese, was briefly employed for kinetoscope experiments.

24. Thomas Edison, Caveat 117, 2 November 1889, filed 16 December 1889, NjWOE.

25. Dickson, *The Life and Inventions of Thomas Alva Edison*, p. 305; Hendricks, *The Edison Motion Picture Myth*, pp. 84–86.

26. Notes in Legal Files, Box 71, NjWOE; André Millard, *Edison and the Business of Innovation* (Baltimore: Johns Hopkins University Press, 1990), chap. 7.

27. Dickson offers this chronology and Hendricks (pp. 99–100) follows it. Why Dickson and Heise persisted with the cylinder approach is puzzling. Perhaps they were trying to avoid duplicating Marey's methods or perhaps Edison was so committed to parallels with the phonograph that he refused to give them up. Yet even here the historical record is not entirely clear. Dickson ordered six

strips of ¾-inch film, each fifty-four feet long. While he claimed these were for astronomical experiments, they may well have been used then or subsequently for motion-picture experiments (Dickson to Eastman Co., 21 November 1889, reprinted in *American Cinematographer*, July 1989, p. 59).

28. William Friese-Greene to Thomas A. Edison, 18 March 1890, NjWOE.

29. "Mr. Edison's New Invention in Electrical Photography," *Phonogram*, May 1891, pp. 122–123. This visit by the clubwomen was not mentioned in any of the Orange newspapers and the precise date remains somewhat speculative ("Notable Gathering of Women," *Orange Journal*, 23 May 1891, p. 7).

30. "The Kinetograph," *New York Sun*, 28 May 1891, p. 2.

31. Notes in legal files, Box 71, NjWOE.

32. Terry Ramsaye (*A Million and One Nights*, pp. 74–79) perpetuates the myth of Edison's shortsighted decision. Instead, one might argue that his decision to not pursue overseas patents was astute (at least in the long run), since patent defeats overseas would have inevitably impacted on decisions made in the courts at home.

33. W. K. L. Dickson to Eastman Dry Plate and Film Co., 2 November 1891; 7 December 1891; 13 January 1892; W. K. L. Dickson to Messers Zeiss, 29 December 1891 and 4 January 1892; W. K. L. Dickson to Columbia Rubber Co., 12 November 1891 (all NjWOE).

34. "The Kinetograph," *Phonogram*, October 1892, pp. 217–218

35. Alfred O. Tate to Thomas A. Edison, 31 October 1892, NjWOE; John F. Randolph, testimony, 3 February 1900, *Edison* v. *American Mutoscope Co.*; "First Public Exhibition of Edison's Kinetograph," *Scientific American*, 20 May 1893, 310.

36. The presence or absence of the kinetoscope at the fair has been a topic of considerable historical controversy. Terry Ramsaye claimed, quoting Norman Raff, that no Edison peephole kinetoscope was shown at the Columbian Exposition (*A Million and One Nights*, p. 85). Gordon Hendricks suggests that at least one machine—the model shown at the Brooklyn Institute—was part of the Edison phonograph exhibit (*The Kinetoscope*, pp. 40–45). A careful review of the available evidence indicates that Ramsaye was correct.

37. "Mr. Edison Wants to Fly," *Albany* (N.Y.) *Telegram*, 3 November 1893, clipping (incorrectly filed under "1895 Motion Pictures"), NjWOE.

38. J. F. Randolph, testimony, 3 February 1900, *Edison* v. *American Mutoscope Co.*

39. *New York World*, 18 March 1894, p. 21; "Edison and the Kinetoscope," *Photographic Times*, 6 April 1894, pp 209–212; "Edison's Kinetoscope Perfected," *Orange* (N.J.) *Journal*, 8 March 1894, p. 5.

40. Raff & Gammon, *Price List of Films*, n.d. [*ca.* late June 1895], in MH-BA and Charles Musser *et al.*, *Motion Picture Catalogs by American Producers and Distributors, 1894–1908: A Microfilm Edition* (Frederick, Md.: University Publications of America, 1985), frames A005–A007; *Brooklyn Citizen*, 16 August 1894, cited in Hendricks, *The Kinetoscope*, p. 113; Kinetoscope Company, *Bulletin* no. 2, January 1895, MH-BA. All catalogs cited in this volume can be found in the Musser *et al.* microfilm edition.

41. Hendricks, *The Kinetoscope*, pp. 78–79.

42. "Signor Caicedo's Fine Exhibition," *Orange Chronicle*, 28 July 1894, p. 5.

43. As serious filmmaking commenced, the task of finding performers and the expense of taking films was assigned to Edison's kinetoscope sales agents rather than the Edison Company itself. These agents effectively owned the negatives, which remained at the laboratory under Edison control. By September 1894 identifying the owner of these subjects was becoming a problem; as a result, small signs were placed in the scenes being photographed. "R" indicated a film was produced by Raff & Gammon, "MB" by Maguire & Baucus. In early 1895 the "MB" was apparently replaced by a "C," standing for the Continental Commerce Company, which was owned by Maguire and Baucus.

44. A. O. Tate to Thomas Edison, 13 February 1894, NjWOE; Randolph, testimony, *Edison* v. *American Mutoscope Co.*; Alfred O. Tate, *Edison's Open Door* (New York: Dutton, 1938).

45. Kinetoscope Company, financial statement, 1 April 1895, in Ramsaye, *A Million and One Nights*, pp. 836–837.

46. Edison Manufacturing Company, Cash Book No. 2, pp. 92, 102, 108, 110, 116 and 118; "Kinetoscope at Eagle Rock," *Orange Journal*, 12 July 1894, p. 7; Thomas A. Edison, Norman Raff, Frank Gammon, agreement, 18 August 1894, NjWOE; Raff & Gammon invoices, vol. 1., MH-BA.

47. Edison Manufacturing Company, Cash Book No. 2, entry for 11 July 1894, received $1,275.00; Thomas Edison to Maguire & Baucus, 3 September 1894, NjWOE; Continental Commerce Company, certificate of incorporation, filed 10 September 1894, NNNCC-Ar; F. Z. Maguire to Thomas A. Edison, 9 November 1894, NjWOE.

48. Otway Latham to William Gilmore, 16 May 1894, NjWOE.

49. Enoch J. Rector to Edison Manufacturing Company, 30 July 1894, NjWOE; Edison Manufacturing Company, Cash Book No. 2, entry for 6, 16 and 20 August 1894, pp. 110, 114, 116; Thomas A. Edison to Otway Latham, 18 August 1894, NjWOE.

50. *New York Herald*, 8 September 1894, p. 11; *Phonoscope*, March 1898, p. 9; "Inventor Edison and the Grand Jury," *New York Times*, 14 September 1894, p. 9; Hendricks, *The Kinetoscope*, pp. 108–109.

51. Otway Latham to William Gilmore, 14 and 24 September 1894, NjWOE; letterhead, Kinetoscope Exhibition Company, NjWOE; *Phonoscope*, March 1898, p. 9.

52. Edison Manufacturing Company, Cash Book No. 2, entries for November 1893–1 March 1895, NjWOE. The sales figures for the Kinetoscope Company include purchases by the Holland brothers and the International Novelty Company for their own use. Unaccounted sales were those initially made to unaffiliated individuals. Kinetoscope Company, financial statement, 1 April 1895, in Ramsaye, *A Million and One Nights*, p. 836. Operating expenses were $7,282.37, yielding a profit of $21,984.25. Other substantial revenues came from Kinetoscope Company parlors. Edison Manufacturing Company, statement of profit and loss, NjWOE.

53. Hendricks, *The Kinetoscope*, p. 132; Alfred Clark, oral history, NjWOE. These reverted to tried and true scenes of dancing girls (e.g. UMBRELLA DANCE).

54. James H. White, deposition, 9 February 1900, Edison p. 165.

55. Raff to Dickson, 20 January 1896, 3:204, MH-BA.

56. James H. White, testimony, 9 February 1900; Charles Webster, testimony, 9 February 1900, *Edison v. American Mutoscope Co.*

CHAPTER 3. Projecting Motion Pictures: Invention and Innovation

1. Macgowan, *Behind the Screen*, pp. 80–81; John Barnes, *The Beginnings of the Cinema in England* (London: David and Charles, 1976), p. 41.

2. Woodville Latham, testimony, 4 December 1897, *Woodville Latham v. Thomas Armat*, Patent Appeal Docket No. 153, printed record, p. 8. The case was originally begun as *Thomas Armat v. Herman Casler v. Edward H. Amet v. Woodville Latham*, Patent Interference No. 18,461. Patent-interference cases were created by the U.S. Patent office when two or more inventors made competing or overlapping claims. The resulting process ascertained which inventor had priority to which claims so that the appropriate patents could then be issued. Much of the testimony for this case was subsequently reprinted in *Motion Picture Patents Company v. Independent Moving Picture Company*, No. 5–157, District Court, Southern District of New York, filed 10 February 1910, NjBAR. For biographies of the Lathams see Hendricks, *The Kinetoscope*, pp. 147–153 and Woodville Latham, testimony, 4 December 1897, *Latham v. Armat*, pp. 20–21.

3. Otway Latham, testimony, 13 December 1897, *Latham v. Armat*.

4. Merritt Crawford, biography of Eugène Lauste, unpublished manuscript, Merritt Crawford Collection, NNMOMA.

5. Woodville Latham, testimony, p. 71.

6. Latham, pp. 13, 72; Eugène Lauste, testimony, 29 April 1898, *Latham v. Armat*.

7. Woodville Latham, testimony, p. 19; Lauste, testimony.

8. Woodville Latham, testimony, pp. 75–76.

9. *Brooklyn Eagle*, 8 May 1895, p. 4. Although tentatively called the pantoptikon in the *New York Sun* (22 April 1895, p. 2), the machine had not been given an official name by the time of the filming on 4 May.

10. Ramsaye, *A Million and One Nights*, p. 136, gives the address as 153 Broadway, a minor inaccuracy perpetuated by others. The correct address is given in the patent-interference testimonies of Woodville and Otway Latham (pp. 20, 149).

11. Otway Latham, testimony, p. 147.

12. Ramsaye, *A Million and One Nights*, pp. 182–183; *Chicago Inter-Ocean*, 25 August 1895, p. 33, and 15 September 1895, p. 37. Ramsaye incorrectly implies that the eidoloscope was opening in many major cities, including Boston, at the time of the Chicago opening. This is not supported by the testimony in Patent Interference No. 18,461 nor by searches through the *Boston Herald* and other newspapers of the period.

13. Ramsaye, *A Million and One Nights*, pp. 183–184; *Philadephia Record*, 22 December 1895, p. 10. George Pratt, "Firsting the Firsts," in Marshall Deutelbaum, ed., *"Image" on the Art and Evolution of the Film* (New York: Dover, 1979), pp. 20–22, provides a useful look at the eidoloscope and important information on New York State exhibitions.

14. C. Francis Jenkins and J. P. Freeman, contract, 17 January 1893, PPS; "Some Cooking Recipes," *Washington Star*, 15 November 1894, p. 9.
15. Thomas Armat, testimony, 10 August 1911, *Motion Picture Patents Company* v. *Independent Moving Picture Company*, No. 5–167, District Court, Southern District of New York, 3 vols. 1:544, 546, 600; Armat-Jenkins Agreement, 25 March 1895, *Animated Projecting Company* v. *American Mutoscope Company and Benjamin Keith Company*, No. 7130, Circuit Court, Southern District of New York, filed 31 December 1898, NjBaFAR. Normal procedure for a patent application required the machine to be built before an application was applied for. Ramsaye (*A Million and One Nights*, p. 142) dates this contract a year earlier, perhaps in an attempt to validate Armat as sole inventor.
16. Jenkins to Murphy, 8 and 30 August 1895 and 7 September 1895, *Motion Picture Patents Co.* v. *Independent Moving Picture Co.*, 1:553–559. Charles Francis Jenkins and Thomas Armat, patent specification, filed 28 August 1895 and granted 20 July 1897 as Patent No. 586,953; Lumière Patent No. 592,882 filed 6 September 1895, granted 30 March 1897; Parker W. Page, question, 9 February 1900, *Animated Projecting Co.* v. *American Mutoscope Co.*, p. 23. For additional information on the Jenkins-Armat collaboration see Gene G. Kelkres, "A Forgotten First: The Armat-Jenkins Partnership and the Atlanta Projection," *Quarterly Review of Film Studies* 9 (Winter 1984), pp. 45–58.
17. Thomas Armat, C. Francis Jenkins, Chris Armat, S. Brooke Armat, and J. Hunter Armat, agreement, 16 September 1895, *Animated Projecting Co.* v. *American Mutoscope Co.* exhibit; Thomas Armat, testimony, 1:550.
18. Thomas Armat, testimony, *Motion Picture Patents Co.* v. *Independent Moving Picture Co.*, 1:586.
19. *Ibid.*, 1:549.
20. C. Francis Jenkins, testimony, 17 January 1911, *Motion Picture Patents Co.* v. *Independent Moving Picture Co.*, 2:140.
21. Thomas Armat, testimony, 1:600–601; *idem*, testimony, 10 October 1901, *Animated Projecting Co.* v. *American Mutoscope Co.*, p. 87; Gray Latham, testimony, 17 December 1897, *Latham* v. *Armat*, pp. 217–218.
22. *Richmond* (Indiana) *Daily Times*, 30 October 1895, PPS; *Atlanta Journal*, 15 October 1895, PPS; *Atlanta Constitution*, 16 October 1895.

CHAPTER 4. The Vitascope

1. *Phoenix Gazette*, 17 and 18 May 1897, courtesy George C. Hall; *Honolulu Evening Bulletin*, 4 February 1897, p. 5 and 6 February 1897, p.1, cited in Robert C. Schmitt, "Movies in Hawaii, 1897–1932," *Hawaiian Journal of History* 1 (1967).
2. Ramsaye, *A Million and One Nights*; Hendricks, *The Edison Motion Picture Myth*, pp. viii, 4; Robert C. Allen, "Vitascope/Cinematographe: Initial Patterns of Film Industrial Practice," in Fell, ed., *Film Before Griffith*, pp. 144–152.
3. Raff & Gammon to Daniel and Armat, n.d. [*ca.* 26 December 1895], 3:179, 181, MH-BA.
4. Armat–Raff & Gammon contract, exhibit, *Animated Projecting Co.* v. *American Mutoscope Co.*
5. Raff & Gammon to Daniel and Armat, 17 January 1896, 3:201; Raff & Gammon to W. K. L. Dickson, 20 January 1896, 3:204, MH-BA.
6. Armat to Raff & Gammon, 10 February 1896, and Raff & Gammon to Armat, 13 February 1896, exhibits, *Animated Projecting Co.* v. *American Mutoscope Co.*; Raff & Gammon to Armat, 5 March 1896, 3:289–290, MH-BA.
7. F. R. Gammon to Thomas Armat, 5 March 1896, 3:285, MH-BA; Kinetoscope Co. to Armat, 3 March 1896, 3:274, MH-BA; Armat to Raff & Gammon, 27 March 1896, exhibit, Equity No. 7130; Raff & Gammon to Armat, 28 March 1896, exhibit, *Animated Projecting Co.* v. *American Mutoscope Co.*
8. Raff & Gammon to Armat, 4 March 1896, 3:279, MH-BA; Raff & Gammon to Armat, 17 March 1896, 3:368, MH-BA; Raff & Gammon to Armat, 19 March 1896, 3:379, MH-BA.
9. Raff & Gammon to Armat, 16 March 1896, exhibit, *Animated Projecting Co.* v. *American Mutoscope Co.*; Raff & Gammon to Armat, 21 March 1896, 3:390, MH-BA; Raff & Gammon to Armat, 26 March 1896, 3:409, MH-BA.
10. Raff & Gammon to Armat, 17 March 1896, 3:367, MH-BA.
11. Raff & Gammon to Peter Bacigalupi, 5 February 1896, 3:212; The Kinetoscope Company to Lyman H. Howe, 17 February 1896, 3:215; Raff & Gammon to T. L. Tally, 4 April 1896, 2:58, all MH-BA.
12. For the following information see correspondence files for the vitascope entrepreneurs (the W. R. Miller file, Robert Fischer file, and so forth) in the Raff & Gammon Collection, MH-BA. Much is

revealed by letterheads. See the following correspondence in particular: A. F. Rieser to Raff & Gammon, 28 March 1896; Thomas J. Ryan to Raff & Gammon, 26 May 1896; C. O. Richardson to Vitascope Company, 13 November 1896; Llewellyn to Vitascope Company, 28 June 1896. Additional information came from "Death of William T. Rock," *Moving Picture World*, 12 August 1916, p. 1078; New York City directories, 1895–1897; *Wilkes-Barre City Directory*, 1896; Rev. Horace Edwin Hayden, Hon. Alfred Hand and John W. Jordan, *Geneaological and Family History of the Wyoming and Lackawanna Valleys* (New York: Lewis, 1906), vol. 2, p. 596.

13. For a detailed look at this group's activities see Musser, *Before the Nickelodeon*, pp. 75–94.

14. Raff & Gammon, invoice, 27 February 1897, 1:336, MH-BA.

15. Raff & Gammon to Cinquevalli, 17 March 1896, 3:373, MH-BA; Raff & Gammon to Armat, 16 March 1896, exhibit, *Animated Projecting Co. v. American Mutoscope Co.*; Raff & Gammon to E. Kuhn, 18 April 1896, 2:258, MH-BA; Charles Webster to Raff & Gammon, 31 April 1896, reprinted in Ramsaye, *A Million and One Nights*, pp. 240–241; Raff & Gammon to J. H. White, 10 April 1896, 2:135–136, MH-BA; Vitascope Company, certificate of incorporation, 5 May 1896, NNNCC-Ar.

16. Raff & Gammon to Daniel and Armat, n.d. [*ca.* 26 December 1895], 3:180, MH-BA.

17. Raff & Gammon to Albert Bial, 23 March 1896, 3:402; Raff & Gammon to Albert Bial, 7 April 1896, 2:108, MH-BA. This figure is extremely difficult to decipher and may have been three hundred dollars per week.

18. *New York Dramatic Mirror*, 2 May 1896, p. 19 (hereafter *NYDM*).

19. E. Kuhn to Frank Gammon, 28 July 1896, incoming letters, July 1896, MH-BA.

20. *New York Mail and Express*, 24 April 1896, p. 12.

21. Barnes, *The Beginnings of the Cinema in England*, pp. 58–59; Albert Bial to Raff & Gammon, 26 March 1896, MH-BA; *Boston Herald*, 31 May 1896, p. 27.

22. Raff & Gammon to P. W. Kiefaber, 6 May 1896, 2:477, MH-BA; "Herald Square Vitascoped," *New York Herald*, 12 May 1896, p. 9.

23. "The Vitascope at Keith's," *Boston Herald*, 19 May 1896, p. 9.

24. "Keith's New Theatre," *Boston Herald*, 26 May 1896, p. 7.

25. P. W. Kiefaber to Vitascope Company, 25 May 1896, MH-BA; *Boston Herald*, 23 June 1896, p. 9.

26. *Boston Herald*, 28 June 1896, p. 11, 12 July 1896, p. 11; *Philadelphia Record*, 19 July 1896, p. 11; *Boston Herald*, 28 July 1896, p. 7, 4 August 1896, p. 7.

27. *Phonoscope*, November 1896, p. 16.

28. *Mail and Express*, 15 September 1896, p. 5.

29. Keith's Union Square Theater, program, 22 February 1897; *Boston Herald*, 6 July 1897, p. 9.

30. A. F. Rieser to Raff & Gammon, 8 May 1896; W. R. Miller to Raff & Gammon, 19 May 1896, MH-BA.

31. *Chicago Tribune*, 26 July 1896, p. 34. "Ten-Twenty-Thirty" refers to vaudeville admissions prices ranging from ten cents in the gallery to thirty cents in the orchestra.

32. *Louisville Courier-Journal*, 20 September 1896, p. 6B; *Cleveland Plain-Dealer*, 12 July 1896, p. 15.

33. *New Haven Journal-Courier*, 29 May 1896, p. 7; *New Haven Register*, 5 June 1896, p. 2; *St. Louis Republic*, 16 June 1896, p. 11; *Albany Times-Union*, 18 August 1896, p. 1; *Atlanta Constitution*, 21 November 1896, p. 7.

34. *Providence Journal*, 7 June 1896, p. 8. Edmund McLoughlin to Raff & Gammon, 3 September 1896; Edmund McLoughlin to Raff & Gammon, 12 September 1896, MH-BA; *Utica Observer*, 29 December 1896, p. 1.

35. Miller to Vitascope Co., 21 June 1896; Miller to Vitascope Co., 14 June 1896, MH-BA; *Asbury Park Dail Press*, 17 July 1896, p. 4.

36. *Philadelphia Record*, 9 August 1896, p. 11; *Baltimore Sun*, 23 June 1896, p. 10; P. W. Kiefaber to Raff & Gammon, 31 March 1896, MH-BA; *Atlantic City Daily Union*, 19 August 1896, p. 1; *Brooklyn Eagle*, 21 June 1896, p. 23. Hotaling eventually became a prominent producer-director for Sigmund Lubin.

37. E. Hopkins, Jr., to Raff & Gammon, 2 June 1896; W. R. Miller to Raff & Gammon, 24 May 1896, MH-BA.

38. Robert C. Allen, *Vaudeville and Film, 1895–1915*, pp. 97–98; J. Hunter Armat to P. W. Kiefaber, 17 June 1896; P. W. Kiefaber to Vitascope Company, 11 June 1896; Andrew Holland to Raff, 8 September 1896, MH-BA.

39. Holland to Gammon, 26 September 1896, MH-BA.

40. H. R. Kiefaber to Raff & Gammon, 29 July 1896; Purdy & Kiefaber to Vitascope Company, 17 August 1896; A. F. Rieser to Raff & Gammon, 25 September 1896; Edmund McLoughlin to Raff & Gammon, 4 August 1896, MH-BA.

41. C. O. Richardson to Vitascope Company, 4 October 1896; 13 November 1896, MH-BA; W. R. Miller to Raff & Gammon, 14 August 1896, MH-BA.

42. Holland to Raff, 28 December 1896, MH-BA.

CHAPTER 5. Early Motion Picture Companies

1. *New York World*, 19 April 1896, p. 14.

2. Thomas Armat, testimony, 11 August 1911, *Motion Picture Patents Company* v. *Independent Moving Picture Company*, No. 5–167, NjBAR.

3. "Eidoloscope Attachment," *New York Tribune*, 3 September 1896, p. 13; "A Spaniard's Delight," *Detroit Free Press*, 29 May 1896, p. 5; "Eidoloscope Al Fresco," *ibid.*, 2 July 1896, p. 10; *Atlantic City Dail Union*, 2 July 1896, p. 4; Purdy & Kiefaber to Vitascope Company, 8 July 1896, MH-BA.

4. "Museum—Yankee Cruiser," *Boston Herald*, 21 June 1896, p. 10; Ramsaye, *A Million and One Nights*, p. 292; *NYDM*, 23 May 1896, p. 19, cited in Pratt, "Firsting the Firsts"; *NYDM*, 6 June 1896, p. 17.

5. *New York Times*, 12 May 1896, p. 5; *New York Mail and Express*, 12 May 1896, p. 7.

6. When Patent Interference No. 18,461 (*Latham* v. *Armat*) was resolved, this became Patent No. 707,934, submitted 1 June 1896, granted 26 August 1902. This patent involved the famous "Latham loop," which was the center of later controversy. See "Biograph Company Defines Its Position in Fight," *Variety*, 14 March 1908, p. 12; "Latham Loop Patent Adjudicated," *MPW*, 21 August 1912, p. 747.

7. Woodville Latham, testimony, 8 December 1897, *Latham* v. *Armat*, p. 81.

8. Otway Latham, testimony, 13 December 1897, *Latham* v. *Armat*, p. 172; *Atlanta Constitution*, 24 November 1896, p. 3; *NYDM*, 19 December 1896, p. 9. Early motion-picture exhibitions were far more common than some surveys suggest. Burnes St. Patrick Hollyman, "The First Picture Shows: Austin, Texas," in John Fell, ed., *Film Before Griffith*, pp. 188–206, is notably incomplete, placing the first exhibition of projected motion pictures in Austin during 1900.

9. Richard A. Anthony, testimony, 10 December 1897, *Latham* v. *Armat*, pp. 110–119. Ramsaye (*A Million and One Nights*, pp. 292–294) suggests that Anthony loaned Woodville Latham a thousand dollars against his patents in 1898. The family was never able to repay, and Anthony finally took control.

10. Eidoloscope films were apparently shown in New York City at Hermann's Theater on Broadway between Twenty-eighth and Twenty-ninth streets in the spring or early summer of 1897 (Otway Latham, testimony, *Latham* v. *Armat*, p. 172); see also Pratt, "Firsting the Firsts," in Deutelbaum, ed., *"Image,"* pp. 20–22.

11. The Lumières had filed for French patents on their cinématographe during February 1895. In April they made similar applications throughout Europe, including Belgium, England, Austria, and Spain. The brothers failed, however, to apply for U.S. patents until 6 September 1895 (Patent No. 579,882, granted 30 March 1897), a week after Jenkins and Armat submitted their claim. As the United States Patent Office then operated, the Jenkins–Armat patent application was given priority for its various claims. Ironically, the shortsighted "mistake" of failing to take out key patents in foreign countries has been attributed to Edison (for the most part inappropriately since his sweeping claims would never have been sustained in Europe as they often were in United States). In contrast, this "oversight" was much more costly for the Lumières.

12. Alan Williams, "The Lumière Organization and Documentary Realism," in Fell, ed. *Film Before Griffith*, pp. 153–161; See also Deslandes and Richard, *Histoire comparée du cinéma*, vol. 1. The wisdom of the Lumières' approach contrasts with the example of Jenkins and Armat, whose rapid and unsuccessful deployment of their phantoscope was a failure of marketing rather than hardware.

13. The cinématographe, which generally used a calcium light, was adapted to Keith's large Union Square Theatre by the addition of an electric arc lamp that provided a much brighter image.

14. *New Haven Register*, 19 September 1896, p. 2; Keith advertisement, *New York World*, 28 June 1896, p. 14; *NYDM*. 4 July 1896, p. 17; 11 July 1896, p. 18.

15. *NYDM*, 11 July 1896, p. 18; *Mail and Express*, 4 July 1896, p. 5; *NYDM*, 16 July 1896, p. 17; *Clipper*, 11 July 1896, p. 296. English titles of French subjects varied widely and will here be used as first cited or most commonly employed. THE ARRIVAL OF THE MAIL TRAIN was almost certainly the well-known L'ARRIVÉE D'UN TRAIN EN GARE.

16. *Philadelphia Record*, 16 August 1896, p. 11; Albee to Kiefaber, 29 July 1896, MH-BA; *Boston Herald*, 4 August 1896, p. 7.

17. "Vaudeville Jottings," *NYDM*, 8 August 1896, p. 18; *Clipper*, 10 April 1897, p. 100; Félix Mesguich, *Tours de manivelle: Souvenirs d'un chasseur d'images* (Paris: Bernard Grasset, 1933), pp. 8–9. The

prominent role that Mesguich assigns himself in this professional memoir does not appear warranted on the basis of newspaper accounts. Moreover, his assertion that the cinématographe opened at Koster & Bial's rather than Keith's suggests that he was not even present during the first month of cinématographe activity in the U.S.

18. *Pittsburgh Dispatch*, 6 September 1896, p. 21; *New Haven Evening Register*, 7 November 1896, p. 9; 8 October 1896, p. 4. The total population of New Haven in 1900 was 108,027.

19. *Clipper*, 7 November 1896, p. 570; Mesguich, *Tours de manivelle*, p. 13.

20. *Brooklyn Eagle*, 15 August 1895, p. 2; 25 October 1896, p. 24; 1 November 1896, p. 17. Nizier Delorme, who first projected at Keith's Union Square Theater, was later based at the Brooklyn store show—before being sent to exhibit in Syracuse, New York. (Nizier Delorme, testimony, 20 June 1907, *Armat Moving Picture Company* v. *Edison Manufacturing Company*).

21. Lumière advertisement, *Hartford Courant*, 3 December 1896, p. 5; Holland to Raff, 23 September 1896, MH-BA.

22. Film No. 1168, in Maguire & Baucus, Ltd., *Lumière Films, Edison Films, International Films*, Fall 1897, p. 3 ("Showing the long trough in the barracks at which a large number of cavalry men are watering their horses"); *Philadelphia Record*, 6 September 1896, p. 10. Bonheur's *The Horse Fair* (1848) was in the collection of the Metropolitan Museum of Art in New York and was certainly Bonheur's best-known painting in the United States, but *Chevaux sortant de l'abreuvoir* (1843) also seems possible.

23. "Keith's Union Square," *NYDM*, 11 July 1896, p. 17; *New Haven Register*, 19 October 1896, p. 9.

24. *Philadelphia Record*, 9 August 1896, p. 11; 23 August 1896, p. 11; "The Cinématographe at Keith's," *NYDM*, 4 July 1896, p. 17; *Philadelphia Record*, 30 August 1896, p. 11.

25. *Philadelphia Record*, 23 August 1896, p. 11; *New Haven Evening Register*, 29 September 1896, p. 10.

26. Mesguich, *Tours de manivelle*, p. 7; *Brooklyn Eagle*, 6 September 1896, p. 13; *Brooklyn Eagle*, 27 September 1896, p. 24; *Philadelphia Record*, 22 November 1896, p. 10; *New Haven Register*, 10 October 1896, 6. The Lumières may have been reluctant to print and develop films in the United States until they regained control of their concession.

27. For example, Robert C. Allen, "Vitascope/Cinématographe: Initial Patterns of American Film Industrial Practice," in Fell, ed., *Film Before Griffith*, pp. 144–152.

28. *New York World*, 21 February 1896, p. 15; 28 February 1896, p. 15; 7 March 1896, p. 15; *Cleveland Plain Dealer*, 28 March 1897, p. 7; Proctor's Pleasure Palace, programs, 15 February 1897, 15 and 29 March 1897; *New York World*, 19 July 1896, p. 13.

29. Gordon Hendricks, *Beginnings of the Biograph*, provides the basis for much of this section.

30. Patent No. 509,841, photographic camera shutter, filed 1 March 1893, issued 28 November 1893. The patent was granted to Casler, while Marvin was assigned half ownership (thus Marvin logically received one-half the royalties, not Dickson, as Hendricks suggests). Since Dickson claimed to have invented the device, he was clearly linked to the enterprise (*Orange Chronicle*, 16 December 1893).

31. Patent No. 549,309, mutoscope, filed 21 November 1894 and issued 5 November 1895.

32. Harry Marvin, testimony, *Latham* v. *Armat*, cited in Hendricks, *Beginnings of the Biograph*, p. 14.

33. Patent No. 629,063, kinetographic camera, filed 26 February 1896, issued 18 July 1899 ("kinetographic camera" was the descriptive title assigned to the mutograph by the U.S. Patent Office).

34. G. W. Bitzer, *Billy Bitzer: His Story* (New York: Farrar, Straus and Giroux, 1973), p. 18. The "projecting mutoscope" was actually offered for sale by the Biograph Company in 1897 (*Clipper*, 11 September 1897, p. 470).

35. Herman Casler, Patent No. 666,495, consecutive-view apparatus, applied 26 February 1896, granted 22 January 1901.

36. American Mutoscope Company, certificate of organization, filed 30 December 1895, Hudson County Clerk's Office, New Jersey; Dun & Company, "American Mutoscope Company, 10 February 1897, NjWOE; Transfer of Patents, vol. J-52, cited in Hendricks, *Beginnings of the Biograph*, p. 31; George R. Blanchard obituary, *New York Times*, 9 October 1900, p. 7; Ramsaye, *A Million and One Nights*, p. 216.

37. American Mutoscope and Biograph, photo catalogs. These catalogs provide a key resource in tracing Biograph's production history. They can be found in Musser *et al.*, *A Microfilm Edition of Motion Picture Catalogs by American Producers and Distributors, 1894–1909*. In this volume, all Biograph films will be listed with their production number to provide the reader with a stronger sense of production chronology. The vast majority of surviving Biograph films from this period are in the Paper Print Collection at the Library of Congress.

38. Bitzer, *Billy Bitzer*, pp. 8–13; "New York on Wheels," *New York World*, 7 June 1896, p. 5; *Canastoda Bee*, quoted in Hendricks, *Beginnings of the Biograph*, p. 44. Production nos. 77–81 were undoubtedly all taken on the same filming trip. No. 81 survives in the Paper Print Collection.

39. *Pittsburgh Post*, 15 September 1896; *Philadelphia Record*, 22 September 1896, p. 2; *Philadelphia Times*, 22 September 1896; *New York World*, 31 August 1896, p. 1.

40. *Brooklyn Eagle*, 29 September 1896, p. 7; "Sandow's Olympia to Close," *New York Herald*, 6 October 1896, p. 9.

41. *New York Mail and Express*, 3 November 1896, p. 4. "Popocrat" is an amalgam of Populist and Democrat, the two parties that had nominated Bryan.

42. *New York Mail and Express*, 7 November 1896, p. 13.

43. "Vaudeville," *New York Mail and Express*, 17 October 1896, p. 13.

44. *New Haven Evening Register*, 1 December 1896, p. 8; 8 December 1896, p. 9; 16 December 1896, p. 7.

45. At Willard's Hall in Washington, D.C., the cinématographe closed one week and the biograph opened the next. In Hartford, the Biograph Company opened at Unity Hall on 4 February, less than three weeks after the Lumière cinématographe completed a six-week run. For four weeks the Biograph Company presented a screen program consisting of a stereopticon lecture on Cuba and a selection of films (*Hartford Courant*, 5 February 1897, p. 5).

CHAPTER 6. The Proliferation of Motion-Picture Companies and an Assessment of the Novelty Year

1. Edward D. Easton, deposition, 24 December 1902, *Armat Moving Picture Company* v. *Edison Manufacturing Company*, No. 8303, Circuit Court, Southern District of New York, filed 28 November 1902, NjBaFAR; *T. Cushing Daniel et al.* v. *C. Francis Jenkins*, No. 17,416, Supreme Court for District of Columbia, filed 27 May 1896, MdSuFR; T. Cushing Daniel, testimony, 26 December 1902, *Armat Moving Picture Co.* v. *Edison Manufacturing Co.*

2. "Living Pictures Stopped," *Brooklyn Eagle*, 14 July 1896, p. 14. The article uses both spellings; it is unclear which is correct.

3. J. D. Hopkins to Vitascope Company, 3 and 7 August 1896, MH-BA; *Vitascope Company* v. *Chicago Talking Machine Company*, No. 24,219, Circuit Court, Northern District of Illinois, ICAR; *Chicago Inter-Ocean*, 9 August 1896 cited in Ramsaye, *A Million and One Nights*, p. 273; *Chicago Tribune*, 11 August 1896, p. 7; Hopkins to Vitascope Company, August 1896, quoted in Ramsaye, *A Million and One Nights*, p. 273; *St. Louis Republic*, 23 August 1896, p. 13; P. W. Kiefaber to Vitascope Company, 2 September 1896, MH-BA.

4. Barnes, *The Beginnings of the Cinema in England*, pp. 66–67; *Clipper*, 12 September 1896, p. 450; 26 September 1896, p. 480; 19 September 1896, p. 462.

5. Raff and Gammon to Amet Talking Machine Company, 7 March 1896, 3:302; Ramsaye, *A Million and One Nights*, pp. 300–302; "Kinodrome Making Is an Art," *Show World*, 10 August 1907, p. 14; *Clipper*, 14 November 1896, p. 595. The Chicago-based Western Phonograph Company began soliciting engagements for its magniscope in November and claimed responsibility for the exhibitions at Schiller's Theater (*Clipper*, 28 November 1896, p. 627, and 23 April 1897, p. 134). It is not known whether George Spoor was involved in obtaining any of the Chicago engagements.

6. Maguire & Baucus to customers, 25 August 1896, MH-BA; *Rochester Post-Express*, 13 October 1896, p. 8.

7. James White, testimony, 9 February 1900, *Edison* v. *American Mutoscope Co.*, Paul Spehr, "Edison Films in the Library of Congress," in Iris Newsom, ed., *Wonderful Inventions: Motion Pictures, Broadcasting, and Recorded Sound at the Library of Congress* (Washington, D.C.: Library of Congress, 1985), pp. 34–50; Edison Manufacturing Company, journal, 1897–1904. Vitascope entrepreneurs generally felt abandoned and betrayed by Edison's independent activities. As rival machines grew in numbers, they painfully discovered that Armat's patent applications offered them no protection for the foreseeable future. Moreover, Maguire & Baucus sold Edison films for 25 percent less than Raff & Gammon, from whom states rights owners were contractually bound to purchase their films (A. F. Rieser to Vitascope Company, 9 November 1896, MH-BA). "You sold goods that you have been unable to deliver; your franchise, as most franchises are, [is] like the old woman's passage (principally wind)," M. M. Hixson penned Raff. "The money I have paid to you was the hard earnings of a 'Country Doctor' and paid according to agreement and in good faith. It matters not to us what your difficulties have been. We are the ones suffering" (M. M. Hixson to N. C. Raff, 23 November 1896,

MH-BA). As I am situated today," Peter Kiefaber wrote Raff & Gammon, "you have all my good money in addition to the hard year's work done on my part, for which I do not have a cent to show for my services" (P. W. Kiefaber to Vitascope Company, 31 October 1896, MH-BA).

8. "Manager Foley's Treat," *Harrisburg Patriot*, 1 December 1896, p. 1; Maguire & Baucus, *Preliminary Circular, Edison Perfected Projecting Kinetoscope*, 16 February 1897, NN; Maguire & Baucus, *Edison Films*, 20 January 1897, NN; Maguire & Baucus, *Lumière Films, Edison Films, International Films*, Fall 1897, NjWOE; Edison Manufacturing Company, statements of profit and loss, NjWOE.

9. *Phonoscope*, November 1896, p. 15; *Clipper*, 7 November 1896, p. 576. The company's "cinagraph" projector was advertised later in the theatrical season (*Clipper*, 24 April 1897, p. 133).

10. *Phonoscope*, December 1896, p. 13.

11. *New Haven Register*, 16 April 1897, p. 2; *Phonoscope*, December 1896, p. 13; January–February 1897, p. 12; Barnes, *The Beginnings of the Cinema in England*, pp. 130–131.

12. *Clipper*, 17 October 1896, p. 522; *New York Mail and Express*, 21 November 1896, p. 14; *Clipper*, 14 November 1896, p. 595; "Dangers in X-Rays," *Phonoscope*, January–February 1897, p. 15; *New York World*, 21 March 1897, p. 15; *Clipper*, 3 April 1897, p. 84.

13. Ramsaye, *A Million and One Nights*, pp. 304–307; *Lexington Herald*, 15 September 1897, p. 30.

14. *Phonoscope*, November 1896, p. 15; *San Francisco Chronicle*, 14 December 1896, p. 10; 20 December 1896, p. 13; *Phonoscope*, January–February 1897, p. 14.

15. *Clipper*, 6 March 1897, p. 15; 16 January 1897, p. 739; Edison Manufacturing Company, Cash Book Nos. 3 and 4, NjWOE; "The Real Corbett," *Philadelphia Record*, 30 March 1897, p. 2; *Clipper*, 1 May 1897, p. 150.

16. *Clipper*, 24 April 1897, p. 125; Jacob B. Smith, testimony, 27 March 1903, *Thomas A. Edison v. Siegmund Lubin*, Nos. 24 and 25, October Sessions 1902, Circuit Court, Eastern District of Pennsylvania, PPFAR; *Clipper*, 1 May 1897, p. 141; *Clipper*, 24 April 1897, p. 125; *Phonoscope*, August–September 1897, p. 9.

17. "American Mutoscope Company," Dun & Company, 16 October 1897, NjWOE; *Clipper*, 13 February 1897, p. 794, and 15 May 1897, p. 168. Whiting Allen not only managed the show in February and early March but gave a brief spiel during the screenings ("The Biograph," *Washington Star*, 22 February 1897, p. 24).

18. *Boston Herald*, 20 April 1897, p. 9; 11 April 1896, p. 11.

19. Herman Casler, testimony, 24 March 1897, *Latham* v. *Armat*; " 'Biographing' Jumbo," *Hartford Times*, 8 April 1897, p. 1; "Fine Day for Biograph," *ibid.*, 12 April 1897, p. 1.

20. Barnes, *The Beginnings of the Cinema in England* (London: Bishopsgate Press, 1983), pp. 143–144; *Orange Chronicle*, 15 May 1897, p. 6; Merritt Crawford, "Eugène Augustin Lauste," pp. 34–35, *New York Mail and Express*, 15 July 1897, p. 7; Rachel Low and Roger Manvell, *The History of British Film, 1896–1906* (London: Allen and Unwin, 1948), pp. 15–16, 30.

21. Bitzer, *Billy Bitzer*, pp. 9, 21.

22. Dun & Company, "American Mutoscope Company," 16 October 1897; "Another 'Scope," *New York Herald*, 7 February 1897, p. 9D.

23. *Clipper*, 10 April 1897, p. 100.

24. Mesguich, *Tours de manivelle*, pp. 15–16.

25. *Clipper*, 10 April 1897, p. 100; Barnes, *The Beginnings of the Cinema in England*, p. 122.

26. *Boston Herald*, 11 April 1897, p. 10, and 2 May 1897, p. 10; *Phonoscope*, May 1897, p. 9.

27. *Boston Herald*, 19 May 1896, p. 9; 26 May 1896, p. 7; "Union Square," *New York Mail and Express*, 4 July 1896, p. 5.

28. Raff & Gammon, *The Vitascope*, p. 5; *Port Jervis Evening Gazette*, 12 December 1896, HPS; "Mr. Howe's Fine Entertainment," *Wilkes-Barre Record*, 9 January 1897, p. 5; *Geneva* (N.Y.) *Advertiser*, 6 April 1897, p. 3.

29. *Boston Herald*, 23 June 1896, p. 9; *Philadelphia Record*, 19 July 1896, p. 11.

30. Proctor's 23rd Street Theater, program for week of 8 March 1897, MH-TT.

31. Koster & Bial's Music Hall, program for week of 2 November 1896, MH-TT.

32. "Jubilee Pictures," *Boston Herald*, 1 August 1897, p. 10; *ibid.*, 10 August 1897, p. 6.

33. Bitzer, *Billy Bitzer*, p. 22.

34. "A Cinematograph Fire," *Danbury Evening News*, 6 September 1897, p. 8; "Fire and Panic," *New Brunswick* (N.J.) *Daily Times*, 30 September 1897, p. 1; "Fire and Panic," *ibid.*, 29 September 1897, p. 1. Other pre-nickelodeon-era fires that have been located include 3–4 February 1898: YMCA, Scranton, Pa.; 8 November 1899: Lyman Howe's Moving Pictures at Wilson Opera House, Oswego, New York; 26 February 1900: vitagraph at Miner's Harlem Theater, New York City; 22 October 1901:

Selig's polyscope at Temple Theater, Louisville, Kentucky; 18 November 1901: Paley's kalatechno-scope at Proctor's 58th Street Theater, New York City; 3 October 1903: Landsburg Department Store, New Brunswick, N.J.; 19 October 1903: Metropolis Theater, New York City; 25 November 1903: cinématograph at Harry Davis' Avenue Theater, Pittsburgh, Pa.

35. Robert Snyder, *The Voice of the City: Vaudeville and Popular Culture in New York* (New York: Oxford University Press, 1990).
36. *Philadelphia Record*, 6 September 1896, p. 10.
37. *New York Journal*, 4 April 1896, clipping, MH-BA.
38. Brooklyn Institute of Arts and Science, ticket No. 14, 1896–1897.
39. "An Illustrated Lecture," *Brooklyn Eagle*, 9 March 1897, p. 7.
40. *Utica Observer*, 31 March 1898, p. 1; "Picture Machines Raided," *Brooklyn Eagle*, 30 July 1897, p. 1.

CHAPTER 7. Full-Length Programs: Fights, Passion Plays, and Travel

1. *Clipper*, 24 August 1895, p. 391. Jeffrey T. Sammons, *Beyond the Ring: The Role of Boxing in American Society* (Urbana: University of Illinois Press, 1988), provides an insightful account of prize-fighting in this era but ignores the crucial importance of motion pictures.
2. Raff & Gammon made several films of unpublicized bouts for its kinetoscopes, but these commanded little attention and modest sales.
3. "The Eden Musee," *Pittsburgh Dispatch*, 2 February 1897, p. 9.
4. "Prize Fighting Legal in Texas," *Clipper*, 28 September 1895, p. 473; 12 October 1895, p. 508.
5. "The World's Championship," *Clipper*, 29 February 1896, p. 829.
6. *Phonoscope*, January 1898, p. 8; Ramsaye (*A Million and One Nights*, p. 286) is probably incorrect when he asserts that each fighter received 25 percent of the profits.
7. *Clipper*, 6 February 1897, p. 783; Ramsaye, *A Million and One Nights*, pp. 296–297.
8. "The Prize Fight Bill," *Brooklyn Eagle*, 28 February 1897, p. 4.
9. *Boston Herald*, 17 March 1897, p. 1; 16 March 1897, p. 1; *Clipper*, 27 March 1897, p. 64.
10. *New York World*, 14 March 1897, p. 15; "Prize Ring vs. Woman Suffrage," *Boston Herald*, 18 March 1897, p. 3; "Corbett Hasn't a 1 to 10 Chance," *New York World*, 18 March 1897, p. 4.
11. "A Gratifying Exposure," *New Haven Evening Register*, 16 March 1897, p. 6; *Utica Observer*, 10 April 1897, p. 6; *Phonoscope*, July 1899, p. 9; "Want No Fight Pictures," *New Haven Evening Register*, 20 March 1897, p. 7. "Bonheur Notes," *Clipper*, 11 May 1897, p. 141; *Phonoscope*, May 1897, p. 9.
12. "The Veriscope Shows the Fight," *New York Tribune*, 23 May 1897, p. 8; "The Record by the Veriscope of the Corbett–Fitzsimmons Fight at Carson City," *New York World*, 22 May 1897, pp. 3–4; "Fitzsimmons Cries Fraud," *ibid.*, 23 May 1897, p. 4.
13. *Chicago Tribune*, 20 June 1897, p. 32; *Boston Herald*, 26 April 1898, p. 9. Although not playing New Haven, Connecticut, until 15 November, the veriscope attracted immense crowds at Poli's Wonder-land, where it remained for one week. Admission was pegged at Poli's regular ten- and twenty-cent fees, with four daily shows, including some vaudeville (*New Haven Evening Register*, 15 November 1897, p. 7).
14. *Phonoscope*, July 1899, p. 9; "Veriscope Pictures," *Boston Herald*, 26 April 1898, p. 9; *Philadelphia Record*, 9 November 1897, p. 2; *Baltimore Sun*, 18 April 1898, p. 1; *Phonoscope*, July 1898, p. 9.
15. "Does Its Work Well," *Boston Herald*, 1 June 1897, p. 7; *Phonoscope*, June 1897, p. 11; *Boston Herald*, 30 May 1897, p. 10; 1 June 1897, p. 7; 8 June 1897, p. 9.
16. "Park Theater," *Boston Herald*, 10 May 1898, p. 9; Ramsaye, *A Million and One Nights*, p. 288.
17. *Phonoscope*, June 1897, p. 12; August–September 1897, p. 8.
18. "Opening of Poli's," *New Haven Journal-Courier*, 4 September 1899, p. 3.
19. *New York Evening Telegram*, 8 June 1899; *New York World*, 10 June 1899, pp. 1, 8; *Clipper*, 19 August 1899, p. 504, 9 September 1899, p. 571.
20. "Fighters Bothered by Intense Heat," *New York Herald*, 4 November 1899, p. 4; "New York," *Clipper*, 25 November 1899, p. 814; "Fight Pictures," *Philadelphia Record*, 19 December 1899, p. 8.
21. Colin Young, "Observational Cinema," in Paul Hockings, ed., *Principles of Visual Anthropology* (The Hague: Mouton, 1975), pp. 65–88.
22. "The Passion," *San Francisco Chronicle*, 4 March 1879, p. 3.
23. "Mr. Abbey's Decision," *New York Times*, 28 November 1880, p. 7; "Aldermanic Virtue Aroused," *ibid.*, 24 November 1880, p. 8; "The Passion Play Denounced," *ibid.*, 16 November, 1880, p. 2;

"Pastors to Their Flocks," *ibid.*, 29 November 1880, p. 2; "The Passion Play Read," *ibid.*, 4 December 1880, pp. 2, 4 (editorial).

24. "Ober-Ammergau's Passion Play," *New York Times*, 12 December 1880, p. 5; "The Lecture Platform," *New York Tribune*, 12 December 1880, p. 2. Actual photographs of the play had been taken for the king of Bavaria. Taylor, *John L. Stoddard*, p. 98.

25. Thomas Armat to Raff & Gammon, 24 February 1896, exhibit, *Animated Photo Projecting Company* versus *American Mutoscope Company*, No. 7130, Circuit Court, District of Southern New York, filed 31 December 1898, NjWOE; *Boston Herald*, 2 January 1898, p. 10; Sadoul, *L'Invention du cinéma*, pp. 368–369. Unlike Sadoul, Zdenek Stabla correctly dates the Lumière PASSION PLAY as 1898 rather than 1897 (*Queries Concerning the Hořice Passion Film* [Prague: Film Institute, 1971]).

26. Stabla, *Queries*, pp. 10–16. Hurd is usually given the initials "W.B.," but the only source for this appears to be Terry Ramsaye (*A Million and One Nights*, p. 367). It is likely that Ramsaye or his informant was misinformed, since a Charles Hurd was in Horitz during the filming and subsequently involved with contractual matters involving the Horitz play (C. S. Hurd to Edison Manufacturing Co., 8 August 1901, NjWOE). Of course, it is quite possible that there was a W. B. as well as a Charles S. Hurd, but no contemporaneous evidence of this has been found.

27. *Phonoscope*, November–December 1897, p. 9; "The Passion Play at Horticultural Hall," *Philadelphia Record*, 28 November 1898, p. 16; "The Passion Play," *Boston Herald*, 2 January 1898, p. 10; "Passion Play in Pictures," *New York Times*, 15 March 1898, p. 7; *New York Herald*, 13 March 1898, p. 9.

28. Kemp Niver with Bebe Bergsten, *Klaw & Erlanger Present Famous Plays in Pictures* (Los Angeles: Locare Research Group, 1976), includes useful information about the exhibition of THE HORITZ PASSION PLAY and reprints several complete reviews.

29. "The Passion Play," *Philadelphia Inquirer*, 23 November 1897, p. 5; "The Passion Play at Daly's," *New York Herald*, 15 March 1898, p. 13; *Rochester Post-Express*, 22 February 1898, p. 7; *Pittsburgh Post*, 24 May 1898, p. 4.

30. "The Passion Play," *Boston Herald*, 2 January 1898, p. 10; "Inspired Peasant Actors," *ibid.*, 2 January 1898, p. 32. Lacy had written *Chatterton* for Julia Marlowe, and his play in blank verse, *Rinaldo*, had enjoyed critical acclaim in Boston and other cities.

31. "Passion Play Given Here in Boston," *Boston Herald*, 4 January 1898, p. 6.

32. Thomas Edison, Marc Klaw, Abraham L. Erlanger, Walter W. Freeman, William Harris, and Franck Z. Maguire, contract, 7 April 1898, NjWOE; " 'Passion Play' Scenes," *Baltimore Sun*, 8 February 1898, p. 7.

33. For more information on the Eden Musee see Musser, *Before the Nickelodeon*, pp. 118–144.

34. "Scenes on Bible Subjects," *New York Tribune*, 29 January 1898, p. 9; *Moving Picture World*, 22 February 1908, p. 132; Ramsaye, *A Million and One Nights*, pp. 370–371.

35. "Crowds at the Musee," *New York Mail and Express*, 5 February 1898, p. 15; "Passion Play at the Eden Musee," *ibid.*, 1 February 1898, p. 3.

36. Madison C. Peters to Hollaman, 1 April 1898, reprinted in *MPW*, 22 February 1908, p. 133. Peters was subsequently to become active in the film industry as a religious adviser.

37. *Mail and Express*, 19 February 1898, p. 15, 26 March 1898, p. 15; *New Haven Journal-Courier*, 15 March 1898, p. 5. Two years later, Thompson lectured with the same program for three weeks during Lent at Willard's Hall in Washington, D.C.

38. *New Haven Journal-Courier*, 8 March 1898, p. 3; 7 March 1898, p. 6.

39. Ramsaye, *A Million and One Nights*, pp. 374–376; "Moving Pictures in Church," *Danbury News*, 9 November 1898, p. 8.

40. *New York World*, 27 February 1898, p. 15; *Clipper*, 28 May 1898, p. 222; Selig Polyscope Company, *Films of the Passion Play* (*ca.* 1900).

41. W. K. L. Dickson, "The Man Who Took the Pope's Pictures Tells How He Did It," *St. Louis Republic*, 4 December 1898, p. 2B; "Pope Leo XIII as He Is," *New York Mail and Express*, 15 December 1898, p. 7; "Moving Pictures of the Pope," *New York Tribune*, 15 December 1898, p. 7; "Biograph Views of the Pope," *New York Times*, 15 December 1898, p. 5.

42. *Boston Herald*, 1 January 1899, pp. 14–15.

43. *Hartford Courant*, 19 March 1898, p. 5, 28 March 1898, p. 5; *Rochester Democrat and Chronicle*, 6 November 1899, p. 10; *New York World*, 31 December 1899, p. 3E; *Utica Observer*, 31 May 1898, p. 8, and 3 June 1898, p. 5.

44. E. Burton Holmes, *The Burton Holmes Lectures, 1897–98*, p. 3 (courtesy Burton Holmes International [hereafter BHI]; Oscar A. Depue, "My First 50 Years in Motion Pictures," *American Cinematographer*, April 1948, pp. 124–126; E. Burton Holmes, account book, 16 March 1898, BHI.

45. "Tour Through Thessaly with Burton Holmes," *Boston Herald*, 6 January 1898, p. 9; "The First Lenten Lecture," *New York Tribune*, 25 February 1898, p. 7; "A Successor to Stoddard," *Brooklyn Eagle*, 13 March 1898, p. 32. The *New York World*, however, criticized Holmes for the "hard and wooden and somewhat monotonous" quality of his delivery (25 February 1898, p. 9).

46. E. Burton Holmes, account book, 4 to 16 March 1898, BHI; *New York Tribune*, 25 February 1898, p. 7.

47. E. Burton Holmes, program, 1898–99, BHI; "Holmes Lecture on Hawaii," *Brooklyn Eagle*, 28 December 1899, p. 13; "Manila and the Philippines," *ibid.*, 30 December 1899, p. 4.

48. "Brooklyn Institute News," *Brooklyn Eagle*, 1 December 1900, p. 9; 8 February 1898, p. 12; 17 January 1899, p. 6; *New York Clipper*, 4 March 1899, p. 8; *Philadelphia Record*, 19 February 1899, p. 9.

49. Of the three genres, the fight film was clearly a new element in nonfiction screen practice—a genre that has never really been seen as part of "the documentary tradition." The passion play as an oeuvre, on the other hand, emerged out of the travel lecture, and in some cases travel lecturers continued to give programs on that subject. THE HORITZ PASSION PLAY and THE PASSION PLAY OF OBERAMMERGAU, however, were distinctive in their production methods and came to be seen as part of a separate religious genre.

CHAPTER 8. Commercial Warfare and the Spanish-American War: 1897–1898

1. *Phonoscope*, June 1897, p. 7.

2. *Orange* (N.J.) *Chronicle*, 15 May 1897, p. 7; *Boston Herald*, 30 May 1897, p. 11; 13 June 1897, p. 14; 6 July 1897, p. 9.

3. "Keith Theatre," *Boston Herald*, 17 August 1897, p. 6.

4. Tom Gunning, "The Cinema of Attractions," *Wide Angle* 8, no. 3–4 (Fall 1986), pp. 63–70; *Boston Herald*, 21 September 1897, p. 9; "Life on Canvas," *New York Mail and Express*, 21 September 1897, p. 2.

5. *Boston Herald*, 14 December 1897, p. 9.

6. *Boston Herald*, 6 June 1897, p. 11; 16 January 1898, p. 10; "The First Photoplaywright," *MPW*, 14 December 1912, p. 1075.

7. *Boston Herald*, 1 August 1897, p. 10.

8. *San Francisco Chronicle*, 31 October 1897, p. 5; *Clipper*, 21 May 1898, p. 200; "Reouverture du Casino de Paris," *Le Figaro*, 17 September 1897, p. 5.

9. Based on copyright records and, prior to September 1896, newspaper information. While these comparisons are revealing, they are not precise since Edison not only made films it did not copyright but copyrighted films it did not make.

10. While this film was not copyrighted until 16 December 1898, Heise apparently completed it sometime in 1897, since a notice reading "copyrighted 1897" is on a surviving copy of the film.

11. *Phonoscope*, July 1897, p. 14; "Dime Museum," *Philadelphia Record*, 5 September 1897, p. 9; 14 November 1897, p. 16; *Phonoscope*, November–December 1897, p. 13.

12. *Clipper*, 4 December 1897, p. 666; 4 September 1897, p. 446; 13 August 1898, p. 398; and 23 October 1897, p. 566. "Arthur Hotaling Recalls the 'Good Old Days,' " *MPW*, 15 July 1916, p. 380; Jacob Blair Smith, testimony, 27 March 1903, *Thomas A. Edison* v. *Siegmund Lubin*, Nos. 24 and 25, October Sessions 1902, Circuit Court, Eastern District of Pennsylvania, filed 6 November 1902, PPFAR. Hotaling, who often operated a projector for Lubin's cineograph service during the 1890s and early 1900s, went on to become one of Lubin's major directors.

13. *Phonoscope*, July 1897, p. 14; September 1897, p. 15; October 1897, p. 13.

14. Maguire & Baucus, *Lumière Films, Edison Films, International Films*, pp. 7–8.

15. Hendricks, *The Edison Motion Picture Myth*, p. 133; Commissioner Benjamin Butterworth, decision, 31 July 1897, in *Decisions of Patents and of United States Courts in Patent and Trade-mark Cases 1897* (Washington: Government Printing Office, 1898); Harry N. Marvin, answer, 15 July 1898, *Thomas A. Edison* v. *American Mutoscope Company*, NjBaFAR.

16. *Thomas A. Edison* v. *Charles H. Webster, individually and as a member of the International Film Company, and Edmund Kuhn, individually and as a member of the International Film Company*, Nos. 6795 and 6796, Circuit Court, Southern District of New York, filed 7 December 1897, NjBaFAR; *Thomas A. Edison* v. *Maguire & Baucus, Limited, Joseph D. Baucus, individually and as President of said Maguire & Baucus, Limited, Franck Z. Maguire, individually and as Vice-President and Managing Director of said Maguire & Baucus Limited and William M. Paxton, Jr., individually*

and as Secretary of said Maguire & Baucus, Nos. 6797 and 6798, Circuit Court, Southern District of New York, filed 7 December 1897, NjBaFAR; *Thomas Edison v. Siegmund Lubin*, No. 50, October Sessions, 1897, Circuit Court, Eastern District of Pennsylvania, filed 10 January 1898, PPFAR; *Thomas A. Edison v. Edward Amet*, No. 24,753, Circuit Court, Northern District of Illinois, filed 10 January 1898, ICFAR; *Phonoscope*, March 1898, p. 11, April 1898, p. 6; Siegmund Lubin, answer, 19 March 1898, *Edison v. Lubin*, October Sessions, 1897, PPFAR.

17. *Thomas A. Edison v. Eden Musee American Company, Ltd., and Richard G. Hollaman, individually and as President of Said Company*, Nos. 6845 and 6846, Circuit Court, Southern District of New York, filed 7 February 1898, NjBaFAR; *Thomas A. Edison v. Marc Klaw and Abraham Erlanger, individually and as members of the firm of Klaw and Erlanger and W. W. Freeman*, Nos. 6853 and 6854, Circuit Court, Southern District of New York, filed 15 February 1898, NjBaFAR; Edison to F. Z. Maguire & Co., 26 February 1898, printed in *Clipper*, 5 March 1898, p. 15; *Thomas A. Edison v. Augustin C. Daly*, No. 6877, Circuit Court, Southern District of New York, filed 14 March 1898, NjBaFAR; *Thomas A. Edison, Marc Klaw, Abraham L. Erlanger, Walter W. Freeman, William Harris, and Franck Z. Maguire*, agreement, 7 April 1898, NjWOE.

18. *Clipper*, 11 December 1897, p. 686; Ramsaye, *A Million and One Nights*, p. 363; *Thomas A. Edison v. Water L. Isaacs*, Nos. 6882 and 6883, Circuit Court, Southern District of New York, filed 22 March 1898, NjBaFAR; *Thomas A. Edison v. the Veriscope Company, Daniel A. Stuart, individually and as President of the company, and Frank C. Meehan, individually and as Secretary of the company*, No. 6857, Circuit Court, Southern District of New York, filed 19 February 1898, NjBaFAR.

19. *Thomas A. Edison v. American Mutoscope Company and Benjamin Franklin Keith*, No. 6928, U.S. Circuit Court, Southern District of New York, filed 13 May 1898, NjBaFAR.

20. *Decisions of the Commissioner of Patents and of the United States Courts in Patent and Trade-mark Cases 1897* (Washington: Government Printing Office, 1898), pp. 202–203; *T. Cushing Daniel, Trustee, Christopher Armat, John H. Armat, and Selden B. Armat v. American Mutoscope Company and Benjamin Keith*, No. 6753, Circuit Court, Southern District of New York, filed 11 October 1897, NjBaFAR; *Casler v. Armat*, Patent Interference No. 18,461, MdSuFR.

21. "Chicago Enthusiasts," *New York World*, 24 February 1898, p. 3; *Clipper*, 5 March 1898, p. 6.

22. *Philadelphia Record*, 31 July 1898, p. 9; "Proctor's Pleasure Palace," *Clipper*, 19 March 1898, p. 42.

23. *Rochester Post Express*, 5 April 1898; *Boston Herald*, 27 March 1898, p. 10; *Philadelphia Record*, 3 April 1898, pp. 16–17.

24. F. Z. Maguire to William Gilmore, 20 April 1898, NjWOE.

25. *Clipper*, 9 April 1898, p. 92; *New York World*, 31 March 1898, p. 7; *Utica Observer*, 9 May 1898, p. 6.

26. *Clipper*, 21 May 1898, p. 200. Four other cities where substantial runs had recently been completed were also listed. In addition to the locations specified in Biograph's ads, its machine was attached to a few traveling theatrical companies like Hallen and Fuller's First Prize Ideals (*Baltimore Sun*, 31 January 1898, p. 1). A handful of machines were also engaged for brief runs, playing for instance at Hyde & Behman's Brooklyn vaudeville house for one week in late March and the Shuberts' Utica Opera House, where the biograph showed films between theater acts for two weeks (*Brooklyn Eagle*, 27 March 1898, p. 25; *Utica Observer*, 10 May 1898, p. 6).

27. "Extending the Keith Circuit," *NYDM*, 12 March 1898, p. 19.

28. *Phonoscope*, February 1898, p. 8.

29. W. E. Gilmore to William Paley, 7 March 1898, NjWOE.

30. *Philadelphia Record*, 31 July 1898, p. 9.

31. Patrick Loughney, "A Descriptive Analysis of the Library of Congress Paper Print Collection and Related Copyright Records" (Ph.D. diss., George Washington University, 1988), p. 223.

32. "Bill Paley, the Kinetoscope Man," *Phonoscope*, August 1898, pp. 7–8; G. W. Bitzer, *Billy Bitzer*, pp. 38–40.

33. *Philadelphia Record*, 27 March 1898, p. 17; *NYDM*, 9 March 1898, p. 3; *New York Mail and Express*, 2 April 1898, p. 14; *New York World*, 1 May 1898, p. 15, and 19 June 1898, p. 15.

34. *Baltimore Sun*, 25 April 1898, p. 1; *Reading Eagle*, 21 August 1898 through 2 October 1898. Schneider later claimed that he was the first to have such a device and that this "trade secret" had been stolen by American Vitagraph. Although hard evidence is lacking, the general popularity of Schneider's exhibition service makes the statement credible ("Correspondence," *MPW*, 10 August 1907, p. 360).

35. Patent No. 673,329, kinetoscope, filed 15 March 1900, granted 30 April 1901; and Albert E. Smith, deposition, 9 April 1900, *Thomas A. Edison v. J. Stuart Blackton, and Albert E. Smith, individually and as co-partners trading under the name and style of Commercial Advertising Bureau and Amer-*

ican Vitagraph, Nos. 6990 and 6991, Circuit Court, Southern District of New York, filed 12 July 1898, NjBaFAR. Commercial Advertising Bureau, account books, Albert Smith Collection, CLU. Albert Smith filed a patent application for the reframing device well after it was in general use. Later he not only claimed this improvement as his own idea but enjoyed a royalty of one dollar per machine under the arrangements with the Motion Picture Patents Company. (See Volume 2 of this series.)

36. *New York Clipper*, 4 June 1898, p. 234; *Thomas A. Edison v. J. Stuart Blackton and Albert E. Smith, individually and as co-partners trading under the name and style of Commercial Advertising Bureau and American Vitagraph*, Nos. 6989, 6990, and 6991, Circuit Court, Southern District of New York, filed 12 July 1898, NjBaFAR.

37. Thomas Armat to William T. Rock, 18 August 1898, Armat Letter Book, 1898. Thomas A. Armat/ Glenn E. Mathews Collection, NR-GE.

38. *Chicago Tribune*, 15 May 1898, p. 42; *Chicago Inter-Ocean*, 17 May 1898, p. 6. These subjects seem to coincide with titles listed in Selig Polyscope Company, *1903 Complete Catalogue of Films and Moving Picture Machines*, pp. 2–3, 47. At the same time the American War Film Company of Chicago, which was selling Amet's films, did offer a series called "Life in Camp," which could conceivably have been these films (*Clipper*, 2 July 1898, p. 302).

39. See Ramsaye's account in *A Million and One Nights*, pp. 390–391.

40. *Clipper*, 6 August 1898, p. 379.

41. *Clipper*, 30 April 1898, p. 154; *Philadelphia Record*, 29 May 1898, p. 17; *Clipper*, 11 June 1898, p. 254.

42. *Clipper*, 25 June 1898, p. 286.

43. *Clipper*, 12 March 1898, p. 33; 19 March 1898, p. 65; 11 June 1898, p. 254; *Boston Herald*, 13 February 1898, p. 10; 27 February 1898, p. 11; *Philadelphia Record*, 27 March 1898, p. 17.

44. *Clipper*, 13 November 1897, p. 617; 11 December 1897, p. 686; 12 March 1898, p. 33; and 19 March 1898, p. 65.

45. *Reading Eagle*, 28 August 1898, p. 2. Schneider's programs at Proctor's Pleasure Palace are likewise exemplary in this regard.

46. *New Haven Journal-Courier*, 22 April 1898, p. 3; *Philadelphia Record*, 31 July 1898, p. 9, 27 March 1898, p. 17; *New York Mail and Express*, 21 May 1898, p. 14, 22 November 1898, p. 7.

47. Lyman H. Howe, program, fall 1898, reprinted in Musser and Nelson, *High-Class Moving Pictures*.

CHAPTER 9. The Film Industry Achieves Modest Stability: 1898–1901

1. *NYDM*, 22 October 1898, p. 22; "American Mutoscope & Biograph Company to Our Patrons," 22 December 1900, reprinted in Niver, ed., *Biograph Bulletins*, p. 54.

2. *Phonoscope*, May 1898, p. 11; "Commercial Features of the Mutoscope," American Mutoscope Company, n.d. [1898], CLAc; "The Mutoscope," *Philadelphia Record*, 26 February 1899, p. 9; "New Corporations," *Phonoscope*, February 1899, p. 14.

3. American Mutoscope & Biograph Company, "The American Biograph," July 1899, reprinted in Niver, ed., *Biograph Bulletins*, p. 45.

4. "The Biograph in Venice," *New York Mail and Express*, 1 April 1899, *Illustrated Magazine*, p. 13; "Taking the Dewey Pictures," *Boston Herald*, 24 September 1899, p. 47.

5. William Kennedy Laurie Dickson, *The Biograph in Battle* (London: Fisher Unwin, 1901); "The War in China," *Boston Herald*, 10 March 1901, p. 17.

6. American Mutoscope Company, "Biograph Operator's Instructions," 12 October 1898, CLCM; Bitzer, *Billy Bitzer*, p. 27.

7. Bordwell, Thompson, and Staiger, *The Classical Hollywood Cinema*, pp. 116–117.

8. "Keith's Union Square Theatre," *Clipper*, 11 June 1898, p. 244; 3 September 1898, p. 444.

9. *Boston Herald*, 1 November 1898, p. 9. When the biograph was at Keith's new vaudeville theater in Providence, Rhode Island, a local critic reported, "The biograph pictures were warmly applauded, especially one showing the Providence pets, the First Rhode Island Volunteers, at Camp Meade" (*NYDM*, 5 November 1898, p. 21).

10. Bitzer, *Billy Bitzer*, pp. 45–46; American Mutoscope & Biograph Company, production records, production nos. 1376 and 1378, NNMOMA.

11. When these were sold later (in 1902) as 35-mm films, their length came to about 28 feet, or half the length of short comedies made by 35-mm producers. These negatives were printed optically, not only to reduce the frame from 70 mm to 35 mm but apparently so that only every other frame was used. (See films taken from paper prints that Biograph submitted for copyright purposes in 1902–1903.) Free-lance exhibitors could thus show them at about fifteen frames per second rather than thirty.

12. Deslandes and Richard, *Histoire comparée du cinéma*, vol. 2, p. 282. Although McCutcheon was credited as cameraman, it seems unlikely that he was in the booth.

13. These films differed from earlier efforts such as the scenes from *Rip Van Winkle*, which had not been shown—as far as is known—as part of a single sequence. The Christmas series of 1897 had used only a single set and camera position, but, more important, it had not been repeated.

14. Albert F. McLean, Jr., *American Vaudeville as Ritual* (Lexington: University of Kentucky Press, 1965).

15. *Clipper*, 10 September 1898, p. 412; *NYDM*, 19 November 1898, p. 20.

16. *Thomas A. Edison v. Eberhard Schneider*, Nos. 7124 and 7125, Circuit Court, Southern District of New York, filed 21 December 1898, NjBaFAR; *Thomas A. Edison v. George Huber*, No. 7224, Circuit Court, Southern District of New York, filed 28 April 1899, NjBaFAR. See Germain Lacasse, *L'historiographe: Les débuts du spectacle cinématographique au Québec* (Montreal: Cinémathèque Québequois, 1985) for a rigorous though partial history of these French showmen operating in North America.

17. *Clipper*, 24 June 1899, p. 328.

18. *Clipper*, 7 October 1899, p. 652. However, not all the Dewey films shown at Pastor's were taken by Vitagraph employees.

19. *New Orleans Picayune*, 9 October 1899, p. 7.

20. *NYDM*, 14 October 1899, p. 18.

21. *New York World*, 5 November 1899, p. 8E; 19 November 1899, p. 6E.

22. Photograph, Twenty-third Street, New York City, fall 1900, NNMus; *Clipper* 19 May 1900, p. 264; "A Big Pictorial Melodrama at the Garden Theatre," *New York Times*, 22 February 1900, p. 7. George Pratt has reported that this play also marked Cecil B. DeMille's professional debut as an actor.

23. *James H. White and John Schermerhorn v. Percival Waters*, Supreme Court, New York County, NNNCC-Ar. The case focused on the nature of this partnership with its obvious conflict-of-interest implications.

24. Robert Grau, *Theatre of Science* (New York: Broadway Publishing Co., 1914), p. 26. Accepted at face value by most survey histories, the issue has been explored in greater depth in Joseph H. North, *The Early Development of the Motion Picture: 1887–1909* (New York: Arno Press, 1973), pp. 187–188; Allen, *Vaudeville and Film*, pp. 167–172; Charles Musser "Another Look at the Chaser Theory," *Studies in Visual Communication* 10 (Fall 1984), p. 51.

25. *Providence Journal*, 23 February 1901, cited in Allen, *Vaudeville and Film*, p. 175.

26. American Mutoscope & Biograph Company, announcement, 5 March 1901, reprinted in Niver, *Biograph Bulletins*, p. 55.

27. Such overstatement is characteristic of both Grau's *The Theatre of Science* and Ramsaye's *A Million and One Nights*, which devotes entire chapters to such relatively minor events. The distortions must be corrected, yet the specific incidents are ignored or dismissed only at the contemporary historian's peril.

28. *Wilkes-Barre Record*, 26 October 1899, p. 5; *Mail and Express*, 8 April 1899, p. 11; *Philadelphia Record*, 18 April 1899, p. 2; 29 October 1899, p. 9. The trick films were promoted under the "Houdin" brand name, which referred to Méliès's famous Théâtre Robert-Houdin in Paris.

29. *NYDM*, 7 April 1900, p. 11; "News and Gossip of the Players," *Utica Observer*, 18 February 1899, p. 9.

30. Ramsaye, *A Million and One Nights*, p. 384.

31. *Pittsburgh Post*, 5 November 1899, p. 7; "Exposition Esplanade—Lubin's Cineograph," *Philadelphia Record*, 26 November 1899, p. 9.

32. This film was advertised in F. M. Prescott, *Catalogue of New Films* (New York, 20 November 1899), p. 4.

33. A New York bias has dominated news-gathering in the United States since 1849, when the city's newspapers formed the Associated Press (see Daniel J. Czitrom, *Media and the American Mind: From Morse to McLuhan* [Chapel Hill: University of North Carolina Press, 1982], pp. 16–29).

34. Amet films were still for sale in the fall of 1899 (*Clipper*, 23 September 1899, p. 619) and still being shown by Vitagraph the following year (Blackton and Smith to Edison Manufacturing Co., 10 September 1900), but there the trail stops. Further research remains to be done on Amet.

35. *Memphis Commercial Appeal*, 20 January 1901, p. 19.

36. Selig Polyscope Company, certificate of incorporation, filed 21 November 1900, incorporated 4 December 1900, ICC; *Thomas A. Edison v. William N. Selig*, No. 25,761, Circuit Court, Northern District of Illinois, filed 5 December 1900, ICFAR; Selig Polyscope Company, minutes, 1900–, CLac.

37. Selig Polyscope Company, minutes, pp. 9–29.
38. *Ibid.*, pp. 21, 26.
39. Selig Polyscope Company, *1903 Complete Catalogue*, p. 43.
40. *Ibid.*, p. 27.
41. Selig Polyscope Company, Minutes, p. 8.
42. Patent No. 628,413, kinetoscopic apparatus, applied 25 February 1898, granted 4 July 1899; Patent No. 632,472, kinetoscopic apparatus, applied 16 March 1899, granted 5 September 1899. Roebuck had left Sears, Roebuck & Company and was a principal owner of the Enterprise Optical Company (Enterprise Optical Company, certificate of incorporation, filed 27 December 1900, ICC).
43. *Thomas A. Edison v. Sears, Roebuck and Co.*, Nos. 25,552 and 25,553, Circuit Court, Northern District of Illinois, filed 30 April 1900; *Thomas A. Edison v. Stereopticon and Film Exchange, and William B. Moore individually and as Treasurer and Manager of said Company*, Nos. 25,808 and 25,809, Circuit Court, Northern District of Illinois, filed 5 February 1901; *Thomas A. Edison v. The Enterprise Optical Mfg. Company and Frank McMillan, individually and as President and Manager of said Company*, Nos. 25,993 and 25,994, Circuit Court, Northern District of Illinois, filed 14 September 1901; *Thomas A. Edison v. Edward D. Otis and N. M. Kent individually and as co-partners trading under the firm name and style of Chicago Projecting Company*, No. 25,996, Circuit Court, Northern District of Illinois, filed 16 September 1901, ICFAR.
44. These sweeping statements, of course, require nuance and some qualification. Since vaudeville managers made their selections from among the most successful firms, their choices were necessarily limited. Paley would falter, while Spoor would seek a new partner as he moved into production. But Eberhard Schneider could have been among these leaders if he had found the support of a vaudeville manager.

CHAPTER 10. A Period of Commercial Crisis: 1900–1903

1. In fact, George Pratt's research indicates that no films of any kind were shown in Rochester theaters from March 1901 to March 1903 ("No Magic, No Mystery, No Sleight of Hand," in Deutlebaum, ed., *"Image,"* pp. 39–46).
2. "Revival of Moving Picture Craze," *Pittsburgh Post*, 23 February 1902, p. 6C.
3. M. J. Keating, "Boston Show," *Keith Reports* 1:73 (week of 24 November 1902), IaU. See also Musser, "Another Look at the 'Chaser Theory.'"
4. *Clipper*, 24 March 1906, p. 134; *Film Index*, 12 May 1906, p. 4, 29 September 1906, p. 4; *Manchester* (N.H.) *Mirror*, quoted in *Moving Picture World*, 26 October 1907, p. 541.
5. "Miles Brothers Made Early Start," *MPW*, 15 July 1916, p. 399; "Halls of the Ancients," *Washington Evening Star*, 10 September 1901, p. 16.
6. *Los Angeles Times*, 16 April 1902, p. 1; "Clever Moving Pictures," *ibid.*, 11 October 1903, p. 2F.
7. Searchlight Theater, account book and broadsides, 1900–1902, DLC.
8. Reese V. Jenkins, *Images and Enterprise: Technology and the American Photographic Industry, 1839–1925* (Baltimore: Johns Hopkins University Press, 1975), p. 279. Unfortunately figures are not available for the 1903–1905 period. A further check of the Kodak Company Archive proved unproductive: apparently the company has a policy of destorying virtually all records after five years.
9. *Clipper*, 29 December 1900, p. 986; 11 May 1901, p. 265.
10. 110 *Federal Reporter*, pp. 660–664.
11. H. J. Collins, deposition, 2 August 1901, *Edison v. American Mutoscope Company*, NjBaFAR. Note that "Biograph Earnings" + "Mutoscope Earnings" = Net Earnings.
12. 110 *Federal Reporter*, pp. 664–665; Dyer, Edmonds, and Dyer to Kerr, Page, and Cooper, 3 December 1901; and Dyer, Edmonds, and Dyer to William Gilmore, 18 December 1901, NjWOE. The Warwick Trading Company was owned by Maguire & Baucus and managed by Charles Urban.
13. 114 *Federal Reporter*, p. 934.
14. H. J. Collins, monthly income reports, 16 September 1901 to March 1902, *Edison v. American Mutoscope Co.*, NjBaFAR.
15. See the paper prints of Biograph films produced between 1896 and 1902 at the Library of Congress. They give very little idea of the quality of the original 68-mm productions, however. Biograph had developed the ability for optical printing early on since its mutoscope cards were enlarged from the negatives.
16. *Clipper*, 29 March 1902, p. 110.
17. *Thomas A. Edison v. American Mutoscope & Biograph Company*, Nos. 8289 and 8290, Circuit Court,

Southern District of New York, filed 7 November 1902, NjBaFAR. This important case, which gradually worked its way through the courts over the next several years, will be considered further in chapter 14.

18. *Clipper*, 28 March 1903, p. 128.

19. *Clipper*, 30 August 1902, p. 616; *Keith Reports* 1:73 (week of 24 November 1902), 1:26 (week of 20 October 1902), 1:443 (week of 5 January 1903), IaU.

20. *Keith Reports* 1:217 (week of 23 March 1903), IaU; Keith's Union Square Theatre, program, 23 March 1903, Theater Collection, PP; *Keith Reports* 1:227, 228, 231 (week of 30 March 1903), 1:236, 241 (week of 6 April 1903), IaU.

21. *San Francisco Chronicle*, 7 June 1903, p. 30. Biograph also made a short film of Sid Grauman bowing to the audience, perhaps as a way to introduce the pictures in his theaters.

22. *Clipper*, 2 March 1901, p. 24.

23. *New Haven Journal Courier*, 29 October 1901. It is also possible that Poli arranged for an Edison cameraman to take the film.

24. *La Presse*, 23 and 30 March 1901, cited in Lacasse, *L'historiographe*, p. 25. THE GREAT ALBANY CAR STRIKE, which Paley took for Proctor's Albany house in May, was immediately offered for sale by Edison but never copyrighted (*Albany Evening Journal*, 20 May 1901, p. 10; *Clipper*, 25 May 1901, p. 292).

25. Tom Gunning, "The Non-Continuous Film," in Holman, *Cinema, 1900–1906*.

26. *Clipper*, 8 June 1901, p. 336, and 29 June 1901, p. 396.

27. Bruno Bettelheim, *The Uses of Enchantment* (New York: Alfred A. Knopf, 1976), pp. 183–195.

28. *Edison Films*, February 1903, pp. 2–3; *Clipper*, 31 January 1903, p. 1100; both reprinted in Musser, *Before the Nickelodeon*.

29. *Clipper*, 2 March 1901, p. 24.

30. *Clipper*, 25 May 1901, p. 312; 29 June 1901, p. 396; Oscar T. Taylor to Dyer, Edmonds, and Dyer, 13 June 1901, NjWOE.

31. Lubin Cineograph- und Film-Fabrik, advertisement, legal files, NjWOE.

32. Dun & Company, "Siegmund Lubin," 5 May 1902 and 29 May 1902, legal files, NjWOE; *Thomas A. Edison v. Siegmund Lubin*, No. 25, October Sessions 1902, Circuit Court, Eastern District of Pennsylvania, filed 6 November 1902, PPFAR.

33. *Thomas A. Edison v. Siegmund Lubin*, No. 36, April Sessions 1902, Circuit Court, Eastern District of Pennsylvania, filed 6 June 1902, PPFAR.

34. *Clipper*, 5 April 1902, p. 140, and 12 July 1902, p. 444; Selig Polyscope Company, *Special Supplement of Colorado Films* (November 1902).

35. *Clipper*, 3 May 1902, p. 256, 2 August 1902, p. 504, 27 September 1902, p. 688; S. Lubin, *Lubin's Films*, January 1903, p. 36.

36. *Clipper*, 1 November 1902, p. 808; S. Lubin, *Lubin's Films*, January 1903, p. 55.

37. *Clipper*, 6 December 1902, p. 920; S. Lubin, *The Holy City and Other Illustrated Songs in Life Motion Pictures* (1905). The later catalog raised the cost to $5,000.

38. *Clipper*, 28 February 1903, p. 36; Thomas A. Edison and Siegmund Lubin, memorandum of agreement, 15 October 1902, legal files, NjWOE.

39. "Armat Moving Picture Company to Exhibitors of and Dealers in Moving Picture Machines, Films, and Supplies," 25 March 1902, reprinted in *United States v. Motion Picture Patents Company*, pp. 2127–2133; 118 *Federal Reporter*, pp. 840–850; *Armat Moving Picture Company v. Edison Manufacturing Company*, No. 8303, Circuit Court, Southern District of New York, filed 28 November 1902, NjBaFAR.

40. Armat Moving Picture Company and E. Burton Holmes, agreement, 12 December 1900, reprinted in Thomas Armat, testimony, *United States v. Motion Picture Patents Company*, pp. 2119–2121; "Armat Moving Picture Company to Exhibitors of and Dealers in Motion Picture Machines, Films, and Supplies," 25 March 1902; *Armat Moving Picture Company v. Eden Musee American Company, Ltd.*, No. 8361, Circuit Court, Southern District of New York, filed 5 February 1903, NjBaFAR; Edison Manufacturing Company, circular letter form, *ca.*, August 1903, NjWOE. See also B. B. H. Lawrence to W. E. Gilmore, 16 May 1903, NjWOE.

41. *Louisville Courier-Journal*, 24 September 1901, p. 4; "Men Fought Women in Temple Theater Panic," *Louisville Courier-Journal*, 23 October 1901, pp. 1, 2; "Theater Panic," *ibid.*, 24 October 1901, p. 4.

42. *Clipper*, 9 March 1902, p. 109; Selig Polyscope Company, *New Films*, 2 February 1903; *Thomas A. Edison v. Selig Polyscope Company*, No. 26,512, Circuit Court, Northern District of Illinois, filed 7 November 1902, ICFAR.

43. "Now a Vaudeville Trust," *Chicago Tribune*, 15 July 1901, p. 2; "Vaudeville Theaters Effect a Combine," *San Francisco Chronicle*, 15 July 1915, p. 6.

44. Edwin S. Porter, affidavit, *ca.* 1907, legal files, NjWOE; American Vitagraph Company, *New Vitagraph Features!* p. 10; *New Haven Journal Courier*, 28 December 1902, p. 3.

45. *Clipper*, 14 March 1903, pp. 65–73; *Keith Reports* 1:25 (week of 27 April 1903), 1:247 (week of 20 April 1903), IaU.

46. The others were from late 1895 to early 1896, late 1897 to early 1898, and late 1898 to early 1899. The last two, however, were subject to considerable regional variation.

CHAPTER 11. The Transition to Story Films: 1903–1904

1. American Mutoscope & Biograph Company, "Select Comedy Films," 12 September 1904, reprinted in Niver, ed., *Biograph Bulletins*, p. 126.

2. American Mutoscope & Biograph Company, *Bulletin* no. 6 (1 June 1903), in Niver, *Biograph Bulletins*, pp. 83, 84; M. J. Keating, *Keith Reports* 1:312 (week of 17 August 1903), IaU.

3. The number of films made at Edison that were neither copyrighted nor entered in its catalog is uncertain since comprehensive production records like those of Biograph are lacking. Thomas Edison copyrighted 90 films between 1 July 1903 and 1 July 1904, while Biograph listed 529 productions in its catalog for the same period. Copyright registration offers only a partial picture of any company's filmmaking activities, since films were often made for clients or did not merit the expense of copyrighting. Moreover, Biograph often listed scenes for a single subject separately. Although the differences are not as extreme as these figures suggest, it is clear that Edison's three cinematographers did not match Biograph's output.

4. The 1900 census reports that McCutcheon and Marion (both married with children and both at Biograph) shared living quarters in Manhattan.

5. American Mutoscope & Biograph Company, *Bulletin* no. 5 (14 May 1903) and *Bulletin* no. 9 (29 August 1903), reprinted in Niver, ed., *Biograph Bulletins*, pp. 82, 88. The first shot of *The Haymarket*, photographed on a studio set, shows people waiting outside the street entrance. A sign reads "Doors open at 8:45," providing a time frame as people begin to go inside, including a man and a prostitute he picks up by the front door. The next shot shows the dance floor and the Haymarket's denizens executing various popular steps. People in the first shot appear in the second, but considerable time has presumably elapsed. The third shot takes place in another part of the Haymarket— according to the catalog description, the wine room—where a fight starts. The manager, who has already appeared in shot 2, intervenes. The fourth shot returns to the opening camera position, an exterior of the Haymarket, as the bouncer and waiter throw out the two fighters. The fifth scene occurs on the dance floor as the police raid the hall. The final scene returns to the exterior view as the patrons are loaded into a paddy wagon. It is likely that each shot was introduced by a title.

6. *Ibid.*, 29 August 1903, p. 90.

7. The ability to replace one cameraman with the other and achieve the same result reveals the extent of the teamwork at Biograph.

8. American Mutoscope & Biograph Company, *Bulletin* no. 14 (21 September 1903), reprinted in Niver, ed., *Biograph Bulletins*, p. 102.

9. Low and Manvell, *The History of British Film 1896–1906*, p. 16.

10. Patent No. 722,382, animated picture apparatus, issued 10 March 1903 to John A. Pross, assignor to American Mutoscope & Biograph Company. The company also apparently shared the technology with Charles Urban, providing him with one of the key assets that launched his business.

11. *Keith Reports* 1:301 (week of 27 July 1903), 1:305, 306 (week of 3 August 1903), IaU.

12. A scene-by-scene Edison catalog description of this film can be found in Jacobs, *The Rise of the American Film*, pp. 43–46.

13. Andre Gaudreault, "Detours in Film Narrative: The Development of Cross-Cutting," *Cinema Journal* (Fall 1979), pp. 39–59.

14. David Levy, "The Fake Train Robbery," in Holman, *Cinema, 1900–1906*.

15. Temporality and some plot elements of *Out in the Streets* are only made explicit in the catalog description, which would have been the basis for a showman's lecture or his title slides, *Biograph Bulletin* no. 55 (27 November 1905), reprinted in Niver, ed., *Biograph Bulletins*, p. 217.

16. See, for example, "The Awful Battle of the Yalu Fiercely Fought by Boys of a Military School in Front of the Mutoscope-Biograph Camera," *San Francisco Examiner*, 10 April 1904, magazine section.

17. *Clipper*, 9 January 1904, p. 1113.

18. *Boston Herald,* 26 January 1904, p. 11.

19. *Clipper* 12 September 1903, p. 692.

20. *Clipper,* 19 December 1903, p. 1040.

21. S. Lubin, *The Holy City and Other Illustrated Songs in Life Motion Pictures* (1905) and *Illustrated Song Slides,* 1905.

22. *Clipper,* 30 April 1904, p. 233.

23. Selig Polyscope Company, *Complete 1903 Catalogue,* pp. 46, 48.

24. Selig Polyscope Company, "Special President Roosevelt Circular" and *The New Bull Fight; Clipper,* 2 July 1904, p. 450.

25. American Vitagraph Company, *New Vitagraph Features!* (1903) p. 11; *Rochester Democrat and Chronicle,* 6 March 1904, p. 16. The film of the Rochester fire may have been purchased from a local cinematographer (perhaps associated with Kodak) and was eventually sold by the Edison Manufacturing Company.

26. William T. Rock and J. Stuart Blackton to Albert E. Smith, 27 February 1908, CLU.

27. Gaston Méliès, testimony, 29 December 1909, *Georges Méliès Company* v. *Motion Picture Patents Company and Edison Manufacturing Company,* No. 15-5826, District Court, District of New Jersey, filed 21 May 1909, NjWOE; Georges Méliès, *Complete Catalogue of Genuine and Original Star Films* (New York, 1903), p. 5; William Rock and J. Stuart Blackton to Albert E. Smith, 27 February 1908, CLU. Since Biograph retained an agency for Méliès films for a period of time, it seems that the company told Gaston about copyright procedures. Méliès, however, ceased submitting paper prints in 1904. Balshofer reports that Lubin, at least, was duplicating Méliès productions during 1905–1906 (Fred J. Balshofer and Arthur C. Miller, *One Reel a Week* [Berkeley: University of California Press, 1967], pp. 5–9).

28. *Bulletins* 10 [*sic* 11], 12, 14 (3, 18, and 21 September 1903), reprinted in Niver, *Biograph Bulletins,* pp. 95, 98–99, 107.

29. Low and Manvell, *The History of British Film, 1896–1906,* pp. 17–22.

30. *Boston Herald,* 9 February 1904, p. 9. See also 27 March 1904, p. 6.

31. *Rochester Democrat and Chronicle,* 14 February 1904, p. 16.

32. Musser and Nelson, *High-Class Moving Pictures.*

33. *Clipper,* 8 August 1903, p. 572. Of course, it is highly unlikely that he had that many takers. Even so, Lubin's contribution to this industry-wide shift may not have been properly credited because he was not directly competing in the key New York market.

34. *Clipper,* 5 December 1903, p. 992; Herbert L. Miles, testimony, February 1911, *Motion Picture Patents Company* v. *Independent Moving Picture Company,* no. 5–167, NjBaFAR; Albert E. Smith, testimony, 14 November 1913, *U.S.* v. *Motion Picture Patents Company,* pp. 1702–1703. Albert E. Smith remembered that the Kinetograph Company made the move before the Miles Brothers, while the Miles Brothers always claimed to be the first to open a rental exchange. Who came first seems less important than the fact that both made the move at about the same time.

35. *Clipper,* 9 January 1904, p. 1113; 5 March 1904, p. 36; 30 April 1904, pp. 232, 238. At this point, the National Film Renting Bureau was simply named the Film Rental Bureau.

36. "Burton Holmes Lectures," *Boston Herald,* 29 November 1903, p. 17.

37. "Lenten Lectures on Distant Lands and People," *New York World,* 28 February 1904, p. 4M.

38. " 'Give Us the Bull Fight,' Cried Men and Women," *Brooklyn Eagle,* 13 November 1904, p. 1.

CHAPTER 12. Cinema Flourishes Within Its Existing Commercial Framework: 1904–1905

1. *Film Index,* 21 November 1908, p. 3; *Clipper,* 30 September 1905, p. 824.

2. "Plimton in on Ground Floor," *MPW,* 15 July 1916, p. 389; Adolph Zukor with Dale Kramer, *The Public Is Never Wrong* (New York: G. P. Putnam's Sons, 1953), pp. 36–37; "Zukor Quits Furs for Films," *MPW,* 15 July 1916, p. 415; Automatic Vaudeville Company, certificate of incorporation, 4 March 1904, and related documents, NNNCC-Ar; "Another Amusement Project," *Pittsburgh Dispatch,* 16 November 1905, p. 14.

3. *Biograph Bulletin* no. 28 (15 August 1904), reprinted in Niver, ed., *Biograph Bulletins,* p. 121.

4. Loughney, "The Suburbanite," in Leyda and Musser, eds., *Before Hollywood,* p. 119.

5. *New York World,* 17 July 1904, Sunday magazine section.

6. Academy Theater advertisement, *Washington Star,* 29 November 1902, p. 21.

7. *Bulletin* no. 39, reprinted in Niver, *Biograph Bulletins,* p. 142.

8. *Bulletin* no. 55 (27 November 1905), p. 28, reprinted in Niver, ed., *Biograph Bulletins*, p. 218.

9. Noël Burch, "Primitivism and the Avant-Gardes: A Dialectical Approach," in Philip Rosen, ed., *Narrative, Apparatus, Ideology* (New York: Columbia University Press, 1986), p. 502.

10. *Keith Reports* 3:166 (week of 3 October 1904), IaU.

11. G. H. Fleming, ed., *The Unforgettable Season* (New York: Holt, Rinehart, and Winston, 1981), p. 209.

12. *American Mutoscope & Biograph Company* v. *Edison Manufacturing Company*, No. 10-221, Circuit Court, District of New Jersey, filed 12 November 1904, NjWOE. (Court records for the District of New Jersey were lost in a fire; some pertinent records survive at the Edison National Historic Site.)

13. Gene Gauntier, "Blazing the Trail," unpublished manuscript, NNMOMA; Edison Manufacturing Company, payroll book, 1895–1906, NjWOE.

14. *Clipper*, 3 June 1905, p. 392; "Defendant's Brief on Demurrer to Bill," 18 April 1905, *American Mutoscope & Biograph Company* v. *Edison Manufacturing Company*; *Clipper*, 1 July 1905, p. 488. INTERIOR NEW YORK SUBWAY, 14TH STREET TO 42ND STREET (No. 3031) was also sold and shown separately.

15. *Clipper*, 17 December 1904, p. 1020.

16. In the later part of 1904, both A. C. Abadie and J. Blair Smith left Edison's employ. For a more detailed account of Edison's hirings and firings see Musser, *Before the Nickelodeon*.

17. See Richard Hofstadter, ed., *The Progressive Movement, 1900–1915* (Englewood Cliffs, N.J.: Prentice-Hall, 1963).

18. This animation was probably done by shooting the titles upside down. The titles were first shot in their final position and then scattered by moving them slightly between single-frame exposures. After development, the negative was turned so that the tail became the head, and vice versa.

19. Lubin, *Meet Me at the Fountain*, p. 10, and *Lubin Films* (1905), pp. 7–9, CLAc. Like other surviving catalogs of this era, these may be found in Musser *et al.*, eds., *Motion Picture Catalogs by American Producers and Distributors, 1894–1908*.

20. *Billboard*, 11 November 1905, p. 30; Paul Hammond, ed., *The Shadow and Its Shadow: Surrealist Writing on Cinema* (London: British Film Institute, 1978), pp. 8–9.

21. *Clipper*, 1 October 1904, p. 752.

22. *Clipper*, 30 April 1904, p. 240; *Billboard*, 11 November 1905, p. 5.

23. *Clipper*, 27 August 1904, p. 613. The record producer, Victor, was based in Camden, New Jersey, and, paralleling Lubin's situation, was in direct competition with Edison's phonograph operations.

24. *Clipper*, 9 July 1904, p. 450.

25. "Stage Coach Held-up Within Mile of the City," *Colorado Springs Gazette*, 3 October 1904, p. 3.

26. *Moving Picture World*, 3 July 1909, p. 15.

27. "New Ways for Girls to Make Money," *San Francisco Examiner*, 23 October 1904, magazine section; *Chicago Tribune*, 16 October 1904, magazine section.

28. *Billboard*, 2 September 1905, p. 47; Selig Polyscope Company, *The Gay Deceivers*; CLAc; *Billboard*, 28 October 1905, p. 40.

29. *Clipper*, 25 March 1905, p. 134; Selig Polyscope Company, *Samoa and the Fiji Islands* (1905), CLAc.

30. *Clipper*, 29 October 1904, p. 837. Short fragments of these pictures survive in the Paper Print Collection at the Library of Congress and provide tentative information about their form and subject matter.

31. *Clipper*, 28 January 1905, p. 1188; Ramsaye, *A Million and One Nights*, p. 424.

32. *Thomas A. Edison* v. *William Paley and William F. Steiner, doing business under the name Paley & Steiner*, No. 8911, Circuit Court, Southern District of New York, filed 23 November 1904, NjBaFAR; *Clipper*, 12 August 1905, p. 636.

33. Troy, N.Y., *Northern Budget*, 22 October 1905, p. 6; 29 October 1905, p. 6.

34. *Clipper*, 29 April 1905, p. 268, 23 September 1905, p. 795; *Norwalk Hour*, 7 October 1904, p. 7; *New Britain Record*, 25 November 1904, p. 3.

35. *Thomas Edison* v. *American Vitagraph Company, William T. Rock, J. Stuart Blackton, and Albert E. Smith*, No. 9,035, Circuit Court, Southern District of New York, filed 13 March 1905, NjBaFAR; Edwin S. Porter, unused deposition, *ca.* 1907, NjWOE.

36. Gartenberg, "Vitagraph Before Griffith: Forging Ahead in the Nickelodeon Era."

37. *Clipper*, 23 September 1905, p. 795; E. W. Hornung, *Raffles* (New York: Charles Scribner's Sons, 1901) and *The Amateur Cracksman* (New York: Charles Scribner's Sons, 1902); *Clipper*, 7 October 1905, p. 852, 9 December 1905, p. 1072, 16 March 1907, p. 124. American Vitagraph Company

remained the name for Blackton, Smith, and Rock's exhibition-rental entity until it was sold to the General Film Company on 15 August 1910 (*U.S. v. Motion Picture Patents Company*, p. 191).

38. *Clipper*, 6 January 1906, p. 1188.

39. *Clipper*, 21 October 1905, p. 906.

40. NYDM, 3 May 1911, p. 34; Max Hollander, "Recollections of an Old-Timer," *Motion Picture Projectionist*, October 1927, p. 10; William Basil Courtney, "History of Vitagraph," *Moving Picture News*, 21 March 1925, p. 1222.

41. The Vitagraph partners had learned from past mistakes; unlike Paley & Steiner, they contested Edison's patent-infringement suits and prospered.

42. *Clipper*, 27 August 1904, p. 613.

43. Alex T. Moore to James White, 10 October 1904, NjWOE.

44. *Clipper*, 3 May 1905, p. 290.

CHAPTER 13. Nickels Count: Storefront Theaters, 1905–1907

1. The nickelodeon era of storefront motion-picture theaters has been a subject of considerable study and debate. Robert Sklar provides an excellent overview of the positions taken by a range of scholars in "Oh! Althusser!: Historiography and the Rise of Cinema Studies," *Radical History Review* 41 (1988), pp. 11–35. Besides those articles mentioned elsewhere in this chapter, the interested reader is referred to Garth Jowett, *Film: The Democratic Art* (Boston: Little, Brown, 1976); Elizabeth Ewen, "City Lights: Immigrant Women and the Rise of the Movies," *Signs* 5, no. 3 Supplement (1980), pp. S45–65; Judith Mayne, "Immigrants and Spectators," *Wide Angle* 5, no. 2 (1982), pp. 32–40; Miriam Hansen, "Early Silent Cinema: Whose Public Sphere?" *New German Critique* 29 (Winter 1983), pp. 147–184.

2. *Clipper*, 30 September 1905, p. 824; Roy Rosenzweig, *Eight Hours for What We Will: Workers and Leisure in an Industrial City* (Cambridge: Cambridge University Press, 1983), pp. 191–221.

3. *Clipper*, 15 July 1905, p. 540; *Billboard*, 23 September 1905, p. 48. The Miles Brothers indicated that they would rent films with changes "oftener" than once a week as early as May 1905 (*Clipper*, 27 May 1905, p. 368).

4. "Among the Picture Theaters," *MPW*, 11 January 1913, p. 163; "Our Head Office Boy Wants to be a Reporter," *Film Index*, 5 May 1906, p. 11; "Will Enforce Sunday Laws," *Pittsburgh Post*, 2 May 1904, p. 8; "Soda Fountains Exempt in New Sunday Closings," *Pittsburgh Dispatch*, 12 May 1905, p. 14.

5. *Pittsburgh Post*, 4 September 1904, p. 6B; and 11 October 1904.

6. "Alvin Becomes Property of B. F. Keith," *Pittsburgh Post*, 1 May 1904, p. 2C; "The Stage and Its People," *ibid.*, 12 June 1904, p. 5C; "The Star Theater," *ibid.*, 16 October 1904, p. 3B; *Clipper*, 27 February 1904, p. 18; *Pittsburgh Dispatch*, 4 June 1905, p. 5; *Pittsburgh Moving Picture Bulletin*, 23 April 1914, p. 4. Royer ran as many as twelve houses at one time with George Balsdon.

7. "Record Pay in Towns of the Monongahela," *Pittsburgh Dispatch*, 16 April 1905, p. 1B; 4 June 1905, p. 5B; 24 August 1905, p. 12; and 28 October 1905, p. 16.

8. "Amusement Is Turned to Horror," *Pittsburgh Post*, 19 November 1905, p. 1; "Picture Machine Gets Afire in Packed Room and Many Are Injured," *Pittsburgh Dispatch*, 19 November 1905, p. 2; "Inspect Nickelodians," *Pittsburgh Post*, 23 November 1905, p. 3.

9. *Film Index*, 30 June 1906, p. 6.

10. "Rochester," *Billboard*, 27 June 1908, p. 36; "The First Nickelodeon in the States," *MPW*, 30 November 1907, p. 629; "Pittsburgh, Pa., Has a Record Date for 'Store Shows,' " *ibid.*, 15 July 1916, p. 405; "The Situation in Philadelphia," *ibid.*, 26 October 1907, p. 540.

11. *Billboard*, 27 January 1906, p. 7; and 27 June 1908, p. 13; and 31 August 1907, p. 5.

12. "New Orleans Records Wonderful Development," *MPW*, 15 July 1916, p. 403; *Billboard*, 29 December 1906, p. 41, and 15 December 1906, p. 32.

13. "Zanesville," *Billboard*, 27 June 1908, p. 36.

14. *Wilkes-Barre Record*, 30 March 1906, p. 5.

15. "Chicago Reports Many Variations in Picture Shows," *MPW*, 15 July 1916, pp. 413–414. The Cline theater goes unmentioned in this account.

16. Carl Laemmle, "This Business of Motion Pictures," *n.d.*, CBevA; "Carl Laemmle Made Start in Chicago Storefront," *MPW*, 15 July 1916, p. 420.

17. "Our Head Office Boy Wants to Be a Reporter," *Film Index*, 5 May 1906, p. 11; "An Unexploited Field and Its Possibilities," *ibid.*, 6 October 1906, p. 3; *Variety*, 16 December 1905, p. 4.

18. *Film Index*, 6 October 1906, p. 3. This article indicates that Bowery film theaters drew most of their patrons from the Lower East Side and that Italians from this area were important moviegoers, contrary to the claims made in Robert C. Allen, "Motion Picture Exhibition in Manhattan, 1906–1912," in Fell, ed., *Film Before Griffith*, pp. 166, 169–170.

19. *Billboard*, 12 May 1906, p. 9; *Topeka State Journal*, 1 December 1906, p. 7, 9 March 1907, p. 5; "Moving Pictures at Dallas," *MPW*, 23 March 1907, p. 40; *Billboard*, 13 October 1906, p. 20.

20. "New Theatre Comique Is Crowded All First Day," *Boston Herald*, 31 August 1906, 7; *ibid.*, 2 April 1907, p. 10; *MPW*, 13 April 1907, p. 88. Russell Merritt thus incorrectly dates the first Boston nickelodeons. In various other ways, his Boston-based study is not typical of developments in other parts of the nation (Merritt, "Nickelodeon Theaters, 1905–1914: Building an Audience for the Movies," in Tino Balio, ed., *The American Film Industry* [Madison: University of Wisconsin Press, 1976], pp. 50–82).

21. Rosenzweig, *Eight Hours for What We Will*, p. 192.

22. William John Mann, "The Movies Come to Middletown: The Cinematic Experience of a Small Town, 1897–1917" (M.A. thesis, Wesleyan University, Middletown, Conn., 1987), pp. 45–46.

23. "Pictures and Vaudeville," *Oswego Palladium*, 19 November 1906, p. 5; "At Wonderland," *ibid.*, 3 December 1906, p. 1.

24. *Troy Daily Times*, 20 December 1906, p. 6; 9 March 1907, p. 2; and 21 March 1907, p. 6.

25. *Lewiston Evening Journal*, 7 January 1907, p. 3; *Pawtucket Evening Times*, 5 June 1906, p. 7.

26. "In the New Nickel," *Manchester Union*, 2 April 1907, p. 3.

27. *Billboard*, 13 December 1906, pp. 32–33; *Show World*, 23 June 1907, p. 20; *Billboard*, 6 July 1907, p. 33.

28. *Billboard*, 16 March 1907, p. 32. *Show World* (29 June 1907, p. 28) claimed 160 Chicago theaters were showing only films and another 20 theaters had them on their bill. In August 1907 *Moving Picture World* reported that Chicago had 116 five-cent picture shows and 18 ten-cent vaudeville/motion-picture theaters (10 August 1907, p. 359). Such discrepancies are common.

29. "Heaven Save Us from More," *Akron Beacon-Journal*, 15 February 1907, p. 4; *Billboard*, 2 March 1907, p. 34; *ibid.* 25 May, p. 39; *Moving Picture World*, 8 July 1907, p. 214.

30. "Electric Theaters and Nickelodeons," *Billboard*, 15 December 1906, pp. 32–33.

31. *Moving Picture World*, 15 July 1916, p. 421; *Variety*, 30 May 1908, p. 11.

32. *Billboard*, 15 December 1906, pp. 32–33.

33. Raymond Fielding, "Hale's Tours: Ultrarealism in the Pre-1910 Motion Picture," in Fell, ed., *Film Before Griffith*, pp. 116–130, provides an excellent study of this subject.

34. Deslandes and Richard, *Histoire comparée de cinéma*, vol. 2, pp. 44–50.

35. "Chief Hale's New Concession at Electric Park," *Kansas City Star*, 28 May 1905, p. 7B; *Film Index*, 5 May 1906, p. 4; *Pittsburgh Post*, 27 August 1905, p. 3B; *Billboard*, 9 September 1905, p. 29; Brady–Grossman Company, certificate of incorporation, filed 2 March 1906, NNNCC-Ar; *Bulletin No. 73*, 30 June 1906, reprinted in Niver, ed., *Biograph Bulletins*, pp. 250–251; *Film Index*, 23 June 1906, p. 6; 30 June 1906, p. 4. Historians have incorrectly asserted that Hale's Tours was at the St. Louis World's Fair in 1904. Advertisements and promotional material make it clear that the Electric Park show was the first.

36. *Film Index*, 21 July 1906, p. 6; 7 July 1906, p. 2; 19 May 1906, p. 7.

37. Peiss, *Cheap Amusements*, p. 152; Manchester, N.H., *Union*, 27 November 1906, p. 12; *MPW*, 23 March 1907, p. 40; *Lewiston Evening Journal*, 14 January 1907, p. 2; "Teddy Bear Souvenir Reception at Bijou, Friday," *ibid.*, 29 May 1907, p. 2; 5 June 1907, p. 2.

38. "Amusement Is Turned to Horror," *Pittsburgh Post*, 19 November 1905, p. 1; "New Pictures at the Nickel," *Lewiston Evening Journal*, 11 January 1907, p. 2.

39. *Film Index*, 28 July 1906, p. 3; 1 December 1906, p. 3; *Billboard*, 18 May 1907, p. 43; *Variety*, 6 July 1907, p. 5.

40. *Billboard*, 16 March 1907, p. 33; *Clipper*, 7 October 1905, p. 842; "Large Profits in Motion Views," *Show World*, 6 July 1907, p. 16; "Moving Pictures in the Parlor," *ibid.*, 20 July 1907, p. 16; *Billboard*, 16 June 1906, p. 26; *MPW*, 15 July 1916, pp. 413–414; Swanson, testimony, *U.S.* v. *Motion Picture Patents Company*, p. 650; *Film Index*, 24 November 1906, p. 8; *Billboard*, 15 June 1907, p. 18.

41. *Billboard*, 27 October 1906, p. 24; Laemmle, "This Business of Motion Pictures," p. 63.

42. Theater Film Service Company, certificate of incorporation, filed 9 January 1907, ICC.

43. *Film Index*, 1 December 1906, p. 6; *Billboard*, 8 December 1906, p. 28.

44. Greater New York Film Rental Company, certificate of incorporation, filed 25 March 1907, NNNCC-Ar; William Fox to Selig Polyscope Company, 5 April 1907, CLAc; *MPW*, 27 April 1907, p. 113.

45. *MPW*, 15 July 1916, 405; *Film Index*, 1 September 1906, p. 10; *ibid.*, 2 March 1907, p. 6; Harry Warner to Selig Polyscope Company, 22 April 1907, CLAc; *MPW*, 15 July 1916, p. 395; *Clipper*, 16 February 1907, p. 1372; *MPW*, 15 July 1916, p. 389; Josiah Pearce & Sons to Selig Polyscope Company, 15 March 1907, CLAc; Marcus Loew to Selig Polyscope Company, 11 March 1907, CLAc.

46. *Baltimore Sun*, 4 August 1907, p. 1.

47. This dearth of opportunities soon changed: after late 1907 many managers would add vaudeville acts to their bills and eventually a theater's staff would even condense or re-edit films to "improve" their shows and keep up the pace. See Eileen Bowser, *The Transformation of Cinema*, chap. 1; Richard Koszarski, *An Evening's Entertainment*, chap. 6; and Miriam Hansen, *Babel and Babylon: Spectatorship in American Silent Film* (Cambridge: Harvard University Press, forthcoming).

48. *Billboard*, 16 March 1907, p. 80; *Film Index*, 16 March 1907, p. 6.

49. *Billboard*, 13 April 1907, p. 53.

50. This copy of the film is at NNMOMA.

51. *MPW*, 30 March 1907, p. 59.

52. H. S. Lewis, *MPW*, 4 May 1907, p. 133.

53. *MPW*, 7 September 1907, p. 422; "What Is an Operator?" *ibid.*, 6 June 1908, p. 495. Operators at vaudeville houses or those with traveling showmen may have often worked similar hours, but their responsibilities were diverse and the amount of time spent projecting films and slides seldom totaled more than two or three hours per day. For the traveling operator, much time was spent traveling, setting up and breaking down the projector, and so forth. In vaudeville, operators working for an exhibition service might perform a variety of jobs between their stints projecting films.

54. "New Moving Picture Theater a Decided Success," *MPW*, 6 June 1908, p. 492; "The Health of the Operator," *ibid.*, 29 February 1908, p. 165; "Moving Picture Shows Have Resumed," *Akron Beacon-Journal*, 20 December 1906, p. 4; "Asbestos Booths Now the Order," *MPW*, 21 March 1908, p. 267; "Hero Loses Life in Theatre Fire," *ibid.*, 6 April 1907, p. 72; "As They Appeal to the Fire Fighters," *ibid.*, 2 November 1907, p. 561; "Singer Falls to Death in Panic," *Cleveland Plain Dealer*, 19 December 1906, p. 1. (The singer was projecting the films when the fire occurred.)

55. "A Plea for Fair Treatment of the Operator," *MPW*, 9 March 1907, p. 10; "Moving Pictures," *Clipper*, 2 February 1907, p. 1321; "An Operators' League and Why?" *MPW*, 9 March 1907, p. 11; "I.B.E.W." *ibid.*, 30 March 1907, p. 52; *Variety* 31 August 1907, p. 9.

56. *MPW*, 24 August 1907, p. 392; *Akron Beacon-Journal*, 1 October 1907, p. 6; "Explosion of Moving Picture Films," *Fireman's Herald* (*ca.* October 1907) cited in *MPW*, 2 November 1907, p. 561; "Picture Men Before Officials," *Akron Beacon-Journal*, 19 December 1906, p. 9; *MPW*, 24 August 1907, p. 391. By this date, Milwaukee and Cleveland had each suffered at least two significant film fires during the previous eight months.

57. *MPW*, 23 March 1907, p. 36; 24 August 1907, p. 391; 18 May 1907, p. 169; 24 August 1907, p. 391.

58. "The Projectoscope," *Film Index*, 23 June 1906, p. 5.

59. *Meriden Journal*, 18 October 1906, p. 14; *Los Angeles Times*, 2 March 1906, p. 2; Thomas L. Tally to Selig Polyscope Company, 17 November 1906, CLAc; *Film Index*, 2 June 1906, p. 10.

60. Hollander, "Recollections of An Old-Timer," pp. 10–11.

61. W. C. Pflueger to J. J. Shubert, 5 March 1909, Shubert Archives.

62. "Ed Howe Lecture," *Topeka Daily Journal*, 19 January 1907, p. 1; "E. S. Curtis' Lecture," *Brooklyn Eagle*, 29 April 1907, p. 6; Bill Holm and George Irving Quimby, *Edward S. Curtis in the Land of the War Canoes: A Pioneer Cinematographer in the Pacific Northwest* (Seattle: University of Washington Press, 1980).

CHAPTER 14. Production as the Nickelodeon Era Begins: 1905–1907

1. *Film Index*, 26 May 1906, p. 4; Musser *et al.*, *Motion Picture Catalogs by American Producers and Distributors, 1894–1908*; *Film Index*, 23 June 1906, p. 5; *Billboard*, 21 September 1907, p. 28. On the other hand, motion-picture cameras continued to be made almost exclusively in Europe—a legacy of Edison's patent suits.

2. This estimate was based on a survey of the *New York Clipper*, adjusted to account for films unsuitable for nickelodeon use and for some European productions that were not advertised.

3. Figures combine *MPW*, 4 May 1907, p. 134, and *Billboard*, 24 August 1907, p. 4. Kleine appears to be the source in both instances. In mid March 1907, however, *Billboard* estimated the supply of films at approximately two thousand feet a week or ten thousand feet per month (16 March 1907, p. 33).

4. 144 *Federal Reporter*, pp. 121–128; 151 *Federal Reporter*, pp. 767–774. Patents continued to play a

crucial role in the motion-picture industry during the next eight years and will be discussed in the second volume of this series. Edison's central, ongoing role in these legal and commercial maneuvers is also examined in Musser, *Before the Nickelodeon,* pp. 379–386, 437–450.

5. Gauntier, "Blazing the Trail." "Mr. Harrington" was probably either Edward M., who later helped to establish the Actograph Company, or George, who worked at Edison as a director in 1909. Relations between Marion and his directors were neither equal nor ongoing; thus the organization of production at Biograph looked toward a more modern producer-based cinema.

6. *Bulletin* no. 77, 6 August 1906, reprinted in Niver, ed., *Biograph Bulletins,* p. 256.

7. Elsie Clews Parsons, *The Family: An Ethnological and Historical Outline with Descriptive Notes,* (New York: G. P. Putnam's Sons, 1906); *New York American,* 16 November 1906, p. 1; "Trial Marriages by Two Women Who Have Tried It," *ibid.,* 2 December 1906, magazine section, p. 2; 8 December 1906, p. 12. Among Frederick Oppers' political cartoons, there was one that proposed "a Realistic Moving Picture Entitled 'Our National Trial Marriage,'" in which "The Trusts" go to bed with "The Common People."

8. *Bulletin* no. 58, 21 November 1905, reprinted in Niver, ed., *Biograph Bulletins,* p. 232.

9. "Academy of Music," *Washington Evening Star,* 29 November 1902, p. 20.

10. "Thieves Carry Out Safe," *New York Herald,* 31 August 1905, p. 7.

11. "Do Moving Pictures Breed Immorality?" *Film Index,* 22 September 1906, p. 3.

12. In this respect, the Biograph *Bulletin* for THE TUNNEL WORKERS tells a completely different story from that of the intertitles. In the *Bulletin* the men are both engineers and equals, while the wife's friendship with the other man is totally innocent.

13. *Billboard,* 10 November 1906, p. 15; 16 March 1907, p. 32; 13 October 1906, p. 21.

14. *Clipper,* 19 January 1907, p. 1266; *Variety,* 16 February 1907, p. 8.

15. *Billboard,* 16 March 1907, p. 32.

16. *MPW,* 7 August 1909, p. 209.

17. *MPW,* 27 July 1907, p. 327; *Billboard,* 3 August 1907, p. 17; *MPW,* 12 October 1908, p. 502, 16 November 1907, p. 598; A. W. Koenig to Delos Holden, 9 April 1908, NjWOE.

18. In addition, the Edison Company was commissioned to make COLONIAL VIRGINIA: HISTORICAL SCENES AND INCIDENTS CONNECTED WITH THE FOUNDING OF JAMESTOWN, VIRGINIA for presentation at the Jamestown Exposition. Shot in May, the negative measured 2,285 feet and cost the client $1,866.24. Other films were also commissioned, but no others are known to be "features."

19. *Billboard,* 13 October 1906, p. 21.

20. The narrative of *Life of a Cowboy* may have had well-known antecedents that have yet to be identified. Porter later argued that this film was "the first Western," even though his THE GREAT TRAIN ROBBERY is now assigned that honor. In fact, the earlier picture was made and initially seen within the context of the crime genre.

21. *Billboard,* 24 August 1907, p. 5.

22. For a provocative reading of this film see Miriam Hansen, "Adventures of Goldilocks: Spectatorship, Consumerism, and Public Life," *Camera Obscura* 21 (Spring 1990).

23. *Pittsburgh Post,* 11 November 1906, p. 6G.

24. Jon Gartenberg, "Vitagraph Before Griffith: Forging Ahead in the Nickelodeon Era," *Studies in Visual Communications* 10 (Fall 1984), pp. 7–22, provides a fine analysis of Vitagraph's activities during this period.

25. "Moving Pictures Amuse and Instruct," *Brooklyn Eagle,* 9 September 1906, p. 1D.

26. *Clipper,* 13 January 1906, p. 1207.

27. *Billboard,* 27 October 1906, pp. 18–19.

28. *Billboard,* 16 March 1907, p. 32; *Film Index,* 18 August 1906, p. 11, 16 February 1907, p. 6.

29. George E. Stevens, unfiled deposition [April 1907], NjWOE; Hollander, "Recollection of an Old-Timer," pp. 9–10.

30. J. Stuart Blackton to Albert E. Smith, 15 February 1908, CLU; Elmer MacIntosh, affidavit, 26 April 1911, *Motion Picture Patents Co. v. Independent Moving Picture Co.* pp. 48–50, NjBaFAR; Albert E. Smith, affidavit, 25 March 1911, *Motion Picture Patents Co. v. Carl Laemmle and Independent Moving Picture Co. of America,* NjBaFAR.

31. A. W. Koenig to Delos Holden, 3 April 1908, NjWOE.

32. Ramsaye, *A Million and One Nights,* pp. 386–387.

33. *Film Index,* 18 August 1906, p. 9. Anderson claimed responsibility for GIRL FROM MONTANA and HIS FIRST RIDE in an advertisement for his and George K. Spoor's Essanay Film Manufacturing Company (*MPW,* 27 July 1907, p. 335).

34. "Manufacture of Moving Pictures Is a Science," *Show World*, 6 July 1907, p. 17.

35. *Billboard*, 24 August 1907, p. 39. For frame enlargements of these films, see Selig catalogs, CLAc.

36. *MPW*, 7 November 1908, p. 361, provides a retrospective, detailed account of the making of Selig's FOUR-FOOTED HERO in late 1907.

37. Selig Polyscope Company, *Catalog of the Selig Polyscope and Library of Selig Films* (1907); *MPW*, 12 October 1907, p. 503.

38. *Variety*, 2 February 1907, p. 11; *Catalog of the Selig Polyscope and Library of Selig Films* (1907), p. 46.

39. *Show World*, 6 July 1907, p. 9.

40. "Houston Authorities Object to Picture of Thaw–White Tragedy," *MPW*, 20 April 1970, p. 102; Sigmund Lubin, *John D. —— and the Reporter*, CLAc.

41. Sigmund Lubin, *When Women Vote*, CLAc.

42. *Billboard*, 21 September 1907, p. 28; 27 June 1908, p. 13; *Baltimore Sun*, 2 April 1907, p. 12.

43. *MPW*, 19 August 1911, p. 441; *New York World*, 4 September 1906, p. 1; *Film Index*, 15 December 1906, p. 4; Balshofer and Miller, *One Reel a Week*, pp. 11–13; Fred A. Dobson, affidavit, 9 December 1909, *Motion Picture Patents Company* v. *Carl Laemmle and Independent Moving Picture Company*, No. 5-167, NjBaFAR.

44. "How Moving Pictures Are Made in Pittsburgh for Amusement, Practical, and Scientific Purposes," *Pittsburgh Post*, 9 December 1906, p. 4G. The film survives in the Kleine Collection at DLC but is undated and is improperly attributed to the Edison Company.

45. "The Life Story of Harry Davis," *Pittsburgh Sun-Telegraph*, 3 January 1940, clipping, University of Pittsburgh, Theater Collection; *Billboard*, 15 December 1906, p. 12.

46. *Billboard*, 3 August 1907, p. 32; Kalem Company, certificate of incorporation, filed 2 May 1907, NNNCC-Ar; *MPW*, 8 June 1907, p. 223; Gauntier, "Blazing the Trail."

47. *Billboard*, 14 December 1907, p. 5.

48. Peerless Film Manufacturing Company, certificate of incorporation, filed 29 April 1907, incorporated 21 May 1907, ICC; *Billboard*, 24 August 1907, p. 4; Gilbert P. Hamilton, affidavit, 13 April 1911, *Motion Picture Patents Company* v. *Laemmle and Independent Moving Picture Company*, No. 7-151, NjBaFAR.

49. *Clipper*, 10 August 1907, p. 674; Balshofer and Miller, *One Reel a Week*, pp. 11–13; Actograph Company, certificate of doing business under an assumed name, 12 June 1907, NNNCC-Ar; *MPW*, 31 August 1907, p. 406; *Film Index*, 7 September 1907, p. 6; *Billboard*, 7 December 1907, p. 74. Mosher co-owned the dog with his wife, Laura Comstock.

50. *MPW*, 20 July 1907, p. 311, 7 September 1907, p. 424; *Show World*, 2 November 1907, p. 11.

51. Lawrence Karr, "Introduction," in Rita Horwitz, *An Index to Vol. 1 of "The Moving Picture World and View Photographer"* (Washington, D.C.: American Film Institute, 1974); "The Pictures from the Standpoint of One Who Shows Them," *Film Index*, 19 May 1906, p. 6.

52. *Film Index*, 19 May 1906, p. 8; *Billboard*, Oct 13, 1906, p. 21; Charles Pathé, *De Pathé Frères à Pathé Cinéma* (Nice, 1940; Paris: Premier plan, 1970), p. 62.

53. "Burglars Break In and Steal," *MPW*, 25 May 1907, p. 188.

54. *MPW*, 18 May 1907, p. 172; *Billboard*, 13 April 1907, p. 53; *MPW*, 4 May 1907, p. 136.

CHAPTER 15. Concluding Remarks

1. Miriam Hansen, "Adventures of Goldilocks: Spectatorship, Consumerism, and Public Life," *Camera Obscura* 21 (Spring 1990).

Bibliography

BOOKS

Allen, Robert C. *Vaudeville and Film, 1895–1915: A Study in Media Interaction.* New York: Arno Press Dissertation Series, 1980.

Allen, Robert C., and Douglas Gomery. *Film History: Theory and Practice.* New York: Alfred A. Knopf, 1985.

Altick, Richard D. *The Shows of London.* Cambridge: Harvard University Press, 1978.

Anderson, Robert J. "The Motion Picture Patents Company." Ph.D. dissertation, University of Wisconsin—Madison, 1983.

André, Jacques, and Marie André. *Une saison Lumiére.* Perpignan: Institut Jean Vigo, 1987.

Auerbach, Erich. *Mimesis.* Princeton: Princeton University Press, 1953.

Balio, Tino, ed. *The American Film Industry.* Madison: University of Wisconsin Press, 1976.

Balshofer, Fred J., and Arthur C. Miller. *One Reel a Week.* Berkeley: University of California Press, 1967.

Barber, Xenophon Theodore. "Evenings of Wonders: A History of the Magic Lantern Show in America." Ph.D. dissertation, New York University, 1993.

Barnes, John. *The Beginnings of the Cinema in England.* New York: Barnes and Noble, 1976.

———. *The Rise of the Cinema in Great Britain: Jubilee Year 1897.* London: Bishopsgate Press, 1983.

———. *Pioneers of the British Film, 1898: The Rise of the Photoplay.* London: Bishopsgate Press, 1989.

Barnouw, Erick. *The Magician and the Cinema.* New York: Oxford University Press, 1981.

———. *Documentary.* New York: Oxford University Press, 1974.

Bell, Geoffrey. *The Golden Gate and the Silver Screen.* Cranbury, N.J.: Associated University Presses, 1984.

Bettelheim, Bruno. *The Uses of Enchantment.* New York: Alfred A. Knopf, 1976.

Bitzer, G. W. *Billy Bitzer: His Story.* New York: Farrar, Straus, and Giroux, 1973.

Black, Alexander. *Photography Indoors and Out: A Book for Amateurs.* Boston: Houghton Mifflin, 1893.

———. *A Capital Courtship.* New York: Charles Scribner's Sons, 1897.

———. *Miss Jerry.* New York: Charles Scribner's Sons, 1897.

———. *Time and Chance.* New York: Farrar and Rinehart, 1937.

Bordwell, David. *The Films of Carl-Theodor Dreyer.* Berkeley: University of California Press, 1981.

Bordwell, David, Janet Staiger, and Kristin Thompson. *The Classical Hollywood Cinema: Film Style and Mode of Production to 1960.* New York: Columbia University Press, 1985.

Bowser, Eileen, ed. *Biograph Bulletins, 1908–1912.* New York: Farrar, Straus, and Giroux, 1973.

———, ed. *Film Notes.* New York: Museum of Modern Art, 1969.

Braverman, Harry. *Labor and Monopoly Capital: The Degradation of Work in the Twentieth Century*. New York: Monthly Review Press, 1974.

Brownlow, Kevin. *The Parade's Gone By. . . .* New York: Alfred A. Knopf, 1969.

————. *Hollywood: The Pioneers*. New York: Alfred A. Knopf, 1979.

Burch, Noël. *Theory of Film Practice*. New York: Praeger, 1969.

————. *Correction Please: A Study Guide*. London: Arts Council of Great Britain, 1980.

————. *To the Distant Observer*. Berkeley: University of California Press, 1982.

————. *In and Out of Sync*. Aldershot, England: Gower, 1990.

————. *Life to Those Shadows: Contributions to the History of Film Language, 1902–1914*. Berkeley: University of California Press, forthcoming.

Caldwell, Genoa. *The Man Who Photographed the World: Burton Holmes, Travelogues, 1886–1938*. New York: Harry N. Abrams, 1977.

Carmen, Ira H. *Movies, Censorship, and the Law*. Ann Arbor: Univ. of Michigan Press, 1966.

Caughie, John, ed. *Theories of Authorship*. London: Routledge and Kegan Paul, 1981.

Ceram, C. W. [Kurt Wilhelm Marek]. *Archaeology of the Cinema*. New York: Harcourt, Brace, 1965.

Chanan, Michael. *The Dream That Kicks*. London: Routledge and Kegan Paul, 1980.

Cherchi-Usai, Paolo., ed. *Vitagraph Company of America: Il cinema prima di Hollywood*. Pordenone: Edizioni Studio Tesi, 1987.

Conant, Michael. *Antitrust in the Motion Picture Industry: Economic and Legal Analysis*. Berkeley: University of California Press, 1960.

Conot, Robert. *A Streak of Luck: The Life and Legend of Thomas Alva Edison*. New York: Seaview Books, 1979.

Cook, David A. *A History of Narrative Film*. New York: W. W. Norton, 1990.

Cook, Olive. *Movement in Two Dimensions*. London: Hutchinson, 1963.

Crafton, Donald. *Before Mickey: The Animated Film (1898–1928)*. Boston: MIT Press, 1982.

Cripps, Thomas. *Slow Fade to Black: The Negro in American Film, 1900–1942*. London: Oxford University Press, 1977.

Czitrom, Daniel J. *Media and the American Mind: From Morse to McLuhan*. Chapel Hill: University of North Carolina, 1982.

Defleur, Melvin L., and Everette Dennis. *Understanding Mass Communication*. Boston: Houghton Mifflin, 1981.

Deslandes, Jacques. *Le boulevard du cinéma*. Paris: Éditions du Cerf, 1963.

————. *Histoire comparée du cinéma*. Vol. 1, *De la cinématique au cinématographe, 1826–1896*. Tournai: Casterman, 1966.

Deslandes, Jacques, and Jacques Richard. *Histoire comparée du cinéma*. Vol. 2, *Du cinématographe au cinéma*. Tournai: Casterman, 1968.

Deutelbaum, Marshall A., ed. *"Image": On the Art and Evolution of the Film*. New York: Dover, 1979.

Dickson, William Kennedy Laurie. *Biograph in Battle*. London: Fisher Unwin, 1901.

————. *History of the Kinetograph and Kinetophonograph*. 1895. Reprint, New York: Arno, 1970

Dickson, William Kennedy Laurie, and Antonia Dickson. *The Life and Inventions of Thomas Alva Edison*. New York: Thomas Y. Crowell, 1894.

Dyer, Frank, Thomas Martin, and William Meadowcroft. *Edison: His Life and Inventions*. New York: Harper and Brothers, 1929.

Eckhardt, Joseph P. and Linda Kowall. *Peddler of Dreams: Siegmund Lubin and the Creation of the Motion Picture Industry 1896–1916*. Philadelphia: National Museum of American Jewish History, 1984.

Eisenstein, Sergei. *Film Form: Essays in Film Theory*. Translated and edited by Jay Leyda. New York: Harcourt, Brace, and World, 1949.

Elsaesser, Thomas. *Early Cinema*. London: British Film Institute, 1990.

Everson, William K. *American Silent Film*. New York: Oxford University Press, 1978.

Fell, John L. *Film and the Narrative Tradition*. Norman: University of Oklahoma Press, 1974.

———, ed. *Film Before Griffith*. Berkeley: University of California Press, 1983.

Fenin, George N., and William K. Everson. *The Western from Silents to Cinerama*. New York: Bonanza Books, 1972.

Fielding, Ray, ed. *A Technological History of Motion Pictures and Television*. Berkeley: University of California Press, 1967.

Fleming, G. H., ed. *The Unforgettable Season*. New York: Holt, Rinehart, and Winston, 1981.

Frohman, Daniel. *Daniel Frohman Presents: An Autobiography*. New York: Claude Kendall & Willoughby Sharp, 1935.

Frazer, John. *Artificially Arranged Scenes: The Films of Georges Méliès*. Boston: G. K. Hall, 1979.

Gaudreault, André, ed. *Ce que je vois de mon ciné: La réprésentation du régard dans le cinéma des premiers temps*. Saint-Étienne: Impression Dumas, 1988.

Gauntier, Gene. "Blazing the Trail," unpublished manuscript, NNMOMA.

Gelatt, Roland. *The Fabulous Phonograph 1877–1977*, 2d revised edition. New York: Collier Books, 1977.

Grau, Robert. *The Business Man in the Amusement World*. New York: Broadway, 1910.

———. *Theatre of Science*. New York: Broadway, 1914.

Green, Abel, and Joe Laurie, Jr. *Show Biz: From Vaude to Video*. New York: Henry Holt, 1951.

Guibbert, Pierre, ed. *Les premiers ans du cinéma français*. Perpignan: Institut Jean Vigo, 1985.

A Guide to Cromwell's Stereopticon. Introduction by A. C. Wheeler. New York, *ca.* 1869.

Gunning, Thomas. "D. W. Griffith and the Narrator-System: Narrative Structure and Industry Organization in Biograph Films (1908–09)." Ph.D. dissertation: New York University, 1985.

———. *D. W. Griffith and the Rise of the Narrative Film*. Urbana: University of Illinois Press, forthcoming.

Gutman, Herbert G. *Work, Culture, and Society in Industrializing America*. New York: Vintage Books, 1977.

Guy, Alice. *Autobiographie d'une pionnière du cinéma*. Paris: Éditions Denoël, 1976.

Haas, Robert Bartlett. *Muybridge: Man in Motion*. Berkeley: University of California Press, 1976.

Hales, Peter Bacon. *Silver Cities: The Photography of American Urbanization, 1839–1915*. Philadelphia: Temple University Press, 1984.

Hall, Stuart, and Paddy Whannel. *The Popular Arts*. New York: Pantheon Books, 1964.

Hampton, Benjamin B. *A History of the Movies*. New York: Covici, 1931. Reprint (as *A History of the American Film Industry from Its Beginnings to 1931*, ed. Richard Griffith), New York: Dover Books, 1970.

Hammond, Paul. *Marvellous Méliès*. New York: St. Martin's Press, 1975.

———, ed. *The Shadow and Its Shadow: Surrealist Writing on Cinema*. London: British Film Institute, 1978.

Hansen, Miriam. *Babel and Babylon: Spectatorship in American Silent Film*. Cambridge: Harvard University Press, forthcoming.

Harris, Neil. *Humbug: The Art of P. T. Barnum*. Boston: Little, Brown, 1973.

Hawaii Film Board. *Celebration of the 80th Anniversary of the First Film Showing in Hawaii*. Honolulu, 1977.

Heider, Karl G. *Ethnographic Film*. Austin: University of Texas Press, 1976.

Hemphill, William Despard. *Stereoscopic Illustrations of Clonmel and the Surrounding Countryside*. Dublin: William Curry, 1860.

Henderson, Robert M. *D. W. Griffith: The Years at Biograph*. New York: Farrar, Straus, and Giroux, 1970.

Hendricks, Gordon. *The Edison Motion Picture Myth*. Berkeley: University of California Press, 1961. Reprint, New York: Arno, 1972.

————. *Beginnings of the Biograph: The Story of the Invention of the Mutoscope and the Biograph and Their Supplying Camera*. 1964. Reprint, New York: Arno, 1972.

————. *The Kinetoscope: America's First Commercially Successful Motion Picture Exhibitor*. 1966. Reprint, New York: Arno, 1972.

————. *Eadweard Muybridge: The Father of the Motion Picture*. New York: Grossman, 1975.

Hepworth, Cecil M. *Came the Dawn: Memories of a Film Pioneer*. London: Phoenix House, 1951.

————. *Animated Photography: The ABC of the Cinematograph*. 1900. Reprint, New York: Arno, 1970.

Hepworth, Thomas Cradock. *The Book of the Lantern*. 1899. Reprint, New York: Arno, 1978.

Hill, Christopher. *The Pelican Economic History of England: Reformation to Industrial Revolution*. London: Weidenfeld and Nicolson, 1967.

History of Coney Island. New York: Burroughs, 1905.

Hobsbawm, E. J. *The Age of Revolution*. London: Weidenfeld and Nicolson, 1962.

Hockings, Paul, ed. *Principles of Visual Anthropology*. The Hague: Mouton, 1975.

Hofstadter, Richard. *The Age of Reform from Bryan to F.D.R.* New York: Alfred A. Knopf, 1955.

————, ed. *The Progressive Movement: 1900–1915*. Englewood Cliffs, N.J.: Prentice-Hall, 1963.

Holman, Roger, comp. *Cinema 1900–1906: An Analytical Study by the National Film Archive (London) and the International Federation of Film Archives*. 2 vols. Vol. 1, *Brighton Symposium, 1978*. Vol. 2, *Analytical Filmography (Fiction Films), 1900–1906*. Brussels: Fédération internationale des archives du film, 1982.

Hone, William. *Ancient Mysteries Described*. London, 1823.

Hopwood, Henry V. *Living Pictures*. 1899. Reprint, New York: Arno, 1970.

Horn, Maurice, ed. *World Encyclopedia of Comics*. New York: Chelsea House, 1976.

Horwitz, Rita. *An Index to Volume 1 of "The Moving Picture World and View Photographer."* Introduction by Lawrence Karr. American Film Institute, 1974.

Horwitz, Rita, and Harriet Harriman. *The George Kleine Collection of Early Motion Pictures in the Library of Congress: A Catalog*. Washington, D.C.: Library of Congress, 1980.

Hoyt, Harlowe R. *Town Hall Tonight*. Englewood Cliffs, N.J.: Prentice-Hall, 1955.

Hulfish, David. *The Motion Picture: Its Making and Its Theater*. Chicago: Electricity Magazine Corporation, 1909.

Irwin, Will. *The House That Shadows Built*. Garden City, N.Y.: Doubleday, Doran, 1928.

Jacobs, Lewis. *The Rise of the American Film*. New York: Harcourt, Brace, 1939. Rev. ed., New York: Teachers College Press, 1967.

Jeffreys, Thomas E., *et al*. *Thomas A. Edison Papers: A Selective Microfilm Edition*. Part I, *1850–1878*. Part II, *1878–1886*. Frederick, Md.: University Publications of America, 1985.

Jenkins, C. Francis. *Picture Ribbons*. Washington, D.C.: H. L. McQueen, 1897.

————. *Animated Pictures*. Washington, D.C.: H. L. McQueen, 1898.

Jenkins, C. Francis, and Oscar B. Depue. *Handbook for Motion Picture and Stereopticon Operators*. Washington, D.C.: Knega, 1908.

Jenkins, Reese V. *Images and Enterprise: Technology and the American Photographic Industry, 1839–1925*. Baltimore: Johns Hopkins University Press, 1975.

Jenkins, Reese V., *et al*. *The Papers of Thomas A. Edison*. Vol. 1, *The Making of an Inventor, February 1847–June 1873*. Baltimore: Johns Hopkins University Press, 1989.

Jones, John. *Wonders of the Stereoscope*. New York: Alfred A. Knopf, 1976.

Jordan, John W., and James Hadden, eds. *Genealogical and Personal History of Fayette County*. New York: Lewis Historical Publishing Company, 1912.

Josephson, Matthew. *Edison*. New York: McGraw-Hill, 1959.

Jowett, Garth. *Film: The Democratic Art*. Boston: Little, Brown, 1975.

Julius Cahn's Official Theatrical Guide. New York, 1896.

Kindem, Gorham. *The Amerian Movie Industry: The Business of Motion Pictures*. Carbondale: Southern Illinois University Press, 1982.

Kircher, Athanasius. *Ars magna lucis et umbrae*. Rome, 1646. 2d ed., rev., Amsterdam, 1671.

Kolko, Gabriel. *The Triumph of Conservatism: A Re-interpretation of American History*. New York: Free Press of Glencoe, 1963.

Koszarski, Richard, ed. *Hollywood Directors, 1914–1940*. New York: Oxford University Press, 1976.

Kuleshov, Lev. *Kuleshov on Film*. Edited and translated by Ronald Levaco. Berkeley: University of California Press, 1974.

Lacasse, Germain. *L'historiographe: Les débuts du spectacle cinématographique au Québec*. Montreal: Cinémathèque Québécoise, 1985.

Laemmle, Carl. "The Business of Motion Pictures." Unpublished manuscript, CBevA.

Lahue, Kalton C., ed. *Motion Picture Pioneer: The Selig Polyscope Company*. South Brunswick, N.J.: A. S. Barnes, 1973.

Levy, David. "Edwin S. Porter and the Origins of the American Narrative Film, 1894–1907." Ph.D. dissertation, McGill University, 1983.

Leyda, Jay. *Kino*. London: Allen and Unwin, 1960.

Leyda, Jay, and Charles Musser, eds. *Before Hollywood*. New York: American Federation of the Arts, 1986.

Liesegang, Franz Paul. *Dates and Sources: A Contribution to the History of the Art of Projection and to Cinematography*. London: The Magic Lantern Society of Great Britain, 1986.

Loughney, Patrick. "A Descriptive Analysis of the Library of Congress Paper Print Collection and Related Copyright Records." Ph.D. dissertation, George Washington University, 1988.

Low, Rachel. *The History of the British Film, 1906–1914*. London: Allen and Unwin, 1949.

Low, Rachel, and Roger Manvell. *The History of the British Film, 1896–1906*. London: George Allen and Unwin, 1948.

McAllister, T. H. *Catalogue and Price List of Stereopticons*. New York, 1885.

Macgowan, Kenneth. *Behind the Screen*. New York: Delacorte Press, 1965.

Macgowan, Kenneth, and William Melnitz. *The Living Stage: A History of the World Theater*. Englewood Cliffs, N.J.: Prentice-Hall, 1955.

Mann, William John. "The Movies Come to Middletown: The Cinematic Experience of a Small Town, 1897–1917." M.A. thesis, Wesleyan University, 1987.

Marcy, L. J. *The Sciopticon Manual*. Philadelphia, 1871.

———. *The Sciopticon Manual: Explaining Marcy's New Magic Lantern and Light, Including Lantern Optics, Experiments, Photographing and Coloring Slides, etc.* 5th ed. Philadelphia: Sherman, 1874.

———. *Marcy's Sciopticon: Priced Catalogue of Sciopticon Apparatus and Magic Lantern Slides*. 6th ed. Philadelphia, ca. 1878.

Mast, Gerald. ed. *The Movies in Our Midst: Documents in the Cultural History of Film in America*. Chicago: University of Chicago Press, 1982.

———. *A Short History of the Movies*. 4th ed. New York: Macmillan, 1986.

May, Lary Linden. *Screening the Past: The Birth of Mass Culture and the Motion Picture Industry*. New York: Oxford University Press, 1980.

McLean, Albert F. Jr. *American Vaudeville as Ritual*. Louisville: University of Kentucky Press, 1965.

Mesguich, Félix. *Tours de manivelle: Souvenirs d'un chasseur d'images*. Paris: Bernard Grassett, 1933.

Metz, Christian. *Film Language*. New York: Oxford University Press, 1974.

Millard, André. *Edison and the Business of Innovation*. Baltimore: Johns Hopkins University Press, 1990.

Mitry, Jean. *Histoire du cinéma*. Vol. 1. Paris: Éditions universitaires, 1967.

Montgomery, David. *Workers' Control in America: Studies in the History of Work, Technology, and Labor Struggles*. Cambridge: Cambridge University Press, 1979.

Mozley, Anita V. *Eadweard Muybridge: The Stanford Years*. Palo Alto, Calif.: Stanford University, Department of Art, 1972.

Musser, Charles. *Before the Nickelodeon: Edwin S. Porter and the Edison Manufacturing Company*. Berkeley: University of California Press, 1991.

Musser, Charles, with Carol Nelson. *High-Class Moving Pictures: Lyman H. Howe and the Forgotten Era of Traveling Exhibition*. Princeton, N.J.: Princeton University Press, 1990.

Musser, Charles, *et al*. *Motion Picture Catalogs by American Producers and Distributors, 1894–1908: A Microfilm Edition*. Frederick, Md.: University Publications of America, 1985.

————. *A Guide to "Motion Picture Catalogs by American Producers and Distributors, 1894–1908: A Microfilm Edition."* Frederick, Md.: University Publications of America, 1985.

Newsom, Iris, ed. *Wonderful Inventions: Motion Pictures, Broadcasting, and Recorded Sound at the Library of Congress*. Washington, D.C.: Library of Congress, 1985.

Niver, Kemp R. *Motion Pictures from the Library of Congress Paper Print Collection, 1894–1912*. Berkeley: University of California Press, 1967.

————. *The First Twenty Years: A Segment of Film History*. Los Angeles: Locare Research Group, 1968.

————. *Klaw and Erlanger Present Famous Plays in Pictures*. Edited by Bebe Bergsten. Los Angeles: Locare Research Group, 1976.

————. *Early Motion Pictures: The Paper Print Collection in the Library of Congress*. Washington, D.C.: Library of Congress, 1985.

————, ed. *Biograph Bulletins, 1896–1908*. Los Angeles: Locare Research Group, 1971.

Nochlin, Linda. *Realism*. Harmondsworth, England: Penguin, 1971.

North, Joseph H. *The Early Development of the Motion Picture: 1887–1909*. New York: Arno, 1973.

Pathé, Charles. *De Pathé Frères à Pathé Cinéma*. Nice, 1940; Paris: Premier plan, 1970.

Pearson, Roberta. "The Modesty of Nature: Performance in Griffith's Biographs." Ph.D. dissertation, New York University, 1986.

Pecor, Charles Joseph. *The Magician and the American Stage*. Washington, D.C.: Emerson and West, 1977.

Peiss, Kathy. *Cheap Amusements: Working Women and Leisure in Turn-of-the-Century New York*. Philadelphia: Temple University Press, 1986.

Pratt, George C. *Spellbound in Darkness: A History of the Silent Film*. Greenwich, Conn.: New York Graphic Society, 1966.

Proceedings of the 1890 Convention of Local Phonograph Companies of the United States Held at Chicago, May 28 and 29, 1890. Milwaukee: Phonograph Printing Company, 1890.

Proceedings of Second Annual Convention of Local Phonograph Companies of the United States, 16–18 June 1891.

Ramsaye, Terry. *A Million and One Nights*. New York: Simon and Schuster, 1926.

Richardson, F. H. *Motion Picture Handbook, 1910*. New York: Moving Picture World, 1910.

Riis, Jacob. *How the Other Half Lives*. New York: Charles Scribner's Sons, 1890.

Rittaud-Hutinet, Jacques. *Le cinéma des origines: Les frères Lumiére et leurs opérateurs*. Seyssel: Éditions du Champ Valon, 1985.

Robertson, E[tienne] G[aspar] [Robert]. *Mémoires récréatifs, scientifiques et anecdotiques*. 2 vols. Paris: Chez l'auteur et Librairie de Wurtz, 1831–1833.

Rosen, Philip, ed. *Narrative, Apparatus, Ideology*. New York: Columbia University Press, 1986.

Rosenzweig, Roy. *Eight Hours for What We Will: Workers and Leisure in an Industrial City, 1870–1920*. Cambridge: Cambridge University Press, 1983.

Sadoul, Georges. *Histoire générale du cinéma*. Vol. 1, *L'invention du cinéma, 1832–1897*. Vol. 2, *Les pionniers du cinéma: De Méliès à Pathé, 1897–1909*. Paris: Éditions Denoël, 1947–1948.

———. *British Creators of Film Technique*. London: British Film Institute, 1948.

———. *Louis Lumière*. Paris: Éditions Seghers, 1964.

———. *Lumière et Méliès*. Revised by Bernard Eisenhitz. Paris: L'Herminer, 1985.

Salt, Barry. *Film Style and Technology: History and Analysis*. London: Starwood, 1983.

Sammons, Jeffrey T. *Beyond the Ring: The Role of Boxing in American Society*. Urbana: University of Illinois Press, 1988.

Sanderson, Richard Arlo. "A Historical Study of the Development of American Motion Picture Content and Techniques Prior to 1904." Ph.D. dissertation, University of Southern California, 1961.

Schivelbusch, Wolfgang. *The Railway Journey: Trains and Travel in the 19th Century*. New York: Urizen Books, 1977.

Seldes, Gilbert. *The Great Audience*. New York: Viking Press, 1950.

Sitney, P. Adams, ed. *The Essential Cinema: Essays on Film in the Collection of Anthology Film Archives*. New York: New York University Press, 1975.

Sklar, Robert. *Movie-Made America: A Cultural History of American Movies*. New York: Random House, 1975.

Slide, Anthony. *Early American Cinema*. New York: A. S. Barnes, 1970.

Slide, Anthony, with Alan Gevison. *The Big V: A History of the Vitagraph Company*. 2nd ed. Metuchen, N.J.: Scarecrow Press, 1987.

Smith, Albert E., with Phil A. Koury. *Two Reels and a Crank*. Garden City, N.Y.: Doubleday, 1952.

Snyder, Robert. *The Voice of the City: Vaudeville and Popular Culture in New York*. New York: Oxford University Press, 1990.

Spehr, Paul C. *The Movies Begin: Making Movies in New Jersey, 1887–1920*. Newark: Newark Museum—Morgan and Morgan, 1977.

Stabla, Zdenek. *Queries Concerning the Hořice Passion Film*. Prague: Film Institute, 1971.

Stoddard, John L. *John L. Stoddard's Lectures*. 10 vols. Boston: Balch Brothers, 1897–1898.

———. *Red Letter Days Abroad*. New York, 1884.

Talbot, Daniel, ed. *Film: An Anthology*. New York: Simon and Schuster, 1959.

Tate, Alfred O. *Edison's Open Door*. New York: Dutton, 1938.

Taylor, Daniel Crane. *John L. Stoddard: Traveller, Lecturer, Litterateur*. New York: P. J. Kennedy, 1935.

Thompson, Kristin. *Exporting Entertainment: America in the World Film Market, 1907–1934*. London: British Film Institute, 1985.

Toulet, Émmanuelle. *Domitor Bibliographie internationale du cinéma des premiers temps: Travaux des members*. Quebec: Domitor, 1987.

———. *Cinématographe: Invention du siècle*. Paris: Gallimard, 1988.

Trachtenberg, Alan. *The Incorporation of America: Culture and Society in the Gilded Age*. New York: Hill and Wang, 1982.

Vardac, A. Nicholas. *Stage to Screen: Theatrical Methods from Garrick to Griffith*. Cambridge, Mass.: Harvard University Press, 1949.

Walls, Howard Lamarr. *Motion Pictures, 1894–1912*. Washington, D.C.: Library of Congress, 1953.

Welling, William. *Photography in America: The Formative Years, 1839–1900.* New York: Thomas Y. Crowell, 1983.

White-Hensen, Wendy, and Veronica M. Gillespie. *The Theodore Roosevelt Association Film Collection: A Catalog.* Washington: Library of Congress, 1986.

Williams, Raymond. *Marxism and Literature.* New York: Oxford University Press, 1977.

Wilson, Edward. *Wilson's Lantern Journeys.* 3 vols. Philadelphia: By the author, 1874–1886.

Zukor, Adolph, with Dale Kramer. *The Public Is Never Wrong.* New York, G. P. Putnam's Sons, 1953.

ARTICLES

Allen, Robert C. "Film: The Narrow Discourse." *Film Studies Annual,* 1977: 9–17.

———. "Looking at 'Another Look at the Chaser Theory.'" *Studies in Visual Communication* 10 (Fall 1984): 45–50.

Black, Alexander. "Photography in Fiction." *Scribner's Magazine* 18 (September 1895): 348–360.

Bottomore, Stephen. "Joseph Rosenthal." *Sight and Sound* 52, no. 3 (Summer 1983): 152–153.

———. "The Most Glorious Profession." *Sight and Sound* 52, no. 4 (Autumn 1983): 260–265.

Brewster, Ben. "A Scene at the 'Movies.'" *Screen* 23 (July–August 1982): 4–15.

———. *The Big V: A History of the Vitagraph Company.* 2d ed. Metuchen, N.J.: Scarecrow Press, 1987.

Burch, Noël. "Porter, or Ambivalence." *Screen* 19 (Winter 1978–1979): 91–105.

———. "Charles Baudelaire v. Dr. Frankenstein." *Afterimage* 8–9 (Spring 1981): 4–21.

———. "How We Got into Pictures: Notes Accompanying *Correction Please.*" *Afterimage* 8–9 (Spring 1981): 22–38.

———. "Un mode de représentation primitif." *Iris* 2 (Spring 1984): 113–124.

Carroll, Noel. "Film History and Film Theory: An Outline for an Institutional Theory of Film." *Film Reader* 4 (1979): 81–96.

———. "Art, Film, and Ideology." *Millennium* 13 (1983): 120–32.

Cassady, Ralph. "Monopoly in Motion Picture Production and Distribution, 1908–1915." *Southern California Law Review* 32 (Summer 1959).

Coulson, Thomas. "Philadelphia and the Development of the Motion Picture." *Journal of the Franklin Institute* 262 (July 1956): 1–16.

Comolli, Jean-Louis. "Technique and Ideology: Camera, Perspective, Depth of Field." In *Film Reader* 2 (1977): 128–140.

Cosandey, Roland. "Revoir Lumière." *Iris* 2 (Spring 1984): 71–82.

Czitrom, Daniel. "The Redemption of Leisure: The National Board of Censorship and the Rise of Motion Pictures in New York City, 1900–1920." *Studies in Visual Communication* 10 (Fall 1984): 2–5.

Depue, Oscar A. "My First 50 Years in Motion Pictures," *American Cinematographer,* April 1948: 124–127.

Dickson, Antonia. "Wonders of the Kinetoscope." *Leslie's Monthly,* February 1895, pp. 245–251.

Engberg, Marguerite. "Le cinéma de fiction au Danemark avant 1908." *Iris* 2 (Spring 1984): 125–137.

Ewen, Elizabeth. "City Lights: Immigrant Women and the Rise of the Movies." *Signs* 5, no. 3, supplement (1980): S45–65.

Fell, John L. "L'articulation des rapports spatiaux." *Les cahiers de la Cinémathèque* 29 (Winter 1979): 81–87.

Field, Simon. "Beginning . . . and Beginning Again." *Afterimage* 8–9 (Spring 1981): 2–3.

Gartenberg, Jon. "Camera Movement in Edison and Biograph Films, 1900–1906." *Cinema Journal* 19 (Spring 1980): 1–16.

———. "Vitagraph Before Griffith: Forging Ahead in the Nickelodeon Era." *Studies in Visual Communication* 10 (Fall 1984): 7–23.

———. "The Brighton Project: The Archives and Research." *Iris* 2 (Spring 1984): 5–16.

Gaudreault, André. "Detours in Film Narrative: The Development of Cross-Cutting." *Cinema Journal* 19 (Fall 1979): 39–59.

———. "Un cinéma sans foi ni loi." *Iris* 2 (Spring 1984): 2–4.

———. "Film, récit, narration: Le cinéma des frères Lumière." *Iris* 2 (Spring 1984): 61–70.

———. "La transgression des lois du copyright aux débuts du cinéma: Consequences pratiques et séquelles théoriques." *Film échange* 28 (1984): 41–49.

———. "The Infringement of Copyright Laws and Its Effects, 1900–1906." *Framework* 29 (1985): 2–14.

Gosser, H. Mark. "Kircher and the Lanterna Magica: A Reexamination." *Journal of Society of Motion Pictures and Television Engineers* 90 (October 1981): 972–978.

———. "The Literature of the Archeology of Cinema." *Quarterly Review of Film Studies* 9 (Winter 1984): 3–10.

Guillaudeau, Thomas. "Les productions Pathé et Méliès en 1905–1906 (notes préliminaires)." *Iris* 2 (Spring 1984): 33–46.

Gunning, Tom. "Le style non-continu du cinéma des premiers temps." *Les cahiers de la Cinématheque* 29 (Winter 1979): 24–34.

———. "Weaving a Narrative: Style and Economic Background in Griffith's Biograph Films." *Quarterly Review of Film Studies* 6 (Winter 1981): 11–26.

———. "Non-continuity, Continuity, Discontinuity: A Theory of Genres in Early Films." *Iris* 2 (Spring 1984): 101–112.

———. "The Cinema of Attractions: Early Cinema, Its Spectators, and the Avant-Garde." *Wide Angle* 8, no. 3–4 (Fall 1986): 63–70.

Hagan, John. "L'érotisme des premiers temps." *Les cahiers de la Cinématheque* 29 (Winter 1979): 72–79.

Hammond, John H. "Movement, Color, and Sound in a Darke Roome." *Quarterly Review of Film Studies* 9 (Winter 1984): 33–41.

Hammond, Paul. "Georges, This Is Charles." *Afterimage* 8–9 (Spring 1981): 39–49.

Hansen, Miriam. "Early Silent Cinema: Whose Public Sphere?" *New German Critique* 29 (Winter 1983): 147–184.

———. "Adventures of Goldilocks: Spectatorship, Consumerism, and Public Life." *Camera Obscura* 21 (Spring 1990).

Harris, Adrienne. "Women, Baseball, and Words." *PsycheCritique* 1 (1985): 35–54.

Hendricks, Gordon. "A New Look at an Old Sneeze." *Film Culture* 22/23 (1961): 90–95.

Herzog, Charlotte. "The Archeology of Cinema Architecture: The Origins of the Movie Theatre." *Quarterly Review of Film Studies* 9 (Winter 1984): 11–32.

Jenkins, Reese V. "Elements of Style: Continuities in Edison's Thinking," *Annals of the New York Academy of Sciences* 424 (1984): 149–162.

———. "Words, Images, Artifacts, and Sound: Documents for the History of Technology." *British Journal of History and Science* 20 (January 1987): 39–56.

Kelkres, Gene G. "A Forgotten First: The Armat–Jenkins Partnership and the Atlanta Projection." *Quarterly Review of Film Studies* 9 (Winter 1984): 45–58.

"The Kineto-Phonograph." *Electrical World*, 16 June 1894, pp. 799–801.

Levy, David. "The 'Fake Train Robbery': Les reportages simulés, les réconstitutions et le film narratif américain." *Les cahiers de la Cinémathèque* 29 (Winter 1979): 42–56.

Loughney, Patrick G. "In the Beginning Was the Word: Six Pre-Griffith Motion Picture Scenarios." *Iris* 2 (Spring 1984): 17–32.

———. "Still Images in Motion: The Influence of Photography on Motion Pictures in the Early Silent Period," in Annette Michelson *et al.*, *The Art of Moving Shadows*. Washington: National Gallery of Art, 1989. Pp. 31–47.

Maguire, Thomas. "The Kinetograph." *Frank Leslie's Weekly*, 5 April 1894, pp. 224–226.

Mayne, Judith. "Immigrants and Spectators." *Wide Angle* 5:2 (1982): 32–40.

Mottet, Jean. "Le cinéma des débuts, ou l'ambiguité révélatrice." *Iris* 2 (Spring 1984): 91–100.

Musser, Charles. "The Early Cinema of Edwin S. Porter." *Cinema Journal* 19 (Fall 1979): 1–38.

———. "American Vitagraph: 1897–1901." *Cinema Journal* 22 (Spring 1983): 4–46.

———. "The Travel Genre in 1903–4: Moving Toward Fictional Narrative." *Iris* 2 (Spring 1984): 47–60.

———. "Another Look at the Chaser Theory." *Studies in Visual Communication* 10 (Fall 1984): 24–44, 51–52.

Pryluck, Calvin. "The Itinerant Movie Show and the Development of the Film Industry." *Journal of the University Film and Video Association* 36 (Fall 1983): pp. 11–22.

Sadoul, Georges. "English Influence on the Work of Edwin S. Porter." *Hollywood Quarterly* 3 (Fall 1947): 41–50.

Salt, Barry. "Film Form, 1900–1906." *Sight and Sound* 47 (Summer 1978): 148–153.

———. "What Can We Learn from the First Twenty Years of Cinema?" *Iris* 2 (Spring 1984): 83–90.

Schmitt, Robert C. "Movies in Hawaii, 1897–1932." *Hawaiian Journal of History* 1 (1967).

Sipley, Louis Walton. "The Magic Lantern." *Pennsylvania Arts and Sciences* 4 (December 1939): 39–43.

———. "W. and F. Langenheim—Photographers." *Pennsylvania Arts and Sciences* (193-), pp. 25–31.

Sklar, Robert. "Oh! Althusser!: Historiography and the Rise of Cinema Studies." *Radical History Review* 41 (1988): 11–35.

Sopocy, Martin. "A Narrated Cinema: The Pioneer Story Films of James A. Williamson." *Cinema Journal* 18 (Fall 1978): 1–28.

Spears, Jack. "Edwin S. Porter." *Films in Review* 31 (June–July 1970): 327–354.

Spehr, Paul C. "Filmmaking at the American Mutoscope and Biograph Company, 1900–1906." *Quarterly Journal of the Library of Congress* 37 (Summer–Fall 1980): 413–421.

Staiger, Janet. "Combination and Litigation: Structures of U.S. Film Distribution, 1891–1917." *Cinema Journal* 23 (Winter 1984): 41–72.

———. "The Eyes Are Really the Focus." *Wide Angle* 6, no. 4 (1985): 14–23.

Stoneman, Rod. "Perspective Correction: Early Cinema to the Avant-Garde." *Afterimage* 8–9 (Spring 1981): 50–63.

Toulet, Emmanuelle. "Le cinéma à l'Exposition Universelle de 1900." *Revue d'histoire moderne et contemporaine* 33 (April–June 1986): 179–209.

Waller, Gregory A. "Introducing the 'Marvellous Invention' to the Provinces: Film Exhibition in Lexington, Kentucky, 1896–1897." *Film History* 3 (1989): 223–234.

Walton, Kendall. "Categories of Art." *Philosophical Review* 74 (1970): 334–367.

FILMOGRAPHY

A significant group of films, primarily documentaries, have been made about screen practices prior to 1907. These include:

Andersen, Thom. EADWEARD MUYBRIDGE, ZOOPRAXOGRAPHER, 1975. Distributed by New Yorker Films.

Burch, Noël. CORRECTION PLEASE; OR, HOW WE GOT INTO PICTURES, 1979. Distributed by the Museum of Modern Art.

———. WHAT DO THOSE OLD FILMS MEAN?, 1986. Television series; episode four, "Tomorrow the World: USA, 1902–1914."

Musser, Charles. BEFORE THE NICKELODEON, 1982. Distributed by First-Run Features.

Nekes, Werner. FILM BEFORE FILM, 1983.

Nelson, Carol, and Ben Levin. LYMAN H. HOWE'S HIGH-CLASS MOVING PICTURES, 1983.

NEWSPAPERS AND PERIODICALS

The following trade periodicals and local newspapers were used extensively for the dates indicated in brackets:

Trade Periodicals

Billboard [1904–1906]
Magic Lantern [1874–1878]
Moving Picture News [1911]
Moving Picture World [1907–1917]
New York Clipper [1895–1909]
New York Dramatic Mirror [1896–1909]
Optical Magic Lantern Journal [1895–1901]
Philadelphia Photographer [1864–1888]
Phonogram [1891–1893]
Phonograph Monthly [1903–1907]
Phonoscope [1896–1900]
Photographic Times, [1888–1900]
Show World [1907–1909]
Variety [1905–1909]
Views and Film Index [1906–1910]

Daily and Weekly Newspapers

Albany Times-Union [1895–1906]
Asbury Park (N.J.) *Daily Press* [1895–1900]
Atlanta Constitution [1895–1897]
Atlantic City Daily Union [1896–1900]
Baltimore Sun [1895–1907]
Boston Gazette [1804–1807]
Brooklyn Eagle [1863–1907]
Boston Herald [1894–1907]
Chicago Inter-Ocean [1895–1901]
Chicago Tribune [1896–1907]
Cleveland Plain Dealer [1896–1907]
Danbury (Ct.) *Evening News* [1896–1904]
Detroit Free Press [1896–1907]
Harrisburg Patriot [1896–1897]
Hartford Courant [1896–1907]
Independent Chronicle (Boston) [1804–07]
Lewiston (Me.) *Evening Journal* [1903–1907]
Louisville Courier-Journal [1896–1902]
New Haven Evening Register [1896–1904]
New Haven Journal-Courier [1896–1907]
New Orleans Picayune [1896–1905]
New York Daily Tribune [1863–1904]
New York Evening Post [1803–1826]
New York Herald [1896–1907]
New York Journal and Advertiser [1896–1906]
New York Mail and Express [1896–1901]
New York Sun [1891–1896]
New York Times [1880–1907]
New York World [1894–1907]

Troy, N.Y. *Northern Budget* [1896–1907]
Orange (N.J.) *Chronicle* [1888–1907]
Orange (N.J.) *Journal* [1888–1907]
Pawtucket (R.I.) *Evening Times* [1901–1907]
Philadelphia Record [1895–1906]
Pittsburgh Dispatch [1896–1906]
Pittsburgh Post [1896–1907]
Providence Journal [1896–1907]
Reading (Pa.) *Eagle* [1896–1907]
Rochester (N.Y.) *Democrat and Chronicle* [1896–1906]
San Francisco Chronicle [1879–1907]
San Francisco Examiner [1876–1904]
St. Louis Republic [1896–1906]
Utica (N.Y.) *Observer* [1896–1907]
Washington Evening Star [1894–1906]
Wilkes-Barre Record [1896–1907]

ARCHIVAL COLLECTIONS

Academy of Motion Picture Arts and Sciences, Margaret Herrick Library. (CLAc)
  1. J. Searle Dawley Collection.
  2. William Selig Collection.
  3. Charles Clark Collection.

American Film Institute, Los Angeles. (CBevA)
  1. Library.

Cook County Clerk's Office, Chicago. (ICC)
  1. Incorporation Records.

Edison National Historic Site. (NjWOE)

Federal Archive and Record Center, Bayonne, New Jersey. (NjBaFAR)
  1. Court Cases for the U.S. Circuit Court, Southern District of New York.
    A. Equity No. 6753, T. Cushing Daniel, Trustee, Christopher Armat, John H. Armat, and Selden B. Armat v. American Mutoscope Company and Benjamin F. Keith, filed 11 October 1897.
    B. Equity No. 6761, American Mutoscope Company v. Walter L. Isaacs, filed 18 October 1897.
    C. Equity No. 6762, American Mutoscope Company v. Robert H. Ingersoll and Charles H. Ingersoll, filed 18 October 1897.
    D. Equity Nos. 6795 and 6796, Thomas A. Edison v. Charles H. Webster, individually and as a member of the International Film Company, and Edmund Kuhn, individually and as a member of the International Film Company, filed 7 December 1897.
    E. Equity Nos. 6797 and 6798, Thomas A. Edison v. Maguire & Baucus, Limited, Joseph D. Baucus, individually and as President of said Maguire & Baucus, Limited, Frank Z. Maguire, individually and as Vice-President and Managing Director of said Maguire & Baucus, Limited, and William M. Paxton, Jr., individually and as Secretary of said Maguire & Baucus, filed 7 December 1897.
    F. Equity Nos. 6845 and 6846, Thomas A. Edison v. Eden Musee American Company, Ltd., and Richard G. Hollaman, individually and as President of Said Company, filed 7 February 1898.
    G. Equity Nos. 6852 and 6853, Thomas A. Edison v. Marc Klaw and Abraham Erlanger, individually and as members of the firm of Klaw & Erlanger, and W. W. Freeman, filed 15 February 1898.

H. Equity No. 6857, Thomas A. Edison v. the Veriscope Company, Daniel A. Stuart, individually and as President of the company, and Frank C. Meehan, individually and as Secretary of the company, filed 19 February 1898

I. Equity Nos. 6876 and 6877, Thomas A. Edison v. Augustin C. Daly, filed 14 March 1898.

J. Equity Nos. 6882 and 6883, Thomas A. Edison v. Water L. Isaacs, filed 22 March 1898.

K. Equity No. 6928, Thomas Edison v. American Mutoscope Company and Benjamin Franklin Keith, filed 13 May 1898.

L. Equity Nos. 6989, 6990, and 6991, Thomas A. Edison v. J. Stuart Blackton and Albert E. Smith, individually and as co-partners trading under the name and style of Commercial Advertising Bureau and American Vitagraph, filed 12 July 1898.

M. Equity Nos. 7124 and 7125, Thomas A. Edison v. Eberhard Schneider, filed 21 December 1898.

N. Equity No. 7130, Animated Projecting Company v. American Mutoscope Company and Benjamin Keith, filed 31 December 1898.

O. Equity Nos. 7224 and 7225, Thomas A. Edison v. George Huber, filed 28 April 1899.

P. Equity Nos. 7275 and 7276, Thomas A. Edison v. Frederick M. Prescott, filed 9 June 1899.

Q. Equity Nos. 7521 and 7522, Thomas A. Edison v. the Enterprise Optical Manufacturing Company and William J. Fry individually and as Manager trading under the name and style of Entertainment Supply Company, filed 31 May 1900.

R. Equity Nos. 7596 and 7597, Thomas A. Edison v. American Vitagraph Company and Walter Arthur individually and as General Manager of said Company, filed 13 September 1900.

S. Equity Nos. 7598 and 7599, Thomas A. Edison v. William T. Rock, filed 13 September 1900.

T. Equity Nos. 7649 and 7650, Thomas A. Edison v. the "Farmer" Dunn Moving Picture Machine Company and Elias B. Dunn, individually and as President of said Company, filed 15 November 1900.

U. Equity Nos. 8289 and 8290, Thomas A. Edison v. American Mutoscope & Biograph Company, filed 7 November 1902.

V. Equity No. 8303, Armat Moving Picture Company v. Edison Manufacturing Company, filed 28 November 1902.

W. Equity No. 8317, Thomas A. Edison v. Arthur D. Hotaling, filed 4 December 1902.

X. Equity No. 8361, Armat Moving Picture Company v. Eden Musee American Company, Ltd., filed 5 February 1903.

Y. Richard F. Outcault v. Edison Manufacturing Company and Percival L. Waters, filed 6 May 1904.

Z. Equity No. 8911, Thomas A. Edison v. William Paley and William F. Steiner, doing business under the name Paley & Steiner, filed 23 November 1904.

AA. Equity No. 8912, Thomas A. Edison v. Compagnie Generale de Phonographes, Cinématographes, et Appareils de Precision, and J. A. Berst, doing business under the name Pathé Cinématographe Co., filed 23 November 1904.

BB. Equity No. 8913, Thomas A. Edison v. Georges Méliès and Gaston Méliès, doing business under the name of Georges Méliès, filed 23 November 1904.

CC. Equity No. 8914, Thomas A. Edison v. Eberhard Schneider, doing business as American Cinematograph Company and German-American Cinematograph and Film Co., filed 23 November 1904.

DD. Equity Nos. 9034 and 9035, Thomas Edison v. American Vitagraph Company, William T. Rock, J. Stuart Blackton and Albert E. Smith, filed 13 March 1905.

2. Court Cases for the U.S. Circuit Court, Eastern District of New York.
3. Court Cases for the U.S. Circuit Court, District of New Jersey.
 A. Equity No. 10-221, American Mutoscope & Biograph Company v. Edison Manufacturing Company, filed 12 November 1904. Documentation at NjWOE.
4. Court Cases for the U.S. District Court, Southern District of New York.
 A. Equity No. 5-95, Motion Picture Patents Company v. Carl Laemmle and Independent Moving Picture Company of America, filed 11 December 1909.
 B. Equity No. 5-167, Motion Picture Patents Company v. Independent Moving Picture Company, filed 10 February 1910.
 C. Equity No. 7-151, Motion Picture Patents Company v. Independent Moving Picture Company, filed 27 March 1911.
5. Court Cases for the U.S. District Court, Eastern District of New York.
6. Court Cases for the U.S. District Court, District of New Jersey.
 A. Equity No. 15-5826, Georges Méliès v. Motion Picture Patents Company and Edison Manufacturing Company, filed 21 May 1909. Documentation at NjWOE.

Federal Archive and Record Center, Chicago, Illinois. (ICFAR)
1. Court Cases for the U.S. Circuit Court, Northern District of Illinois.
 A. Equity No. 24,219, Vitascope Company v. Chicago Talking Machine Company, filed 13 August 1896.
 B. Equity No. 24,579, Veriscope Company v. John W. White, filed 4 August 1897.
 C. Equity No. 24,753, Thomas A. Edison v. Edward Amet, filed 10 January 1898.
 D. Equity Nos. 25,552 and 25,553, Thomas A. Edison v. Sears, Roebuck, and Company, filed 30 April 1900.
 E. Equity Nos. 25,760 and 25,761, Thomas A. Edison v. William N. Selig, filed 5 December 1900.
 F. Equity Nos. 25,808 and 25,809, Thomas A. Edison v. Stereopticon and Film Exchange and William B. Moore individually and as Treasurer and Manager of said Company, filed 5 February 1901.
 G. Equity Nos. 25,993 and 25,994, Thomas A. Edison v. the Enterprise Optical Mfg. Company and Frank McMillan, individually and as President and Manager of said Company, filed 14 September 1901.
 H. Equity Nos. 25,995 and 25,996, Thomas A. Edison v. Edward D. Otis and N. M. Kent individually and as co-partners trading under the firm name and style of Chicago Projecting Company, filed 16 September 1901.
 I. Equity Nos. 26,512 and 26,513, Thomas A. Edison v. Selig Polyscope Company, filed 7 November 1902.
 J. Equity No. 28,856, Vitagraph Company of America v. 20th Century Optiscope Company and Robert Bachman, filed 25 October 1907.

Federal Archive and Record Center, Philadelphia. (PPFAR)
1. Court Cases for the U.S. Circuit Court, Eastern District of Pennsylvania.
 A. Equity No. 50, October Sessions, 1897, Thomas A. Edison v. Siegmund Lubin, filed 10 January 1898.
 B. Equity No. 59, April Sessions, 1901, Armat Moving Picture Company v. Siegmund Lubin, filed 1902.
 C. Equity No. 36, April Sessions, 1902, Thomas A. Edison v. Siegmund Lubin, 6 June 1902.
 D. Equity Nos. 24 and 25, October Sessions, 1902, Thomas A. Edison v. Siegmund Lubin, filed 6 November 1902.
 E. Equity No. 27, October Sessions, 1903, American Mutoscope and Biograph Company v. Siegmund Lubin, filed 24 November 1903.
2. Court Cases for the District Court, Eastern District of Pennsylvania.

    A. Equity No. 889, September Sessions, 1912, United States of America v. Motion
    Picture Patents Company *et al.*, filed 16 August 1912.

Franklin Institute of Arts and Sciences, Philadelphia. (PPS)
  1. C. Francis Jenkins Collection.

George Eastman House. (NR-GE)
  1. Glenn Matthews/Thomas Armat Collection.
  2. Film Collections.

Harvard Business School, Baker Library, Boston. (MH-BA)
  1. Manuscript Collection.
      A. Dun and Company Collection.
      B. Raff & Gammon Collection.

Harvard Theater Collection, Cambridge, Mass. (MH-TT)

Library of Congress, Washington, D.C. (DLC)
  1. Motion Picture, Television, and Recorded Sound Division.
      A. Paper Print Collection.
      B. AFI Collection.
      C. Searchlight Theatre Collection.
  2. Manuscript Division.
      A. George Kleine Collection.

Los Angeles County Museum of Natural History. (CLCM)
  1. Thomas Armat Collection.
  2. Miscellaneous catalogs.

Museum of the City of New York. (NNMus)
  1. Theater Collection.
  2. Photograph Collection.

Museum of Modern Art, New York City. (NNMOMA)
  1. Film Study Center
      A. Merritt Crawford Collection.
      B. Edison Collection.
      C. Film collections.
  2. Library.
      A. American Mutoscope and Biograph Company records.

National Archives, Washington, D.C. (DNA)
  1. Motion Picture Section.

New-York Historical Society. (NNHi)
  1. Bella Landour Collection.

New York Public Library. (NN)
  1. Newspaper and Periodical Collection.
  2. Billy Rose Theater Collection.

New York County Clerk's Office. (NNNCC-Ar)
  1. Court cases for the Supreme Court of New York State.
  2. Partnership and incorporation records.

Free Library of Philadelphia. (PP)
  1. Theater Collection.

University of California at Los Angeles. (CLU)
   1. Albert Smith Collection.
   2. UCLA Film and Television Archive.

University of Iowa at Iowa City. (IaU)
   1. Special Collections
      A. Edward Albee Papers.

Washington National Record Center, Suitland, Md. (MdSuFR)
   1. Cases for the Supreme Court, District of Columbia.
      A. Equity No. 17,416, T. Cushing Daniel *et al.* v. C. Francis Jenkins, filed 27 May 1896.
      B. Equity No. 19,962, the Animated Photo Projecting Company v. N. Dushane Cloward *et al.*, filed 30 November 1898.
      C. Equity No. 22,103, Armat Moving Picture Co. v. Plimpton B. Chase, filed 7 March 1901.
      D. Equity No. 22,448, Armat Moving Picture Co. v. Plimpton B. Chase, filed 9 July 1901.
      E. Equity No. 27,419, Armat Moving Picture Company v. Interstate Amusement Co., filed 18 October 1907.
   2. Cases for the Court of Appeals for the District of Columbia.
      A. Patent Appeal Docket No. 153, Patent Interference No. 18,461, Box 720 of Accession No. 53DOO37.

Wyoming Historical and Geological Society, Wilkes-Barre, Pa. (PW-bH)
   1. Robert Gillaum Collection.

Picture Sources

Unless indicated otherwise, the photographer is an in-house service or the author.

Anthology Film Archives: 144
Marc Wanamaker/Bison Archives:
  163, 274, 284, 431, 434, 445, 469,
  475
Circus World: 202
*Theater Collection, Philadelphia Free
  Library:* 237; courtesy Linda
  Kowall: 285
*Federal Archive and Record Center,
  Bayonne:* 253, 260
Lake County Museum: courtesy L.
  Carey Williams: 261
Richard M. Bueschel: 262, 296

UCLA Film and Television Archive:
  279
*Academy of Motion Picture Arts and
  Sciences:* 338
*Lewis Walpole Library, Yale
  University:* 384 (top)
Bobst Library, New York University:
  419, 437, 487
Chicago Historical Society: 423
David Bowers: 427, 433, 440
*Theodore Roosevelt Collection,
  Harvard College Library:* 464

General Index

Italic numerals signify illustrations.

Index of Films

When an indexed film exists in its entirety (or nearly so), its title is preceded by an asterisk (*). Virtually all of these films are preserved in American film archives, notably the Museum of Modern Art (New York City), the Library of Congress (Washington, D.C.), the George Eastman House (Rochester, New York), the University of California at Los Angeles Film and Television Archives (Los Angeles), and the Anthology Film Archives (New York City). Doubtless, additional surviving films will be discovered or made available after publication of this book. My notations are thus meant to serve only as an informal guide to what the author was able to record in 1990, not a definitive source. The reader should also recognize that many noteworthy films are not mentioned in the text, and therefore are not listed in this index, on account of constraints of space and readability. Italic numerals signify illustrations.